Enterprise Development with Flex

Enterprise Development with Flex

Yakov Fain, Victor Rasputnis, and Anatole Tartakovsky

O'REILLY®

Beijing • Cambridge • Farnham • Köln • Sebastopol • Taipei • Tokyo

Enterprise Development with Flex
by Yakov Fain, Victor Rasputnis, and Anatole Tartakovsky

Published by O'Reilly Media, Inc., 1005 Gravenstein Highway North, Sebastopol, CA 95472.

O'Reilly books may be purchased for educational, business, or sales promotional use. Online editions are also available for most titles (*http://my.safaribooksonline.com*). For more information, contact our corporate/institutional sales department: (800) 998-9938 or *corporate@oreilly.com*.

Editor: Mary E. Treseler
Development Editor: Linda Laflamme
Production Editor: Adam Zaremba
Copyeditor: Nancy Kotary
Proofreader: Sada Preisch
Indexer: Ellen Troutman Zaig
Cover Designer: Karen Montgomery
Interior Designer: David Futato
Illustrator: Robert Romano

Printing History:
March 2010: First Edition.

RepKover™

This book uses RepKover™, a durable and flexible lay-flat binding.

ISBN: 978-0-596-15416-5

[M] [8/10]

1281316883

Adobe Developer Library, a copublishing partnership between O'Reilly Media Inc., and Adobe Systems, Inc., is the authoritative resource for developers using Adobe technologies. These comprehensive resources offer learning solutions to help developers create cutting-edge interactive web applications that can reach virtually anyone on any platform.

With top-quality books and innovative online resources covering the latest tools for rich-Internet application development, the *Adobe Developer Library* delivers expert training straight from the source. Topics include ActionScript, Adobe Flex®, Adobe Flash®, and Adobe Acrobat®.

Get the latest news about books, online resources, and more at *http://adobedeveloperlibrary.com*.

Table of Contents

Preface

Four years ago, the authors of this book were looking for a solid platform and a robust component framework to develop rich Internet applications (RIAs) for enterprises. We worked with AJAX. We worked with Java Swing. But when Adobe released the alpha version of Flex 2, we realized that this was exactly what we'd been looking for. To prove our convictions, we even created a company, Farata Systems, dedicated to the creation of enterprise solutions that utilize Adobe Flex on the frontend.

Since then, we have worked on lots of large- and small-scale projects that involved either Adobe Flex or Adobe Integrated Runtime (AIR) technologies. During these years, we have faced recurring issues and have been able to apply the same or similar solutions over and over again. Many solutions involved adding missing features to the user interface (UI) components that came with Flex SDK. In some cases, we had to enhance the communication layer of BlazeDS or LiveCycle Data Services (LCDS). All these enhancements were possible because the Flex framework was well designed as an open framework that allowed customization of its parts that didn't meet specific needs.

We've always shared our findings in the form of technical blogs or articles, but when the amount of accumulated materials reached critical mass, it was clear that the time was ripe for a book targeting enterprise RIA developers and managers.

Having O'Reilly as a publisher of your book is an honor in itself, but you might not know that to get this little "Adobe Developer Library" logo on the cover, our book outline had to get approval from Adobe Flex team members—the most respected software engineers in the field.

Typically, technical books on a particular software include the appropriate version number in the title. This book is different, however; it doesn't focus on an application programming interface (API) that's specific to any version of the software. Rather, it explains the approach to efficient design of scalable Flex applications, building component libraries, and dealing with performance issues. Code examples from the book will work in Flex 3 and Flex 4 (in beta at the time of this writing).

The last chapter of the book is dedicated to LCDS 3.0, which was released just before press time and offers a new model-driven approach to developing data-intensive applications. Though the chapter on AIR is based on AIR 1.5, it offers a unique and original solution for data synchronization using AIR and BlazeDS, which will work just fine with AIR 2.0, which, as we write, is currently in beta.

Who Is This Book For?

This book is intended for Flex and Java application architects, team leaders, and senior developers who are interested in getting to know:

- How the Flex framework works under the hood
- The pros and cons of some of the third-party libraries
- How to build reusable component libraries for their enterprises
- How to select and improve (if need be) Flex-to-Java communication
- What to watch for from a performance perspective
- How to modularize the Flex RIA
- Which design patterns to apply
- How to select third-party frameworks

This book will be very useful for Java Enterprise Edition (JEE) developers who are still not sure whether the Flex SDK is a good fit for their cross-platform RIAs. We are positive that after reading the first several chapters, you will appreciate the power and flexibility of the open source Flex SDK, third-party libraries, and their server-side tools.

This is not an introductory book, and we assume that the reader already has some experience with developing Flex applications and a good understanding of object-oriented design principles.

How the Book Is Organized

Even though the chapters in this book don't have to be read in any particular order, in some places we develop code samples or custom components based on materials presented earlier. Following is a brief book outline, from which you can decide your own starting point:

Chapter 1, *Comparing Selected Flex Frameworks*
: The goal of any framework is to make the process of software development and maintenance easier; however, the ways of achieving this goal differ. Some people prefer working with frameworks that are based on the Model-View-Controller (MVC) pattern, and others like dealing with class libraries of components. Each approach has its pros and cons. In this chapter, you'll learn how to build the same application using the MVC frameworks Cairngorm 2, Mate, and PureMVC. You'll also see a different, non-MVC approach for generating the code of a create, read, update, and delete (CRUD) application with components from the open source framework Clear Toolkit.

Chapter 2, *Selected Design Patterns*
Design patterns suggest solutions to common problems that arise during software development. Flex is a domain-specific tool that's aimed at creating a rich UI for the Web, and in this chapter we'll discuss the specifics of selected design patterns when applied to the creation of a UI with Flex, namely:

- Singleton
- Proxy
- Mediator
- Data transfer object
- AsyncToken
- Class factory

Chapter 3, *Building an Enterprise Framework*
For the majority of the enterprise applications, development comes down to a few major activities:

- Creating data grids
- Working with forms
- Validating data

In this chapter, you'll learn how to build components for your enterprise framework that simplify dealing with these activities. We'll identify some of the issues with Flex 3 SDK components and show you how to extend and enhance them.

Chapter 4, *Equipping Enterprise Flex Projects*
Typical enterprise RIA projects are developed by mixed teams of client- and server-side developers. This chapter is essentially a laundry list of topics that development managers and team leaders face:

- What skillsets are required for the project
- How to automate creation of build and deployment scripts
- What tools to use for testing
- What continuous integration is
- How to arrange for logging
- Which third-party component libraries might come in handy

Chapter 5, *Customizing the Messaging Layer of LCDS or BlazeDS*
This chapter starts with a quick example of how to perform the push by making a direct call to a `MessageBroker`, which comes with LCDS and BlazeDS. It continues with a discussion of the existing world of custom adapters and message channels. You'll see how to implement a messaging layer with guaranteed message delivery and take care of the proper sequencing of messages using BlazeDS implementation of the Action Message Format (AMF) protocol.

Chapter 6, *Open Source Networking Solutions*
: Open sourcing of Flex framework in general, and its communication protocols and server-side components in particular, play an important role in the adoption of Flex by enterprises. Although large-scale applications are most likely powered by LCDS, smaller ones will find open source server-side components very useful. This chapter will unleash the power of AMF and provide illustrations of how to create a robust platform for development of a modern RIA without paying hefty licensing fees. It will discuss polling and server-side push techniques for client-server communications, as well as how to extend the capabilities of BlazeDS. You'll also learn how to create a BlazeDS-based solution similar to LCDS's Data Management Services, where you'll be creating `ChangeObject`, `Assembler`, and `DAO` classes that will take care of automated data synchronization between Flex clients and Java servers.

Chapter 7, *Modules, Libraries, Applications, and Portals*
: This chapter suggests an approach to creating every Flex application as a modularized portal that loads and communicates with independently built and compiled modules and subapplications. You'll learn how to work with module loaders and the difference between application, child, and sibling domains. We'll explain how to properly design module-to-module communications. You'll get familiar with an original technique for compiling Runtime Shared Libraries (RSLs) that are self-initialized, and finally, you will learn how to integrate existing Flex applications as legacy JEE portals.

Chapter 8, *Performance Improvement: Selected Topics*
: This chapter continues the conversation started in Chapter 7. We'll talk about actual versus perceived performance of RIA and discuss the use of application preloaders to make the first page of your RIA appear as soon as possible. We'll also describe how to improve the process of initial loading of RSLs, which serves the same goal: minimizing the amount of code that travels from the server to the client computer. You'll learn how to build every application as a portal while providing an independent testing environment for multideveloper teams. The chapter ends by focusing on issues that affect the performance of most Flex applications.

Chapter 9, *Working with Adobe AIR*
: Adobe AIR is a cross-platform development environment and runtime that adds an API required for desktop applications, comes with a local database management system (DBMS), and substantially simplifies embedding HTML into RIA by offering a full-featured embedded web browser engine. This chapter starts by covering the basics of AIR development, but quickly turns into a project for a fictitious pharmaceutical company that demonstrates a solution for data synchronization between local and remote databases when the network is not always available but the application must remain operational. This solution works with occasionally connected AIR/BlazeDS as well as AIR/LCDS applications. As a bonus, the sample application also demonstrates how to integrate Google Maps into an AIR application.

Chapter 10, *Developing Flex Applications for LiveCycle Enterprise Suite*
: LiveCycle is an service-oriented architecture (SOA) platform that runs on Java EE application servers, and this chapter is about creating enterprise workflows using this tool. You will learn how to use a web browser–based UI written in Flex to streamline the part of the workflow that requires user interaction. We'll cover the process of extending LiveCycle with your application-specific services and the creation of complex PDF documents. The larger portion of this chapter explains how to integrate LiveCycle ES functionality with your existing Flex-based applications.

Chapter 11, *Printing with Flex*
: Printing is often one of the most time-consuming tasks in developing Flex enterprise applications. Just using the Flex printing API would require allocation of substantial budget and human resources. In this chapter, we'll discuss an open source solution for generating PDF documents on the client. This printing functionality will be applied to the sample pharmaceutical application introduced in Chapter 9.

Chapter 12, *Model-Driven Development with LCDS ES2*
: In this chapter, you'll see how to create a CRUD application in which Flex talks to a remote database via recently released LCDS 3.0. The good part is that no programming is required. You'll create a data model and the rest of the code will be generated automatically.

Conventions Used in This Book

The following typographical conventions are used in this book:

Italic
: Indicates new terms, URLs, email addresses, filenames, and file extensions.

`Constant width`
: Used for program listings, as well as within paragraphs to refer to program elements such as variable or function names, databases, data types, environment variables, statements, and keywords.

`Constant width bold`
: Shows commands or other text that should be typed literally by the user.

`Constant width italic`
: Shows text that should be replaced with user-supplied values or by values determined by context.

This icon signifies a tip, suggestion, or general note.

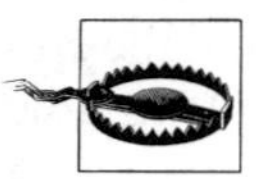

This icon signifies a warning or caution.

Using Code Examples

This book is here to help you get your job done. In general, you may use the code in this book in your programs and documentation. You do not need to contact us for permission unless you're reproducing a significant portion of the code. For example, writing a program that uses several chunks of code from this book does not require permission. Selling or distributing a CD-ROM of examples from O'Reilly books *does* require permission. Answering a question by citing this book and quoting example code does not require permission. Incorporating a significant amount of example code from this book into your product's documentation *does* require permission.

We appreciate, but do not require, attribution. An attribution usually includes the title, author, publisher, and ISBN. For example: "*Enterprise Development with Flex*, by Yakov Fain, Victor Rasputnis, and Anatole Tartakovsky. Copyright 2010 Yakov Fain, Victor Rasputnis, and Anatole Tartakovsky, 978-0-596-15416-5." If you feel your use of code examples falls outside fair use or the permission given here, feel free to contact us at *permissions@oreilly.com*.

The source code for this book is available online; each chapter is in a single zipped folder. To download the sample code for a chapter, enter the directory URL followed by the name of the chapter with the extension *.zip*. For example, the code for Chapter 5 can be accessed at the following URL:

> *http://faratasystems.com/entflex_sc/chapter5/chapter5.zip*

If you see a directory called *Flex4* in some of the *.zip* files, it contains a port of the Flex 3 code samples. Please note that the folder for Chapter 4 doesn't exist, as there is no sample code in that chapter. The folder for Chapter 6 doesn't exist either, because all of the source code for enhanced Flex components is included in the *clear.swc* library in the Clear Toolkit Concurrent Versions System (CVS) repository at SourceForge. To save space, Chapters 7 and 10 contain only manually written code.

Most of the chapters contain Flex projects copied from the workspaces of the authors of this book. In certain cases, supporting libraries were not included (such as Chapter 8), as some of the projects were more than 300 MB! To use the code in these cases, create a new project in Flash Builder and copy the source code into the newly created project.

How to Contact Us

Please address comments and questions concerning this book to the publisher:

O'Reilly Media, Inc.
1005 Gravenstein Highway North
Sebastopol, CA 95472
800-998-9938 (in the United States or Canada)
707-829-0515 (international or local)
707-829-0104 (fax)

We have a web page for this book, where we list errata, examples, and any additional information. You can access this page at:

http://oreilly.com/catalog/9780596154165

To comment or ask technical questions about this book, send email to:

bookquestions@oreilly.com

For more information about our books, conferences, Resource Centers, and the O'Reilly Network, see our website at:

http://oreilly.com

Safari® Books Online

Safari Books Online is an on-demand digital library that lets you easily search over 7,500 technology and creative reference books and videos to find the answers you need quickly.

With a subscription, you can read any page and watch any video from our library online. Read books on your cell phone and mobile devices. Access new titles before they are available for print, and get exclusive access to manuscripts in development and post feedback for the authors. Copy and paste code samples, organize your favorites, download chapters, bookmark key sections, create notes, print out pages, and benefit from tons of other time-saving features.

O'Reilly Media has uploaded this book to the Safari Books Online service. To have full digital access to this book and others on similar topics from O'Reilly and other publishers, sign up for free at *http://my.safaribooksonline.com*.

Acknowledgments

Writing a book requires very serious support from family members, and we'd like to thank them—especially our children, who got used to the idea that after coming home from work, dads still had to be glued to those computers to work on some boring technical book.

We'd like to thank all the members of the Flex community who appreciated our work in the past and encouraged us to continue sharing every little bit of knowledge we've gained.

We are grateful to the excellent software engineers from the Adobe Flex team, who put their trust in our ability to write such a complex and advanced book. Our special thanks to one unknown member of the Flex team who allegedly said during the book approval process something like, "I don't agree with many of the things that these authors write about Flex, and I'd rather not approve them, but I will because there are not many people in the industry who are capable of writing such a book." We don't know your name, but we consider this assessment to be the best compliment we've received so far.

Our praise goes to the cover designers, who correctly visualized the authors of this book without ever seeing them.

We'd like to thank Aliaksandr Yuzafovich for his research and contribution to the data synchronization solution described in Chapter 9.

Our hats off to Linda Laflamme, an excellent development editor from O'Reilly. After reading some of her comments, we had the feeling that she understands technical materials better than we do.

And mainly, we thank you, our readers, for reading this book.

—Yakov Fain, Victor Rasputnis, and Anatole Tartakovsky

Technical Editor Bios

Kaushik Datta is currently working at Mercedes-Benz USA, LLC, where he and his team have built Flex-based web applications. He has been using Flex since the Beta Royale days. Kaushik spends his off-hours reading blogs on various other Adobe products and looking for better designer–developer workflows. He also enjoys cricket and theater. You can reach him at *kaudata@yahoo.com*.

Greg Jastrab is presently a technical project manager at SmartLogic Solutions in Baltimore, MD. He's been using Flex since version 1.5 and occasionally speaks at local Adobe user groups. Outside of work, Greg enjoys relaxing with his wife and dog, and playing the guitar, video games, and poker. You can follow him at *http://blog.smartlogicsolutions.com* and on Twitter at *@gjastrab*.

Igor Lachter is currently a senior developer at SAIC, where he is involved in developing a procurement system using Flex technology. He's been working with Flex since version 3, utilizing many of the approaches described in this book. When not programming, he tutors SAT math and plays soccer with his three daughters. You can reach him online at *igor_gl@yahoo.com*.

CHAPTER 1

Comparing Selected Flex Frameworks

The first 90% of the code accounts for the first 90% of the development time. The remaining 10% of the code accounts for the other 90% of the development time.

—Tom Cargill

Frameworks Versus Component Libraries

Whenever the subject of third-party architectural frameworks is raised at a gathering of Flex developers, the developers are quick to start explaining how they use and like a particular framework. But a simple question like, "Why do you use this framework?" often catches them off guard. Many enterprise developers, especially those who came to Flex after spending some time developing Java EE applications, just know that using these frameworks is the right thing to do. Is it so? What are the benefits of using architectural frameworks? This chapter offers some answers as to what you should expect of a framework built on top of the Flex framework.

The goal of any well-designed framework is to make the process of software development and maintenance easier. There are different ways of achieving this goal. Some people prefer working with frameworks that are based on the Model-View-Controller pattern; others like dealing with libraries of components. Each approach has its benefits and costs. In this chapter, you will learn how to build the same application using several frameworks or component libraries used by Flex developers.

First, let's define the term *framework* versus *component library*. Imagine a new housing development. For some pieces of property, the builder has already erected the frames for certain house models, but other pieces of property have only piles of construction materials guarded by specially trained dogs. By the entrance to the new community, you see a completely finished model house with lots of upgrades.

You have three options:

- Purchase the model house and move in in a month.

- Purchase one of five prearchitected models (see those houses that are framed?). The frames are pretty much ready; you just need to select windows, flooring, and kitchen appliances.
- Purchase a custom house using a mix of the builder's and your own materials.

Now, to draw some analogies to the software engineering world, Case A is the equivalent of purchasing an all-encompassing enterprise software package that comes with 2,000 database tables and thousands of lines of code, with a promise to cover all the needs of your organization.

Case B is the equivalent of a software framework that you must code in ways that operate by the rules of the framework, adding your own application-specific logic where appropriate. Often such frameworks are intrusive—you have to include in your application code hooks to build your software on the pillars of the selected framework.

Case C gives you complete freedom of choice, as long as you have all the components and the know-how to put them together. For some people, it's the most appealing option, but for others it is the most intimidating option, because it has such freedom; these people select option B to ensure that their house will not be blown away by the Big Bad Wolf, as in the fairy tale "The Three Little Pigs (*http://en.wikipedia.org/wiki/Three_Little_Pigs*)."

Adobe Flex provides you with an extendable framework that you can use as a solid starting point for your business application. Along with that, there are a number of third-party frameworks and component libraries created with the same noble goal: *to make your life easier*.

As Flex is already a framework, you should have very strong reasons to create another one. Flex has extendable components and events, and when you work in a team of developers, each of them may have a different understanding of how custom components should find and communicate with each other, how to properly organize the project, and how to make a team work more productively. At the time of this writing, there are about a dozen Flex frameworks from which you can choose to help you organize your Flex project. Each of these frameworks has the same goal: to increase each developer's productivity.

In this chapter, you'll get familiar with three architectural frameworks and one toolkit, which includes additional productivity plug-ins and a component library. Of course, as the readers of this book may have a different understanding of what *easy* means, the authors decided to show you how you can build the same application using each of the frameworks or libraries. (Each of the reviewed products is offered at no charge.)

The sample application that you will build is based on Café Townsend, a small program that was originally developed by creators of the Cairngorm framework. This application allows the end user to maintain data for Café Townsend's employees. The application reads data from the database, displays a list of employees, and allows the user to add a new employee or edit an existing employee.

The chapter starts by introducing the original Cairngorm Café Townsend application on the Adobe website (*http://www.adobe.com/go/cairngorm*). Next, it explores the version of the application written in the Mate framework and published on the AsFusion website (*http://mate.asfusion.com*). The chapter then analyzes the version of the application written in Cliff Hall's PureMVC framework (*http://www.puremvc.org*). Finally, you'll explore a version of the Café Townsend application generated with the help of the open source Clear Toolkit (*http://sourceforge.net/projects/cleartoolkit*). The Café Townsend application versions are posted on each framework's corresponding website, which is the best place to download the sample application and the given framework, as it's safe to assume that the authors of the frameworks in each case have either written or approved the code.

Each of the following sections starts with a brief introduction of the framework or library, followed by a code walkthrough and conclusions. Each framework will be explored, followed by a report card evaluation of the framework's pros and cons.

Introducing Café Townsend

The original Café Townsend application consists of three views (Figures 1-1, 1-2, and 1-3). These views allow the user to log in, display the list of employees, and add a new employee of the Café. The application also has one image (the Café Townsend logo) and a CSS file, *main.css*, for styling.

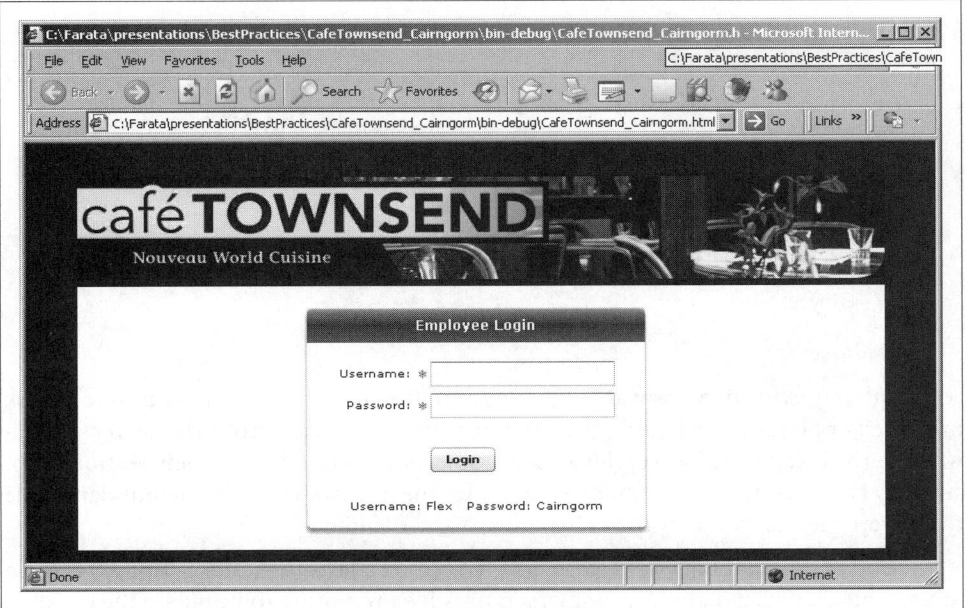

Figure 1-1. Café Townsend Employee Login view

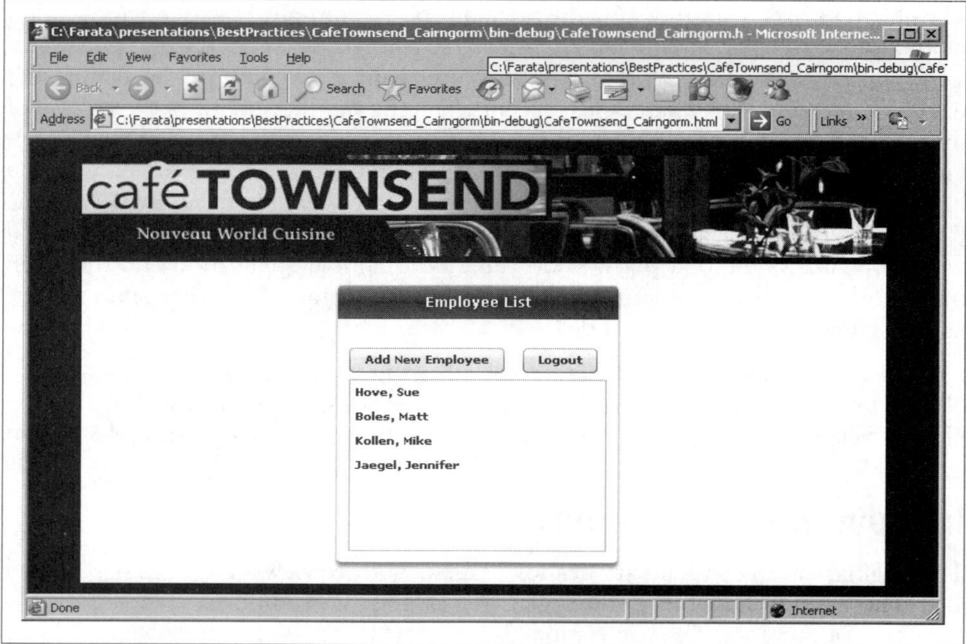

Figure 1-2. Café Townsend Employee List view

The application retrieves data from *Employee.xml*, as shown in the following code snippet:

```
<?xml version="1.0" encoding="utf-8"?>
<employees>
  <employee>
    <emp_id>1</emp_id>
    <firstname>Sue</firstname>
    <lastname>Hove</lastname>
    <email>shove@cafetownsend.com</email>
    <startdate>01/07/2006</startdate>
  </employee>
    ...
</employees>
```

Although retrieving data from an XML file simplifies the explanation of this framework in this example, it is preferable that you pass the typed data from the server in real-world projects, for example, Java value objects converted into their ActionScript strongly typed peers. This technique eliminates the need to write a lot of mundane code to convert the `startdate` from `String` to `Date` and the like.

At the end of this chapter, you'll learn how to include a Java-to-ActionScript 3.0 version of the Café Townsend application, which uses Flex remoting to populate the data.

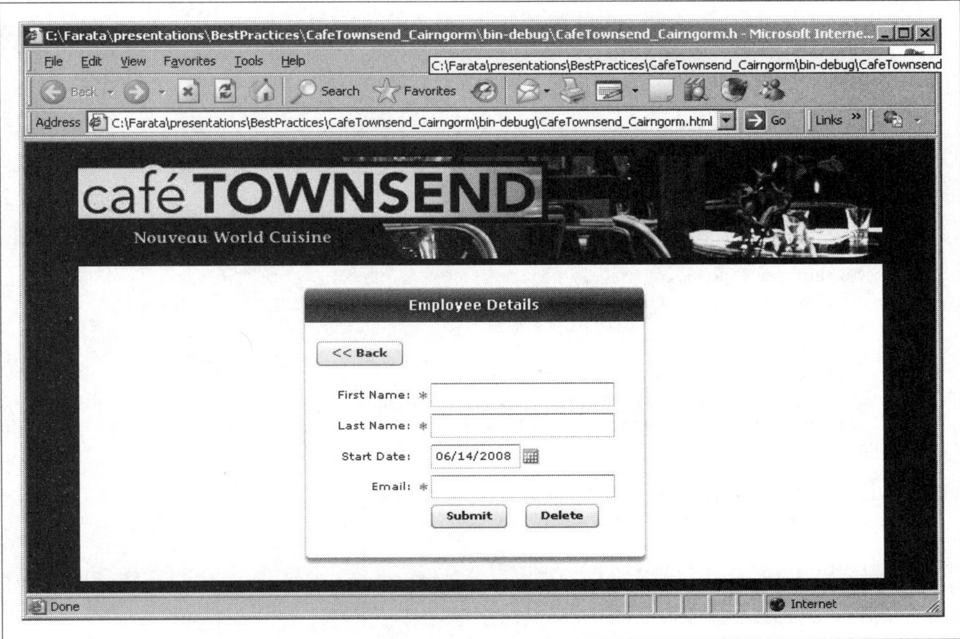

Figure 1-3. Café Townsend Employee Details view

Employee List Without Frameworks

The title of this section is a bit of a misnomer, because Flex itself is a framework. But we wanted to stress that you can create an application that reads XML and displays the data in a list control without the use of any additional third-party framework or component library.

The Flex framework already supports the MVC pattern by separating the View (the `List` control) and the data that can be stored in a nonvisual data provider such as `ArrayCollection`. Let's write a quick-and-dirty version of the `EmployeeList` component that does not use any frameworks.

This Café application uses `HTTPService` to read the file *Employees.xml* located in the folder *assets*, and a `List` component displays the full name of the employee using the label function `fullName()`.

The data is stored in the data provider `employees` (a.k.a. MVC's Model), and the `List` controls play the role of MVC's View. For simplicity, this version does not have error processing, and the Add Employee and Logout buttons are nonfunctional.

The following application (Example 1-1) reads the list of employees using just the Flex framework.

Example 1-1. EmployeeList using the Flex framework

```
<?xml version="1.0" encoding="utf-8"?>
<!-- The service call empService.send() plays the role of MVC Controller -->
<mx:Application xmlns:mx="http://www.adobe.com/2006/mxml" layout="absolute"
   creationComplete="empService.send()">

   <mx:Panel title="Employee List" horizontalCenter="0">
      <mx:HBox paddingTop="25">
         <mx:Button label="Add New Employee" />
         <mx:Spacer width="100%" />
         <mx:Button label="Logout" />
         <mx:Spacer width="100%" height="20" />
      </mx:HBox>

     <!-- List of Employees a.k.a. View-->
      <mx:List id="employees_li" dataProvider="{employees}"
         labelFunction="fullName" width="100%"/>
   </mx:Panel>

   <mx:HTTPService id="empService" url="assets/Employees.xml"
      result="employeeDataHandler(event)" />

   <mx:Script>
      <![CDATA[
      import mx.rpc.events.ResultEvent;
      import mx.collections.ArrayCollection;

      //data provider for the list is an ArrayCollection a.k.a. model
      [Bindable]
      private var employees: ArrayCollection=new ArrayCollection;

      private function employeeDataHandler(event:ResultEvent):void{
         employees=event.result.employees.employee;
      }
      // format the names to display last and first names in the List
      public function fullName( empItem : Object ) : String {
         return empItem.lastname + ", " + empItem.firstname;
      }
      ]]>
   </mx:Script>
</mx:Application>
```

Because real-world RIAs are a lot more complex than this simple application and may contain a hundred or more different views created by multiple developers with data coming from different sources, consider using one of the additional frameworks or component libraries to simplify the programming of similar tasks and to better organize the project.

Now let's consider the Café application rewritten in Cairngorm, Mate, PureMVC, and the Clear Toolkit.

Cairngorm

The architectural framework Cairngorm was created by Alistair McLeod and Steven Webster while they were working at the company iteration::two (they are presently employed by Adobe Consulting). Cairngorm implements several design patterns such as MVC, Command, and Delegate. It was open sourced in the summer of 2008.

Cairngorm was designed to ensure that UI components do not need to know where data is located. The business layer retrieves data from the servers and stores it in the memory objects that represent the data model, which use binding to notify the UI components about data arrival or changes. On the same note, changes in the UI are propagated to the server side through this business layer.

The Cairngorm framework promotes the use of the MVC design pattern in the client portion of your RIA. It offers a number of classes implementing Model, View, and Controller tiers, and interaction between them.

The Model tier is represented by the class `ModelLocator`, which stores the application-specific data (these are often collections of *value objects*, a.k.a. *data transfer objects*). `ModelLocator`'s data is bound to the View controls.

The View portion contains visual components required by your application, value objects, and Cairngorm-specific event classes used for communication with the Model and Controller tiers.

The Controller tier is responsible for invoking appropriate code containing the business logic of your application, which is implemented by using global `FrontController` and `ServiceLocator` classes as well as additional `Command` and `Delegate` classes.

The Cairngorm framework's documentation and sample applications are located at *http://www.cairngormdocs.org*.

As this chapter was being written, Adobe decided to rebrand Cairngorm; instead of a mere framework, Adobe is promoting it as a set of tools and methodologies containing various frameworks, including what has been earlier known as the "Cairngorm framework." You can read about this Cairngorm 3 initiative at *http://opensource.adobe.com/wiki/display/cairngorm/Cairngorm+3*. In this chapter, we refer to Cairngorm 2, which is an MVC Flex framework and nothing else.

Café Townsend with Cairngorm

The "pure Flex" code shown in Example 1-1 includes representatives of each MVC tier. The code knows that the data will be loaded into an `ArrayCollection` (the Model) by the HTTP service pointing at the *Employees.xml* file by calling a `send()` method on the `creationComplete` event (the Controller) of the application. The `List` component (the View) knows about its model and is bound to it directly via its `dataProvider` property.

The data flow between Cairngorm components while displaying a list of Café employees is depicted in Figure 1-4.

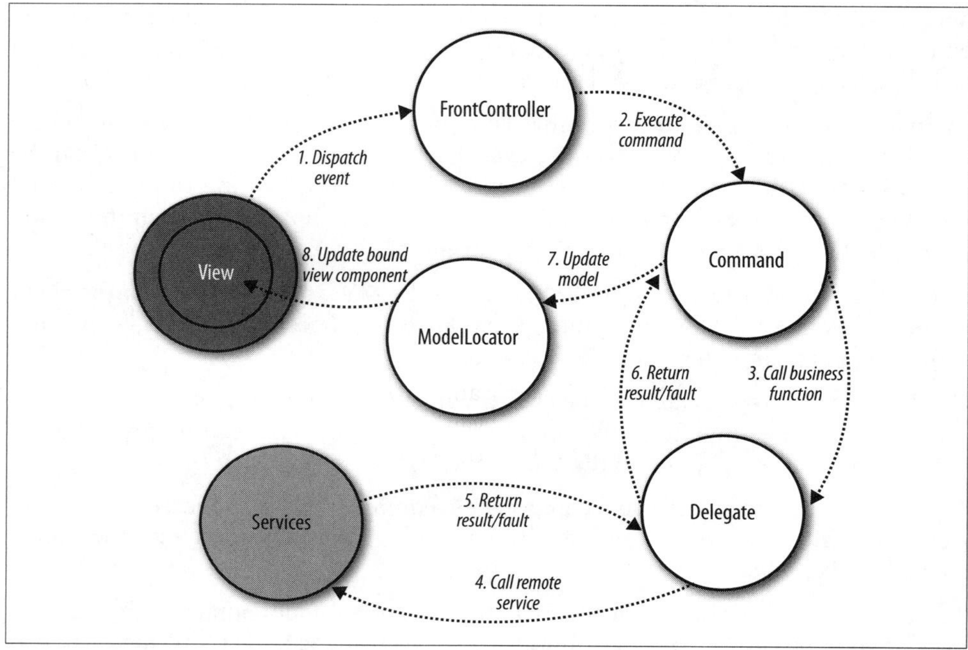

Figure 1-4. Cairngorm employee list data flow

The Cairngorm version of this application has the following six major participants:

Services
: The UI portion does not know about implementation of services and can't call them directly, so you must move the `HTTPService` object into a special file called *Services.mxml*.

`FrontController`
: The View and the service layer can't send events to each other directly, but rather have to be registered with a singleton `FrontController` that maps all application events to appropriate actions (commands).

`Command`
: When a `View` component fires an event, `FrontController` finds the `Command` class that was registered with this event and calls its method `execute()`.

`Delegate`
: The method `execute()` of the `Command` class creates an instance of the `Delegate` class that knows which service to call (`HTTPService`, `RemoteObject`, `WebService`) and returns the result or fault to the `Command` class.

`ModelLocator`
: The `Command` class updates the data in the model (typically, a collection of value objects) defined in the global `ModelLocator`.

`View`
: Because each model located inside the `ModelLocator` is bound to a UI control, its content gets updated automatically.

Use the source code of the Café Townsend Multi-View Contact Management application that was converted to Cairngorm 2 by Darren Houle and is available under the Creative Commons license (*http://creativecommons.org/licenses/by/2.5/*). You can download the source code of this application at *http://cairngormdocs.org/blog/?p=19*.

Figure 1-5 is a screenshot of the Café Townsend Flash Builder project. Please note that the code for the six participants mentioned earlier is organized in separate packages (folders). The *business* folder is for delegates and service components. The *command* folder is for `Command` classes; *control* is for events and `FrontController`; the `ModelLocator` is located in the *model* folder; and the *view* folder has visual components as shown in Figures 1-1 through 1-3. The value objects of the application have been placed in the folder called *vo*. Regardless of what framework you are going to use, separating various application components in project subfolders helps make the project more organized.

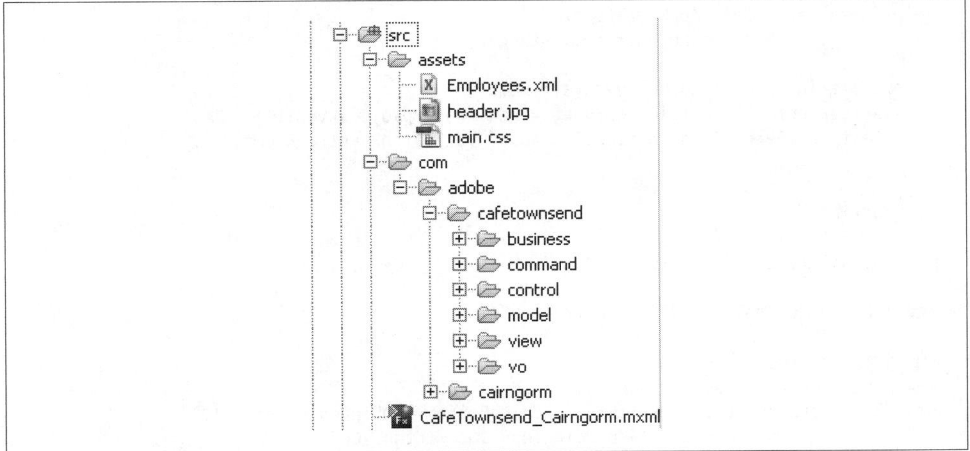

Figure 1-5. Café Townsend Cairngorm project structure

To make Cairngorm classes available to your application, just download Cairngorm's compiled version (binary) and add *cairngorm.swc* to the Library path of your Flex project (use the Flex Build Path menu under your project's properties).

Let's get familiar with the Cairngorm workflow by tracing the data and events starting from the main application object of Café Townsend, shown in Example 1-2. Please note the use of four global objects: AppModelLocator, Services, AppController, and CairngormEventDispatcher.

Example 1-2. The application file of Café Townsend

```
<?xml version="1.0" encoding="utf-8" standalone="no"?>
<!--
  Cafe Townsend MVC Tutorial © 2006 Adobe
  Converted to Cairngorm 2 by Darren Houle
   lokka_@hotmail.com   http://www.digimmersion.com
  This is released under a Creative Commons license.
  http://creativecommons.org/licenses/by/2.5/
-->
<mx:Application xmlns:mx="http://www.adobe.com/2006/mxml"
xmlns:business="com.adobe.cafetownsend.business.*"
   xmlns:control="com.adobe.cafetownsend.control.*"
  xmlns:view="com.adobe.cafetownsend.view.*" backgroundColor="#000000"
  creationComplete="loadEmployees();" layout="vertical
   viewSourceURL="srcview/index.html">

   <mx:Script>
      <![CDATA[
      import com.adobe.cairngorm.control.CairngormEventDispatcher;
      import com.adobe.cafetownsend.control.LoadEmployeesEvent;
      import com.adobe.cafetownsend.model.AppModelLocator;

      [Bindable]
      private var model: AppModelLocator =
                  AppModelLocator.getInstance();

      private function loadEmployees() : void {
       var cgEvent : LoadEmployeesEvent = new LoadEmployeesEvent();
        CairngormEventDispatcher.getInstance().dispatchEvent(cgEvent);
      }
      ]]>
   </mx:Script>

   <business:Services id="services"/>

   <control:AppController id="appController"/>

   <mx:Style source="assets/main.css"/>
   <mx:Image source="assets/header.jpg" width="700"/>
   <mx:HBox backgroundColor="#ffffff" paddingBottom="10" paddingLeft="10"
              paddingRight="10" paddingTop="10" width="700">
   <mx:VBox paddingRight="10" verticalScrollPolicy="off" width="100%">
    <mx:ViewStack paddingBottom="10" paddingTop="10" resizeToContent="true"
               selectedIndex="{model.viewing}" width="100%">
      <view:EmployeeLogin/>
      <view:EmployeeList/>
      <view:EmployeeDetail/>
    </mx:ViewStack>
   </mx:VBox>
  </mx:HBox>
</mx:Application>
```

In the example code, CairngormEventDispatcher dispatches the cgEvent:

```
CairngormEventDispatcher.getInstance().dispatchEvent(cgEvent);
```

Cairngorm's front controller (AppController) creates an instance of a command class that was registered to process this event (see Example 1-4 later).

To eliminate the need to import CairngormEventDispatcher in every view, starting from Cairngorm 2.2 you can call the dispatch() method on the event itself, which uses CairngormEventDispatcher internally, that is:

```
cgEvent.dispatch();
```

The three views of the Café Townsend application object are implemented as components located in the ViewStack container.

On the application startup, the code dispatches LoadEmployeesEvent and, as if by magic, the EmployeeList gets populated from *Employees.xml*. How did it happen? LoadEmployeesEvent is a subclass of CairngormEvent (Example 1-3).

Example 1-3. The class LoadEmployeesEvent

```
package com.adobe.cafetownsend.control {

   import com.adobe.cairngorm.control.CairngormEvent;
   import com.adobe.cafetownsend.control.AppController;

   public class LoadEmployeesEvent extends CairngormEvent {

      public function LoadEmployeesEvent() {
         super( AppController.LOAD_EMPLOYEES_EVENT );
         }
      }
}
```

This class creates an event with an ID AppController.LOAD_EMPLOYEES_EVENT, which among other events has been registered and mapped to the command LoadEmployeesCommand in the global AppController implementation shown in Example 1-4.

Example 1-4. The AppController implementation

```
package com.adobe.cafetownsend.control {

   import com.adobe.cairngorm.control.FrontController;
   import com.adobe.cafetownsend.command.*;

   public class AppController extends FrontController {

      public static const LOAD_EMPLOYEES_EVENT : String =
         "LOAD_EMPLOYEES_EVENT";
      public static const LOGIN_EMPLOYEE_EVENT : String =
         "LOGIN_EMPLOYEE_EVENT";
      public static const ADD_NEW_EMPLOYEE_EVENT : String =
        "ADD_NEW_EMPLOYEE_EVENT";
      public static const UPDATE_EMPLOYEE_EVENT : String =
```

```
        "UPDATE_EMPLOYEE_EVENT";
      public static const LOGOUT_EVENT : String =
        "LOGOUT_EVENT";
      public static const CANCEL_EMPLOYEE_EDITS_EVENT : String =
        "CANCEL_EMPLOYEE_EDITS_EVENT";
      public static const DELETE_EMPLOYEE_EVENT : String =
        "DELETE_EMPLOYEE_EVENT";
      public static const SAVE_EMPLOYEE_EDITS_EVENT : String =
        "SAVE_EMPLOYEE_EDITS_EVENT";

  public function AppController() {
   addCommand( AppController.LOAD_EMPLOYEES_EVENT, LoadEmployeesCommand );
   addCommand( AppController.LOGIN_EMPLOYEE_EVENT, LoginEmployeeCommand );
   addCommand( AppController.ADD_NEW_EMPLOYEE_EVENT, AddNewEmployeeCommand );
   addCommand( AppController.UPDATE_EMPLOYEE_EVENT, UpdateEmployeeCommand );
   addCommand( AppController.LOGOUT_EVENT, LogoutCommand );
   addCommand( AppController.CANCEL_EMPLOYEE_EDITS_EVENT,
                        CancelEmployeeEditsCommand );
   addCommand( AppController.DELETE_EMPLOYEE_EVENT, DeleteEmployeeCommand );
   addCommand( AppController.SAVE_EMPLOYEE_EDITS_EVENT,
                       SaveEmployeeEditsCommand );
  }
  }
}
```

The next point of interest is the class `LoadEmployeesCommand`. This command class implements the `Command` implementation (Example 1-5), which forces you to implement the method `execute()`, which can invoke the right delegate class that has the knowledge of "who to talk to" when a specific command has been received. The method `execute()` must have an argument—the instance of the `CairngormEvent` object that may or may not encapsulate some application data (for example, some value object that is not used in our scenario).

It also implements the interface `IResponder`, which requires you to add the `result()` and `fault()` methods. By using these callbacks the delegate will return to the command class the result (or error information) of the execution of the command in question.

Example 1-5. The Command implementation

```
package com.adobe.cafetownsend.command {

   import mx.rpc.IResponder;
   import com.adobe.cairngorm.commands.Command;
   import com.adobe.cairngorm.control.CairngormEvent;
   import com.adobe.cafetownsend.business.LoadEmployeesDelegate;
   import com.adobe.cafetownsend.model.AppModelLocator;

 public class LoadEmployeesCommand implements Command, IResponder {

   private var model : AppModelLocator = AppModelLocator.getInstance();

   public function execute( cgEvent:CairngormEvent ) : void {
```

```
    // create a worker who will go get some data
    // pass it a reference to this command so the delegate
    // knows where to return the data
     var delegate : LoadEmployeesDelegate = new LoadEmployeesDelegate(this);

    // make the delegate do some work
    delegate.loadEmployeesService();
    }

    // this is called when the delegate receives a result from the service
    public function result( rpcEvent : Object ) : void {
    // populate the employee list in the model locator with
    // the results from the service call
     model.employeeListDP = rpcEvent.result.employees.employee;
    }

    // this is called when the delegate receives a fault from the service
    public function fault( rpcEvent : Object ) : void {
    // store an error message in the model locator
    // labels, alerts, etc. can bind to this to notify the user of errors
     model.errorStatus = "Fault occured in LoadEmployeesCommand.";
    }
  }
}
```

Because this version of the Café Townsend application uses the `HTTPService` request for retrieval, Flex automatically converts *Employees.xml* into `ArrayCollection` and does not use the value object *Employee.as*. This leads to the need for additional coding to convert the data to appropriate types. For example, employee `startDate` will be stored as a string and will require code to convert it to `Date` if any date manipulations will be needed.

If you'll be using Cairngorm in your projects, consider simplifying the application design by eliminating the delegate classes. Just move the business logic from the delegate right into the `execute()` method of the command class itself.

Create a common ancestor to all your commands and define the fault method there to avoid repeating the same code in each command class.

To load the employees, the `Command` class creates an instance of the proper delegate passing the reference to itself (this is how the delegate knows where to return the data) and calls the method `loadEmployeesService()`:

```
var delegate : LoadEmployeesDelegate = new LoadEmployeesDelegate(this);
delegate.loadEmployeesService();
```

Have you noticed that the `Command` class has also reached for the `AppModelLocator` to be able to update the model?

```
private var model : AppModelLocator = AppModelLocator.getInstance();
...
model.employeeListDP = rpcEvent.result.employees.employee;
...
 model.errorStatus = "Fault occured in LoadEmployeesCommand.";
```

Now, let's take a peek into the `Delegate` class from Example 1-6. It gets a hold of the global `ServiceLocator` class, the only player who knows about who's hiding behind the mysterious name `loadEmployeesService`. The method `loadEmployeesService()` sends the request to the execution and assigns the responder (the instance of `LoadEmployeesCommand`), engaging the `AsyncToken` design pattern described in Chapter 2.

Example 1-6. The Delegate implementation

```
package com.adobe.cafetownsend.business {

   import mx.rpc.AsyncToken;
   import mx.rpc.IResponder;
   import com.adobe.cairngorm.business.ServiceLocator;

 public class LoadEmployeesDelegate {

       private var command : IResponder;
   private var service : Object;

   public function LoadEmployeesDelegate( command : IResponder ) {
    //constructor will store a reference to the service we're going to call
    this.service = ServiceLocator.getInstance().getHTTPService(
                         'loadEmployeesService' );
    // and store a reference to the command that created this delegate
    this.command = command;
   }

   public function loadEmployeesService() : void {
    // call the service
    var token:AsyncToken = service.send();
    // notify this command when the service call completes
    token.addResponder( command );
   }
 }
}
```

As mentioned previously, each Cairngorm application has a central registry that knows about each and every service that may be used by the application (Example 1-7).

Example 1-7. The Services implementation

```
<?xml version="1.0" encoding="utf-8"?>
<cairngorm:ServiceLocator
   xmlns:mx="http://www.adobe.com/2006/mxml"
   xmlns:cairngorm="com.adobe.cairngorm.business.*">

   <mx:HTTPService id="loadEmployeesService" url="assets/Employees.xml" />

</cairngorm:ServiceLocator>
```

In our case it's just one `HTTPService`, but in a real-world scenario, the *Services.mxml* file may list dozens of services. As every service must have a unique ID (in our case, it's `loadEmployeesService`), the delegate class was able to find it by using the following line:

```
this.service = ServiceLocator.getInstance().getHTTPService(
                                'loadEmployeesService' );
```

If you'd need to call a service implemented as RemoteObject, the delegate would be calling the method getRemoteObject() instead of getHTTPService(). For web services, call the method getWebService().

Those who work with Data Management Services can use Cairngorm's EnterpriseServiceLocator and its method getDataService().

ServiceLocator can be used not only as a repository of all services, but also as an authorization mechanism that restricts access to certain application services based on specified credentials. See its methods setCredentials() and setRemoteCredentials() for details.

The final portion of the loading employees process goes as follows:

1. The loadEmployeesService class reads *Employees.xml*
2. The delegate gets the result and passes it to the result() method of the Command class (see Example 1-5)
3. The Command class updates the model.employeeListDP via ModelLocator
4. The List component on the View gets automatically updated, because it's bound to model.employeeListDP (see Example 1-8)

Example 1-8. The View: EmployeesList.mxml

```
<?xml version="1.0" encoding="utf-8"?>
<mx:VBox xmlns:mx="http://www.adobe.com/2006/mxml" xmlns="*" width="100%"
   horizontalAlign="center">

   <mx:Script>
      <![CDATA[
   import com.adobe.cairngorm.control.CairngormEventDispatcher;
   import com.adobe.cafetownsend.control.AddNewEmployeeEvent;
   import com.adobe.cafetownsend.control.UpdateEmployeeEvent;
   import com.adobe.cafetownsend.control.LogoutEvent;
   import com.adobe.cafetownsend.model.AppModelLocator;

   [Bindable]
   private var model : AppModelLocator = AppModelLocator.getInstance();

   // mutate the add new employee button's click event
   public function addNewEmployee() : void {
      // broadcast a cairngorm event
      var cgEvent : AddNewEmployeeEvent = new AddNewEmployeeEvent();
      CairngormEventDispatcher.getInstance().dispatchEvent( cgEvent );

       //de-select the list item
       clearSelectedEmployee();
   }

   // mutate the List's change event
   public function updateEmployee() : void {
```

```
    //broadcast a cairngorm event that contains selectedItem from the List
    var cgEvent : UpdateEmployeeEvent = new UpdateEmployeeEvent(
                                    employees_li.selectedItem );
    CairngormEventDispatcher.getInstance().dispatchEvent( cgEvent );

    // de-select the list item
    clearSelectedEmployee();
  }

  // mutate the logout button's click event
  private function logout() : void {
    // broadcast a cairngorm event
    var cgEvent : LogoutEvent = new LogoutEvent();
    CairngormEventDispatcher.getInstance().dispatchEvent( cgEvent );
  }

  // format the names that are displayed in the List
  public function properName( dpItem : Object ) : String {
    return dpItem.lastname + ", " + dpItem.firstname;
  }

  // de-select any selected List items
 private function clearSelectedEmployee() : void {
     employees_li.selectedIndex = -1;
  }
     ]]>
  </mx:Script>

  <mx:Panel title="Employee List" horizontalCenter="0">
     <mx:HBox paddingTop="25">
     <mx:Button label="Add New Employee" click="addNewEmployee()" />
     <mx:Spacer width="100%" />
     <mx:Button label="Logout" click="logout()" />
     <mx:Spacer width="100%" height="20" />
     </mx:HBox>
     <!-- data provider for the list is an ArrayCollection stored in
     the centralized model locator -->
     <mx:List id="employees_li" dataProvider="{ model.employeeListDP }"
     labelFunction="properName" change="updateEmployee()" width="100%"
     verticalScrollPolicy="auto"/>
  </mx:Panel>
</mx:VBox>
```

We're almost there, but let's not forget about the `ModelLocator`, the storage of your application's data. At the time of this writing, the code of the Café Townsend application published at *http://cairngormdocs.org* still implements the `ModelLocator` interface, but recently has been renamed `IModelLocator`.

In Example 1-9 the class `AppModelLocator` implements `IModelLocator`.

Example 1-9. The ModelLocator of Café Townsend Cairngorm

```
package com.adobe.cafetownsend.model {

  import mx.collections.ArrayCollection;
```

```
import com.adobe.cairngorm.model.ModelLocator;
import com.adobe.cafetownsend.vo.Employee;
import com.adobe.cafetownsend.vo.User;

 [Bindable]
public class AppModelLocator implements ModelLocator {

   // this instance stores a static reference to itself
   private static var model : AppModelLocator;

   // available values for the main viewstack
   // defined as constants to help uncover errors at compile time
   public static const EMPLOYEE_LOGIN : Number =   0;
   public static const EMPLOYEE_LIST : Number =   1;
   public static const EMPLOYEE_DETAIL : Number =   2;
   // viewstack starts out on the login screen
   public var viewing : Number = EMPLOYEE_LOGIN;

   // user object contains uid/passwd
   // its value gets set at login and cleared at logout but nothing
   // binds to it or uses it retained since it was used in the
   // original Adobe CafeTownsend example app
   public var user : User;

   // variable to store error messages from the httpservice
   // nothing currently binds to it, but an Alert or the login box
   // could to show startup errors
   public var errorStatus : String;

   // contains the main employee list, which is populated on startup
   // mx:application's creationComplete event is mutated into a
   // cairngorm event that calls the httpservice for the data
   public var employeeListDP : ArrayCollection;

   // temp holding space for employees we're creating or editing
   // this gets copied into or added onto the main employee list
   public var employeeTemp : Employee;

   // singleton: constructor only allows one model locator
   public function AppLocator(){
   if ( AppModelLocator.model != null )
      throw new Error(
      "Only one ModelLocator instance should be instantiated" );
   }

   // singleton always returns the only existing instance to itself
   public static function getInstance() : AppModelLocator {
      if ( model == null )
         model = new AppModelLocator();
      return model;
      }
   }
}
```

This model locator stores the data and the state of this application—in particular, the variable `employeeListDP`, which is the place where the list of employees is being stored.

Please note that as ActionScript 3 does not support private constructors, the public constructor of this class throws an error if someone tries to improperly instantiate it (i.e., using the `new` command) but the instance of this object already exists.

We went through the entire process of displaying the initial list of employees, but just to ensure that the Cairngorm data flow is clear, we'll include a brief explanation of yet another use case from Café Townsend.

The user presses the Add New Employee button (see Figure 1-2), enters the detail info for a new employee on the View component shown in Figure 1-3, and presses the Submit button. This is what's happening between this button click and the moment when the new employee appears in the employee list:

If you want to follow along, please download the source code of Café Townsend and start from *EmployeeDetail.mxml* on the following line:

```
<mx:Button label="Submit" click="saveEmployeeEdits()"
id="submit" />
```

1. The `SaveEmployeeEditsEvent` event is dispatched:

   ```
   var cgEvent : SaveEmployeeEditsEvent = new
         SaveEmployeeEditsEvent(model.employeeTemp.emp_id, firstname.text,
               lastname.text,startdate.selectedDate, email.text );

   CairngormEventDispatcher.getInstance().dispatchEvent( cgEvent );
   ```

   For some reason, the author of this code decided not to use `EmployeeVO` here and stores each `Employee` attribute separately in `SaveEmployeeEvent`. This is not the best way of encapsulating data inside a custom event, but let's keep the original code intact.

2. The `FrontController` receives this event and passes it to the registered command `SaveEmployeeEditsCommand` (see Example 1-4 earlier) for execution.

3. The `execute()` method of `SaveEmployeeEditsCommand` does not use any delegates, as it just needs to add a newly inserted `Employee` to the model. Because this application does not save modified data anywhere other than in memory, no other service calls are made to pass the changed data to the server side for persistence.

4. The View portion of the employee list gets updated automatically as a result of data binding.

While planning for your application with Cairngorm, think of all events, services, value objects, and business services and then create appropriate classes similarly to the way it was done in the Café Townsend example.

To Use or Not to Use Cairngorm?

Online, you may encounter lots of debate regarding whether Cairngorm should be used in Flex projects. With all due respect to the creators of Cairngorm, we don't believe that Cairngorm makes a Flex team more productive and that most enterprise projects would not benefit from it. We prefer working with frameworks that offer enhanced Flex components rather than just separation of work among team members. If you have to develop a project without experienced Flex developers on your team, however, Cairngorm can give your project a structure that will prevent it from failing.

So, is Cairngorm right for your project? Read Chapters 2, 3 and 6, and then decide whether you prefer working with the components described there or one of the architectural MVC frameworks. Meanwhile, keep these observations about Cairngorm in mind:

- Cairngorm's architecture is based on components dispatching events to a global event handler without knowing what the latter will do with them. The problem with this approach is in the global nature of such an event handler. The `FrontController` object serves as a central registry of all Cairngorm events. Although keeping all application events in one place simplifies their maintenance, it leads to tighter coupling of the application components.
- Using a centralized `ModelLocator` also makes multiple components dependent on the knowledge of the properties of the model. If your project will start growing, the `ModelLocator` may not scale well.
- Modularizing Flex applications is one of the major ways of minimizing the size of the downloadable Shockwave Flash (SWF) files. The other benefit is reusability of the modules. Now imagine a midsize web application that consists of 10 modules. If this application has been built using Cairngorm, each of these modules becomes dependent on the central `FrontController` located in the main *.swf* file.
- Application developers have to write lots of boilerplate code. For example, you have to create additional event and command classes for every event that can be dispatched in your application. Even in a midsize application this can translate to a hundred or more additional Cairngorm-specific classes. To minimize the amount of manually written code, consider using Cairngen, an open source code generator for Cairngorm. It's available at *http://code.google.com/p/cairngen/*.
- `FrontController` allows you to map only one command per event, yet your application may need to have several event listeners per command.
- Even though data binding can help in writing less code, because Cairngorm enforces data binding as the only mechanism of updating the views, it makes them nonreusable. For example, you can't just simply reuse the *EmployeeList.mxml* from Example 1-8 in another application, because it has an intimate knowledge of the internals of the model and relies on the fact that the model has a public variable

`employeeListDP`. Just simply renaming this variable in the `ModelLocator` will require changes in one or more views that are bound to it.

- Having no other choice but data binding for updating the UI may cause performance problems. The global `ModelLocator` object defines multiple bindable variables representing different models, and the Flex compiler may generate additional `EventDispatcher` objects on the class level (this depends on the types of the variables). Suppose you have 10 `[Bindable] String` variables in the `ModelLocator`. If one of them will get updated, not only will its listener get notified to update the view, but the other 9 will get this event, too.
- The fact that Cairngorm is built around a Command pattern with a centrally located command repository can be very convenient for some projects that require audit or undo functionality. Every command arrives at the same place, and you can conditionally hook up, say, an undo module that remembers old/new states of some data or logs every user request (this can be a must in some financial trading applications).
- Cairngorm has been around longer than any other Flex framework. As of today, it's the most popular framework, and many Flex developers around the world already know it, which may be an important factor for development managers who put together large project teams, especially when the teams consist of a large number of junior Flex developers.

Report Card: Cairngorm

Cairngorm separates business- and UI-related work into different layers, which means that the work of the project team can be split between developers responsible for the visual portion and those who are coding just the business logic of the application. The fact that all services are located in a central place allows us to quickly reconfigure the data sources, i.e., switch to quality assurance (QA) or production servers.

Development managers who have to work with distributed teams of beginner or mid-level Flex developers and need a safety net to split the project work into smaller controllable tasks (e.g., John works on the server side and Srinivas works only on the views) may consider using Cairngorm. Here's the report card followed by more detailed explanations.

The pros are:

- It's a popular framework—many Flex developers know it.
- It allows separate responsibilities of developers.
- It lowers the requirements for developers' skillsets.

The cons are:

- It requires developers to write lots of additional classes, which adds to project timeline.

- It's built on global singletons, which complicates modularization.
- It allows only one-to-one mapping between events and commands.
- The framework design is based on singletons, which leads to tight object coupling.

Mate

Mate is an event- and tag-based Flex framework. The API is in MXML tags. Mate-based applications are built using implicit invocation caused by dispatching and dependency injection of the results into views.

With implicit invocation, any interested object can listen to the events that are listed (with their handlers) in one or more MXML components of type `<EventMap>`. Any important action in the application should generate one of the events listed in this map. In Mate, as opposed to Cairngorm, an application developer can configure multiple handlers for each event and specify the sequence in which they should be invoked by assigning priorities in the event handler.

This section walks you through the Mate framework by analyzing its version of Café Townsend, created by the Mate team, which we encourage you to download from *http://mate.asfusion.com/page/examples/cafe-townsend*.

The data flow between Mate components while displaying a list of Café employees is depicted in Figure 1-6.

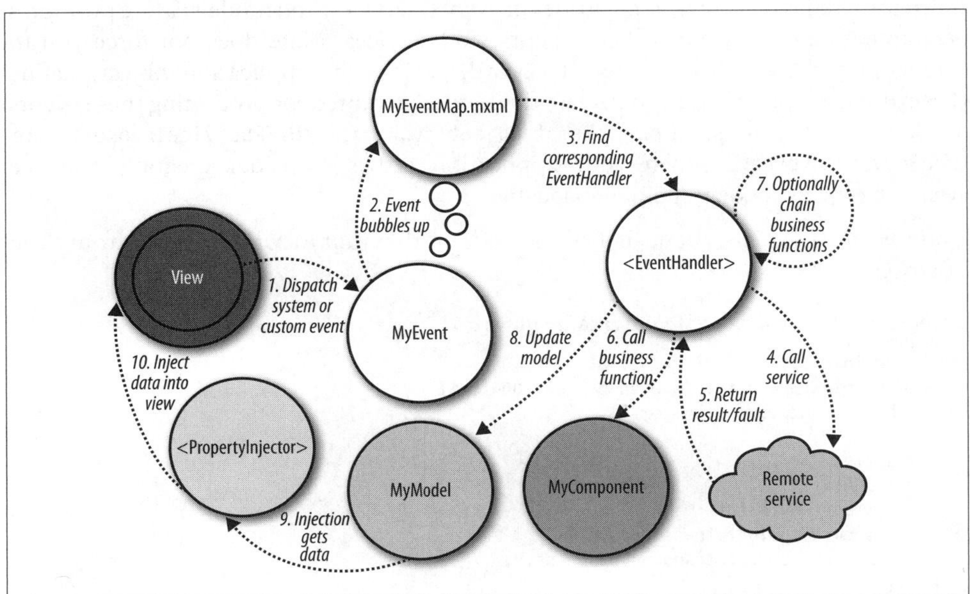

Figure 1-6. Bringing a list of employees with Mate

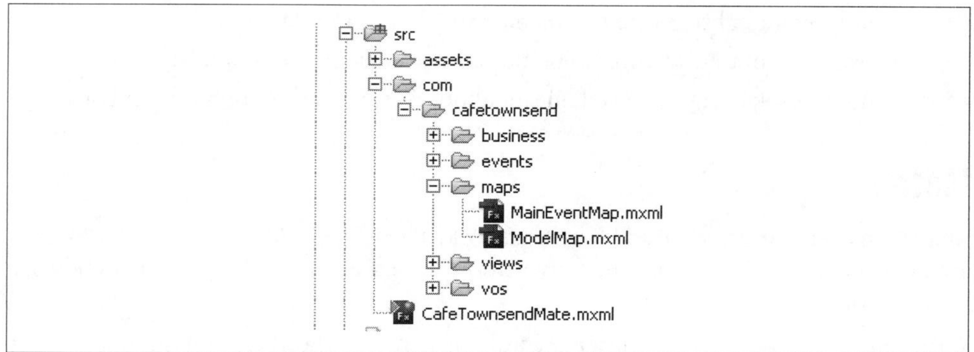

Figure 1-7. Café Townsend Mate project structure

Mate is a much less intrusive framework than Cairngorm, as it does not force developers to add lots of boilerplate code in their applications. Figure 1-7 shows the project structure of the Café. The folder *maps* contains objects added to the Café project because it's written using Mate (at least one event map is required). These objects are included in the main application as follows:

```
<maps:MainEventMap />
<maps:ModelMap />
```

All events that bubble up in Café will reach these map objects, which will process them according to the event handlers defined in these event maps.

Cairngorm relies on central repositories of events, services, and models; Mate promotes decoupling among business logic, events, and services. Mate does not force you to extend any classes. Just create an `<EventMap>` in your application object, define `<EventHandler>` tags there, and declare the services required for processing these events inside the handlers, i.e., `<RemoteObjectInvoker>`, `<HTTPServiceInvoker>`, or `<WebServiceInvoker>`. When your application grows, consider creating multiple `EventMap` objects to keep them manageable.

Example 1-10 depicts about half of the code of the *MainEventMap.mxml* from Café Townsend.

Example 1-10. Fragment of MainEventMap.mxml

```
<?xml version="1.0" encoding="utf-8"?>
<EventMap xmlns:mx="http://www.adobe.com/2006/mxml"
xmlns="http://mate.asfusion.com/">

   <mx:Script>
      <![CDATA[
         import mx.events.*;
         import com.cafetownsend.events.*;
         import com.cafetownsend.business.*;
      ]]>
   </mx:Script>
```

```
    <!-- FlexEvent.PREINITIALIZE -->

    <EventHandlers type="{FlexEvent.PREINITIALIZE}">
       <ObjectBuilder generator="{AuthorizationManager}"
              constructorArguments="{scope.dispatcher}" />
    </EventHandlers>

    <!-- FlexEvent.APPLICATION_COMPLETE -->

    <EventHandlers type="{FlexEvent.APPLICATION_COMPLETE}">

       <HTTPServiceInvoker instance="{employeesService}">
          <resultHandlers>
             <MethodInvoker generator="{EmployeeParser}"
                method="loadEmployeesFromXML"
                    arguments="{resultObject}" />

             <MethodInvoker generator="{EmployeeManager}"
             method="saveEmpoyeeList" arguments="{lastReturn}" />
          </resultHandlers>
       </HTTPServiceInvoker>

    </EventHandlers>

    <!-- LoginEvent.LOGIN -->

    <EventHandlers type="{LoginEvent.LOGIN}">
       <MethodInvoker generator="{AuthorizationManager}" method="login"
               arguments="{[event.username, event.password]}" />

 <!-- Because there is no server request, we just send the response right away.
    Normally, we would do this inside the resultSequence -->
       <ResponseAnnouncer type="loginResultResponse">
          <Properties loginResult="{lastReturn}"/>
       </ResponseAnnouncer>
    </EventHandlers>

    <!-- EmployeeEvent.SAVE -->

    <EventHandlers type="{EmployeeEvent.SAVE}">
       <MethodInvoker generator="{EmployeeManager}"
             method="saveEmployee" arguments="{event.employee}"/>
       <!-- assume everything was ok, make employee list show up -->
       <EventAnnouncer generator="{NavigationEvent}"
                 type="{NavigationEvent.EMPLOYEE_LIST}"/>
    </EventHandlers>

...
    <mx:HTTPService id="employeesService" url="assets/data/Employees.xml"
                         resultFormat="e4x" />
</EventMap>
```

In the example code, note the declaration of the handler of the system Flex event `APPLICATION_COMPLETE` with nested `HttpServiceInvoker` to get the data from *Employees.xml* via `employeesService`, which is defined at the very end of this map using the familiar <mx:HTTPService> tag. EventHandler objects match the type of the received event with the one specified in the type attribute in the map file.

When your application receives the result of the call to employeesService, it invokes the functions defined in the resultHandlers nested inside the service invoker. In our case, two methods listed in the result handler section are called sequentially: EmployeeParser.loadEmployeesForXML() and EmployeeManager.saveEmployeeList():

```
<resultHandlers>
      <MethodInvoker generator="{EmployeeParser}"
         method="loadEmployeesFromXML"
             arguments="{resultObject}" />

      <MethodInvoker generator="{EmployeeManager}"
            method="saveEmpoyeeList" arguments="{lastReturn}" />
  </resultHandlers>
```

The first method, loadEmployeeList(), gets the resultObject returned by the HTTPService. The second one, saveEmployeeList(), gets the value returned by the first method via a predefined Mate variable called lastReturn. This way you can chain several method calls if needed.

Example 1-11 shows that the method loadEmployees() converts XML into an ActionScript Array object and returns it to Mate, which, according to the event map, forwards it to the method saveEmployeeList() for further processing (see Example 1-12). The name saveEmployeeList() is a bit misleading, because this method does not persist data, but rather stores it in memory in an ArrayCollection object.

Example 1-11. EmployeeParser.as

```
package com.cafetownsend.business{
   import com.cafetownsend.vos.Employee;

   public class EmployeeParser {
    public function loadEmployeesFromXML(employees:XML):Array {
      var employeeList:Array = new Array();

      for each( var thisEmployee:XML in employees..employee ){
         var employee:Employee = new Employee();
         employee.email = thisEmployee.email;
         employee.emp_id = thisEmployee.emp_id;
         employee.firstname = thisEmployee.firstname;
         employee.lastname = thisEmployee.lastname;
         employee.startdate = new
         Date(Date.parse(thisEmployee.startdate));
         employeeList.push(employee);
      }
      return employeeList;
    }
  }
}
```

The EmployeeManager plays the role of the model here—it stores employees in the collection employeeList and information about the selected/new employee in the variable employee.

Example 1-12. The model: EmployeeManager.as

```
package com.cafetownsend.business{
   import com.cafetownsend.vos.Employee;
   import flash.events.Event;
   import flash.events.EventDispatcher;
   import mx.collections.ArrayCollection;

   public class EmployeeManager extends EventDispatcher {

   private var _employeeList:ArrayCollection;
   private var _employee:Employee;

   [Bindable (event="employeeListChanged")]
   public function get employeeList():ArrayCollection{
      return _employeeList;
   }

   [Bindable (event="employeeChanged")]
   public function get employee():Employee{
      return _employee;
   }

   public function saveEmpoyeeList(employees:Array):void {
      _employeeList = new ArrayCollection(employees);
      dispatchEvent(new Event('employeeListChanged'));
   }

   public function selectEmployee(employee:Employee):void {
      _employee = employee;
      dispatchEvent(new Event('employeeChanged'));
   }

   public function deleteEmployee (employee:Employee) : void {
     _employeeList.removeItemAt(_employeeList.getItemIndex(employee));
     selectEmployee(null);
   }

   public function saveEmployee (employee:Employee) : void {
     var dpIndex : int = -1;

    for ( var i : uint = 0; i < employeeList.length; i++ ) {
    // does the the incoming emp_id exist in the list
      if ( employeeList[i].emp_id == employee.emp_id ) {
      // set our ArrayCollection index to that employee position
         dpIndex = i;
      }
    }

   if ( dpIndex >= 0 ) {
      // update the existing employee
```

```
        (employeeList.getItemAt(dpIndex) as Employee).copyFrom(employee);
     } else {
        // add the employee to the ArrayCollection
        var tempEmployee:Employee = new Employee();
        tempEmployee.copyFrom(employee);
        employeeList.addItem(tempEmployee);
     }
     // clear out the selected employee
     selectEmployee(null);
    }
  }
}
```

So far, so good. The array of employees will be passed to the `saveEmployeeList()` function and placed for storage in the `employeeList` collection. But where's the link between the Model and the View?

EmployeeList.mxml, located in the package view, has the fragment shown in Example 1-13.

Example 1-13. Fragment from the View: EmployeeList.mxml

```
 [Bindable]
public var employees:ArrayCollection = null;
...
<mx:List id="employees_li" dataProvider="{employees}"
labelFunction="properName" change="updateEmployee()" width="100%" />
```

And now let's take a peek at the content of the second mapping object, called *ModelMap.mxml*, shown in Example 1-14. It uses Mate's `PropertyInjector` object, which "injects" the value into the variable `EmployeeList.employee` from `EmployeeManager.employeeList` (there is one more `PropertyInjector`, which is irrelevant for our discussion).

Example 1-14. ModelMap.mxml

```
<?xml version="1.0" encoding="utf-8"?>
<EventMap xmlns:mx="http://www.adobe.com/2006/mxml" xmlns="http://mate.asfusion.com/">
 <mx:Script>
   <![CDATA[
   import com.cafetownsend.business.*;
   import com.cafetownsend.views.*;
   ]]>
</mx:Script>

 <Injectors target="{EmployeeDetail}" >
   <PropertyInjector targetKey="selectedEmployee"
      source="{EmployeeManager}" sourceKey="employee" />
 </Injectors>

 <Injectors target="{EmployeeList}">
   <PropertyInjector targetKey="employees"
      source="{EmployeeManager}" sourceKey="employeeList" />
```

```
  </Injectors>
</EventMap>
```

If you sense a *Dependency Injection design pattern*, you're right.

This pattern really helps you create loosely coupled components. Let's revisit the code fragment of the view shown in Example 1-13. It's written "assuming" that some outsider object will populate the variable employees. This code does not reach out for another specific component, demanding, "Give me the data!" It waits until someone injects the data.

And this someone is declared in *ModelMap.mxml* as follows:

```
<PropertyInjector targetKey="employees"
    source="{EmployeeManager}" sourceKey="employeeList" />
```

At this point, software developers familiar with Java Spring framework should feel at home. It's the same concept. Objects never reach out for other object's data—the plumbing is done in third-party declarative components (XML in Spring and MXML in Mate). The benefits are obvious: components don't depend on one another. Just write the mapping file like *ModelMap.mxml* and specify the source and target for the data.

Another benefit is simplified testing—if the real data feed is not ready, create a mock model object and use it in the `PropertyInjector` tag. Switching to a real data model is just a matter of changing a couple of properties in this injector.

Creators of the Mate version of the Café Townsend application have decided to use `EmployeeParser` and `EmployeeManager` objects, but the Mate framework does not force you to separate parsing or any other business logic from the model. In this case, the parser could have injected the data directly to the View without even performing this loop converting XML into an array.

In the case of Cairngorm, a view that needs some data would reach out for the model by making a call like `ModelLocator.getModelLocator().employeeList`, which means that the view is tightly coupled with a `ModelLocator` object.

In the case of Mate injectors, the view waits to receive `employeeList` without making any remote procedure calls (RPCs).

Report Card: Mate

Mate is a nonintrusive MXML framework that offers flexible separation of the application views and processing logic. The application developers are not forced to do all of their plumbing exclusively via Mate and are free to use standard Flex event processing along with the `EventMap` object offered by Mate. Because it is tag-based, Flex developers will find it easy to program with. The learning curves of Mate and Cairngorm are comparable. Here's the report card.

The pros are:

- Mate is nonintrusive—Mate-specific code can be encapsulated in a handful of objects.
- It's MXML-based and allows you to keep using the Flex event model.
- It promotes loose coupling between components by implementing dependency injection.
- It's well documented.

The cons are:

- It hasn't been officially released yet.
- It doesn't support working with Data Management Services offered by LCDS, and because of this you'd need to code this part manually.

As opposed to Cairngorm, using Mate in your application does not require developers to create many additional classes or components just to support the life cycle of the framework itself. This explains why the Mate version of the released Café Townsend SWF is about 10 percent smaller.

Mate promotes loose coupling between components by implementing a Dependency Injection design pattern. But loose coupling comes at a price—all communications in Mate are done via events, which have more overhead compared to direct function calls. Events require additional object instances to be created, as you don't just call a function on some component, but have to create an instance of some event and dispatch it to that component. The receiving party has to create additional event listeners, which may become a source of memory leaking.

Function calls do not have these issues and offer additional benefit-type checking of arguments and returned values.

Mate also uses singletons, but they do not have to be instantiated by application developers. Application components are also instantiated by the framework as per MXML tags included in the `EventMap` object, which also performs the role of a class factory with lazy instantiation—if the event that required an instance of `EmployeeManager` was never triggered, the instance is not created. A special `Boolean` attribute cache on `MethodInvoker` and `ObjectBuilder` ensures that the instance will be garbage-collected.

Currently, Mate offers over 30 MXML tags, but this number can be increased by application developers. For example, by subclassing Mate's `AbstractServiceInvoker` class, you can create a new tag that implements a service that's specific to your application and can be invoked from `EventMap`, the same way other services can.

If your application uses Flex modules, Mate documentation suggests that you can place `EventMap` objects in the main application as well as in modules. But as with any framework that uses global objects (`EventMap` in this case), you can run into conflicts between events defined in the module's map and the main application's map. Of course, if modules are created to be used with only one application, you can come up with some naming conventions to ensure that every event has a unique name, but this may cause issues if you'd like to treat modules as functional black boxes that can be reused in multiple applications.

Mate does not offer UI controls; it does not include code generators to automate the development process. It does not support automatic data synchronization between the client and the server (LCDS Data Management Service) and would require manual programming in this area.

Mate is the youngest of all frameworks reviewed in this chapter. But even though (at the time of this writing) Mate hasn't been released yet, it's well documented.

PureMVC

PureMVC is not Flex but rather an ActionScript (AS) framework. PureMVC concentrates on the task of creating a generic framework for low-level AS objects; Flex comes with "prebuilt suggestions" for how a Model-View-Controller might work—and it offers lots of hooks throughout the data and UI classes that help implement MVC. But because Flex, AIR, and Flash understand this language, PureMVC can be used in any applications built in any of these environments.

Similarly to Cairngorm, PureMVC is built on singletons. The `Model`, `View`, `Controller`, and `Facade` classes are singletons. In Cairngorm, developers need to write code to instantiate each singleton; in PureMVC, only the `Facade` class has to be instantiated in the application code and creation of the `Model`, `View`, and `Controller` classes is done by the `Facade` class itself.

In Cairngorm, you create an application-specific `FrontController` and register event-command pairs; in PureMVC, you create a `Facade` class and register notification-command pairs there. With PureMVC, you can execute multiple commands as a reaction to a notification.

Object-oriented programming languages arrange event-driven communication between the objects by implementing the Observer design pattern. An observer object is registered with one or more observable objects that generate notifications to be consumed by the observer.

Cliff Hall, the author of PureMVC, went the same route to ensure that this framework can be used even in non-Flash environments that don't offer `flash.events.Event` and `EventDispatcher` classes.

Views are controlled by their mediator objects, which maintain maps of notifications and their observers.

Notifications are a PureMVC implementation of event-driven communication between application components. The author of PureMVC wanted to make this framework portable to other languages; hence standard Flash events are not used in the framework, even though Flex developers still can use regular events to process, say, button clicks.

Although flash.events.Event is not leveraged by the PureMVC framework, the Notification class has the property called body typed as Object, which is a place for storing application-specific data that may need to be carried by a notification object. In pure ActionScript, you'd have to create a custom event object providing a placeholder for the custom data (on the other hand, in custom ActionScript events, the data can be strongly typed as opposed to being just Objects).

Café Townsend with PureMVC

To better understand this framework, take a walk through the code of Café Townsend that was ported to PureMVC by Michael Ramirez. Please download this application at *http://trac.puremvc.org/Demo_AS3_Flex_CafeTownsend*.

The data flow between PureMVC components while displaying a list of Café employees is depicted in Figure 1-8.

Your goal remains the same: walk the route that would display the list of Café employees. Figure 1-9 shows the structure of this application in Flash Builder.

The code of the *CafeTownsend.mxml* application is shown in Example 1-15. You'll see a familiar ViewStack container that holds employee login, list, and detail views. It declares the variable facade, which holds the reference to the ApplicationFacade singleton that is created during initializing the value of this variable. Then the method startup() is called on this ApplicationFacade object inherited from PureMVC's Facade class.

Example 1-15. CafeTownsend.mxml—the application

```
<?xml version="1.0"?>
<!-- PureMVC AS3 Demo - Flex CafeTownsend
 Copyright (c) 2007-08 Michael Ramirez <michael.ramirez@puremvc.org>
 Parts Copyright (c) 2005-07 Adobe Systems, Inc.
 Your reuse is governed by the Creative Commons Attribution 3.0 License -->

<mx:Application xmlns:mx="http://www.adobe.com/2006/mxml"
   xmlns:view="org.puremvc.as3.demos.flex.cafetownsend.view.components.*"
   xmlns:mvc="org.puremvc.as3.demos.flex.cafetownsend.*"
   layout="vertical" backgroundColor="#000000"
   creationComplete="facade.startup(this)">

   <mx:Script>
      <![CDATA[
      import org.puremvc.as3.demos.flex.cafetownsend.*;
      private var facade:ApplicationFacade =
                 ApplicationFacade.getInstance();
      ]]>
   </mx:Script>

   <mx:Style source="assets/main.css" />
   <mx:Image source="@Embed('assets/header.jpg')" width="700" />
   <mx:HBox paddingBottom="10" paddingLeft="10" paddingRight="10"
```

```
        paddingTop="10" backgroundColor="#ffffff" width="700">
    <mx:VBox width="100%" verticalScrollPolicy="off"
                          paddingRight="10">
      <mx:ViewStack id="vwStack" width="100%" paddingBottom="10"
     paddingTop="10" resizeToContent="true" creationPolicy="all">
         <view:EmployeeLogin id="employeeLogin" />
         <view:EmployeeList id="employeeList" />
         <view:EmployeeDetail id="employeeDetail" />
      </mx:ViewStack>
    </mx:VBox>
  </mx:HBox>
</mx:Application>
```

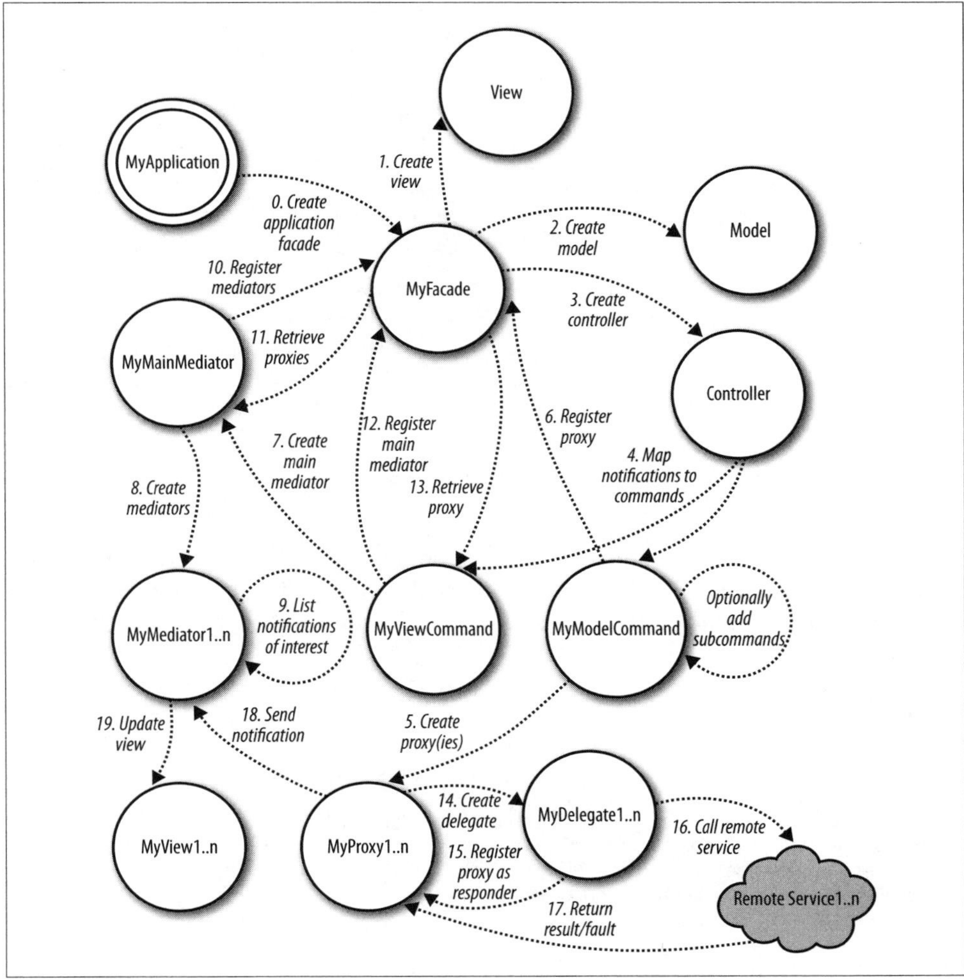

Figure 1-8. Bringing the employee list with PureMVC

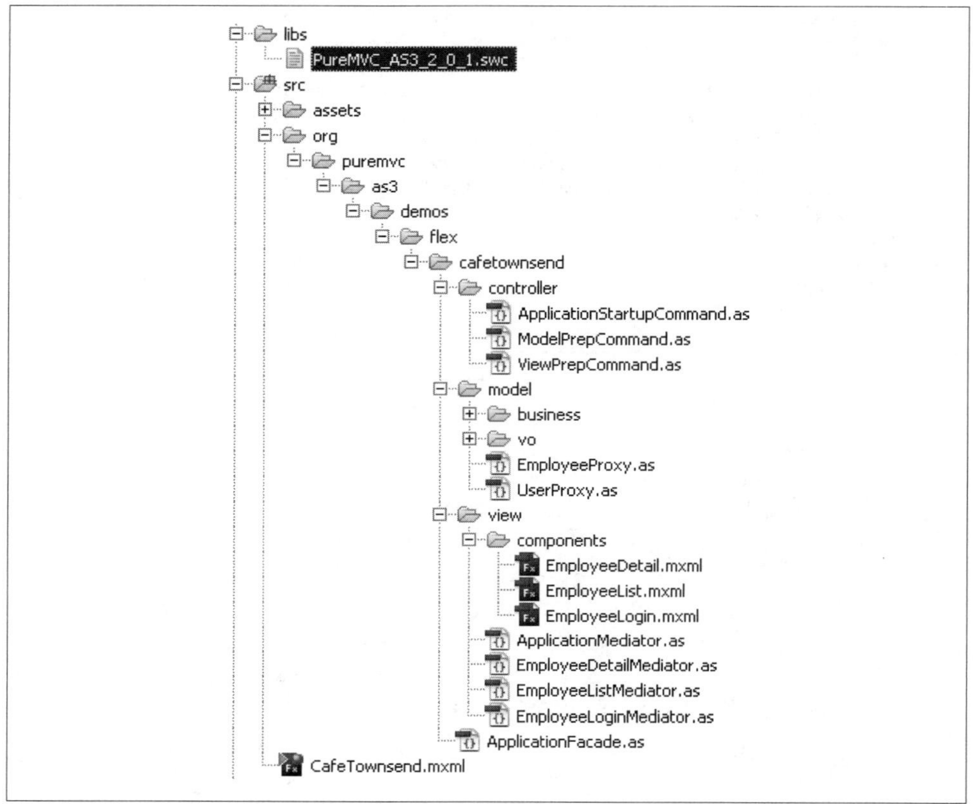

Figure 1-9. Café Townsend with PureMVC—the project structure

During creation of the `Facade` instance (see Example 1-16), PureMVC automatically initializes the instances of `Model`, `View`, and `Controller` classes, and if you need to execute application-specific code during this process, override the appropriate initialize method.

Example 1-16. ApplicationFacade.as

```
/* PureMVC AS3 Demo - Flex CafeTownsend
 Copyright (c) 2007-08 Michael Ramirez <michael.ramirez@puremvc.org>
 Parts Copyright (c) 2005-07 Adobe Systems, Inc.
 Your reuse is governed by the Creative Commons Attribution 3.0 License */
package org.puremvc.as3.demos.flex.cafetownsend{
  import org.puremvc.as3.interfaces.*;
  import org.puremvc.as3.patterns.proxy.*;
  import org.puremvc.as3.patterns.facade.*;

  import org.puremvc.as3.demos.flex.cafetownsend.view.*;
  import org.puremvc.as3.demos.flex.cafetownsend.model.*;
  import org.puremvc.as3.demos.flex.cafetownsend.controller.*;
```

```
/**
 * A concrete <code>Facade</code> for the <code>CafeTownsend</code>
   application.
 * The main job of the <code>ApplicationFacade</code> is to act as a single
 * place for mediators, proxies, and commands to access and communicate
 * with each other without having to interact with the Model, View, and
 * Controller classes directly. All this capability it inherits from
 * the PureMVC Facade class.</P>
 * This concrete Facade subclass is also a central place to define
 * notification constants which will be shared among commands, proxies, and
 * mediators, as well as initializing the controller with Command to
 * Notification mappings.</P>
 */
public class ApplicationFacade extends Facade
{
// Notification name constants
public static const STARTUP:String= "startup";
public static const SHUTDOWN:String= "shutdown";
public static const APP_LOGOUT:String= "appLogout";
public static const APP_LOGIN:String= "appLogin";
public static const LOAD_EMPLOYEES_SUCCESS:String="loadEmployeesSuccess";
public static const LOAD_EMPLOYEES_FAILED:String="loadEmployeesFailed";
public static const VIEW_EMPLOYEE_LOGIN:String= "viewEmployeeLogin";
public static const VIEW_EMPLOYEE_LIST:String= "viewEmployeeList";
public static const VIEW_EMPLOYEE_DETAIL:String= "viewEmployeeDetail";
public static const ADD_EMPLOYEE:String= "addEmployee";
public static const UPDATE_EMPLOYEE:String= "updateEmployee";
public static const SAVE_EMPLOYEE:String= "saveEmployee";
public static const DELETE_EMPLOYEE:String   = "deleteEmployee";
  /**
   * Singleton ApplicationFacade Factory Method
   */
public static function getInstance() : ApplicationFacade{
    if ( instance == null ) instance = new ApplicationFacade( );
    return instance as ApplicationFacade;
}
  /**
   * Register Commands with the Controller
   */
override protected function initializeController( ) : void {
    super.initializeController();
    registerCommand( STARTUP, ApplicationStartupCommand );
}

public function startup( app:CafeTownsend ):void{
     sendNotification( STARTUP, app );
  }
 }
}
```

In Example 1-16, during controller initialization, the STARTUP notification is registered with the command class `ApplicationStartupCommand`. So far it looks pretty similar to Cairngorm's `FrontController` from Example 1-4, doesn't it?

But PureMVC allows you to invoke more than one command as a response to a notification. For example, the author of this version of Café Townsend decided to invoke two commands during the application startup—`ModelPrepCommand` and `ViewPrepCommand`. When your command class extends `MacroCommand`, you are allowed to register a sequence of subcommands, and the `ApplicationStartupCommand` looks like Example 1-17.

Example 1-17. ApplicationStartupCommand.as

```
/* PureMVC AS3 Demo - Flex CafeTownsend
 Copyright (c) 2007-08 Michael Ramirez <michael.ramirez@puremvc.org>
 Parts Copyright (c) 2005-07 Adobe Systems, Inc.
 Your reuse is governed by the Creative Commons Attribution 3.0 License*/
package org.puremvc.as3.demos.flex.cafetownsend.controller
{
  import org.puremvc.as3.patterns.com7mand.*;
  import org.puremvc.as3.interfaces.*;
  /**
   * A MacroCommand executed when the application starts.
   */
  public class ApplicationStartupCommand extends MacroCommand {
    override protected function initializeMacroCommand() :void{
      addSubCommand( ModelPrepCommand );
      addSubCommand( ViewPrepCommand );
    }
  }
}
```

We'll follow the model preparation route at this point, but we'll get back to `ViewPrepCommand` in Example 1-22.

After the controller tier that routes commands come the proxy classes that deal with both—data models and the service calls if need be. Let's follow the `ModelPrepCommand` (Example 1-18). It registers employee and user proxy classes with the `Facade` class, so they know where to send notifications.

Example 1-18. ModelPrepCommand.as

```
/*PureMVC AS3 Demo - Flex CafeTownsend
 Copyright (c) 2007-08 Michael Ramirez <michael.ramirez@puremvc.org>
 Parts Copyright (c) 2005-07 Adobe Systems, Inc.
 Your reuse is governed by the Creative Commons Attribution 3.0 License */
package org.puremvc.as3.demos.flex.cafetownsend.controller {
  import org.puremvc.as3.interfaces.*;
  import org.puremvc.as3.patterns.command.*;
  import org.puremvc.as3.patterns.observer.*;
  import org.puremvc.as3.demos.flex.cafetownsend.*;
  import org.puremvc.as3.demos.flex.cafetownsend.model.*;
  /**
   * Create and register <code>Proxy</code>s with the <code>Model</code>.
   */
  public class ModelPrepCommand extends SimpleCommand{
    override public function execute( note:INotification ) :void{
```

```
        facade.registerProxy(new EmployeeProxy());
        facade.registerProxy(new UserProxy());
      }
   }
}
```

We are about halfway through the process of getting the employee list with PureMVC. This time, we'll just get familiar with a fragment of the code for the `EmployeeProxy` class (Example 1-19).

Example 1-19. A fragment of EmployeeProxy.as

```
public class EmployeeProxy extends Proxy implements IResponder {
   public static const NAME:String = "EmployeeProxy";
   public var errorStatus:String;

   public function EmployeeProxy ( data:Object = null ){
      super ( NAME, data );
   }

   public function loadEmployees():void{
   // create a worker who will go get some data; pass it a reference to
  // this proxy so the delegate knows where to return the data
   var delegate : LoadEmployeesDelegate =new LoadEmployeesDelegate(this );

   // make the delegate do some work
   delegate.loadEmployeesService();
  }

   // this is called when the delegate receives a result from the service
   public function result( rpcEvent : Object ) : void{

   // populate the employee list in the proxy with the results
   // from the service call
    data = rpcEvent.result.employees.employee as ArrayCollection;
    sendNotification( ApplicationFacade.LOAD_EMPLOYEES_SUCCESS );
  }

   // this is called when the delegate receives a fault from the service
   public function fault( rpcEvent : Object ) : void {
      data = new ArrayCollection();
    // store an error message in the proxy
    // labels, alerts, etc can bind to this to notify the user of errors
    errorStatus = "Could Not Load Employee List!";
    sendNotification( ApplicationFacade.LOAD_EMPLOYEES_FAILED );
   }
```

Proxies link the data model with services. The model is represented by the variable data that's predefined in the superclass. The service is available via the delegate class, which in this version of Café Townsend is called `LoadEmployeesDelegate`. Because `EmployeeProxy` implements the `IResponder` interface, it must include the methods `result()` and `fault()`. In the case of success, the variable data is populated with the retrieved list of employees and notification `LOAD_EMPLOYEES_SUCCESS` is sent to whoever is interested in hearing about it—you can take a peek at the method `listNotificationInterests()` in Example 1-21. In the case of failure, this version of Café Townsend just assigns a value to the variable `errorStatus` and sends the notification `LOAD_EMPLOYEES_FAILED`.

As you can see in Example 1-20, the delegate class to load employees has nothing specific to PureMVC—it just sets the responder and uses `HTTPService` to read the file *Employees.xml*.

Example 1-20. LoadEmployeesDelegate.as

```
 /*
 PureMVC AS3 Demo - Flex CafeTownsend
 Copyright (c) 2007-08 Michael Ramirez <michael.ramirez@puremvc.org>
 Parts Copyright (c) 2005-07 Adobe Systems, Inc.
 Your reuse is governed by the Creative Commons Attribution 3.0 License
 */
package org.puremvc.as3.demos.flex.cafetownsend.model.business
{
   import mx.rpc.AsyncToken;
   import mx.rpc.IResponder;
   import mx.rpc.http.HTTPService;

   public class LoadEmployeesDelegate{
      private var responder : IResponder;
      private var service : HTTPService;

      public function LoadEmployeesDelegate( responder : IResponder ) {
         this.service = new HTTPService();
         this.service.url="assets/Employees.xml";

         // store a reference to the proxy that created this delegate
         this.responder = responder;
      }

      public function loadEmployeesService() : void {
         // call the service
         var token:AsyncToken = service.send();

         // notify this responder when the service call completes
         token.addResponder( responder );
      }
   }
}
```

Now trace how the employees will arrive to the View. The view tier in PureMVC has two players: the UI component and the *mediator class*. Chapter 2 discusses the Mediator pattern, but in general, its role is to arrange the communication of two or more components without them knowing about each other. For example, an application container has a shopping cart component and a product list component. When the user makes a selection, the product component sends an event carrying the selected product to the mediator (e.g., an application), which forwards it to the shopping cart component.

But PureMVC mediators play the role of middlemen between the UI components and proxy objects (not controllers), and the need for these middlemen is questionable. In our opinion, it would be cleaner to introduce a value object and pass it directly (in the body of `Notification`) between the view and its controller rather than having the mediator reaching out to internals of both the proxy and the view. But it is what it is, and the `EmployeeList` view interacts with the `EmployeeListMediator`, and the latter deals with the controller's notifications.

In Example 1-21, note the method `listNotificationInterests()`, where you, the developer, have to list all events this mediator is interested in (similar to a subscription in messaging). The method `handleNotification()` will process notifications when they arrive.

Example 1-21. EmployeeListMediator.as

```
/*
 PureMVC AS3 Demo - Flex CafeTownsend
 Copyright (c) 2007-08 Michael Ramirez <michael.ramirez@puremvc.org>
 Parts Copyright (c) 2005-07 Adobe Systems, Inc.
 Your reuse is governed by the Creative Commons Attribution 3.0 License
 */
package org.puremvc.as3.demos.flex.cafetownsend.view{
   import flash.events.Event;
  import org.puremvc.as3.interfaces.*;
   import org.puremvc.as3.patterns.mediator.Mediator;

  import org.puremvc.as3.demos.flex.cafetownsend.ApplicationFacade;
   import org.puremvc.as3.demos.flex.cafetownsend.view.components.*;
   import org.puremvc.as3.demos.flex.cafetownsend.model.EmployeeProxy;
  /**
   * A Mediator for interacting with the EmployeeList component
   */
 public class EmployeeListMediator extends Mediator{

   public static const NAME:String = "EmployeeListMediator";
   public function EmployeeListMediator( viewComponent:Object ){
    // pass the viewComponent to the superclass where
    // it will be stored in the inherited viewComponent property
    super( NAME, viewComponent );

     employeeProxy = EmployeeProxy( facade.retrieveProxy(
                         EmployeeProxy.NAME ) );

     employeeList.addEventListener( EmployeeList.APP_LOGOUT, logout );
     employeeList.addEventListener( EmployeeList.ADD_EMPLOYEE,
                            addEmployee );
     employeeList.addEventListener( EmployeeList.UPDATE_EMPLOYEE,
                           updateEmployee );
  }
    /**
     * List all notifications this Mediator is interested in.
     * Automatically called by the framework when the mediator
     * is registered with the view.
```

```
    * @return Array the list of Notification names
    */
  override public function listNotificationInterests():Array{
     return [ ApplicationFacade.LOAD_EMPLOYEES_SUCCESS,
              ApplicationFacade.LOAD_EMPLOYEES_FAILED ];
}

   /**
    * Handle all notifications this Mediator is interested in.
    * <P>
    * Called by the framework when a notification is sent that
    * this mediator expressed an interest in when registered
    * (see <code>listNotificationInterests</code>.</P>
    *
    * @param INotification a notification
    */
  override public function handleNotification(note:INotification ):void{
     switch ( note.getName() ) {
      case ApplicationFacade.LOAD_EMPLOYEES_SUCCESS:
         employeeList.employees_li.dataProvider =
                  employeeProxy.employeeListDP;
        break;
       case ApplicationFacade.LOAD_EMPLOYEES_FAILED:
         employeeList.error.text = employeeProxy.errorStatus;
         break;
     }
  }
   /**
    * Cast the viewComponent to its actual type.
    *
    * This is a useful idiom for mediators. The
    * PureMVC Mediator class defines a viewComponent
    * property of type Object. </P>
    *
    * @return EmployeeList the viewComponent cast to EmployeeList
    */
  protected function get employeeList():EmployeeList{
     return viewComponent as EmployeeList;
  }

   private function logout( event:Event = null ):void{
        sendNotification( ApplicationFacade.APP_LOGOUT );
   }

   private function addEmployee( event:Event = null ):void{
        sendNotification( ApplicationFacade.ADD_EMPLOYEE );
   }

   private function updateEmployee( event:Event = null ):void{
     sendNotification( ApplicationFacade.UPDATE_EMPLOYEE,
             employeeList.employees_li.selectedItem);
   }

   private var employeeProxy:EmployeeProxy;
```

```
  }
}
```

The code of `handleNotification()` directly manipulates the internals of the view components (e.g., `employeeList.employees_li`), which leads to tight coupling between the mediator and the view. If the next version of the `employeeList` component will use a `DataGrid` instead of the `List` component, the mediator's code has to be refactored, too.

The previous discussion of Example 1-17 did not cover the process of preparing the view for receiving the events. Handling that process is the branch of code originated by the following call:

```
addSubCommand( ViewPrepCommand );
```

Shown in Example 1-22, the `ViewPrepCommand` class registers the main application mediator (you'd have to write it), and asks the proxy to load the employee list.

Example 1-22. ViewPrepCommand.as

```
/* PureMVC AS3 Demo - Flex CafeTownsend
 Copyright (c) 2007-08 Michael Ramirez <michael.ramirez@puremvc.org>
 Parts Copyright (c) 2005-07 Adobe Systems, Inc.
 Your reuse is governed by the Creative Commons Attribution 3.0 License
 */
package org.puremvc.as3.demos.flex.cafetownsend.controller{
  import org.puremvc.as3.interfaces.*;
  import org.puremvc.as3.patterns.command.*;
  import org.puremvc.as3.patterns.observer.*;
  import org.puremvc.as3.demos.flex.cafetownsend.*;
  import org.puremvc.as3.demos.flex.cafetownsend.model.*;
  import org.puremvc.as3.demos.flex.cafetownsend.view.ApplicationMediator;
  /**
   * Prepare the View for use.
   * The Notification was sent by the Application, and a reference to that
   * view component was passed on the note body.
   * The ApplicationMediator will be created and registered using this
   * reference. The ApplicationMediator will then register
   * all the Mediators for the components it created.
   */
  public class ViewPrepCommand extends SimpleCommand{
    override public function execute( note:INotification ) :void{
    // Register your ApplicationMediator
    facade.registerMediator( new ApplicationMediator( note.getBody()));

    // Get the EmployeeProxy
    var employeeProxy:EmployeeProxy = facade.retrieveProxy(
                 EmployeeProxy.NAME ) as EmployeeProxy;
    employeeProxy.loadEmployees();

    sendNotification( ApplicationFacade.VIEW_EMPLOYEE_LOGIN );
    }
  }
}
```

This command class issues a request to load employees without even waiting for the successful logon of the user. At the end of the `execute()` method, this code sends the `VIEW_EMPLOYEE_LOGIN` notification, which displays the logon view.

For brevity, Example 1-23 does have most of the comments from the code of `ApplicationMediator`. It builds all view components and registers the mediators for each of them.

Example 1-23. ApplicationMediator.as

```
/* PureMVC AS3 Demo - Flex CafeTownsend
 Copyright (c) 2007-08 Michael Ramirez <michael.ramirez@puremvc.org>
 Parts Copyright (c) 2005-07 Adobe Systems, Inc.
 Your reuse is governed by the Creative Commons Attribution 3.0 License*/
package org.puremvc.as3.demos.flex.cafetownsend.view {
  public class ApplicationMediator extends Mediator{
    public static const NAME:String = "ApplicationMediator";
    public static const EMPLOYEE_LOGIN : Number =   0;
    public static const EMPLOYEE_LIST : Number =   1;
    public static const EMPLOYEE_DETAIL : Number =   2;

    public function ApplicationMediator( viewComponent:Object )
    {
      // pass the viewComponent to the superclass where
      // it will be stored in the inherited viewComponent property
      super( NAME, viewComponent );

      // Create and register Mediators for the Employee
      // components that were instantiated by the mxml application
      facade.registerMediator( new EmployeeDetailMediator(
                          app.employeeDetail ) );
      facade.registerMediator( new EmployeeListMediator(
                           app.employeeList ) );
        facade.registerMediator( new EmployeeLoginMediator(
             app.employeeLogin ) );

      // retrieve and cache a reference to frequently accessed proxys
      employeeProxy = EmployeeProxy( facade.retrieveProxy(
                              EmployeeProxy.NAME ) );
        userProxy = UserProxy( facade.retrieveProxy( UserProxy.NAME ) );
    }

    override public function listNotificationInterests():Array
    {

      return [ ApplicationFacade.VIEW_EMPLOYEE_LOGIN,
               ApplicationFacade.VIEW_EMPLOYEE_LIST,
               ApplicationFacade.VIEW_EMPLOYEE_DETAIL,
               ApplicationFacade.APP_LOGOUT,
               ApplicationFacade.UPDATE_EMPLOYEE
              ];
    }
    /**
     * Handle all notifications this Mediator is interested in.
```

```
     */
    override public function handleNotification( note:INotification
                              ):void{
      switch ( note.getName() ){
              case ApplicationFacade.VIEW_EMPLOYEE_LOGIN:
                app.vwStack.selectedIndex = EMPLOYEE_LOGIN;
                break;
            case ApplicationFacade.VIEW_EMPLOYEE_LIST:
                employeeProxy.employee = null;
                app.vwStack.selectedIndex = EMPLOYEE_LIST;
                break;
            case ApplicationFacade.VIEW_EMPLOYEE_DETAIL:
                app.vwStack.selectedIndex = EMPLOYEE_DETAIL;
                break;
            case ApplicationFacade.APP_LOGOUT:
                app.vwStack.selectedIndex = EMPLOYEE_LOGIN;
                break;
            case ApplicationFacade.UPDATE_EMPLOYEE:
                app.vwStack.selectedIndex = EMPLOYEE_DETAIL;
                break;
      }
    }
    /**
     * Cast the viewComponent to its actual type.
     * The PureMVC Mediator class defines a viewComponent
     * property of type Object.
     */
    protected function get app():CafeTownsend{
      return viewComponent as CafeTownsend
    }
      // Cached references to needed proxies
      private var employeeProxy:EmployeeProxy;
      private var userProxy:UserProxy;
  }
}
```

The `ApplicationMediator` is also a central repository of all proxies that know how to get the data (`EmployeeProxy` and `UserProxy` in our case). So the `ViewPrepCommand` creates an instance of the `ApplicationMediator` (which creates other mediators and proxies to be cached), registers it with the facade, and asks the facade for a newly created instance of the `EmployeeProxy`, and calls its `loadEmployees()` method.

If the `EmployeeProxy` successfully retrieves the employee, it triggers the notification `LOAD_EMPLOYEES_SUCCESS`, which the `EmployeeMediator` processes, putting the data in the data provider of the `EmployeeList` (see Example 1-21 earlier):

```
case ApplicationFacade.LOAD_EMPLOYEES_SUCCESS:
 employeeList.employees_li.dataProvider = employeeProxy.employeeListDP;
```

The circle is closed. As you can see, the PureMVC way to bring Café Townsend's employee list is a lot more complicated than the Cairngorm or Mate way.

Still, if you work with an application built on the PureMVC framework, consider using a freeware product by Kap IT called PureMVC Console, available at *http://lab.kapit.fr/display/puremvcconsole/PureMVC+Console*. This tool comes in handy if you've joined a PureMVC project and need to hit the ground running. This console allows you to monitor the internal flow of this framework in real time. The creators of PureMVC Console offer a nice demo of monitoring Café Townsend—check it out at the website.

The MultiCore version of PureMVC supports modular programming where singletons are replaced with so-called Multiton Core actors.

We are having difficulty finding reasons for recommending an architectural framework that requires developers to replace 20 lines of code from Example 1-1 with all the code shown in Examples 1-15 through 1-23 to achieve the same goal: display the list of employees from an XML file in a list control.

Report Card: PureMVC

The author of PureMVC wanted to create a framework that could have been ported to other programming languages, and this approach inadvertently delivers a product that underutilizes benefits offered by language-specific constructs. Because PureMVC was not created specifically for Flex, it doesn't take advantage of the declarative nature of MXML, which would've substantially minimized the amount of handwritten code by application developers. For the same reason, PureMVC doesn't use standard Flex events and data binding. As an old saying goes, "When in Rome, speak Latin." It can be rephrased as, "When in Flex, speak MXML and ActionScript."

The pros are:

- It's well documented.
- It supports working with Flex modules.
- It's available for developers who want to use only ActionScript (e.g., Flash programmers). For Flex programmers, though, that can't be considered a benefit.

The cons are:

- It's not a framework written for Flex, and thus does not use features offered by MXML.
- It has too many layers, which are tightly coupled.
- It requires staffing projects with more senior developers.
- Developers have to write lots of additional classes, which adds to the project timeline.
- Its standard version is built on singletons, and application code becomes cluttered by making multiple calls to them.

One of the main Flex selling points is its MXML-to-ActionScript code generator, which spares application developers from manually writing lots of code. PureMVC doesn't use MXML and forces developers to write more code, which makes them less productive.

PureMVC notifications are more flexible than event maps of Mate, in that the latter relies on the enabled event bubbling, and if the `EventMap` object is not located in the ancestor of the object that triggers the event, it won't get it. As a workaround, Mate offers a special `Dispatcher` class to trigger events, say from a pop-up window that is not a descendant of an `Application` object. But in PureMVC, any object can subscribe for any other object's notifications regardless of their relations. Also, since the `Notification` class already has the property `body` to carry additional payload, application developers don't need to create subclasses for each notification object.

PureMVC has too many layers, dependencies, and singletons, and as a result has a steeper learning curve than Cairngorm or Mate. Managers on the projects that use PureMVC would need to hire more experienced developers than managers on projects using Mate or Cairngorm.

PureMVC Console is a convenient tool allowing you to monitor the Cairngorm and PureMVC applications; see *http://lab.kapit.fr*. To monitor the PureMVC version of Café Townsend, click on the image of the Café at *http://lab.kapit.fr/display/puremvcconsole/PureMVC+Console*.

PureMVC documentation states, "The PureMVC framework has a very narrow main goal: to help you separate your application's coding concerns into three discrete tiers; Model, View, and Controller." The framework attempts to achieve this goal by forcing application developers to write a lot of additional ActionScript code.

Unit testing of separate parts of the PureMVC application is nontrivial, because each test case would require additional work to register notifications, mediators, and other objects.

Clear Toolkit

So far, each framework that was reviewed in this chapter is an MVC-based architectural framework. They try to achieve the goal of separating the data flow into different tiers or classes based on the assumption that this would simplify the project management. In Flex project teams, these frameworks help to ensure that the person who creates the view doesn't need to know where its model is. Why? Is this a real-world situation or an artificial prerequisite that results in additional overhead in your application?

Clear Toolkit is not an architectural framework; it is a set of open source Flex components and utilities that may be called an application framework. As opposed to architectural frameworks, application frameworks don't just have a goal to organize developer's code into tiers, but rather offer a set of enhanced classes and methodologies to make application developers more productive. Good examples of application frameworks are Microsoft Foundation Classes, Ruby on Rails, Swing Application Framework (JSR-296), and Powersoft Foundation Classes.

You can download all or some of the Clear Toolkit components at *http://sourceforge.net/projects/cleartoolkit/*, and see the interface in Figure 1-10.

The main goals of Clear Toolkit are:

- To make software developers write less code by offering automatic code generation
- To give enterprise developers a set of smart data-driven components (e.g., advanced data grid and form, explained in Chapter 3) that would help developers in achieving the first goal—to write less code

The first version of this free and open source toolkit was developed by Farata Systems in 2006. It wasn't branded as Clear Toolkit back then, but the authors of this book were using these components internally in multiple consulting projects. Two years later, we decided to document these tools so that other Flex developers could also benefit from them.

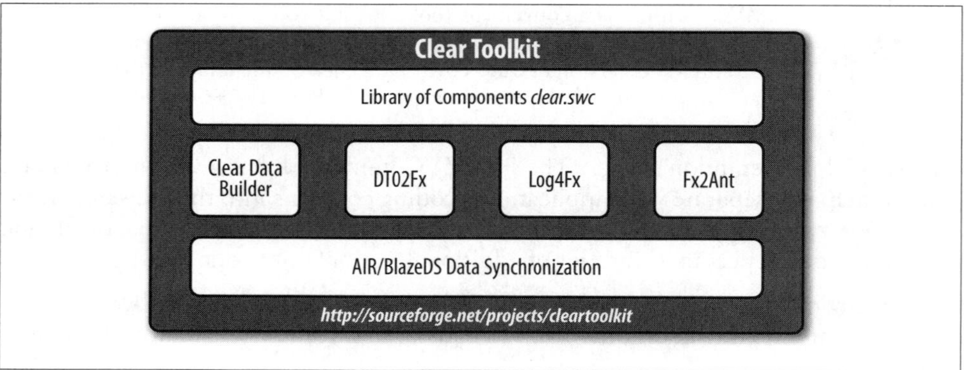

Figure 1-10. Components of Clear Toolkit

The components library is packaged in a *clear.swc* file that includes a number of enhanced Flex components such as `Datagrid`, `ComboBox`, et al. Also included are:

Clear Data Builder
: An Eclipse plug-in that can generate CRUD applications for BlazeDS or LCDS based on a SQL statement or a Java data transfer object (DTO)

DTO2Fx
: A utility that automatically generates ActionScript classes based on their Java peers

Log4Fx
: An advanced logger (Eclipse plug-in) that is built on top of the Flex logging API but automates and make the logging process more flexible and user-friendly

Fx2Ant
: A generator of optimized Ant build scripts for Flash Builder projects

Clear Toolkit 3.2.1 includes the following additions:

- Flex UI controls to support PDF generation on the client
- A data synchronization solution for AIR/BlazeDS applications

Café Townsend with Clear Toolkit

This section demonstrates how to use CDB to generate an application working with Café Townsend employees. In Chapter 3, you'll learn how to enhance some of the Flex components and work with those that are already included in *clear.swc*.

We haven't included a diagram for the Café application generated by Clear Data Builder (CDB), because it just uses a `DataCollection` object with an encapsulated Flex `RemoteObject`—no additional singletons, proxies, commands, or delegates are needed.

Before taking a deep dive into yet another version of Café Townsend, remember that neither Mate nor PureMVC support autosynchronization of the data offered by Data Management Services that are included in LiveCycle Data Services.

Using *Employee.xml* as a data source simplifies the explanation of the framework's basics, but in real-world situations, more often than not, you need to persist the data on the server. If you've added a new employee, adding a new value object to an `ArrayCollection` in memory is not enough. You need to persist it in a medium that survives computer reboots and electrical blackouts.

Clear Data Builder offers automatic code generation for both retrieval and persistence of the data, and to illustrate this, we'll be populating Café Townsend's employee list not with the data from an XML file but from a MySQL Server employee table stored in DBMS (Figure 1-11).

Installing the software for the CRUD example

At the time of this writing, the latest version of CDB is 3.2.1; it requires Eclipse JEE, which comes with productivity plug-ins for web developers. You can download Eclipse JEE at *http://www.eclipse.org/downloads/*. Installing Eclipse JEE is just a matter of unzipping the downloaded file to a folder on your hard disk.

Installation of the plug-in version of Flex Builder 3 is also easy. Just go to *http://www.adobe.com/products/flex/features/flex_builder/* and select the plug-in version of Flex Builder.

Get a free CDB license at the Clear Toolkit website. The latest CDB installation instructions can be found in the CDB User Guide (*http://www.myflex.org/documentation/CDB3.pdf*).

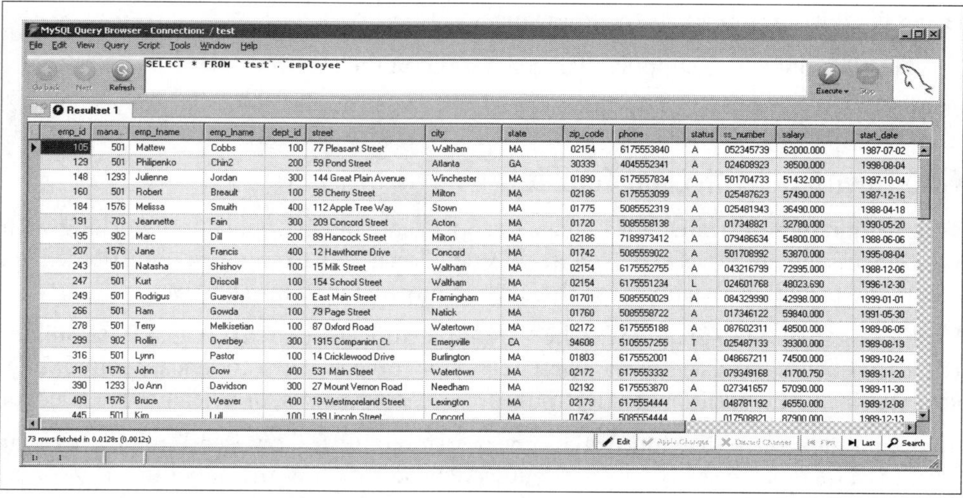

emp_id	mana...	emp_fname	emp_lname	dept_id	street	city	state	zip_code	phone	status	ss_number	salary	start_date
105	501	Mattew	Cobbs	100	77 Pleasant Street	Waltham	MA	02154	6175553840	A	052345739	62000.000	1987-07-02
129	501	Philipenko	Chin2	200	59 Pond Street	Atlanta	GA	30339	4045552341	A	024608923	38500.000	1998-08-04
148	1293	Julienne	Jordan	300	144 Great Plain Avenue	Winchester	MA	01890	6175557834	A	501704733	51432.000	1997-10-04
160	501	Robert	Breault	100	58 Cherry Street	Milton	MA	02186	6175553099	A	025487623	57490.000	1987-12-16
184	1576	Melissa	Smuith	400	112 Apple Tree Way	Stown	MA	01775	5085552319	A	025481943	36490.000	1988-04-18
191	703	Jeannette	Fain	300	209 Concord Street	Acton	MA	01720	5085558138	A	017348821	32780.000	1990-05-20
195	902	Marc	Dill	200	89 Hancock Street	Milton	MA	02186	7189973412	A	079486634	54800.000	1988-06-06
207	1576	Jane	Francis	400	12 Hawthorne Drive	Concord	MA	01742	5085559022	A	501708992	53870.000	1995-08-04
243	501	Natasha	Shishov	100	15 Milk Street	Waltham	MA	02154	6175552755	A	043216799	72995.000	1988-12-06
247	501	Kurt	Driscoll	100	154 School Street	Waltham	MA	02154	6175551234	L	024601768	48023.690	1996-12-30
249	501	Rodrigus	Guevara	100	East Main Street	Framingham	MA	01701	5085550029	A	084329990	42998.000	1999-01-01
266	501	Ram	Gowda	100	79 Page Street	Natick	MA	01760	5085558722	A	017346122	59840.000	1991-05-30
278	501	Terry	Melkisetian	100	87 Oxford Road	Watertown	MA	02172	6175555188	A	087602311	48500.000	1989-06-05
299	902	Rollin	Overbey	300	1915 Companion Ct.	Emeryville	CA	94608	5105557255	T	025487133	39300.000	1989-08-19
316	501	Lynn	Pastor	100	14 Cricklewood Drive	Burlington	MA	01803	6175552001	A	048667211	74500.000	1989-10-24
318	1576	John	Crow	400	531 Main Street	Watertown	MA	02172	6175553332	A	079349168	41700.750	1989-11-20
390	1293	Jo Ann	Davidson	300	27 Mount Vernon Road	Needham	MA	02192	6175553870	A	027341657	57090.000	1989-11-30
409	1576	Bruce	Weaver	400	19 Westmoreland Street	Lexington	MA	02173	6175554444	A	048781192	46550.000	1989-12-08
445	501	Kim	Lull	100	199 Lincoln Street	Concord	MA	01742	5085554444	A	017508821	87900.000	1989-12-13

Figure 1-11. Employee table in MySQL Server database test

To ensure that you have the latest instructions for installing CDB and running a sample application, we highly recommend that you read the appropriate section of the CDB User Guide.

To generate this version of Café, you'll also need to download and install three more pieces of software:

- The binary edition of Adobe BlazeDS 3.0 (*http://opensource.adobe.com/wiki/display/blazeds/download+blazeds+3*); unzip it into some folder, for example, *C:\blazeds*
- Apache Tomcat 6 (select Windows Service Installer from the Core Downloads section at *http://tomcat.apache.org/download-60.cgi*)
- MySQL Community Server (*http://dev.mysql.com/downloads/mysql/5.0.html#downloads*)

In addition, you must create a sample database called *test* using the SQL script provided in the accompanying files for this chapter. Create a user called `dba` with the password `sql` and grant this user full access to the test database.

Important: CDB requires JDK 1.5 or later (note: JDK, not JRE). Select the Eclipse menu Window → Preferences → Java → Installed JREs and point it to your JDK installation directory, as shown in Figure 1-12.

The last preparation step is installing DBMS—we use MySQL Community Server. During the installation, we've entered `dba` as a user ID and `sql` as a password.

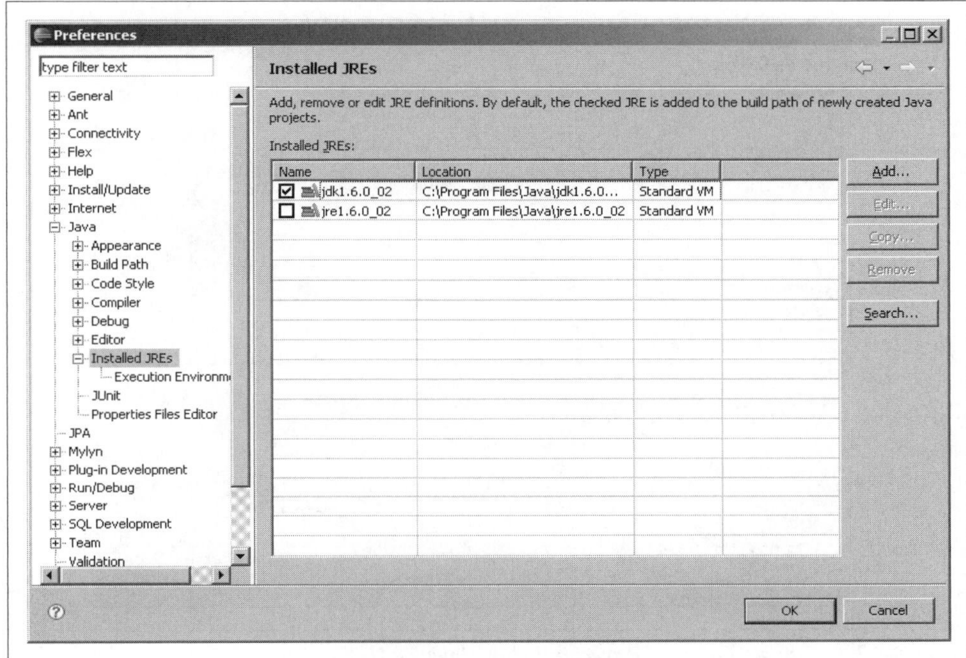

Figure 1-12. Selecting installed JDK

Creating an Eclipse Dynamic Web Project with CDB facets

The first step in creating an Eclipse Dynamic Web Project is to start Eclipse JEE integrated development environment (IDE) and create a new instance of the Tomcat 6 server (File → New → Other → Server). Create a new Dynamic Web Project in Eclipse (File → New → Other → Web → Dynamic Web Project) and name it Café Townsend CDB. Specify the Target Runtime as Apache Tomcat 6.0 in the Dynamic Web Project configuration screen (Figure 1-13).

If you use Eclipse 3.4 or later, click the Modify button in the Configurations section (not shown) and select the checkboxes in the MyFlex section to include MyFlex facets required for proper code generation.

Click the Next button. Select the Clear Data Builder and Flex Web Project facets as shown in Figure 1-14, then click Next.

In the next window, leave unchanged the next screen that suggests *RIA_CRUD* as a context, *WebContent* as a content directory, and *src* as a directory for the Java code; then click Next.

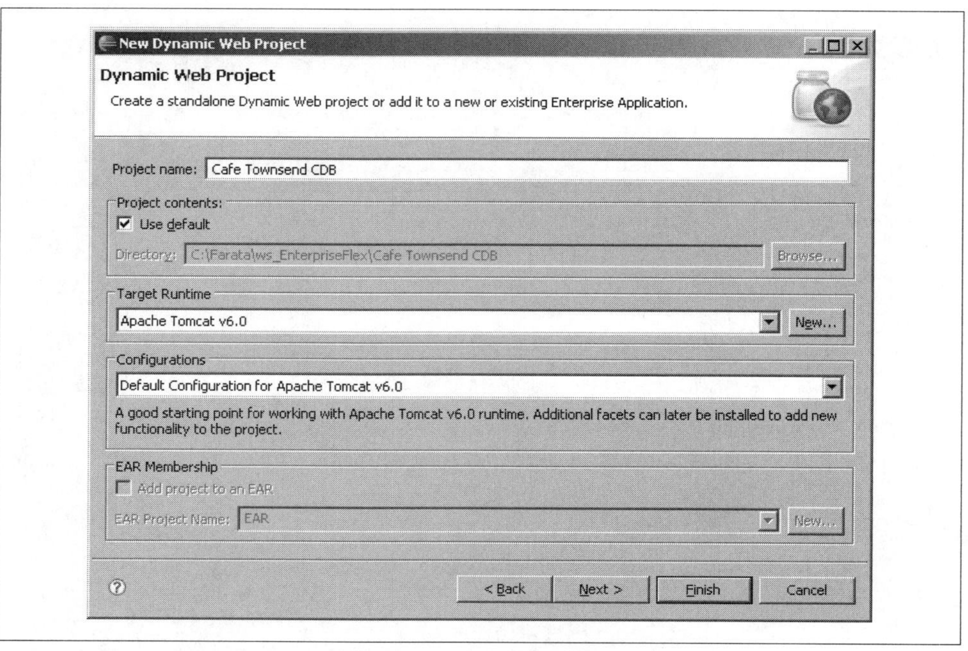

Figure 1-13. Creating a Dynamic Project in Eclipse Java EE IDE

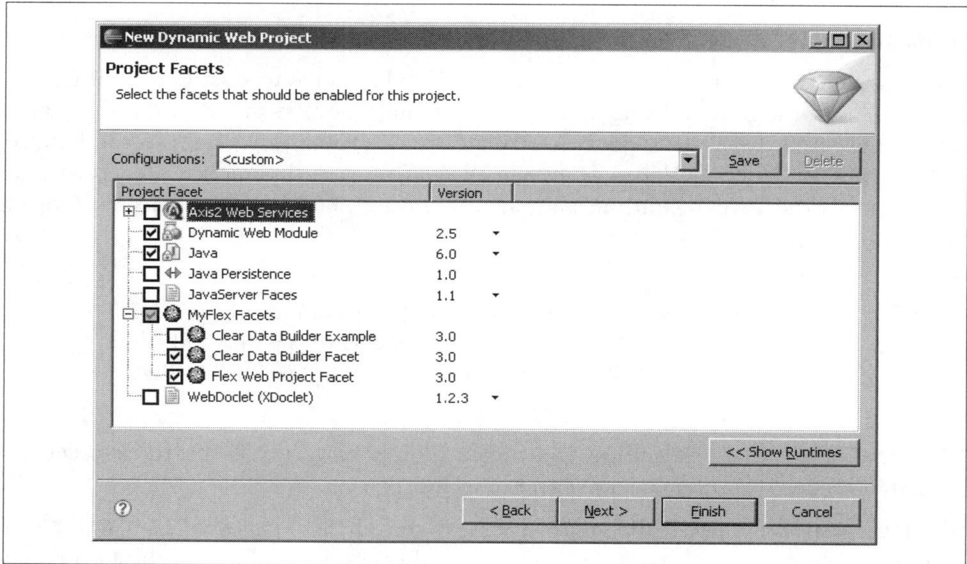

Figure 1-14. Adding CDB facets to the project

Specify that you are going to use BlazeDS on the server side, and specify the location of your *blazeds.war*, which in this case is *C:\BlazeDS\blazeds.war* (Figure 1-15). Click Next.

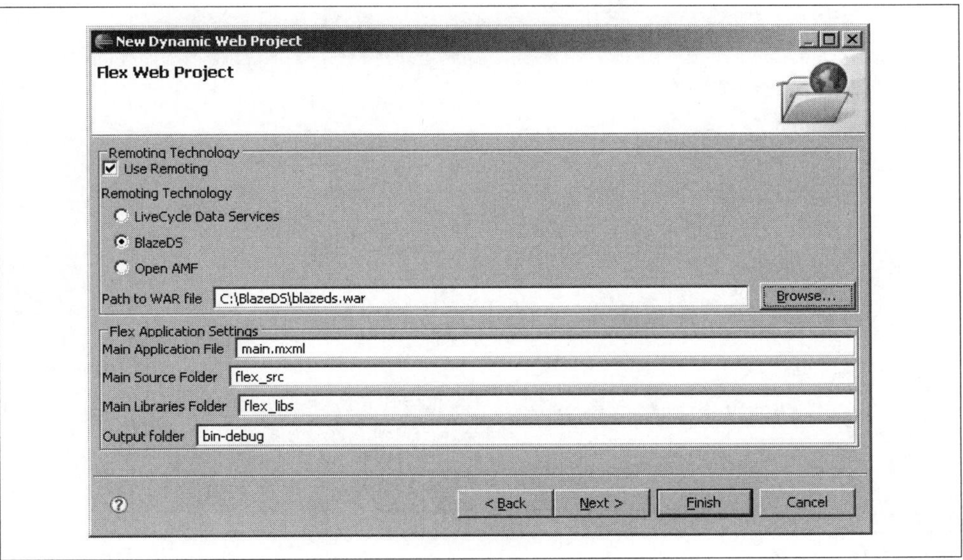

Figure 1-15. Adding blazeds.war to the project

Specify that the application will be deployed under Tomcat, and select and configure the database connection (Figure 1-16). Important: your database server has to be up and running. Select the database DBMS, the driver, specify any name for your connection pool, and enter the URL of your database. By default, MySQL Server runs on port 3306, and the name of our sample database is *test*.

Don't forget to press the Test Connection button to ensure that there are no problems in that department. If you don't see a message about successful connection, ensure that you've started an instance of MySQL Server and that it runs on the same port specified in the screen shown in Figure 1-16. Also, make sure that the test database exists.

Click the Finish button, and the new Dynamic Web Project will be created. This project will contain both Flex and Java code. The DTO objects were autogenerated by CDB. The *resources* folder contains special resource files, explained in Chapter 3. The folder *script* has SQL scripts required to create a sample test database for various DBMSs (Figure 1-17).

All these goodies were created based on the class *Employee.java*, explained next.

Now you need to create a small abstract class `Employee` with defined method signatures that are to be used for retrieval of the employee data. Right-click on the folder

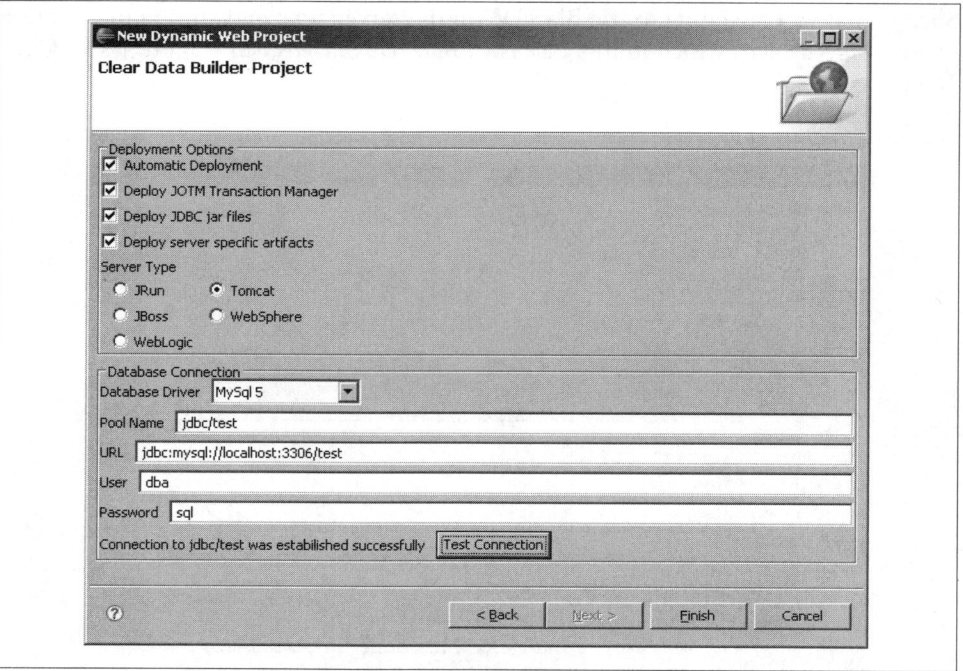

Figure 1-16. Configuring DBMS

Java Resources:src, select New → Class, enter the package name *com.farata*, and select the abstract checkbox.

The code of the generated Java class `Employee` will look like this:

```
package com.farata;

public abstract class Employee {

}
```

Specify the data location within CDB. For our Café project, we will add to *Employee.java* a couple of method signatures, annotated (we use doclets) with SQL statements that will bring the data. We'll need to specify what table is to be updated and the primary key there. For example, we'll define where to get the data on employees and departments (see Example 1-24).

Example 1-24. Employee.java

```
package com.farata;
import java.util.List;
/**
 * @daoflex:webservice
 *  pool=jdbc/test
 */
```

```
public abstract class Employee{
 /**
 * @daoflex:sql
 * pool=jdbc/test
 * sql=:: select * from employee
 * ::
 * transferType=EmployeeDTO[]
 * keyColumns=emp_id
 * updateTable=employee
 */

 public abstract List getEmployees();
 /**
 * @daoflex:sql
 * sql=:: select * from department
 * ::
 * transferType=DepartmentDTO[]
 */
 public abstract List getDepartments();

}
```

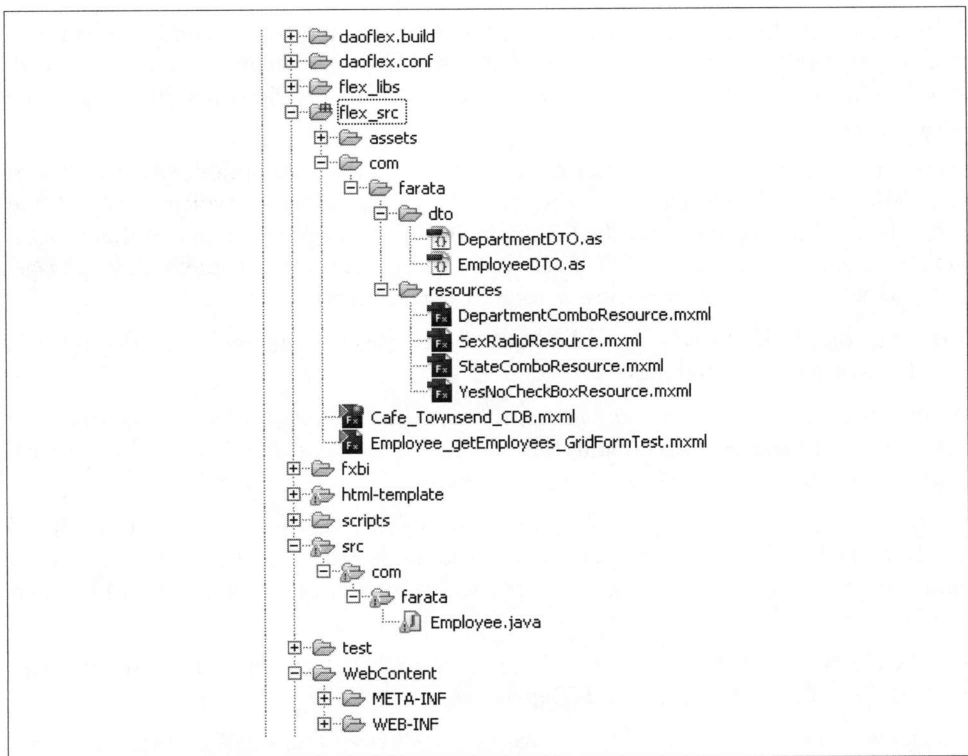

Figure 1-17. Generated Flex/Java Dynamic Web Project

Double colons are used to specify the start and the end of the SQL statement. CDB can help you with the syntax—just right-click inside the curly braces in the class `Employee`, and you'll see the menu shown in Figure 1-18.

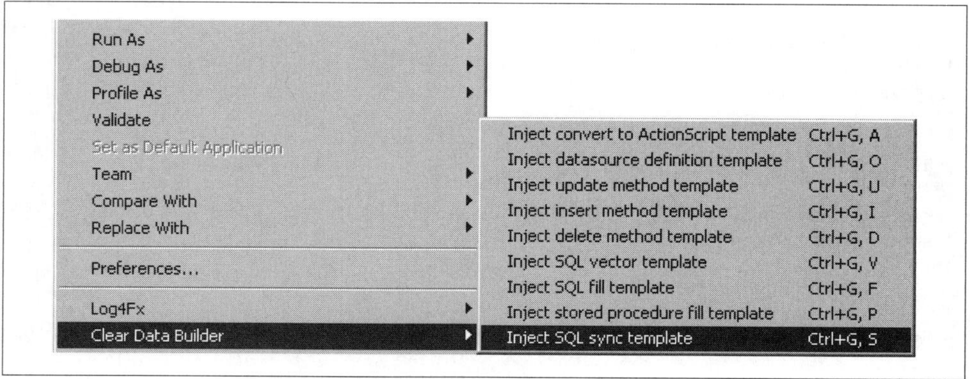

Figure 1-18. CDB helps insert the right code templates

You can select "Inject SQL sync template" if you need to generate code that can read and update the data, or "Inject SQL fill template" if you are planning to create a read-only application. CDB will insert commented code that will help you write similar code on your own.

Now we can go to Eclipse's Project menu and select the Clean option, which will start the CDB code generation and build process. The Clean process invokes the Ant build script located under the folder *daoflex.build*. The only proper outcome of this process is the message BUILD SUCCESSFUL in Eclipse console. If you do not see this message, most likely you've done something wrong or in the wrong order.

After this build, the Java DTO and data access classes are generated and deployed in our Tomcat servlet container.

Now run the Ant script *daoflex-build.xml* located in the *daoflex.build* directory. You can find the generated Java code in the folder *.daoflex-temp\gen*. If you don't see this folder immediately, refresh your Eclipse project.

Technically, you do not need to keep these source files, as they are going to be jarred by the CDB build process and deployed in the *lib* directory of your servlet container under *WEB-INF\lib* in the files *daoflex-runtime.jar*, *services-generated.jar*, and *services-original.jar*.

On the client side, CDB has generated the *EmployeeDTO.as*, which is an ActionScript peer of the generated *EmployeeDTO.java*.

To deploy the application, add the project Café Townsend CDB to the configured Tomcat server, using the Server view of the Eclipse JEE IDE. Right-click in the Server view on Tomcat Server, select Add or Remove Projects, and add the project Café

Townsend CDB to the Configured Projects panel. Start the server by using its right-click menu.

CDB also generates a number of reference client Flex applications, which can be used as the frontend of our Café application. We'll use the one called *Employee_getEmployees_GridFormTest.mxml*, which not only creates a data grid, but also generates master/detail support and opens a form view when the user selects and double-clicks on a grid row.

Switch to Flex perspective, copy *Employee_getEmployees_GridFormTest.mxml* from *test/rpc/com/farata/* to *flex_src*, and set it as the default application (right-click menu).

Create one small MXML file to support population of the `Departments` drop-down using the function `getDepartments()` that we've declared in *Employee.java*, as shown previously in Example 1-24.

Programming with resource files will be explained in Chapter 3. For now, just create a new MXML file called *DepartmentComboResource.mxml* in the directory *flex_src/com/farata/resources* (see Example 1-25).

Example 1-25. DepartmentComboResource.mxml

```
<?xml version="1.0" encoding="utf-8"?>
<resources:ComboBoxResource
   xmlns="com.farata.resources" xmlns:mx="http://www.adobe.com/2006/mxml"
   xmlns:resources="com.theriabook.resources.*"
   width="160"
   dropdownWidth="160"
   destination="com.farata.Employee"
   keyField="DEPT_ID"
   labelField="DEPT_NAME"
   autoFill="true"
   method="getDepartments"
   >
</resources:ComboBoxResource>
```

Compile and run *Employee_getEmployees_GridFormTest.mxml*. Figure 1-19 shows the resulting output window.

This window has been automatically generated based on the Java class `Employee` shown in Example 1-24. If you select and double-click any row in this grid, you'll see details in a form window (Figure 1-20).

A very solid foundation for Café Townsend is ready, and the only code you had to write was shown in Examples 1-24 and 1-25.

Example 1-26 provides the code snippet of the generated *Employee_getEmployees_GridFormTest.mxml*.

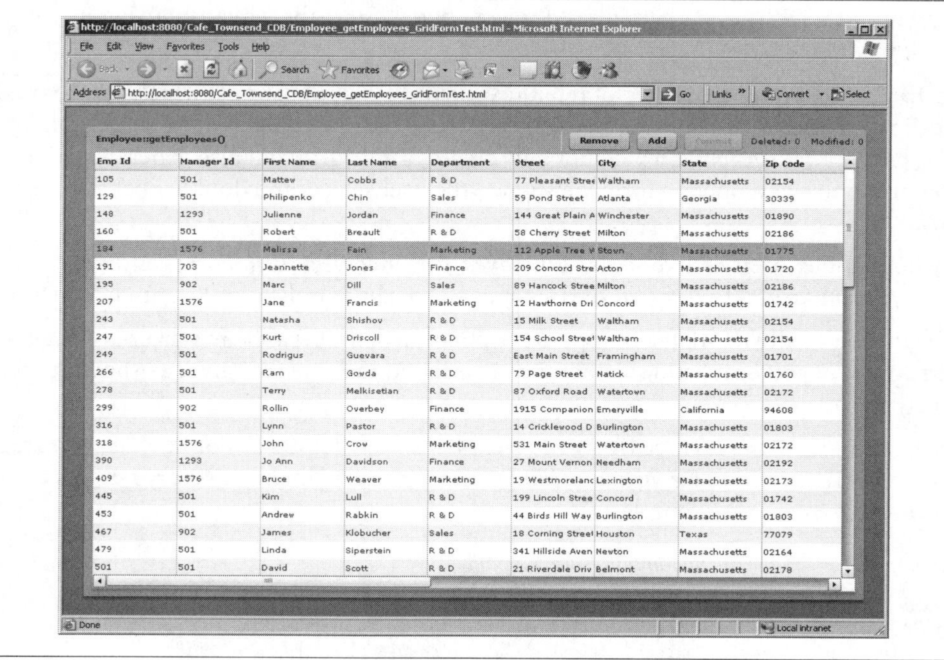

Emp Id	Manager Id	First Name	Last Name	Department	Street	City	State	Zip Code
105	501	Mattew	Cobbs	R & D	77 Pleasant Stree	Waltham	Massachusetts	02154
129	501	Philipenko	Chin	Sales	59 Pond Street	Atlanta	Georgia	30339
148	1293	Julienne	Jordan	Finance	144 Great Plain A	Winchester	Massachusetts	01890
160	501	Robert	Breault	R & D	58 Cherry Street	Milton	Massachusetts	02186
184	1576	Melissa	Fain	Marketing	112 Apple Tree W	Stown	Massachusetts	01775
191	703	Jeannette	Jones	Finance	209 Concord Stre	Acton	Massachusetts	01720
195	902	Marc	Dill	Sales	89 Hancock Stree	Milton	Massachusetts	02186
207	1576	Jane	Francis	Marketing	12 Hawthorne Dri	Concord	Massachusetts	01742
243	501	Natasha	Shishov	R & D	15 Milk Street	Waltham	Massachusetts	02154
247	501	Kurt	Driscoll	R & D	154 School Street	Waltham	Massachusetts	02154
249	501	Rodrigus	Guevara	R & D	East Main Street	Framingham	Massachusetts	01701
266	501	Ram	Gowda	R & D	79 Page Street	Natick	Massachusetts	01760
278	501	Terry	Melkisetian	R & D	87 Oxford Road	Watertown	Massachusetts	02172
299	902	Rollin	Overbey	Finance	1915 Companion	Emeryville	California	94608
316	501	Lynn	Pastor	R & D	14 Cricklewood D	Burlington	Massachusetts	01803
318	1576	John	Crow	Marketing	531 Main Street	Watertown	Massachusetts	02172
390	1293	Jo Ann	Davidson	Finance	27 Mount Vernon	Needham	Massachusetts	02192
409	1576	Bruce	Weaver	Marketing	19 Westmorelanc	Lexington	Massachusetts	02173
445	501	Kim	Lull	R & D	199 Lincoln Stree	Concord	Massachusetts	01742
453	501	Andrew	Rabkin	R & D	44 Birds Hill Way	Burlington	Massachusetts	01803
467	902	James	Klobucher	Sales	18 Corning Street	Houston	Texas	77079
479	501	Linda	Siperstein	R & D	341 Hillside Aven	Newton	Massachusetts	02164
501	501	David	Scott	R & D	21 Riverdale Driv	Belmont	Massachusetts	02178

Figure 1-19. Generated CRUD application to maintain employees

Example 1-26. The code fragment of Employee_getEmployees_GridFormTest.mxml

```
<?xml version="1.0" encoding="UTF-8"?>
<mx:Application xmlns:mx="http://www.adobe.com/2006/mxml"
   xmlns:lib=" http://www.faratasystems.com/2008/components"
         creationComplete="onCreationComplete()">

<mx:ViewStack id="vs" height="100%" width="100%" >
<mx:Canvas height="100%" width="100%">
 <mx:Panel title="Employee::getEmployees()" width="100%"
                         height="100%">
 <lib:DataGrid doubleClick="vs.selectedIndex=1" doubleClickEnabled="true"
     horizontalScrollPolicy="auto" width="100%" id="dg"
     dataProvider="{collection}" editable="true" height="100%">
   <lib:columns>
    <lib:DataGridColumn dataField="EMP_ID" editable="false"
                        headerText="Emp Id"/>
    <lib:DataGridColumn dataField="MANAGER_ID" editable="false"
                        headerText="Manager Id"/>
   <lib:DataGridColumn dataField="EMP_FNAME" editable="false"
                        headerText="First Name"/>
   <lib:DataGridColumn dataField="EMP_LNAME" editable="true"
                         headerText="Last Name"/>
   <lib:DataGridColumn dataField="DEPT_ID" editable="false"
    headerText="Department"
       resource="{com.farata.resources.DepartmentComboResource}"/>
```

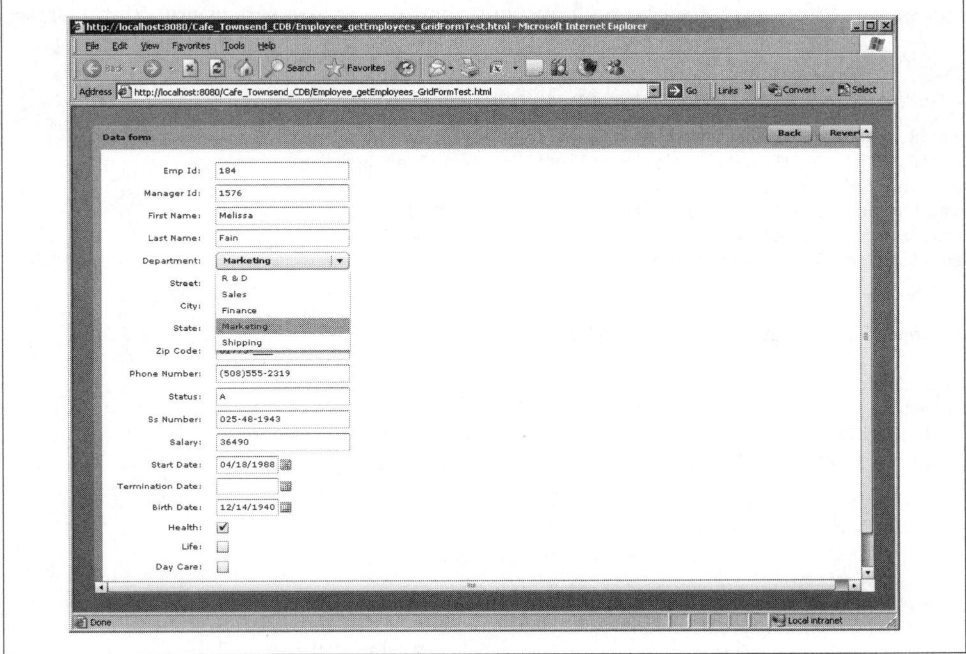

Figure 1-20. Detailed employee information

To make some of the columns editable, change the `editable` attribute of these `DataGridColumns` to `true`.

The code in Example 1-26 uses the `DataGrid` object from the Clear Toolkit component library *clear.swc*. The `Department` column (and the drop-down in Figure 1-19) has been populated by the function `getDepartments()` declared in *Employee.java* without the need to do any additional coding on your part.

The server-side code is deployed under the Tomcat server. While generating this project, CDB has added a library, *clear.swc*, to the build path. It includes a number of handy components that enhance the standard controls of the Flex framework and a number of classes simplifying communication with the database layer.

The following autogenerated code illustrates another example of a useful component from *clear.swc*. It uses a `DataCollection` object, which is a subclass of the Flex class `ArrayCollection`. You can read more about `DataCollection` in Chapter 6.

Look at the code in the `onCreationComplete()` function shown in Example 1-27. `DataCollection` is a smart, data-aware class that combines the functionality of Flex's `ArrayCollection` and `RemoteObject`, and some functionality of the Data Management Services without the need for LCDS. Just set the values in the `DataCollection` properties `destination` and the `method` to call, and call its method `fill()` or `sync()`. No need to define the `RemoteObject` with result and fault handlers, as no server-side configuration is required.

Example 1-27. Using DataCollection object from clear.swc

```
<mx:Button label="Fill" click="fill_onClick()"/>
<mx:Button label="Remove" click="collection.removeItemAt(dg.selectedIndex)"
enabled="{dg.selectedIndex != -1}"/>
<mx:Button label="Add" click="addItemAt(Math.max(0,dg.selectedIndex+1)) "/>
<mx:Button label="Commit" click="collection.sync()"
enabled="{collection.commitRequired}"/>
...

   import com.farata.dto.EmployeeDTO;

  Bindable]
   public var collection:DataCollection ;
   [Bindable]
   private var log : ArrayCollection;

   private function onCreationComplete() : void {
      collection = new DataCollection();
      collection.destination="com.farata.Employee";
      collection.method="getEmployees";
      //getEmployees_sync is the default for collection.syncMethod
      log = new ArrayCollection();
      collection.addEventListener( CollectionEvent.COLLECTION_CHANGE,
                                   logEvent);
      collection.addEventListener("fault", logEvent);
      fill_onClick();
   }
   private function fill_onClick():void {
      collection.fill();
   }

   private function addItemAt(position:int):void    {
      var item:EmployeeDTO = new EmployeeDTO();
      collection.addItemAt(item, position);
      dg.selectedIndex = position;
   }

  private function logEvent(evt:Event):void {
      if (evt.type=="fault") {
         logger.error(evt["fault"]["faultString"]);
      } else {
         if (evt.type=="collectionChange") {
            logger.debug(evt["type"] + " " + evt["kind"]);
         } else {
            logger.debug(evt["type"]);
         }
      }
   }
```

To finalize Café Townsend, we'll steal (copy) the *assets* folder from the original Café to display the logo on top, apply the styles defined in *main.css*, and make just a couple of cosmetic changes:

- Remove the `Application` tag from Example 1-26, moving the declaration of namespaces and the `creationComplete()` event to its MXML tag `ViewStack` (you'll also need to remove three references to the autogenerated variable `vs` that was referring to this `ViewStack`):

```
<mx:ViewStack height="100%" width="100%"
      xmlns:mx="http://www.adobe.com/2006/mxml"
      xmlns:lib="http://www.faratasystems.com/2008/components"
      creationComplete="onCreationComplete()">
```

- Create a small application *Café_Townsend_CDB* to include the styles, the logo, and the main view (see Example 1-28).

Example 1-28. Café_Townsend_CDB.mxml

```
<?xml version="1.0" encoding="utf-8" standalone="no"?>
<mx:Application xmlns:mx="http://www.adobe.com/2006/mxml" xmlns:views="*"
            backgroundColor="#000000" layout="vertical">
  <mx:Style source="assets/main.css"/>
  <mx:Image source="assets/header.jpg" width="700"/>
  <views:Employee_getEmployees_GridFormTest selectedIndex="0"/>
</mx:Application>
```

Compile and run the application, just to ensure that Café Townsend CDB looks as good as possible (Figure 1-21).

The entire process of creating Café Townsend with Clear Data Builder has been prerecorded, and you can find this screencast in the Demos section at *http://www.faratasystems.com*.

Report Card: Clear Toolkit

Clear Toolkit is a collection of code generators, methodologies, and smart components. Its components may be used either as an alternative to architectural frameworks or together with them. If you are a development manager starting a Flex project with a team that has at least one senior Flex architect, using Clear Toolkit is the productive way to go.

If you have to deal with a number of junior developers, consider using the Mate framework with some of the Clear Toolkit components, e.g., enhanced `DataGrid`, `DataForm`, and a number of enhanced UI controls. Besides, having a good reporter, logger, Ant script, and DTO generators is quite handy regardless of whether you use architectural frameworks.

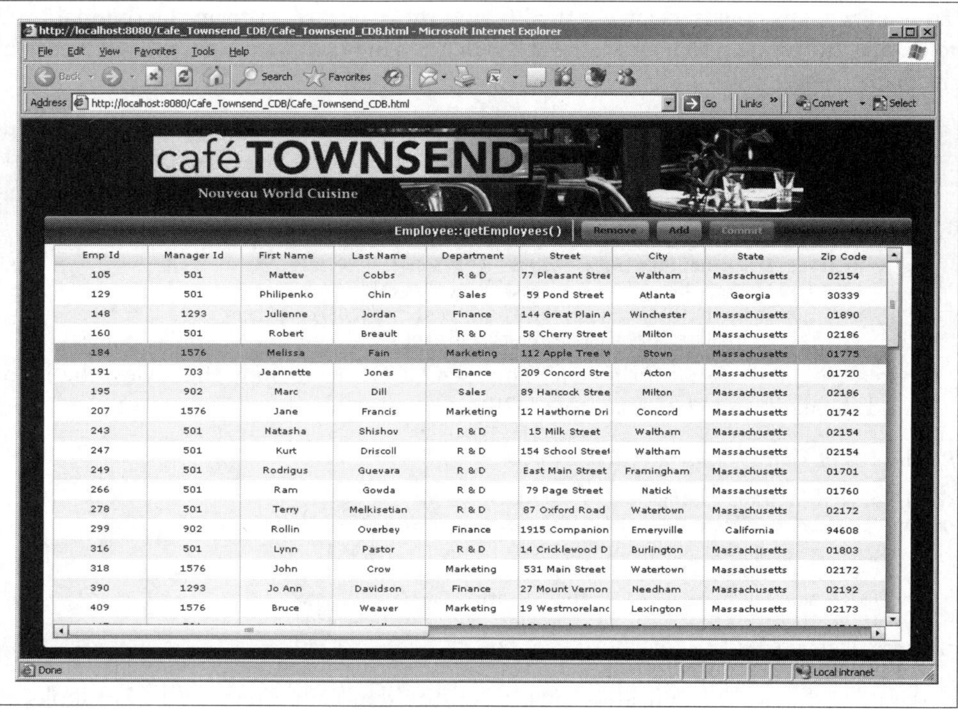

Figure 1-21. Café Townsend, as generated by Clear Data Builder

The pros are:

- It offers a library of enriched Flex components (supergrid, data-aware components, etc.).
- It automatically generates code, which minimizes the amount of code to be written by application developers.
- It offers data synchronization functionality in free BlazeDS, similar to Data Management Services from LCDS.
- Its components can be used à la carte on an as-needed basis.
- It automates creation of Ant build scripts.
- It automates creation of ActionScript data transfer objects.

The cons are:

- It doesn't help in separating work among team members.
- Data exchange between the application's views and modules must be coded manually.

Final Framework Selection Considerations

If you are a Flex architect or a development manager in charge of selecting a third-party Flex framework, ask yourself these questions: "Do I want to use intelligent objects that encapsulate most of the framework functionality, or do I prefer to deal with simple objects and do explicit coding for each instance? Will I have senior developers in the project team? Do I need to modularize the application to be developed? Do I trust code generators?"

After answering these questions, take a detailed look at the implementation of several frameworks, assess the benefits each of them brings to your application, and pick the most appealing one that will give you confidence that it—given the project's size/nature/deliverables/available human resources—has the least probability of failing.

Always keep in mind that your application may grow and you'll need to redesign it into modules. Will your selected framework become your friend or foe in a modularized application? In general, if you are going with modules, you need a multilayered framework and intelligent registration services that are written specifically for the task.

Cairngorm, Mate, and PureMVC are architectural frameworks that utilize global objects. These may simplify project management by providing a structure and separating developers' work on the Model, View, and Controller. All these singletons, managers, and event maps are a way to establish communication between the application parts. By making this process more formal, you can build much smaller chunks, communicating with each other, and in your mind the more formal process will yield better maintainability. On the other hand, it will create more parts in your application that require maintenance and testing.

Clear Toolkit is an application framework that consists of a mix of enhanced components and code generators. Its goal is to make the development process more productive by substantially reducing the need to write code manually.

If the word *global* gives you goosebumps, but you are uncomfortable with code generators too, consider Joe Berkovitz's MVCS approach (see "References" on page 61) as a middle ground between the two. This may work better for medium to large teams that would have no access to code generators and data-driven/factories-based architecture.

This book targets enterprise developers whose main concern is data processing. But there are legions of Flex developers who do not care about `DataGrid` and the like. They are into the creation of small visual components and do not need to use any application frameworks. For example, if you Google *image viewer Cairngorm*, you'll find an example of a small application to display images built with this framework. This is clearly overkill and an example of bad practice, because if you are the only developer working on a small one-view application, introducing any architectural framework is plain wrong. For these kinds of applications, all you need is the Flex framework and possibly one or two self-contained components.

Large projects are different animals. Six months into the project, the functional specification may change. This can happen for a variety of reasons, for example:

- The business analyst realizes that she made a mistake.
- The business process changes.
- Another department needs some of your application's functionality.
- Another line of business has to be handled by your application.

If this happens, commands need to be amended and recoded, views redesigned, and events integrated with a different workflow. Now you are thinking to yourself, "Why didn't I go with code generators that could've made my application more agile?"

Using code generators and components is a way to get you through the "implementation" part faster while giving you maximum flexibility on the "design and functionality" part. If you don't have 80 percent of your application built in 20 percent of the time, you will be late with the remaining 20 percent.

Flex itself is more of an application framework. It is not a library of patterns, but rather a set of objects that are built to communicate and react. The Flex framework itself uses code generators. The key here is automation of implementation tasks by minimizing the amount of manually written code. That is done by explicitly checking the "related" objects for specific interfaces. By not adhering to the implementation of these interfaces, the external frameworks require serious application development effort to support them.

After rebuilding Café Townsend, we decided to compare the sizes of the produced *.swf* file. We've been using Flex Builder 3's Project→Export Release Build option with all default settings. These are the results:

Cairngorm	409 KB
Mate	368 KB
PureMVC	365 KB

The total size of the Café Townsend application produced by Clear Toolkit is 654 KB on the client and 30 KB of Java JARs (Java ARchives) deployed on the server. The size is larger, but this application includes full CRUD functionality; Cairngorm, Mate, and PureMVC don't. And you've had to write just a dozen lines of code manually. This is a reasonable size for an application that has full CRUD functionality.

Of course, you can further reduce the size of the business portion of the Café written with any of the frameworks by linking the Flex SDK as an RSL.

When making your selection, consider the benefits you'll be getting from the framework of your choice. From the learning curve perspective, none of the reviewed frameworks is overly difficult to master. You may spend a day or two with the manuals. But ask yourself, "What will be different in my project development if I use this particular framework?" Are you adding a small library to your project that helps you organize your project better, but still requires you to write a lot of code? Or are you adding a larger library that makes you write less code and be more productive?

Of course we are biased—we created Clear Toolkit to help us develop the types of applications we work on with our business clients, and it serves us well. Before making your final decision on a framework for your application (especially if it's not as small as Café Townsend), ask yourself one more question: "If three months down the road I realize that I've selected the wrong framework, how much time/money would it take to remove it?" The answer to this question may be crucial in the selection process.

If you decide to use one of the architectural frameworks, it doesn't mean that you can't throw in a couple of useful components from Clear Toolkit or other libraries mentioned in the following section. You can also find some brief reviews and recommendations of third-party libraries and tools that will make your Flex ecosystem more productive.

References

Due to space constraints, we reviewed only some of the Flex frameworks in this chapter. What other Flex MVC frameworks would we have reviewed if space allowed? We recommend you to take a close look at Swiz and Parsley, which are light MVC frameworks that implement the Inversion of Control design pattern. Here is a comprehensive list of Flex frameworks and component libraries, in alphabetical order:

- as3corelib (*http://code.google.com/p/as3corelib/*)
- Cairngen (*http://code.google.com/p/cairngen/*)
- Cairngorm (*http://opensource.adobe.com/wiki/display/cairngorm/Cairngorm*)
- Cairngorm extensions (*http://code.google.com/p/flexcairngorm/*)
- Clear Toolkit (*http://sourceforge.net/projects/cleartoolkit/*)
- EasyMVC (*http://projects.simb.net/easyMVC/*)
- Flextras (*http://www.flextras.com*)
- FlexLib Components (*http://code.google.com/p/flexlib/*)
- FlexMDI (*http://code.google.com/p/flexmdi/*)
- Guasax (*http://www.guasax.com/guasax/web/en/index.php*)
- Mate (*http://mate.asfusion.com/*)
- MVCS (*http://www.joeberkovitz.com/blog/reviewtube/*)
- Parsley (*http://spicefactory.org/parsley/*)
- PureMVC (*http://www.puremvc.org*)
- Spring ActionScript (*http://www.springactionscript.org/*)
- Swiz (*http://code.google.com/p/swizframework/*)
- Tweener (*http://code.google.com/p/tweener/*)

While analyzing frameworks, fill out the following questionnaire for each candidate:

- Will using this framework reduce the time required for development of my project?
- Does it offer enhanced Flex components or just help with separation of responsibilities of developers?
- Is it well documented?
- Is it easy to master for developers that were assigned to this project?
- Is technical support available? If yes, is it provided by creators of this framework or is it available via an online community?
- If I make the wrong choice, how long will it take to remove this framework from the application code?
- Does it support modularized applications?
- How long has this framework been around? Has it been released or is it still in beta?

This chapter was a brief comparison of selected frameworks. If you'd like to get a better understanding of how things work in Flex and maybe consider creating your own framework of rich and reusable components, we encourage you to study Chapters 2, 3, and 6. The authors sincerely hope that after reading this book, you'll be able to pick the right Flex framework for your project!

CHAPTER 2

Selected Design Patterns

Life is like an ever-shifting kaleidoscope—a slight change, and all patterns alter.

—Sharon Salzberg

Design patterns suggest an approach to common problems that arise during software development regardless of programming language. For example, when you need to ensure that your application allows only one instance of a particular class, you need to implement a singleton design pattern. If you need to pass the data between different objects, you create data transfer objects (a.k.a. value objects). There are a number of books written about design patterns and their implementation in different programming languages, including ActionScript 3.0; see *ActionScript 3.0 Design Patterns (http://oreilly.com/catalog/9780596528461/)* by William Sanders and Chandima Cumaranatunge (O'Reilly). This chapter is not yet another tutorial on patterns. The goal of this chapter is to highlight selected patterns, as you (the developer) may implement them to take advantage of the Flex framework.

While going through the examples shown in this chapter, please keep in mind that Flex is a domain-specific tool that's aimed at creating rich UI for the Web and providing efficient communication with the server-side systems.

We realize that there are people who don't like using the dynamic features of ActionScript, arguing that it makes the code less readable. In our opinion, there are lots of cases when dynamic features of the language can make the code concise and elegant.

All code examples from this chapter are located in two Flash Builder projects: *Patterns* and a Flex library project called *Patterns_lib*. You'll need to import them from the code accompanying this book.

In the previous chapter, you saw that each version of Café Townsend was built implementing some of design patterns. After reading this chapter, you may want to revisit the code of Chapter 1—you may have some new ideas about how to build yet another version of Café.

Singleton

As the name *singleton* implies, only one instance of such a class can be instantiated, which makes such classes useful if you'd like to create some kinds of global repositories of the data so that various objects of your application can access them. In Chapter 1, you saw examples of their use by various architectural Flex frameworks. For example, `ModelLocator` from Cairngorm provides a repository for the data that was retrieved by delegates so that the views can properly display it. But to get access to the data stored in this singleton, your application class has to first get a hold of this singleton:

```
var model: AppModelLocator = AppModelLocator.getInstance();
```

After this is done, you can access the data stored in various properties of the object to which the variable `model` refers.

If you need a Cairngorm singleton that can communicate with the server side, write the following code:

```
service = ServiceLocator.getInstance().getHTTPService(
                                  'loadEmployeesService');
```

Pretty soon, your application code gets polluted with similar lines of code that try to get a reference to one of the singletons.

Here's the idea. Why not just use a singleton that already exists in any Flex application instead of introducing new ones? This is a Flex Application object that's always there for you because it is part of the Flex framework. Thus you can be fairly sure that there is only one instance of it.

The problem is that the `Application` class was not created as dynamic, and you need to either extend it to act as a singleton with specific properties, or make it dynamic to be able to add to the application singleton any properties dynamically. Example 2-1's dynamic class `DynamicApplication` is a subclass of the Flex class `Application`. It implements a `Dictionary` that allows you to register your services with the application.

Example 2-1. DynamicApplication class

```
package com.farata.core{
    import flash.utils.Dictionary;
    import mx.core.Application;

public dynamic class DynamicApplication extends Application implements
                                                IApplicationFacade{
    public function DynamicApplication(){
            super();
    }
    public static var services:Dictionary =
                                          new Dictionary();

// Consider using getter and setter if you need to override behavior
// but a workaround with "static" problem in Flex
    public function getService(name:String) : Object {
```

```
        return services[name];
    }
    public function addService(name:String,value: Object): void {
        services[name] = value;
    }
    public function removeService(name:String) : void {
            delete services[name];
    }

    public function getServices() : Dictionary {
            return services;
    }
  }
}
```

This singleton class implements the `IApplicationFacade` interface (Example 2-2), which defines the methods to add, remove, and get a reference to the objects that are required by your application. The main reason to use the `IApplicationFacade` interface here is that when you typecast an `Application` with this interface in your code, you get Flash Builder's "intellisense" support and compile-time error checking.

Example 2-2. IApplicationFacade interface

```
package com.farata.core
{
    import flash.utils.Dictionary;

    public interface IApplicationFacade    {
    function getService(name:String) : Object ;
    function addService(name:String,value:Object):void ;
    function removeService(name:String) : void ;
    function getServices() : Dictionary ;
    }
}
```

Note that the test program shown in Example 2-3 is no longer a regular `<mx:Application>`, but rather an instance of the dynamic class shown in Example 2-1 and is located in the *Patterns_lib* project. Upon application startup, it calls the function `addAllServices()`, which dynamically adds `myModel` and `myServices` properties to the application object. Now any other object from the application can access this global repository just by accessing `DynamicApplication.services` followed by the property you are trying to reach. This is illustrated in the functions `getData()` and `setData()` used in Example 2-3.

Example 2-3. The application Singleton.mxml

```
<?xml version="1.0" encoding="utf-8"?>
<fx:DynamicApplication xmlns:mx="http://www.adobe.com/2006/mxml" layout="absolute"
xmlns:fx="http://www.faratasystems.com/2009/components"
creationComplete="addAllServices();">
<mx:Script>
    <![CDATA[
    import com.farata.core.DynamicApplication;
```

```
    import mx.core.Application;

// Add required services to the Application object.
// For illustration purposes, we'll add myModel and
// myServices

private function addAllServices() :void {

// Add the model repository to the application object
DynamicApplication.services["myModel"]= new Object();

// Add the services to the application object
DynamicApplication.services["myServices"] = new Object();
}

private function getData(serviceName:String,
key:Object):Object{

return DynamicApplication.services[serviceName][key];
}

private function setData(serviceName:String, key:Object,
value:String):void{
            DynamicApplication.services[serviceName][key]=
new String(value);
}

]]>
</mx:Script>

<!--Adding values to myModel -->
<mx:Button label="Add to myModel" x="193" y="59"
click="setData('myModel',key.text, value.text)"/>

<mx:Label x="14" y="42" text="Key" fontWeight="bold"/>
<mx:Label x="14" y="14" fontWeight="bold" fontSize="14">
<mx:text>
Add one or more key/value pairs to the object MyModel
</mx:text>
</mx:Label>
<mx:Label x="91" y="42" text="Value" fontWeight="bold"/>
<mx:TextInput x="8" y="59" id="key" width="75"/>
<mx:TextInput x="89" y="59" id="value" width="96"/>

<!--Retrieving the value from a Singleton. -->
<mx:Button label="Show the value" x="8" y="122" click=
"retrievedValue.text=getData('myModel', key.text) as String"/>
<mx:Label x="135" y="121" width="95" id="retrievedValue" fontWeight="bold"
fontSize="15"/>
<mx:Label x="10" y="94" fontWeight="bold" fontSize="14">
<mx:text>
Retrieve and display the value from MyModel bykey
</mx:text>
</mx:Label>
</fx:DynamicApplication>
```

As Figure 2-1 shows, this application displays a window in which a user can add any key/value pairs to the `myModel` object located in the singleton `DynamicApplication`. Then you can access them by key by clicking on the button labeled "Show the value."

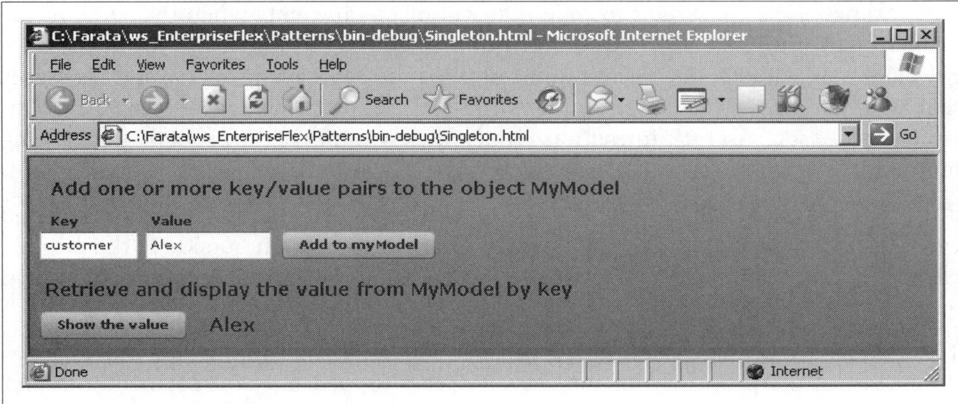

Figure 2-1. Running Singleton.mxml

The point of this exercise was to show how you can use a somewhat modified Flex `Application` object to create a global repository (a singleton) without the need to implement the singleton design pattern on your own.

Proxy

A *proxy* is an object that represents another object and controls access to it. Think of someone's spokesperson or a secretary. If someone brings a package to a big shot, the package is taken by the secretary, who would inspect the contents and then either deliver the package to the boss or delegate its further processing to someone else (e.g., security personnel).

In object-oriented programming in general and in ActionScript specifically, you can wrap the class XYZ in `mx.util.ObjectProxy`, which will be a proxy that controls access to XYZ's properties.

Let's think of some concrete Flex examples that illustrate how proxies can control access to object properties by dispatching `propertyChange` events. As a matter of fact, your Flex programs that use data binding already implement a similar mechanism of event notifications under the hood.

Data binding is a very useful technique that substantially increases the productivity of Flex developers. If you start the declaration of a variable or a class with the meta tag `[Bindable]`, all of a sudden the variable starts emitting events about all changes that can happen to it. The syntax to make this happen is very simple:

```
[Bindable]
var lastName:String;
```

How does this event notification mechanism get engaged by simply adding the magic word [Bindable]? You are all seasoned programmers and don't believe in the tooth fairy. Someone has to write the code that will dispatch events when the value of the property lastName changes. The compiler does it behind the scenes by creating a wrapper class that implements a getter and setter for the lastName property and then uses that wrapper class. The setter contains the code-dispatching **propertyChange** event, which carries such useful information as old and new values of the property that's being modified.

But you don't always have to depend on the Flex compiler when you need to create an event notification or any other customization or generalization outside of the original class. For that, you create a proxy on your own using the class ObjectProxy as shown in the following examples.

To illustrate the work of ObjectProxy, we have created a small application that changes the values of the properties of the class Person wrapped into an instance of ObjectProxy (Example 2-4).

Example 2-4. Class Person

```
package com.farata{
    public dynamic class Person    {
          public var lastName:String="Johnson";
          public var salary:Number=50000;
    }
}
```

The application code illustrating the use of ObjectProxy is shown in Example 2-5.

Example 2-5. PersonProxy.mxml

```
<?xml version="1.0" encoding="utf-8"?>
<mx:Application xmlns:mx=http://www.adobe.com/2006/mxml
creationComplete="personProxy.addEventListener(PropertyChangeEvent.PROPERT
Y_CHANGE, changeHandler)"
layout="absolute">

<mx:Script>
<![CDATA[
import mx.events.PropertyChangeEvent;
import mx.utils.ObjectProxy;
import com.farata.Person;

var person:Person = new Person;
var personProxy:ObjectProxy = new ObjectProxy(person);

function changeHandler(event:PropertyChangeEvent):void{
    log.text+="event.kind: "+ event.kind + " property :"
+ event.property +" old value:" + event.oldValue +
" new value: " + event.newValue +"\n";
```

```
    }
  ]]>
</mx:Script>
<mx:Button x="46" y="31" label="Increase Salary by $3K"
       click="personProxy.salary += 3000;"/>

<mx:Button x="211" y="31" label="Change Last Name toMcCartney"
click="personProxy.lastName='McCartney'"/>

<mx:Button x="428" y="31" label="Directly Change Last Name to Allen"
click="person.lastName='Allen';"/>

<mx:Label x="47" y="61" text="Change Log" fontWeight="bold"
fontSize="14"/>
<mx:TextArea id="log" x="46" y="91" width="600"
height="250" fontWeight="bold" fontSize="14"/>

<mx:Button x="50" y="357" label="Add pension property "
       click="personProxy.pension='yes'"/>
<mx:Button x="216" y="357" label="Delete pension property"
       click="delete personProxy.pension"/>
<mx:Label text="{personProxy.lastName}"  x="428" y="359"
       fontSize="14" fontWeight="bold"/>
</mx:Application>
```

There is one line in *PersonProxy.mxml* that wraps up the instance of the class `Person` into an `ObjectProxy`:

```
var personProxy:ObjectProxy = new ObjectProxy(person);
```

This is all it takes to ensure that all changes to `PersonProxy` will be announced—the `PropertyChangeEvent` will be triggered, and as you've added an event listener to the instance of the `Person` class, notifications are being sent about every little change that happens to that instance.

Figure 2-2 shows the output generated by this event handler after six sequential clicks: top buttons one, two, three, two, followed by the clicks on the two buttons at the bottom.

After the first click, the salary is increased by $3K, and the `ObjectProxy` notification conveniently offers the old and the new values of the property salary. The click on the second button changes the last name from Johnson to McCartney. The click on the third button quietly changes the last name from McCartney to Allen, because you applied this change not to the `personProxy` instance, but directly to the `Person`. To make sure that the value has been changed, you click button two again, which goes through the `ObjectProxy` and properly reports that the name has been changed from Allen to McCartney.

The two buttons at the bottom just illustrate that because the class `Person` has been declared as dynamic, you can add and remove properties on the fly and the `personProxy` will properly report on these events, too.

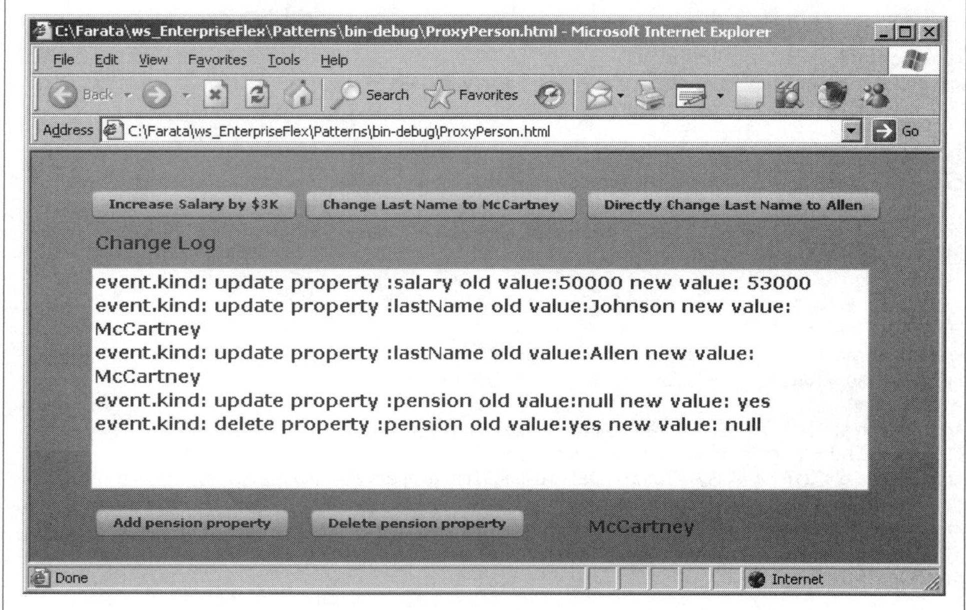

Figure 2-2. Changing Person's properties via ObjectProxy

Notice the addition of property change notifiers to the class `Person` without changing a single line of this code. This technique may also become handy when you don't have the source code of a class but need to enable property change notifications. In other words, you can enable data binding on a class that you did not create. If you've had a chance to deal with aspect-oriented programming, this may sound familiar—you add the functionality to the application without changing the application objects.

To give this example more business context, create a custom class `MyPersonProxy` by subclassing `ObjectProxy` and adding some application logic to it. If the salary of a person increases over $55K, say, that employee becomes entitled to the pension in the amount of 2 percent of the salary. You want to add this functionality without touching the code of the class `Person`.

When you create a subclass of `ObjectProxy`, you'll be overriding at least two methods: `getProperty()` and `setProperty()` from the namespace `flash_proxy`, the reason being that if you write `MyPersonProxy.lastName="McCartney"`, this object will call its own method `setProperty("lastName", "McCartney")` and if you want to intercept this call and add some additional processing to it, you just add it to the overridden method `setProperty()`. The method `getProperty()` is being called when you are trying to read a property of a Proxy object. The Proxy class defines a number of other useful functions, but discussing them is out of the scope of this book.

Our class MyPersonProxy (see Example 2-6) is derived from ObjectProxy. Its constructor receives and stores the instance of the Person class, and its setProperty() method is overridden to add a new property pension as soon as the salary of the person goes over $55K. Obviously, you can use any business logic to intercept the moment when some "important" properties are being changed in your application and react accordingly.

Example 2-6. MyPersonProxy.as

```
package com.farata
{
    import mx.utils.ObjectProxy;
    import flash.utils.*;

use namespace flash_proxy;

    public dynamic class MyPersonProxy extends ObjectProxy
    {
    // The object to wrap up
    private var person:Person;

        public function MyPersonProxy(item:Person){
            super(item);
            person=item;
        }

      flash_proxy override function setProperty(name:*, value:*):void {

if ( name == 'salary'&& value>55000) {
    // add a new property to this instance of the
    // class Person, which can be used in the calculations
    // of the total compensation
                setProperty("pension", 0.02);
            }
super.setProperty(name, value);
        }
      }
    }
```

In Example 2-7, the program CustomProxy illustrates the use of the MyPersonProxy class.

Example 2-7. CustomProxy.mxml

```
<?xml version="1.0" encoding="utf-8"?>
<mx:Application xmlns:mx="http://www.adobe.com/2006/mxml" layout="absolute"

creationComplete="personProxy.addEventListener(PropertyChangeEvent.PROPERTY_CHANGE,
changeHandler)">
    <mx:Script>
        <![CDATA[
import mx.events.PropertyChangeEvent;
//import mx.utils.ObjectProxy;
```

```
import com.farata.MyPersonProxy;
import com.farata.Person;

var person:Person = new Person;
var personProxy:MyPersonProxy = new MyPersonProxy(person);

function changeHandler(event:PropertyChangeEvent):void   {
    log.text+="event.kind: "+ event.kind + " property :" + event.property +
    " old value:" + event.oldValue + " new value: " + event.newValue +"\n";
   }
  ]]>
    </mx:Script>
    <mx:Button x="46" y="31" label="Increase Salary by $3K"
        click="personProxy.salary += 3000;"/>
    <mx:Label x="47" y="61" text="Change Log" fontWeight="bold" fontSize="14"/>
    <mx:TextArea id="log" x="46" y="91" width="600" height="250" fontWeight="bold"
fontSize="14"/>

</mx:Application>
```

Run this program and you'll see the output in Figure 2-3 after making three clicks on the Increase Salary button. The second click properly reports the addition of the `pension` property as well as the salary change. The third click doesn't report the change—the `pension` property was being assigned the same value on the third click; the proxy did not dispatch a `PropertyChangeEvent` regarding the pension.

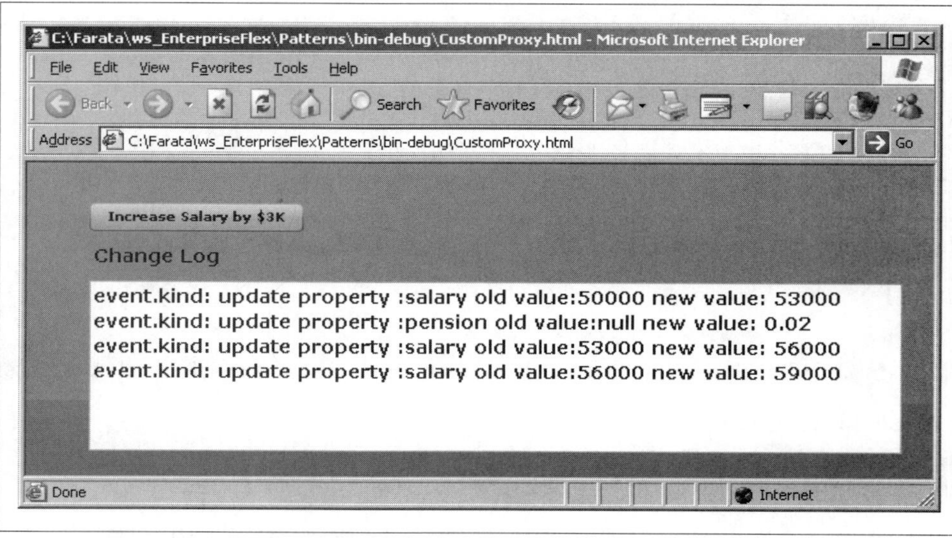

Figure 2-3. Output of CustomProxy.mxml

Here's another example, `RemoteObject`:

```
<mx:RemoteObject id="ro" destination="MyEmployees" />
```

What exactly happens when you call a method on a remote destination that goes by the nickname `MyEmployees`?

```
MyEmployees.getEmployees();
```

Flex is client software that does not need to know what powers the `MyEmployees` function has on the server side. Is there a ColdFusion or a Java object that has the function `getEmployees()` implemented? Flex doesn't need to know or care.

In the Java world, if you want to implement client/server communication using Remote Method Invocation between objects located in different Virtual Machines (VMs), you'd have to explicitly define a *stub* class on the client (a proxy) that represents its peer *skeleton* class on the server on the remote VM.

Flex spares you from creating stubs, automatically wraps these remote calls into proxy objects, and internally uses the `invoke()` method call to pass the name of the remote method and its parameters.

Flex's ability to declaratively define a reaction to the changes in the data or components state greatly simplifies programming and reduces errors related to low-level coding.

In order for binding to work, you need to make sure that the Flex framework knows when the data changes. Unlike most dynamic language implementations, ActionScript 3.0 is built for speed and heavily utilizes direct access to properties and methods. In this situation, the only way for data to notify the world about the changes is to embed the code to fire change events.

The Flex compiler helps in a big way by introducing `[Bindable]` and `[Managed]` tags. If you prefix your variable with the `[Bindable]` tag, the compiler does the following:

- Inspects every public property and setter of your variables class and generates wrapper getters/setters that add event notification
- References these getters/setters instead of original properties every time a "bindable" property is being used

Having a wrapper with a setter and a getter is technically the same as creating a proxy; that is, the setter can include and execute additional code every time the value of this specific property changes. Obviously, it does not work with untyped data coming from the server. Such data is converted to a dynamic `Object` type. The problem is alleviated a bit by the fact that the Flex framework would automatically wrap the `Object` in the `ObjectProxy` if the default property of the `RemoteObject makeObjectBindable=true` were not modified.

However, Flex will wrap only the top level and not the individual array members, making changes to those undetectable. For example, say you are passing a set of the objects from a remote Java assembler class that sends data transfer objects (DTOs) that may include an array property. These DTOs will eventually become rows in a `DataGrid`. The changes to these array elements are not going to dispatch change events unless you explicitly wrap each array element in the `ObjectProxy`, for example:

```
private function onResult(r:ResultEvent) : void {
    var quotes:ArrayCollection = r.result.quotes;
    var wrappedQuotes = new ArrayCollection();

    for each (var quote in quotes)
    wrappedQuotes.addItem(new ObjectProxy(quote))
    view.dataProvider = wrappedQuotes;
}
```

`ObjectProxy` can make the code development process more productive, but keep in mind that you are going to pay a high price for this as it introduces additional processing during the runtime—dynamic objects are much slower than strongly typed ones. Even more important, because of automatic wrapping the code might dispatch an event on each data change. Data binding is great, but if you need to process larger data sets and really need to use data binding, consider strongly typed classes that will support `[Bindable]` on the class members level and even optimize dispatching of the events. If you are doing massive updates of data, using `ObjectProxy` or any other form of data binding can substantially affect performance and the ability to trace your applications.

The bottom line is this: implement the proxy design pattern whenever you need to monitor the changes that are happening to a particular object. Yet another advantage of using proxies is that you can modify the behavior of an object without the need to modify its code.

Mediator

Almost any complex screen of a business application consists of a number of containers and components. The era of developers being responsible for both functionality and visuals is coming to an end, and a large portion of the enterprise RIA is created in a collaboration between professional UI designers and developers.

Typically, a UI designer gives you a UI wireframe that he puts together using one of the design tools. In the best-case scenario, the UI designer knows how to use Flash Builder in the design mode or even uses Adobe Flash Catalyst to autogenerate MXML for the UI. But even in this case, you, the developer, will need to rip this code apart and decide what components to build to create this view and how they are going to communicate with each other—you need to refactor the code.

Let's see how you can arrange communication between custom Flex components. The diagram in Figure 2-4 consists of a number of nested components and containers that are numbered for easier reference.

For simplicity and better abstraction, this example does not use the actual components, like panels and drop-downs, but you can extrapolate this image onto the wireframe of the actual view you are about to start developing.

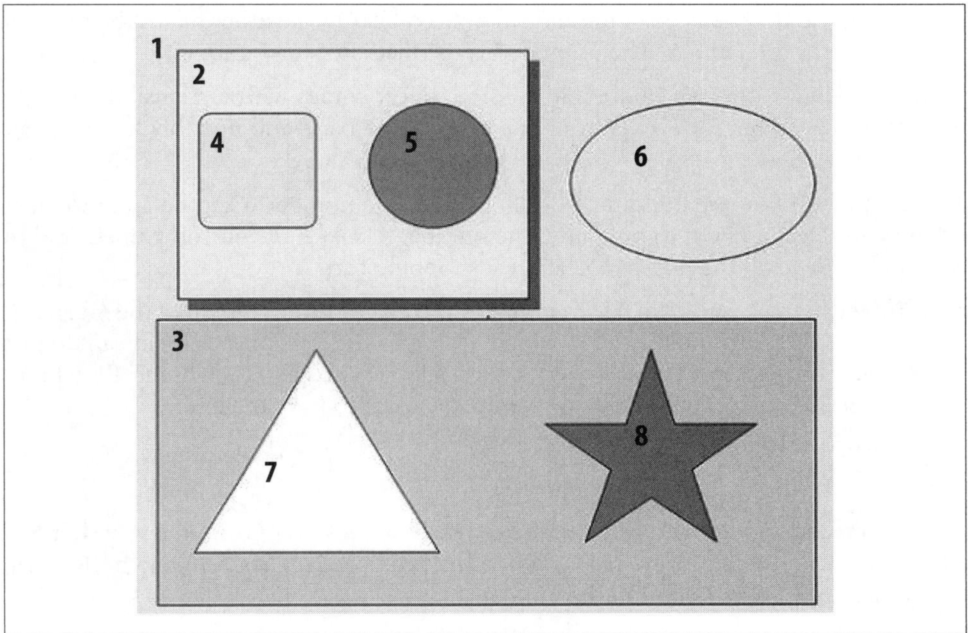

Figure 2-4. An abstract UI design that includes eight custom components

A simple (but wrong) approach is to just put all these components in one container (number 1 in Figure 2-4), program the business logic and communications among these components, and be done with it. This would produce a monolithic application with tightly coupled components that know about each other and where removal of one component would lead to multiple code changes in the application. Talk about strings attached!

The better approach is to create loosely coupled custom components that are self-contained, do not know about one another's existence, and can communicate with the "outside world" by sending and receiving events.

Adobe Flex was designed for creating event-driven applications, and it has a good component model, allowing you to create custom components if need be. But after custom components are designed, they need to communicate with each other. This section covers the use of the *Mediator design pattern* as it applies to UIs created with Flex.

Think of a single Lego from a Lego toy set. Now, some kid (i.e., the mediator) may decide to use that Lego piece to build a house. Tomorrow, the mediator may decide to use that same Lego piece in a boat.

In the diagram from Figure 2-4, containers play the role of the mediators. The top-level mediator is the container marked as 1, which is responsible for making sure that the components 2, 3, and 6 can communicate if need be. On the other hand, the number 2 is a mediator for 4 and 5. The number 3 is the mediator for 7 and 8.

Being a mediator is a very honorable mission, but it comes with responsibilities. The mediator must listen for events from one of the Lego parts and possibly fire an event on the other one(s).

For example, if you are building an online store, the number 6 can be a component where you select an item to purchase, the number 4 can be the button named Add to Shopping Cart, and the number 5 can be a shopping cart.

Let's forget about the number 6 for a moment and examine the content of the mediator, number 2. It contains the button 4, which has a specific look and feel and can do just one thing—broadcast a custom event called `AddItemClicked`. To whom? To whomever's interested in receiving such an event. So expect to have the line:

```
dispatchEvent(new Event("AddItemClicked"))
```

somewhere inside the code of the component 4.

Because mediator number 2 is interested in receiving this event from number 4, it will define an event listener for such an event, which will receive the event and in turn will dispatch another event right on the number 5:

```
addEventListener("AddItemClicked", addItemClickedEventHandler)
...
private function addItemClickedEventHandler ():void{
    Number5.dispatchEvent(new Event("Add2ShoppingCart"));
}
```

In this pseudocode, the mediator is choreographing the show by defining how its components will communicate.

We'd like to stress that in the previous example, the number 4 is like shooting an event up into the sky—anyone who wants to can listen. On the other hand, the number 5 is just sitting quietly and listening to the incoming event. From whom? It has no idea. This is what loose coupling of components means. The number 4 mediator does not know about the number 5, but they talk anyway through the mediator.

But as a developer of this screen, you have to take care of mediator-to-mediator communications as well. For instance, if the number 6 is a widget where you can select your Sony TV, the mediator 1 will be notified about it and need to talk to the mediator 2, which in turn will arrange the flow between 4 and 5.

Let's build a concrete example showing how to build these components and establish their communication using the Mediator design pattern. This is an oversimplified trading screen to buy/sell equities at the stock market. This application will have price and order panels. In the real world, the price panel would get an external feed about the prices and deals for all securities that are being traded on the market.

The web designer might give you the two screenshots shown in Figures 2-5 and 2-6 (we hope that your designer has better artistic talent than we do).

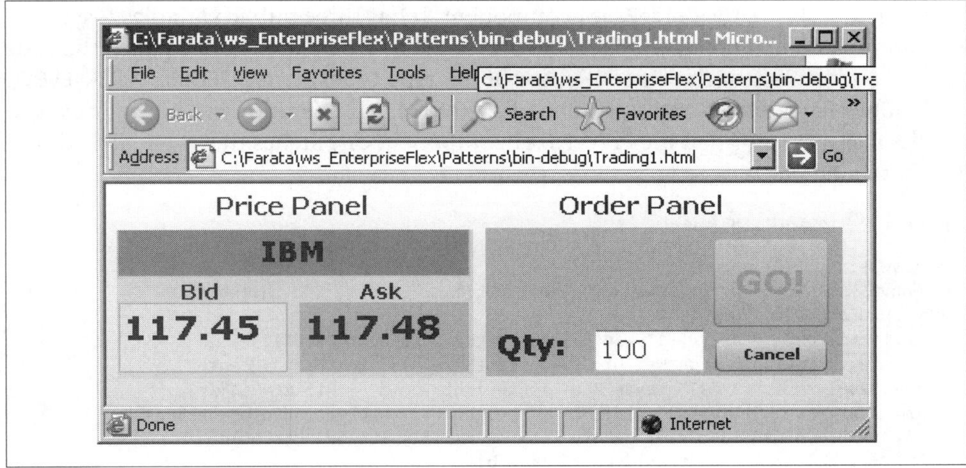

Figure 2-5. Before the trader clicked on the price panel

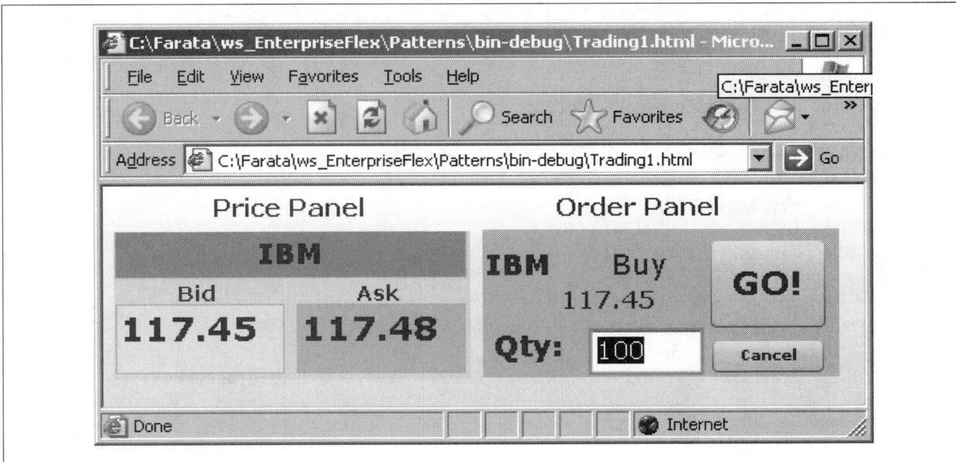

Figure 2-6. After the trader clicked on the bid number

This is a pretty simple window. You will design it as two components that communicate with each other without having any knowledge about each other. The Flex application will play role of the mediator here. When the user sees the right price to buy or sell IBM shares, she clicks on the bid or ask price; this action will create a custom event with the current data from the price panel bid and ask prices, the stock symbol, and whether this is a request to buy or sell.

In brokerage, *bid* means the highest price that the trader is willing to pay for the stock or other financial product, and *ask* is the lowest price the seller is willing to accept.

Example 2-8 shows the PricePanel component. It has three public variables—symbol, bid, and ask. When the trader clicks on one of the numbers in the price panel, the code creates an instance of the custom event of the type OrderEvent.PREPARE_ORDER_EVENT, and all public variables and the name of the requested operation are nicely packaged inside of this event. Then the PricePanel component dispatches this event. To whom? It has no idea.

Example 2-8. PricePanel.mxml

```
<?xml version="1.0" encoding="utf-8"?>
<mx:Canvas xmlns:mx="http://www.adobe.com/2006/mxml" width="230" height="100"
backgroundColor="#D4E5D9">
    <mx:TextInput x="0" y="-1" width="228" backgroundColor="#0DF113"
        text="{symbol}" fontWeight="bold" fontSize="19" textAlign="center"/>
    <mx:Label x="39" y="31" text="Bid" fontWeight="bold" fontSize="14"/>
    <mx:TextArea x="1" y="49" width="109" height="47" backgroundColor="#EBF4A2"
        text="{bid}" fontSize="22" fontStyle="normal" fontWeight="bold"
        click="placeOrder(true)" editable="false"    />

<mx:Label x="154" y="31" text="Ask" fontWeight="bold" fontSize="14"/>
    <mx:TextArea x="118" y="49" width="109" height="47"
        backgroundColor="#A2BFF4" text="{ask}" fontSize="22" fontStyle="normal"
fontWeight="bold" click="placeOrder(false)" editable="false"/>
<mx:Script>
    <![CDATA[
        import com.farata.events.OrderEvent;

    public var symbol:String;
    [Bindable]
        public var bid:String;
        [Bindable]
        public var ask:String;

        // Dispatch the OrderEvent to be picked by a Mediator
        private function placeOrder(buy:Boolean):void {
           dispatchEvent(new
               OrderEvent(OrderEvent.PREPARE_ORDER_EVENT,symbol,bid,ask,buy));
        }
    ]]>
</mx:Script>

</mx:Canvas>
```

And Example 2-9 shows the definition of the custom OrderEvent. In this version, it declares several variables for storing the order data, but the section on data transfer objects simplifies this event a little bit.

Please note that this event defines two event types. The OrderEvent of the type PREPARE_ORDER_EVENT is being sent by the PricePanel; the mediator receives it and forwards it to the OrderPanel as PLACE_ORDER_EVENT.

Example 2-9. OrderEvent.as

```
package com.farata.events{

import flash.events.Event;
public class OrderEvent extends Event {

public var symbol:String;
public var bid:String;
public var ask:String;
public var buy:Boolean;
public var eventType:String;

public static const PREPARE_ORDER_EVENT:String ="OrderEvent";
public static const PLACE_ORDER_EVENT:String   ="PlaceOrderEvent";

public function OrderEvent(eventType:String, symbol:String, bid:String,
ask:String, buy:Boolean ){

    super(eventType,true, true);  // let it bubble
    this.symbol=symbol;
    this.bid=bid;
    this.ask=ask;
    this.buy=buy;
    this.eventType=eventType;
  }

override public function clone():Event{
    return new OrderEvent(eventType,symbol, bid, ask,buy);
  }
 }
}
```

The `OrderPanel` shown in Example 2-10 listens to the event of the `OrderEvent.PLACE_ORDER_EVENT` type. When this event arrives (this panel has no idea from whom), the `OrderPanel` populates the fields with the order data extracted from the event object.

Example 2-10. OrderPanel.mxml

```
<?xml version="1.0" encoding="utf-8"?>
<mx:Canvas xmlns:mx="http://www.adobe.com/2006/mxml" width="230" height="100"
backgroundColor="#4CF3D2" creationComplete=
"this.addEventListener(OrderEvent.PLACE_ORDER_EVENT,orderEventHandler)">
    <mx:Text id="sym" x="0" y="10"  width="61" fontWeight="bold" fontSize="19"/>
    <mx:Text id="operation" x="81" y="10"  fontSize="19"/>
    <mx:Text id="price" x="48" y="37"  width="91" fontWeight="bold" fontSize="16"/>
    <mx:Label x="5" y="65" text="Qty:" fontSize="19" fontWeight="bold"/>
    <mx:TextInput id="qty" x="70" y="69" width="71" text="100"
        fontSize="16" selectionBeginIndex="0" selectionEndIndex="5"/>
    <mx:Button id="go" x="147" y="7" label="GO!" height="60" width="74"
        fontSize="22" click="placeOrder()" enabled="false"/>
    <mx:Button x="148" y="75" label="Cancel" width="72"
        click="cancelOrder()"/>
```

```
    <mx:Script>
        <![CDATA[
        import mx.controls.Alert;
        import com.farata.events.OrderEvent;

        private function orderEventHandler(evt:OrderEvent){
            go.enabled=true;
            sym.text=evt.symbol;
            operation.text=evt.buy?"Buy":"Sell";
            price.text=operation.text=="Buy"?evt.bid:evt.ask;
            qty.setFocus();
        }

        private function placeOrder():void{

            Alert.show(operation.text + " " + qty.text +
            " shares of " + sym.text +
            " at" + price.text + " per share", "Placing order");

            // call a remote service to place this order
        }

        private function cancelOrder():void{
            sym.text="";
            operation.text="";
            price.text="";
            go.enabled=false;
        }

        ]]>
    </mx:Script>

</mx:Canvas>
```

Here comes the mediator (Example 2-11), which includes two components—`PricePanel` and `OrderPanel`. The mediator listens to the event from the `PricePanel` and forwards it to the `OrderPanel` in the function `orderEventHandler`.

Example 2-11. A test application: Trading1.mxml

```
<?xml version="1.0" encoding="utf-8"?>
<mx:Application xmlns:mx="http://www.adobe.com/2006/mxml" layout="absolute"
    xmlns:comp="com.farata.components.*" backgroundColor="white"
    applicationComplete=
"this.addEventListener(OrderEvent.PREPARE_ORDER_EVENT,orderEventHandler)">
<mx:Label text="Price Panel" y="4" height="23" x="69" fontSize="16"
fontWeight="bold"/>
<mx:Label text="Order Panel" y="4" height="23" x="290" fontSize="16"
fontWeight="bold"/>
<comp:PricePanel symbol="IBM" bid="117.45" ask="117.48" y="31" x="7"/>
<comp:OrderPanel id="ordPanel" x="245" y="30"/>

<mx:Script>
    <![CDATA[
        import mx.controls.Alert;
```

```
        import com.farata.events.OrderEvent;

        private function orderEventHandler(evt:OrderEvent):void{
            // The mediator decides what to do with the received event.
            // In this case it forwards the order received
            // from PricePanel to OrderPanel
            var orderEvt: OrderEvent= new
            OrderEvent(OrderEvent.PLACE_ORDER_EVENT,
            evt.symbol, evt.bid, evt.ask, evt.buy);
            ordPanel.dispatchEvent(orderEvt);
        }
    ]]>
</mx:Script>
</mx:Application>
```

Once again, components don't know about one another and can be reused in another context, too.

The mediator is one of the most useful patterns for any programming environment that includes components communicating with each other—even more so if you program in an event-driven environment such as Flex. Use this pattern before implementing the UI design. Identify your mediators and custom reusable components and decide what events these components will broadcast or listen to.

After you have made all these decisions, select the format of the data that will travel between the components. This is where the data transfer pattern comes into the picture.

Data Transfer Object

Data transfer objects are also known as *value objects* (*VOs*) and are used for data exchanges between various application components, which can be either colocated in the same process or on remote computers. These DTOs can even be written in different programming languages, for example, Java and ActionScript.

First, modify the application from the previous section and encapsulate the order details in a simple `OrderDTO` that will be placed in the event object and will happily travel between price and order panels. When this is done, you will spend some time with more advanced DTOs that you may want to use in Flex remoting.

Example 2-12 is a simple *OrderDTO.as* that will be passed between the price and order panels.

Example 2-12. OrderDTO.as

```
package com.farata.dto{
    // [RemoteClass] meta tag goes here if this DTO
    // is used in Flex Remoting
    [Bindable]
    public class OrderDTO{
    public var symbol:String;
        public var bid:String;
```

```
        public var ask:String;
        public var buy:Boolean; //a buy/sell flag

         public function OrderDTO(symbol:String, bid:String, ask:String,
                                                        buy:Boolean=false){
        this.symbol=symbol;
        this.bid=bid;
        this.ask=ask;
        this.buy=buy;
    }
  }
}
```

In Example 2-13's second version of the price panel, add a function `startDataFeed()`, emulating the real data feed that may be bringing the market data to the pricing panel. Please note that the `PricePanel` now displays the data from this "external" feed by binding the UI controls to the properties of the `currentData` object "received" from a remote server.

Example 2-13. PricePanel2.mxml

```
<?xml version="1.0" encoding="utf-8"?>
<mx:Canvas xmlns:mx="http://www.adobe.com/2006/mxml" width="230" height="100"
backgroundColor="#D4E5D9">
    <mx:TextInput x="0" y="-1" width="228" backgroundColor="#0DF113"
        text="{currentData.symbol}" fontWeight="bold" fontSize="19"
textAlign="center"/>
    <mx:Label x="39" y="31" text="Bid" fontWeight="bold" fontSize="14"/>
    <mx:TextArea x="1" y="49" width="109" height="47" backgroundColor="#EBF4A2"
        text="{currentData.bid}" fontSize="22" fontStyle="normal" fontWeight="bold"
        click="placeOrder(true)" editable="false"
        creationComplete="startDataFeed()"/>

<mx:Label x="154" y="31" text="Ask" fontWeight="bold" fontSize="14"/>
    <mx:TextArea x="118" y="49" width="109" height="47"
        backgroundColor="#A2BFF4" text="{currentData.ask}" fontSize="22"
        fontStyle="normal" fontWeight="bold"
        click="placeOrder(false)" editable="false"/>
<mx:Script>
    <![CDATA[
        import com.farata.dto.OrderDTO;
        import com.farata.events.OrderEvent2;

        [Bindable]
    private var currentData:OrderDTO;

    private function startDataFeed():void{
        // the code for getting the real data feed goes here
        currentData = new OrderDTO("ADBE","40.47", "40.51");
        }

        // Create the OrderEvent and place the DTO there
        // Dispatch the event to be picked by a mediator
```

```
        private function placeOrder(buy:Boolean):void {
           currentData.buy=buy; // set the flag to buy or sell

           dispatchEvent(new
               OrderEvent2(OrderEvent2.PREPARE_ORDER_EVENT,currentData));
        }
    ]]>
</mx:Script>

</mx:Canvas>
```

In Example 2-14, the function `placeOrder()` dispatches the `OrderEvent2` with a packaged DTO inside. There is no need to declare multiple variables, as this was done in Example 2-9.

Example 2-14. OrderEvent2.as

```
package com.farata.events{

import com.farata.dto.OrderDTO;
import flash.events.Event;

public class OrderEvent2 extends Event {

public var orderInfo: OrderDTO;
public var eventType:String;

public static const PREPARE_ORDER_EVENT:String ="OrderEvent";
public static const PLACE_ORDER_EVENT:String   ="PlaceOrderEvent";

public function OrderEvent2(eventType:String, order:OrderDTO ){
    super(eventType,true, true);  // let it bubble
    this.orderInfo=order;         // store the orderDTO

    this.eventType=eventType;
  }

override public function clone():Event{
    return new OrderEvent2(eventType,orderInfo);
  }
 }
}
```

The new version of your driving application, *Trading2.mxml* (Example 2-15), does not assign the symbol, bid, and ask values to the price panel, as this was done for simplicity in Example 2-11. Now the `PricePanel` is being populated by its own data feed.

Example 2-15. The driving application, Trading2.mxml

```
<?xml version="1.0" encoding="utf-8"?>
<mx:Application xmlns:mx="http://www.adobe.com/2006/mxml" layout="absolute"
    xmlns:comp="com.farata.components.*" backgroundColor="white"
    applicationComplete="this.addEventListener(
OrderEvent2.PREPARE_ORDER_EVENT,orderEventHandler)" >
```

```
<mx:Label text="Price Panel" y="4" height="23" x="69" fontSize="16"
fontWeight="bold"/>
<mx:Label text="Order Panel" y="4" height="23" x="290" fontSize="16"
fontWeight="bold"/>
<comp:PricePanel2 y="31" x="7"/>
<comp:OrderPanel2 id="ordPanel" x="245" y="30"/>
<mx:Script>
    <![CDATA[
        import mx.controls.Alert;
        import com.farata.events.OrderEvent2;

        private function orderEventHandler(evt:OrderEvent2):void{
            // The mediator decides what to do with the received event
            // In this case it forwards the order received
            // from PricePanel to OrderPanel

            var orderEvt: OrderEvent2= new
            OrderEvent2(OrderEvent2.PLACE_ORDER_EVENT,evt.orderInfo);
            ordPanel.dispatchEvent(orderEvt);
        }
    ]]>
</mx:Script>
</mx:Application>
```

Even though you haven't yet seen the code of the `OrderPanel2`, you can still use it, as long as its API is known—in this case, you know that it listens to the `OrderEvent2`. As a matter of fact, in many cases you'll be using components without having any knowledge about how they operate inside.

But to go easy on you, Example 2-16 shows you the source code of *OrderPanel2.mxml*, which receives the `OrderEvent2`, extracts the `OrderDTO`, and populates its UI controls.

Example 2-16. OrderPanel2.mxml

```
<?xml version="1.0" encoding="utf-8"?>
<mx:Canvas xmlns:mx="http://www.adobe.com/2006/mxml" width="230" height="100"
backgroundColor="#4CF3D2"
creationComplete="this.addEventListener(OrderEvent2.PLACE_ORDER_EVENT,orderEventHan
dler)">
    <mx:Text id="sym" x="0" y="10"  width="61" fontWeight="bold" fontSize="19"/>
    <mx:Text id="operation" x="81" y="10"  fontSize="19"/>
    <mx:Text id="price" x="48" y="37"  width="91" fontWeight="bold" fontSize="16"/>
    <mx:Label x="5" y="65" text="Qty:" fontSize="19" fontWeight="bold"/>
    <mx:TextInput id="qty" x="70" y="69" width="71" text="100"
        fontSize="16" selectionBeginIndex="0" selectionEndIndex="5"/>
    <mx:Button id="go" x="147" y="7" label="GO!" height="60" width="74"
        fontSize="22"
        click="placeOrder()" enabled="false"/>
    <mx:Button x="148" y="75" label="Cancel" width="72"
        click="cancelOrder()"/>
    <mx:Script>
        <![CDATA[
            import com.farata.dto.OrderDTO;
```

```
        import mx.controls.Alert;
        import com.farata.events.OrderEvent2;

        private var orderInfo:OrderDTO;  // the order packaged in the DTO

        private function orderEventHandler(evt:OrderEvent2){
            go.enabled=true;

            orderInfo=evt.orderInfo;  // extract the DTO from the event object

            sym.text=orderInfo.symbol;
            operation.text=orderInfo.buy?"Buy":"Sell";
            price.text=operation.text=="Buy"?orderInfo.bid:orderInfo.ask;
            qty.setFocus();
        }

        private function placeOrder():void{

            Alert.show(operation.text + " " + qty.text +
            " shares of " + sym.text +
            " at" + price.text + " per share", "Placing order");

            // call a remote service to place this order
        }

        private function cancelOrder():void{
            sym.text="";
            operation.text="";
            price.text="";
            go.enabled=false;
        }

        ]]>
    </mx:Script>

</mx:Canvas>
```

Examples 2-12 through 2-16 illustrated an application that used a DTO as a sort of exchangeable currency in the interaction between colocated Flex components.

But DTOs also play an important role during the exchange of data with the server-side application using Flex remoting or Data Management Services. In such enterprise applications, the server-side team provides a DTO coded in one of the programming languages (this example uses Java), and the Flex team has to provide a similar ActionScript DTO.

Flex `RemoteObject` or `DataService` classes will serialize/deserialize these DTOs into each other, regardless of which direction they travel.

If you don't define DTOs on the Flex side, the data will be wrapped into `ObjectProxy` instances, which has a negative effect on performance. If you do, annotate Flex DTOs with the `[RemoteClass...]` meta tag or via the `registerClassAlias()` function call.

We highly recommend using strongly typed data transfer objects, as opposed to dynamic objects or XML for data exchange between the client and server tiers. If you are working with a Java Server, make your Java (methods) accept/return custom classes and not generic map objects.

The following list gives you some generic recommendations about creating DTOs that are meant for communication with a remote subsystem, and then offers a solution that can automate the process of creating ActionScript DTOs from their Java peers.

- Define similar classes in Java and ActionScript languages.
- If you envision dynamic updates to the data on the client (e.g., the data feed of new stock prices constantly updating the data), declare these classes with the meta tag `[Bindable]`. Use collections of these bindable instances as data providers for Flex `List`-based controls like `DataGrid`, and Flex will ensure that all changes to the data will be reflected by the visual control. Remember, the `[Bindable]` meta tag results in autogeneration of the code dispatching events on every property change.

  Use an `ArrayCollection` of such bindable DTOs as a `dataProvider` in your `DataGrid`, `List`, and similar components.

  Imagine a collection of objects with complex structure, with class variables of non-primitive data types—for example, a collection of `Employee` objects in which each object has a variable of type `WorkHistory`, which is a class with its own properties. If a variable declared in the `WorkHistory` class gets modified, the collection of `Employee` objects won't know about this change unless you explicitly dispatch the `propertyChange` event.
- Make sure that both server-side and client-side DTOs provide a *unique* property `uuid`. Flex uses this property to uniquely identify the data elements of the `List`-based controls. You will find numerous uses for this property, too.

  For instance, instead of sorting orders by the DTO's property `symbol`, you'd sort by `symbol` and `uuid`. In this case, the autogenerated hash value of each DTO will be unique for each record, which will result in better performance.
- Don't try to intercept the changed values on the visual controls (a.k.a. View). This task belongs to the data layer (a.k.a. Model).
- Consider replacing each public property with the getter and setter. This will allow you to have more control over the modifications of these properties. You can add code to these setters/getters that will intercept the action of data modification and perform additional processing based on what's being changed. Then, the setter can dispatch the event `PropertyChange` as illustrated in this code snippet:

  ```
  [Bindable(event="propertyChange")]
      public dynamic class OrderDTO extends EventDispatcher{
          private  var _bid:Number;
          public  function set bid( value : Number):void{
              var oldValue:Object = _bid;
              if (oldValue !== value)   {
                   lastPrice = value;
  ```

```
                dispatchUpdateEvent("bid", oldValue, value);
            }
        }

    public function get bid() : String{
            return _bid;
    }

     private function dispatchUpdateEvent(propertyName:String, oldValue:Object,
                                                                value:Object):void
{
      dispatchEvent(
        PropertyChangeEvent.createUpdateEvent(this, propertyName, oldValue,
                                                                   value));
     }

     }
```

This is yet another technique (remember wrapping up an object in a proxy?) for customizing the behavior of the objects when the data is being changed. Imagine that you need to create your own version of a data management service and want to maintain a collection of changed objects that remember all modifications in a DataGrid that uses a collection of OrderDTO objects as a data provider. You can maintain a collection of changed objects that remember all old and new values.

There's a difference between the [Bindable(event="propertyChange")] and [Bindable] meta tags. The former syntax instructs the Flex compiler to generate code watching the propertyChange events. The latter syntax forces the Flex compiler to generate the event—it replaces the property with a setter/getter pair in which the setter's role is to dispatch the event. But if your code has taken care of event dispatching already, you may wind up with events being dispatched twice!

- Over your project's life span, you will see many additional uses for DTOs: custom serialization and custom toString() and toXML() methods, for example.
- Create a basic OrderDTO as in Example 2-12 and subclass it. This way, the superclass OrderDTO maintains its original structure while its subclass allows you to add some new functionality like notifying a third party about properties' changes or adding new properties like total order amount, which is a result of the multiplication of total shares by price per share:

```
[Bindable(event="propertyChange"]
public function get totalOrderAmount():Number {
    return price*totalShares;
}
```

If you are creating DTOs for the data exchange between Java and ActionScript classes using subclassing, both ActionScript classes will have the meta tag [RemoteClass] pointing to the same Java DTO. This won't be an issue; Flex is smart enough to use the subclass for serialization.

In the real world, an enterprise project's Flex and Java developers often belong to different teams and if Java folks change the structure of their DTOs, Flex developers need to ensure that the structure of their classes is updated accordingly. There are different ways of automating this process, as shown in Example 2-17.

DTO2Fx is a free plug-in that's available at *http://www.myflex.org*. It generates ActionScript DTO classes using the subclassing technique described earlier.

Consider the Java DTO in Example 2-17.

Example 2-17. Annotated OrderDTO2.java

```
package com.farata.dto;
import com.farata.dto2fx.annotations.FXClass;

@FXClass
publicclass OrderDTO2 {
public String symbol;
public String bid;
public String ask;
public Boolean buy;

public OrderDTO2(String symbol, String bid,String ask, Boolean buy){
    this.symbol=symbol;
    this.bid=bid;
    this.ask=ask;
    this.buy=buy;
 }
}
```

The DTO2Fx plug-in uses Java annotations in the process of generating ActionScript classes, and `@FXClass` is such an annotation. The rest of the process is simple. As soon as you create or modify this class, it automatically regenerates a couple of ActionScript classes: *_OrderDTO2.as* and *OrderDTO2.as*. You can find more details about this process in the User Guide of DTO2Fx, but for now just examine the generated code in Example 2-18.

Example 2-18. Superclass _OrderDTO2.as

```
package com.farata.dto {


import mx.events.PropertyChangeEvent;

import flash.events.EventDispatcher;
import mx.core.IUID;
import mx.utils.UIDUtil;

/* [ExcludeClass] */
public class _OrderDTO2 extends flash.events.EventDispatcher implements
```

```
mx.core.IUID {

/* Constructor */
  public function _OrderDT02():void {
    super();
    }

// implementors of IUID must have a uid property
    private var _uid:String;

    [Transient]
    [Bindable(event="propertyChange")]
    public function get uid():String {
    // If the uid hasn't been assigned a value, just create a new one.
    if (_uid == null) {
        _uid = mx.utils.UIDUtil.createUID();
      }
    return _uid;
    }

    public function set uid(value:String):void {
     const previous:String = _uid;
     if (previous != value) {
        _uid = value;
        dispatchEvent(
          mx.events.PropertyChangeEvent.createUpdateEvent(
                              this, "uid", previous, value
          )
        );
      }
    }

/* Property "ask" */
    private var _ask:String;

    [Bindable(event="propertyChange")]
    public function get ask():String {
       return _ask;
    }
    public function set ask(value:String):void {
       const previous:String = this._ask;
    if (previous != value) {
        _ask = value;
    const ev:mx.events.PropertyChangeEvent =
        mx.events.PropertyChangeEvent.createUpdateEvent(
        this, "ask", previous, _ask
        );
        dispatchEvent(ev);
      }
    }

/* Property "bid" */
    private var _bid:String;

    [Bindable(event="propertyChange")]
```

```
    public function get bid():String {
      return _bid;
    }
    public function set bid(value:String):void {
      const previous:String = this._bid;
      if (previous != value) {
        _bid = value;
      const ev:mx.events.PropertyChangeEvent =
        mx.events.PropertyChangeEvent.createUpdateEvent(
                            this, "bid", previous, _bid);
        dispatchEvent(ev);
      }
    }

/* Property "buy" */
    private var _buy:Boolean;

    [Bindable(event="propertyChange")]
    public function get buy():Boolean {
      return _buy;
    }

    public function set buy(value:Boolean):void {
       const previous:Boolean = this._buy;
       if (previous != value) {
        _buy = value;
      const ev:mx.events.PropertyChangeEvent =
      mx.events.PropertyChangeEvent.createUpdateEvent(
      this, "buy", previous, _buy );
        dispatchEvent(ev);
      }
    }

/* Property "symbol" */
     private var _symbol:String;

    [Bindable(event="propertyChange")]
    public function get symbol():String {
       return _symbol;
    }

   public function set symbol(value:String):void {
       const previous:String = this._symbol;
       if (previous != value) {
         _symbol = value;
         const ev:mx.events.PropertyChangeEvent =
         mx.events.PropertyChangeEvent.createUpdateEvent(
         this, "symbol", previous, _symbol);
        dispatchEvent(ev);
      }
    }

  }

}
```

Example 2-18 is a superclass that will always be regenerated by DTO2Fx anytime the Java class changes. This class has a unique object identifier (`uid`) and includes getters and setters that will dispatch `propertyChange` events when the time comes.

The code of the class `OrderDTO2` is shown in Example 2-19. This class is generated only once and is a subclass of *_OrderDTO2.as*. This is a place for an application developer to add application-specific customization, such as the addition of new properties and/ or functions. This class will never be overridden by DTO2Fx, regardless of what was changed in `OrderDTO2.java`.

Example 2-19. Subclass OrderDTO2.as

```
package com.farata.dto {

  [RemoteClass(alias="com.farata.dto.OrderDTO2")]

public class OrderDTO2 extends com.farata.dto._OrderDTO2 {

/* Constructor */
   public function OrderDTO2():void {
     super();
    }
  }
}
```

We hope that our message to you is clear now: the use of DTOs is a preferred way of designing interobject communications.

Asynchronous Token

Consider an enterprise application in which a user can place purchase orders for some parts and request price quotes from various suppliers. In this case, the user may click several buttons, resulting in server-side calls to one or more destinations. On each click event of the button, a `RemoteObject` sends a new request to the server.

The user hits this button several times to place several orders, which in turn initiates the same number of remote calls. The user can also click different buttons, initiating calls to different destinations. Because of the asynchronous nature of remote calls in Flex, the results from each call can arrive at random times.

When each result arrives to the client, it triggers a `result` event, which obediently calls the result handler function written by an application programmer. So far, so good. Here's the million-dollar question: how can the application code map arriving result objects back to the initial requesters if they can come back to the client in an arbitrary order? The fact that you place an order to purchase a Sony TV first and a DVD player 10 seconds afterward doesn't guarantee that results will arrive to your Flex application in the same order.

The goal of the *Asynchronous Token pattern* is to properly route the processing on the client in response to the data arriving asynchronously from the server.

Because `AsyncToken` is a dynamic class, you can add any properties to this class during runtime, as is done with `orderNumber` in Example 2-20. You can also add one or more responders that will provide the result handling. Adding responders on the token level simplifies memory management.

Example 2-20. Using the AsyncToken class

```
<mx:RemoteObject id="ord" destination="Orders" />
 ...
private function sendOrder(/*arguments go here*/):void{
    var token: AsyncToken = ord.placeOrder({item:"Sony TV"});
    token.orderNumber="12345";
    token.responder = new Responder(processOrderPlaced, processOrderFault);
    token.addResponder(new Responder(createShipment,processOrderFault));
}
```

`AsyncToken` is a local object. It is identified by a `messageId` that is passed with the request to the server. When the server responds, it includes a `correlationId` property in the message header, and Flex automatically calls the appropriate `AsyncToken` responders in the order they were defined. Example 2-20 calls the function `send()`, which starts with creating the `AsyncToken` instance. Then, you'll attach as many properties to this instance as you need. You may get the impression that something is not right—the values are being assigned to the instance of the token *after* the request has been sent to the server for execution. If so, when the result in the form of an `AsyncToken` comes back, it shouldn't contain values such as `orderNumber` and references to the responders, right? Wrong.

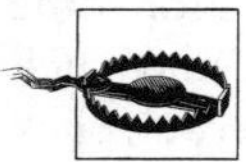

Flash Player executes your application's requests in cycles driven by frame events. First, it performs the requests related to the modifications of the UI, then it gives a slice of time to process the application's ActionScript code, and only after that does it take care of the network requests, if any. This means that all the code in the previous snippet will complete before the call `ord.placeOrder({item:"Sony TV"})` is made. Always remember that from the developer's perspective, Flex applications are single-threaded and responses are handled within each such cycle—even if the underlying communications are multithreaded.

In Example 2-20, two responders were added to the `placeOrder()` request. In the case of successful order placement, two functions will be called: `processOrderPlaced()` and `createShipment()`. In the case of errors, the function `processOrderFault()` will be called.

You can add an instance of a `Responder` object to a token on the fly, as was done in the earlier code snippet, or your can provide an existing instance of a class that implements the `IResponder` interface—that is, that has the functions `result()` and `fault()`.

To see a different way of assigning a responder, please revisit the code in Example 1-6 that demonstrates how Cairngorm's `Delegate` class adds a `Command` object as a responder. Sure enough, the `Command` object implements `result()` and `fault()` methods.

In the more traditional way of programming client/server communications, you define the handlers for results and faults:

```
<mx:RemoteObject id="ord" destination="Orders" result="processOrderPlaced(event)"
fault="processOrderFault(event)"/>
```

But using `AsyncToken`, you can assign the handlers during runtime as was done in Example 2-20, which gives your application additional flexibility.

At some point in time, the result will come back to the client and you can retrieve the token from the property `ResultEvent.token` and examine its dynamic properties (just the `orderNumber` in your case) that were originally added to the token:

```
private function processOrderPlaced(event:ResultEvent):void {
    myOrderNumber:Object = event.token.orderNumber;
    // if myOrderNumber is 12345, process it accordingly
}
```

Using the Asynchronous Token design pattern allows Flex to efficiently map associated requests and responses without the need to introduce a multithreaded environment and create some mapping tables to avoid mixing up requests and responses.

Class Factory

Flex offers you various ways to create an instance of a component. For example, in MXML, you can create an instance of `MyObject` and initialize its property description as follows:

```
<comp:MyObject id="order" description="Sony TV" />
```

You can achieve the same result (i.e., create an instance of `MyObject` and initialize the description) in ActionScript:

```
var order:MyObject = new MyObject();
order.description="Sony TV";
```

This code works fine as long as `MyObject` is the only possible component that can be placed in this particular screen location. But what if you need more flexibility—for example, under certain conditions you need to create either `MyObject` or `HisObject` at this location?

Instead of using the `new` operator, you can introduce a class with a function that will build different objects for your application based on a specified parameter. In this case, you need to implement the Class Factory design pattern—the object that will create and return either an instance of `MyObject` or `HisObject`.

You can easily find code samples of how to create class factories. Some of them are very basic, so that you just provide the name of the object you need to a factory method that has a switch statement, and it returns the proper instance of the object based on the provided name. More advanced factories are programmed to interfaces, which allows you to add new types of objects to the factory without the need to use and modify the switch each time a new object type is introduced.

A Class Factory from the Flex Framework

The Flex framework includes an implementation of the Class Factory pattern in the mx.core.ClassFactory class. Let's quickly review its code; see Example 2-21 (we've removed some of the comments for brevity).

Example 2-21. mx.core.ClassFactory.as

```
////////////////////////////////////////////////////////////////////////////////
//  ADOBE SYSTEMS INCORPORATED                                                //
//  Copyright 2005-2006 Adobe Systems Incorporated                            //
//  All Rights Reserved.                                                      //
//                                                                            //
//  NOTICE: Adobe permits you to use, modify, and distribute this file        //
//  in accordance with the terms of the license agreement accompanying it.    //
////////////////////////////////////////////////////////////////////////////////

package mx.core{

/**
 *  A ClassFactory instance is a "factory object" which Flex uses
 *  to generate instances of another class, each with identical properties.
 *
 *  You specify a generator class when you construct the factory object.
 *  Then you set the properties property on the factory object.
 *  Flex uses the factory object to generate instances by calling
 *  the factory object's newInstance() method.
 *
 *  The newInstance() method creates a new instance
 *  of the generator class, and sets the properties specified
 *  by properties in the new instance.
 *  If you need to further customize the generated instances,
 *  you can override the newInstance() method.
 *
 *  The ClassFactory class implements the IFactory interface.
 *  Therefore it lets you create objects that can be assigned to properties
 *  of type IFactory, such as the itemRenderer property of a List control
 *  or the itemEditor property of a DataGrid control.
 *
 *  For example, suppose you write an item renderer class named ProductRenderer
 *  containing a showProductImage property which can be true or false.
 *  If you want to make a List control use this renderer, and have each renderer
 *  instance display a product image, you would write the following code:
 *
 *  var productRenderer:ClassFactory = new ClassFactory(ProductRenderer);
```

```
 *  productRenderer.properties = { showProductImage: true };
 *  myList.itemRenderer = productRenderer;
 *
 *  The List control calls the newInstance() method on the
 *  itemRenderer to create individual instances of ProductRenderer,
 *  each with showProductImage property set to true.
 *  If you want a different List control to omit the product images, you use
 *  the ProductRenderer class to create another ClassFactory
 *  with the properties property set to { showProductImage: false }.
 *
 *  Using the properties property to configure the instances
 *  can be powerful, since it allows a single generator class to be used
 *  in different ways.
 *  However, it is very common to create non-configurable generator classes
 *  which require no properties to be set.
 *  For this reason, MXML lets you use the following syntax:
 *
 *  <mx:List id="myList" itemRenderer="ProductRenderer"/>
*/

public class ClassFactory implements IFactory
{

    include "../core/Version.as";

    public function ClassFactory(generator:Class = null){
        super();
        this.generator = generator;
    }

    public var generator:Class;

    /**
     * An Object whose name/value pairs specify the properties to be set
     *  on each object generated by the newInstance() method.
     *
     *  For example, if you set properties to
     *  { text: "Hello", width: 100 }, then every instance
     *  of the generator class that is generated by calling
     *  newInstance() will have its text set to
     *  "Hello" and its width set to 100.
     */
    public var properties:Object = null;

    /**
     *  Creates a new instance of the generator class,
     *  with the properties specified by properties.
     *
     *  This method implements the newInstance() method
     *  of the IFactory interface.
     *
     *  @return The new instance that was created.
     */
    public function newInstance():* {
        var instance:Object = new generator();
```

```
        if (properties != null){
            for (var p:String in properties){
                instance[p] = properties[p];
        }
        }
      return instance;
    }
  }
}
```

Please read the comments for this class and pay attention to the following section:

```
var productRenderer:ClassFactory = new ClassFactory(ProductRenderer);
productRenderer.properties = { showProductImage: true };
myList.itemRenderer = productRenderer;
```

The first line of this code instructs `ClassFactory` to create an instance of the class `ProductRenderer`; it's stored in the `generator` property of this class. The second line initializes the property `showProductImage` of the newly created `ProductRenderer`. You can initialize more than one property of the object that you create by assigning to the `properties` variable an object containing several key/value pairs. If you are instantiating a sealed class, make sure that the properties you are initializing exist in the class being instantiated. In the case of a dynamic object, you can initialize/create any properties on the fly.

The function `newInstance()` copies all properties that need to be initialized from the `properties` object to the corresponding properties of the newly created instance. But the earlier code example doesn't call `newInstance()`; is this a mistake?

No, this code is correct, and here's why. The data type of the variable `itemRenderer` (as well as `itemEditor`) of the Flex `List` component is `IFactory`, the interface that declares just one method: `newInstance()`. `List`-based components know how to instantiate objects that implement the `IFactory` interface, and the previous `ClassFactory` does implement it.

This also means that instead of providing a concrete object as an `itemRenderer`, you may specify a subclass of `ClassFactory` with the overridden method `newInstance()` that will be supplying the appropriate object instance.

If you'll be using this `ClassFactory` in other situations of the application code, you may need to call `newInstance()` explicitly.

Although `mx.core.ClassFactory` and item renderers are a very powerful combination when you need to customize the appearance of the data in `List`-based components, the `ClassFactory` shown in Example 2-21 has the following restrictions:

- The Flex 3 SDK class `mx.core.ClassFactory` can create a factory only for a class; it can't create a factory for a class name that is being provided as a `String`. It can't build instances of objects based on a return of a function—a class is required.
- Building UI objects on the fly may require applying dynamic data-driven styles. Styles are not properties, and `mx.core.ClassFactory` would not know what to do with them if you used them in the `properties` variable.
- If you use UI components as renderers or editors, they may need to process events. It would be nice if event listeners could be attached by a class factory, and the created object would dispatch events when properties are changing. The class `mx.core.ClassFactory` doesn't know how to do it.

In the Flex 4 SDK, `ClassFactory` allows you to dynamically assign item renderers to `List`-based components based on the name of the class provided in a string variable:

```
<s:List itemRendererFunction="myRendererFunc">
...
private function myRenderedFunc (item:Object): ClassFactory{
     var myRenderer:Class;

    switch (item.membershipType){
        case "Trial":  myRenderer=TrialMemberRenderer;
          break;
       case "Basic":
          myRenderer=BasicMemberRenderer;
          break;
       case "Premium":
         myRenderer=TrialMemberRenderer;
          break;
    }
   return new ClassFactory(myRenderer);
}
```

Creating UIStaticClassFactory

This final section offers you a more advanced implementation of the Class Factory pattern that is specifically created for the UI components, especially item renderers in `List`-based Flex components. Please read the description of this implementation, called `UIStaticClassFactory`, in the code comments of Example 2-22.

Example 2-22. UIStaticClassFactory.as

```
////////////////////////////////////////////////////////////////////////////////
//                                                                            //
//  Copyright 2009 Farata Systems LLC                                         //
//  All Rights Reserved.                                                      //
//                                                                            //
//  NOTICE: Farata Systems permits you to use, modify, and distribute this file  //
//  in accordance with the terms of the license agreement accompanying it.    //
//                                                                            //
////////////////////////////////////////////////////////////////////////////////
```

```
package com.farata.core{
/**
 *  UIStaticClassFactory is an implementation of the Class Factory design pattern
 *  for dynamic creaion of UI components. It allows dynamic passing of the
 *  properties, styles and event listeners during the object creation.
 *  It's implemented as a wrapper for mx.core.ClassFactory and can
 *  be used as a class factory not just for classes, but for functions
 *  and even strings.
 *
 *  @see mx.core.IFactory
 */
    import flash.utils.describeType;
    import flash.utils.getDefinitionByName;
    import mx.controls.dataGridClasses.DataGridColumn;
    import mx.core.ClassFactory;
    import mx.core.IFactory;
    import mx.events.FlexEvent;
    import mx.styles.StyleProxy;
    import mx.logging.Log;
    import mx.logging.ILogger;
    import mx.logging.LogEventLevel;


    public class UIStaticClassFactory implements IFactory{

        // A class factory object that serves as a wrapper
        // for classes, functions, strings, and even class factories
        private var _wrappedClassFactory : ClassFactory;

        // A reference to a function if the object instances are
        // to be created by a function
        private var factoryFunction : Function = null;

        // Styles for the UI object to be created
        public var styles:Object;

        // Event Listeners for the UI object to be created
        public var eventListeners:Object;


        private static const logger:ILogger =
                    Log.getLogger ("com.farata.core.UICassFactory");

        public function set properties(v:Object):void    {
            _wrappedClassFactory.properties = v;
        }
        public function get properties():* {
            return _wrappedClassFactory.properties ;
        }

        public function get wrappedClassFactory():ClassFactory {
            return _wrappedClassFactory;
        }
        /**
```

```
 * Constructor of UIClassFactory takes four arguments
 * cf   -  The object to build. It can be a class name,
 *         a string containing the class name, a function,
 *         or another class factory object;
 * props - inital values for some or all properties if the object;
 * styles - styles to be applied to the object being built
 * eventListeners - event listeners to be added to the object being built
 */
function UIStaticClassFactory( cf: * , props:Object = null,
          styles:Object = null, eventListeners:Object = null ) {

    var className:String;// if the class name was passed as a String

    if ( cf is UIStaticClassFactory) {
        _wrappedClassFactory =
                 UIStaticClassFactory(cf).wrappedClassFactory;
    } if ( cf is ClassFactory) {
        _wrappedClassFactory = cf;
    } else if (cf is Class) {
        _wrappedClassFactory = new ClassFactory(Class(cf));
    } else if (cf is String) {
        className = String(cf);
        try {
            var clazz:Class = getDefinitionByName(className) as Class;
            _wrappedClassFactory = new  ClassFactory(clazz);
        } catch (e:Error)     {
            trace(" Class '"+ className + "' can't be loaded
                 dynamically. Ensure it's explicitly referenced in the
                          application file or specified via @rsl.");
        }
    } else if (cf is Function) {
        factoryFunction = cf;
    } else {
            className = "null";
            if (cf!=null)
                className = describeType(cf).@name.toString();
            trace("'" + className + "'" +
                  " is invalid parameter for UIClassFactory constructor.");
    }

    if (!_wrappedClassFactory) {
        _wrappedClassFactory = new ClassFactory(Object);
    }

    if (props != null) _wrappedClassFactory.properties = props;
    if (styles != null) this.styles = styles;
    if (eventListeners != null) this.eventListeners = eventListeners;
}

/**
* The implementation of newInstance is required by IFactory
*/
public function newInstance():* {
    var obj:*;
    if (factoryFunction!=null){
```

```
                // using a function to create an object
                 obj = factoryFunction();
                 // Copy the properties to the new object
                 if (properties != null)  {
                     for (var p:String in properties) {
                         obj[p] = properties[p];
                     }
                    }
            } else
                 obj = _wrappedClassFactory.newInstance();

            // Set the styles on the new object
            if (styles != null)  {
                for (var s:String in styles) {
                    obj.setStyle(s,  styles[s]);
                }
            }

            //add event listeners, if any
            if (eventListeners != null)  {
                for (var e:String in eventListeners) {
                    obj.addEventListener(e,  eventListeners[e]);
                }
            }
            return obj;
        }
    }
}
```

Let's examine the constructor of this class factory. It has four arguments, described in the comments. In the first argument, the code of this constructor checks the type of the object to build the factory for. In particular, if it's a class, it just instantiates `mx.core.ClassFactory`.

More interestingly, if it finds that the type of the first argument is a `String`, it'll load the class specified in this `String` and build a factory for this class, too.

One more scenario: if you'd like to specify not a class but just a function for the class factory, it can accommodate this request as well.

Example 2-23 shows you a test application that uses this class factory to dynamically build item renderers for a `DataGrid` not on a *per-column* basis but on a *per-cell* basis.

Example 2-23. ClassFactoryDemo.mxml

```
<?xml version="1.0" encoding="utf-8"?>
<mx:Application xmlns:mx="http://www.adobe.com/2006/mxml"
    xmlns:fx="http://www.faratasystems.com/2009/components"
    layout="vertical" creationComplete="init()">
    <mx:HDividedBox width="100%" height="100%">
        <fx:DataGrid   id="dg" dataProvider="{dp}"  editable="true" height="100%"
            showHeaders="false"  alternatingItemColors="[#869CA7,#869CA7]"
            verticalGridLines="false"  variableRowHeight="true"
            preventRendererReuse="columnValue">
```

```
        <fx:columns>
            <mx:Array>
                <mx:DataGridColumn width="120"  dataField="columnLabel"
                    headerText="Field"  textAlign="right"   editable="false"/>
                <mx:DataGridColumn width="150"    textAlign="left"
                     dataField="columnValue"   headerText="Value"
                     wordWrap="true"  rendererIsEditor="true"
                     itemRenderer="{new UIStaticClassFactory(function():* {
                         return switcher(dg.rendererData)})}"/>
            </mx:Array>
        </fx:columns>
    </fx:DataGrid>

    <mx:DataGrid editable="true" dataProvider="{dp}" height="100%" >
    </mx:DataGrid>

</mx:HDividedBox>
    <mx:Script>
    <![CDATA[
        import mx.controls.Label;
        import mx.collections.ArrayCollection;
        import mx.controls.RadioButtonGroup;
        import mx.controls.TextInput;
        import com.adobe.flex.extras.controls.MaskedTextInput;
        import com.farata.core.UIStaticClassFactory;
        [Bindable]
        private var dp:ArrayCollection;
        private function init() :void {
            dp= new ArrayCollection ([
                new ColumnRecord("First Name: ", "text", "John" ),
                new ColumnRecord("Last Name: ", "text", "Smith" ),
                new ColumnRecord("SSN#: ", "ssn", "123704523" ),
            ]);
        }
        private function switcher(data:Object = null) :*{
            if (data == null) return new  Label();
            switch(data.columnType) {
            case "ssn":
                var mi:MaskedTextInput = new MaskedTextInput();
                mi.inputMask = "###-##-####";
                return mi;
            }
            return new  TextInput();
        }
    ]]>
    </mx:Script>
</mx:Application>
```

The ColumnRecord in the previous example is just a little DTO (see Example 2-24).

Example 2-24. ColumnRecord.as

```
package
{
    public class ColumnRecord
```

```
    {
        public  var columnLabel:String;
        public  var columnType:String;
        public  var columnValue:*;

        public function ColumnRecord(l:String, t:String, v:*) {
            columnLabel=l;
            columnType=t;
            columnValue=v;
        }
    }
}
```

The *ClassFactoryDemo* application generates the view in Figure 2-7, which at first sight looks like a form and a DataGrid.

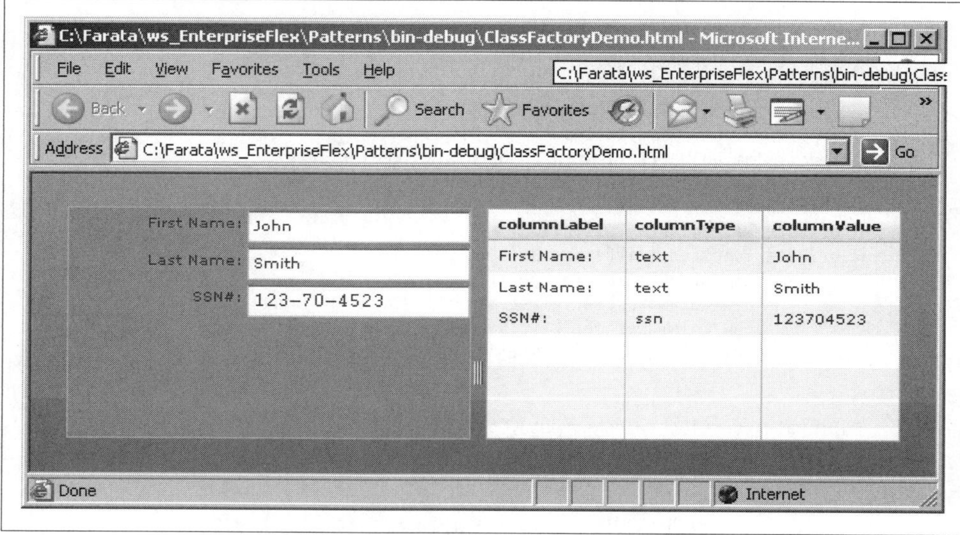

Figure 2-7. A DataGrid with dynamic item renderers

But this is a container with two DataGrid objects pointing to the same data provider—a simple array that contains both the data (columnValue) and the metadata (the label, and the type of the data).

On the righthand side, it's a regular <mx:DataGrid> from the Flex framework.

On the left is your 50-line extension of the original data grid, <fx:DataGrid>, which has a small addition—it cures the limitation of <mx:DataGrid> that reuses the same itemRenderer for the entire column (its source code comes with this book).

Our goal was to create a class factory that would supply different item renderers based on some criteria:

```
itemRenderer="{new UIStaticClassFactory(function():*
              return switcher(dg.rendererData)})}"/>
```

The left data grid gives the closure function to `UIStaticClassFactory`, which calls another function, `switcher()`, which analyzes the metadata (the column type). If it's simple text, it just renders it as a `Label`, but if the type of the column is `ssn`, it renders it as a `MaskedTextInput`.

Please note that this class factory does not know in advance what to build, as you don't use static linkage here.

This example kills two birds with one stone. First, it shows a more advanced class factory, and second, it illustrates how you can build dynamic forms having a `DataGrid` with dynamic data renderers under the hood.

In general, using components for item renderers and editors may be challenging. When you use a renderer as an editor, you have at your disposal powerful control with a built-in mask. In the earlier view, if a user decides to change the value of SSN#, he will be restricted by the mask `MaskedTextInput`.

Even though having many different item renderers may be a bit expensive from the performance view, it brings you a lot of flexibility and a nicer-looking UI.

The authors of this book use item renderers as item editors and have a single point of customization for controls.

Using class factories allows you to make grids that do not look like grids but rather like dynamic forms. They can support runtime properties, styles, and other types of plug-ins either via MXML or—even better—via well-structured ActionScript.

OK, this can't all be that rosy, and there is a little issue—you can't declare properties needed for these custom renderer components on the `DataGridColumn` tag. When you write in MXML something like `itemRenderer="MyClassFactory"`, there is no room for you to specify properties of the renderer component. You have to use the `<mx:Component>` tag in order to "embed" them into a class.

Creating UIClassFactory

Using the class `UIStaticClassFactory` with item renderers is a good idea, but let's have a little more fun with factories. This new demo application uses another version of class factory first. The source code of the more advanced `UIClassFactory` will follow.

This version of the factory shows you how you can create dynamic styles, properties, and events in a declarative way. The demo application looks like Example 2-25.

Example 2-25. ClassFactoryDemo2.mxml

```
<?xml version="1.0" encoding="utf-8"?>
<mx:Application xmlns:mx="http://www.adobe.com/2006/mxml"
    xmlns:fx="http://www.faratasystems.com/2009/components"
    layout="vertical" creationComplete="init()">
    <mx:DataGrid horizontalScrollPolicy="auto" width="100%" id="dg"
            editable="true" height="100%">
        <mx:columns>
         <mx:DataGridColumn dataField="EMP_FNAME"  headerText="First Name"/>
         <mx:DataGridColumn dataField="EMP_LNAME"  headerText="Last Name"/>
         <mx:DataGridColumn dataField="DEPT_ID" editable="false"
                                                headerText="Department" />
        <mx:DataGridColumn dataField="PHONE"  rendererIsEditor="true"
                                               headerText="Phone Number" >
            <mx:itemRenderer>
                <fx:UIClassFactory>
                    <fx:generator>
                        {MaskedTextInput}
                    </fx:generator>
                    <fx:properties>
                        <mx:Object inputMask = "###-###-####" />
                    </fx:properties>
                </fx:UIClassFactory>
            </mx:itemRenderer>
        </mx:DataGridColumn>
       <mx:DataGridColumn dataField="STATUS" headerText="Status"
                                            rendererIsEditor="true"  />
        <mx:DataGridColumn dataField="SS_NUMBER"  rendererIsEditor="true"
                                                        headerText="SSN#" >
            <mx:itemRenderer>
                <fx:UIClassFactory>
                    <fx:generator>
                        {MaskedTextInput}
                    </fx:generator>
                    <fx:properties>
                        <mx:Object inputMask = "###-##-####" />
                    </fx:properties>
                </fx:UIClassFactory>
            </mx:itemRenderer>
        </mx:DataGridColumn>

        <mx:DataGridColumn dataField="SALARY" editable="false" headerText="Salary"
                                    textAlign="right" rendererIsEditor="true">
            <mx:itemRenderer>
                <fx:UIClassFactory>
                    <fx:generator>
                        {TextInput}
                    </fx:generator>
                   <fx:runtimeStyles>
                      <mx:Object
                      fontWeight="{function(d:*):String { return
                                            d.SALARY>50000?'normal':'bold'}}"
                           backgroundColor="{function(d:*):String { return
                                          d.SALARY>30000?'green':'red'}}"/>
                   </fx:runtimeStyles>
```

```
                </fx:UIClassFactory>
            </mx:itemRenderer>
        </mx:DataGridColumn>

        <mx:DataGridColumn dataField="START_DATE" headerText="Start Date"
              itemRenderer="mx.controls.DateField" editorDataField="selectedDate"
                                                       rendererIsEditor="true" />
        <mx:DataGridColumn dataField="BENE_HEALTH_INS" editable="false"
                                                            headerText="Health" >

            <mx:itemRenderer>
                <fx:UIClassFactory>
                    <fx:generator>
                        {CheckBox}
                    </fx:generator>
                    <fx:runtimeProperties>
                        <mx:Object
                        selected="{function(d:*):Boolean { return
                                                  d.BENE_HEALTH_INS=='Y'}}"/>
                    </fx:runtimeProperties>

                    <fx:eventListeners>
                        <mx:Object
                        click="{function (e:MouseEvent): void {
                                          trace('hello:'+e);
                                          beneHealthClick(e);
                                          }
                                 }"/>
                    </fx:eventListeners>
                </fx:UIClassFactory>
            </mx:itemRenderer>
        </mx:DataGridColumn>

        <mx:DataGridColumn dataField="SEX" editable="false" headerText="Sex"  />
          </mx:columns>
    </mx:DataGrid>

<mx:Script>
<![CDATA[
    import mx.controls.Label;
    import mx.collections.ArrayCollection;
    import mx.controls.RadioButtonGroup;
    import mx.controls.TextInput;
    import com.farata.core.UIClassFactory;
    import com.adobe.flex.extras.controls.MaskedTextInput;
    import mx.controls.CheckBox;
    private function init() :void {
        var dp:Array = [
            {EMP_ID:1,MANAGER_ID:200,EMP_FNAME:"John",
                EMP_LNAME:"Smith",DEPT_ID:100,STREET:"10 Baker Str",
                CITY:"New York",STATE:"NY",SALARY:25000,
                ZIP_CODE:"10001",PHONE:"2125551111",STATUS:"A",
                SS_NUMBER:"123456789", START_DATE:new Date("10/1/1998"),
                BENE_HEALTH_INS:"Y",SEX:"M"},
```

```
            {EMP_ID:2,MANAGER_ID:200,EMP_FNAME:"Jane",
                EMP_LNAME:"Smith",DEPT_ID:100,STREET:"10 Baker Str",
                CITY:"New York",STATE:"NY",SALARY:75000,
              ZIP_CODE:"10001",PHONE:"2121115555",STATUS:"A",
                SS_NUMBER:"987654321",START_DATE:new Date("10/1/1997"),
                BENE_HEALTH_INS:"N",SEX:"F"},

            {EMP_ID:3,MANAGER_ID:200,EMP_FNAME:"Count",
                EMP_LNAME:"Dracula",DEPT_ID:100,STREET:"10 Baker Str",
                CITY:"New York",STATE:"NY",SALARY:175000,
              ZIP_CODE:"10001",PHONE:"2121117777",STATUS:"A",
                SS_NUMBER:"321654321",START_DATE:new Date("10/1/1908"),
                BENE_HEALTH_INS:"Y",SEX:"F"}
        ];

        dg.dataProvider = dp;
    }
    private function beneHealthClick(e : MouseEvent ) : void {
        e.currentTarget.data.BENE_HEALT_INS = e.currentTarget.selected?"Y":"N";
    }
]]>
</mx:Script>
</mx:Application>
```

If you run this application, you'll see the window shown in Figure 2-8 with item renderers assigning dynamic properties, styles, and event listeners (as this book is printed in black, keep in mind that the actual background color of the salary in the first row is red, and in the other two is green):

Here's how simple and sweet it is:

```
<mx:itemRenderer>
        <fx:UIClassFactory>
            <fx:generator>
                {MaskedTextInput}
            </fx:generator>
            <fx:properties>
                <mx:Object inputMask = "###-###-####" />
            </fx:properties>
        </fx:UIClassFactory>
</mx:itemRenderer>
```

We declare that this item renderer will use the class factory that should build an instance of `MaskedTextInput`, and the `inputMask` property of this class to be generated is **"###-###-####"**.

Now you can assign values to the properties of the instances-to-be of a class factory!

The next code snippet shows you how to dynamically change the `fontWeight` styles and background column depending on the value of the `Salary` in each row:

```
<fx:runtimeStyles>
  <mx:Object
   fontWeight="{function(d:*):String { return
                                   d.SALARY>50000?'normal':'bold'}}"
```

```
        backgroundColor="{function(d:*):String { return
                          d.SALARY>30000?'green':'red'}}"/>
</fx:runtimeStyles>
```

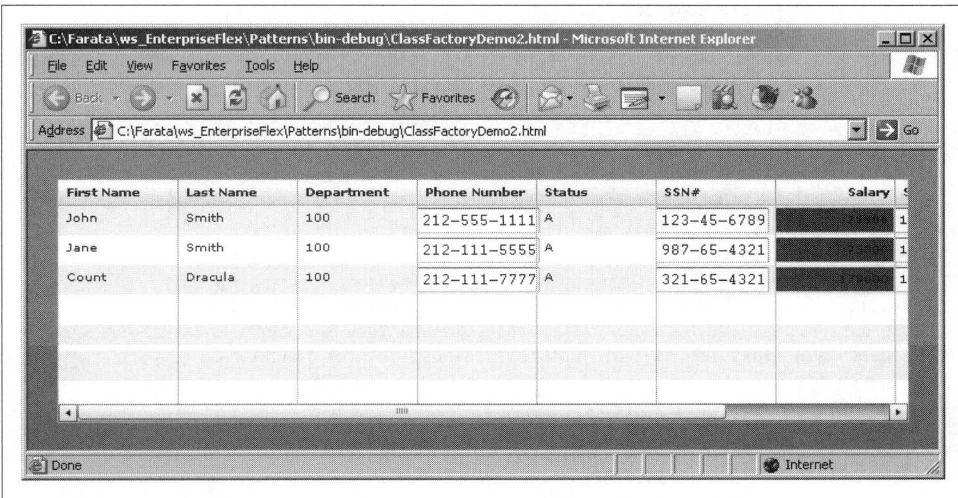

Figure 2-8. Output of ClassFactoryDemo2

The next code fragment renders the health insurance data as `CheckBox`, sets its `selected` property based on the data value (Y or N), and adds an event listener to process clicked events of this `CheckBox`:

```
<mx:itemRenderer>
    <fx:UIClassFactory>
        <fx:generator>
            {CheckBox}
        </fx:generator>
        <fx:runtimeProperties>
            <mx:Object
            selected="{function(d:*):Boolean { return
                                       d.BENE_HEALTH_INS=='Y'}}"/>
        </fx:runtimeProperties>

        <fx:eventListeners>
            <mx:Object
            click="{function (e:MouseEvent): void {
                                trace('hello:'+e);
                                beneHealthClick(e);
                                }
                    }"/>
        </fx:eventListeners>
    </fx:UIClassFactory>
</mx:itemRenderer>
```

We hope you've enjoyed this sample application. To examine the source code of the all-new `UIClassFactory`, see Example 2-26.

Example 2-26. UIClassFactory.as

```
////////////////////////////////////////////////////////////////////////////////
//                                                                            //
//  Copyright 2009 Farata Systems LLC                                         //
//  All Rights Reserved.                                                      //
//                                                                            //
//  NOTICE: Farata Systems permits you to use, modify, and distribute this file  //
//  in accordance with the terms of the license agreement accompanying it.    //
//                                                                            //
////////////////////////////////////////////////////////////////////////////////

package com.farata.core{
/**
 *  UIClassFactory is an implementation of the Class Factory design pattern
 *  for dynamic creaion of UI components. It allows dynamic passing of the
 *  propeties, styles and event listeners during the object creation.
 *  It's implemented as a wrapper for mx.core.ClassFactory and can
 *  be used as a class factory not just for classes, but for functions
 *  and even strings.
 *
 *  @see mx.core.IFactory
 */
    import flash.utils.describeType;
    import flash.utils.getDefinitionByName;

    import mx.controls.Label;
    import mx.core.ClassFactory;
    import mx.core.IFactory;
    import mx.events.FlexEvent;
    import mx.logging.ILogger;
    import mx.logging.Log;

    public class UIClassFactory implements IFactory{

        // A class factory object that serves as a wrapper
        // for classes, functions, strings, and even class factories
        private var _wrappedClassFactory : ClassFactory;

        // A reference to a function if the object instances are
        // to be created by a function
        private var factoryFunction : Function = null;

        // Styles for the UI object to be created
        public var styles:Object;

        // Runtime Styles for the UI object to be created
        public var runtimeStyles:Object;

        // Runtime Properties for the UI object to be created
        public var runtimeProperties:Object;

        // Event Listeners for the UI object to be created
        public var eventListeners:Object;

        private static const logger:ILogger =
```

```
                    Log.getLogger ("com.farata.core.UICassFactory");

public var properties:Object = {};

public function get wrappedClassFactory():ClassFactory {
    return _wrappedClassFactory;
}

public function set generator (cf:Object) : void {
    var className:String;// if the class name was passed as a String
    if (cf == null)
       cf = Label;
    if ( cf is UIClassFactory) {
        _wrappedClassFactory = UIClassFactory(cf).wrappedClassFactory;
    } if ( cf is ClassFactory) {
        _wrappedClassFactory = cf as ClassFactory;
    } else if (cf is Class) {
        _wrappedClassFactory = new ClassFactory(Class(cf));
    } else if (cf is String) {
        className = String(cf);
        try {
            var clazz:Class = getDefinitionByName(className) as Class;
            _wrappedClassFactory = new  ClassFactory(clazz);
        } catch (e:Error)     {
            trace(" Class '"+ className + "' can't be loaded
                      dynamically. Ensure it's explicitly referenced
                      in the application file or specified via @rsl.");
        }
    } else if (cf is Function) {
        factoryFunction = cf as Function;
    } else {
            className = "null";
            if (cf!=null)
                className = describeType(cf).@name.toString();
            trace("'" + className + "'" + " is invalid parameter for
                                        UIClassFactory constructor.");
    }

    if (!_wrappedClassFactory) {
        _wrappedClassFactory = new ClassFactory(Object);
    }

}
/**
 * Constructor of UIClassFactory takes four arguments
 * cf   -  The object to build. It can be a class name,
 *         a string containing the class name, a function,
 *         or another class factory object;
 * props - inital values for some or all properties if the object;
 * styles - styles to be applied to the object being built
 * eventListeners - event listeners to be added to the object being built
 */
public function UIClassFactory( cf: Object = null , props:Object = null,
                   styles:Object = null, eventListeners:Object = null ) {
```

```
        generator = cf;
        if (props != null) this.properties = props;
        if (styles != null) this.styles = styles;
        if (eventListeners != null) this.eventListeners = eventListeners;
    }

    /**
    * The implementation of newInstance is required by IFactory
    */
    public function newInstance():* {
        var obj:*;
        if (factoryFunction!=null){
           // using a function to create an object
            obj = factoryFunction();
        } else
            obj = _wrappedClassFactory.newInstance();

        // Copy(aggregate) the properties to the new object
        if (properties != null)  {
            for (var p:String in properties) {
                obj[p] = properties[p];
            }
            }
        // Set the styles on the new object
        if (styles != null)  {
            for (var s:String in styles) {
                obj.setStyle(s,  styles[s]);
            }
        }

        // add event listeners, if any
        if (eventListeners != null)  {
            for (var e:String in eventListeners) {
                obj.addEventListener(e,  eventListeners[e]);
            }
        }

        // Watch data modifications
        obj.addEventListener(FlexEvent.DATA_CHANGE, onDataChange);
        return obj;
    }

    /**
    * onDataChange is the handler for the DATA_CHANGE events. It uses
    * runtimeStyles and runtimeProperties, which were added to Clear Toolkit's
    * version of the DataGridColumn to handle styles and properties that were
    * added dynamically.
    *
    * If you'll use this UIClassFactory with regular DataGridColumns that does
    * not support dynamic styles, the onDataChange function won't find any
    * runtimeStyles or runtimeProperties and won't do anything.
    */
    private function onDataChange(event:FlexEvent):void{

        // Skip this call if caused by header renderers
```

```
            var renderer:Object = event.currentTarget;
            var functionObject:Function;
            var value:*;
            // Act only on 'dynamic style' columns
            for (var style:String in runtimeStyles) {
                functionObject = null;
                value = runtimeStyles[style];

                if (value is Function){
                    functionObject = value as Function;
                }

                if (null != functionObject) {
                    try {
                        value =
                        functionObject(renderer.data) ;
                        renderer.setStyle(style, value);
                    } catch (e:Error) {
                        logger.error(e.message);
                    }
                } else
                    renderer.setStyle(style, value);
            }
            for (var prop:String in runtimeProperties) {
                functionObject = null;
                value = runtimeProperties[prop];

                if ( value is Function ){
                    functionObject = value as Function;
                }

                if (null != functionObject ) {
                    try {
                        value =functionObject(renderer.data) ;
                         renderer[prop] = value;
                    } catch (e:Error) {
                        logger.error(e.message);
                    }
                } else
                    renderer[prop] = value;
            }
        }
    }
}
```

If you compare the code of the UIStaticClassFactory with the code of UIClassFactory, you'll notice that the latter introduces the property generator—an object to be created by the factory.

The function onDataChange() is a handler for the DATA_Change events. However, this function is relevant only if you are going to use UIClassFactory with the DataGrid from the Clear Toolkit's component library.

This concludes a brief overview of selected design patterns and shows how they can make your Flex programming more efficient. This chapter covered selected design patterns used in Flex applications. In many cases, Flex gives you a hand, allowing you to use a particular design pattern based on some of the existing elements of the Flex framework. For example, instead of creating a new singleton class and finding references to it with a number of `getInstance()` function calls, you can reuse the readily available singleton application, available in the Flex framework. The proxy pattern used in this chapter is based on `ObjectProxy`, which is also a part of the Flex SDK.

A creative approach to class factories can make your application a lot more flexible. In Chapter 4, you'll see how you can use factories to integrate BlazeDS and the Spring framework.

Design patterns is a lingua franca, understood by all software developers in general and Flex developers in particular. By the end of this book, you will be more comfortable speaking this language, too.

CHAPTER 3

Building an Enterprise Framework

Programming today is a race between software engineers striving to build bigger and better idiot-proof programs, and the Universe trying to produce bigger and better idiots. So far, the Universe is winning.

—Rich Cook

There is no such thing as perfect design. The Flex framework is evolving, and we are grateful that software engineers from the Flex team made this framework extendable. Because this book covers the use of the Flex framework in enterprise software development, we will identify and enhance those components that are widely used in business RIA.

For the majority of the enterprise applications, development comes down to a few major activities:

- Creating data grids
- Working with forms
- Validating data
- Printing

If you, the architect, can achieve improvements in each of these areas by automating common tasks, application developers will spend less time writing the same mundane code over and over again. The key is to encapsulate such code inside reusable Flex components, to create smarter components that can be collected into libraries.

Chapter 1 reviewed such architectural frameworks as Cairngorm, PureMVC, and Mate, which mainly helped with separating the code into tiers, but now you'll learn how to build another type of framework by enhancing existing Flex components. Specifically, this chapter demonstrates how to build a framework that radically simplifies creation of data entry applications by:

- Identifying common reusable components, which in turn reduces the number of errors inevitably introduced during manual coding

- Encapsulating implementation of architectural patterns inside selected components
- Defining best practices and implementing them in concrete components rather than just describing them on paper

You'll learn how to inherit your components from the existing ones, starting with the basic techniques, while extending a simple `CheckBox`, then approaching the more complex `ComboBox` component. The remainder of the chapter is devoted to extending components that every enterprise application relies on, namely `DataGrid`, `Form`, and `Validator`.

By providing a framework that integrates the work of programmers, business analysts, designers, and advanced users, you can drastically simplify the development of enterprise applications.

Every web developer is familiar with Cascading Style Sheets (CSS), which let designers define and change the look and feel of the applications without the need to learn programming. As you'll learn in this chapter, *Business Style Sheets* (*BSS*) serve a similar role for enterprise application developers, enabling software developers to attach a remote data set to a component with minimum coding. For example, you'll see how a simple resource file can instruct a `ComboBox` (or any other component) on where to get and how to display the data. Think of it as a data skinning. With BSS, you can develop artifacts that are highly reusable across enterprise applications.

Along the way, you'll learn more about BSS and other techniques for enhancing and automating Flex components. Although you won't be able to build an entire framework here (the challenges of printing and reporting are covered in the last chapter), you'll get a good start in mastering valuable skills that any Flex architect and component developer must have.

Upgrading Existing Flex Components

Flex evolved as a Flash framework from the HTML object model, and the base set of Flex controls capitalized on the simplicity of HTML. The price that Flex developers have to pay for this is that each control has its own (different) set of properties and behaviors. This can make building an enterprise framework a challenge. Consider a `CheckBox` control as an example. To quickly and easily integrate `CheckBox` into a variety of frameworks, developers would prefer the component to have a unified property value (*on* or *off*) that's easily bindable to application data. Currently, Flex's `CheckBox` has a property called `selected` and developers need to write code converting *Yes/No* data into the `true` or `false` that the `selected` property expects. If you later use another control, you must then convert these *Yes/No* values into the form that the new control requires. Clearly some common ground would reduce the amount of redundant coding.

The sections that follow will take a closer look at the `CheckBox` as well as other major Flex components that every application needs, and identify what they are missing and how to enhance them.

Introducing Component Library clear.swc

As you may remember from Chapter 1, Clear Toolkit's component library, *clear.swc*, contains a number of enhanced Flex components (Figure 3-1). Specifically, this component library consists of three packages:

- *com.farata.components*
- *com.farata.grid*
- *com.farata.printing*

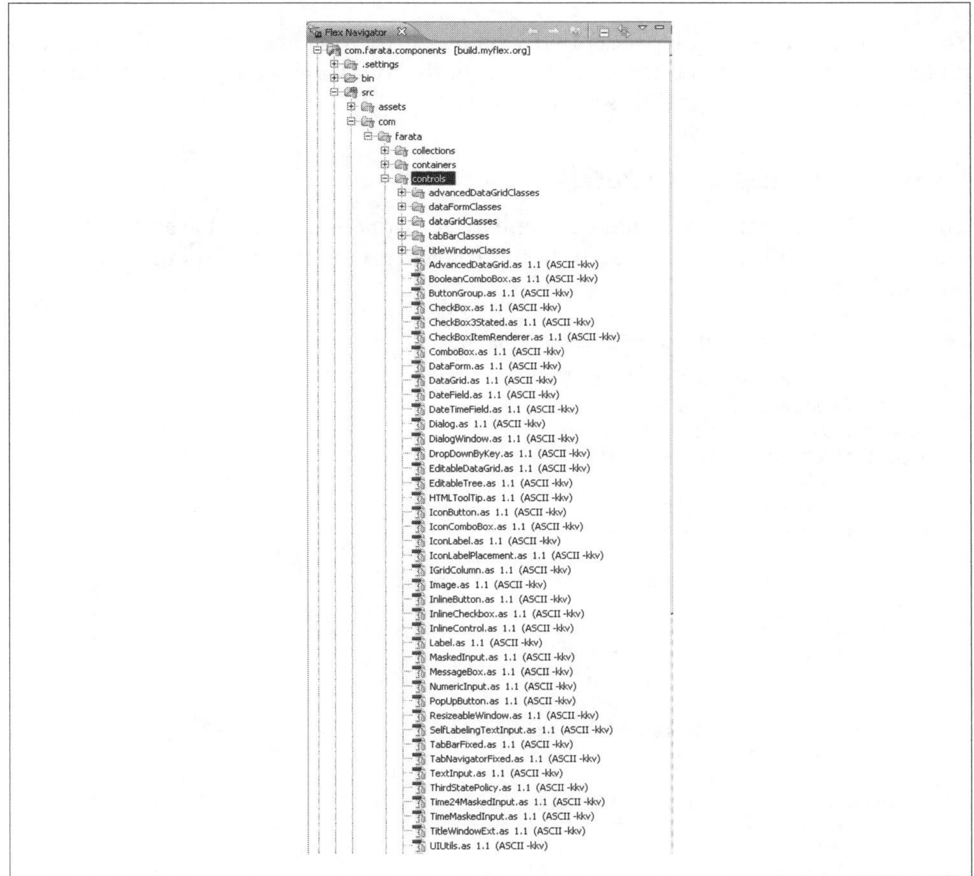

Figure 3-1. The com.farata.components package from clear.swc

To demonstrate how you can extend components, in the following sections we'll explain how we built some of the components from the package *com.farata.components*. Later you can use these discussions for reference, if you decide to build a similar (or better) library of components. (Some of the classes from the other two packages will be discussed in Chapter 11 of this book.)

You can find the source code of all components described in this chapter in the *clear.swc* component library. The code of some of the components explained here was simplified to make explanations of the process of extending Flex components easier. Neither this chapter nor the book as a whole is meant to be a manual for the open source *clear.swc* library. If you just want to use *clear.swc* components, refer to *https://sourceforge.net/projects/cleartoolkit/*, where the ASDoc-style API and the source code of each component from *clear.swc* are available.

You can use *clear.swc* independently by linking it to your Flex project. To help you understand how its components can help you, the following sections examine simplified versions of some of the library's controls.

Creating a Value-Aware CheckBox

The `CheckBox` in Example 3-1 has been enhanced with additional `value` and `text` properties. You can specify which value should trigger turning this control into the on/off position.

Example 3-1. CheckBox with value and text properties

```
package com.farata.controls {
    import flash.events.Event;
    import flash.events.KeyboardEvent;
    import flash.events.MouseEvent;

    import mx.controls.CheckBox;
    import mx.events.FlexEvent;

    public class CheckBox extends mx.controls.CheckBox {

        public var onValue:Object=true;
        public var offValue:Object=false;
        private var _value:*;

        public function set text(o:Object):void {
            value = o;
        }
        public function get text():Object {
            return value;
        }

        [Bindable("valueCommit")]
```

```
        public function set value(val:*) :void {
            _value = val;
            invalidateProperties();
            dispatchEvent(new FlexEvent (FlexEvent.VALUE_COMMIT));
        }

        public function get value():Object  {
           return selected?onValue:offValue;
        }

        override protected function commitProperties():void {
            if (_value!==undefined)
                selected = (_value == onValue);
            super.commitProperties();
        }
    }
}
```

This `CheckBox` will automatically switch itself into a selected or unselected state: just add it to your view, set the on and off values, and either assign a string or an `Object` value to it. You should note that the `value` setter calls the function `invalidateProperties()`, which internally schedules the invocation of the function `commitProperties()` on the next UI refresh cycle.

The `commitProperties()` function enables you to make changes to all the properties of a component in one shot. That's why we set the value of the selected property based on the result of the comparison of `_value` and `onValue` in this function.

Example 3-2 is a test application illustrating how to use this `CheckBox`, with the resulting interface shown in Figure 3-2. To run a test, click the first `Set OnValue=` button to teach the `CheckBox` to turn itself *on* when the value *Male* is assigned, and *off* when its property text has the value of *Female*. Then, click the first or second `cbx_test.text` button to assign a value to the newly introduced property text of this `CheckBox`, and watch how its state changes.

Example 3-2. Test application for the value-aware CheckBox

```
<?xml version="1.0" encoding="utf-8"?>
<mx:Application xmlns:mx="http://www.adobe.com/2006/mxml"
    xmlns:clear="com.farata.controls.*" layout="vertical">

    <clear:CheckBox id="cbx_test" label="Assign me a value" />

    <mx:Button label="Set OnValue='Male' and offValue='Female'"
         click="cbx_test.onValue='Male';cbx_test.offValue='Female';"/>

    <mx:Button label="cbx_test.text='Male'" click="cbx_test.text='Male'" />
    <mx:Button label="cbx_test.text='Female'" click="cbx_test.text='Female'" />

    <mx:Button label="Set OnValue=Number('1') and offValue=Number('0')"
         click="cbx_test.onValue=Number('1');cbx_test.offValue=Number('0');"/>

    <mx:Button label="cbx_test.value='Number('1')'"
```

```
        click="cbx_test.value =new Number('1')" />
    <mx:Button label="cbx_test. value='Number('0')"
        click="cbx_test.value =new Number('0')" />

</mx:Application>
```

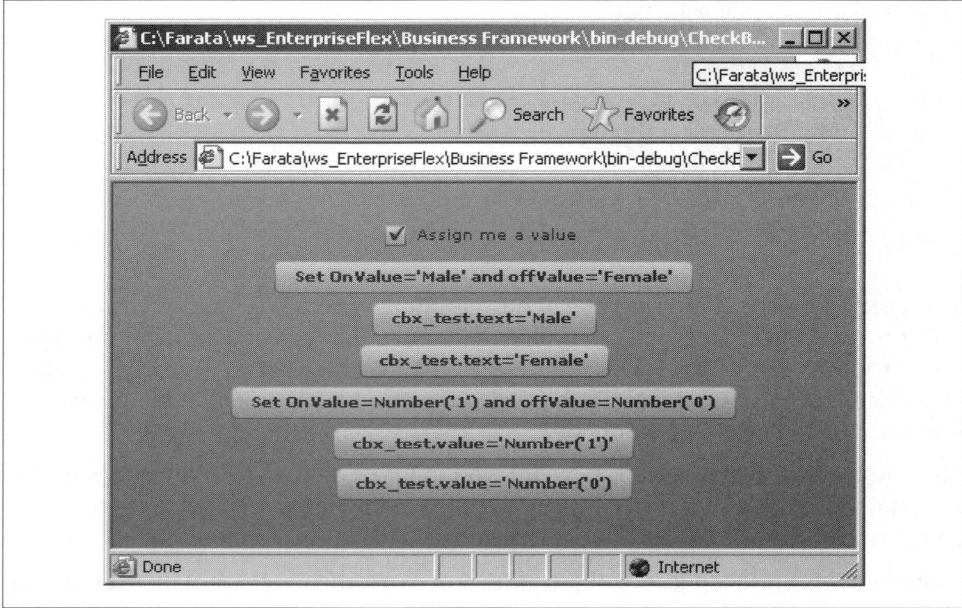

Figure 3-2. Testing the value-aware CheckBox

Creating a Centered CheckBox

This example demonstrates how to create a `CheckBox` that can center itself horizontally in any container, including a data grid cell.

Although you could introduce an item renderer that uses a `CheckBox` inside an `HBox` with the style `horizontalAlign` set to `center`, using a container inside the item rendered negatively affects the data grid control's performance.

The better approach is to extend the styling of the `CheckBox` itself. Example 3-3 is a code extension that "teaches" a standard Flex `CheckBox` to respond to the `textAlign` style if the `label` property of the `CheckBox` is not defined.

Example 3-3. Self-centering solution for CheckBox

```
override protected function updateDisplayList(unscaledWidth:Number,
      unscaledHeight:Number):void {

    super.updateDisplayList(unscaledWidth, unscaledHeight);
    if (currentIcon) {
```

```
        var style:String = getStyle("textAlign");
        if ((!label) && (style=="center") ) {
            currentIcon.x = (unscaledWidth - currentIcon.measuredWidth)/2;
    }
            }
        }
```

In the example code, the x coordinate of the CheckBox icon will always be located in the center of the enclosing container. Because no additional container is introduced, you can use this approach in the DataGridColumn item renderer, which is a style selector. When you use this enhanced CheckBox as a column item renderer, textAlign automatically becomes a style of this style selector, and you can simply set textAlign=center on DataGridColumn.

While developing enhanced components for the enterprise business framework, concentrate on identifying reusable functionality that application developers often need, program it once, and incorporate it in the component itself.

Creating a Protected CheckBox

The standard Flex CheckBox has a Boolean property called enabled that is handy when you want to disable the control. Unfortunately, a disabled CheckBox is rendered as grayed out. What if you want to use a CheckBox in some noneditable container, say in a DataGridColumn, and you want it to be nonupdateable but look normal?

The answer is to use a new class called CheckBoxProtected, which includes an additional property updateable. Its trick is to suppress standard keyboard and mouse-click processing. Overriding event handlers by adding the following:

```
if (!updateable) return;
```

works like a charm! Example 3-4 lists the complete code.

Example 3-4. Class CheckBoxProtected

```
package com.farata.controls
{
    import flash.events.Event;
    import flash.events.KeyboardEvent;
    import flash.events.MouseEvent;
    import mx.controls.CheckBox;

    public class CheckBoxProtected extends mx.controls.CheckBox {

    public var updateable:Boolean = true;

    public function CheckBoxProtected() {
        super();
        addEventListener(MouseEvent.CLICK, onClick);
    }
```

```
    private function onClick (event:MouseEvent):void {
        dispatchEvent(new Event(Event.CHANGE));
    }
    override protected function keyDownHandler(event:KeyboardEvent):void {
            if (!updateable) return;
            super.keyDownHandler(event);
    }
    override protected function keyUpHandler(event:KeyboardEvent):void {
            if (!updateable) return;
            super.keyUpHandler(event);
    }
    override protected function mouseDownHandler(event:MouseEvent):void {
           if (!updateable)return;
           super.mouseDownHandler(event);
    }
    override protected function mouseUpHandler(event:MouseEvent):void {
             if (!updateable)return;
            super.mouseUpHandler(event);
    }
    override protected function clickHandler(event:MouseEvent):void {
            if (!updateable)return;
            super.clickHandler(event);
        }
    }
}
```

To test the protected CheckBox, use Example 3-5.

Example 3-5. Test application for CheckBoxProtected

```
<?xml version="1.0" encoding="utf-8"?>
<mx:Application xmlns:mx="http://www.adobe.com/2006/mxml"
    xmlns:clear="com.farata.controls.*" layout="vertical">

 <clear:CheckBoxProtected updateable="false"
               label="I am protected" fontSize="18"/>
 <mx:CheckBox enabled="false"
               label="I am disabled" fontSize="18"/>

</mx:Application>
```

Running this application produces the results in Figure 3-3, which shows the difference between the protected and disabled checkboxes.

Why not use the extensibility of the Flex framework to its fullest? This chapter is about what you *can* do with Flex components. Armed with this knowledge, you'll make your own decisions about what you *want* to do with them.

For example, think of a CheckBox with a third state. The underlying data can be Yes, No, or null. If the value is null (the third state), the CheckBox needs to display a different image, such as a little question mark inside. In addition to supporting three states (selected, unselected, and null), this control should allow an easy switch from one state to another. Such an enhancement includes a skinning task—create a new skin (with a

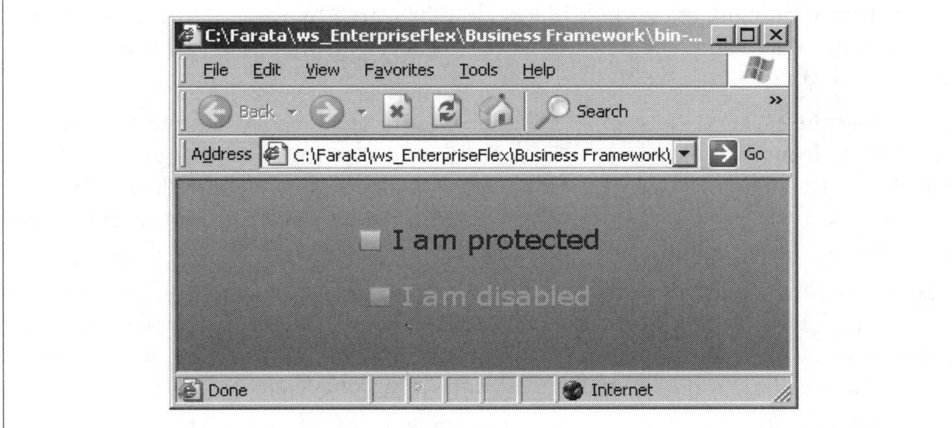

Figure 3-3. Running the CheckBoxProtected application

question mark) in Photoshop and ensure that the control switches to this state are based on the underlying data. For a working example, see `CheckBox3Stated` in the *clear.swc* component library.

Upgrading ComboBox

The `CheckBox` is easiest to enhance because it's one of the simplest controls, having only two states (`on` or `off`). You can apply the same principles to a more advanced `ComboBox`, however. Identify reusable functionality, program it once, and incorporate it into the component.

What if, for example, you need to programmatically request a specific value to be selected in a `ComboBox`? The traditional approach is to write code that loops through the list of items in the `ComboBox` data provider and manually works with the `selectedIndex` property. To set `Texas` as a selected value of a `ComboBox` that renders states, you could use:

```
var val:String; val= 'Texas' ;
for (var i: int = 0; i < cbx.dataProdider.length; i++) {
 if ( val == cbx_states.dataProvider[i].[cbx_states.labelField])
 {
      cbx_states.selectedIndex = i;
      break;
  }
}
```

The downside of this approach is that if your application has 50 `ComboBox` controls, several developers will be writing similar loops instead of a single line, such as `cbx_states.value="Texas"`.

Unfortunately, `ComboBox` does not provide a specific property that contains the selected value. It has such properties as `labelField`, `selectedIndex`, and `selectedItem`. Which one of them is actually a data field? How do you search by value? Do you really care about the number of the selected row in the ComboBox? Not at all—you need to know the selected value.

Let's revisit the earlier code snippet. The labelField of a ComboBox knows the name of the property from the objects stored in the backing collection. But what about the data field that corresponds to this label (in the case of Texas, a good candidate to be considered as the ComboBox data could be TX)? Currently, finding such data is the application programmer's responsibility.

Even if you are OK with writing these loops, considering the asynchronous nature of populating data providers, this code may need to wait until the data arrives from the server. It would be nice, though, if you could simply assign the value to a ComboBox without the need to worry about asynchronous flows of events.

Consider a List control, the brother of the ComboBox. Say the user selected five items, and then decided to filter the backing data collection. The user's selections will be lost. The List could benefit from yet another property that would remember selected values and could be used without worrying about the time of the data arrival.

Example 3-6 offers a solution: the class ComboBoxBase, which extends ComboBox by adding the value property (don't confuse it with <mx:ComboBoxBase>). After introducing the value property, it uses the dataField property to tell the ComboBox the name of the data field in the object of its underlying data collection that corresponds to this value. The new dataField property enables you to use any arbitrary object property as ComboBox data.

You'll also notice one more public property: keyField, which is technically a synonym of dataField. You can use keyField to avoid naming conflicts in situations where the ComboBoxBase or its subclasses are used inside other objects (say, DataGridColumn) that also have a property called dataField.

Example 3-6. Class com.farata.control.ComboBoxBase

```
package com.farata.controls {
    import flash.events.Event;

    import mx.collections.CursorBookmark;
    import mx.collections.ICollectionView;
    import mx.collections.IViewCursor;
    import mx.controls.ComboBox;
    import mx.controls.dataGridClasses.DataGridListData;
    import mx.controls.listClasses.ListData;
    import mx.core.mx_internal;
    use namespace mx_internal;

    public class ComboBoxBase extends ComboBox {

    public function ComboBoxBase() {
        super();
        addEventListener("change", onChange);
```

```
}

// Allow control to change dataProvider data on change
private function onChange(event:Event):void {
     if (listData is DataGridListData) {
         data[DataGridListData(listData).dataField] = value;
     }else if (listData is ListData && ListData(listData).labelField in data) {
         data[ListData(listData).labelField] = value;
     }
}

protected function applyValue(value:Object):void {
   if ((value != null) && (dataProvider != null)) {
         var cursor:IViewCursor = (dataProvider as ICollectionView).createCursor();
            var i:uint = 0;
            for (cursor.seek( CursorBookmark.FIRST ); !cursor.afterLast;
                                                    cursor.moveNext(), i++) {
                var entry:Object = cursor.current;
                if ( !entry ) continue;
                if ( (dataField in entry && value == entry[dataField])) {
                    selectedIndex = i;
                    return;
                }
            }
        }
        selectedIndex = -1;
    }

private var _dataField:String = "data";
private var _dataFieldChanged:Boolean = false;

[Bindable("dataFieldChanged")]
[Inspectable(category="Data", defaultValue="data")]

public function get dataField():String { return _dataField; }
public function set dataField(value:String):void {
    if ( _dataField == value)
    return;

    _dataField = value;
    _dataFieldChanged = true;
    dispatchEvent(new Event("dataFieldChanged"));
    invalidateProperties();
}

public function get keyField():String { return _dataField; }

public function set keyField(value:String):void {
    if ( _dataField == value)
        return;
    dataField = value;
}

private var _candidateValue:Object = null;
private var _valueChanged:Boolean  = false;
```

```
[Bindable("change")]
[Bindable("valueCommit")]
[Inspectable(defaultValue="0", category="General", verbose="1")]

public function set value(value:Object) : void {
        if (value == this.value)
            return;

     _candidateValue = value;
     _valueChanged = true;
     invalidateProperties();
}

override public function get value():Object {
     if (editable)
        return text;

     var item:Object = selectedItem;

     if (item == null )
        return null;

     return dataField in item ? item[dataField] : null/*item[labelField]*/;
}

override public function set dataProvider(value:Object):void {
       if ( !_valueChanged ) {
           _candidateValue = this.value;
           _valueChanged = true;
       }
       super.dataProvider = value;
}

override public function set data(data:Object):void {
     super.data = data;
     if (listData is DataGridListData) {
       _candidateValue = data[DataGridListData(listData).dataField];
       _valueChanged = true;
       invalidateProperties();
     }else if (listData is ListData && ListData(listData).labelField in data) {
       _candidateValue = data[ListData(listData).labelField];
       _valueChanged = true;
       invalidateProperties();
     }
    }

override protected function commitProperties():void {
     super.commitProperties();
     if (_dataFieldChanged) {
           if (!_valueChanged && !editable)
           dispatchEvent( new Event(Event.CHANGE) );

            _dataFieldChanged = false;
     }
```

```
        if (_valueChanged) {
            applyValue(_candidateValue);
            _candidateValue = null;
            _valueChanged = false;
        }
    }

    public function lookupValue(value:Object, lookupField:String = null):Object {
      var result:Object = null;
      var cursor:IViewCursor = collectionIterator;
      for (cursor.seek(CursorBookmark.FIRST);!cursor.afterLast;cursor.moveNext()) {
           var entry:Object = cursor.current;
           if ( value == entry[dataField] ) {
              result = !lookupField ? entry[labelField] : entry[lookupField];
              return result;
           }
      }
      return result;
    }
  }
}
```

The new property value is assigned in the following setter function:

```
[Bindable("change")]
[Bindable("valueCommit")]
[Inspectable(defaultValue="0", category="General", verbose="1")]
 public function set value(value:Object) : void {
    if (value == this.value)
       return;

   _candidateValue = value;
   _valueChanged = true;
   invalidateProperties();
}
```

Notice that when the function turns on the flag `_valueChanged`, `invalidateProperties()` internally schedules a call to the method `commitProperties()` to ensure that all changes will be applied in the required sequence. In the example, the code in the `commitProperties()` function ensures that the value of the `dataField` is processed before explicit changes to the `value` property, if any.

`ComboBox` is an asynchronous control that can be populated by making a server-side call. There is no guarantee that the remote data has arrived by the time that you assign some data to the `value` property. The `_candidateValue` in the `value` setter is a temporary variable supporting deferred assignment in the method `commitProperties()`.

The function `commitProperties()` broadcasts the notification that the `value` has been changed (in case some other application object is bound to this value) and passes the `_candidateValue` to the method `applyValue()`:

```
override protected function commitProperties():void {
        super.commitProperties();
```

```
            if (_dataFieldChanged) {
                 if (!_valueChanged && !editable)
                dispatchEvent( new Event(Event.CHANGE) );

                 _dataFieldChanged = false;
            }

            if (_valueChanged) {
                applyValue(_candidateValue);
                _candidateValue = null;
                _valueChanged = false;
            }
    }
```

The method applyValue() loops through the collection in the dataProvider using the IViewCursor iterator. When this code finds the object in the data collection that has a property specified in the dataField with the same value as the argument of this function, it marks this row as selected:

```
    protected function applyValue(value:Object):void {
           if ((value != null) && (dataProvider != null)) {
               var cursor:IViewCursor = (dataProvider as ICollectionView).createCursor();
                    var i:uint = 0;
                    for (cursor.seek( CursorBookmark.FIRST ); !cursor.afterLast;
                                                    cursor.moveNext(), i++) {
                        var entry:Object = cursor.current;
                        if ( !entry ) continue;
                        if ( (dataField in entry && value == entry[dataField])) {
                            selectedIndex = i;
                            return;
                        }
                    }
           }
           selectedIndex = -1;
    }
```

Tags such as:

```
[Inspectable(defaultValue="0",category="General", verbose="1")]Inspectable tag
```

ensure that corresponding properties will appear in property sheets of ComboBoxBase in Flash Builder's design mode (in this case, under the category *General* with specified initial values in defaultValue and verbose).

Meta tags such as [Bindable("dataFieldChanged")] ensure that the dataFieldChange event will be dispatched (to those who care) whenever the value of the dataField changes.

In Example 3-7, the small application *TestComboBoxApp.mxml* demonstrates the use of the ComboBoxBase component.

Example 3-7. Using the ComboBoxBase component

```
<?xml version="1.0" encoding="utf-8"?>
<mx:Application xmlns:mx="http://www.adobe.com/2006/mxml"
```

```
    xmlns:clear="com.farata.controls.*" layout="vertical">
    <mx:ArrayCollection id="cbData">
        <mx:Array>
            <mx:Object label="Adobe" data="ADBE" taxID="1111"/>
            <mx:Object label="Microsoft" data="MSFT"  taxID="2222"/>
            <mx:Object label="Farata Systems" data="FS"  taxID="3333"/>
        </mx:Array>
    </mx:ArrayCollection>

    <clear:ComboBoxBase  dataProvider="{cbData}" value="FS"/>

    <clear:ComboBoxBase  dataProvider="{cbData}" dataField="taxID" value="3333"/>

</mx:Application>
```

Both drop-downs use the same `dataProvider`. When you run Example 3-7's application, you'll see a window similar to Figure 3-4.

Figure 3-4. Running an application with two ComboBoxBase components

The first `ComboBoxBase` shows "Farata Systems" because of the assignment `value="FS"`, which compares it with values in the `data` field of the objects from the `cbData` collection.

The second drop-down sets `dataField="taxID"`, which instructs the `ComboBox` to use the value of the `taxID` property in the underlying data collection. If the code assigns a new value to `taxID`—e.g., an external data feed—the selection in the `ComboBox` will change accordingly. This behavior better relates to the real-world situations in which a collection of DTOs with multiple properties arrives from the server and has to be used with one or more `ComboBox` controls that may consider different DTO properties as their data.

Resources As Properties of UI Controls

An even more flexible solution for enhancing components to better support your enterprise framework is the use of a programming technique that we call *data styling* or Business Style Sheets (BSS), as mentioned earlier. The basic process is to create small files, called *resources*, and attach them as a property to a regular UI component as well as a `DataGrid` column.

Example 3-8 illustrates this BSS technique and contains a small MXML file called *YesNoCheckBoxResource.mxml*.

Example 3-8. A CheckBox resource (see YesNoCheckBoxResource.mxml)

```
<?xml version="1.0" encoding="utf-8"?>
<fx:CheckBoxResource
    xmlns="com.farata.resources" xmlns:mx="http://www.adobe.com/2006/mxml"
    xmlns:resources="com.theriabook.resources.*"
    offValue = "N"
    onValue = "Y"
    textAlign="center"
    >

</fx:CheckBoxResource>
```

Doesn't it look like a style to you? You can easily make it specific to a locale by, for example, changing the on/off values of Y/N to Д/Н, which mean **Да/Нет** (which you might be more familiar with as Da/Nyet) in Russian, or Si/No for Spanish. When you think of such resources as entities that are separate from the application components, you begin to see the flexibility of the technique. Isn't such functionality similar to what CSS is about?

As a matter of fact, it's more sophisticated than CSS, because this resource is a mix of styles and properties, as illustrated in Example 3-9. Called *StateComboBoxResource.mxml*, this resource demonstrates using properties (e.g., `dataProvider`) in a BSS. Such a resource can contain a list of values, such as names and abbreviations of states.

Example 3-9. StateComboBoxResource with hardcoded states

```
<?xml version="1.0" encoding="utf-8"?>
<fx:ComboBoxResource
    xmlns="com.farata.resources" xmlns:mx="http://www.adobe.com/2006/mxml"
    xmlns:resources="com.theriabook.resources.*"
    dropdownWidth="160"
    width="160"
    >
    <fx:dataProvider>
        <mx:Array>
            <mx:Object data="AL" label="Alabama" />
            <mx:Object data="AZ" label="Arizona" />
            <mx:Object data="CA" label="California" />
            <mx:Object data="CO" label="Colorado" />
            <mx:Object data="CT" label="Connecticut" />
            <mx:Object data="DE" label="Delaware" />
            <mx:Object data="FL" label="Florida" />
            <mx:Object data="GA" label="Georgia" />
            <mx:Object data="WY" label="Wyoming" />
        </mx:Array>
    </fx:dataProvider>
</fx:ComboBoxResource>
```

Yet another example of a resource, Example 3-10 contains a reference to a remote destination for automatic retrieval of dynamic data coming from a DBMS.

Example 3-10. Sample DepartmentComboResource configured for a remote destination

```
<?xml version="1.0" encoding="utf-8"?>
<fx:ComboBoxResource
    xmlns="com.farata.resources" xmlns:mx="http://www.adobe.com/2006/mxml"
    xmlns:resources="com.theriabook.resources.*"
    width="160"
    dropdownWidth="160"
    destination="Employee"
    keyField="DEPT_ID"
    labelField="DEPT_NAME"
    autoFill="true"
    method="getDepartments"
    >
</fx:ComboBoxResource>
```

As a matter of fact, you can't tell from this code whether the data is coming from a DBMS or from somewhere else. That data is cleanly separated from the instances of the `ComboBox` objects associated with this particular resource and can be cached either globally (if the data needs to be retrieved once) or according to the framework caching specifications. When developing a business framework, you may allow, for example, lookup objects to be loaded once per application or once per view. This flexibility doesn't exist in singleton-based architectural frameworks. Frameworks built using the resource technique/BSS, however, do allow the flexibility to look up objects.

Based on this resource file, you can say only that the data comes back from a remote destination called `Employee`, which is either a name of a class or a class factory. You can also see that the method `getDepartments()` will return the data containing `DEPT_ID` and `DEPT_NAME`, which will be used with the enhanced `ComboBox` described earlier in this chapter (Example 3-6).

In addition to such resources, however, you need a mechanism of attaching them to Flex UI components. To teach a `ComboBox` to work with resources, add a `resource` property to it:

```
private var _resource:Object;
public function get resource():Object
{
    return _resource;
}

public function set resource(value:Object):void {
    _resource = value;
    var objInst:*  = ResourceBase.getResourceInstance(value);
    if(objInst)
        objInst.apply(this);
}
```

The section "The Base Class for Resources" on page 131 will describe in detail the ResourceBase class. For now, concentrate on the fact that the resource property enables you to write something like this:

```
<fx:ComboBox resource="{DepartmentComboResource}"
```

Each of the enhanced UI components in your framework should include such a property. Because interfaces don't allow default implementation of such a setter and getter and because ActionScript does not support multiple inheritances, the easiest way to include this implementation of the resource property to each control is by using the language compile-time directive #include, which includes the contents of the external file—say, *resource.as*—into the code of your components:

```
#include "resource.as"
```

Styles Versus Properties

Before going too deep into the BSS and resources approach, you need to understand some key differences between styles and properties. For instance, although simple dot notation (myObject.resource=value) is valid Flex syntax for properties, it is not allowed for styles. Instead, application programmers have to use the function setStyle(). Suffice it to say that the StyleManager handles styles that can be cascading, yet properties can't cascade. From the framework developer's point of view, properties allow defining classes with getters and setters and take advantage of inheritance. With styles, you can't do this. On the other hand, you can't add properties (i.e., value and destination) to styles.

The designers of the Flex framework separated styles from properties for easier separation of internal processes; if an application code changes the style, the Flex framework performs some underground work to ensure that cascading style conventions are properly applied—for example, a global style that dictates that the Verdana font family is properly *overridden* by the style applied to a Panel or its child.

From an enterprise framework designer's perspective, this means that if you create a base class for the styles, and some time later decide to change it, the change may affect all derived classes. Suppose that you subclass ComboBox and define some new styles in the derived MyComboBox and then later change the style of the ComboBox. For the descendant class, this means that now code changes are required to properly (according to the changed rules) apply the overridden and added styles.

All this explains why every book and product manual keeps warning that styles are expensive and you should limit the use of the setSyle() function during runtime. With properties, life is a lot easier.

A beneficial framework would allow application programmers to define a small named set of application-specific styles and properties and the ability to govern the work of the UI control with selectors.

To accomplish this, get into the DataGrid state of mind. Have you ever thought of how a DataGridColumn object sets its own width, height, and other values? The DataGridColumn class is a descendant of a style selector called CSSStyleSelector, which means that it can be used to modify styles but not properties.

DataGrid examines every DataGridColumn and asks itself, "Do I have the same as this column object in my cache?" If it does not, it answers, "Nope, there's nothing I can reuse. I need to create a new class factory to supply a new item renderer." After this is done, the DataGrid code assigns the supplied DataGridColumn to the item renderer as a style. (Search for renderer.styleName=c in the code of *DataGridBase.as* to see for yourself.) At this point, all the specified column's styles (height, width, color, and text alignment) are applied as styles to the item renderer.

Treat DataGridColumn as a CSS style selector that also includes a limited number of properties (i.e., itemRenderer). DataGrid creates one instance of such a selector object and then reapplies it to every cell in this column.

Unfortunately, designing a DataGrid this way makes it next to impossible to externalize this CSS style selector, and you can't extend the properties of the data grid column to make them specific to the item renderer. Say you wanted to use a CheckBox with a property value (on/off) as an item renderer. Tough luck—DataGridColumn is not a dynamic object and you can't just add this as a new property.

Flex is an extendable framework, however, and what you *can* add is a new resource class with behaviors more to your liking. In fact, that's exactly what the ResourceBase class does, and it's described next.

The Base Class for Resources

Example 3-11 depicts the class ResourceBase, which serves as a base class for all resources for all components. This class can tell properties from styles. In Chapter 2, you learned about a class factory that accepts a class or a function name to create instances of objects. We applied that same technique here: with ResourceBase, a resource instance can be created from a class factory or a class.

Technically, the ResourceBase class applies specified values as either properties or resources.

Example 3-11. The ResourceBase class

```
package com.farata.resources {
    import com.farata.controls.TextInput;

    import flash.system.ApplicationDomain;

    import mx.core.ClassFactory;
    import mx.core.UIComponent;
    import mx.utils.StringUtil;
```

```
public dynamic class ResourceBase {
    public var resourceProps:Array = [];
    public var resourceStyles:Array = [];

public function load(source:Object):void {
    for each(var propName:String in resourceProps) {
        try    {
            if( source[propName])
                this[propName]= source[propName] ;
        }
        catch (e:Error) {}
    }
    for each(var styleName:String in resourceStyles){
        try    {
            if(source.getStyle(styleName))
                this[styleName] = source.getStyle(styleName);
        }
        catch (e:Error){}
    }
}

public function apply(target:Object):void         {
    try {
        for each(var propName:String in resourceProps)
            if (this[propName]!=undefined)
                target[propName] = this[propName];
    } catch (e:Error) {
        var error:String = mx.utils.StringUtil.substitute(
      "Incompatible resource class. Can not apply
         property {0} of {1} to {2}",
          [propName,this.toString(), target.toString()]    );
       throw new Error(error);
    }
    try {

        for each(var styleName:String in resourceStyles)
            if(this[styleName])
                target.setStyle(styleName, this[styleName]);
}

public static function getResourceInstance(value:Object,
                            styleOwner:Object=null):*    {
    var resClass:Object;
    if(value is Class) {
        resClass = Class(value);
        if (styleOwner) {
            try     {
                var result:* = new resClass(styleOwner);
                return result;
            }
            catch (e:Error) {
                return new resClass();
            }
        }
        else
```

```
            return new resClass();
    }
    else if(value is ResourceBase)
        return value;
    else if(value is ClassFactory)
        return ClassFactory(value).newInstance();
    else  if (value != null)     {
        var v:String = String(value).replace(/{/,"");
        v = v.replace(/}/,"");
        resClass = ApplicationDomain.currentDomain.getDefinition(v);
        if (styleOwner) {
            try    {
                var result2:* = new resClass(styleOwner);
                return result2;
            }
            catch (e:Error)    {
                return new resClass();
            }
        }
        else
            return new resClass();
    }
}
public function get itemEditor() : UIComponent {
    return new TextInput();
}
}
}
```

When application programmers design a resource for a particular type of Flex UI control, they simply extend it from a `ResourceBase` class (or build an MXML component based on it) and specify the names of the variables and their default values, if need be.

The `ResourceBase` class relies on two arrays: `resourceProps` and `resourceStyles`. When application developers create concrete resources, they also must populate these arrays. Example 3-12 illustrates the implementation of a sample class called `ComboBoxResource`. Note how the array `resourceProps` is populated with the data in the constructor.

Example 3-12. Sample ComboBoxResource class

```
package com.farata.resources {
    import mx.core.IFactory;
    import mx.core.UIComponent;
    import mx.styles.CSSStyleDeclaration;
    import mx.styles.StyleManager;
    import com.farata.controls.ComboBox;

    dynamic public class ComboBoxResource extends ResourceBase {
        public var autoFill :Boolean = false;
        public var keyField : String = "data";
        public var destination:String=null;
        public var dropdownWidth : int = 0;
        public var editable:Boolean = false;
```

```
        public var itemRenderer:IFactory = null;
        public var labelFunction : Function = null;
        public var labelField : String = "label";
        public var dataField : String = "label";
        public var method : String = null;
        public var width:int=-1;
        public var dataProvider : Object;

        public function ComboBoxResource(styleOwner:Object=null) {
            resourceProps.push("autoFill", "keyField", "destination",
              "dropdownWidth", "editable","itemRenderer", "labelField",
           "labelFunction","method", "dataProvider", "width");

            var sd:CSSStyleDeclaration =
                  StyleManager.getStyleDeclaration(".comboBoxResource");
            if (!sd)        {
                sd = new CSSStyleDeclaration();
                StyleManager.setStyleDeclaration(".comboBoxResource",
                   sd, false);
                sd.setStyle("paddingBottom", 0);
                sd.setStyle("paddingTop", 0);
            }
            if ( styleOwner!= null )
                load( styleOwner );
        }
        override public function get itemEditor() :UIComponent {
                return new ComboBox();
        }
    }
}
```

This class has to be written once for your enterprise framework, and after that any junior programmer can easily create and update resources such as `StateComboResource` or `DepartmentComboResource`, shown earlier in this chapter in Examples 3-9 and 3-10.

Similarly to CSS, resources should be compiled into a separate *.swf* file. They can be loaded and reloaded during the runtime. You can find out more about class loaders in Chapter 7.

DataGrid with Resources

The most interesting part about these resources is that you can attach them not only to regular controls, but also to such dynamic controls as `DataGridColumn`. For example, the following code snippet instructs the `DataGridColumn` (it was also enhanced and is available in *clear.swc*) to turn itself into a `ComboBox` and populate itself based on the configured resource `DepartmentComboResource` shown in Example 3-10:

```
<fx:DataGridColumn dataField="DEPT_ID" editable="false"
headerText="Department"
resource="{com.farata.resources.DepartmentComboResource}"/>
```

A resource attached to a DataGridColumn not only sets a column's properties but also identifies the item renderer and editor for this column.

As discussed in Chapter 2, class factories become extremely powerful if you use them as item renderers for a data grid column. Using this methodology, you can also encapsulate a number of properties and styles in the object provided by the factory. For example, you can enable the support of resources on the enhanced DataGridColumn object by adding the code fragment in Example 3-13.

Example 3-13. Enabling resources support in DataGridColumn

```
private var _resource:Object;
public function set resource(value:Object):void{
    _resource = ResourceBase.getResourceInstance(value, this);
    if(labelFunction==null) {
        getLabelFunctionByResource(_resource, this);
    }
}

public function get resource():Object{
    return _resource;
}
public static function getLabelFunctionByResource(resourceRef:Object,
                                                  column:Object):void {
    var resource:ResourceBase = resourceRef as ResourceBase;
    if (resource) {
        if(resource.hasOwnProperty("destination") &&
                                        resource["destination"])
            CollectionUtils.getCollection(
                function(ev:Event, collection:Object):void {
                    collectionLoaded(collection, column);
                },
                resource.destination,
                resource.method
            );
        else if (resource.hasOwnProperty("dataProvider") &&
                                    resource["dataProvider"]) {
            collectionLoaded(
                resource.dataProvider,
                column,
                safeGetProperty(resource, "labelField", "label"),
                safeGetProperty(resource, "keyField", "data")
            );
        }
    }
}
private static function collectionLoaded(collection:Object, column:Object,
                    labelField:String = null, dataField:String = null):void {
    if (null == collection) return;
    labelField =
        labelField ?
            labelField :
            (column["labelField"] != null ?
                column.labelField :
```

```
                (column.resource.labelField ?
                    column.resource.labelField : "label"));

    if (!dataField)
        dataField = column.resource.keyField ?
                    column.resource.keyField : column.dataField;

    collection = CollectionUtils.toCollection(collection);

    const options:Dictionary = new Dictionary();

    // copy only when collection is non empty
    if (collection != null && collection.length > 0 ) {
        const cursor:IViewCursor = collection.createCursor();
        do {
    options[cursor.current[dataField]] =
                                        cursor.current[labelField];
        } while(cursor.moveNext())
    }

    column.labelFunction = function(data:Object, col:Object):String {
        var key:* = data is String || data is Number ? data :
                                                data[col.dataField];
        var res:String = options[key];
        return res != null ? res : '' + key;
    };
}
```

Suppose that you have a DataGrid and a ComboBox with the values 1, 2, and 3 that should be displayed as John, Paul, and Mary. These values are asynchronously retrieved from a remote DBMS. You can't be sure, however, whether John, Paul, and Mary will arrive before or after the DataGrid gets populated. The example code extends the DataGrid Column with the property resource and checks whether the application developer supplied a labelFunction. If not, the code tries to "figure out" the labelFunction from the resource itself.

If resource has the destination set and the method is defined as the Department ComboResource as in Example 3-10, the code loads the Collection and after that, creates the labelFunction (see the collectionLoaded() method) based on the loaded data.

The resource may either come with a populated dataProvider as in Example 3-9, or the data for the dataProvider may be loaded from the server. When the dataProvider is populated, the collectionLoaded() method examines the dataProvider's data and creates the labelFunction. The following code attaches a labelFunction on the fly as a dynamic function that gets the data and, by the key, finds the text to display on the grid:

```
column.labelFunction = function(data:Object, col:Object):String {
        var key:* = data is String || data is Number ? data :
                                                data[col.dataField];
var res:String = options[key];
        return res != null ? res : '' + key;
        };
```

This closure uses the dictionary `options` defined outside. The code above this closure traverses the data provider and creates the following entries in the dictionary:

1, John
2, Paul
3, Mary

Hence the value of the `res` returned by this label function will be John, Paul, or Mary.

These few lines of code provide a generic solution for the real-life situations that benefit from having asynchronously loaded code tables that can be programmed by junior developers. This code works the same way as translating the `data` value into John and Mary, Alaska and Pennsylvania, or department names.

With resources, the properties and styles of UI controls become available not only to developers who write these classes but also to outsiders, in a fashion similar to CSS. The examples of resources from the previous section clearly show that they are self-contained, easy-to-understand artifacts that can be used by anyone as BSS.

You can create a resource as a collection of styles, properties, and event listeners that also allows the provision of a class name to be used with it. You can also create a class factory that will produce instances of such resources.

Technically, any resource is an abstract class factory that can play the same role that XML-based configurable properties play in the Java EE world. But this solution requires compilation and linkage of all resources, which makes it closer to configuring Java objects using annotations. Just to remind you, in Flex, CSS also get compiled.

To summarize, resources offer the following advantages:

- They are compiled and work fast.
- Because they are simple to understand, junior programmers can work with them.
- You can inherit one resource from another; Flash Builder will offer you context-sensitive help, and Flex compiler will help you to identify data type errors.
- You can attach resources to a `DataGridColumn` and use them as a replacement for item renderers.

Resources are a good start for automation of programming. In Chapter 6, you'll get familiar with yet another useful Flex component: `DataCollection`, a hybrid of `ArrayCollection` and `RemoteObject`, which is yet another step toward reducing manual programming.

Data Forms

In this section, you'll continue adding components to the enterprise framework. It's hard to find an enterprise application that does not use forms, which makes the Flex form component a perfect candidate for possible enhancements. Each form has some underlying model object, and the form elements are bound to the data fields in the model. Flex 3 supports only one-way data binding: changes on a form automatically propagate to the fields in the data model. But if you want to update the form when the data model changes, you have to manually program it using the curly braces syntax in one direction and `BindingUtils.bindProperty()` in another.

Flex 4 introduces a new feature: two-way binding. Add an @ sign to the binding expression (`@{expression}`) and notifications about data modifications are sent in both directions—from the form to the model and back. Although this helps in basic cases where a text field on the form is bound to a text property in a model object, two-way binding doesn't have much use if you'd like to use data types other than `String`.

For example, two-way binding won't help that much in forms that use the standard Flex `<mx:CheckBox>` component. What are you going to bind here? The server-side application has to receive 1 if the `CheckBox` was selected and 0 if not. You can't just bind its property `selected` to a numeric data property on the underlying object. To really appreciate two-way binding, you need to use a different set of components, similar to the ones that you have been building in this chapter.

Binding does not work in cases when the model is a moving target. Consider a typical master/detail scenario: the user double-clicks on a row in a `DataGrid` and details about the selected row are displayed in a form. Back in Chapter 1, you saw an example of this: double-clicking a grid row in Figure 1-19 opened up a form that displayed the details for the employee selected in a grid. This magic was done with the enhanced form component that you are about to review.

The scenario with binding a form to a `DataGrid` row has to deal with a moving model; the user selects another row. Now what? The binding source is different now and you need to think of another way of refreshing the form data.

When you define data binding using an elegant and simple notation with curly braces, the compiler generates additional code to support it. But in the end, an implementation of the *Observer design pattern* is needed, and "someone" has to write the code to dispatch events to notify registered dependents when the property in the object changes. In Java, this someone is a programmer; in Flex it's the compiler, which also registers event listeners with the model.

Flex offers the `Form` class, which an application programmer binds to an object representing the data model. The user changes the data in the UI form, and the model gets changed, too. But the original `Form` implementation does not have a means of tracking the data changes.

It would be nice if the Form control (bound to its model of type DataCollection) could support similar functionality, with automatic tracking of all changes compatible with the ChangeObject class that is implemented with remote data service. Implementing such functionality is the first of the enhancements you'll make.

The second improvement belongs to the domain of data validation. The enhanced data form should be smart enough to be able to validate not just individual form items, but the form in its entirety, too. The data form should offer an API for storing and accessing its validators *inside* the form rather than in an external global object. This way the form becomes a self-contained black box that has everything it needs. (For details on what can be improved in the validation process, see the section "Validation" on page 151.)

During the initial interviewing of business users, software developers should be able to quickly create layouts to demonstrate and approve the raw functionality without waiting for designers to come up with the proper pixel-perfect controls and layouts. Hence your third target will be making the prototyping of the views developer-friendly. Besides needing to have uniform controls, software developers working on prototypes would appreciate not being required to give definitive answers as to which control to put on the data form. The first cut of the form may use a TextInput control, but the next version may use a ComboBox instead. You want to come up with some UI-neutral creature (call it a *data form item*) that will allow a lack of specificity, like, "I'm a TextInput", or "I'm a ComboBox". Instead, developers will be able to create prototypes with generic data items with easily attachable resources.

The DataForm Component

The solution that addresses your three improvements is a new component called DataForm (Example 3-14). It's a subclass of a Flex Form, and its code implements two-way binding and includes a new property, **dataProvider**. Its function **validateAll()** supports data validation, as explained in the next sections. This DataForm component will properly respond to data changes, propagating them to its data provider.

Example 3-14. Class DataForm

```
package com.farata.controls{
import com.farata.controls.dataFormClasses.DataFormItem;

import flash.events.Event;

import mx.collections.ArrayCollection;
import mx.collections.ICollectionView;
import mx.collections.XMLListCollection;
import mx.containers.Form;
import mx.core.Container;
import mx.core.mx_internal;
import mx.events.CollectionEvent;
import mx.events.FlexEvent;
import mx.events.ValidationResultEvent;
```

```
public dynamic class DataForm extends Form{
    use namespace mx_internal;
    private var _initialized:Boolean = false;
    private var _readOnly:Boolean = false;
    private var _readOnlySet:Boolean = false;

    public function DataForm(){
        super();
        addEventListener(FlexEvent.CREATION_COMPLETE, creationCompleteHandler);
    }

    private var collection:ICollectionView;
    public function get validators() :Array {
        var _validators :Array = [];
        for each(var item:DataFormItem in items)
            for (var i:int=0; i < item.validators.length;i++)    {
                _validators.push(item.validators[i]);
            }
        return _validators;
    }
    public function validateAll(suppressEvents:Boolean=false):Array {
        var _validators :Array = validators;
        var data:Object = collection[0];
        var result:Array = [];
        for (var i:int=0; i < _validators.length;i++) {
            if ( _validators[i].enabled ) {
                var v : * = _validators[i].validate(data, suppressEvents);
                if ( v.type != ValidationResultEvent.VALID)
                    result.push( v );
            }
        }
        return result;
    }

    [Bindable("collectionChange")]
    [Inspectable(category="Data", defaultValue="undefined")]

    /**
     *  The dataProvider property sets of data to be displayed in the form.
     *  This property lets you use most types of objects as data providers.
     */
    public function get dataProvider():Object{
        return collection;
    }

    public function set dataProvider(value:Object):void{
        if (collection){
            collection.removeEventListener(CollectionEvent.COLLECTION_CHANGE,
                                                           collectionChangeHandler);
        }

        if (value is Array){
            collection = new  ArrayCollection(value as Array);
        }
        else if (value is ICollectionView){
```

```
        collection = ICollectionView(value);
    }
    else if (value is XML){
        var xl:XMLList = new XMLList();
        xl += value;
        collection = new XMLListCollection(xl);
    }
    else{
        // convert it to an array containing this one item
        var tmp:Array = [];
        if (value != null)
        tmp.push(value);
        collection = new ArrayCollection(tmp);
    }

    collection.addEventListener(CollectionEvent.COLLECTION_CHANGE,
                                            collectionChangeHandler);
    if(initialized)
        distributeData();
}

public function set readOnly(f:Boolean):void{
    if( _readOnly==f ) return;
    _readOnly = f;
    _readOnlySet = true;
    commitReadOnly();
}

public function get readOnly():Boolean{
    return _readOnly;
}

 /**
 *  This function handles CollectionEvents dispatched from the data provider
 *  as the data changes.
 *  Updates the renderers, selected indices and scrollbars as needed.
 *
 *  @param event The CollectionEvent.
 */
protected function collectionChangeHandler(event:Event):void{
    distributeData();
}

private function commitReadOnly():void{
    if( !_readOnlySet ) return;
    if( !_initialized ) return;
    _readOnlySet = false;
    for each(var item:DataFormItem in items)
        item.readOnly = _readOnly;
}

private function distributeData():void {
    if((collection != null) && (collection.length < 0)) {
        for (var i:int=0; i<items.length; i++)    {
            DataFormItem(items[i]).data = this.collection[0];
```

```
            }
        }
    }

    private var items:Array = new Array();
    private function creationCompleteHandler(evt:Event):void{
        distributeData();
        commitReadOnly();
    }

    override protected function createChildren():void{
        super.createChildren();
        enumerateChildren(this);
        _initialized = true;
        commitReadOnly();
    }
    private function enumerateChildren(parent:Object):void{
        if(parent is DataFormItem){
            items.push(parent);
        }
        if(parent is Container){
            var children:Array = parent.getChildren();
            for(var i:int = 0; i < children.length; i++){
                enumerateChildren(children[i]);
            }
        }
    }
  }
}
```

Let's walk through the code of the class `DataForm`. Examine the setter `dataProvider` in the example code. It always wraps up the provided data into a collection. This is needed to ensure that the `DataForm` supports working with remote data services the same way that `DataGrid` does. It checks the data type of the value. It wraps an `Array` into an `ArrayCollection`, and XML turns into `XMLListCollection`. If you need to change the backing collection that stores the data of a form, just point the collection variable at the new data.

If a single object is given as a `dataProvider`, turn it into a one-element array and then into a collection object. A good example of such case is an instance of a `Model`, which is an `ObjectProxy` (see Chapter 2) that knows how to dispatch events about changes of its properties.

Once in a while, application developers need to render noneditable forms; hence, the `DataForm` class defines the `readOnly` property.

The changes of the underlying data are propagated to the form in the method `collectionChangeHandler()`. The data can be modified either in the `dataProvider` or from the UI, and the `DataForm` ensures that each visible `DataFormItem` object (`items[i]`) knows about it. This is done in the function `distributeData()`:

```
    private function distributeData():void {
        if((collection != null) && (collection.length < 0)) {
```

```
            for (var i:int=0; i<items.length; i++)    {
                DataFormItem(items[i]).data = this.collection[0];
            }
        }
    }
```

This code always works with the element 0 of the collection, because the form always has one object with data that is bound to the form. Such a design resembles the functionality of the `data` variable of the Flex `DataGrid`, which for each column provides a reference to the object that represents the entire row.

Again, we need the data to be wrapped into a collection to support `DataCollection` or `DataService` from LCDS.

Technically, a `DataForm` class is a `VBox` that lays out its children vertically in two columns and automatically aligns the labels of the form items. This `DataForm` needs to allow nesting—containing items that are also instances of the `DataForm` object. A recursive function, `enumerateChildren()`, loops through the children of the form, and if it finds a `DataFormItem`, it just adds it to the array `items`. But if the child is a container, the function loops through its children and adds them to the same `items` array. In the end, the property `items` contains all `DataFormItems` that have to be populated.

Notice that the function `validateAll()` is encapsulated inside the `DataForm`; in the Flex framework, it is located in the class `Validator`. There, the validation functionality was external to `Form` elements and you'd need to give an array of validators that were tightly coupled with specific form fields.

Our `DataForm` component is self-sufficient; its validators are embedded inside, and reusing the same form in different views or applications is easier compared to the original Flex `Form` object, which relies on external validators.

The DataFormItem Component

The `DataFormItem`, an extension of the Flex `FormItem`, is the next component of the framework. This component should be a bit more humble than its ancestor, though. The `DataFormItem` should not know too much about its representation and should be able to render any UI component. The design of new Flex 4 components has also been shifted toward separation between their UI and functionality.

At least half of the controls on a typical form are text fields. Some of them use masks to enter formatted values, like phone numbers. The rest of the form items most likely are nothing but checkboxes and radio buttons. For these controls (and whatever else you may need), just use resources. Forms also use combo boxes. The earlier section "DataGrid with Resources" on page 134 showed you how class factory–based resources can be used to place combo boxes and other components inside the `DataGrid`. Now you'll see how to enable forms to have flexible form items using the same technique.

The DataFormItem is a binding object that is created for each control placed inside the DataForm. It has functionality somewhat similar to that of BindingUtils to support two-way binding and resolve circular references. The DataFormItem has two major functions:

- Attach an individual control internally to the instance of DataFormItemEditor to listen to the changes in the underlying control
- Create a UI control (either a default one, or according to the requested masked input or resource)

The first function requires the DataFormItem control to support the syntax of encapsulating other controls, as it's implemented in FormItem, for example:

```
<lib:DataFormItem dataField="EMP_ID" label="Emp Id:">
  <mx:TextInput/>
</lib:DataFormItem>
```

In this case, the DataFormItem performs binding functions; in the Flex framework, <mx:FormItem> would set or get the value in the encapsulated UI component, but now the DataFormItem will perform the binding duties. Assignment of any object to the dataField property item of the DataFormItem will automatically pass this value to the enclosed components. If an application developer decides to use a chart as a form item, for example, the data assigned to the DataFormItem will be given for processing to the chart object. The point is that application developers would use this control in a uniform way regardless of what object is encapsulated in the DataFormItem.

The second function, creating a UI control, is implemented with the help of resources, which not only allow specifying the styling of the component, but also can define what component to use. If you go back to the code of the class ResourceBase, you'll find a better itemEditor that can be used for the creation of controls. Actually, this gives you two flexible ways of creating controls for the form: either specify a resource name, or specify a component as itemEditor=myCustomComponent. If neither of these ways is engaged, a default TextInput control will be created.

The previous code looks somewhat similar to the original FormItem, but it adds new powerful properties to the component that represents the form item. The data of the form item is stored in the EMP_ID property of the data collection specified in the dataProvider of the DataForm. The label property plays the same role as in FormItem.

The source code of the DataFormItem component is shown in Example 3-15. It starts with defining properties, as in DataGrid: dataField, valueName, and itemEditor. The DataGridItem can create an itemEditor from a String, an Object, or a class factory. It also defines an array validator, which will be described later in this chapter.

Example 3-15. Class DataFormItem

```
package com.farata.controls.dataFormClasses {
    import com.farata.controls.DataForm;
    import csom.farata.controls.MaskedInput;
```

```
import com.farata.core.UIClassFactory;
import com.farata.resources.ResourceBase;
import com.farata.validators.ValidationRule;

import flash.display.DisplayObject;
import flash.events.Event;
import flash.events.IEventDispatcher;
import flash.utils.getDefinitionByName;

import mx.containers.FormItem;
import mx.events.FlexEvent;
import mx.validators.Validator;

dynamic public class DataFormItem extends FormItem {
    public function DataFormItem()    {
        super();
    }

    private var _itemEditor:IEventDispatcher; //DataFormItemEditor;

    [Bindable("itemEditorChanged")]
    [Inspectable(category="Other")]
    mx_internal var owner:DataForm;

    private var _dataField:String;
    private var _dataFieldAssigned:Boolean = false;
    private var _labelAssigned:Boolean = false;
    private var _valueName:String = null;
    private var _readOnly:Boolean = false;
    private var _readOnlySet:Boolean = false;

    public function set readOnly(f:Boolean):void{
        if( _readOnly==f ) return;
        _readOnly = f;
        _readOnlySet = true;
        commitReadOnly();
     }

    public function get readOnly():Boolean {
        return _readOnly;
    }

    public function set dataField(value:String):void {
        _dataField = value;
        _dataFieldAssigned = true;
    }

    public function get dataField():String{
        return _dataField;
    }

    override public function set label(value:String):void  {
        super.label = value;
        _labelAssigned = true;
    }
```

```
public function set valueName(value:String):void {
    _valueName = value;
}

public function get valueName():String {
    return _valueName;
}

override public function set data(value:Object):void {
    super.data = value;
    if(_itemEditor)
        if (_itemEditor["data"] != value[_dataField])
            _itemEditor["data"] = value[_dataField];

    for ( var i : int = 0; i < validators.length; i++) {
        if ( validators[i] is ValidationRule && data)
            validators[i]["data"]= data;
        validators[i].validate();
    }
}

override protected function createChildren():void{
    super.createChildren();
    if(this.getChildren().length > 0) {
        _itemEditor = new DataFormItemEditor(this.getChildAt(0), this);
        _itemEditor.addEventListener(Event.CHANGE, dataChangeHandler);
        _itemEditor.addEventListener(FlexEvent.VALUE_COMMIT,
                                              dataChangeHandler);
    }
}

public function get itemEditor():Object {
    return _itemEditor;
}

private var _validators :Array = [];

public function get validators() :Array {
    return _validators;
}
public function set validators(val :Array ): void {
    _validators = val;
}

public var _dirtyItemEditor:Object;

public function set itemEditor(value:Object):void{
    _dirtyItemEditor = null;
 if(value is String){
   var clazz:Class = Class(getDefinitionByName(value as String));
      _dirtyItemEditor = new clazz();
    }
    if(value is Class)
        _dirtyItemEditor = new value();
```

```
        if(value is UIClassFactory)
            _dirtyItemEditor = value.newInstance();
        if(value is DisplayObject)
            _dirtyItemEditor = value;
}

private function dataChangeHandler(evt:Event):void{
    if (evt.target["data"]!==undefined)    {
        if (data != null) {
            data[_dataField] = evt.target["data"];
            }
    }
}

private var _resource:Object;
public function set resource(value:Object):void {
    _resource = ResourceBase.getResourceInstance(value);
    invalidateProperties();
}

public function get resource():Object{
    return _resource;
}

private function commitReadOnly():void{
    if( _itemEditor==null ) return;
    if( !_readOnlySet ) return;
if( Object(_itemEditor).hasOwnProperty("readOnly") )
{
    Object(_itemEditor).readOnly = _readOnly;
    _readOnlySet = false;
}
}

override protected function commitProperties():void{
    super.commitProperties();
    if(itemEditor == null) //no child controls and no editor from resource
    {
        var control:Object = _dirtyItemEditor;
        if(!control && getChildren().length > 0)
            control = getChildAt(0);  //user placed control inside
        if(!control)
            control = itemEditorFactory(resource as ResourceBase);

        if(resource)
            resource.apply(control);
        if( (control is MaskedInput) && hasOwnProperty("formatString"))
            control.inputMask = this["formatString"];

        addChild(DisplayObject(control));
        //Binding wrapper to move data back and force
        _itemEditor = new
                DataFormItemEditor(DisplayObject(control),this);
        _itemEditor.addEventListener(Event.CHANGE, dataChangeHandler);
        _itemEditor.addEventListener(FlexEvent.VALUE_COMMIT,
```

```
                                                    dataChangeHandler);
} else
        control = itemEditor.dataSourceObject;

 commitReadOnly();

for ( var i : int = 0; i < validators.length; i++) {
    var validator : Validator = validators[i] as Validator;
    validator.property = (_itemEditor as DataFormItemEditor).valueName;
    validator.source = control;
    if ( validator is ValidationRule && data)
        validator["data"]= data;
    validator.validate();
}
}
protected function itemEditorFactory(resource : ResourceBase =
                                                   null):Object{
    var result:Object = null;
    if (resource && ! type)
        result = resource.itemEditor;
    else {
        switch(type)    {
        case "checkbox":
            result = new CheckBox();
            if (!resource) {
                resource = new CheckBoxResource(this);
                resource.apply(result);
            }
            break;
        case "radiobutton":
            result = new RadioButtonGroupBox();
            if (!resource) {
                resource = new RadioButtonGroupBoxResource(this);
                resource.apply(result);
            }
            break;
        case "combobox":
            result = new ComboBox();
            if (!resource) {
                resource = new ComboBoxResource(this);
                resource.apply(result);
            }
            break;
        case "date":
            result = new DateField();
            if (formatString) (result as DateField).formatString =
                                                          formatString;
            break;
        case "datetime":
            result = new DateTimeField();
            if (formatString) (result as DateTimeField).formatString =
                                                          formatString;
            break;
        case "mask":
            result = new MaskedInput();
```

```
                break;
            }
        }
        if(result == null && formatString)
            result = guessControlFromFormat(formatString);
        if(result == null)
            result = new TextInput();
        return result;
    }

    protected function guessControlFromFormat(format:String):Object{
        var result:Object = null;
        if(format.toLowerCase().indexOf("currency") != -1)
            result = new NumericInput();
        else if(format.toLowerCase().indexOf("date") != -1){
            result = new DateField();
            (result as DateField).formatString = format;
        }
        else{
            result = new MaskedInput();
            (result as MaskedInput).inputMask = format;
        }
        return result;
    }
  }
}
```

You'll see in the example code that you can use an instance of a `String`, an `Object`, a class factory, or a UI control as an `itemEditor` property of the `DataFormItem`. The function `createChildren()` adds event listeners for `CHANGE` and `VALUE_COMMIT` events, and when any of these events is dispatched, the `dataChangeHandler()` pushes the provided value from the data attribute of the UI control used in the form item into the `data.dataField` property of the object in the underlying collection.

The `resource` setter allows application developers to use resources the same way as was done with a `DataGrid` earlier in this chapter.

The function `commitReadonly()` ensures that the `readOnly` property on the form item can be set only after the item is created.

The function `itemEditorFactory()` supports creation of the form item components from a resource based on the value of the variable `type`. The `guessControlFromFormat()` is a function that can be extended based on the application needs, but in the previous code, it just uses a `NumericInput` component if the *currency* format was requested and `DateField` if the *date* format has been specified. If an unknown format was specified, this code assumes that the application developer needs a mask; hence the `MaskedInput` will be created.

Remember that Flex schedules a call to the function `commitProperties()` to coordinate modifications to component properties when a component is created. It's also called as a result of the application code calling `invalidateProperties()`. The function `commitProperties()` checks whether the `itemEditor` is defined. If it is not, it'll be created and the event listeners will be added. If the `itemEditor` exists, the code extracts from it the UI control used with this form item.

Next, the data form item instantiates the validators specified by the application developers. This code binds all provided validators to the data form item:

```
for ( var i : int = 0; i < validators.length; i++) {
    var validator : Validator = validators[i] as Validator;
    validator.property = (_itemEditor as DataFormItemEditor).valueName;
    validator.source = control;
    if ( validator is ValidationRule && data)
        validator["data"]= data;
    validator.validate();
}
```

The next section discusses the benefits of hiding validators inside the components and offers a sample application that shows how to use them and the functionality of the `ValidationRule` class. Meanwhile, Example 3-16 demonstrates how an application developer could use the `DataForm`, the `DataFormItem`, and resources. Please note that by default, `DataFormItem` renders a `TextInput` component.

Example 3-16. Code fragment that uses DataForm and DataFormItem

```
<lib:DataForm dataProvider="employeeDAO">
    <mx:HBox>
        <mx:Form>
            <lib:DataFormItem dataField="EMP_ID" label="Emp Id:"/>
            <lib:DataFormItem dataField="EMP_FNAME" label="First Name:"/>
            <lib:DataFormItem dataField="STREET" label="Street:"/>
            <lib:DataFormItem dataField="CITY" label="City:"/>
            <lib:DataFormItem dataField="BIRTH_DATE" label="Birth Date:"
                                         formatString="shortDate"/>
            <lib:DataFormItem dataField="BENE_HEALTH_INS" label="Health:"
                    resource="{com.farata.resources.YesNoCheckBoxResource}"/>
            <lib:DataFormItem dataField="STATUS" label="Status:"
                    resource="{com.farata.resources.StatusComboResource}"/>
        </mx:Form>

        <mx:Form>
            <lib:DataFormItem dataField="MANAGER_ID" label="Manager Id:"/>
            <lib:DataFormItem dataField="EMP_LNAME" label="Last Name:"/>
            <lib:DataFormItem dataField="STATE" label="State:"
                    resource="com.farata.resources.StateComboResource"/>
            <lib:DataFormItem dataField="SALARY" label="Salary:"
                    formatString="currency" textAlign="right"/>
            <lib:DataFormItem dataField="START_DATE" label="Start Date:"
                    formatString="shortDate"/>
            <lib:DataFormItem dataField="BENE_LIFE_INS" label="Life:"
                    resource="{com.farata.resources.YesNoCheckBoxResource}"/>
            <lib:DataFormItem dataField="SEX" label="Sex:"
                    resource="{com.farata.resources.SexComboResource}"/>
        </mx:Form>

        <mx:Form>
           <lib:DataFormItem dataField="DEPT_ID" label="Department:"
```

```
            resource="{com.farata.resources.DepartmentComboResource}"/>
         <lib:DataFormItem dataField="SS_NUMBER" label="Ss Number:"
         itemEditor="{com.theriabook.controls.MaskedInput}" formatString="ssn"/>
         <lib:DataFormItem dataField="ZIP_CODE" label="Zip Code:"
                                                formatString="zip"/>
         <lib:DataFormItem dataField="PHONE" label="Phone Number:"
        itemEditor="{com.theriabook.controls.MaskedInput}" formatString="phone">

       <lib:validators>
           <mx:Array>
               <mx:PhoneNumberValidator  wrongLengthError="keep typing"/>
           </mx:Array>
       </lib:validators>
        </lib:DataFormItem>
       <lib:DataFormItem dataField="TERMINATION_DATE"
                label="Termination Date:" formatString="shortDate"/>
       <lib:DataFormItem dataField="BENE_DAY_CARE" label="Day Care:"
               resource="{com.farata.resources.YesNoCheckBoxResource}"/>
       </mx:Form>
   </mx:HBox>
</lib:DataForm>
```

This code is an extract from the Café Townsend application (Clear Data Builder's version) from Chapter 1. Run the application *Employee_getEmployees_GridFormTest.mxml*, double-click on a grid row, and you'll see the `DataForm` in action. In the next section of this chapter, you'll see other working examples of `DataForm` and `DataGrid` with validators.

Validation

Like data forms and components in general, the Flex `Validator` could use some enhancement to make it more flexible for your application developers. In Flex, validation seems to have been designed with an assumption that software developers will mainly use it with forms and that each validator class will be dependent on and attached to only one field. Say you have a form with two email fields. The Flex framework forces you to create two instances of the `EmailValidator` object, one per field.

In real life, though, you may also need to come up with validating conditions based on relationships between multiple fields, as well as to highlight invalid values in more than one field. For example, you might want to set the date validator to a field and check whether the entered date falls into the time interval specified in the start *and* end date fields. If the date is invalid, you may want to highlight all form fields.

In other words, you may need to do more than validate an object property. You may need the ability to write validation rules in a function that can be associated not only with the UI control but also with the underlying data, that is, with data displayed in a row in a `DataGrid`.

Yet another issue of the Flex `Validator` is its limitations regarding view states of automatically generated UI controls. Everything would be a lot easier if validators could live inside the UI controls, in which case they would be automatically added to view states along with the hosting controls.

Having a convenient means of validation on the client is an important part of the enterprise Flex framework. Consider, for example, an RIA for opening new customer accounts in a bank or an insurance company. This business process often starts with filling multiple sections in a mile-long application form. In Flex, such an application may turn into a `ViewStack` of custom components with, say, 5 forms totaling 50 fields. These custom components and validators are physically stored in separate files. Each section in a paper form can be represented as the content of one section in an `Accordion` or other navigator. Say you have total of 50 validators, but realistically, you'd like to engage only those validators that are relevant to the open section of the `Accordion`.

If an application developer decides to move a field from one custom component to another, she needs to make appropriate changes in the code to synchronize the old validators with a relocated field.

What are some of the form fields that are used with view states? How would you validate these moving targets? If you are adding three fields when the `currentState="Details"`, you'd need to write `AddChild` statements manually in the state section `Details`.

Say 40 out of these 50 validators are permanent, and the other 10 are used once in a while. But you don't want to use even these 40 simultaneously; hence you need to create, say, 2 arrays having 20 elements each, and keep adding/removing temporary validators to these arrays according to view state changes.

Even though it seems that Flex separates validators and field to validate, this is not a real separation but rather a tight coupling. What's the solution? For the customer accounts example, you want a `ViewStack` with 5 custom components, each of which has 1 `DataForm` whose elements have access to the entire set of 50 fields, but that validates only its own set of 10. In other words, all 5 forms will have access to the same 50-field `dataProvider`. If during account opening the user entered 65 in the field *age* on the first form, the fifth form may show fields with options to open a pension plan account, which won't be visible for younger customers.

That's why each form needs to have access to all data, but when you need to validate only the fields that are visible on the screen at the moment, you should be able to do this on behalf of this particular `DataForm`. To accomplish all this, we created a new class called `ValidationRule`. Our goal is not to replace existing Flex validation routines, but rather to offer you an alternative solution that can be used with forms and list-based controls. The next section demonstrates a sample application that uses the class `ValidationRule`. After that, you can take a look at the code under the hood.

Sample Application: DataFormValidation

The *DataFormValidation.mxml* application (Figure 3-5) has two `DataForm` containers located inside the `HBox`. Pressing the Save button initiates the validation of both forms and displays the message regardless of whether the entered data is valid.

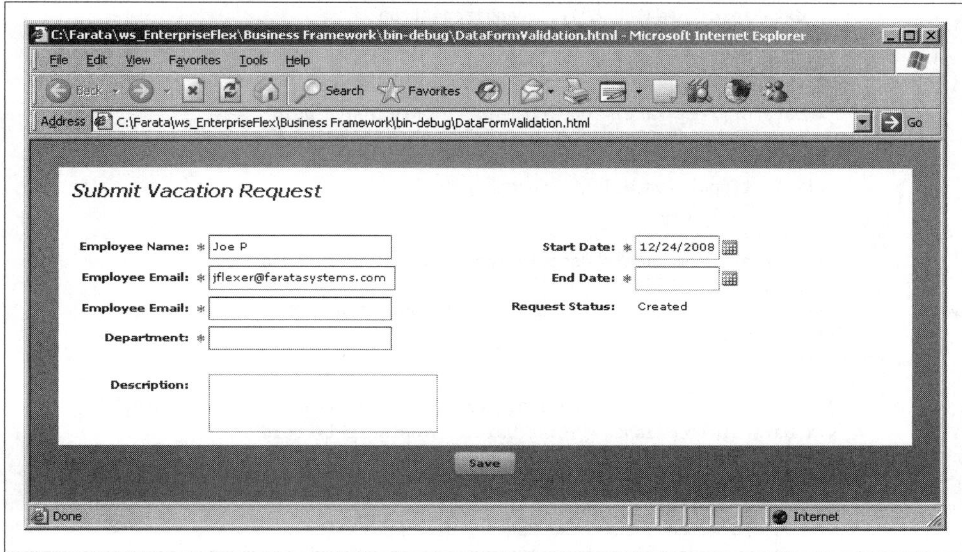

Figure 3-5. Running the DataFormValidation application

Example 3-17 shows the code of the *DataFormValidation.mxml* application that created these forms.

Example 3-17. DataFormValidation.mxml

```
<?xml version="1.0" encoding="utf-8"?>
<mx:Application width="100%" height="100%" layout="vertical"
    xmlns:mx="http://www.adobe.com/2006/mxml"
    xmlns:fx="http://www.faratasystems.com/2008/components"
    creationComplete="onCreationComplete()"
    >
    <mx:VBox width="100%" height="100%" backgroundColor="white">
         <mx:Label text="Submit Vacation Request"
            fontWeight="bold" fontSize="16" fontStyle="italic"
            paddingTop="10" paddingBottom="5" paddingLeft="10"
            />

        <mx:HBox width="100%" height="100%" >
        <fx:DataForm id="left" width="100%" dataProvider="{vacationRequestDTO}">
          <fx:DataFormItem label="Employee Name: " fontWeight="bold"
             dataField="EMPLOYEE_NAME" required="true"
             validators="{[nameValidator, requiredValidator]}">
            <mx:TextInput  fontWeight="normal" />
```

```
        </fx:DataFormItem>
        <fx:DataFormItem label="Employee Email: " fontWeight="bold"
            dataField="EMPLOYEE_EMAIL" required="true"
            validators="{[emailValidator]}">
              <mx:TextInput   fontWeight="normal"/>
         </fx:DataFormItem>
         <fx:DataFormItem label="Employee Email: " fontWeight="bold"
             dataField="MANAGER_EMAIL" required="true"
             validators="{[emailValidator]}">
           <mx:TextInput   fontWeight="normal"/>
         </fx:DataFormItem>
         <fx:DataFormItem label="Department: " fontWeight="bold"
            dataField="DEPARTMENT" required="true"
            validators="{[requiredValidator]}">
           <fx:TextInput fontWeight="normal"/>
         </fx:DataFormItem>
         <mx:Spacer height="10"/>
         <fx:DataFormItem label="Description: " fontWeight="bold"
             dataField="DESCRIPTION">
          <mx:TextArea width="200"  height="80" fontWeight="normal" />
        </fx:DataFormItem>
      </fx:DataForm>

      <fx:DataForm id="right" width="100%" dataProvider="{vacationRequestDTO}">
          <fx:DataFormItem label="Start Date: " fontWeight="bold"
              dataField="START_DATE"  valueName="selectedDate" required="true">
              <mx:DateField fontWeight="normal"/>
          </fx:DataFormItem>
          <fx:DataFormItem label="End Date: " fontWeight="bold"
               dataField="END_DATE" valueName="selectedDate" required="true">
              <fx:DateField  fontWeight="normal"/>
                <fx:validators>
                  <mx:Array>
                    <fx:ValidationRule
                      rule="{afterStartDate}"
                       errorMessage="End Date ($[END_DATE]) must be later
                           than Start Date $[START_DATE]">
                  </fx:ValidationRule>
                  <fx:ValidationRule
                      rule="{afterToday}"
                       errorMessage="End Date ($[END_DATE]) must be later
                           than today">
                  </fx:ValidationRule>
                  </mx:Array>
              </fx:validators>
          </fx:DataFormItem>
          <fx:DataFormItem label="Request Status: " fontWeight="bold"
                    dataField="STATUS">
              <mx:Label  fontWeight="normal"/>
          </fx:DataFormItem>
         </fx:DataForm>
      </mx:HBox>
  </mx:VBox>
  <mx:Button label="Save" click="onSave()"/>
```

```
<mx:Script>
    <![CDATA[
        import com.farata.datasource.dto.VacationRequestDTO;
        import mx.utils.UIDUtil;

        [Bindable] private var vacationRequestDTO:VacationRequestDTO ;
        private function afterToday( val: Object) : Boolean {
            var b : Boolean = val.END_DATE > new Date();
            return b;
        }
        private function afterStartDate( val: Object) : Boolean {
            var b : Boolean = val.END_DATE > val.START_DATE;
            return b;
        }

        private function onCreationComplete():void {
            // create a new vacation request
            vacationRequestDTO = new VacationRequestDTO;
            vacationRequestDTO.REQUEST_ID = UIDUtil.createUID();
            vacationRequestDTO.STATUS = "Created";
            vacationRequestDTO.START_DATE =
                          new Date(new Date().time + 1000 * 3600 * 24);
            vacationRequestDTO.EMPLOYEE_NAME = "Joe P";
            vacationRequestDTO.EMPLOYEE_EMAIL = "jflexer@faratasystems.com";
            vacationRequestDTO.VACATION_TYPE = "L"; //Unpaid leave - default
        }

        private function onSave():void    {
            if (isDataValid()) {
                mx.controls.Alert.show("Validation succeeded");
            } else {
                mx.controls.Alert.show("Validation failed");
            }
        }

        private function isDataValid():Boolean {
            var failedLeft:Array = left.validateAll();
            var failedRight:Array = right.validateAll();
            return ((failedLeft.length == 0)&&(failedRight.length == 0));
        }
    ]]>
</mx:Script>

<mx:StringValidator id="nameValidator" minLength="6"
              requiredFieldError="Provide your name, more than 5 symbols" />
<mx:EmailValidator id="emailValidator"
              requiredFieldError="Provide correct email" />
<mx:StringValidator id="requiredValidator"
              requiredFieldError="Provide non-empty value here" />
</mx:Application>
```

On the `creationComplete` event, this application creates an instance of the `vacationRequestDTO` that is used as a `dataProvider` for both left and right data forms.

This code uses a mix of standard Flex validators (`StringValidator`, `EmailValidator`) and subclasses of `ValidatorRule`. Note that both email fields use the same instance of the `EmailValidator`, which is not possible with regular Flex validation routines:

```
<fx:DataFormItem label="Employee Email: " fontWeight="bold"
              dataField="EMPLOYEE_EMAIL" required="true"
              validators="{[emailValidator]}">
                <mx:TextInput    fontWeight="normal"/>
           </fx:DataFormItem>
           <fx:DataFormItem label="Employee Email: " fontWeight="bold"
               dataField="MANAGER_EMAIL" required="true"
               validators="{[emailValidator]}">
             <mx:TextInput    fontWeight="normal"/>
           </fx:DataFormItem>
```

Notice that these validators are encapsulated inside the `DataFormItem`. If application programmers decide to add or remove some of the form item when the view state changes, they don't need to program anything special to ensure that validators work properly! The form item *end date* encapsulates two validation rules that are given as the closures `afterStartDate` and `afterToday`:

```
<fx:DataFormItem label="End Date: " fontWeight="bold"
                 dataField="END_DATE" valueName="selectedDate" required="true">
                <fx:DateField  fontWeight="normal"/>
                  <fx:validators>
                    <mx:Array>
                      <fx:ValidationRule
                        rule="{afterStartDate}"
                         errorMessage="End Date ($[END_DATE]) must be later
                             than Start Date $[START_DATE]">
                    </fx:ValidationRule>
                    <fx:ValidationRule
                        rule="{afterToday}"
                         errorMessage="End Date ($[END_DATE]) must be later
                             than today">
                    </fx:ValidationRule>
                    </mx:Array>
                </fx:validators>
            </fx:DataFormItem>

...

private function afterToday( val: Object) : Boolean {
    var b : Boolean = val.END_DATE > new Date();
    return b;
}

private function afterStartDate( val: Object) : Boolean {
    var b : Boolean = val.END_DATE > val.START_DATE;
    return b;
}
```

The example code does not include standard Flex validators inside `<fx:validators>`, but this is supported, too. For example, you can add the following line in the `validators` section of a `DataFormItem` right under the `<mx:Array>` tag:

```
<mx:StringValidator id="requiredValidator"
                    requiredFieldError="Provide non-empty value here" />
```

If you do it, you'll have three validators bound to the same form item, `End Date`: one standard Flex validator and two functions with validation rules.

From the application programmer's perspective, using such validation rules is simple. It allows reusing validators, which can be nicely encapsulated inside the form items.

For brevity, the function `onSave()` just displays a message box stating that the validation failed:

```
mx.controls.Alert.show("Validation failed");
```

But if you run this application through a debugger and place a breakpoint inside the function `isDataValid()`, you'll see all validation errors in the `failedLeft` and `failedRight` arrays (Figure 3-6).

The next question is, "How does all this work?"

⊞ this	DataFormValidation (@2c8a0a1)
⊟ failedLeft	Array (@2e10389)
⊟ [0]	mx.events.ValidationResultEvent (@2e100e9)
⊞ [inherited]	
field	null
message	"This string is shorter than the minimum allowed length. This must be at least 6 characters long."
⊞ results	Array (@2e102a9)
⊟ [1]	mx.events.ValidationResultEvent (@2e100b1)
⊞ [inherited]	
field	null
message	"Provide non-empty value here"
⊞ results	Array (@2e10121)
⊞ [2]	mx.events.ValidationResultEvent (@2e10201)
⊞ [3]	mx.events.ValidationResultEvent (@2e10549)
⊞ [4]	mx.events.ValidationResultEvent (@2e343c1)
length	5
⊟ failedRight	Array (@2e34e09)
⊟ [0]	mx.events.ValidationResultEvent (@2e10e09)
⊟ [inherited]	
bubbles	false
cancelable	false
⊞ currentTarget	com.farata.validators.ValidationRule (@2b90681)
eventPhase	2
⊞ target	com.farata.validators.ValidationRule (@2b90681)
type	"invalid"
field	null
message	"End Date (Sat Dec 6 00:00:00 GMT-0500 2008) must be later than Start Date Wed Dec 10 00:00:00 GMT-0500 2008"

Figure 3-6. Debugger's view of validation errors

The ValidationRule Class Explained

Enhancing the original Flex validators, the new `ValidationRule` extends the Flex `Validator` and is known to *clear.swc*'s UI controls. With it, developers can attach any number of validation rules to any field of a form or a list-based component. This means you can attach validation rules not only on the field level, but also on the parent level, such as to a specific `DataGrid` column or to an entire row.

When we designed the class, our approach was to separate (for real) validation rules from the UI component they validate. We also made them reusable to spare application developers from copy/pasting the same rule repeatedly. With the `ValidationRule` class, you can instantiate each rule once and reuse it across the entire application. Our goal was to move away from one-to-one relationships between a validator and a single property of a form field, to many-to-many relationships where each field can request multiple validators and vice versa.

If you don't need to perform cross-field validation in the form, you can continue using the original Flex validator classes. If you need to validate interdependent fields—if, say, the amount field has a value greater than $10K, and you need to block overnight delivery of the order field until additional approval is provided—use our more flexible extension, `ValidationRule`.

We still want to be able to reuse the validators (`EmailValidator`, `StringValidator`, etc.) that come with Flex, but they should be wrapped in our `ValidationRule` class. On the other hand, with the `ValidationRule` class, the application developers should also be able to write validation rules as regular functions, which requires less coding.

The source code of the `ValidationRule` class that supports all this functionality is listed in Example 3-18.

Example 3-18. The ValidationRule class

```
package com.farata.validators{
    import mx.controls.Alert;
    import flash.utils.describeType;

    import mx.events.ValidationResultEvent;
    import mx.validators.ValidationResult;
    import mx.validators.Validator;

    public class ValidationRule   extends Validator{
        public var args:Array = [];
        public var wrappedRule:Function ;
        public var errorMessage : String = "[TODO] replace me";
        public var data:Object;

        public function ValidationRule() {
            super();
            required = false;
        }
        private function combineArgs(v:Object):Array {
                var _args:Array = [v];
                if( args!=null && args.length>0 )
                    _args["push"].apply(_args, args);
                return  _args;
        }
```

```
public function set rule(f:Object) : void {
      if (!(f is Function)){
        Alert.show(""+f, "Incorrect Validation Rule" );
      return; // You may throw an exception here
    }

      wrappedRule = function(val:Object) :Boolean {
     return f(val);
      }
}

 private function substitute(...rest):String {
      var len:uint = rest.length;
     var args:Array;
     var str:String = "" + errorMessage;
     if (len == 1 && rest[0] is Array){
         args = rest[0] as Array;
         len = args.length;
     }
     else{
         args = rest;
     }

     for (var i:int = 0; i < len; i++){
         str = str.replace(new RegExp("\\$\\["+i+"\\]", "g"), args[i]);
     }
     if ( args.length == 1 && args[0] is Object) {
         var o:Object = args[0];
         for each (var s:*  in o){
             str = str.replace(new RegExp("\\$\\["+s+"\\]", "g"), o[s]);
         }

         var classInfo:XML = describeType(o);
         // List the object's variables, their values, and their types.
         for each (var v:XML in classInfo..variable) {
             str = str.replace(new RegExp("\\$\\["+v.@name+"\\]", "g"),
                                                            o[v.@name]);
         }

     // List accessors as properties
         for each (var a:XML in classInfo..accessor) {
         // Do not get the property value if it is write-only
             if (a.@access != 'writeonly') {
                  str = str.replace(new RegExp("\\$\\["+a.@name+"\\]",
                                                       "g"), o[a.@name]);
             }
           }
     }
     return str;
 }

override protected function doValidation(value:Object):Array{
         var results:Array = [];
```

```
            if (!wrappedRule(data))
               results.push(new ValidationResult(true, null, "Error",
                       substitute(combineArgs(data))));

            return results;
        }
       override public function validate(value:Object = null,
                  suppressEvents:Boolean = false):ValidationResultEvent{
        if (value == null)
            value = getValueFromSource();

        // If the required flag is true and there is no value,
        // we need to generate a required field error
        if (isRealValue(value) || required){
            return super.validate(value, suppressEvents);
        }
        else {
            // Just return the valid value
            return new ValidationResultEvent(ValidationResultEvent.VALID);
        }
      }
    }
}
```

The superclass `Validator` has two methods that will be overridden in its descendants: `doValidation()`, which initiates and performs the validation routine, and the function `validate()`, which watches required arguments and gets the values from the target UI control.

Notice that this code fragment from the *DataFormValidation.mxml* application:

```
<fx:ValidationRule rule="{afterStartDate}"
 errorMessage="End Date ($[END_DATE]) must be later than Start Date $[START_DATE]">
</fx:ValidationRule>
```

mentions the name of the function `afterStartDate` that alternatively could have been declared inline as a closure. The function ensures that the date being validated is older than the `END_DATE`:

```
private function afterToday( val: Object) : Boolean {
    var b : Boolean = val.END_DATE > new Date();
    return b;
}
```

In this code, `val` points at the `dataProvider` of the form, which, in the sample application, is an instance of the `vacationRequestDTO`. An important point is that both the `DataForm` and the `ValidationRule` see the same `dataProvider`.

The value of the `errorMessage` attribute includes something that looks like a macro language: `($[END_DATE])`. The function `substitute()` finds and replaces via regular expression the specified name (e.g., `END_DATE`) in all properties in the `dataProvider` with their values.

If `dataProvider` is a dynamic object, the function `ValidationRule.substitute()` enumerates all its properties via a `for each` loop. For regular classes, Flex offers a reflection mechanism using the function `describeType()`; give it a class name and it'll return a definition of this class in a form of XML. Then the function `substitute()` gets all class variables and *accessors* (getters and setters) and applies the regular expression to the `errorMessage` text.

For example, if you deal with a dynamic object `o` that has a property `END_DATE`, the following line will replace `($[END_DATE])` in the error text with the value of this property `o[s]`:

```
str = str.replace(new RegExp("\\$\\["+s+"\\]", "g"), o[s]);
```

The method `substitute()` is called from `doValidate()`, and if the user enters invalid dates (for example, if the start date is 12/10/2008 and the end date 12/06/2008), the validator will find the properties called `END_DATE` and `START_DATE` and turn this error text:

```
"End Date ($[END_DATE]) must be later than Start Date $[START_DATE]"
```

into this one:

```
"End Date (12/06/2008) must be later than Start Date 12/10/2008"
```

In Chapter 2, you learned how to write class factories that can wrap functions and return them as objects. This technique is applied in the `ValidationRule` class, too, which supports functions as validators. If the application code uses the setter `rule`, the function with business-specific validation rules is expected.

The class `ValidationRule` has this setter:

```
public function set rule(f:Object) : void {
            if (!(f is Function)){
               Alert.show(""+f, "Incorrect Validation Rule" );
            return;
         }

            wrappedRule = function(val:Object) :Boolean {
         return f(val);
            }
}
```

In the application *DataFormValidation.mxml*, you can easily find that this setter has been used (we already discussed the function `afterStartDate` earlier):

```
<fx:ValidationRule
    rule="{afterStartDate}"
    errorMessage="End Date ($[END_DATE]) must be later
                    than Start Date $[START_DATE]">
</fx:ValidationRule>
```

We hope you like the simplicity that `ValidationRule` offers to application developers who have to validate forms. The next section examines a sample application that demonstrates the use of this class in a `DataGrid` control.

Embedding Validation Rules into a DataGrid

As opposed to component libraries, classes in a framework depend on each other. In this context, this means that the `ValidationRule` class requires an enhanced `DataGrid` component.

Please note that the sample application shown next uses `DataGrid` and `DataGridItem` from a different namespace. These classes are included in the *clear.swc* library and come with the source code accompanying the book, but due to space constraints, we won't include the source code of these objects here.

This example is yet another version of the Café Townsend application from Chapter 1. For simplicity, the employee data hardcoded, and to run this application you don't need to do any server-side setup.

This application is an example of a master/detail window with validators embedded inside a data grid. Figure 3-7 shows the phone number having the wrong number of digits in the first row of our `DataGrid` component. The embedded validation rule properly reports an error message that reads, "Wrong length, need 10 digit number."

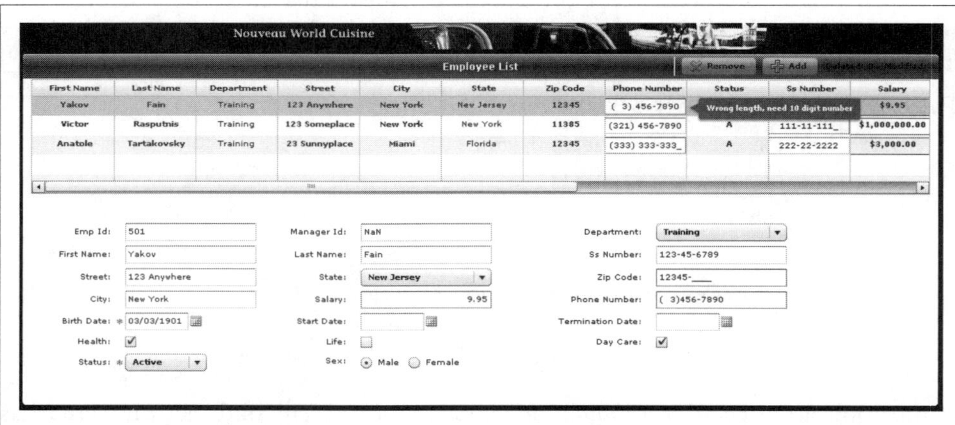

Figure 3-7. Validating the phone DataGridColumn

You can also assign validation rules to the form items that show details of the selected row. In Figure 3-8 you can see a validation error message stating that "Salary (9.95) is out of reasonable range." All fields that have invalid values have red borders. While examining the source code, please note that the drop-down box "Department" was populated using a resource file.

The version of the Café Townsend application in Example 3-19 uses the custom object `Employee_getEmployees_gridFormTest`.

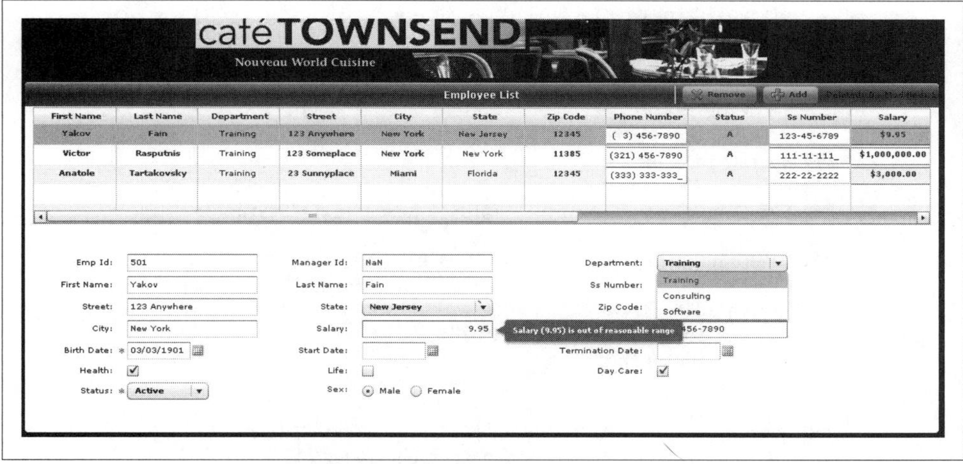

Figure 3-8. Validating the salary DataGridColumn

Example 3-19. Code of Café Townsend with validations

```
<?xml version="1.0" encoding="UTF-8"?>
<mx:ViewStack height="100%" width="100%" xmlns:mx="http://www.adobe.com/2006/mxml"
    xmlns:fx="http://www.faratasystems.com/2008/components"  creationPolicy="all"
    creationComplete="fill_onClick()">
<fx:DataCollection id="collection" destination="com.farata.datasource.Employee"
        method="getEmployees"  collectionChange="trace(event)"
                                                fault="trace(event)" />
<mx:Canvas height="100%" width="100%">
    <mx:Panel title="Employee List" width="100%" height="100%">
        <fx:DataGrid id="dg"
            itemRenderer="{new
      UIClassFactory(com.farata.controls.dataGridClasses.DataGridItemRenderer)}"
        horizontalScrollPolicy="auto" width="100%" dataProvider="{collection}"
            editable="true" height="100%" rowHeight="25">
           <fx:columns>
            <fx:DataGridColumn dataField="EMP_FNAME"  headerText="First Name"/>
            <fx:DataGridColumn dataField="EMP_LNAME"  headerText="Last Name"/>
            <fx:DataGridColumn dataField="DEPT_ID"  editable="false"
                  headerText="Department"
                  resource="{com.farata.resources.DepartmentComboResource}"/>
            <fx:DataGridColumn dataField="STREET"  headerText="Street"/>
            <fx:DataGridColumn dataField="CITY"  headerText="City"/>
            <fx:DataGridColumn dataField="STATE"  editable="false"
                  headerText="State"
                  resource="{com.farata.resources.StateComboResource}"/>
            <fx:DataGridColumn dataField="ZIP_CODE"  headerText="Zip Code"
                  formatString="zip" >
                <fx:validators>
                    <mx:ZipCodeValidator />
                </fx:validators>
            </fx:DataGridColumn>
            <fx:DataGridColumn dataField="PHONE" headerText="Phone Number"
                  formatString="phone"  >
```

```
    <fx:validators>
        <mx:Array>
            <mx:PhoneNumberValidator  wrongLengthError="Wrong
                    length, need 10 digit number"/>
        </mx:Array>
    </fx:validators>
</fx:DataGridColumn>

<fx:DataGridColumn dataField="STATUS"  headerText="Status"/>

<fx:DataGridColumn dataField="SS_NUMBER" headerText="Ss Number"
                                              formatString="ssn" >
    <fx:validators>
        <mx:SocialSecurityValidator/>
    </fx:validators>
</fx:DataGridColumn>

<fx:DataGridColumn dataField="SALARY" headerText="Salary"
                     formatString="currency(2)">
    <fx:validators>
        <mx:Array>
          <fx:ValidationRule
                rule="{function(data:Object):Boolean
                      { return (data &amp;&amp;data.SALARY > 10000
                      &amp;&amp; data.SALARY < 500000);}}"
             errorMessage="Salary ($[SALARY]) is out of reasonable
                                                          range"/>
       </mx:Array>
   </fx:validators>
</fx:DataGridColumn>

<fx:DataGridColumn dataField="START_DATE"  headerText="Start Date"
    itemEditor="mx.controls.DateField" editorDataField="selectedDate"
    formatString="shortDate"/>

<fx:DataGridColumn dataField="TERMINATION_DATE"
      headerText="Termination Date" itemEditor="mx.controls.DateField"
      editorDataField="selectedDate" formatString="shortDate">
    <fx:validators>
        <fx:ValidationRule
            rule="{afterStartDate}"
             errorMessage="End Date ($[TERMINATION_DATE]) must be
                                   later than Start Date $[START_DATE]">
       </fx:ValidationRule>
    </fx:validators>
</fx:DataGridColumn>

<fx:DataGridColumn dataField="BIRTH_DATE" headerText="Birth Date"
      itemEditor="mx.controls.DateField" editorDataField="selectedDate"
      formatString="shortDate"/>

   <fx:DataGridColumn dataField="BENE_HEALTH_INS"  headerText="Health"
      resource="{YesNoCheckBoxResource}" rendererIsEditor="true"/>

<fx:DataGridColumn dataField="BENE_LIFE_INS"  headerText="Life"
```

```
            resource="{YesNoCheckBoxResource}"   rendererIsEditor="true"/>

          <fx:DataGridColumn dataField="BENE_DAY_CARE"  headerText="Day Care"
            resource="com.farata.resources.YesNoCheckBoxResource"
            rendererIsEditor="true"/>

          <fx:DataGridColumn dataField="SEX"  headerText="Sex"
            resource="{SexRadioResource}" rendererIsEditor="true"/>
      </fx:columns>
</fx:DataGrid>

<fx:DataForm dataProvider="{dg.selectedItem}">
    <mx:HBox>
        <mx:Form>
            <fx:DataFormItem dataField="EMP_ID" label="Emp Id:"/>
             <fx:DataFormItem dataField="EMP_FNAME" label="First Name:"/>
            <fx:DataFormItem dataField="STREET" label="Street:"/>
            <fx:DataFormItem dataField="CITY" label="City:"/>
            <fx:DataFormItem dataField="BIRTH_DATE" label="Birth Date:"
                  formatString="shortDate" required="true"/>
            <fx:DataFormItem dataField="BENE_HEALTH_INS" label="Health:"
                  resource="{com.farata.resources.YesNoCheckBoxResource}"/>
            <fx:DataFormItem dataField="STATUS" label="Status:"
                  resource="{com.farata.resources.StatusComboResource}"
                  required="true"/>
        </mx:Form>

        <mx:Form>
            <fx:DataFormItem dataField="MANAGER_ID" label="Manager Id:"/>
            <fx:DataFormItem dataField="EMP_LNAME" label="Last Name:"/>
            <fx:DataFormItem dataField="STATE" label="State:"
                  resource="com.farata.resources.StateComboResource"/>
            <fx:DataFormItem dataField="SALARY" label="Salary:"
                  formatString="currency" textAlign="right">
                <fx:validators>
                 <fx:ValidationRule rule="{function(data:Object):Boolean {
                        return (data &amp;&amp;data.SALARY > 10000 &amp;&amp;
                               data.SALARY < 500000);}}"
                    errorMessage="Salary ($[SALARY]) is out
                                                   of reasonable range"/>
                 </fx:validators>
            </fx:DataFormItem>
            <fx:DataFormItem dataField="START_DATE" label="Start Date:"
                              formatString="shortDate"/>
            <fx:DataFormItem dataField="BENE_LIFE_INS" label="Life:"
                      resource="{YesNoCheckBoxResource}"/>
            <fx:DataFormItem dataField="SEX" label="Sex:"
                      resource="{SexRadioResource}"/>
        </mx:Form>
        <mx:Form>
            <fx:DataFormItem dataField="DEPT_ID" label="Department:"
                      resource="{DepartmentComboResource}"/>
            <fx:DataFormItem dataField="SS_NUMBER" label="Ss Number:"
                      itemEditor="{com.farata.controls.MaskedInput}"
                                                  formatString="ssn">
```

```
                    <fx:validators>
                        <mx:SocialSecurityValidator/>
                    </fx:validators>
                  </fx:DataFormItem>
                   <fx:DataFormItem dataField="ZIP_CODE" label="Zip Code:"
                                     formatString="zip">
                    <fx:validators>
                        <mx:ZipCodeValidator />
                    </fx:validators>
                  </fx:DataFormItem>
                 <fx:DataFormItem dataField="PHONE" label="Phone Number:"
                         itemEditor="{com.farata.controls.MaskedInput}"
                                    formatString="phone">
                     <fx:validators>
                         <mx:PhoneNumberValidator
                                         wrongLengthError="keep typing"/>
                     </fx:validators>
                 </fx:DataFormItem>
                 <fx:DataFormItem dataField="TERMINATION_DATE"
                        label="Termination Date:" formatString="shortDate">
                     <fx:validators>
                         <fx:ValidationRule
                         rule="{afterStartDate}"
                          errorMessage="End Date ($[TERMINATION_DATE]) must be
                                later than Start Date $[START_DATE]">
                        </fx:ValidationRule>
                 </fx:validators>
                   </fx:DataFormItem>
                 <fx:DataFormItem dataField="BENE_DAY_CARE" label="Day Care:"
                        resource="{YesNoCheckBoxResource}"/>
             </mx:Form>
         </mx:HBox>
    </fx:DataForm>
</mx:Panel>

<mx:HBox horizontalScrollPolicy="off" verticalAlign="middle" height="30"
                                                          width="100%">
 <mx:Spacer width="100%"/>
 <mx:VRule strokeWidth="2" height="24"/>
 <mx:Button enabled="{dg.selectedIndex != -1}"
           click="collection.removeItemAt(dg.selectedIndex)" label="Remove"
           icon="@Embed('/assets/delete_16x16.gif')"/>
 <mx:Button click="addItemAt(Math.max(0,dg.selectedIndex+1)) " label="Add"
           icon="@Embed('/assets/add_16x16.gif')" />
 <mx:Label text="Deleted: {collection.deletedCount}"/>
 <mx:Label text="Modified: {collection.modifiedCount}"/>
</mx:HBox>
</mx:Canvas>

<mx:Script>    <![CDATA[
    import com.farata.controls.dataGridClasses.DataGridItemRenderer;
    import com.farata.core.UIClassFactory;
    import com.farata.collections.DataCollection;
    import mx.collections.ArrayCollection;
    import mx.controls.dataGridClasses.DataGridColumn;
```

```
    import mx.events.CollectionEvent;
    import com.farata.datasource.dto.EmployeeDTO;
    import com.farata.resources.*;
    import mx.validators.*;

    private var linkage:EmployeeDTO = null;

     private function fill_onClick():void {
        collection.source = Test.data;
        dg.selectedIndex=0;
    }

    private function addItemAt(position:int):void    {
        var item:EmployeeDTO = new EmployeeDTO();
        collection.addItemAt(item, position);
        dg.selectedIndex = position;
    }

    import com.farata.resources.*;
    import com.farata.controls.*;
    private function afterStartDate( val: Object) : Boolean {
        return !val.TERMINATION_DATE || val.TERMINATION_DATE > val.START_DATE;
    }
    ]]>
  </mx:Script>
</mx:ViewStack>
```

When you review the code in Example 3-19, you'll find different flavors of validation rules inside the data grid columns in this implementation of the Café Townsend application. For example, the following rule is defined as an anonymous function for the data grid column `SALARY`:

```
<fx:DataGridColumn dataField="SALARY" headerText="Salary"
                               formatString="currency(2)">
               <fx:validators>
                   <mx:Array>
                     <fx:ValidationRule
                           rule="{function(data:Object):Boolean
                                  { return (data &amp;&amp;data.SALARY > 10000
                                  &amp;&amp; data.SALARY < 500000);}}"
                        errorMessage="Salary ($[SALARY]) is out of reasonable
                                                                      range"/>
                  </mx:Array>
               </fx:validators>
            </fx:DataGridColumn>
```

If the data grid is populated and the salary in a particular cell does not fall into the range between 10,000 and 500,000, this function returns `false` and this data value is considered invalid. Such cell(s) will immediately get the red border, and the error message will report the problem in the red error tip right by this cell.

Some of the validation rules were repeated both in the `DataGrid` and `DataForm`, but this doesn't have to be the case. The same instances of the `ValidationRule` class can be reused as in the `DataFormValidation` application.

The data for this sample application is hardcoded in *Test.as*, which starts as follows:

```
public class Test{

        public function Test(){
        }
        static public function get data() : Array {
            var e : EmployeeDTO = new EmployeeDTO;
            e.EMP_FNAME = "Yakov";
            e.EMP_LNAME = "Fain";
            e.BENE_DAY_CARE = "Y";
            e.BENE_HEALTH_INS = "Y";
            e.BENE_LIFE_INS = "N";
              ...
```

If you'd like to have a deeper understanding of how `<fx:DataGridColumn>` works with embedded validators, please examine the source code of the classes **`com.farata.controls.dataGridClasses.DataGridItem`** and **`com.farata.controls.DataGrid`** that are included with the source code accompanying this chapter.

We had to jump through a number of hoops to allow Flex validators to communicate with the `DataGrid`, as the `Validator` class expects to work only with subclasses of the `UIComponent` that are focusable controls with borders. It's understandable—who needs to validate, say, a `Label`?

But we wanted to be able to display a red border around the cell that has an invalid value and a standard error tip when the user hovers the mouse pointer over the `DataGrid` cell. Hence we had to make appropriate changes and replace the original `DataGrid.itemRenderer` with our own, which implements the `IValidatorListener` interface. An `itemRenderer` on the `DataGrid` level affects all its columns:

```
<fx:DataGrid id="dg"
    itemRenderer="{new UIClassFactory(
com.farata.controls.dataGridClasses.DataGridItemRenderer)}"
```

We've included this replacement of the `DataGridItemRenderer` in the demo application just to show that you can substitute the base classes from the Flex framework with your own. But as a developer of a business framework, you should hide such code in the base components, which in this case would have been a constructor of your enhanced `DataGrid`.

Besides validation rules, it is worth noting how master/detail relationships are implemented with just one line:

```
<fx:DataForm dataProvider="{dg.selectedItem}">
```

A selected row in a `DataGrid` (master) is a `dataProvider` for a `DataForm` (detail). With original Flex `DataGrid` and `Form` components, it would take a lot more coding to properly rebind the object representing a selected row that changes whenever the user selects a different one.

Once again, a well-designed framework should allow application developers to write less code. The code of this version of Café Townsend is an example of what can be done in only about 160 lines of code. It implements master/detail relationships, performs a lot of custom validations, and uses Business Style Sheets. Adding a couple dozen lines of code can turn this application into a CRUD built on the powerful `DataCollection` class that will be discussed in Chapter 6.

Minimizing the Number of Custom Events

Until now, you've concentrated on building rich components for a business framework. We Flex architects also recommend some coding techniques that serve the same goal as these components: enabling application developers to write less code. In this section, you'll see how to minimize the number of custom event classes in any application.

Flex is all about event-driven development. Create loosely coupled custom components and let them send events to each other, as in the mediator pattern example from Chapter 2. You can create new events for every occasion. If an event does not need to carry any additional data, just give it a name, specify its type as `flash.events.Event`, and define the meta tag to help Flash Builder list this event in its type-ahead prompts and dispatch it when appropriate. If your new event needs to carry some data, create an ActionScript class extending `flash.events.Event`, define a variable in this subclass to store application data, and override the method `clone()`.

Currently, for a midsize Flex application that includes about 30 views, where each view has two components that can send/receive just one custom event, for example, you face the need to write 60 custom event classes that look pretty much the same. We'll show you how to get away with just *one* custom event class for the *entire* application.

To illustrate the concept, we've created a simple application that defines one event class that can serve multiple purposes. This application consists of two modules (`GreenModule`, shown in Figure 3-9, and `RedModule`) that are loaded in the same area of the main application upon the click of one of the load buttons. It also has one universal event class called `ExEvent`.

Clicking any Send button creates an instance of this event that's ready to carry an application-specific payload: a DTO, a couple of `String` variables, or any other object.

Figure 3-9's example uses an ActionScript class called `GirlfriendDTO`. No Cairngorm-style mapping is required between the event being sent and the modules. For example, if you send a `Green` event to the `RedModule`, nothing happens, as the latter is not listening to the `Green` event.

This application and its source code are deployed at *http://tinyurl.com/5n5qkg*.

Flash Builder's project has a folder called *modules* that contains two modules: `RedModule` and `GreenModule`. The red one is listening for the arrival of the girlfriend's

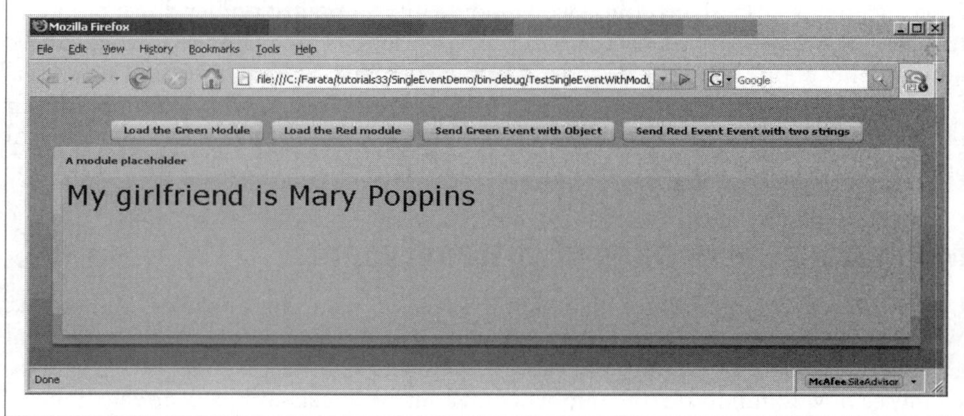

Figure 3-9. The GreenModule is loaded

first and last name, packaged in our single event class as the two separate strings listed in Example 3-20.

Example 3-20. RedModule.mxml

```
<?xml version="1.0" encoding="utf-8"?>
<mx:Module xmlns:mx="http://www.adobe.com/2006/mxml" layout="absolute"
    width="100%" height="100%" creationComplete="onCreationComplete(event)">
    <mx:TextArea id="display" backgroundColor="#FF4949"  width="100%" height="100%"
                                                fontSize="28"/>
    <mx:Script>
    <![CDATA[
    private function onCreationComplete(evt:Event):void{
        this.addEventListener("RedGirlfriend", onRedGirlfriend);
    }

    private function onRedGirlfriend(evt:ExEvent):void{
        display.text="My girlfriend is "+ evt.fName+ " " + evt.lName ;
    }
    ]]>
    </mx:Script>
</mx:Module>
```

The green module (Example 3-21) expects the girlfriend's name in the form of `GirlfriendDTO` (Example 3-22).

Example 3-21. GreenModule.mxml

```
<?xml version="1.0" encoding="utf-8"?>
<mx:Module xmlns:mx="http://www.adobe.com/2006/mxml" layout="absolute"
   width="100%" height="100%" creationComplete="onCreationComplete(event)">
    <mx:TextArea id="display" backgroundColor="#9CE29C" width="100%"
                height="100%" color="#070707" fontSize="28"/>
    <mx:Script>
        <![CDATA[
        import dto.GirlfriendDTO;
```

```
        private function onCreationComplete(evt:Event):void{
          this.addEventListener("GreenGirlfriend", onGreenGirlfriend);
        }

        private function onGreenGirlfriend(evt:ExEvent):void{
         var myGirlfriend:GirlfriendDTO=evt["girlfriend"];

         display.text="My girlfriend is "+ myGirlfriend.fName+ " " +
                                                myGirlfriend.lName ;

         }
        ]]>
    </mx:Script>
</mx:Module>
```

The `GirlfriendDTO` is pretty straightforward, too, as Example 3-22 shows.

Example 3-22. GirlfriendDTO

```
package dto
/**
 * This is a sample data transfer object (a.k.a. value object)
 */
{
    public class GirlfriendDTO {
         public var fName:String; // First name
         public var lName:String; // Last name
    }
}
```

The next step is to create a single but universal event class. It will be based on the `DynamicEvent` class, which allows you to add any properties to the event object on the fly. For the example, `GirlfriendDTO` is the object. Here's how a dynamic event can carry the `GirlfriendDTO`:

```
var myDTO:GirlfriendDTO=new GirlfriendDTO();
myDTO.fName="Mary";
myDTO.lName="Poppins";

var greenEvent:ExEvent=new ExEvent("GreenGirlfriend");
greenEvent.girlfriend=myDTO;
someObject.dispatchEvent(greenEvent);
```

Sending any arbitrary variables with this event will be straightforward:

```
var redEvent:ExEvent=new ExEvent("RedGirlfriend");

redEvent.fName="Mary";
redEvent.lName="Poppins";
someObject.dispatchEvent(redEvent);
```

The `ExEvent` is a subclass of `DynamicEvent`, which has a little enhancement eliminating manual programming of the property `Event.preventDefault`:

```
package{
    import mx.events.DynamicEvent;
```

```
    public dynamic class ExEvent extends DynamicEvent{
        private var m_preventDefault:Boolean;

        public function ExEvent(type:String, bubbles:Boolean = false,
                                          cancelable:Boolean = false)     {
            super(type, bubbles, cancelable);
            m_preventDefault = false;
        }

         public override function preventDefault():void        {
            super.preventDefault();
            m_preventDefault = true;
        }

        public override function isDefaultPrevented():Boolean     {
            return m_preventDefault;
        }
    }
}
```

The function `preventDefault()` is overridden, because the class `DynamicEvent` does not automatically process `preventDefault` in cloned events.

The code of the following test application loads modules, and then the user can send any event to whatever module is loaded at the moment. Of course, if the currently loaded module does not have a listener for the event you're sending, tough luck. But the good news is that it won't break the application either, as shown in Example 3-23.

Example 3-23. An application that tests the generic event ExEvent

```
<?xml version="1.0" encoding="utf-8"?>
<mx:Application xmlns:mx="http://www.adobe.com/2006/mxml" layout="vertical"
viewSourceURL="srcview/index.html">
 <mx:HBox>
    <mx:Button label="Load the Green Module"
          click="loadMyModule('modules/GreenModule.swf')"/>
    <mx:Button label="Load the Red module"
          click="loadMyModule('modules/RedModule.swf')"/>
    <mx:Button label="Send Green Event with Object" click="sendGreen()"/>
    <mx:Button label="Send Red Event Event with two strings" click="sendRed()"/>

 </mx:HBox>

<mx:Panel width="100%" height="100%" title="A module placeholder"
                                                 layout="absolute">
  <mx:ModuleLoader id="theModulePlaceholder" width="100%" height="100%"/>
</mx:Panel>
<mx:Script>
    <![CDATA[
        import dto.GirlfriendDTO;
        //Load the module specified in the moduleURL
        private function loadMyModule(moduleURL:String):void{
            theModulePlaceholder.url=moduleURL;
            theModulePlaceholder.loadModule();
        }
```

```
        // Sending generic ExEvent, adding an object that contains
        // the name of the girlfriend
        private function sendGreen():void{

            // Strongly typed DTO - better performance and readability,
            // but its structure has to be known for both parties -
            // the main application and the module
            var myDTO:GirlfriendDTO=new GirlfriendDTO();
            myDTO.fName="Mary";
            myDTO.lName="Poppins";

            if (theModulePlaceholder.child !=null){
                var greenEvent:ExEvent=new
                                          ExEvent("GreenGirlfriend");
                greenEvent.girlfriend=myDTO;

                theModulePlaceholder.child.dispatchEvent(greenEvent);
            }
        }

    // Sending a generic ExEvent that holds the name of the girlfriend
    // as two separate variables
        private function sendRed():void{
                var redEvent:ExEvent=new ExEvent("RedGirlfriend");

                redEvent.fName="Angelina";
                redEvent.lName="YouKnowWho";

                if (theModulePlaceholder.child !=null){
                theModulePlaceholder.child.dispatchEvent(redEvent);
                }
        }
    ]]>
</mx:Script>
</mx:Application>
```

The function `sendGreen()` sends an instance of `ExEvent`, carrying the DTO inside. The `sendRed()` function just adds two properties, `fName` and `lName`, to the instance of `ExEvent`.

Instead of using a DTO, you could've used a weakly typed data transfer object:

```
var myDTO:Object={fname:"Mary",lname:"Poppins"};
```

But this approach might result in a slightly slower performance and the code would be less readable. On the plus side, there would be no need to explicitly define and share the class structure of the DTO between the application (the mediator) and the module. You can use this technique for creating quick-and-dirty prototypes.

To summarize, using a single dynamic event spares you from the tedious coding of dozens of similar event classes. On the negative side, because this solution does not use the meta tag `Event` declaring the names of the events, Flash Builder won't be able to help you with the name of the event in its type-ahead help.

In the vast majority of RIAs, you can afford to lose a couple of milliseconds caused by using a dynamic event. Using a single dynamic event is one more step toward minimizing the code to be written for your project.

Summary

In this chapter, you learned by example how to start enhancing the Flex framework with customized components and classes, such as `CheckBox`, `ComboBox`, `DataGrid`, `DataForm`, `DataFormItem`, and `ValidationRule`. You also saw how to use these components in your applications. The source code for this chapter comes as two Flash Builder projects—the Business Framework, which includes the sample applications discussed in this chapter, and the Business Framework Library, which includes a number of enhanced Flex components (some of them were shown here in simplified form) that can be used in your projects as well.

The *clear.swc* component library is offered for free under the MIT license as a part of the open source framework Clear Toolkit—just keep the comments in the source code giving credit to Farata Systems as the original creator of this code. You can find the up-to-date information about all components included in Clear Toolkit by visiting the popular open source repository SourceForge, or, to be more specific, the following URL: *https://sourceforge.net/projects/cleartoolkit*. Make sure that you've tested these components thoroughly before using them in production systems.

In this chapter, we reviewed and explained why and how we extended several Flex components. We started with simpler `CheckBox` and `ComboBox` components, just because it was easier to illustrate the process of extending components. But then we did some heavy lifting and extended such important components as `Form` and `Validator`. You've seen a working example application that would integrate validators into `DataForm` and `DataGrid` components.

Besides extending components, we've shown you some best practices (using resources and writing applications) that use only one `event` class and thus greatly minimize the amount of code that Flex developers have to write.

You'll see more of extended components in Chapters 6, 9, and 11. Next we'll discuss convenient third-party tools that can be handy for any Flex team working on an enterprise project.

CHAPTER 4

Equipping Enterprise Flex Projects

"Excuse me, where can I find For Sale signs?"

"Probably they are in the Hardware section."

"Why there?"

"If we don't know where to shelve an item, we put it in Hardware."

—A conversation in a home remodeling store

For a successful project, you need the right mix of team members, tools, and techniques. This chapter covers a variety of topics that are important for development managers and enterprise and application architects who take care of the ecosystem in which Flex teams operate. The fact that Flex exists in a variety of platforms and that BlazeDS and LCDS can be deployed under any Java servlet container sounds great. But when you consider that today's enterprise development team often consists of people located all around the globe, such flexibility can make your project difficult to manage.

This chapter is not as technical as the others. It's rather a grab bag of little things that may seem unrelated, but when combined will make your development process smoother and the results of your development cycle more predictable.

Specifically, you'll learn about:

- Staffing enterprise Flex projects
- Working with the version control repository
- Stress testing
- Creating build and deployment scripts
- Continuous integration
- Logging and tracing
- Open source Flex component libraries
- Integration with Spring and Hibernate

The chapter's goal is to give you a taste of your options and help make your Flex team more productive. Without further ado, let's start building a Flex team.

Staffing Considerations

Any project has to be staffed first. Developers of a typical enterprise RIA project can be easily separated into two groups: those who work on the client tier and those who work on the server-side components. You can further divide this latter group into those who develop the middle tier with business logic and those who take care of the data. In all cases, however, how does a project manager find the right people?

The number of formally trained Flex programmers is increasing daily, but the pool of Flex developers is still relatively small compared to the multimillion legions of Java and .NET professionals.

The main concern of any project manager is whether enough people with Flex skills can be found to staff, but what does the title of "Flex developer" mean? In some projects, you need to develop a small number of Flex views, but they have very serious requirements for the communication layer. In other projects, you need to develop lots of UI views (a.k.a. screens) supported by standard LCDS or BlazeDS features. Any of these projects, however, require the following Flex personnel:

- UI developers
- Component developers
- Architects

For the sake of simplicity, this discussion assumes that the project's user interface design is done by a professional user experience designer.

The better you understand these roles, the better you can staff your project.

GUI and Component Developers

GUI developers create the view portion of an RIA. This is the easiest skill to acquire if you already have some programming language under your belt. The hard work of the Adobe marketing force and technical evangelists did a good job in creating the impression that working with Flex is easy: just drag and drop UI components on the what-you-see-is-what-you-get (WYSIWYG) area in Flash Builder, align them nicely, and write the functions to process button clicks or row selections in the data grid—sort of a Visual Basic for the Web.

The GUI development skillset is low-hanging fruit that many people can master pretty quickly. Savvy project managers either outsource this job to third-party vendors or send their own developers to a one-week training class. There is rarely a staffing problem here.

GUI developers interact with *user experience designers* who create wireframes of your application in Photoshop, some third-party tool, or even in Flex itself. But even in the Flex case, GUI developers should not start implementing screens until approved by a Flex component developer or an architect.

In addition to having the skills of GUI developers, *Flex component developers* are well versed in object-oriented and event-driven programming.

They analyze each view created by a web designer to decide which Flex components should be developed for this view and how these components will interact with each other (see Figure 2-4). Most likely they will be applying a mediator pattern (described in Chapter 2) to the initial wireframe.

Experienced Flex component developers know that even though the syntax of ActionScript 3 looks very similar to Java, it has provisions for dynamic programming and often they can use this to avoid creating well-defined Java Bean–ish objects.

Flex Architects

Flex architects know everything the GUI and component designers know, plus they can see the big picture. Flex architects perform the following duties:

- Decide which frameworks, component libraries, and utilities should be used on the project
- Decide on communication protocols to be used for communication with the server tier
- Enhance the application protocols if need be
- Decide how to modularize the application
- Arrange for the unit, functional, and stress tests
- Make decisions on application security issues, such as how to integrate with external authentication/authorization mechanisms available in the organization
- Act as a technical lead on the project, providing technical guidance to GUI and component developers
- Coordinate interaction between the Flex team and the server-side developers
- Promote the use of coding best practices and perform code reviews
- Conduct technical job interviews and give recommendations on hiring GUI and component developers

These skills can't be obtained in a week of training. Flex architects are seasoned professionals with years of experience in RIA development. The goal of any project manager is to find the best Flex architect possible. The success of your project heavily depends on this person.

Not every Flex developer can be profiled as a member of one of these three groups. In smaller teams, one person may wear two hats: component developer and architect.

Designopers and Devigners

RIAs require new skills to develop what was previously known as boring-looking enterprise applications. In the past, development of the user interface was done by software developers to the best of their design abilities. A couple of buttons here, a grid there, a gray background—done. The users were happy because they did not see anything better. The application delivered the data. What else was there to wish for? Enterprise business users were not spoiled and would work with whatever was available; they needed to take care of their business. It was what it was.

But is it still? Not anymore. We've seen excellent (from the UI perspective) functional specs for financial applications made by professional designers. Business users are slowly but surely becoming first-class citizens!

The trend is clear: developer art does not cut it anymore. You need to hire a professional user experience designer for your next-generation web application.

The vendors of the tools for RIA development recognize this trend and are trying to bring designers and developers closer to each other. But the main RIA tool vendors, Adobe and Microsoft, face different issues.

Adobe is a well-known name among creative people (Photoshop, Illustrator, Flash); during the last two years, it has managed to convince enterprise developers that it has something for them, too (Flex, AIR). Adobe is trying to win developers' hearts, but it does not want to scare designers either. In addition to various designer-only tools, Adobe's Flash Catalyst tool allows designers create the Flex UI of an application without knowing how to program.

Today, a designer creates artwork in Illustrator or Photoshop, and then developers have to somehow mimic all the images, color gradients, fonts, and styles in Flash Builder. But this process will become a lot more transparent.

A web designer will import his Illustrator/Photoshop creations into Flash Catalyst, then select areas to be turned into Flex components and save the artwork as a new project: a file with extension *.fxp*. Adobe did a good job of maintaining menus and property panes in Flash Catalyst, similar to what designers are accustomed to in Illustrator and Photoshop. The learning curve for designers is not steep at all.

Designers will definitely appreciate the ability to work with Flex view states without the need to write even a line of code. Creating two views for master/detail scenarios becomes a trivial operation.

Flash Catalyst is a handy tool not only for people trained in creating artwork but also for those who need to create wireframe mockups of their application using built-in controls including some dummy data.

Working with Flash Catalyst requires UI designers to use Flash Creative Studio version 4 or later for creation of original artworks. This is needed, because Flash Catalyst internally uses the new *.fxg* format for storing just the graphic part of the Flex controls.

Flash Catalyst will become a valuable addition to the toolbox of a web designer working in the Flex RIA space.

Microsoft comes from quite the opposite side: it has legions of faithful .NET developers, and released Silverlight, which includes great tools for designers creating UI for RIA. Microsoft Expression Design and Expression Blend IDEs take the artwork and automatically generate code for .NET developers and help animate the UI to make it more rich and engaging.

Adobe invests heavily in making the designer/developer workflow as easy and smooth as possible. Adobe's Catalyst generates Flex code based on the artwork created with tools from Creative Studio 4 and later. Most of the work on the application design is done using Adobe Photoshop, Illustrator, or Fireworks, and application interactions you can create in Flash Catalyst. During conversion, the selected piece of the artwork becomes the skin of a Flex component. Figure 4-1 shows how you can convert an area in the artwork into a Flex `TextInput` component.

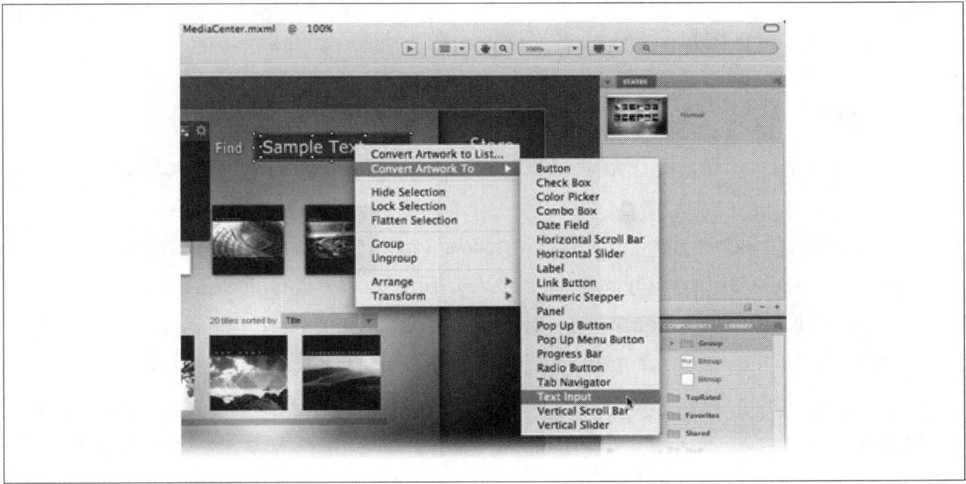

Figure 4-1. Converting artwork into Flex components

Flash Catalyst allows you to create animated transitions between states and, using the timeline, adjust the length and timing of the effects. It allows developers and designers to work on the same project. Designers create the interface of the RIA, and developers add business logic and program communication with the server.

In an effort to foster understanding between the developers and designers, Adobe consults with professors from different colleges and universities on their visual design and software engineering disciplines. The intent is to help designers understand programming better and help software developers get better at designing a user experience. It's a complex and not easily achievable goal, breeding these new creatures called "designopers" and "devigners."

If you are staffing an RIA project and need to make a decision about the position of web designer, you're better off hiring two different talents: a creative person and a web developer. Make sure that each party is aware of decisions made by the other. Invite designers to decision-making meetings. If the project budget is tight, however, you have no choice but to bring on board either a designoper or devigner.

With the right staff on board, you're ready to dig into your project. Even though the Flex SDK includes a command-line compiler and a debugger and you can write code in any plain-text editor of your choice, this is not the most productive approach. You need an IDE—an integrated development environment—and in the next section, you'll get familiar with IDE choices.

Flex Developer's Workstation

While configuring developers' workstations, ensure that each of them has at least 2 GB of RAM; otherwise, compilation by your IDE may take a large portion of your working day. As to what that IDE is, the choice is yours.

IDE Choices

At the time of this writing, enterprise Flex developers can work with one of the following IDEs:

- Flash Builder 3 or 4 Beta (Adobe) (*http://www.adobe.com/products/flex/*)
- RAD 7.5 (IBM) (*http://www.ibm.com/developerworks/downloads/r/rad/*)
- IntelliJ IDEA 9 (JetBrains) (*http://www.jetbrains.com/idea/download/*)
- Tofino 2 (Ensemble) (*http://www.ensemble.com/products/tofino.shtml*)

You can install Flash Builder either as a standalone IDE or as an Eclipse plug-in. The latter is the preferred choice for those projects that use Java as a server-side platform. Savvy Java developers install Eclipse JEE version or MyEclipse from Genuitec; both come with useful plug-ins that simplify development of the Java-based web applications.

Today, Flash Builder is the most popular IDE among Flex enterprise developers. It comes in two versions: Standard and Professional. The latter includes the data visualization package (charting support, `AdvancedDataGrid`, and Online Analytical Processing [OLAP] components). Besides offering a convenient environment for developers, Flash Builder has room for improvement in compilation speed and refactoring.

IBM's RAD 7.5 is a commercial IDE built on the Eclipse platform. RAD feels heavier when compared to Flash Builder. It can substantially slow down your developers if they have desktops with less than 2 GB of RAM.

For many years IntelliJ IDEA was one of the best Java IDEs. IntelliJ IDEA supports Flex development and is more responsive and convenient for Flex/Java developers than Flash Builder. The current version of IDEA, however, does not allow the creation of Flex views in design mode, which is clearly a drawback. It does not include the Flex profiler, which is an important tool for performance tuning of your applications. On the other hand, if you prefer Maven for building projects, you will appreciate the fact that IDEA includes a Maven module.

Tofino is a free plug-in for Microsoft Visual Studio that allows development of a Flex frontend for .NET applications.

At the time of this writing, Flash Builder is the richest IDE available for Flex developers. Flash Builder 4 is going to be released in early 2010. Besides multiple changes in the code of the Flex SDK, it'll have a number of improvements in the tooling department: for example, a wizard for generation of the Flex code for remote data services, project templates, autogeneration of event handlers, integration with Flash Catalyst, a FlexUnit code generator, a Network Monitoring view, better refactoring support, and more.

Preparing for Teamwork

In some enterprises, developers are forced to use specific IDE and application servers for Flex development, such as RAD and WebSphere from IBM. We believe that developers should be able to select the tools that they are comfortable with. Some are more productive with the Flash Builder/Tomcat duo; others prefer RAD/Resin. During development, no such combinations should be prohibited, even if the production server for your application is WebLogic.

Likewise, members of a Flex application group may be physically located in different parts of the world. Third-party consultants may be working in different operational environments, too. They may even install the Flex framework on different disk drives (*C:*, *D:*, etc.).

All this freedom can lead to issues in using version control repositories, because Flash Builder stores the names of physical drives and directories in the property files of the Flash Builder project. Say Developer A has the Flex framework installed in a particular directory on disk drive *D:*. He creates a project pointing at Tomcat and checks it into a source code repository. Developer B checks out the latest changes from the repository and runs into issues, because either her Flex framework was installed on the disk drive *C:* or her project was configured to use WebSphere. In addition to this issue, developers will be reusing specific shared libraries, and each of the Flex modules may depend on other shared libraries as well as the server-side BlazeDS or LCDS components.

To simplify the process of configuring the build path and compile options of the Flex projects (developers may have different deployment directories), use *soft links* rather than hardcoded names of the drives and directories (this is the equivalent of what's known as *symbolic links* in the Unix/Linux OS).

For implementing soft links in the Windows environment, use the *junction* utility, which is available for download at *http://www.microsoft.com/technet/sysinternals/FileAndDisk/Junction.mspx*. This utility is a small executable file that allows the mapping of a soft link (a nickname) to an actual directory on disk.

For example, run the following in the command window:

```
junction c:\serverroot "c:\ Tomcat 6.0\webapps\myflex"
```

It'll create a soft link *C:\serverroot* that can be treated as a directory on your filesystem. In the example, *c:\serverroot* points at the application deployment directory under the Apache Tomcat servlet container. Similarly, another member of your team can map *C:\serverroot* to the deployment directory of WebSphere or any other JEE server.

From now on, all references in the build path and compiler options will start with *C:\serverroot* regardless of what physical server, disk drive, and directory are being used. By following these conventions, all Flash Builder projects will be stored in the source control repositories with the same reference to *C:\serverroot*.

Using soft links simplifies the development of the Ant build scripts, too.

We recommend at least two soft links: *C:\serverroot* and *C:\flexsdk*, where the former is mapped to a document root of the servlet container and the latter is mapped to the installation directory of the Flex SDK. An example of creating a soft link *C:\flexsdk* is shown here:

```
C:\>junction C:\flexsdk "C:\Program Files\Adobe\Flash Builder 3 Plug-in\sdks\3.0.0"
```

When Flex SDK 4.1 or even 5.0 becomes available, this should have minimal effect on your build scripts and Flash Builder projects: just rerun the junction utility to point *C:\flexsdk* to the newly installed Flex framework.

By now, your team has selected the IDE, come to an agreement on the use of soft links, and considered various recommendations regarding Flex code, such as embedding into HTML, testing, build automation, and logging.

Embedding .swf Files into HTML Pages

Flash Builder automatically creates HTML wrappers for embedding Flash Player's content. When you create a new project, it contains a directory called *html-template* that has an HTML wrapper *index.template.html* that Flash Builder uses as a container for your *.swf* and copies into the *bin-debug* (or *bin-release*) folder each time your Flex application is rebuilt.

If you'd like to embed your *.swf* into an HTML page that includes some content specific to one of your existing HTML pages, you'd need to merge your HTML page with the file *index.template.html* and keep it in the *html-template* folder.

If you need to embed this HTML code into another Flex application, you can create an `iFrame`, copy this generated HMTL, specify the coordinates and size of this `iFrame`, and your *.swf* is displayed next to other HTML content that was created in your organization using legacy techniques. Just remember that you are now dealing with two web pages in one, which technically turns it into a portal. The issues of the mixed HTML/Flex portals are described in Chapters 7 and 8.

Adding a .swf to HTML with SWFObject

You can also embed a *.swf* using *SWFObject*, an open source utility (just one small JavaScript file) that offers a simpler way to include *.swf* files into an HTML page. Using Adobe Express Install, SWFObject detects the version of Flash Player installed on the client's machine. SWFObject can work in static HTML using the `<object>` element. It also supports dynamic publishing with JavaScript, which allows passing parameters to a *.swf* file as key/value pairs. Finally, it opens up opportunities for alternative content for the users who have web browsers without Flash Player plug-ins, as well as for added text to be picked up by the search engines.

A simple example contrasts the standard Flash Builder approach and SWFObject. Say you have this application called *HelloSWFObject.mxml*:

```
<?xml version="1.0" encoding="utf-8"?>
<mx:Application xmlns:mx="http://www.adobe.com/2006/mxml" layout="absolute">
   <mx:Text x="24" y="28" text="Hello" fontSize="20"/>
</mx:Application>
```

Flash Builder generates *HelloSWFObject.swf* and automatically embeds it into *HelloSWFObject.html*. Opening *HelloSWFObject.html* reveals more than 50 lines of code that take care of embedding the *.swf*.

Now try the solution offered by SWFObject. First, download and unzip into some folder the file *swfobject_2_2.zip* from *http://code.google.com/p/swfobject/*. Copy *HelloSWFObject.swf* there, too.

To generate an HTML wrapper, download *swfobject_generator_1_2_air.zip*, a handy AIR utility from SWFObject's site. After unzipping, run the application *swfobject_generator* (Figure 4-2).

Select the "Dynamic publishing" method, enter `HelloSWFObject.swf` in the Flash (*.swf*) field, and the name of the HTML container ID that will be used as an ID of the `<div>` area where your *.swf* will reside. In the "Alternative content" section, enter some keywords that you want to expose to search engines, and click the Generate button.

In the lower portion of the window, you'll find HTML that looks like Example 4-1.

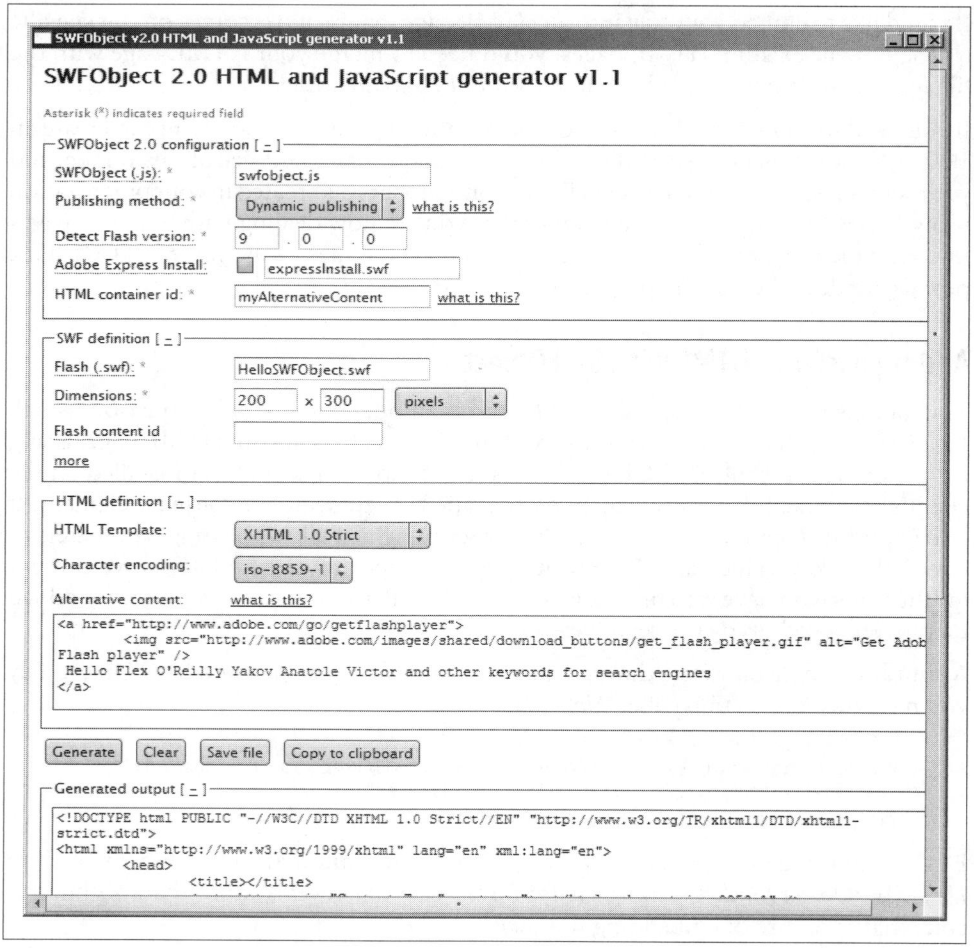

Figure 4-2. SWFObject's HTML generator

Example 4-1. HTML wrapper generated by SWFObject

```
<!DOCTYPE html PUBLIC "-//W3C//DTD XHTML 1.0 Strict//EN"
"http://www.w3.org/TR/xhtml1/DTD/xhtml1-strict.dtd">
<html xmlns="http://www.w3.org/1999/xhtml" lang="en" xml:lang="en">
 <head>
      <title></title>
      <meta http-equiv="Content-Type" content="text/html; charset=iso-8859-1" />
      <script type="text/javascript" src="swfobject.js"></script>
      <script type="text/javascript">
         var flashvars = {};
         var params = {};
         var attributes = {};
         swfobject.embedSWF("HelloSWFObject.swf", "myAlternativeContent",
                  "200", "300", "9.0.0", false, flashvars, params, attributes);
```

```
    </script>
 </head>
 <body>
   <div id="myAlternativeContent">
      <a href="http://www.adobe.com/go/getflashplayer">
           <img
src="http://www.adobe.com/images/shared/download_buttons/get_flash_player.gif"
   alt="Get Adobe Flash player" />
   Hello Flex O'Reilly Yakov Anatole Victor and other keywords for search engines
      </a>
  </div>
  <script type="text/javascript" src="swfobject.js"></script>
  <script type="text/javascript">
     var flashvars = {};
     var params = {};
     var attributes = {};
     swfobject.embedSWF("HelloSWFObject.swf", "myAlternativeContent",
                "200", "300", "9.0.0", false, flashvars, params, attributes);
  </script>
 </body>
</html>
```

Moving the JavaScript to the bottom of the page results in better performance of the page. Look for more tips to improve the performance of a website at *http://developer.yahoo.com/performance/index.html#rules*.

You are ready to run your application. The only issue with this solution is that you've lost the history management that was taken care of by Flash Builder's HTML wrapper. SWFObject 2.2, however, offers support for Flex history and deep linking; you can find an example of this solution published by Oleg Filipchuk at *http://olegflex.blogspot.com/2008/06/swfobject-2-flex-template.html*.

Interacting with HTML and JavaScript

In large enterprises, usually you don't start a new Enterprise Flex project from scratch without worrying about existing web applications written in JSP, ASP, AJAX, and the like.

More often, enterprise architects gradually introduce Flex into the existing web fabric of their organizations. Often, they start with adding a new Flex widget into an existing web page written in HTML and JavaScript, and they need to establish interaction between JavaScript and ActionScript code from the SWF widget.

The ExternalInterface Class

Flex can communicate with JavaScript using an ActionScript class called `ExternalInterface`. This class allows you to map ActionScript and JavaScript functions and invoke these functions either from ActionScript or from JavaScript. The use of the class `ExternalInterface` requires coding in both languages.

For example, to allow JavaScript's function `jsIsCalling()` to invoke a function `asToCall()`, you write in ActionScript:

```
ExternalInterface.addCallback("jsIsCalling", asToCall);
```

Then, you use the ID of the embedded *.swf* (e.g., `mySwfId` set in the HTML object) followed by a JavaScript call like this:

```
if(navigator.appName.indexOf("Microsoft") != -1){
    window["mySwfId"].asToCall();
} else {
document.getElementById("mySwfId").asToCall();
}
```

Flex AJAX Bridge

For the applications that are written by teams of AJAX developers, there is another option for JavaScript/ActionScript interaction. Flex SDK comes with a small library called Flex AJAX Bridge (FABridge).

Say you already have an AJAX application, but want to delegate some input/output (I/O) functionality to Flex or implement some components for the web page (media players, charts, and the like) in Flex. FABridge allows your AJAX developers to continue coding in JavaScript and call the API from within Flex components without the need to learn Flex programming.

With FABridge, you can register an event listener in JavaScript that will react to the events that are happening inside the *.swf* file. For instance, a user clicks the button inside a Flex portlet or some Flex remote call returns the data. Using FABridge may simplify getting notifications about such events (and data) from Flex components into existing AJAX portlets.

You can find a detailed description of how and when to use FABridge versus `ExternalInterface` at *http://bit.ly/aNPxOo*.

The flashVars Variable

A third mechanism of passing data to a *.swf* from the enclosing HTML page is to use the `flashVars` variable.

Consider an assignment: write a Flex application that can run against different servers—development, user acceptance testing (UAT), and production—without the need to recompile the *.swf* file. It does not take a rocket scientist to figure out that the URL of the server should be passed to the *.swf* file as a parameter, and you can do this by using a special variable, `flashVars`, in an HTML wrapper.

While embedding a *.swf* in HTML, Flash Builder includes `flashVars` parameters in the tags `Object` and `Embed`. ActionScript code can read them using `Application.applica tion.parameters`, as shown in the next example.

The script portion of Example 4-2 gets the values of the parameters **serverURL** and **port** (defined by us) using the Flex **Application** object. The goal is to add the values of these parameters to the HTML file via **flashVars**. In a Flex application, these values are bound to the **Label** as a part of the text string.

Example 4-2. Reading flashVars values in Flex

```
<?xml version="1.0" encoding="utf-8"?>
<mx:Application xmlns:mx="http://www.adobe.com/2006/mxml" layout="absolute"
    applicationComplete="initApp()">

  <mx:Label text=
"Will run the app deployed at http://{serverURL}:{port}/MyGreatApp.html" />
  <mx:Script>
      <![CDATA[
          [Bindable]
          var serverURL:String;

          [Bindable]
          var port:String;

          function initApp():void{
              serverURL=Application.application.parameters.serverURL;
              port=Application.application.parameters.port
          }
      ]]>
  </mx:Script>
</mx:Application>
```

Open the generated HTML file, and you'll find the JavaScript function **AC_FL_RunContent** that includes **flashVars** parameters in the form of key/value pairs. For example, in my sample application it looks like this:

```
"flashvars",'historyUrl=history.htm%3F&lconid=' + lc_id +''
```

If you used SWFObject to embed SWF, use different syntax for passing **flashVars** to SWF as shown in Example 4-2.

Add the parameters **serverURL** and **port** to this string to make it look as follows:

```
"flashvars",'serverURL=MyDevelopmentServer&port=8181&historyUrl=history.htm%3F&lconid
='+ lc_id
```

Run the application, and it'll display the URL of the server it connects to, as shown in Figure 4-3. If you'd like to deploy this application on the UAT server, just change the values of the **flashVars** parameters in the HTML file.

There's one last little wrinkle to iron out: if you manually change the content of the generated HTML file, the next time you clean the project in Flash Builder, its content will be overwritten and you'll lose added **flashVars** parameters.

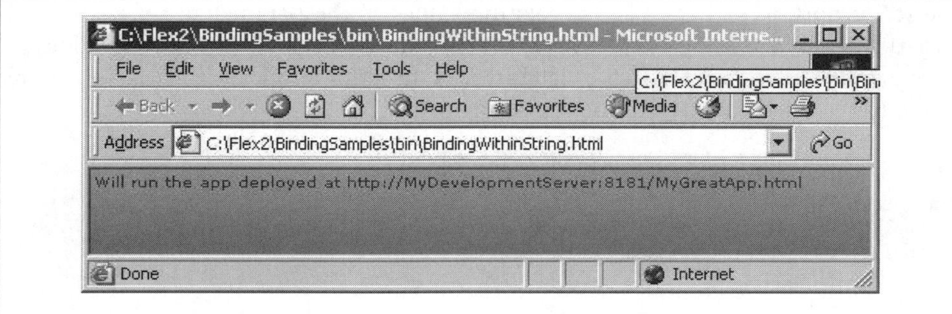

Figure 4-3. Running the flashVars sample—BindingWithString.mxml

There's a simple solution: instead of adding `flashVars` parameters to the generated HTML, add them to the file *index.template.html* from the *html-template* directory.

Of course, this little example does not connect to any server, but it shows how to pass the server URL (or any other value) as a parameter to Flash Player, and how to assemble the URL from a mix of text and bindings.

Testing Flex RIAs

The sooner you start testing your application, the shorter the development cycle will be. It seems obvious, but many IT teams haven't adopted agile testing methodologies, which costs them dearly. ActionScript supports dynamic types, which means that its compiler won't be as helpful in identifying errors as it is in Java. To put it simply, Flex applications have to be tested more thoroughly.

To switch to an agile test-driven development, start with accepting the notion of embedding testing into your development process rather than scheduling testing after the development cycle is complete. The basic types of testing are:

- Unit
- Integration
- Functional
- Load

The sections that follow examine the differences between these testing strategies, as well as point out tools that will help you to automate the process.

Unit and Integration Testing

Unit testing is performed by a developer and is targeted at small pieces of code to ensure, for example, that if you call a function with particular arguments, it will return the expected result.

Test-driven development principles suggest that you write test code even before you write the application code. For example, if you are about to start programming a class with some business logic, ask yourself, "How can I ensure that this function works fine?" After you know the answer, write a test ActionScript class that calls this function to *assert* that the business logic gives the expected result. Only after the test is written, start programming the business logic. Say you are in a business of shipping goods. Create a `Shipment` class that implements business logic and a `ShipmentTest` class to test this logic. You may write a test that will assert that the shipping address is not null if the order quantity is greater than zero.

In addition to business logic, Flex RIAs should be tested for proper rendering of UI components, changing view states, dispatching, and handling events. *Integration testing* is a process in which a developer combines several unit tests to ensure that they work properly with each other. Both unit and integration tests have to be written by application developers.

Several tools can help you write unit and integration tests.

FlexUnit4

FlexUnit4 is a unit testing framework for Flex and ActionScript 3.0 applications and libraries. With FlexUnit4 and Flash Builder, you can generate individual unit tests and combine them into test suites. Flash Builder 4 allows automatic creation of test cases (see New → TestCase Class in the menus). Just enter the name of the class to test, and Flash Builder will generate a test application and a test case class in a separate package.

For each method of your class, say `calculateMonthlyPayment()`, Flash Builder will generate a test method, for example `testCalculateMonthlyPayment()`. You just need to implement it:

```
public function testCalculateMonthlyPayment(){
   //A $200K mortgage at 7% for 30 years should have
   // a monthly payment of $1199.10
   Assert.assertEquals(
    MortgageCalculator.calculateMonthlyPayment (200000, 7,30 ),1199.1 );
}
```

After the test case class is ready, ask Flash Builder to generate the test suite for you (see New → Test Suite Class). To execute your test suite, right-click on the project in Flash Builder and select Execute FlexUnit Tests.

Unit testing of visual components is not as straightforward as unit testing of business logic in ActionScript classes. The Flex framework makes lots of internal function calls to properly display your component on the Flash Player's stage. And if you need to get a hold of a particular UI component to ensure that it's properly created, laid out, and populated, use the `Application.application` object in your tests.

FlexMonkey

A free tool from Gorilla Logic, FlexMonkey is a unit testing framework for Flex applications that also automates testing of Flex UI functionality. FlexMonkey can record and play back UI interactions. For example, Figure 4-4 illustrates the command list that results from the user entering the name of the manager and selecting a date.

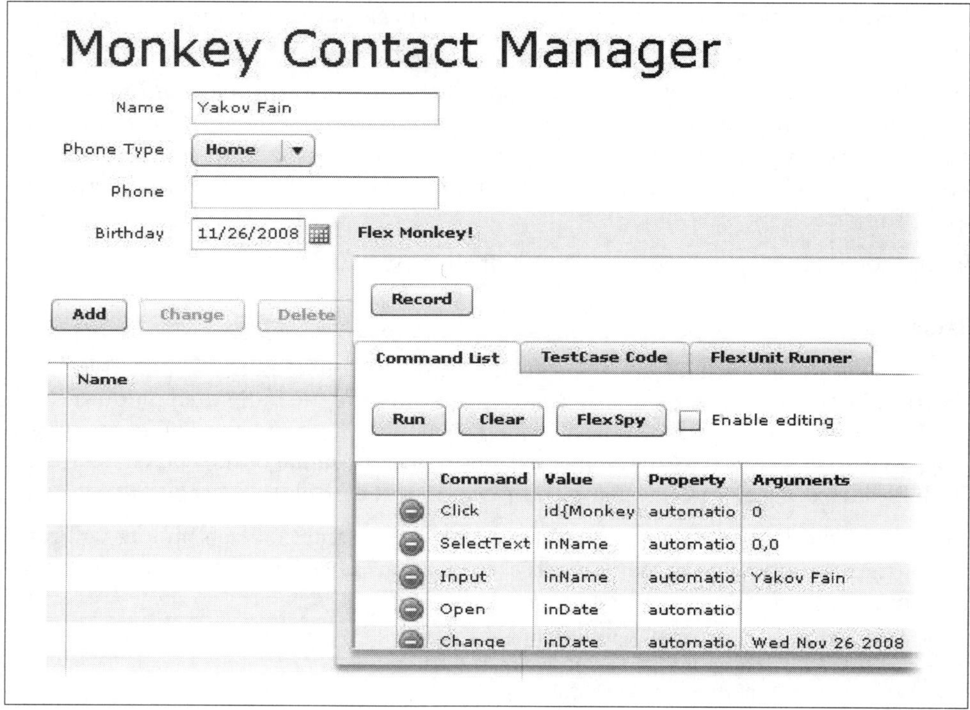

Figure 4-4. Recording command list in FlexMonkey

FlexMonkey not only creates a command list, but also generates ActionScript testing scripts for FlexUnit (Figure 4-5) that you can easily include within a continuous integration process.

Technically, if the test scripts generated by FlexMonkey would allow a programming language simpler than ActionScript, you could consider it both a unit and functional testing framework. In the small IT shops where developers have to perform all kinds of testing, you may use FlexMonkey in this double mode. Even in larger organizations it may be beneficial if a developer runs these prefunctional tests to minimize the number of errors reported by the QA team. For more information on FlexMonkey, see *http://www.gorillalogic.com/flexmonkey*.

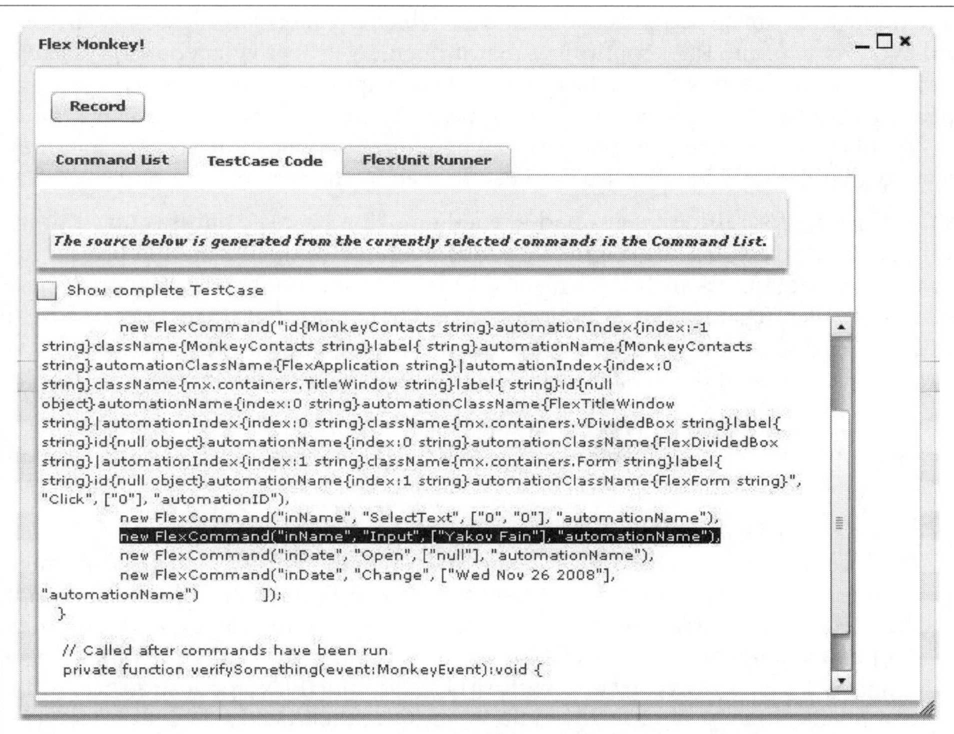

Figure 4-5. Test-generated matching command list

Visual Flex Unit

An open source framework for testing the visual appearance of components, Visual Flex Unit also introduces *visual assertions*, which assert that a component's appearance is identical to a stored baseline image file. Developers can instantiate and initialize UI components, define view states and styles, and test that these components look the same as presaved images of the same. For output, you'll get a report on how many pixels differ. You can run tests in Ant mode and send notifications about the test results. At the time of this writing, Visual Flex Unit is still in alpha version, but you can find more information at *http://code.google.com/p/visualflexunit/*

Functional Testing

Functional testing (a.k.a. black-box, QA, or acceptance testing) is aimed at finding out whether the application properly implements business logic. For example, if the user clicks on a row in the customer data grid, the program should display a form view with specific details about the selected customer. In functional testing business users should define what has to be tested, unlike unit or integration testing where tests are created by software developers.

Functional tests can be performed manually, in which a real person clicks through each and every view of the RIA, confirming that it operates properly or reporting discrepancies with the functional specifications. A better approach, however, is to engage specialized software that allows you to prerecord the sequence of clicks (similar to what FlexMonkey does) and replay these scripts whenever the application has been modified to verify that the functionality has not been broken by the last code changes.

Writing scripts for testing may sound like an annoying process, but this up-front investment can save you a lot of grief and long overtime hours during the project life cycle. Larger organizations have dedicated Quality Assurance teams who write these tests. In smaller IT shops, Flex developers write these tests, but this is a less efficient approach, as developers may not have the correct vision of the entire business workflow of the application and their tests won't cover the whole functionality of the system.

Automated test scripts should be integrated with the build process of your application and run continuously. There are several commercial (and expensive) offerings for automation of functional testing:

QuickTest Professional (QTP) by HP (formerly Mercury)
: During the recording phase, QTP creates a script in the VBScript language in which each line represents an action of the user. The checkpoints included in the script are used for comparison of the current value with expected values of the specified properties of application objects. Flex 3 Professional includes the libraries (*.swc*) required for automated testing with QTP, and your Flex application has to be compiled with these libraries. In addition, the QA testers need to have a commercial license for the QTP itself. The process of installing QTP for testing Flex applications is described at *http://tinyurl.com/5wyqgb*.

Rational Functional Tester by IBM
: Rational Functional Tester supports functional and regression testing of Flex applications. You can see the demo and download a trial version of this product at *http://www-01.ibm.com/software/awdtools/tester/functional/index.html*.

Flex Vulnerability Tests

IBM's Rational AppScan helps test your web application against the threat of SQL injection attacks and data breaches. Staring from version 7.8, AppScan supports a wide array of Flash Player–based applications, including Adobe Flex and Adobe AIR. For more information, visit *http://tinyurl.com/5rswk7*.

RIATest by RIATest
: RIATest (Figure 4-6) is a commercial testing tool for QA teams working with Flex applications. It includes Action Recorder (an RIAScript language similar to ActionScript), a script debugger, and synchronization capabilities.

: Because of the event-driven nature of Flex, UI testing tools need to be smart enough to understand that some events take time to execute and your tests can run only after a certain period of time. RIATest allows you to not only rely on this tool to make such synchronization decisions, but also to specify various wait conditions manually. For example, if a click on the button requires an asynchronous remote call to populate a data grid, RIATest offers you the script command `waitfor`, which won't perform the data verification until the data grid is populated. The Action Recorder creates human-readable scripts. To download a demo, go to *http://riatest.com*.

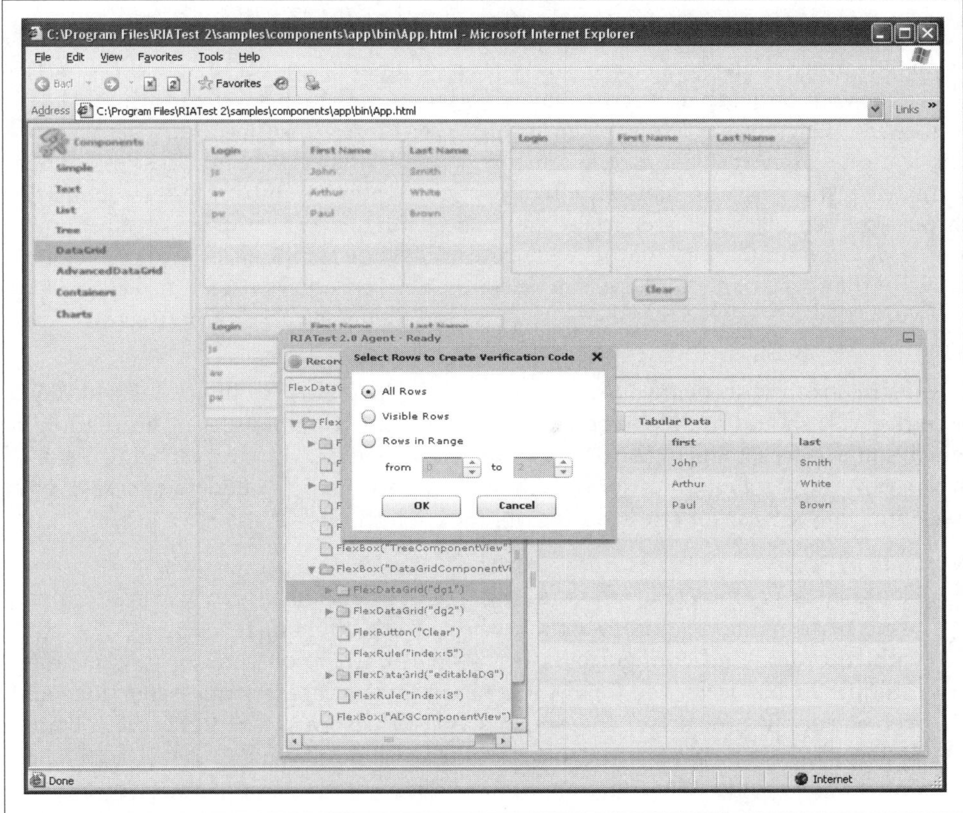

Figure 4-6. RIATest: Visual creation of verification code

Load Testing

While rearchitecting an old-fashioned HTML-based application with RIA, you should not forget that besides looking good, the new application should be at least as scalable as the one you are replacing. Ideally, it should be more scalable than the old one if faster data communication protocols such as AMF and Real Time Messaging Protocol (RTMP) are being used. How many concurrent users can work with your application without bringing your server to its knees? Even if the server is capable of serving a thousand users, will performance suffer? If yes, how bad is it going to be?

It all comes down to two factors: availability and response time. These requirements for your application should be well defined in the *service level agreement* (*SLA*), which should clearly state what's acceptable from the user's perspective. For example, the SLA can include a clause stating that the initial download of your application shouldn't take longer than 30 seconds for users with a slow connection (500 kbps). The SLA can state that the query to display a list of customers shouldn't run for more than five seconds, and the application should be operational 99.9 percent of the time.

To avoid surprises after going live with your new mission-critical RIA, don't forget to include in your project plan a set of heavy stress tests, and do this well in advance before it goes live. Luckily, you don't need to hire 1,000 interns to find out whether your application will meet the SLA requirements. The automated load (a.k.a. stress or performance testing software) allows you to emulate required number of users, set up the throttling to emulate a slower connection, and configure the ramp-up speed. For example, you can simulate a situation where the number of users logged on to your system grows at the speed of 50 users every 10 seconds. Stress testing software also allows you to prerecord the action of the business users, and then you can run these scripts emulating a heavy load.

Good stress-testing software allows simulating the load close to the real-world usage patterns. You should be able to create and run mixed scripts simulating a situation in which some users are logging on to your application while others are retrieving the data and performing data modifications. Each of the following tools understands AMF protocol and can be used for stress testing of Flex applications:

NeoLoad by Neotys
: NeoLoad is a commercial stress-testing tool. It offers analysis of web applications using performance monitors without the need to do manual scripting. You start with recording and configuring a test scenario, then you run the tests creating multiple virtual users, and finally, you monitor client operational system load and web and application server components. As you'll learn in Chapter 6, we at Farata Systems have been using a scalable stress-test solution based on BlazeDS installed under a Jetty server. For more information on NeoLoad, go to *http://neotys.com*.

WebLOAD 8.3 by RadView Software
: A commercial stress-testing software, WebLOAD 8.3 offers similar functionality to NeoLoad. It includes analysis and reporting, and a workflow wizard that helps with building scripts. It also supports AJAX. WebLOAD also allows you to enter SLA requirements right into the tests. To learn more, visit *http://www.radview.com*.

SilkPerformer and SilkTest by Borland
: The commercial Borland test suite includes Borland SilkPerformer, stress-testing software for optimizing performance of business applications, and the functional testing tool Borland SilkTest, among other tools.

SilkPerformer allows you to create thousands of users with its visual scenario modeling tools. It supports Flex clients and the AMF 3 protocol.

SilkTest automates the functional testing process, and supports regression, cross-platform, and localization testing. For more details, see *http://www.borland.com/us/products/index.html*.

Data Services Stress Testing Framework by Adobe (open source)
An open source load-testing tool, Data Services Stress Testing Framework helps developers with stress testing of LiveCycle Data Services ES. This is a tool for putting load on the server and is not meant for stress testing an individual Flex/LCDS application running in the Flash Player. This framework is not compatible with BlazeDS. To download it or learn more, visit *http://labs.adobe.com/wiki/index.php/Flex_Stress_Testing_Framework*. For testing BlazeDS, consider using JMeter as described at the JTeam blog (*http://bit.ly/1cjE78*).

Code Coverage

Even if you are using testing tools, can you be sure that you have tested each and every scenario that may arise in your application?

Code coverage describes the degree to which your code has been tested. It's also known as *white-box testing*, which is an attempt to analyze the code and test each possible path your application may go through. In large projects with hundreds of `if` statements, it's often difficult to cover each and every branch of execution, and automated tools will help you with this.

An open source project, Flexcover is a code coverage tool for Flex and AIR applications. This project provides code coverage instrumentation, data collection, and reporting tools. It incorporates a modified version of the ActionScript 3 (AS3) compiler, which inserts extra function calls in the code within the *.swf* or *.swc* output file. At runtime, these function calls send information on the application's code coverage to a separate tool. The modified compiler also emits a separate coverage metadata file that describes all the possible packages, classes, functions, code blocks, and lines in the code, as well as the names of the associated source code files. For more information, go to *http://code.google.com/p/flexcover/*.

The document "Flex SDK coding conventions and best practices" lays out the coding standards for writing open source components in ActionScript 3, but you can use it as a guideline for writing code in your business application, too. This document is available at the following URL: *http://tinyurl.com/3xphtd*.

FlexPMD (*http://opensource.adobe.com/wiki/display/flexpmd/FlexPMD*) is a tool that helps to improve code quality by auditing any AS3/Flex source directories and detecting common bad practices, such as unused code (functions, variables, constants, etc.), inefficient code (misuse of dynamic filters, heavy constructors, etc.), overly long code (classes, methods, etc.), incorrect use of the Flex component life cycle (`commitProperties`, etc.), and more.

The code coverage tools will ensure that you've tested all application code, and the coding conventions document will help you in adhering to commonly accepted practices, but yet another question to be answered is, "How should you split the code of a large application into a smaller and more manageable modules?" This becomes the subject of the brief discussion that comes next.

Application Modularization from 30,000 Feet

Even a relatively small Flex application has to be modularized. More often than not, a Flex application consists of more than one Flash Builder project. You'll learn more about modularization in Chapter 7; for now, a brief overview will expose you to the main concepts that each Flex developer/architect should keep in mind.

Your main Flash Builder project will be compiled into a main *.swf* application, and the size of this *.swf* should be kept as small as possible. Include only must-have pieces of the application that have to be delivered to the client's computer on the initial application load. The time of the initial application load is crucial and has to be kept as short as possible.

Modularization of the Flex application is achieved by splitting up the code into Flex libraries (*.swc* files) and Flex modules (*.swf* files). Initially, the application should load only the main *.swf* and a set of shared libraries that contain objects required by other application modules. Flex modules are *.swf* files that have `<mx:Module>` as a root tag. They can be loaded and unloaded during the runtime using Flex's `ModuleLoader` loader. If the ability to unload the code during the runtime is important to your Flex application, use modules. If this feature is not important, use Flex libraries, which are loaded in the same application domain and allow direct referencing of the loaded objects in the code with the strong type checking.

Although *.swf* files are created by the *mxmlc* compiler, Flex libraries are compiled into *.swc* files via the *compc* compiler. Flex libraries can be linked to an application in one of three ways:

- Merged into code
- Externally
- Via Runtime Shared Libraries (RSLs)

The linkage type has to be selected based on the needs of the specific application.

Chapter 8 describes pros and cons of each type of linkage, as well as a technique that allows you to create so-called *self-initialized libraries* that can be reused in Flex applications in a loosely coupled fashion.

Application fonts and styles are good candidates for being compiled into a separate *.swf* file that is precompiled and is loaded during the application startup. This will improve the compilation speed of the Flash Builder's projects, because compiling fonts and styles is a lengthy process.

Modularizing the application also simplifies work separation between Flex developers, as each small team can work on a different module. Flex 3.2 has introduced so-called *subapplications*, which are nothing but Flex application *.swf* files that can be compiled in different versions of Flex. `SWFloader` can load this subapplication either in its own or in a separate security sandbox.

Build Scripts and Continuous Integration

A modularized Flex application consists of several Flash Builder projects. Each of the individual projects contains the *build.xml* file that performs the build and deployment of this project. Additionally, one extra file should be created to run individual project builds in an appropriate order and to deploy the entire application in some predefined directory, for example, *C:\serverroot* as described in the section "Flex Developer's Workstation" on page 180.

Such a main build file should account for dependencies that may exist in your project. For example, the application that produces the main *.swf* file can depend on some libraries that are shared by all modules of your application. Hence the main Ant build file needs to have multiple targets that control the order of individual project builds.

In some cases, for auditing purposes, if a build task depends on other builds—i.e., *.swc* libraries—all dependent builds should be rerun even if the compiled version of *.swc* already exists.

Automation of Ant Script Creation

Apache Ant is a popular Java-based tool for automating the software build process. You can run Ant builds of the project either from Flash Builder or from a command line. To run the build script from Flash Builder, right-click on the name of the build file, such as *build.xml*, and choose the Ant Build from the pop-up menu. The build will start and you'll see Ant's output in the Flash Builder console. To build your application from a command line you can use a standalone Ant utility (*http://ant.apache.org/bindownload.cgi*). To be able to run Ant from any directory, add the *bin* directory of Ant's install to the `PATH` environment variable on your computer.

Ant uses the *tools.jar* file that comes with the Java SDK. Modify your environment variable `CLASSPATH` to include the location of *tools.jar* on your PC. For example, if you did a standard install of Java 6 under MS Windows, add the following to the `CLASSPATH` variable: *C:\Program Files \Java\jdk1.6.0_02\lib\tools.jar*.

To run the Ant build from a command line, open a command window, change directory to the project you are planning to build, and enter `ant`, as in:

```
C:\myworkspace> cd my.module.met1
C:\myworkspace\my.module.met1> ant
```

In addition to the developer's workstation, all build scripts need to be deployed under a dedicated server, and developers should run test builds first on their local workstation and then under this server.

Writing Ant build scripts manually is a time-consuming process. To help you, we created *Fx2Ant* (it comes as a part of Clear Toolkit; see *http://sourceforge.net/projects/cleartoolkit/*). After installing the Clear Toolkit Eclipse plug-in, just right-click on "Flash Builder project" and select the menu Generate Build Files, and within a couple of seconds you'll get an Ant build script that reflects all current settings of your Flash Builder project.

There is also an open source project called Antennae that provides templates for building Flex projects with Ant. Antennae can also generate scripts for FlexUnit. It's available at *http://code.google.com/p/antennae/*.

Maven Support

Maven is a more advanced build tool than Ant. Maven supports builds of modules and creation of applications that use the Flex framework RSL. It works with FlexUnit and ASDoc. If your organization uses Maven, get *flex-mojos* at *http://flexmojos.sonatype.org/*. This is a collection of Maven plug-ins to allow Maven to build and optimize Flex and AIR *.swf* and *.swc* files.

You can find an example of configuring a Flex/Maven/Hibernate/Spring/BlazeDS project at *http://www.adobe.com/devnet/flex/articles/fullstack_pt1.html*.

If you use the IntelliJ IDEA IDE, you'll have even more convenient integration of Flex and Maven projects.

Continuous Integration

Introduced by Martin Fowler and Matthew Foemmel, the theory of *continuous integration* recommends creating scripts and running automated builds of your application at least once a day. This allows you to identify issues in the code a lot sooner.

You can read more about the continuous integration practice at *http://www.martinfowler.com/articles/continuousIntegration.html*.

We are successfully using an open source framework called CruiseControl (*http://cruisecontrol.sourceforge.net*) for establishing a continuous build process. When you use CruiseControl, you can create scripts that run either at a specified time interval or on each check-in of the new code into the source code repository. You may also force the build whenever you like.

CruiseControl has a web-based application to monitor or manually start builds (Figure 4-7). Reports on the results of each build are automatically emailed to the designated members of the application group. At Farata Systems, we use it to ensure continuous builds of the internal projects and components for Clear Toolkit.

CruiseControl at build.home *[11/13/08 6:18 AM]*

Project	Status *(since)*	Last failure	Last successful	Label	
FARA-EDEV-force	**modificationset** *(6:12 AM)*		11/10/08	build.1	Build
FARA-EDEV-bymod	queued *(6:14 AM)*	6:06 AM	11/11/08	build.7	Build
FARA-EDEV-daily	*waiting (5:31 AM)*		11/11/08	build.6	Build

Figure 4-7. Controlling CruiseControl from the Web

IT shops that have adopted test-driven development can make the build process even more bulletproof by including test scripts in the continuous integration build process. If unit, integration, and functional test scripts (which automatically run after each successful build process) don't produce any issues, you can rest assured that the latest code changes did not break the application logic.

Hudson (*http://hudson-ci.org*) is yet another popular open source continuous integration server.

Logging with Log4Fx

When you develop distributed applications, you can't overestimate the importance of a good logging facility.

Imagine life without one: the user pressed a button and...nothing happened. Do you know if the client's request reached the server-side component? If so, what did the server send back? Add to this the inability to use debuggers while processing GUI events like focus change, and you may need to spend hours, if not days, trying to spot some sophisticated errors.

That's why a reliable logger is a must if you work with an application that is spread over the network and is written in different languages, such as Adobe Flex and Java.

At Farata Systems, we created a Flash Builder plug-in for Log4Fx, which is available as a part of the open source project Clear Toolkit. This is an advanced yet simple-to-use component for Flex applications. You can set up the logging on the client or the server side (Java), redirect the output of the log messages to local log windows, or make the log output easily available to the production support teams located remotely.

Think of a production situation where a particular client complains that the application runs slowly. Log4Fx allows you to turn on the logging just for this client and you can do it remotely with web browser access to the log output.

Log4Fx comes with several convenient and easy-to-use display panels with log messages. In addition, it automatically inserts the logging code into your ActionScript classes with hot keys (Figure 4-8).

Log4Fx import template	Ctrl+R, M
logger.debug() template	Ctrl+R, D
logger.error() template	Ctrl+R, E
logger.fatal() template	Ctrl+R, F
logger.info() template	Ctrl+R, I
logger.warn() template	Ctrl+R, W

Figure 4-8. Log4Fx hot keys to insert log statements into ActionScript

For example, place the cursor in the script section of your application and press Ctrl-R followed by M to insert the following lines into your program:

```
import mx.logging.Log;
import mx.logging.ILogger;
private var logger:ILogger = Log.getLogger("MyStockPortfolio");
```

Say you are considering adding this trace statement into the function `getPriceQuetes()`:

```
trace("Entered the method getPriceQuotes");
```

Instead of doing this, you can place the cursor in the function `getPriceQuotes()` and press Ctrl-R followed by D. The following line will be added at your cursor location:

```
if (Log.isDebug()) logger.debug("");
```

Enter the text `Entered the method getPriceQuotes()` between the double quotes, and if you've set the level of logging to Debug, this message will be sent to a destination you specified with the Logging Manager.

If a user calls production support complaining about some unexpected behavior, ask her to press Ctrl-Shift-Backspace; the Logging Manager will pop up on top of her application window (Figure 4-9).

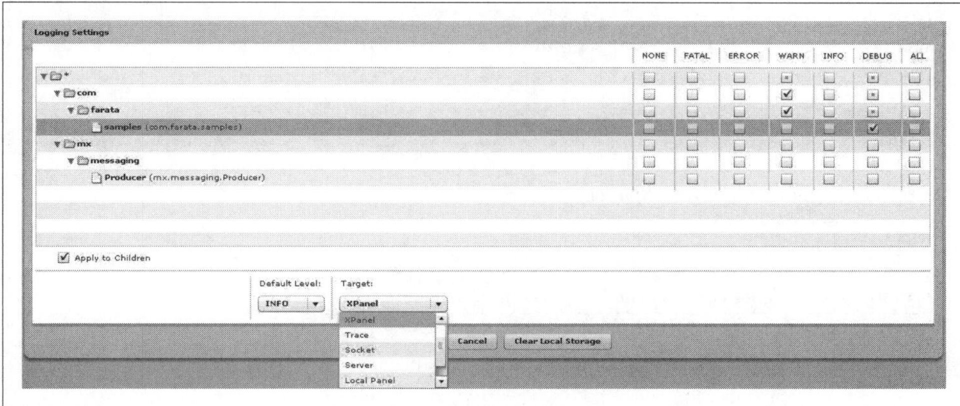

Figure 4-9. A user enables logging

The users select checkboxes to enable the required level of logging, and the stream of log messages is directed to the selected target. You can change the logging level at any time while your application is running. This feature is crucial for mission-critical production applications where you can't ask the user to stop the application (e.g., financial trading systems) but need to obtain the logging information to help the customer on the live system.

You can select a local or remote target or send the log messages to the Java application running on the server side, as shown in Figure 4-10.

Remote Logging with Log4Fx

Log4Fx adds a new application, *RemoteLogReceiver.mxml*, to your Flex project, which can be used by a remote production support crew if need be.

Say the user's application is deployed at the URL *http://230.123.12.10:8080/myapplication.html*. By pressing Ctrl-Shift-Backspace, the user opens the Logging Manager and selects the target Remote Logging (Figure 4-11).

Figure 4-10. Logging in the Local panel

Figure 4-11. Specifying the remote destination for logging

The destination `RemoteLogging` is selected automatically, and the user needs to input a password, which the user will share with the production support engineer.

Because *RemoteLogReceiver.mxml* is an application that sits right next to your main application in Flash Builder's project, it gets compiled into a *.swf* file, the HTML wrapper is generated, and it is deployed in the web server along with your main application. The end users won't even know that it exists, but a production engineer can enter its URL (*http://230.123.12.10:8080/RemoteLogReceiver.html*) in his browser when needed.

Think of an undercover informant who lives quietly in the neighborhood, but when engaged, immediately starts sending information out. After entering the password provided by the user and pressing the Connect button, the production support engineer will start receiving log messages sent by the user's application (Figure 4-12).

Log4Fx is available as a part of the open source project Clear Toolkit at *https://sourceforge.net/projects/cleartoolkit*.

Troubleshooting with Charles

Although lots of programs allow you to trace HTTP traffic, Flex developers need to be able to trace not just HTTP requests, but also AMF calls made by Flash Player to the server. At Farata Systems, we've been successfully using a program called Charles, which is a very handy tool on any Flex project.

Charles is an HTTP proxy and monitor that allows developers to view all of the HTTP traffic between their web browser and the Internet. This includes requests, responses, and HTTP headers (which contain cookies and caching information). Charles allows viewing Secure Sockets Layer (SSL) communication in plain text. Because some users of your application may work over slow Internet connections, Charles simulates various modem speeds by throttling your bandwidth and introducing latency—an invaluable feature.

Charles is not a free tool, but it's very inexpensive. It can be downloaded at *http://www.charlesproxy.com*.

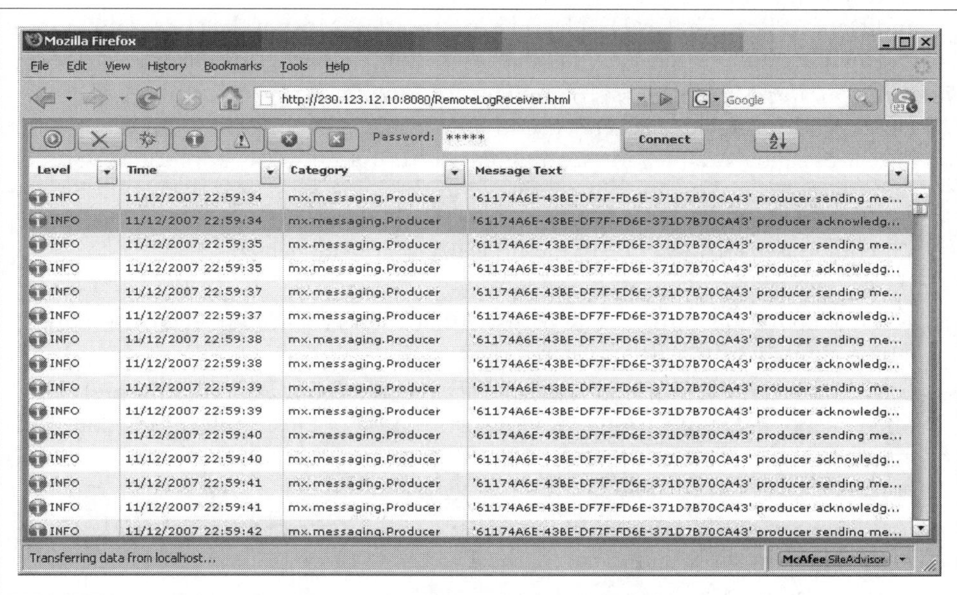

Figure 4-12. Monitoring log output from the remote machine

A Grab Bag of Component Libraries

Regardless of your decision about using Flex frameworks, you should be aware of a number open source libraries of components. The Flex community includes passionate and skillful developers that are willing to enhance and share components that come with the Flex SDK. For example, you may find an open source implementation of the horizontal accordion, autocomplete component, tree grid control, JSON serializer, and much more.

Following you'll find references to some of the component libraries that in many cases will spare you from reinventing the wheel during the business application development cycle:

FlexLib (http://code.google.com/p/flexlib/)
: The FlexLib project is a community effort to create open source user interface components for Adobe Flex 2 and 3. Some of its most useful components are: AdvancedForm, EnhancedButtonSkin, CanvasButton, ConvertibleTreeList, Highlighter, IconLoader, ImageMap, PromptingTextInput, Scrollable Menu Controls, Horizontal Accordion, TreeGrid, Docking ToolBar, and Flex Scheduling Framework.

as3corelib (http://code.google.com/p/as3corelib/)
: as3corelib is an open source library of ActionScript 3 classes and utilities. It includes image encoders; a JSON library for serialization; general String, Number and Date APIs; as well as HTTP and XML utilities. Most of the classes don't even use the Flex framework. AS3corelib also includes AIR-specific classes.

FlexServerLib (http://code.google.com/p/flexserverlib/)
: FlexServerLib includes several useful server-side components: MailAdapter is a Flex Messaging Adapter for sending email from a Flex/AIR application. SpringJmsAdapter is an adapter for sending and receiving messages through a Spring-configured Java Message Service (JMS) destination. EJBAdapter is an adapter allowing the invocation of EJB methods via remote object calls.

asSQL (http://code.google.com/p/assql/)
: asSQL is an ActionScript 3 MySQL driver that allows you to connect to this popular DBMS directly from AIR applications.

Facebook ActionScript API (http://code.google.com/p/facebook-actionscript-api/)
: The Facebook ActionScript API allows you to write Flex applications that communicate with Facebook using the REpresentational State Transfer (REST) protocol.

Twitter ActionScript API (http://apiwiki.twitter.com/Libraries#ActionScript/Flash)
: These libraries allow you to access the Twitter API from ActionScript.

Astra Web API (http://developer.yahoo.com/flash/astra-webapis/), *Google Maps API (http://code.google.com/apis/maps/documentation/flash/)*, *MapQuest Platform (http://platform.mapquest.com/products-free.html)*
: Geographical mapping libraries are quite handy if you'd like your RIA to have the ability to map the location of your business, branches, dealers, and the like. These libraries may be free for personal use, but may require a commercial license to be used in enterprise applications. Please consult the product documentation of the mapping engine of your choice.

  The Astra Web API gives your Flex application access to Yahoo! Maps, Yahoo! Answers, Yahoo! Weather, Yahoo! Search, and a social events calendar. The

Google Maps API for Flash lets Flex developers embed Google Maps in their application. The MapQuest Platform has similar functionality.

as3syndicationlib (http://code.google.com/p/as3syndicationlib/)
: as3syndicationlib parses the Atom format and all versions of Really Simple Syndication (RSS). It hides the differences between the formats of the feeds.

Away3D (http://away3d.com)
: Away3D is a real-time 3D engine for Flash.

Papervision3D (http://code.google.com/p/papervision3d/)
: Papervision3D is a real-time 3D engine for Flash.

YouTube API (http://code.google.com/p/as3youtubelib/)
: The YouTube API is a library for integrating your application with this popular video portal.

as3flickrlib (http://code.google.com/p/as3flickrlib/)
: as3flickrlib is an ActionScript API for Flickr, a popular portal for sharing photographs.

Text Layout Framework (http://labs.adobe.com/technologies/textlayout/)
: Text Layout Framework is a library that supports advanced typographic and text layout features. This library is requires Flash Player 10. It's included in Flex 4, but can be used with Flex 3.2 as well.

To stay current with internal and third-party Flex components and libraries, download and install the AIR application called Tour de Flex (*http://flex.org/tour*). It contains easy-to-follow code samples on use of various components. It's also a place where commercial and noncommercial developers can showcase their work (Figure 4-13).

Although most of the previous components cater to frontend developers, because Flex RIAs are distributed applications, some of the components and popular frameworks will live on the server side. The next two sections will give you an overview of how to introduce such server frameworks as Spring and Hibernate.

Integrating with the Java Spring Framework

The Java Spring framework is a popular server-side container that has its own mechanism of instantiating Java classes—it implements a design pattern called *Inversion of Control*. To put it simply, if an object `Employee` has a property of type `Bonus`, instead of explicit creation of the `bonus` instance in the class `employee`, the framework would create this instance and inject it into the variable `bonus`.

BlazeDS (and LCDS) knows how to instantiate Java classes configured in *remoting-config.xml*, but this is not what's required by the Spring framework.

In the past, a solution based on the Class Factory design pattern was your only option. Both BlazeDS and LCDS allow you to specify not the name of the class to create, but *the name of the class factory* that will be creating instances of this class. An

Figure 4-13. Component explorer Tour de Flex

implementation of such a solution was available in the Flex-Spring library making Spring framework responsible for creating instances of such Java classes (a.k.a. *Spring beans*).

Today, there is a cleaner solution developed jointly by Adobe and SpringSource. It allows you to configure Spring beans in Extensible Markup Language (XML) files, which can be used by the BlazeDS component on the Java EE server of your choice.

James Ward and Jon Rose have published a reference card with code samples on Flex/Spring integration at *http://tinyurl.com/cj3v7b*.

At the time of this writing, the project on the integration of BlazeDS and the Spring framework is a work in progress, and we suggest you to follow the blog (*http://tinyurl.com/noj3nm*) of Adobe's Christophe Coenraets, who publishes up-to-date information about this project.

Integrating with the Hibernate Framework

These days, writing SQL manually is out of style, and lots of software developers prefer using *object-relational mapping* (ORM) tools for data persistence. With ORM, an instance of an object is mapped to a database table. Selecting a row from a database is equivalent to creating an instance of the object in memory. On the same note, deleting the object instance will cause deletion of the corresponding row in a database table.

In the Java community, Hibernate is the most popular open source ORM tool. Hibernate supports lazy loading, caching, and object versioning. It can either create the entire database from scratch based on the provided Java objects, or just create Java objects based on the existing database.

Mapping of Java objects to the database tables and setting their relationships (one-to-many, one-to-one, many-to-one) can be done either externally in XML configuration files or by using annotations right inside the Java classes, a.k.a. *entity beans*. From a Flex remoting perspective, nothing changes: Flex still sends and receives DTOs from a destination specified in *remoting-config.xml*.

After downloading and installing the Hibernate framework under the server with BlazeDS, the integration steps are:

1. Create a server-side entity bean `Employee` that uses annotations to map appropriate values to database tables and specify queries:

   ```
   @Entity
   @Table(name = "employees")
   @NamedQueries( {

   @NamedQuery(name = "employeess.findAll", query = "from Employee"),

   @NamedQuery(name = "employees.byId", query = "select c from Employee e where
   e.employeeId= :employeeId") })
   public class Employee {

    @Id
    @GeneratedValue(strategy = GenerationType.AUTO)
    @Column(name = "employeeId", nullable = false)
    private Long employeeId;

    @Column(name = "firstName", nullable = true, unique = false)
    private String firstName;
   ```

2. Create a file called *persistence.xml* under the *META-INF* directory of your BlazeDS project. In this file, define the database location and connectivity credentials.
3. Write a Java class `EmployeeService` with method `getEmployees()` that retrieves and updates the data using Hibernate—for example:

   ```
   public List<Employee> getEmployees() {

   EntityManagerFactory entityManagerFactory =
            Persistence.createEntityManagerFactory(PERSISTENCE_UNIT);

    EntityManager em = entityManagerFactory.createEntityManager();

    Query findAllQuery = em.createNamedQuery("employees.findAll");

    List<Empoyee> employeess = findAllQuery.getResultList();
   ```

```
    return employees;
  }
```

4. Define a destination in the BlazeDS *remoting-config.xml* file that points at the class `EmployeeService`:

```
<destination id="myEmployee">
 <properties>
  <source>com.farata.EmployeeService</source>
 </properties>
</destination>
```

The rest of the process is the same as in any Flex remoting scenario.

The only issue with this approach is that it has problems supporting lazy loading. BlazeDS uses the Java adapter to serialize Java objects, along with all related objects regardless of whether you want them to be lazy-loaded.

The entire process of the integration of Flex, BlazeDS, Hibernate, and MySQL Server is described in detail in an article published at the Adobe Developer's Connection website. You can find it at *http://www.adobe.com/devnet/flex/articles/flex_hibernate_print.html*.

If your Flex application uses LCDS, this issue is solved by applying special Hibernate adapter for Data Management Services. Digital Primates' dpHibernate is a custom Flex library and a custom BlazeDS Hibernate adapter that work together to give you support for lazy loading of Hibernate objects from inside your Flex applications. You can get dpHibernate at *http://code.google.com/p/dphibernate/*.

There is one more open source product that supports Hibernate. It's called Granite Data Services and is an alternative to BlazeDS.

Project Documentation

Programmers don't like writing comments. They know how their code works. At least, they think they do. Six months down the road, they will be wondering, "Man, did I actually write this myself? What was I planning to do here?"

Program documentation is as important as the code itself. If you are managing the project, make sure that you encourage and enforce proper documentation. Some developers will tell you that their code is self-explanatory. Don't buy this. Tomorrow, these developers won't be around, for whatever reason, and someone else will have to read their code.

Program Documentation with ASDoc

Flex comes with *ASDoc*, a tool that works similarly to JavaDoc, which is well known in the Java community. ASDoc reads the comments placed between the symbols `/**` and `*/`; reads the names of the classes, interfaces, methods, styles, and properties from the code; and generates easily viewable help files.

The source code of the Flex framework itself is available, too. Just Ctrl-click on any class name in Flash Builder, and you'll see the source code of this ActionScript class or MXML object. Example 4-3 is the beginning of the source code of the Flex `Button` component.

Example 4-3. A fragment of the Button source code

```
package mx.controls
{

import flash.display.DisplayObject;
import flash.events.Event;
...

/**
 *  The Button control is a commonly used rectangular button.
 *  Button controls look like they can be pressed.
 *  They can have a text label, an icon, or both on their face.
 *
 *  Buttons typically use event listeners to perform an action
 *  when the user selects the control. When a user clicks the mouse
 *  on a Button control, and the Button control is enabled,
 *  it dispatches a click event and a buttonDown event.
 *  A button always dispatches events such as the mouseMove,
 *  mouseOver, mouseOut, rollOver,rollOut, mouseDown, and
 *  mouseUp events whether enabled or disabled.
 *
 *  You can customize the look of a Button control
 *  and change its functionality from a push button to a toggle button.
 *  You can change the button appearance by using a skin
 *  for each of the button's states.
 */
public class Button extends UIComponent
       implements IDataRenderer, IDropInListItemRenderer,
       IFocusManagerComponent, IListItemRenderer,
       IFontContextComponent, IButton
{
    include "../core/Version.as";

    /**
     *  @private
     *  Placeholder for mixin by ButtonAccImpl.
     */
    mx_internal static var createAccessibilityImplementation:Function;

    /**
     *  Constructor.
```

```
    */
   public function Button(){
       super();

       // DisplayObjectContainer properties. Setting mouseChildren
       // to false ensures that mouse events are dispatched from the
       // button itself, not from its skins, icons, or TextField.
       // One reason for doing this is that if you press the mouse button
       // while over the TextField and release the mouse button while over
       // a skin or icon, we want the player to dispatch a "click" event.
       // Another is that if mouseChildren were true and someone uses
       // Sprites rather than Shapes for the skins or icons,
       // then we we wouldn't get a click because the current skin or icon
       // changes between the mouseDown and the mouseUp.
       // (This doesn't happen even when mouseChildren is true if the skins
       // and icons are Shapes, because Shapes never dispatch mouse events;
       // they are dispatched from the Button in this case.)

       mouseChildren = false;
```

Beside the `/**` and `*/` symbols, you have a small number of the markup elements that ASDoc understands (`@see`, `@param`, `@example`).

The beginning of the Help screen created by the ASDoc utility based on the source code of the `Button` class looks like Figure 4-14.

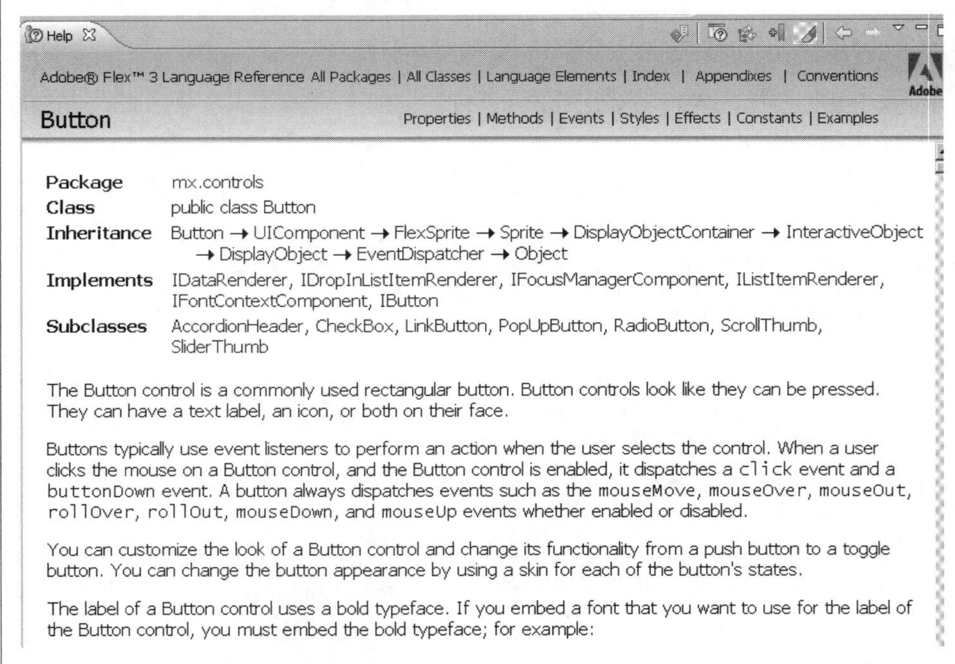

Figure 4-14. A fragment of the Help screen for Button

Detailed information on how to use ASDoc is available at *http://blogs.adobe.com/flexdoc/2009/01/updated_doc_on_using_the_flex_1.html*.

Documenting MXML with ASDoc has not been implemented yet, but is planned to be released with Flex 4. The functional design specifications of the new ASDoc are already published at the Adobe open source site (*http://opensource.adobe.com/wiki/display/flexsdk/ASDoc+in+MXML*).

UML Diagrams

Unified Modeling Language (UML) diagrams are convenient for representing relationships among the components of your application. There are a number of tools that turn the creation of diagrams into a simple drag-and-drop process. After creating a class diagram, these tools allow you to generate code in a number of programming languages.

In a perfect world, any change in the class definition would be done in the UML tool first, followed by the code generation. Future manual additions to these classes wouldn't get overwritten by subsequent code generations if the model changes.

UML tools are also handy in situations where you need to become familiar with poorly commented code written by someone else. In this case, the process of reverse engineering will allow you to create a UML diagram of all the classes and their relationships from the existing code.

There are a number of free UML tools that understand ActionScript 3 (UMLet, VASGen, Cairngen) with limited abilities for code generation.

Commercial tools offer more features and are modestly priced. Figure 4-15 shows a class diagram created by Enterprise Architect from Sparx Systems (*http://www.sparxsystems.com*). This diagram was created by autoreverse engineering of the existing ActionScript classes.

The process is pretty straightforward: create a new project and a new class diagram, then right-click anywhere on the background, select the menu item "Import from source files," and point at the directory where your ActionScript classes are located. The tool supports ActionScript, Java, C#, C++, PHP, and other languages.

Accessibility of Flex RIA

Some users can't see, hear, or move, or have difficulties in reading, recognizing colors, or other disabilities. The World Wide Web Consortium has published a document called Web Content Accessibility Guidelines 1.0 (*http://www.w3.org/TR/WCAG/*), which contains guidelines for making web content available for people with disabilities.

Microsoft Active Accessibility (MSAA) technology and its successor, the UI Automation (UIA) interface, are also aimed at helping such users. Adobe Flex components were designed to help developers in creating accessible applications.

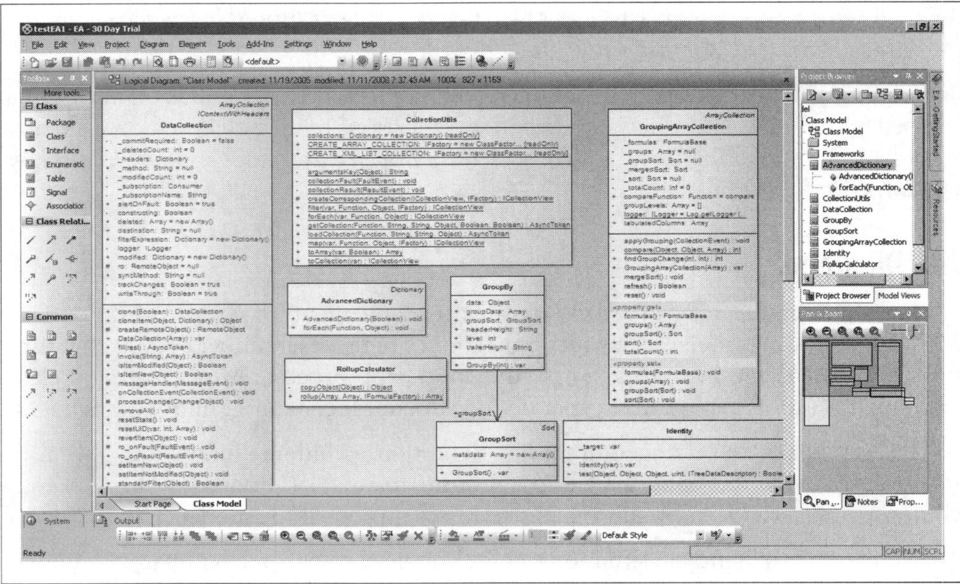

Figure 4-15. Enterprise Architect: a UML class diagram

Did you know that blind users of your RIA mostly use the keyboard as opposed to the mouse? They may interact with your application using special screen readers (e.g., JAWS from Freedom Scientific) or need to hear special audio signals that help them in application navigation.

A screen reader is a software application that tries to identify what's being displayed on the screen, and then reads it to the user either by text-to-speech converters or via a Braille output device.

The computer mouse is unpopular not only among blind people, but also among people with mobility impairments. Are all of the Flex components used in your application accessible by the keyboard?

If your application includes audio, hearing-impaired people would greatly appreciate captions. This does not mean that from now on every user should be forced to watch captions during audio or hear loud announcements of the components that are being displayed on the monitor. But you should provide a way to switch your Flex application into accessibility mode. The Flex compiler offers a special option—*compiler.accessible*—to build an accessible *.swf*.

You can find more materials about Flex accessibility at *http://www.adobe.com/accessibility/products/flex/*.

For testing accessibility of your RIA by visually impaired people, use aDesigner, a disability simulator from IBM. aDesigner supports Flash content and is available at *http://www.eclipse.org/actf/downloads/tools/aDesigner/index.php*.

Summary

This chapter was a grab bag of various recommendations and suggestions that each Flex development manager or architect may find of use over the course of the project. We sincerely hope that materials and leads from this chapter will ensure that your next Flex project is as smooth and productive as possible.

We hope that the variety of commercial and open source tools reviewed in this chapter represent Adobe Flex as a mature and evolving ecosystem, well suited to your next RIA project.

This chapter talked about tools that help in building and testing both the client and server portions of Flex RIA; the next chapter will concentrate on using powerful server-side technology from Adobe, called LiveCycle Data Services.

CHAPTER 5

Customizing the Messaging Layer of LCDS or BlazeDS

There are two ways of constructing a software design: one way is to make it so simple that there are obviously no deficiencies, and the other way is to make it so complicated that there are no obvious deficiencies. The first method is far more difficult.

—Sir Tony Hoare

Flex Messaging Unleashed

People as well as programs receive messages for one of two reasons:

- A message sent to you and your device (e.g., an iPhone or BlackBerry) is configured to work in so-called *push* mode: the other party can push messages for you even if you aren't necessarily eager to get them immediately after they were sent.
- At any given time you decide to check if there messages for you. *You* press the refresh button on your iPhone or your application makes a call from the client to the server. This mode is called *polling*.

This chapter starts with a quick example of how to perform the push by making a direct call to a `MessageBroker`, which comes with LiveCycle Data Services (LCDS) and BlazeDS. Next, it discusses the existing world of custom adapters and message channels. You'll see how to implement a use case with guaranteed message delivery and take care of the proper sequencing of messages.

At this writing, the newly released LCDS 3.0 promises support for reliable messaging to guarantee that no message is lost in case of network failure (check out the `<reliable>` tag in the configuration file for Data Management Services). Data-throttling support will allow you to reduce or increase the amount of data going over the wire based on the speed at which Flash Player processes the data. Adaptive throttling should allow the LCDS server to make such changes automatically.

It's too early to assess whether these new features will fit the bill for some of the very demanding real-time applications. We are pretty confident that Adobe engineers will do a good job in this area.

Not everyone has a commercial LCDS license, however, and there will always be a customer who will come up with that special requirement that none of the existing tools support. Hence, our goal remains the same: to show you how things work under the hood so you can build the software that fits your needs exactly.

After reading this chapter, you won't be intimidated if the need arises to enter the somewhat geeky territory of Flex messaging protocols. You'll learn how to implement clients' heartbeats; create channels and adapters that can acknowledge, receive, and resend lost messages; and more. The best part is that it's not rocket science. Trust us.

Server Messages: Shooting in the Dark

Sending messages from an LCDS or BlazeDS server to a Flex client starts with getting a reference to the `MessageBroker`, which is a Java object deployed in the servlet container where you've installed BlazeDS or LCDS. Then, create an instance of the `AsyncMessage` object, and set the client ID (specific sender) and the destination (an equivalent of a topic in the publish/subscribe messaging terminology). When this is done, place your business-related object inside (e.g., `myOrderInfo`) and call the function `routeMessageToService()`. This process can go like this:

```
MessageBroker msgBroker = MessageBroker.getMessageBroker(null);
String clientID = UUIDUtils.createUUID(false);

AsyncMessage msg = new AsyncMessage();
msg.setDestination("myDestination");
msg.setClientId(clientID);
msg.setMessageId(UUIDUtils.createUUID(false));
msg.setTimestamp(System.currentTimeMillis());

myOrderInfo = new OrderInfo();
// Populate myOrderInfo with some data

msg.setBody(myOrderInfo);
msgBroker.routeMessageToService(msg, null);
```

Here comes the million-dollar question: did the message reach the recipient? Remember, we are talking about the Java server-side code here, not a conventional use of Flex `Producer`/`Consumer` objects that come with acknowledgment event `MessageAckEvent`. This uncertainty explains the need to implement some kind of a *client heartbeat*. A connected client sends a small message to the server, say, every 500 milliseconds. These heartbeats contain delivery confirmations for server messages that successfully arrived at the client within a specified interval.

We will follow up with the message arrivals a bit later, once we deal with the heartbeat itself.

Sending the Client's Heartbeats

To send the client's heartbeats, you need a class to represent the heartbeat and a producer to perform the sending.

The heartbeat message object will leverage available Flex/Java serialization—therefore, you'll need to come up with a pair of almost identical classes: one in Java and the other one in ActionScript. The corresponding classes are presented in Examples 5-1 and 5-2. Notice the array `received`, which will eventually carry delivery confirmations of the latest received messages.

Example 5-1. ClientHeartbeatMessage.as

```
package com.farata.messaging.messages {
import mx.messaging.messages.AbstractMessage;

[RemoteClass(alias="com.farata.messaging.messages.ClientHeartbeatMessage")]
public  class ClientHeartbeatMessage
                  extends mx.messaging.messages.AbstractMessage {

   public var received:Array; //Messages arrived since last heartbeat

    public function ClientHeartbeatMessage() {
      super();
         //TODO - populate array "received" - later...
   }
 }
}
```

Example 5-2. ClientHeartbeatMessage.java

```
package com.farata.messaging.messages;
import flex.messaging.messages.AbstractMessage;

public class ClientHeartbeatMessage extends AbstractMessage {

  public String[] received; // Array of <ClientID>|<MsgNumber> strings
}
```

To periodically send the heartbeat message (Example 5-1) up to the server you need a Flex `Producer` class powered with a `Timer`. Example 5-3 illustrates the custom `ClientHeartbeatProducer` class with the `startHeartbeat()` and `stopHeartbeat()` methods. By default, the heartbeat is sent to the server-side destination `ClientHeartbeat` every second.

Example 5-3. ClientHeartbeatProducer

```
package com.farata.messaging.qos {
   import com.farata.messaging.messages.ClientHeartbeatMessage;
```

```
    import flash.utils.clearInterval;
    import flash.utils.setInterval;

    import mx.messaging.Producer;

    public class ClientHeartbeatProducer extends Producer {
       public function ClientHeartbeatProducer() {
          super();
          destination = "clientHeartbeat";
       }
       public function startHeartbeat( destination:String=null,
                 interval:int=1000) : void {

          if (connected)   this.stopHeartbeat();
          if (destination != null) {
             this.destination = destination;
          }
          connect();
          // The next line can be implemented using Timer class
               processId = setInterval( sendHeartbeat, interval);
       }
       public function stopHeartbeat() : void {
          clearInterval(processId);
       }

       private var processId:int;
       private function sendHeartbeat(): void {
          send(new ClientHeartbeatMessage());
       }
    }
}
```

Note the property `connected` defined in the grandparent of `Producer` (`MessageAgent`); it indicates whether this producer is currently connected to its destination. The function `sendHeartbeat()` will be called multiple times per a specified interval. In this version, the instance of the `ClientHeartBeatMessage` doesn't carry any meaningful information about the specific message being acknowledged.

The heartbeat is being sent—time to look at the receiving end: the server-side Java code.

Heartbeat Adapter

The client sends heartbeats; we need to decide where the right place in the Java server is to intercept these messages. Both the LCDS and BlazeDS architectures provide two logical points to do it: the *adapter* and the *endpoint*. The endpoint is a server-side class that receives the message (see `MessageService` in Example 5-4) and then forwards it for processing to `MessageBroker`, which in turns forwards it to the adapter. Theoretically, if you want to introduce the server-side custom processing into this chain, override either the endpoint or the adapter class.

In our case, the messages are originated on the server and we found empirically that the endpoint doesn't participate in this flow. That's why we decided to customize the adapter class. Later in this chapter, while customizing the client side of the messaging, we'll show you how to customize the endpoint.

By default, the `ActionScriptAdapter` is used for messaging. If you are planning to integrate with third-party middleware via the Java Messaging API, use `JMSAdapter`.

You can read about messaging architecture in the document called the BlazeDS Developer Guide (*http://livedocs.adobe.com/blazeds/1/blazeds_devguide/*). If you use LCDS, refer to the LiveCycle Data Services ES documentation (*http://help.adobe.com/en_US/LiveCycleDataServicesES/3.0/Developing/index.html*).

Example 5-4 illustrates that *clientHeartbeat*, a default heartbeat destination, is configured in *messaging-config.xml* with the custom adapter—`com.farata.messaging.adapters.HeartbeatAdapter`. We'll review it next.

Example 5-4. Heartbeat destination with custom heartbeat adapter

```
<?xml version="1.0" encoding="UTF-8"?>
<service id="message-service"
   class="flex.messaging.services.MessageService">

    <adapters>
        <adapter-definition
      id="actionscript" default="true"
      class="flex.messaging.services.messaging.adapters.
ActionScriptAdapter"/>
        <adapter-definition id="jms"
      class="flex.messaging.services.messaging.adapters.
JMSAdapter"/>

        <adapter-definition
               id="heartbeat"
      class="com.farata.messaging.adapters.HeartbeatAdapter"/>
    </adapters>

    <default-channels>
     <channel ref="my-rtmp" />
   </default-channels>

    <destination id="clientHeartbeat">
       <adapter ref="heartbeat"/>
      <channels>
         <channel ref="my-rtmp" />
      </channels>
    </destination>
</service>
```

Writing custom adapters is not terribly complicated: extend the `MessagingAdapter` class and override the method `invoke()`. Example 5-5 presents our custom `HeartbeatAdapter`. The callback `invoke()` is being called when a client sends a message to the destination.

As per the BlazeDS Developer Guide, a typical `invoke()` method looks as follows:

```
public Object invoke(Message message) {
    MessageService msgService = (MessageService)service;
    msgService.pushMessageToClients(message, true);
    msgService.sendPushMessageFromPeer(message, true);
    return null;
}
```

For this exercise, we don't need to push the message to clients or send it to the peer servers in a cluster. Instead, we merely log the incoming message just to prove that we're getting it. A little later we'll write a more meaningful adapter in which the client's heartbeat will learn how to carry some useful payload.

Example 5-5. Separating transfer of byte code from loading into stage

```
package com.farata.messaging.adapter;

import org.apache.log4j.Logger;

import com.farata.messaging.messages.ClientHeartbeatMessage;
import flex.messaging.messages.Message;
import flex.messaging.services.MessageService;
import flex.messaging.services.messaging.adapters.MessagingAdapter;

public class HeartbeatAdapter extends MessagingAdapter{
    public Object invoke(Message message){

        if ( message instanceof ClientHeartbeatMessage ) {
              logger.info(message);
         }
       return null;
    }
    static Logger logger;
   static   {
           logger = Logger.getLogger(HeartbeatAdapter.class);
   }
}
```

Testing the Client Heartbeat

The next step is to test a simple case where the client sends a dummy heartbeat to the server. The ultimate goal is for the client heartbeat to carry the delivery confirmations so that the server can resend the undelivered messages until they either get delivered or time out.

Figure 5-1 highlights all classes that are involved in sending the client heartbeat. Notice two projects: *com.farata.rtmp.components*, the Flex library project, and *com.farata.rtmp.demo*, a combined Eclipse JEE Flex/Java/Dynamic Web Project. For messaging, we are using RTMP messaging via LiveCycle Data Services.

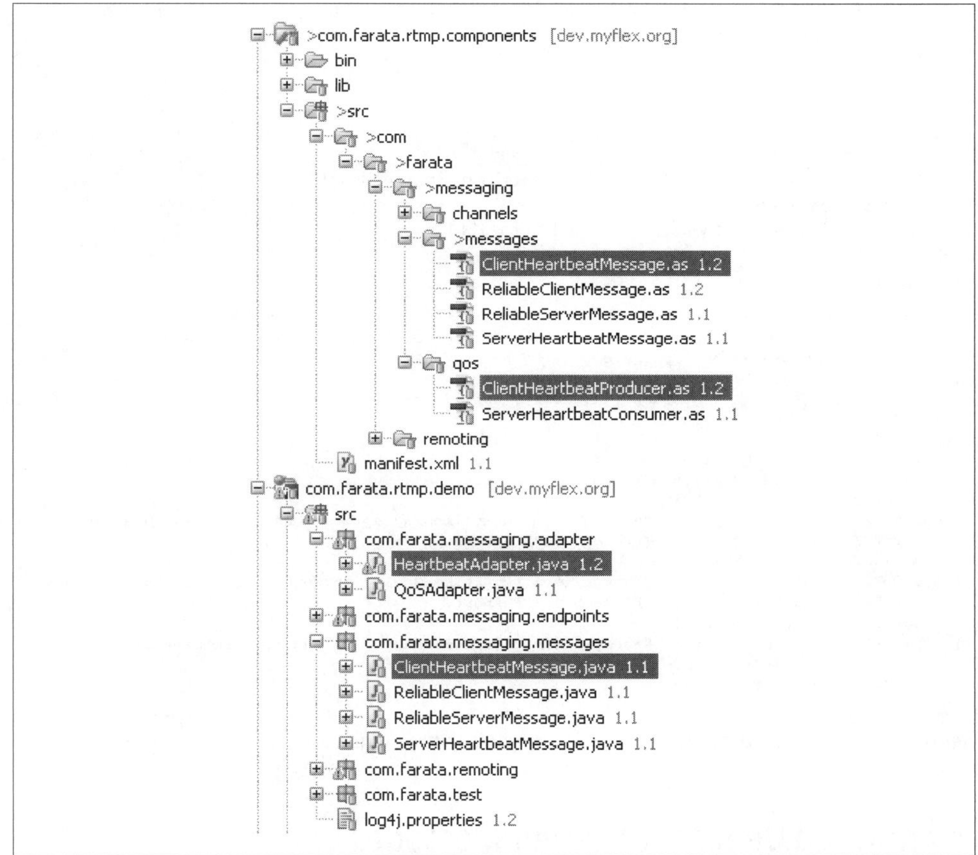

Figure 5-1. Panorama of ClientHeartbeat classes

To test the client heartbeat, run the application *TestClientHeartbeat.mxml* (Example 5-6) and click the Start Client Heartbeat button. Watch how the server log gets populated with the log records made by the custom `HeartbeatAdapter` (Figure 5-2).

Example 5-6. TestClientHeartbeat.mxml

```
<?xml version="1.0" encoding="utf-8"?>
<!--TestClientHeartbeat.mxml -->
<mx:Application xmlns:mx="http://www.adobe.com/2006/mxml"
xmlns:fx="http://www.faratasystems.com/2009/components"
   layout="vertical" frameRate="10">
```

```
    <fx:ClientHeartbeatProducer id="clientHeartbeat" />

    <mx:Script><![CDATA[
       import com.farata.messaging.messages.ClientHeartbeatMessage;

       //Mention the class to ensure that it's linked into SWF
       ClientHeartbeatMessage;
     ]]>
     </mx:Script>

    <mx:HBox>
       <mx:Button label="Start Client Heartbeat"
             click="clientHeartbeat.startHeartbeat('clientHeartbeat')"/>
       <mx:Button label="Stop Client Heartbeat"
             click="clientHeartbeat.stopHeartbeat()"/>
    </mx:HBox>
</mx:Application>
```

```
[LCDS] Starting Adobe LiveCycle Data Services: 2.6.0.201390 Single CPU License
Jun 23, 2009 9:54:50 AM org.apache.coyote.http11.Http11Protocol start
INFO: Starting Coyote HTTP/1.1 on http-8080
Jun 23, 2009 9:54:51 AM org.apache.jk.common.ChannelSocket init
INFO: JK: ajp13 listening on /0.0.0.0:8009
Jun 23, 2009 9:54:51 AM org.apache.jk.server.JkMain start
INFO: Jk running ID=0 time=0/32  config=null
Jun 23, 2009 9:54:51 AM org.apache.catalina.startup.Catalina start
INFO: Server startup in 5470 ms
[2009-06-23 09:55:28,656] Flex Message (com.farata.messaging.messages.ClientHeartbeatMessage)
    hdr(DSId) = 22B6E609-8409-AADC-A809-404DF0AB59EC
    hdr(DSEndpoint) = my-rtmp
[2009-06-23 09:55:29,718] Flex Message (com.farata.messaging.messages.ClientHeartbeatMessage)
    hdr(DSId) = 22B6E609-8409-AADC-A809-404DF0AB59EC
    hdr(DSEndpoint) = my-rtmp
[2009-06-23 09:55:30,718] Flex Message (com.farata.messaging.messages.ClientHeartbeatMessage)
    hdr(DSId) = 22B6E609-8409-AADC-A809-404DF0AB59EC
    hdr(DSEndpoint) = my-rtmp
```

Figure 5-2. ClientHeartbeat logged by the custom HeartbeatAdapter

Guaranteed Delivery of Server Messages

A server can send various types of messages. When a client receives them, we want the client to be able to send back the heartbeat object with delivery confirmations for only some of them, similar to a special treatment that letters with delivery confirmation get in the post office.

Our special messages will be represented by the class `ReliableServerMessage`; only these types of messages will be acknowledged. Java and ActionScript versions of such a class are shown in Examples 5-7 and 5-8.

Example 5-7. ReliableServerMessage.java

```
package com.farata.messaging.messages;
```

```
import flex.messaging.messages.AsyncMessage;
import flex.messaging.util.UUIDUtils;

public class ReliableServerMessage extends AsyncMessage {

   public ReliableServerMessage(Object body) {
      super();
      this.body = body;
      setMessageId(UUIDUtils.createUUID(false));
      timestamp = System.currentTimeMillis();
   }
}
```

Example 5-8. ReliableServerMessage.as

```
package com.farata.messaging.messages {
   import mx.messaging.messages.AsyncMessage;

   [RemoteClass(alias="com.farata.messaging.messages.ReliableServerMessage")]
   public class ReliableServerMessage extends AsyncMessage{
   }
}
```

The easiest way to identify the server-side outgoing message is by assigning some unique sequence number to its header. Just as a reminder, each `AsyncMessage` object has a message *body* and a message *header* and you are allowed to attach any key/value pairs to its header:

```
message = new ReliableServerMessage("Server message #"  + number);
message.setHeader("seqNo", "" + number);
```

On the client side, we receive each message and store the delivery slip until the next heartbeat is generated. For example, if client heartbeats are being sent to the server every 500 milliseconds but the message can arrive at any random time, the delivery slip will have to wait for the next "shuttle" (a.k.a. heartbeat) to the server.

By this time, you already know that a communication channel is represented by the endpoint on the server side. The client side is represented by a channel—an ActionScript class that implements a selected communication protocol. For example, here's the configuration of our `RTMPChannel` in *services-config.xml* in LCDS:

```
<channel-definition id="my-rtmp"
class="mx.messaging.channels.RTMPChannel">
  <endpoint url="rtmp://localhost:2039"
class="flex.messaging.endpoints.RTMPEndpoint"/>
  <properties>
    <idle-timeout-minutes>30</idle-timeout-minutes>
  </properties>
</channel-definition>
```

In this example, the ActionScript class `RTMPChannel` represents the client side of the RTMP channel. But we'll write a custom class as a channel with a special treatment of instances of the `ReliableServerMessage` type. When creating a custom channel, you override its method `receive()`, storing each received message in the `received` array; on the next timer event `receive()` will grab all received but unacknowledged messages, put them in a heartbeat instance, and send them back to the server. Any other messages will just be passed through the channel to the client application without acknowledgments. Figure 5-3 presents such a design, in which our custom channel goes by the working name *AcknowledgingChannel*.

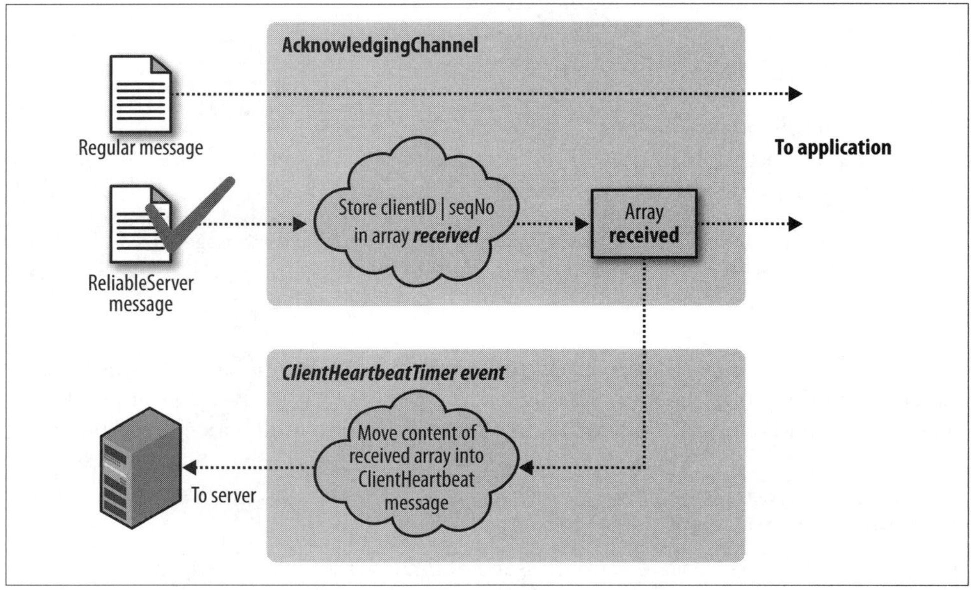

Figure 5-3. Client processing with AcknowledgingChannel

You can say that by adding custom behavior on the protocol level we are enriching the messaging service, or, in other words, adding quality of service (QoS) information to the messages.

Figure 5-4 illustrates the server-side part. Some Java producers generate both regular and reliable messages that go through a custom `QoSAdapter`. The regular messages just go right through to the destination, but the reliable ones are first saved in the `Map` of unconfirmed messages and will stay there until the confirmation from the client arrives.

When the server receives the client heartbeat with the batch of delivery confirmations, the `QoSAdapter` loops through the unconfirmed `Map` and removes the messages that were included in the heartbeat. The messages that haven't been acknowledged by the client can be resent, say, in a three-second interval. In some business cases, you might want to remove the messages that are sitting unconfirmed for more than 20 seconds or any other preferred interval.

All ActionScript and Java classes that support this process are highlighted in Figure 5-5.

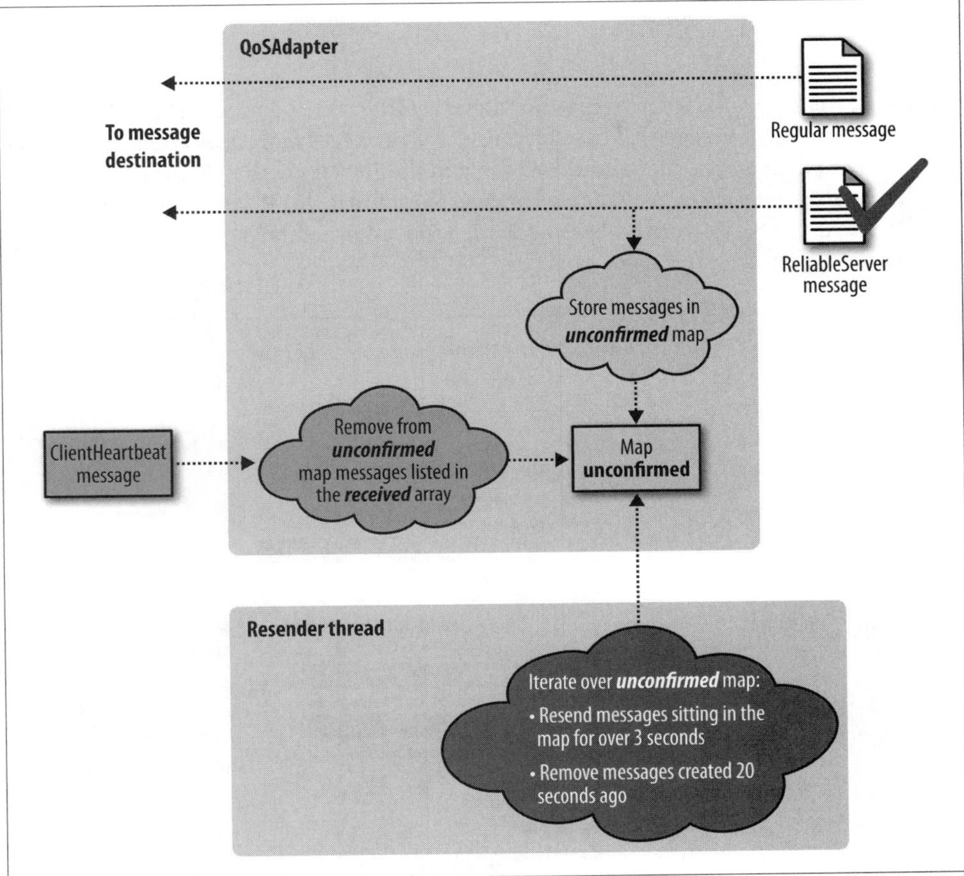

Figure 5-4. Processing acknowledged messages on the server

Building a Custom Acknowledging Channel

In this section, we'll build a custom acknowledging channel for the RTMP protocol, even though you can implement a similar class for AMF-based messaging. The principles of creating custom channels remain the same regardless of the selected protocol. We'll discuss the differences of the communication protocols in Chapter 6.

As stated earlier, you need to overload the `receive()` method and, for each incoming instance of `ReliableServerMessage`, add the `clientId` concatenated with the *message sequence number* to the array called `received`:

```
override public function receive(
 msg:IMessage, ...rest:Array) : void {
 if (msg is ReliableServerMessage) {
   var seqNo : Number = Number(msg.headers["seqNo"]);
   received.push( msg.clientId + "|"+ seqNo);
```

```
    }
    super.receive( msg, rest);
  }
```

Every time the new message arrives from the server, the method `receive()` will be called and a new reliable message will be added to the array `received`. As a reminder, adding a `seqNo` in the message header should be done in the Java code that sends the message. You'll see the use of the message property `clientId` a little later, on the server's `QoSAdapter`; it's used to avoid collision between multiple clients, potentially confirming the same range of message sequences.

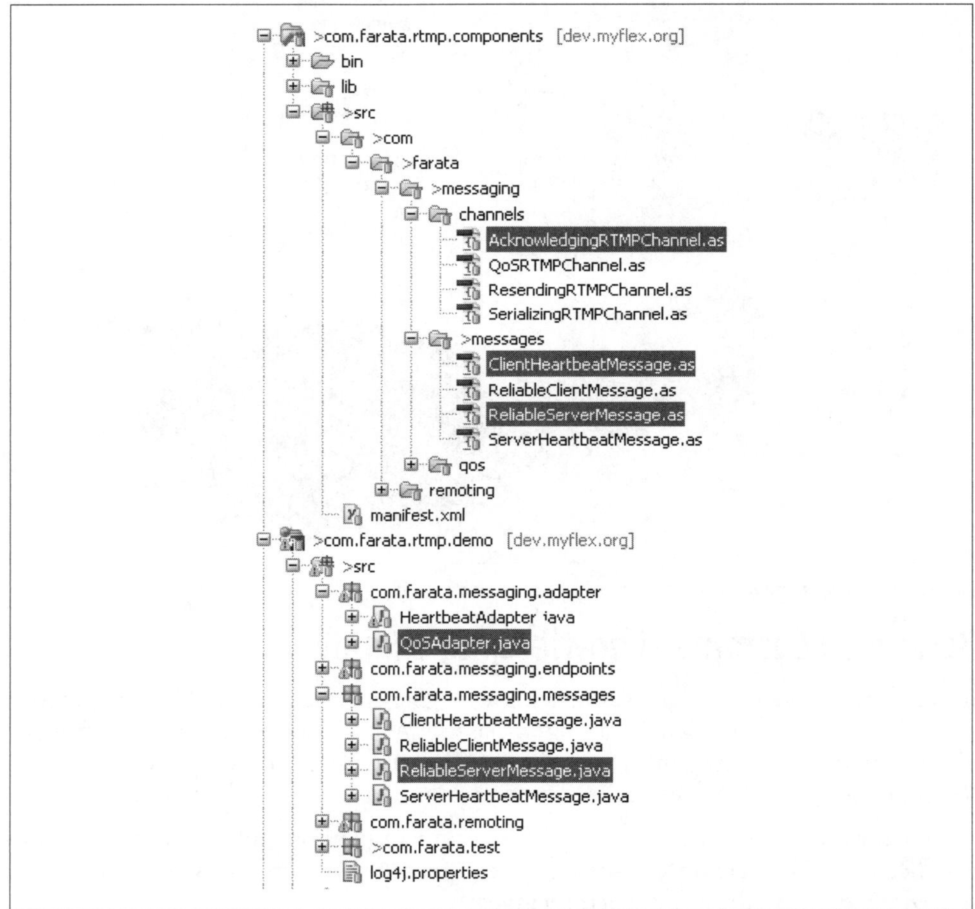

Figure 5-5. Classes involved in the No Server Message Left Behind solution

The code of the client's custom RTMP channel is presented in Example 5-9. Note the method `getConfirmations()`, which will be used to move digests of all recently received but not confirmed messages into yet another property of the `ClientHeartbeatMessage`; it's called `received` and has the type `Array` (Example 5-10).

Example 5-9. AcknowledgingChannel.as

```
package com.farata.messaging.channels {
   import com.farata.messaging.messages.ReliableServerMessage;
   import flash.utils.Dictionary;
   import mx.messaging.channels.RTMPChannel;
   import mx.messaging.messages.IMessage;

   public class AcknowledgingRTMPChannel extends
      mx.messaging.channels.RTMPChannel   {

      public function AcknowledgingRTMPChannel(
      id:String=null, uri:String=null)   {
      super(id, uri);
      }

      override public function receive(
       msg:IMessage, ...rest:Array) : void {
       if (msg is ReliableServerMessage) {
         var seqNo : Number = Number(msg.headers["seqNo"]);
         received.push( msg.clientId + "|"+ seqNo);
       }
       super.receive( msg, rest);
      }

      public static function getConfirmations(result:Array):Array {
       if (result == null) result = [];
       for (var i:int=0;  i < received.length; i++) {
         result.push(received[i]);
       }
       received=[];
       return result;
      }
      private static var received:Array=[];
   }
}
```

Next come the ActionScript and Java versions of the `ClientHeartbeatMessage` (Example 5-10). The ActionScript class has been upgraded from Example 5-1 to populate the `received` array.

Example 5-10. ClientHeartbeatMessage.as and ClientHeartbeatMessage.java

```
package com.farata.messaging.messages{
   import com.farata.messaging.channels.AcknowledgingRTMPChannel;
   import mx.messaging.messages.AbstractMessage;

   [RemoteClass(alias="com.farata.messaging.messages.ClientHeartbeatMessage")]
   public  class ClientHeartbeatMessage extends
                          mx.messaging.messages.AbstractMessage{
      public var received:Array;
      public function ClientHeartbeatMessage() {
```

```
            super();
            received = AcknowledgingRTMPChannel.getConfirmations();
        }
    }
}
```

```
package com.farata.messaging.messages;
     import flex.messaging.messages.AbstractMessage;

     public class ClientHeartbeatMessage extends AbstractMessage {
     public String[] processed;
     public String[] received;
}
```

Resending Messages with QoSAdapter

We have completed the first half of the exercise, in which the heartbeats travel with delivery confirmations via the `AcknowledgingRTMPChannel`. The other half of the solution is:

- To accumulate the delivery confirmations coming from the client with each heartbeat. This will be done in the *QoSAdapter.java* adapter.
- Upon certain timeout, resend unconfirmed messages to the client. This task requires an additional Java `resender` thread, started in *QoSAdapter.java*.

To figure out on the server which messages were confirmed, we need to keep all unconfirmed messages in a safe place—the `unconfirmedMessageMap` in the `QoSAdapter`:

```
     static {
      unconfirmedMessageMap =
          new ConcurrentHashMap<String, ReliableServerMessage>();
    }
```

The data type of this Java map is `ConcurrentHashMap`, which is a `HashMap` that supports concurrent data updates; this is essential in situations in which confirmations can arrive from multiple clients but will all be stored in the same map.

Accordingly, in Example 5-11, the `invoke()` method puts every `Reliable ServerMessage` into the map via a `registerForDeliveryConfirmation()` call.

We also want to emulate the loss of messages on the server by marking about 20 percent (the function `Math.random()` takes care of it) with the header property `tm` for "test mode."

Example 5-11. Method invoke() of QoSAdapter.java

```
public Object invoke(Message message){
 isDebug = logger.isDebugEnabled();
 if ( message instanceof ReliableServerMessage ) {
    registerForDeliveryConfirmation((ReliableServerMessage)message);

    double random = Math.random();
```

```
    if ((random<0.2) && (String)message.getHeader("tm")!=null) {
       String seqNo = (String)message.getHeader("seqNo");
       if (isDebug) logger.debug(
          "QoS adapter emulating loss of message " + seqNo
       );
    } else {
       sendToClient((ReliableServerMessage)message);
    }
 } else if ( message instanceof ClientHeartbeatMessage ) {
     processDeliveryConfirmations((ClientHeartbeatMessage) message);
  }
  return null;
}
```

The complete listing of *QoSAdapter.java* is presented in Example 5-12. The method `registerForDeliveryConfirmation()` adds messages to the map using `clientId + "|"+sequenceNumber` digest as a key, which matches the format in which `AcknowledgingChannel` prepares delivery confirmations. Accordingly, the `processDeliveryConfirmation()` call removes the records from the map.

Both methods lock access to the map with the `synchronized(unconfirmedMessageMap)` Java keyword, not to race with each other but rather to coordinate concurrent access between `QoSAdapter` and the auxiliary `Resender` thread.

Example 5-12. QoSAdapter.java—a resending adapter

```
package com.farata.messaging.adapter;

import java.util.HashSet;
import java.util.Set;
import java.util.concurrent.ConcurrentHashMap;

import org.apache.log4j.Logger;

import com.farata.messaging.messages.ClientHeartbeatMessage;
import com.farata.messaging.messages.ReliableServerMessage;

import flex.messaging.config.ConfigMap;
import flex.messaging.messages.Message;
import flex.messaging.services.MessageService;
import flex.messaging.services.messaging.adapters.MessagingAdapter;

public class QoSAdapter extends MessagingAdapter {
  public void initialize(String id, ConfigMap properties){
    super.initialize(id, properties);

        if( resender == null) {
           resender = new Resender();
           Thread resenderThread =   new Thread(resender, "Resender");
           resenderThread.setDaemon(true);
           resenderThread.start();
      }
   }
```

```
public Object invoke(Message message){
 isDebug = logger.isDebugEnabled();
 if ( message instanceof ClientHeartbeatMessage ) {
     processDeliveryConfirmations((ClientHeartbeatMessage) message);
  } else if ( message instanceof ReliableServerMessage ) {
    registerForDeliveryConfirmation((ReliableServerMessage)message);

    double random = Math.random();
    if ((random<0.2) && (String)message.getHeader("tm")!=null) {
       String seqNo = (String)message.getHeader("seqNo");
       if (isDebug) logger.debug(
          "QoS adapter emulating loss of message " + seqNo
       );
    } else {
       sendToClient((ReliableServerMessage)message);
    }
 }
  return null;
}

private void registerForDeliveryConfirmation( ReliableServerMessage message) {
 String clientId = (String)message.getClientId();
 String seqNo = (String)message.getHeader("seqNo");
 synchronized(unconfirmedMessageMap) {
    message.setHeader("registeredTs", System.currentTimeMillis());
    unconfirmedMessageMap.put(clientId + "|" + seqNo, message);
 }
}

private void sendToClient(ReliableServerMessage message) {
 String seqNo = (String)message.getHeader("seqNo");
 String clientId = (String)message.getClientId();

 MessageService msgService = (MessageService)getDestination().
     getService();
    if (isDebug) logger.debug(
       "QoS adapter is sending through message " + seqNo
    );
    Set<String> subscriberIds = new HashSet<String>();
    subscriberIds.add(clientId);
    msgService.pushMessageToClients(subscriberIds, message, false);
}

private void processDeliveryConfirmations(ClientHeartbeatMessage message) {
 if ((message.received!=null) && (message.received.length>0)) {
   if (isDebug) logger.debug(
    "QoS adapter received delivery confirmations:"
   );
   synchronized(unconfirmedMessageMap) {
     for (int i=0; i <message.received.length; i++) {
     if (isDebug) logger.debug(
       "...and removes (CLIENTID|seqNo)" + message.received[i]
     );
     unconfirmedMessageMap.remove(message.received[i]);
     }
```

```
        }
      }
    }

    private boolean isDebug;
    private Resender resender = null;

    static public ConcurrentHashMap<String, ReliableServerMessage>
unconfirmedMessageMap;
    static Logger logger;
    static {
     unconfirmedMessageMap = new ConcurrentHashMap<String,
        ReliableServerMessage>();
      logger = Logger.getLogger(QoSAdapter.class);
    }
}
```

The code in Example 5-12 uses the class `MessageService`, which manages point-to-point and publish/subscribe messaging. Specifically, `QoSAdapter` uses it to push messages to clients.

The `Resender` thread wakes up every 500 milliseconds and removes all messages that are 20 seconds old from the "unconfirmed" map. For remaining messages that are sitting in the map for as long as three seconds, `Resender` sends another copy of these messages:

```
MessageBroker mb = MessageBroker.getMessageBroker(null);
mb.routeMessageToService(message, null);
```

Example 5-13 presents the `Resender` thread.

Example 5-13. Example of the module

```
package com.farata.messaging.adapter;

import com.farata.messaging.messages.ReliableServerMessage;
import flex.messaging.MessageBroker;
import java.util.Enumeration;
import java.util.concurrent.ConcurrentHashMap;
import org.apache.log4j.Logger;

public class Resender implements Runnable {
  public static int RESENDER_THREAD_SLEEP = 500;
  public static int RESEND_TIMEOUT = 3000; //Resend after 3 sec
  public static int DEAD_CLIENT_TIMEOUT = 20000; //Remove after 20 sec

  protected static Resender resender = null;
  public void run() {
   ConcurrentHashMap<String, ReliableServerMessage> map =
      QoSAdapter.unconfirmedMessageMap;

   while (true) {
      try {
          Thread.sleep(RESENDER_THREAD_SLEEP);
          synchronized (map) {
```

```
        for (Enumeration<String> e = map.keys();e.hasMoreElements();) {

             String key = e.nextElement();
         ReliableServerMessage message = map.get(key);

             String seqNo = (String)message.getHeader("seqNo");
              long nowTs=System.currentTimeMillis();
              long createdTs = message.getTimestamp();
              long registeredTs = (Long)message.getHeader("registeredTs");
              if ((nowTs - createdTs) > DEAD_CLIENT_TIMEOUT) {
                if (logger.isDebugEnabled())logger.debug(
              "Resender thread deletes message  " + seqNo
              );
                map.remove(key);
             } else if ((nowTs - registeredTs) > RESEND_TIMEOUT) {
                  MessageBroker mb = MessageBroker.getMessageBroker(null);
              if (logger.isDebugEnabled())logger.debug(
              "Resender thread resends message " + seqNo
              );

                   mb.routeMessageToService(message, null);
           }
           } //for
        } //synchronized
      } catch (InterruptedException ex){
           if (logger.isInfoEnabled()) logger.info(
           "..in Resender......Interrupted"
      );
      }
    } //while
  }

  static Logger logger;
  static{
      logger = Logger.getLogger(Resender.class);
  }
}
```

Wondering where the message gets timestamped with the `registeredTs` header? After the `routeMessageToService(message, null)` call, the message will be caught by the `QoSAdapter`. `QoSAdapter` will replace the old incarnation of the message in the map and then send the message to the client only with 80 percent probability (if the `tm` header is not null).

Testing Guaranteed Delivery

All the pieces are ready to guarantee that every `ReliableServerMessage` will get delivered to the client. Before testing it, however, specify the acknowledging channel in *services-config.xml* with the code in Example 5-14.

Example 5-14. Registering custom AcknowledgingChannel

```
<channel-definition id="my-acknowledging-client-rtmp"
   class="com.farata.messaging.channels.AcknowledgingRTMPChannel">
      <endpoint uri="rtmp://{server.name}:2040"
      class="flex.messaging.endpoints.RTMPEndpoint"/>
           <properties>
                <idle-timeout-minutes>20</idle-timeout-minutes>
           </properties>
</channel-definition>
```

In *messaging-config.xml*, we direct the custom `QoSAdapter` to intercept messages coming both to `clientHeartbeat` and `serverDeliveryTest` destinations (Example 5-15).

Example 5-15. Configuring destinations for the No Server Message Left Behind test

```
<?xml version="1.0" encoding="UTF-8"?>
<service id="message-service"
   class="flex.messaging.services.MessageService">

    <adapters>
        <adapter-definition
      id="actionscript" default="true"
      class="flex.messaging.services.messaging.adapters.
ActionScriptAdapter"/>
        <adapter-definition id="jms"
      class="flex.messaging.services.messaging.adapters.
JMSAdapter"/>

        <adapter-definition
               id="qos"
      class="com.farata.messaging.adapter.QoSAdapter"/>
    </adapters>

    <default-channels>
     <channel ref="my-rtmp" />
   </default-channels>


    <destination id="clientHeartbeat">
       <adapter ref="qos"/>
      <channels>
         <channel ref="my-rtmp" />
      </channels>
    </destination>

   <destination id="serverDeliveryTest">
       <adapter ref="qos"/>
      <channels>
        <channel ref="my-acknowledging-client-rtmp" />
      </channels>
    </destination>
</service>
```

Once we are done with the messaging configurations, let's look at the Java application class, `ServerMessagingTest`, that we will remote to in order to run the test interactively (Example 5-16). The method `testDeliveryFailure()` sends `messageCount` number of messages sequentially enumerated via the `seqNo` header with `start` as the offset.

Example 5-16. ServerMessagingTest class

```
package com.farata.test;
import java.util.ArrayList;
import com.farata.messaging.messages.ReliableServerMessage;
import flex.messaging.MessageBroker;

public class ServerMessagingTest {
   private static MessageBroker mb;

   private void send(ReliableServerMessage message) {
      if (mb == null) {
         mb = MessageBroker.getMessageBroker(null);
      }
      mb.routeMessageToService(message, null);
   }

   public void testDeliveryFailure(String clientId, int start,
      int messageCount) {

      ReliableServerMessage message;
      for (int i= 0; i < messageCount; i++) {
         message = new ReliableServerMessage(
            "Server message #"  + (i+start)
         );
         message.setHeader("testMode", "true");
         message.setClientId(clientId);
         message.setDestination("serverDeliveryTest");
         message.setHeader("seqNo", "" + (i+start));
         send(message);
      }
   }
   // Other tests
}
```

To remote to this class, we will register it in the *remoting-config.xml* file:

```
<destination id="com.farata.test.ServerMessagingTest">
   <properties>
      <source>com.farata.test.ServerMessagingTest</source>
   </properties>
</destination>
```

The Flex application *TestServerDelivery* will be used as a client portion of the testing setup. This application, besides having an obligatory `ClientHeartbeatProducer`, also has a `Consumer` that listens to the `serverDeliveryTest` destination. Once a `ReliableServerMessage` arrives, the application displays it in the custom control `MessageBar`, as shown in Figure 5-6. The code of the application is presented in Example 5-17; the code of the `MessageBar` we omit for brevity. You can find it in the sample source code accompanying the book.

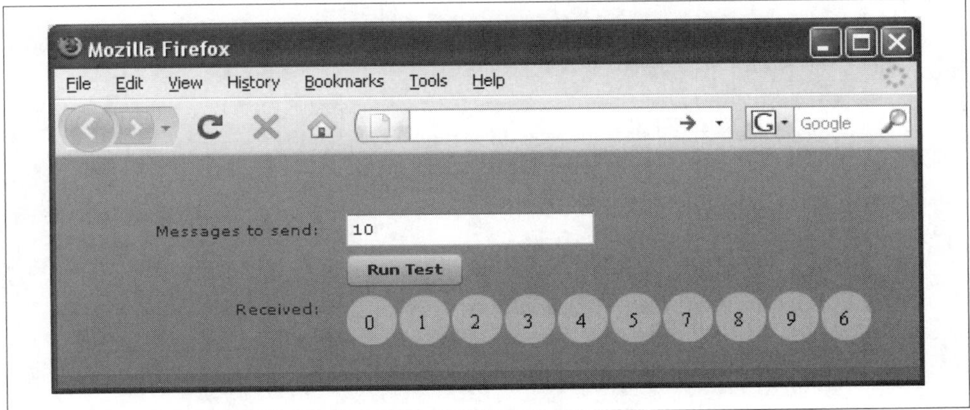

Figure 5-6. Running the TestServerDelivery application

Example 5-17. The TestServerDelivery Flex application

```
<?xml version="1.0" encoding="utf-8"?>
<!--TestServerDelivery.mxml -->
<mx:Application xmlns:mx="http://www.adobe.com/2006/mxml"
   xmlns:fs="http://www.faratasystems.com/2009/components"
   xmlns:local=" *"
   layout="vertical" creationComplete="onCreationComplete()">

   <mx:Form>
      <mx:FormItem label="Messages to send:">
         <mx:TextInput text="10" id="msgCount"/>
         <mx:Button label="Run Test" click="runTest()"/>
      </mx:FormItem>
      <mx:FormItem label="Received:">
         <local:MessageBar id="messageBar" />
      </mx:FormItem>
   </mx:Form>

   <mx:Script>
      <![CDATA[
         import com.farata.messaging.qos.ClientHeartbeatProducer;
         import com.farata.messaging.messages.ReliableServerMessage;
         import mx.messaging.events.MessageEvent;
         import mx.messaging.Consumer;
         [Bindable] public var consumer:Consumer;
```

```
        private var clientHeartbeatProducer:ClientHeartbeatProducer;

     private function onCreationComplete():void {
        clientHeartbeatProducer = new ClientHeartbeatProducer();
        clientHeartbeatProducer.startHeartbeat();

        consumer = new Consumer();
        consumer.destination = "serverDeliveryTest";
        consumer.subscribe();
        consumer.addEventListener(MessageEvent.MESSAGE, onMessage);
     }

     private function onMessage(event:MessageEvent):void {
        var message:ReliableServerMessage = event.message as
                                            ReliableServerMessage;
        var seqNo:Number = Number(message.headers["seqNo"]);
        messageBar.addMessage(messageBar.maxPosition+1, message.headers["seqNo"]);
     }

     private var start:Number=0;
     private function runTest():void {
        messageBar.clean();
        var count:Number = Number(msgCount.text);
        test.testDeliveryFailure(consumer.clientId, start, count);
        start = start + count;
     }

     ]]>
  </mx:Script>
   <mx:TraceTarget />
  <mx:RemoteObject id="test" destination="com.farata.test.ServerMessagingTest" />
</mx:Application>
```

Figure 5-6 illustrates a specific run of the test, where the custom adapter "lost" message #6, which caused the resender thread to resend it later. The corresponding log of the Java server classes is shown in Figure 5-7.

When Message Order Matters

Our guaranteed server message delivery is neglecting the *order* of the messages, which may be an important factor in some business applications. In wide area networks (WANs), messages can be routed in any random way and arrive in any order.

If the order matters in your application, mark the messages with sequence numbers as they get sent and hold on to the "premature" ones on the receiving end. This QoS technique pertains to both server- and client-originated messages. First consider the messages originated on the server; this workflow is shown in Figure 5-8.

```
Jun 23, 2009 6:01:00 PM org.apache.jk.server.JkMain start
INFO: Jk running ID=0 time=0/32  config=null
Jun 23, 2009 6:01:00 PM org.apache.catalina.startup.Catalina start
INFO: Server startup in 2914 ms
[LCDS] Channel endpoint my-amf received request.
[LCDS] Channel endpoint my-amf received request.
[2009-06-23 18:01:10,828] QoS adapter is sending through message 0
[2009-06-23 18:01:10,828] QoS adapter is sending through message 1
[2009-06-23 18:01:10,828] QoS adapter is sending through message 2
[2009-06-23 18:01:10,828] QoS adapter is sending through message 3
[2009-06-23 18:01:10,828] QoS adapter is sending through message 4
[2009-06-23 18:01:10,828] QoS adapter is sending through message 5
[2009-06-23 18:01:10,828] QoS adapter emulating loss of message 6
[2009-06-23 18:01:10,828] QoS adapter is sending through message 7
[2009-06-23 18:01:10,828] QoS adapter is sending through message 8
[2009-06-23 18:01:10,843] QoS adapter is sending through message 9
[2009-06-23 18:01:11,625] QoS adapter received delivery confirmations:
[2009-06-23 18:01:11,625]       ...and removes (CLIENTID|seqNo)26F47B5F-8E1B-1C7D-54FB-9679B5478686|0
[2009-06-23 18:01:11,625]       ...and removes (CLIENTID|seqNo)26F47B5F-8E1B-1C7D-54FB-9679B5478686|1
[2009-06-23 18:01:11,625]       ...and removes (CLIENTID|seqNo)26F47B5F-8E1B-1C7D-54FB-9679B5478686|2
[2009-06-23 18:01:11,625]       ...and removes (CLIENTID|seqNo)26F47B5F-8E1B-1C7D-54FB-9679B5478686|3
[2009-06-23 18:01:11,625]       ...and removes (CLIENTID|seqNo)26F47B5F-8E1B-1C7D-54FB-9679B5478686|4
[2009-06-23 18:01:11,625]       ...and removes (CLIENTID|seqNo)26F47B5F-8E1B-1C7D-54FB-9679B5478686|5
[2009-06-23 18:01:11,625]       ...and removes (CLIENTID|seqNo)26F47B5F-8E1B-1C7D-54FB-9679B5478686|7
[2009-06-23 18:01:11,625]       ...and removes (CLIENTID|seqNo)26F47B5F-8E1B-1C7D-54FB-9679B5478686|8
[2009-06-23 18:01:11,625]       ...and removes (CLIENTID|seqNo)26F47B5F-8E1B-1C7D-54FB-9679B5478686|9
[2009-06-23 18:01:14,171] Resender thread resends message 6
[2009-06-23 18:01:14,171] QoS adapter is sending through message 6
[2009-06-23 18:01:14,734] QoS adapter received delivery confirmations:
[2009-06-23 18:01:14,734]       ...and removes (CLIENTID|seqNo)26F47B5F-8E1B-1C7D-54FB-9679B5478686|6
```

Figure 5-7. Server log of the test illustrated in Figure 5-6

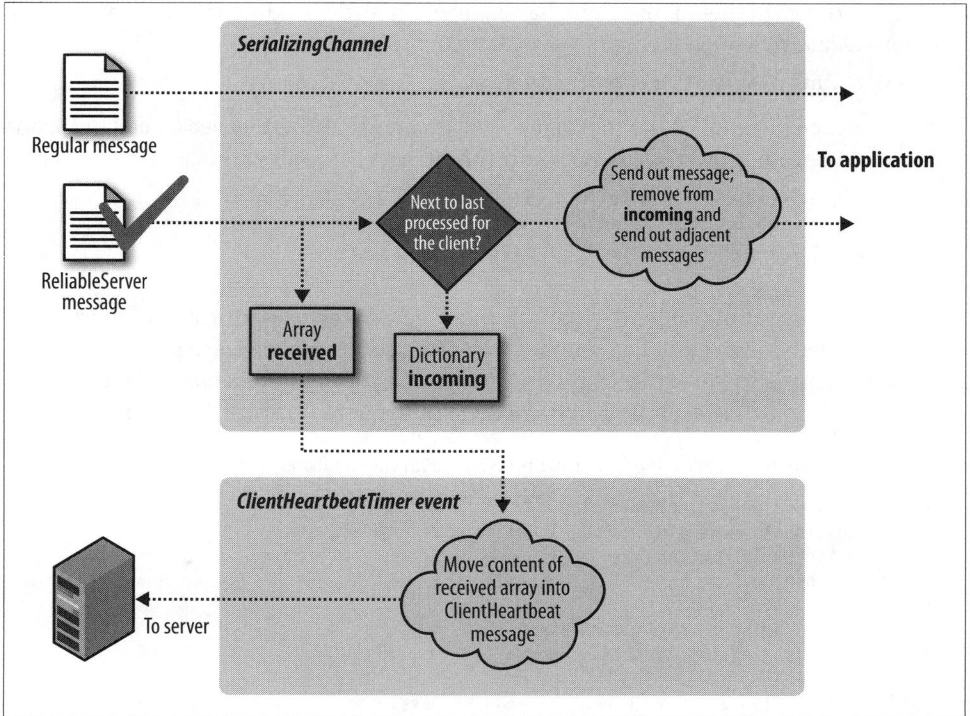

Figure 5-8. Guaranteeing the order of the incoming messages

SerializingChannel

The cornerstone of our design is the `SerializingChannel` class. In addition to the array of *received* message digests described earlier, the channel has to maintain the dictionary of incoming messages for order restoration purposes:

```
private var incoming:Dictionary ;
```

Should a message arrive out of order, the `receive()` method will store it along with the `...rest` arguments:

```
override public function receive(
   msg:IMessage, ...rest:Array
) : void {
   if (msg is ReliableServerMessage) {
      . . .
      // If message is out of order:
      incoming[msg.clientId + '|' + seqNo] = {
         msg:msg, rest:rest
      };
   } else
      super.receive( msg, rest);
}
```

To figure out whether a message has arrived in order, our channel maintains a `lastServedNumber`, which is distinct per each client:

```
public static var lastServedNumber:Dictionary  = new Dictionary();
```

If the sequence number of the message is one greater than `lastServedNumber`, it means that the message has arrived in order and can be sent through with `super.receive()`:

```
if ( seqNo == lastServedNumber[msg.clientId] + 1) {
      super.receive( msg, rest);
      lastServedNumber[msg.clientId]++;
}
```

You also can use the moment when the message arrives to perform one more task: identify stalled messages. The method `findAdjacentBufferedMessages()` in Example 5-18 attempts to yank out of the *incoming* collection all messages delayed by the channel. Example 5-18 has the complete code of the `SerializingRTMPChannel`.

Example 5-18. Custom SerializingRTMPChannel streamlines the order of the messages

```
package com.farata.messaging.channels {
   import com.farata.messaging.messages.ReliableServerMessage;
   import flash.utils.Dictionary;
   import mx.logging.Log;
   import mx.logging.ILogger;
   import mx.messaging.channels.RTMPChannel;
   import mx.messaging.messages.IMessage;

  public class SerializingRTMPChannel extends mx.messaging.channels.RTMPChannel {
   public function SerializingRTMPChannel(
      id:String=null, uri:String=null
```

```
) {
   super(id, uri);
   incoming = new Dictionary();
}

override public function receive(
   msg:IMessage, ...rest:Array
) : void {
   if (msg is ReliableServerMessage) {
      if (Log.isDebug()) logger.debug(msg.body as String);
      var seqNo : Number = Number(msg.headers["seqNo"]);

      received.push( msg.clientId + "|"+ seqNo);

      if (lastServedNumber[msg.clientId]== null) {
         lastServedNumber[msg.clientId]= -1;
      }
      if ( seqNo == lastServedNumber[msg.clientId] + 1) {
            if (Log.isDebug()) logger.debug(
               "Letting out incoming message " + seqNo
            );
            super.receive( msg, rest);
            lastServedNumber[msg.clientId]++;
            seqNo = findAdjacentBufferedMessages(
               msg.clientId, seqNo
            );
      } else if ( seqNo > lastServedNumber[msg.clientId] ) {
         if (Log.isDebug()) logger.debug(
            "Buffering message " + seqNo + " as out of order"
         );
         incoming[msg.clientId + '|' + seqNo] = {
            msg:msg, rest:rest
         };
      }
   } else
      super.receive( msg, rest);
}

private function findAdjacentBufferedMessages(
   clientId:String, seqNo:Number): Number {

   var more:Boolean;
   // We just processed, say, the 3rd message. We may have buffered
   // 5,4,6,7. Internal "for" loop will find 4, then external
   // "while" loop will restart the search and pick 5,6,7.
   do {
      more = false;
      for each(var envelope:Object in incoming){
         var msg:IMessage = envelope.msg;
         if (msg.clientId != clientId)
            continue;
         if (msg.headers["seqNo"] == seqNo + 1) {
            seqNo++;
             lastServedNumber[clientId]++;
            if (Log.isDebug()) logger.debug(
```

```
"Yanking message " + seqNo + " out of the buffer"
            );
            super.receive( msg, envelope.rest);
            delete incoming[seqNo];
            more = true;
         }
      }
   } while (more);
   return seqNo;
}

private var logger:ILogger = Log.getLogger("" +
      "com.farata.messaging.channels.SerializingRTMPChannel"
);
 public static var lastServedNumber:Dictionary  = new Dictionary();
public static var received:Array=[];
private  var incoming:Dictionary ;
 }
}
```

To test the channel, register it in *services-config.xml*, as in Example 5-19.

Example 5-19. Registering SerializingRTMPChannel for the test

```
<channel-definition id="my-serializing-client-rtmp"
   class="com.farata.messaging.channels.SerializingRTMPChannel">
      <endpoint uri="rtmp://{server.name}:2041"
      class="flex.messaging.endpoints.RTMPEndpoint"/>
           <properties>
                <idle-timeout-minutes>20</idle-timeout-minutes>
           </properties>
</channel-definition>
```

Next, add the `serverSequenceTest` destination (Example 5-20) to *messaging-config.xml*.

Example 5-20. Configuring serverSequenceTest messaging destination

```
<destination id="serverSequenceTest">
    <adapter ref="qos"/>
   <channels>
     <channel ref="my-serializing-client-rtmp" />
   </channels>
 </destination>
```

That concludes the configuration work; time to proceed with the test itself. On the server side, we've added the `testSequenceFailure()` method to the class `ServerMessagingTest`. This method randomizes the order of messages prior to sending them, as you can see in Example 5-21.

Example 5-21. Sending test messages in random order

```
package com.farata.test;
import java.util.ArrayList;

import com.farata.messaging.messages.ReliableServerMessage;
import flex.messaging.MessageBroker;
public class ServerMessagingTest {

   . . .
   public void testSequenceFailure(String clientId, int start, int messageCount) {

      ReliableServerMessage message;
      ArrayList<ReliableServerMessage> messages = new
ArrayList<ReliableServerMessage>();
      for (int i= 0; i < messageCount; i++) {
         message = new ReliableServerMessage("Server message #"  + (i+start));
         message.setClientId(clientId);
         message.setDestination("serverSequenceTest");
         message.setHeader("seqNo", "" + (i+start));
         messages.add(message);
      }

      for (long i = 0; i < messageCount; i++) {
         int randomPick = (int )Math.min(
            Math.round(Math.random() * messages.size()),
            messages.size()-1
         );
         message = messages.remove(randomPick);
         send(message);
      }
   }
}
```

When you run the test application *TestServerSequence.mxml*, it will display the messages in perfect order, as shown in Figure 5-9. The code of the testing application is identical to the one presented in Example 5-17 (*TestServerDelivery*), with the exception that line 95 is pointing to the different destination:

```
consumer.destination = "serverSequenceTest";
```

Example 5-22 presents the client-side log of a particular test run. It starts with the remote call, with the following 9 messages out of 10 received out of order. At last comes the message #0; that releases the other nine, and they all get yanked out of the buffer in the right order.

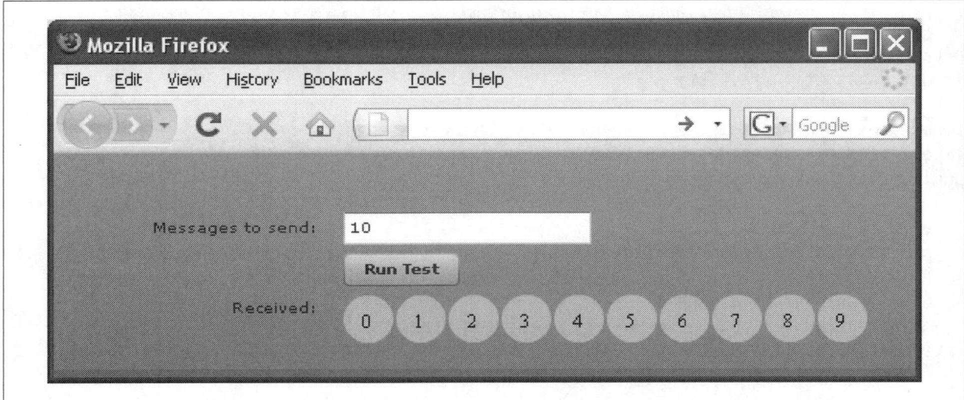

Figure 5-9. Running the TestServerSequence application

Example 5-22. Client-side log of the particular run of the TestServerSequence application

```
14:14:22.062 mx.messaging.Channel 'my-amf' channel sending message:
(mx.messaging.messages::RemotingMessage)#0
  destination = "com.farata.test.ServerMessagingTest"
  operation = "testSequenceFailure"
Buffering message 6 as out of order
Buffering message 3 as out of order
Buffering message 7 as out of order
Buffering message 2 as out of order
Buffering message 9 as out of order
Buffering message 4 as out of order
Buffering message 8 as out of order
Buffering message 5 as out of order
Buffering message 1 as out of order
Letting out incoming message 0
14:14:22.093 mx.messaging.Channel 'my-serializing-client-rtmp' channel
got message (com.farata.messaging.messages::ReliableServerMessage)#0
  body = "Server message #0"
  destination = "serverSequenceTest"
  headers = (Object)#1
    seqNo = "0"

Yanking message 1 out of the buffer
14:14:22.093 mx.messaging.Channel 'my-serializing-client-rtmp' channel
got message (com.farata.messaging.messages::ReliableServerMessage)#0
  body = "Server message #1"
  destination = "serverSequenceTest"
  headers = (Object)#1
    seqNo = "1"

.....

Yanking message 9 out of the buffer
14:14:22.109 mx.messaging.Channel 'my-serializing-client-rtmp' channel
 got message(com.farata.messaging.messages::ReliableServerMessage)#0
```

```
  body = "Server message #9"
  destination = "serverSequenceTest"
  headers = (Object)#1
    seqNo = "9"

14:14:22.328 mx.messaging.Producer 'ED7A14D3-A86A-1C3D-2698-1379B00373E1'
 producer sending message 'FBDFFF8C-8AFD-370C-4768-1379C17883DF'
14:14:22.328 mx.messaging.Channel 'my-rtmp' channel sending message:
(com.farata.messaging.messages::ClientHeartbeatMessage)#0
  body = (Object)#1
  destination = "clientHeartbeat"
  received = (Array)#4
    [0] "318C1775-C11A-E976-FDCD-BB7EA56DAB84|6"
    [1] "318C1775-C11A-E976-FDCD-BB7EA56DAB84|3"
    [2] "318C1775-C11A-E976-FDCD-BB7EA56DAB84|7"
    [3] "318C1775-C11A-E976-FDCD-BB7EA56DAB84|2"
    [4] "318C1775-C11A-E976-FDCD-BB7EA56DAB84|9"
    [5] "318C1775-C11A-E976-FDCD-BB7EA56DAB84|4"
    [6] "318C1775-C11A-E976-FDCD-BB7EA56DAB84|8"
    [7] "318C1775-C11A-E976-FDCD-BB7EA56DAB84|5"
    [8] "318C1775-C11A-E976-FDCD-BB7EA56DAB84|1"
    [9] "318C1775-C11A-E976-FDCD-BB7EA56DAB84|0"
```

As you can see, all 10 messages were reported by the client heartbeat on the next tick. The corresponding server-side log is presented in Example 5-23. Notice that the order of the messages stored/registered by the `QoS adapter` is precisely the same as the order of messages received by our channel.

Example 5-23. Server-side log of this run of TestServerSequence application

```
[LCDS] Channel endpoint my-amf received request.
[LCDS] Channel endpoint my-amf received request.
[14:14:22,078] QoS adapter is sending through message 6
[14:14:22,093] QoS adapter is sending through message 3
[14:14:22,093] QoS adapter is sending through message 7
[14:14:22,093] QoS adapter is sending through message 2
[14:14:22,093] QoS adapter is sending through message 9
[14:14:22,093] QoS adapter is sending through message 4
[14:14:22,093] QoS adapter is sending through message 8
[14:14:22,093] QoS adapter is sending through message 5
[14:14:22,093] QoS adapter is sending through message 1
[14:14:22,093] QoS adapter is sending through message 0
[14:14:22,328] QoS adapter received delivery confirmations:
[4:14:22,328]     ...and removes
      (CLIENTID|seqNo)318C1775-C11A-E976-FDCD-BB7EA56DAB84|6
[14:14:22,328] ...and removes
      (CLIENTID|seqNo)318C1775-C11A-E976-FDCD-BB7EA56DAB84|3
[14:14:22,328] ...and removes
      (CLIENTID|seqNo)318C1775-C11A-E976-FDCD-BB7EA56DAB84|7
[14:14:22,328] ...and removes
      (CLIENTID|seqNo)318C1775-C11A-E976-FDCD-BB7EA56DAB84|2
 [14:14:22,328] ...and removes
......
(CLIENTID|seqNo)318C1775-C11A-E976-FDCD-BB7EA56DAB84|0
```

This concludes our implementation of the guaranteed delivery of messages pushed from the server. What about client messages?

Guaranteed Delivery of Client Messages

Consider the following scenario. A Wall Street trader clicks the Buy button. A Flex message producer sends a message to the remote server over the Internet. You can't afford to lose even one such message, so the rest of this chapter is devoted to implementing guaranteed delivery of messages initiated on the client in the Flash Player.

Because Flex provides an `mx.messaging.events.MessageAckEvent` for every client message, you do not have to worry about acknowledgment. You do still need to take care of the content of the acknowledgment. As you would expect, we are going to enumerate the messages with the `seqNo` header by extending the standard `endpoint` class to return this information inside the `MessageAckEvent` in the form of the `lastProcessedNo` header. This will be a responsibility of the custom `AcknowledgingEndpoint` Java class.

To guarantee message delivery, we will memorize messages as *unconfirmed* prior to sending them out. As soon as the server acknowledgment message comes, we will remove the message from the unconfirmed pool. In parallel, a timer "thread" will be in charge of resending unconfirmed messages in configured intervals. These will be the tasks of the custom ActionScript class `ResendingChannel`. The corresponding design is presented in Figure 5-10.

The top portion of Figure 5-10 represents the client side, and the bottom part is about the server.

The ReliableClientMessage Class

The ActionScript class that knows how to send reliable messages and its Java counterpart are presented in Examples 5-24 and 5-25. Every outgoing `ReliableClientMessage` will have a unique sequential header, `seqNo`.

Example 5-24. ReliableClientMessage.as

```
package com.farata.messaging.messages{
   import mx.messaging.messages.AsyncMessage;

   [RemoteClass(alias="com.farata.messaging.messages.ReliableClientMessage")]
   public class ReliableClientMessage extends AsyncMessage   {

      static public var sequenceNo : int = 0;

      public function ReliableClientMessage(
         body:Object=null, headers:Object=null
      ) {
         if (!headers) {
            headers = [];
```

```
        }
        headers["seqNo"] = sequenceNo++;
        super(body, headers);
      }
    }
}
```

Example 5-25. ReliableClientMessage.java

```
package com.farata.messaging.messages;

import flex.messaging.messages.AsyncMessage;

public class ReliableClientMessage extends AsyncMessage {
}
```

The only reason for creating a subclass of *AsyncMessage.java* is to have a way to separate regular `AsyncMessage` objects that don't require special processing from the reliable ones.

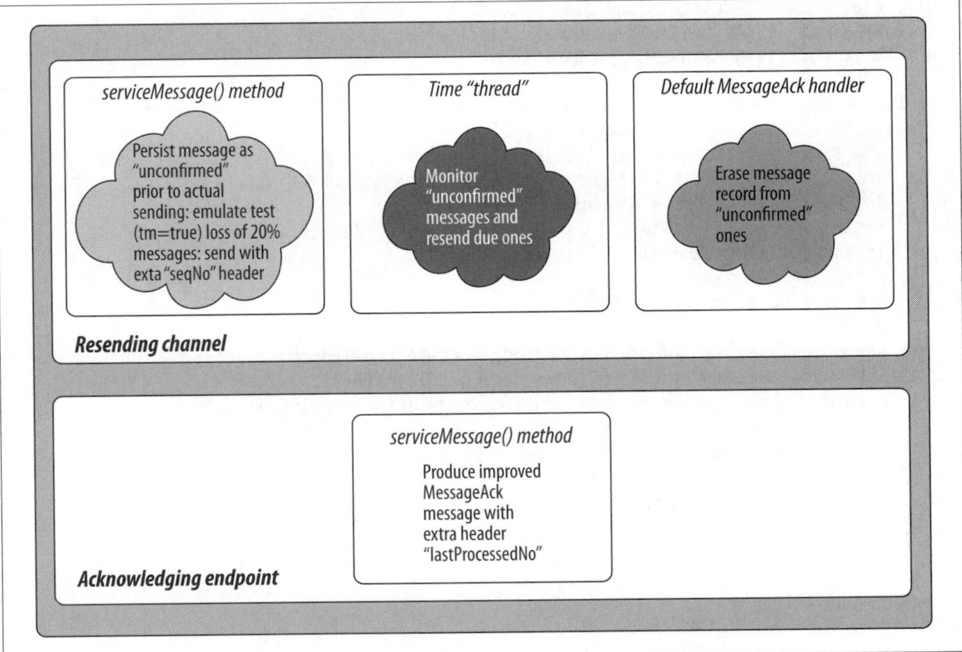

Figure 5-10. Design of the No Client Message Left Behind policy

Acknowledging the Endpoint

Now let's switch to the server side and create a custom endpoint. We need it to beef up the acknowledgment message sent from the server. When the client gets a message, it needs to know the `seqNo` of its last message that was successfully delivered to the server. For now, it will be used only in the testing application. Later, when the order of client messages will be guaranteed, we will use it to determine which ones to put aside and which ones to forward for server processing. As shown in Example 5-26, the proper overloading of the `serviceMessage()` method does the job.

Example 5-26. AcknowledgingRTMPEndpoint.java

```
package com.farata.messaging.endpoints;

import org.apache.log4j.Logger;
import com.farata.messaging.messages.ReliableClientMessage;
import flex.messaging.endpoints.RTMPEndpoint;
import flex.messaging.messages.AcknowledgeMessage;
import flex.messaging.messages.Message;

public class AcknowledgingRTMPEndpoint extends RTMPEndpoint {
  private final String LAST_SERVED_NUMBER="lastServedNumber";
  private final String SEQUENCE_NUMBER="seqNo";

  public Message serviceMessage(Message message) {
   Message m = super.serviceMessage(message);
     if (message instanceof ReliableClientMessage) {
       int sequenceNumber = (Integer)message.getHeader(SEQUENCE_NUMBER) ;
       int lastServedNumber = sequenceNumber;
       String duplicate = (String)message.getHeader("duplicate");
       if (logger.isDebugEnabled()) logger.debug(
         "Received message "+ sequenceNumber +
         ((duplicate!=null)?" (duplicate)":"")
       );
       AcknowledgeMessage acknowledgeMessage = new AcknowledgeMessage();
       acknowledgeMessage.setClientId(message.getClientId());
       acknowledgeMessage.setCorrelationId(message.getMessageId());
       acknowledgeMessage.setHeader(
         LAST_SERVED_NUMBER, (Integer)lastServedNumber
       );
       m = acknowledgeMessage;
     }
     return m;
  }
  static Logger logger;
  static {
    logger = Logger.getLogger(QoSRTMPEndpoint.class);
  }
}
```

This endpoint doesn't touch any messages that are not of the type `ReliableClientMessage`. Note that some of the client messages arrive purposely marked as duplicates; these will just be logged.

Resending Channel Guarantees Delivery

The next customization goes to the client's channel. It has to monitor the server's acknowledgments for each message, and if they are not received in a timely fashion, it must resend the messages. Does this idea sound familiar? The naming convention of the channel also will follow the same pattern as in the server-side adapters and be called `ResendingRTMPChannel`.

This custom channel maintains a `Dictionary` based on the unique `messageId` of the unconfirmed message records:

```
private  var unconfirmed:Dictionary ;
```

Every incoming message stays in this dictionary until acknowledged by the server. If the duration of the stay is longer than a specified timeout, the channel resends the message. The process is spiced up by the fact that the channel is shared by all the client's producers, and during the resend, we need to know which producer has to resend. That is why `unconfirmed` stores the reference to the producer's base class, `MessageAgent`, along with the message itself; the unconfirmed messages that arrived from different clients will be represented by different instances of `MessageAgent`:

```
override public function send(
   agent: MessageAgent, message:IMessage
) : void {

  if (message is ReliableClientMessage) {
    unconfirmed[ message.messageId] = {
       message:message,
      registeredTs: new Date().valueOf(),
      agent:agent
    };
  ...
}
```

To intercept the server's acknowledgment in the Flex application, you can listen to `MessageAckEvent.ACKNOWLEDGE`. To intercept the acknowledgment even earlier, in the channel you need to override `getDefaultMessageResponder()` and also listen to `MessageAckEvent`. Then in the body of the event handler, `onProducerAcknowledge()` removes the corresponding record from the `unconfirmed` collection (Example 5-27).

Example 5-27. Intercepting server's acknowledgment inside custom ResendingRTMPChannel

```
override protected function getDefaultMessageResponder(
   agent:MessageAgent, msg:IMessage
):MessageResponder {

  if (msg is ReliableClientMessage) {
```

```
    if (agent != null && _defaultAgentListener[agent] == null ) {
       _defaultAgentListener[agent] = agent;
       agent.addEventListener(
         MessageAckEvent.ACKNOWLEDGE,
         onProducerAcknowledge
      );
    }
  }
  return super.getDefaultMessageResponder(agent, msg);
}

private function onProducerAcknowledge(event:MessageEvent):void{
  var ackEvent:MessageAckEvent = event as MessageAckEvent;
  var message:ReliableClientMessage = unconfirmed[
     ackEvent.correlationId].message;
  if (Log.isDebug()) logger.debug(
     "ResendingChannel confirms message " + message.headers["seqNo"]
  );
  delete unconfirmed[ackEvent.correlationId];
}
```

Resending of the messages that were not confirmed for three seconds (note `RESEND_TIMEOUT` in Example 5-28) is handled by the timer thread that starts in the channel's constructor.

Example 5-28. Resending of the unconfirmed messages

```
public function ResendingRTMPChannel(id:String=null, uri:String=null) {
  super(id, uri);
  setInterval( resend, RESENDER_SLEEP_INTERVAL);
}

public function resend() : void {
    for each (var record:Object in unconfirmed) {
  if (new Date().valueOf()- record.registeredTs > RESEND_TIMEOUT) {
     var message:IMessage = record.message;
     message.headers["duplicate"]="true";  //for tracing only
     send( record.agent, message);
  }
 }
}
```

The only remaining channel functionality to implement is to deliberately drop about 20 percent of messages (marked with `tm` in the message header) to emulate network problems. Example 5-29 presents the complete code of the *ResendingRTMPChannel.as* file.

Example 5-29. ResendingRTMPChannel.as

```
package com.farata.messaging.channels {
  import com.farata.messaging.messages.ReliableClientMessage;

  import flash.events.IOErrorEvent;
  import flash.utils.Dictionary;
```

```
import flash.utils.setInterval;
import flash.utils.setTimeout;

import mx.logging.ILogger;
import mx.logging.Log;
import mx.messaging.MessageAgent;
import mx.messaging.MessageResponder;
import mx.messaging.channels.RTMPChannel;
import mx.messaging.events.MessageAckEvent;
import mx.messaging.events.MessageEvent;
import mx.messaging.messages.IMessage;

public class ResendingRTMPChannel extends
   mx.messaging.channels.RTMPChannel   {

private  var unconfirmed:Dictionary ;

// Resend unconfirmed message after 3 sec
public static const RESEND_TIMEOUT:int = 3000;
public static const RESENDER_SLEEP_INTERVAL:int = 500;

public function ResendingRTMPChannel(id:String=null, uri:String=null) {
  super(id, uri);
  unconfirmed = new Dictionary();
  setInterval( resendNonDelivered , RESENDER_SLEEP_INTERVAL);
}

override protected function ioErrorHandler(event:IOErrorEvent):void{
  super.ioErrorHandler( event );
  setTimeout(resend, 1);
}

public function resend() : void {

    for each (var record:Object in unconfirmed) {
   if (new Date().valueOf()- record.registeredTs > RESEND_TIMEOUT) {
      var message:IMessage = record.message;
      message.headers["duplicate"]="true";  //for tracing only
      send( record.agent, message);
   }
  }
}

override public function send(
   agent: MessageAgent, message:IMessage
) : void {

  if (message is ReliableClientMessage) {
    unconfirmed[ message.messageId] = {
       message:message,
      registeredTs: new Date().valueOf(),
      agent:agent
    };
   // Emulate 20% of "lost" messages
   if (( message.headers["tm"] != null) && (Math.random()<.2)) {
```

```
            if (Log.isDebug()) logger.debug(
               "ResendingChannel emulates loss of message " + message.headers["seqNo"]
            );
            return;
         } else {
            if (Log.isDebug()) logger.debug(
               "ResendingChannel sends through message " + message.headers["seqNo"]
            );
            super.send( agent, message );
         }
       } else
         super.send( agent, message );
      }

      private var _defaultAgentListener:Dictionary = new Dictionary();

      override   protected function getDefaultMessageResponder(
         agent:MessageAgent, msg:IMessage
      ):MessageResponder {

        if (msg is ReliableClientMessage) {
          if (agent != null && _defaultAgentListener[agent] == null ) {
             _defaultAgentListener[agent] = agent;
             agent.addEventListener(
               MessageAckEvent.ACKNOWLEDGE,
               onProducerAcknowledge
            );
          }
        }
        return super.getDefaultMessageResponder(agent, msg);
       }

      private function onProducerAcknowledge(event:MessageEvent):void{
         var ackEvent:MessageAckEvent = event as MessageAckEvent;
         var message:ReliableClientMessage = unconfirmed[
            ackEvent.correlationId].message;
         if (Log.isDebug()) logger.debug(
            "ResendingChannel confirms message " + message.headers["seqNo"]
         );
         delete unconfirmed[ackEvent.correlationId];
       }

         private var logger:ILogger = Log.getLogger(
         "com.farata.messaging.channels.ResendingRTMPChannel"
      );
     }
   }
```

Our custom channel works in a symmetrical way to the server-side custom endpoint.

Testing Guaranteed Delivery from the Client

To test guaranteed delivery of the messages originated on the client, register `ResendingRTMPChannel` with *service-config.xml* as shown in Example 5-30.

Example 5-30. Endpoint for testing the No Client Message Left Behind solution

```
<channel-definition id="my-resending-client-rtmp"
       class="com.farata.messaging.channels.ResendingRTMPChannel"
  <endpoint uri="rtmp://{server.name}:2042"
       class="com.farata.messaging.endpoints.AcknowledgingRTMPEndpoint"/>
           <properties>
               <idle-timeout-minutes>20</idle-timeout-minutes>
           </properties>
</channel-definition>
```

Next, define the destination `clientDeliveryTest` in *messaging-config.xml* (Example 5-31).

Example 5-31. Messaging destination to test the No Client Message Left Behind solution

```
<destination id="clientDeliveryTest">
    <adapter ref="actionscript"/>
    <channels>
       <channel ref="my-resending-client-rtmp" />
    </channels>
</destination>
```

The testing application *TestClientDelivery* (Example 5-32) displays `seqNo` from the headers of the messages sent by the producer and, separately, `lastProcessedNo` from the headers of the acknowledgment messages that the server replies with. Figure 5-11 illustrates a particular run of the application when messages 7 and 3 were "swallowed" by `ResendingRTMPChannel`, emulating a loss of the messages elsewhere in the network. As a result, these messages were resent by the channel, albeit a bit later. The corresponding server log is presented in Example 5-33.

Example 5-32 lists the source code of the testing application.

Example 5-32. TestClientDelivery application

```
<?xml version="1.0" encoding="utf-8"?>
<!--TestClientDelivery.mxml-->
<mx:Application xmlns:mx="http://www.adobe.com/2006/mxml"
   xmlns:fs="http://www.faratasystems.com/2009/components"
   layout="vertical" xmlns:local="*">
   <mx:Producer id="producer"   acknowledge="onProducerAcknowledge(event)"
      destination="clientDeliveryTest" />
   <mx:Form>
     <mx:FormItem label="Messages to send:">
         <mx:TextInput text="10" id="msgCount"/>
         <mx:Button label="Run Test"
            click="runTest(Number(msgCount.text))"/>
      </mx:FormItem>
```

```
      <mx:FormItem label="Sent:">
         <local:MessageBar id="sentBar" />
      </mx:FormItem>
      <mx:FormItem label="Acknowledged:">
         <local:MessageBar id="ackBar" />
      </mx:FormItem>
   </mx:Form>
   <mx:Script>
      <![CDATA[
   import mx.messaging.messages.IMessage;
   import mx.messaging.events.MessageAckEvent;
   import mx.messaging.Producer;
   import com.farata.messaging.messages.ReliableClientMessage;

   private function runTest(messageCount:int):void {
      var message: ReliableClientMessage;
      var messageSequence:Array = [];
      sentBar.clean();
      ackBar.clean();
      for (var i : int = 0; i < messageCount; i++) {
         message = new ReliableClientMessage(
            // Header "tm" marks this message as a
            // candidate to be lost by the channel
            "Client message #"  + i, {tm:1}
         );
          messageSequence.push( message );
         producer.send( message );
         sentBar.addMessage(i, message.headers["seqNo"]);
      }
   }

   private function onProducerAcknowledge(event:MessageAckEvent):void {

      var message:IMessage = event.acknowledgeMessage as IMessage;
      var servedNumber:Number = message.headers["lastServedNumber"]
      as Number;
      //Assuming messageCount is not changing fast :)
ackBar.appendMessage(servedNumber);      }
      ]]>
   </mx:Script>
   <mx:TraceTarget />
</mx:Application>
```

This application has three buttons labeled Load Module, Modify Content, and Unload Module, each associated with a similarly named function. Example 5-33 is the logfile of a test run.

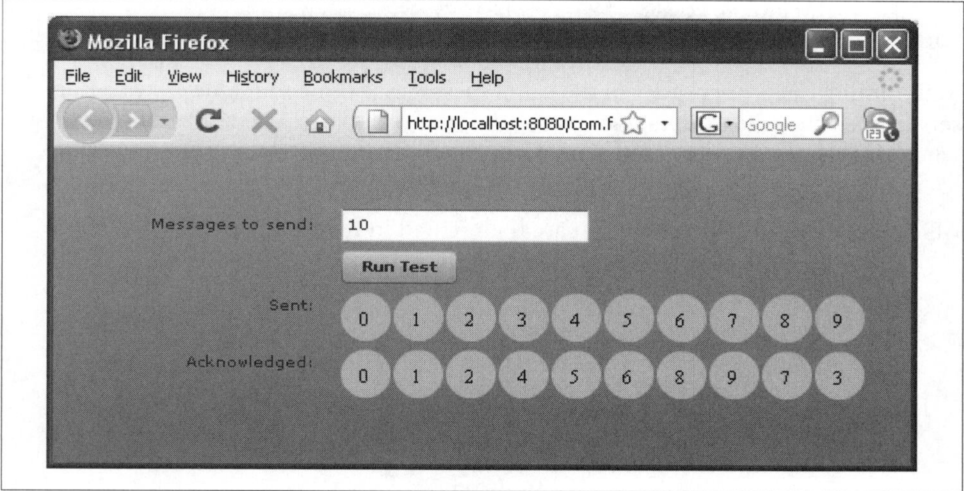

Figure 5-11. Running the TestClientDelivery application

Example 5-33. Server log of the running TestClientDelivery application

```
[2009-06-25 21:16:32,140] Received message 0
[2009-06-25 21:16:32,156] Received message 1
[2009-06-25 21:16:32,156] Received message 2
[2009-06-25 21:16:32,156] Received message 4
[2009-06-25 21:16:32,156] Received message 5
[2009-06-25 21:16:32,171] Received message 6
[2009-06-25 21:16:32,171] Received message 8
[2009-06-25 21:16:32,171] Received message 9
[2009-06-25 21:16:35,234] Received message 7 (duplicate)
[2009-06-25 21:16:38,359] Received message 3 (duplicate)
```

As you can see, the custom `ResendingRTMPChannel` delivers 100 percent of sent messages, although order is not maintained. We will straighten this out in the next section.

Keeping Client Messages in Order

In a WAN environment, neither Flex LCDS nor BlazeDS can guarantee that the messages you are sending are coming in the same order that they were sent. For gaming or trading applications, the consequences can be very serious.

What if your Buy and Modify requests come in the wrong order? How would you feel about placing the straight-up roulette bet at 20, then moving to 21 after the ball stops on 21? Actually, some sequencing mistakes can be beneficial for the gambler and some can cause substantial losses of money. But developers of such client/server communications must remain neutral and ensure that the bets are placed in the right order. Naturally, these things will not happen on the development local area network (LAN), but hey, people want to place bets while sitting in a small Internet café in a French village or from their laptops by the Tiki Bar in Miami Beach.

Maintaining the proper order of the client messages is done the same way it's done for server-born messages: quarantine received out-of-order messages and let them out only when the missing number comes in. The proper place to do this is the server-side custom endpoint: `SerializingRTMPEndpoint` (see Example 5-34).

All classes involved in the solution are highlighted in Figure 5-12.

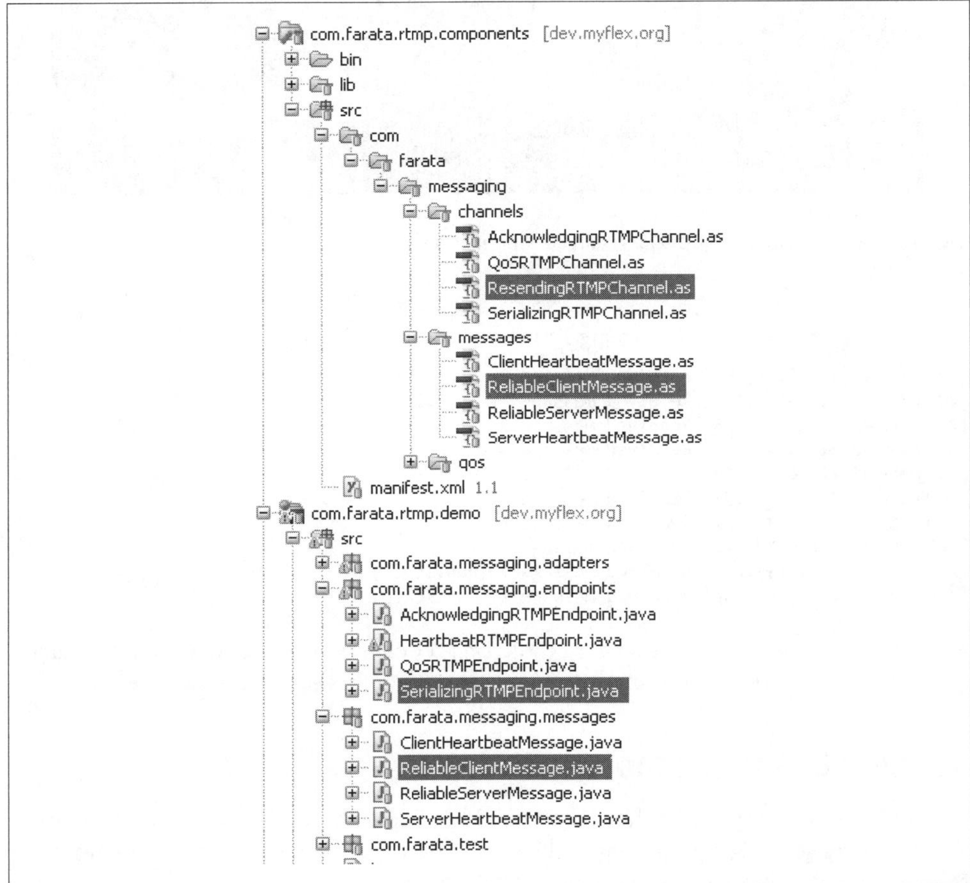

Figure 5-12. Classes involved in guaranteed and orderly delivery of the client-initiated messages

The logic implemented in `SerializingRTMPEndpoint` is similar to that of `SerializingRTMPChannel`. In fact, it's even simpler, because we can accumulate incoming messages and `lastServedNumber` in the `FlexSession` attributes, isolating the processing for different clients.

The FlexSession class is supplied in LCDS and BlazeDS for session management tasks, and we use it here just for illustration purposes. In real life, you may be better off with your own custom-messaging-session mechanism that doesn't interfere with the HTTP domain.

Everything is done inside the overloaded **serviceMessage()** method. If the message sequence number is one greater than **lastServedNumber**, we process it straight through by calling **super.serviceMessage()**. We do not stop, however, because we might have other messages locked in the incoming map. Increment **lastServedNumber** and attempt to find the adjacent message in the map. If found, send it out with **super.serviceMessage()** and keep looping through the incoming map. If the message number is less than **lastServedNumber**, put it in the incoming map, but you should avoid calling **super.serviceMessage()**; the message will remain on hold. The complete code of **SerializingRTMPEndpoint** is shown in Example 5-34.

Example 5-34. SerializingRTMPEndpoint

```
public class SerializingRTMPEndpoint extends RTMPEndpoint {
package com.farata.messaging.endpoints;
import java.util.concurrent.ConcurrentHashMap;

import com.farata.messaging.messages.ReliableClientMessage;
import flex.messaging.FlexContext;
import flex.messaging.FlexSession;
import flex.messaging.endpoints.RTMPEndpoint;
import flex.messaging.messages.AcknowledgeMessage;
import flex.messaging.messages.Message;
import org.apache.log4j.Logger;

public class SerializingRTMPEndpoint extends RTMPEndpoint {
   private final String INCOMING="incomingMessages";
   private final String LAST_SERVED_NUMBER="lastServedNumber";
   private final String SEQUENCE_NUMBER="seqNo";

   @SuppressWarnings("unchecked")
   public Message serviceMessage(Message message)    {
      logger.info(message);

      if ( message instanceof ReliableClientMessage ) {
      FlexSession session =  FlexContext.getFlexSession();
      AcknowledgeMessage acknowledgeMessage = null;
         acknowledgeMessage = new AcknowledgeMessage();
      acknowledgeMessage.setClientId(message.getClientId());
      acknowledgeMessage.setCorrelationId(message.getMessageId());

      if (session.getAttribute(INCOMING) == null)
         session.setAttribute(
            INCOMING,
            new ConcurrentHashMap<Integer,Message>()
         );
      ConcurrentHashMap<Integer,Message> incoming =
```

```
    (ConcurrentHashMap<Integer,Message>) session.getAttribute(
       INCOMING
    );
    int lastServedNumber = -1;
    boolean isDebug=true;logger.isDebugEnabled();

    if ( session.getAttribute(LAST_SERVED_NUMBER) != null )
       lastServedNumber = (Integer)session.getAttribute(
          LAST_SERVED_NUMBER
       );

    int seqNo = (Integer)message.getHeader(SEQUENCE_NUMBER) ;
    String duplicate = (String)message.getHeader("duplicate");
    if ((duplicate!=null) && isDebug)

      if (isDebug) logger.debug(
       "Client sent duplicate to compensate send failure "+ seqNo
      );
      if (seqNo <= lastServedNumber) {
       if (isDebug) logger.debug(
          "Ignoring message " + seqNo + " as already processed"
       );
    } else if (seqNo == lastServedNumber+1){
       if (isDebug) logger.debug(
          "Letting out incoming message " + seqNo
       );
       super.serviceMessage(message);
       lastServedNumber++;

       while
            ((message=(Message)incoming.remove((lastServedNumber+1)))!=null)
           {
          seqNo++;
          if (isDebug) logger.debug(
             "Yanking message " + seqNo + " out of the buffer"
          );
          super.serviceMessage(message);
          lastServedNumber++;
       }
    } else  {
       if (isDebug) logger.debug(
          "Buffering message " + seqNo + " as out of order"
       );
       incoming.put(seqNo, message);
    }

    session.setAttribute(LAST_SERVED_NUMBER,(Integer)lastServedNumber);

    acknowledgeMessage.setHeader(LAST_SERVED_NUMBER,
                                           (Integer)lastServedNumber);
     return acknowledgeMessage;

    } else
    return super.serviceMessage(message);
}
```

```
  static Logger logger;
   static {
           logger = Logger.getLogger(QoSRTMPEndpoint.class);
   }
}
```

We didn't put in much explanation of this code, as it's similar to the example of customizing the server-side message adapter (see the explanation for Example 5-12).

Testing Ordered Delivery of Client Messages

To test ordered delivery of the client messages, register `SerializingRTMPEndpoint` with *services-config.xml* (Example 5-35).

Example 5-35. Channel definition to test ordered delivery of client messages

```
<channel-definition id="my-serializing-server-rtmp"
   class="mx.messaging.channels.RTMPChannel">
   <endpoint uri="rtmp://{server.name}:2043"
      class="com.farata.messaging.endpoints.SerializingRTMPEndpoint"
<properties>
         <idle-timeout-minutes>20</idle-timeout-minutes>
      </properties>
</channel-definition>
```

Then add the destination `clientServiceTest` to *messaging-config.xml* (Example 5-36).

Example 5-36. Messaging destination to test ordered delivery of client messages

```
<destination id="clientSequenceTest">
      <adapter ref="actionscript"/>
   <channels>
        <channel ref="my-serializing-server-rtmp" />
   </channels>
</destination>
```

The code of the testing application *TestClientSequence* is presented in Example 5-37.

The test application sends messages in random order, which is reflected in the Sent bar (Figure 5-13). The application is subscribed to `MessageAckEvent` and displays arrived messages in the Acknowledged bar with circles.

Notice that all messages came acknowledged in the right order, thanks to the housekeeping done by the `SerializingEndpoint`. In Example 5-37, you can also browse the server log produced by this custom endpoint during the specific test run.

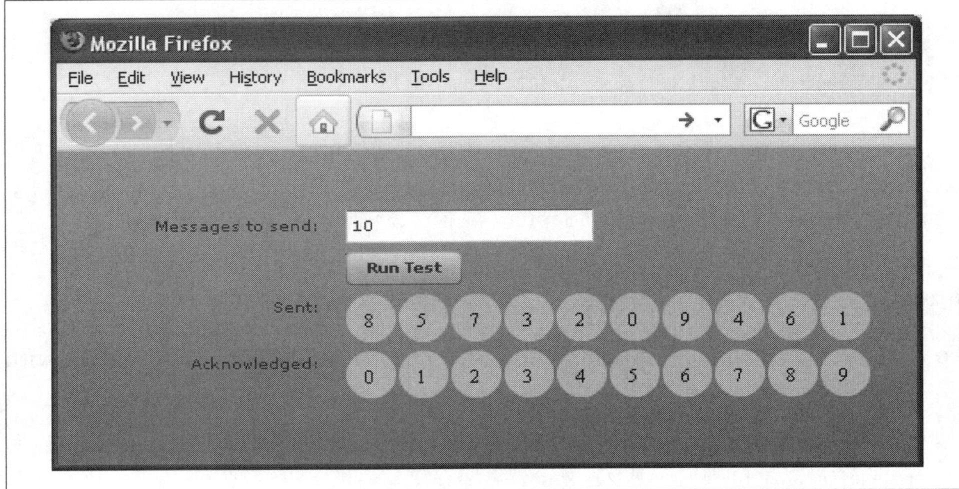

Figure 5-13. Running the TestClientSequence application

The complete code of the test client application is depicted in Example 5-37.

Example 5-37. TestClientSequence application

```
<?xml version="1.0" encoding="utf-8"?>
<!-- TestClientSequence.mxml-->
<mx:Application xmlns:mx="http://www.adobe.com/2006/mxml"
   xmlns:fs="http://www.faratasystems.com/2009/components"
   layout="vertical" xmlns:local="*">
   <mx:Producer id="producer"   acknowledge="onProducerAcknowledge(event)"
      destination="clientSequenceTest" />
   <mx:Form>
      <mx:FormItem label="Messages to send:">
         <mx:TextInput text="10" id="msgCount"/>
         <mx:Button label="Run Test" click="runTest(Number(msgCount.text))"/>
      </mx:FormItem>
      <mx:FormItem label="Sent:">
         <local:MessageBar id="sentBar" />
      </mx:FormItem>
      <mx:FormItem label="Acknowledged:">
         <local:MessageBar id="ackBar" />
      </mx:FormItem>
   </mx:Form>
   <mx:Script>
      <![CDATA[
         import mx.messaging.messages.IMessage;
         import mx.messaging.events.MessageAckEvent;
         import mx.messaging.Producer;
         import com.farata.messaging.messages.ReliableClientMessage;

      private function runTest(messageCount:int):void {
         var message: ReliableClientMessage;
```

```
            var messageSequence:Array = [];
            sentBar.clean();
            ackBar.clean();
            for (var i : int = 0; i < messageCount; i++) {
               messageSequence.push( message );
            }
            for ( i = 0; i < messageCount; i++) {
               var randomPick : int = Math.min( Math.round(Math.random() *
                          messageSequence.length), messageSequence.length - 1);
               message = messageSequence.splice( randomPick, 1 )[0];
               producer.send( message );
               sentBar.addMessage(i, message.headers["seqNo"]);
            }
         }

         private function onProducerAcknowledge(event:MessageAckEvent):void {
            var message:IMessage = event.acknowledgeMessage as IMessage;
            var servedNumber:Number = message.headers["lastServedNumber"] as Number;
            if (servedNumber!=-1)
               ackBar.appendMessageBlock(servedNumber);
         }
         ]]>
   </mx:Script>
</mx:Application>
```

Example 5-38 is the logfile produced by this application.

Example 5-38. Server log of the custom SerializingRTMPEndpoint during the test run pictured in Figure 5-13

```
[2009-06-27 12:54:58,234] Flex Message
(com.farata.messaging.messages.ReliableClientMessage)
    destination = clientSequenceTest
    body = Client message #7
    hdr(seqNo) = 7
    hdr(DSEndpoint) = my-serializing-server-rtmp
[2009-06-27 12:54:58,234] Buffering message 7 as out of order
[2009-06-27 12:54:58,250] Flex Message
(com.farata.messaging.messages.ReliableClientMessage)
    destination = clientSequenceTest
    body = Client message #9
    hdr(seqNo) = 9
    hdr(DSEndpoint) = my-serializing-server-rtmp
[2009-06-27 12:54:58,250] Buffering message 9 as out of order
[2009-06-27 12:54:58,250] Flex Message
(com.farata.messaging.messages.ReliableClientMessage)
    destination = clientSequenceTest
    body = Client message #3
    hdr(seqNo) = 3
    hdr(DSEndpoint) = my-serializing-server-rtmp
[2009-06-27 12:54:58,250] Buffering message 3 as out of order

[2009-06-27 12:54:58,250] Flex Message
(com.farata.messaging.messages.ReliableClientMessage)
    destination = clientSequenceTest
```

```
    body = Client message #0
    hdr(seqNo) = 0
    hdr(DSEndpoint) = my-serializing-server-rtmp
[2009-06-27 12:54:58,250] Letting out incoming message 0

[2009-06-27 12:54:58,250] Flex Message
(com.farata.messaging.messages.ReliableClientMessage)
    destination = clientSequenceTest
    body = Client message #4
    hdr(seqNo) = 4
    hdr(DSEndpoint) = my-serializing-server-rtmp
[2009-06-27 12:54:58,250] Buffering message 4 as out of order
[2009-06-27 12:54:58,250] Flex Message
(com.farata.messaging.messages.ReliableClientMessage)
    destination = clientSequenceTest
    body = Client message #2
    hdr(seqNo) = 2
    hdr(DSEndpoint) = my-serializing-server-rtmp
[2009-06-27 12:54:58,250] Buffering message 2 as out of order
[2009-06-27 12:54:58,250] Flex Message
(com.farata.messaging.messages.ReliableClientMessage)
    destination = clientSequenceTest
    body = Client message #8
    hdr(seqNo) = 8
    hdr(DSEndpoint) = my-serializing-server-rtmp
[2009-06-27 12:54:58,250] Buffering message 8 as out of order
[2009-06-27 12:54:58,250] Flex Message
(com.farata.messaging.messages.ReliableClientMessage)
    destination = clientSequenceTest
    body = Client message #6
    hdr(seqNo) = 6
    hdr(DSEndpoint) = my-serializing-server-rtmp
[2009-06-27 12:54:58,250] Buffering message 6 as out of order
[2009-06-27 12:54:58,250] Flex Message
(com.farata.messaging.messages.ReliableClientMessage)
    destination = clientSequenceTest
    body = Client message #5
    hdr(seqNo) = 5
    hdr(DSEndpoint) = my-serializing-server-rtmp
[2009-06-27 12:54:58,250] Buffering message 5 as out of order

[2009-06-27 12:54:58,250] Flex Message
(com.farata.messaging.messages.ReliableClientMessage)
    destination = clientSequenceTest
    body = Client message #1
    hdr(seqNo) = 1
    hdr(DSEndpoint) = my-serializing-server-rtmp
[2009-06-27 12:54:58,250] Letting out incoming message 1

[2009-06-27 12:54:58,250] Yanking message 2 out of the buffer
[2009-06-27 12:54:58,250] Yanking message 3 out of the buffer
[2009-06-27 12:54:58,250] Yanking message 4 out of the buffer
[2009-06-27 12:54:58,250] Yanking message 5 out of the buffer
[2009-06-27 12:54:58,250] Yanking message 6 out of the buffer
[2009-06-27 12:54:58,250] Yanking message 7 out of the buffer
```

```
[2009-06-27 12:54:58,250] Yanking message 8 out of the buffer
[2009-06-27 12:54:58,250] Yanking message 9 out of the buffer
```

Summary

After reading this chapter, you should have a pretty good understanding of how the process of message customization works in the Flex messaging world. Now roll up your sleeves and see if you can improve the reliability of messages in your application.

Have you noticed that this effort is done in the objects that support the messaging layer, and your application developers don't need to worry about message acknowledgment or out-of-sequence messages in their code? This is the main theme of the entire book: make application developers write less code. We'll keep repeating this mantra in every applicable situation—in the least annoying way possible, of course.

The source code of this chapter comes as two projects:

- A combined Flex/Java project, *com.farata.rtmp.components.demo* (in real-world projects, it's better to separate Java and Flex code into two projects)
- The Flex library project *com.farata.rtmp.components*

But those projects come with a disclaimer: the code used in this chapter is written for illustration purposes only. Although it's conceptually correct, don't treat it as a production-ready solution. We urge you to analyze all specific situations that may arise in your business application and provide their proper processing in custom channels, adapters, and endpoints.

CHAPTER 6

Open Source Networking Solutions

"Ninety-nine percent of the people who reject using the software until it gets open sourced will never even look at its source code when it's done."

"Most people are not planning to use airbags in cars, but they want them anyway."

—A conversation between Yakov and Marat

The selection of a communication protocol can be as crucial for the success of your RIA as a professionally designed UI. LiveCycle Data Services (LCDS) is an excellent solution for building enterprise-grade scalable RIAs, but some enterprises just don't have the budget for it. Many smaller IT organizations still use the more familiar HTTP or SOAP web services, because it's an easy route into the world of RIA with only minor changes on the backend.

Now there's a faster, more powerful open source option. In February 2008, Adobe released BlazeDS in conjunction with open sourcing the specification of the Action Message Format (AMF) communication protocol. Offering many of the same capabilities as LCDS, BlazeDS is a Java-based open source implementation of AMF, which sends the data over the wire in a highly compressed binary form.

Large distributed applications greatly benefit by working with the strongly typed data. Sooner or later developers will need to refactor the code, and if there is no data type information available, changing the code in one place might break the code in another and the compiler might not help you in identifying such newly introduced bugs.

This chapter will unleash the power of AMF and provide illustrations of how to create a robust platform for development of modern RIA without paying hefty licensing fees. It will discuss polling and server-side push techniques for client/server communications, as well as how to extend the capabilities of BlazeDS to bring it closer to LCDS.

BlazeDS Versus LCDS

Prior to Adobe's BlazeDS, Flex developers who wanted to use the AMF protocol to speed up the data communication between Flex and the server side of their application had to select one of the third-party libraries, such as Open AMF, WebORB, or GraniteDS. The release of the open source BlazeDS, however, brought a lot more than just support of AMF. You can think of BlazeDS as a scaled-down version of LCDS. As opposed to LCDS, BlazeDS doesn't support RTMP protocol, Data Management Services, or PDF generation, and has limited scalability. But even with these limitations, its AMF support, ability to communicate with Plain Old Java Objects (POJOs), and support of messaging via integration with the Java Messaging Protocol make BlazeDS a highly competitive player in the world of RIA. These features alone make it a good choice for architecting RIA data communication compared to any AJAX library or a package that just implements the AMF protocol.

Figure 6-1 provides a capsule comparison of BlazeDS and LiveCycle functions. The items shown in regular type represent the features available only in LCDS. The features of BlazeDS are in bold.

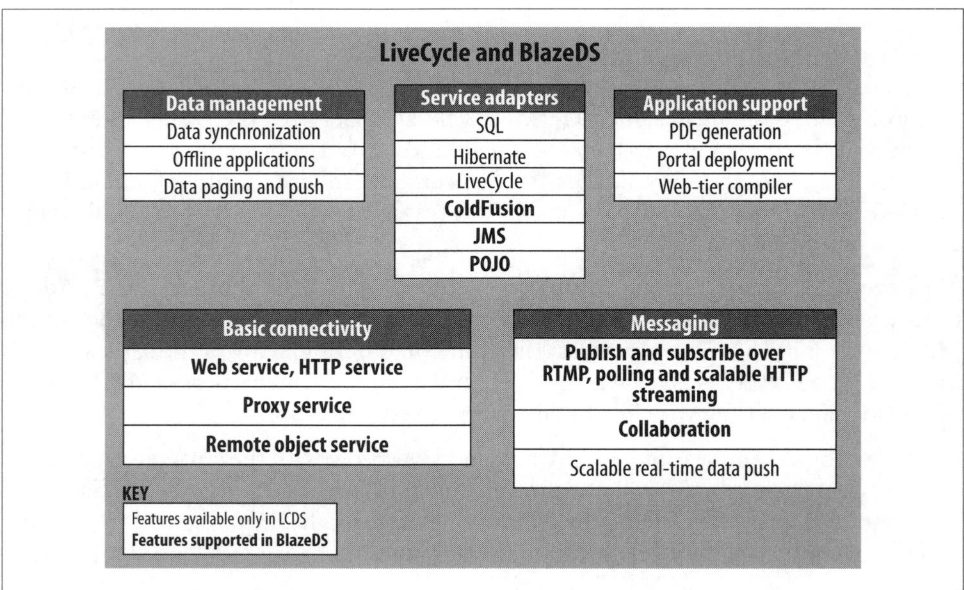

Figure 6-1. Comparing functionality of BlazeDS and LCDS

One limitation of BlazeDS is that its publish/subscribe messaging is implemented over HTTP using long-running connections rather than via RTMP as in LCDS. Under the HTTP approach, the client opens a connection with the server, which allocates a thread that holds this connection on the server. The server thread gets the data and flushes it down to the client but then continues to hold the connection.

You can see the limit right there: because creating each thread has some overhead, the server can hold only a limited number of threads. By default, BlazeDS is configured to hold 10 threads, but it can be increased to several hundred depending on the server being used. Even so, this may not be enough for enterprise-grade applications that need to accommodate thousands of concurrent users.

Real-Time Messaging Protocol (RTMP) is not HTTP-based. It works like a two-way socket channel without having the overhead of AMF, which is built on top of HTTP. One data stream goes from the server to the client, and the other goes in the opposite direction. Because the RTMP solution requires either a dedicated IP address or port, it is not firewall-friendly, which may be a serious drawback for enterprises that are very strict about security. Adobe has announced its plans to open source RTMP.

With a little help, however, BlazeDS can handle this level of traffic, as well as close some of the other gaps between it and LCDS. For example, the section "The Networking Architecture of BlazeDS" on page 277 offers a scalable solution based on the BlazeDS/Jetty server. Also later in this chapter, you'll learn how to enhance BlazeDS to support data synchronization, PDF generation, and scalable real-time data push. In addition to feature support, you'll examine the other piece of the puzzle: increasing the scalability of the AMF protocol in BlazeDS.

Why Is AMF Important?

You may ask, "Why should I bother with AMF instead of using standard HTTP, REST, SOAP, or similar protocols?" The short answer is because the AMF specification is open sourced and publicly available (*http://download.macromedia.com/pub/labs/amf/amf3_spec_121207.pdf*).

The longer answer begins with the fact that AMF is a compact binary format that is used to serialize ActionScript object graphs. An object can include both primitive and complex data types, and the process of serialization turns an object into a sequence of bytes, which contains all required information about the structure of the original object. Because AMF's format is open to all, Adobe as well as third-party developers can implement it in various products to deserialize such pieces of binary data into an object in a different VM (Virtual Machine), which does not have to be Flash Player. For example, both BlazeDS and LCDS implement the AMF protocol to exchange objects between Flash Player and the Java VM. There are third-party implementations of AMF to support data communication between Flash Player and such server-side environments as Python, PHP, .NET, Ruby, and others.

Some of the technical merits of this protocol, when used for the enterprise application, are:

Serialization and deserialization with AMF is fast
: BlazeDS (and LCDS) implementation of AMF is done in C and native to the platform where Flash Player runs. Because of this, AMF has a small memory footprint and is easy on CPU processing. Objects are being created in a single pass—there is no need to parse the data (e.g., XML or strings of characters), which is common for nonnative protocols.

AMF data streams are small and well compressed (in addition to GZip)
: AMF tries to recognize the common types of data and group them by type so that every value doesn't have to carry the information about its type. For example, if there are numeric values that fit in two bytes, AMF won't use four as was required by the variable data type.

AMF supports the native data types and classes
: You can serialize and deserialize any object with complex data types, including the instances of custom classes. Flex uses AMF in such objects as `RemoteObject`, `SharedObject`, `ByteArray`, `LocalConnection`, `SharedObject`, and all messaging operations and any class that implements the `IExternalizable` interface.

Connections between the client and the server are being used much more efficiently
: The connections are more efficient because the AMF implementation in Flex uses automatic batching of the requests and built-in failover policies, providing robustness that does not exist in HTTP or SOAP.

The remainder of the chapter will focus on how you can leverage these merits for your own applications, as well as contrast AMF and the technologies that use it with traditional HTTP approaches.

AMF Performance Comparison

AMF usually consumes half the bandwidth of and outperforms (has a shorter execution time than) other text-based data transfer technologies by 3 to 10 times depending on the amount of data you are bringing to the client. It also usually takes several times less memory compared to other protocols that use untyped objects or XML.

If your application has a server that just sends to the client a couple of hundred bytes once in a while, AMF performance benefits over text protocols are not obvious.

To see for yourself, visit *http://www.jamesward.com/census*, a useful website that enables you to compare the data transfer performance of various protocols. Created by James Ward, a Flex evangelist at Adobe, the test site lets you specify the number of database records you'd like to bring to the client, then graphs the performance times and bandwidth consumed for multiple protocols.

Figure 6-2 shows the results of a test conducted for a medium result set of 5,000 records using out-of-the-box implementations of the technologies with standard GZip compression.

Figure 6-2. James Ward's benchmark site

Visit this website and run some tests on your own. The numbers become even more favorable toward AMF if you run these tests on slow networks and low-end client computers.

The other interesting way to look at performance is to consider what happens to the data when it finally arrives at the client. Because HTTP and SOAP are text-based protocols, they include a parsing phase, which is pretty expensive in terms of time. The RIA needs to operate with native data types, such as numbers, dates, and Booleans. Think about the volume of data conversion that has to be made on the client after the arrival of 5,000 1 KB records.

Steve Souders, a Yahoo! expert in performance tuning of traditional (DHTML) websites, stresses that major improvements can be achieved by minimizing the amount of data processing performed on the client in an HTML page; see *High Performance Web Sites (http://oreilly.com/catalog/9780596529307)* by Steve Souders (O'Reilly). Using the AMF protocol allows you to substantially lower the need for such processing, because the data arrives at the client already strongly typed.

AMF and Client-Side Serialization

AMF is crucial for all types of serialization and communications. All native data serialization is customarily handled by the class `ByteArray`. When serialized, the data type information is marked out by the name included in the metadata tag `RemoteClass`.

Example 6-1 is a small example from the Flash Builder's *NetworkingSamples* project that comes with the book. It includes an application *RegisteredClassvsUnregistered.mxml* and two classes: `RegisteredClass` and `Unregistered`.

Example 6-1. Serialization with and without the RemoteObject meta tag

```
package
{
    [RemoteClass(alias="com.RegisteredClass")]
   public class RegisteredClass{
   }
}

package
{
   public class UnregisteredClass{
   }
}


<?xml version="1.0" encoding="utf-8"?>
<mx:Application xmlns:mx="http://www.adobe.com/2006/mxml"
                                    creationComplete="test()">
<mx:Script>
   <![CDATA[
      import flash.utils.ByteArray

      private function serializeDeserialize(a:Object) : void {
         var ba : ByteArray = new ByteArray();
         ba.writeObject(a);
         ba.position = 0;
         var aa:Object = ba.readObject();
         trace( aa );
      }

      private function test():void {
         serializeDeserialize( new RegisteredClass());
         serializeDeserialize( new UnregisteredClass());
      }
   ]]>
</mx:Script>
</mx:Application>
```

In Example 6-1, the function `serializeDeserialize()` serializes the object passed as an argument into a `ByteArray`, and then reads it back into a variable `aa` of type `Object`. The application makes two calls to this function. During the first call, it passes an object that contains the metadata tag, marking the object with a data type `RegisteredClass`;

the second call passes the object that does not use this metadata tag. Running this program through a debugger displays the following output in the console:

```
[SWF] /NetworkingSamples/NetworkingSamples.swf -
                                        798,429 bytes after decompression
[object RegisteredClass]
[object Object]
```

Annotating a class with the `RemoteClass` metadata tag allows Flash Player to store, send, and restore information in the predictable, strongly typed format. If you need to persist this class, say in AIR disconnected mode, or communicate with another *.swf* locally via the class `LocalConnection`, following the rules of AMF communications is crucial. In the example, `RemoteClass` ensures that during serialization, the information about the class will be preserved.

HTTP Connection Management

To really appreciate the advantages of binary data transfers and a persistent connection to the server, take a step back and consider how web browsers in traditional web applications connect to servers.

For years, web browsers would allow only two connections per domain. Because Flash Player uses the browser's connection for running HTTP requests to the server, it shares the same limitations as all browser-based applications.

The latest versions of Internet Explorer (IE) and Mozilla Firefox increased the default number of simultaneous parallel HTTP requests per domain/window from two to six. It's probably the biggest news in the AJAX world in the last three years. For the current crop of AJAX sites serving real WAN connections it means increasing the load speed and fewer timeouts/reliability issues. By the way, most of the Opera and Safari performance gains over IE and Firefox in the past are attributed to the fact that they allowed and used four connections, ignoring the recommendations of the W3C (which suggested allowing only two connections).

The fact that increasing the number of parallel connections increases network throughput is easy to understand. Today's request/response approach for browser communications is very similar to the village bike concept. Imagine that there are only a couple of bikes that serve the entire village. People ride a bike and come back to give it to the next person in line. People wait for their turns, keeping their fingers crossed that the person in front of them won't get lost in the woods during her ride. If that happens, they need to wait till all hope is gone (i.e., timeout) and the village authorities provide them with a new bike circa 1996.

Pretty often, by the time the new bike arrives it's too late: the person decided to get engaged in a different activity (abandon this site). As the travel destinations become more distant (WAN), people are exposed to real-world troubles of commuting—latency (500 ms for a geostatic satellite network), bandwidth limitations, jitter (errors), unrecoverable losses, etc. Besides that, the users may experience congestion caused by the fact that your ISP decided to make some extra cash by trying to become a TV broadcaster *and* a Voice over Internet Protocol (VoIP) company but lacks the required infrastructure. The applications that worked perfectly on local/fast networks will crumble in every imaginable way.

Obviously, more bikes (browser connections) mean that with some traffic planning you can offer a lot more fun to the bikers (get much better performance and reliability). You might even allocate one bike to a sheriff/firefighter/village doctor so he will provide information on conditions and lost/damaged goods carried by the bikers. You can route important goods in parallel so they will not get lost or damaged that easily.

You can really start utilizing the long-running connection for real data push now. But first, let's go back 10 years and try to figure out how the early adopters of RIAs developed with AJAX survived.

Even though *AJAX* as a term was coined only in 2005, the authors of this book started using the DHTML/`XMLHttpRequest` combo (currently known as AJAX) in the year 2000.

The Hack to Increase a Web Browser's Performance

In the beginning of this century, most of the enterprises we worked with quietly rolled out browser builds/service packs increasing the number of allowed HTTP connections. This was just a hack. For Internet Explorer, the following changes to Windows registry keys would increase the number of the browser connections to 10:

```
HKEY_CURRENT_USER\Software\Microsoft\Windows\CurrentVersion\Internet Settings
MaxConnectionsPer1_0Server    10
MaxConnectionsPerServer       10
```

With Mozilla's Firefox, you has to recompile the source code of the entire browser.

The hack does solve most of the performance and reliability issues for a *short* while. The main reason is that without imposed limits, software increases in size faster than transistor capacity under Moore's Law. And unlike in private networks in enterprises, without a proper "city framework," rampant requests will cause an overall Internet meltdown as the initial rollout of more capable browsers gives them an unfair advantage in terms of bandwidth share.

If a server receives eight connection requests, it'll try to allocate the limited available bandwidth accordingly, and, for instance, Firefox's requests will enjoy better throughput than those of Internet Explorer, which on older and slower networks will cause quality of service (QoS) problems. In other words, this solution has a very real potential to cause more of the same problems it's expected to solve.

Other Ways of Increasing a Web Browser's Performance

Most enterprises have to control QoS of their clients' communications. For example, a company that trades stock has a service level agreement (SLA) with their clients promising to push the new price quotes twice a second. To keep such a promise, the enterprise should create and adopt a number of point-to-point solutions that provide more efficient communication models, which fall into three categories:

HTTP batching and streaming of multiple requests in a single HTTP call and Comet communications
: Comet, a.k.a. reverse AJAX, allows the web server to push data to the web browser, as opposed to a traditional request/response model. AMF performs automatic batching of the requests. If your program executes a loop that generates 50 HTTP requests to the server, AMF will batch them and will send them as one HTTP request.

Imagine that someone wrote a loop in JavaScript that makes an HTTP server request on each iteration. The browser can batch these requests and send, say, 10 requests at a time. This is HTTP batching. In this scenario, the browser would assign a message ID to each request included in the batch, and arriving responses would contain correlation IDs that would allow the browser to find the matching requestors.

Binary components that work with two-directional sockets
: This is the case used in multimedia streaming, where there are two separate channels, and each is used for sending data in one direction: either to or from the server.

Pluggable protocols, which are wrappers for standard protocols
: Say you can develop some custom protocol called HTTPZ, which for the browsers will look like HTTP, but under the hood will use streaming or even a socket-based protocol like RTMP. The browser "believes" that it uses HTTP, the web server receives RTMP, and the translation is done by HTTPZ—every party is happy.

The pluggable protocol option did not become popular, even though it allows moving most of the problems from the browser to the OS level. The batching and streaming options, however, did.

Regular HTTP is based on the request/response model, which has an overhead of establishing a connection (and consequently disconnecting) on each request. In the case of streaming, this connection is opened only once (for more information, see the section "Putting Streaming to Work" on page 274).

HTTP batching and streaming is a combination of a few technologies with a close resemblance to how car traffic is controlled on some highways. There are dedicated lanes for high-occupancy vehicles (HOVs) that move faster during the rush hours. Such

HOV lanes can be compared to the HTTP channels opened for streaming. For example, you can program network communications in such a way that one channel allows only two data pushes per second (a guaranteed QoS), while the other channel will try to push all the data, which may cause network congestion, delays, and queuing.

As an example, the Flex/Flash AMF protocol tries to squeeze out every bit of bandwidth and optimize queuing of the requests in the most efficient way—both on client and server. As a result, your application uses the maximum bandwidth, and request queues are short.

The results of such batching were so good that at Farata Systems, we started recommending AMF to most of our customers (even those that have to use `WebService` or `HTTPService` objects for communication). Using AMF to proxy requests via an AMF-enabled server delivers results from the HTTP servers more efficiently.

> If a client request uses a specific destination on a proxy server, this destination can be configured to use an AMF channel, even if an `HTTPService` object has been used as a means of communications.

With AMF, the data gets loaded faster than with nonbatched requests/responses. And it plays nicely with the typical infrastructures that use firewalls as it piggybacks on the existing browser HTTP requests.

However, for critical applications built on plain infrastructures a problem remains: there is no QoS provided by the HTTP protocol, which may become a showstopper. For example, think of a financial application that sends real-time price quotes to its users. The server keeps sending messages, regardless of the current throughput of the network, which in the case of network congestion will be causing problems with queue overruns or lost packages.

Binary *always on* (re)connected socket protocols are a more logical and efficient solution. Unlike the request/response model, a typical socket connection is like a two-way highway, with data moving in opposite directions independently. But before we fully depart into the Communications 2.0 world, let's make sure that you understand how HTTP is shaping up these days.

The disconnected model of HTTP 1.0 was not practical. The overhead of connecting/disconnecting for each request was not tolerable, and for the last eight years we have not seen a single web browser using it. It has been completely replaced by HTTP 1.1—the protocol that keeps connections open beyond request/response so the next communications with the server happen faster. Under the hood, there are two-way sockets that stay open—but browsers diligently follow the old model. They don't create bidirectional pipe-like connections, as in `flash.net.NetConnection`.

As web browsers started to host business applications, the need to process the real-time data forced people to look into solutions better than polling, and a few server-side push solutions were discovered. Although there were differences in implementations, the main theme remained the same—the server would get requests and hold them for a long time, flushing packages down when it became available.

The packages would reach the browser to be interpreted either by programs upon arrival or executed in the iFrame (if packaged as `<script/>` sections of DHTML). The important part was that people started to see that a server-driven model was valid, and that it was a better fit for some applications. The servers started controlling the clients.

Currently, there are two approaches to breaking the request/response paradigm: the Comet model and the model offered by the creators of the Jetty application server.

When we started writing this book, the draft of the Java Servlet 3.0 specification (JSR-315) was based on asynchronous servlets implemented in the Jetty Servlet container. Then, the public review of JSR-315 was drastically changed. You can read more on the subject in the post titled "JSR-315: JSP Failings (*http://blogs.webtide.com/gregw/entry/servlet_3_0_public_review*)."

What Is Comet?

A number of open source and commercial implementations of Comet exist in Java and Python. They can be very different, capitalizing on nonblocking I/O, using optimized threads, or offering more efficient native sockets support.

A servlet container in Jetty works in a half-duplex mode: it opens a dedicated streaming connection for flushing the data to the client, but also allows request/responses.

The Comet model is a full duplex that uses a two-way socket implementation (like in Apache Tomcat), which extends a conventional request/response model with events that are being sent on an established HTTP connection.

With Comet, the idea is that the server provides a second model for the requests handler in addition to the conventional one. There is a dedicated open connection that receives events related to the requests. If you run a Java servlet, it will receive additional events from the server: `connect`, `read`, `error`, and `disconnect`:

`connect` *and* `disconnect`
: Define the life span of the connection object available for communications.

`error`
: Notifies the servlet of the low-level errors in the transmission protocol.

`read`
: Dispatched when there is a request coming from the client; allows the server to read and process it. The server keeps connection and response objects and writes (flushes) the information to the client as needed.

Adding an event model to the server side brings symmetry to the client/server programming model and greatly simplifies the asynchronous programming. Unfortunately, existing implementations of this model are not overly reliable.

If you want to use the two-way socket model, you will need to write some custom code using the Flash `NetConnection` object to stream the data from the client to the server, too.

Consider how this model is different for fine-grained requests common in today's AJAX applications. Imagine that you're in a coffee shop with a lousy WiFi connection sporting 1-second latency for a typical eBay response implemented as a web device, watching 30 items.

With the current browser settings (two connections per domain), it would take you 15 seconds to refresh all 30 items. With six allowed browser connections, this time is reduced to five seconds, but will require a more powerful infrastructure on the server side.

With the Comet-type requests, you can send all 30 requests without waiting for a single response (the same will be done with AMF HTTP batching) and will receive all 30 responses asynchronously. Meanwhile, with HTTP batching, you would get all 30 responses at once, and need some kind of sorting adapters on both sides to distribute batch members to the proper responders.

Putting Streaming to Work

Imagine a small village by the river. There is one boat, and whoever needs to go to the other bank to buy some food takes this boat. No one in the village can go to the other bank until the boat's back. This is in some sense similar to the HTTP request/response model of communication.

At some point, people who lived in the same village built a two-lane bridge over this river. Each lane allows walking in one direction. All of a sudden you see that lots of people are moving in both directions at the same time. The number of trips to the other riverbank is a lot higher now. Yes, people carrying the shopping bags may go slower, but they are all moving at the same time. And each trip is faster, too; there is no need to embark/disembark from the boat (connect/disconnect). This is streaming.

RTMP implementation offers two-lane traffic (a two-directional socket) and is a lot more efficient than the request/response model. Each connected computer just sends the data in one direction to a dedicated socket, which allows you to measure and estimate delivery metrics in each direction. RTMP is an open protocol available at *http://www.adobe.com/devnet/rtmp/*.

In multimedia applications, having an uninterrupted data delivery is a must, and the request/response model doesn't work here. When you go to *http://www.youtube.com*, you expect to start watching the video immediately, without waiting until the entire file is downloaded to the client. And after seeing the first frames of the video, you'd like to have the rest in a smooth, uninterrupted mode, and this type of playback is supported by buffering of the stream data.

Integrating Multimedia Solutions

For a long time, Flash Player was the de facto standard tool in delivering multimedia—especially video. These capabilities are based on its `NetConnection` object and are embedded in a number of classes, including `Camera`, `Microphone`, and `Video`.

`NetConnection` communicates with the server by establishing a full duplex open connection—the two-way socket—and both the server and the client can initiate the conversation. This is a far simpler programming model, and provides improved performance for intensive two-way communications.

A standard solution is to separate the media portion into an instance (or a farm) of the Flash Media Server. However, some applications might have different licensing and integration requirements. Other alternatives include Red5, an open source server, and Wowza, a commercial Java media server. The advantages of these drop-in servers is the transparency in integration of streaming with the other parts of the application.

With the release of Flash 10, new sound capabilities with high-quality voice codecs and audio capabilities open up a whole new world of human interaction. But the most important feature driving new types of applications will be based on peer-to-peer (P2P) support and User Datagram Protocol (UDP) communications built into Flash Player 10.

Unlike traditional web applications, they require very little infrastructure and bandwidth as they use clients' resources. These applications enable VoIP, teleconferencing, screen sharing, and resource polling of applications on the widest deployment platform.

The users of the business Flex applications want to have the same experience, too. In this case, the stream consists of the Flex code and the data, so it's important to make the right decision about the amount of code that will have to be downloaded to the user's computer.

Consider a few types of web applications that benefit from breaking free from a traditional request/response model:

Applications built on the publish/subscribe model or the server-side push
: In this scenario, the data is being sent to the client as soon as it becomes available on the server. Typical examples of such applications are chat rooms, stock market data feeds, and delivering videos to users.

Online transaction processing, analytical applications, and distributed services that need to extend the request/response model

For example, a call center application has to broadcast the data modifications done by one clerk to another to ensure that the second doesn't work on the stale data. For distributed request/response services, you can't guarantee the response time, because the response may sit on the server just because the client has a very limited set of available connection objects, in which case your application would stall.

Applications that need to force the execution of the code on the client

Some applications benefit from the server-side components being able to directly call methods on the objects that exist on the client side in Flash Player. Typical cases are remote support and administration or workflow systems in which the server needs to force the client to move to a new node of the workflow. BlazeDS needs to be enhanced to support servers that can call clients.

Figure 6-3 illustrates three use cases of enterprise RIA:

Subscribe and publish

You send the data using BlazeDS and improve the scalability of the application. You'll see this demonstrated with the Jetty server scenario in the following section.

Remoting and SOA

A remote object takes care of publishing and subscribing, keeps track of the correlation IDs of the messages received from the clients, and pushes the data to the clients. In the service-oriented architecture (SOA) world, the data returned by the service may change over time, and you can't control it. In this model, you can't control the response time, either. SOA is a good use case for introducing data push to a rich client.

Remote control

You need to push the software or data updates to the client.

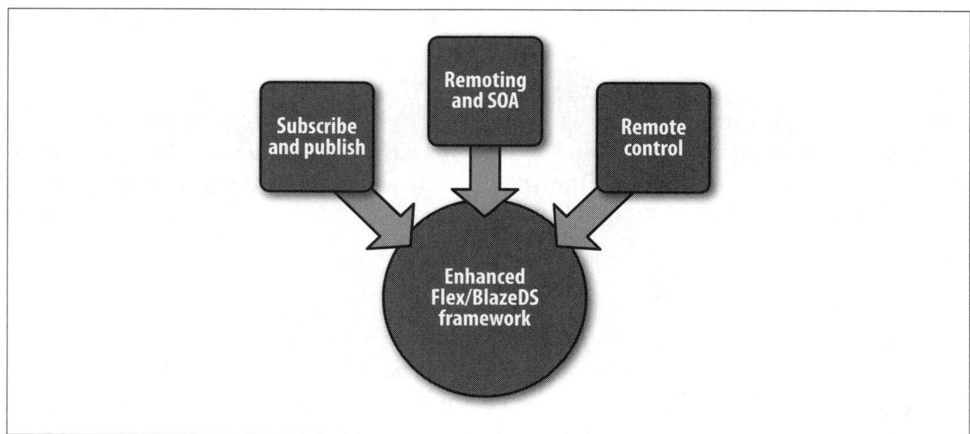

Figure 6-3. Use cases for streaming

To start building streaming solutions, you need to extend BlazeDS to utilize modern JEE technologies. We'll use asynchronous servlets offered by the Jetty server.

JEE stands for Java Enterprise Edition. It was formerly knows as J2EE.

The Networking Architecture of BlazeDS

BlazeDS provides a clean separation of the networking layer (a servlet container) from the actual implementation of server-side services used by Flex clients. To recap what you learned in Chapter 5, the elements that are communicating on the servlet container level and delivering messages to and from services are called *endpoints*. If you open the configuration file *services-config.xml* that comes with BlazeDS, you'll find declarations of several communication channels, for example:

```
<channel-definition id="my-amf" class="mx.messaging.channels.AMFChannel">
 <endpoint
url="http://{server.name}:{server.port}/{context.root}/messagebroker/amf"
class="flex.messaging.endpoints.AMFEndpoint"/>
</channel-definition>
```

By adding new or extending existing endpoints, you can add new or extend existing protocols or even expose the low-level networking in the way required by your application. Figure 6-4 depicts the business part of the application as a service that can be accessed via an endpoint of the protocol being used (a BlazeDS implementation of AMF, in our example). Both your application and BlazeDS live inside the servlet container.

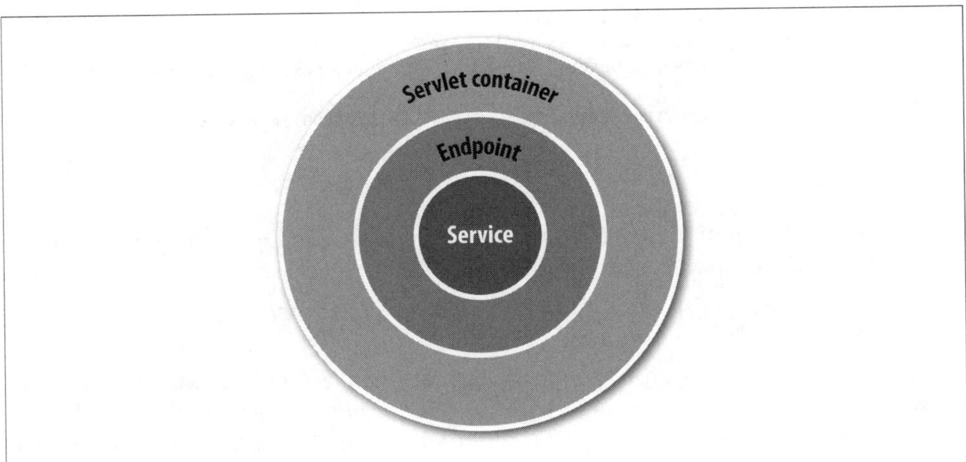

Figure 6-4. Server-side layers

The following sections demonstrate how Farata Systems extended BlazeDS to work with Java nonblocking I/O (NIO) and continuations (suspend/resume mode) offered by the Jetty API.

Setting Up a BlazeDS Sample Application on Jetty

In this exercise, you'll need to use Jetty, as it's the only open source implementation of the asynchronous servlets based on the suspend/resume mode at the time of this writing.

To set up a BlazeDS sample application with Jetty, follow these three steps:

1. Download and install Jetty from *http://dist.codehaus.org/jetty/* according to its installation instructions. The steps assume that you'll install it into the folder */jetty*, but you can use any other folder; just modify the configuration files accordingly.
2. Download the BlazeDS turnkey distribution file from *http://opensource.adobe.com/wiki/display/blazeds/Release+Builds*. Unzip it to a */samples* folder. Locate the file *samples.war* there and unzip it into the */samples* folder under *jetty/webapps-plus/*. Start the *sampledb* database by executing the script provided with this turnkey distro for your OS—for example, */samples/sampledb/startdb.sh*.
3. Uncomment the following section in the file */jetty/etc/jetty-plus.xml* to automatically include all applications located in the folder *webapps-plus*:

```
<Call name="addLifeCycle">
<Arg>
<New class="org.mortbay.jetty.deployer.WebAppDeployer">
    <Set name="contexts"><Ref id="Contexts"/></Set>
    <Set name="webAppDir"><SystemProperty name="jetty.home"
               default="."/>/webapps-plus</Set>
    <Set name="parentLoaderPriority">false</Set>
    <Set name="extract">true</Set>
    <Set name="allowDuplicates">false</Set>
    <Set name="defaultsDescriptor"><SystemProperty name="jetty.home"
    default="."/>/etc/webdefault.xml</Set>
    <Set name="configurationClasses"><Ref id="plusConfig"/></Set>
</New>
</Arg>
</Call>
```

Now you can start Jetty by entering the following command at the prompt (in Windows, replace the `etc/` with another folder):

```
java -DOPTIONS=plus,jsp,ssl -jar start.jar etc/jetty.xml etc/jetty-ssl.xml
etc/jetty-plus.xml
```

Once the server starts, open *http://localhost:8080/samples/* in your web browser and make sure that both the Traders Desktop (*http://localhost:8080/samples/#traderdesktop*) and the Chat sample (*http://localhost:8080/samples/testdrive-chat/index.html*) applications that come with BlazeDS work.

Setting BlazeDS Messaging to Use the Jetty NIO API

Add the NIO messaging endpoint to the BlazeDS configuration:

1. Get the file *http://myflex.org/books/entflex/nioblaze.jar* and copy it into the application's folder, */jetty/webapps-plus/samples/WEB-INF/lib*. This file is also available with this book's samples.
2. Open */jetty/webapps-plus/samples/WEB-INF/flex/services-config.xml* and comment out this section:

```
<!--channel-definition id="my-streaming-amf"
class="mx.messaging.channel.StreamingAMFChannel">
<endpoint
   url="http://{server.name}:{server.port}/{context.root}/messagebroker/
        streamingamf"
   class="flex.messaging.endpoints.StreamingAmfEndpoint"/>
</channel-definition-->
```

3. Add the following section there instead (please note that we are replacing the standard `StreamingAmfEndpoint` with our own `NioAmfEndpoint`):

```
<channel-definition id="my-streaming-amf"
   class="mx.messaging.channel.StreamingAMFChannel">
<endpoint
   url="http://{server.name}:{server.port}/{context.root}/messagebroker/
        streamingamf"
   class="com.farata.nioblaze.messaging.endpoints.NioAmfEndpoint"/>
</channel-definition>
```

4. Restart Jetty. You should be able to run the same Trader Desktop or Chat application, only this time you can support far more concurrent users, and shortly you'll see why.

NIO Performance Test

Jetty itself is powerful enough to support 20,000 connected users. The benchmark tests were performed on a standard Amazon EC2 virtual server, and you can find details about these tests at the site *http://cometdaily.com/2008/01/07/20000-reasons-that-comet-scales/*.

When infused with BlazeDS, however, can Jetty still support thousands of users? We recently put this question to the test at Farata Systems.

The Theory

BlazeDS was offered as a free version of LCDS remoting that also promised scaled-down support of a modest number of concurrent users for data push.

But enterprise IT shops wanted the best of both worlds: an inexpensive but scalable solution. The great part about LCDS and BlazeDS is that their code base is extendable and you can teach these old dogs new tricks. The problem is that their original code is targeting only conventional Java Servlet containers, and that the performance/scalability of BlazeDS also depends on the number of concurrent connections supported by the hosting server, such as Tomcat, JBoss, WebSphere, and so on.

Farata Systems architects started experiments in this area when the prerelease of Jetty 7 was announced (*http://www.mortbay.org/jetty/*).

BlazeDS runs in a servlet container, which maintains a thread pool. A thread is given to a client request and is returned back to the reusable pool after the client has been served. When the client uses a so-called long-running connection, the thread becomes locked by that client until it finishes the request. So the number of the concurrent subscribers in BlazeDS depends on the number of threads that a particular servlet container can hold simultaneously.

Though the source code of BlazeDS has 10 as a default number of simultaneous connections, it can be increased to several hundred, and the actual number depends on the server's threading configuration, CPU, and the size of its Java Virtual Machine (JVM) heap memory. This number can also be affected by the number of messages processed by the server in the unit of time as well as the size of the messages.

Nonblocking I/O combined with Jetty's suspend/resume processing mode allows you to write code that is not tied to available server threads. The servlet container sends a request for execution and puts it in a suspended mode, releasing the thread for other requests. When the result comes back, it resumes the processing of the request, efficiently recycling a smaller number of threads. Because of that, the number of streaming connections can be increased to thousands.

The first goal was to create a module for BlazeDS to support Jetty's suspend/resume mode with the messaging based on AMF streaming. Additional endpoints (components responsible for binding actual application services with the servlet container) were created based on the BlazeDS open source implementation.

Three small changes are required to add NIO endpoints to a standard BlazeDS (or LCDS for that matter) application in the standard Jetty installation:

1. Add Farata's *nioblazeds.jar* to Jetty's *lib* folder.
2. Modify the *services-config.xml* file of BlazeDS to change the standard thread-based endpoint for AMF streaming with Farata's `NioAmfEndpoint`, which supports Jetty's API.
3. Increase the parameter of Jetty's number of open file handlers based on the number of concurrent user requests that you are planning to process.

The Trader Desktop, a sample application that comes with BlazeDS, was successfully deployed under BlazeDS/Jetty and tested without any changes in enhanced endpoints.

The source code of this solution is available in the CVS repository of the Clear Toolkit framework in the NIOBlaze package, available at *http://cleartoolkit.cvs.sourceforge.net/viewvc/cleartoolkit/*.

The next step was to stress-test this application using one of the commercial testing software suites that supports the AMF protocol. Farata engineers teamed up with a company called Neotys (*http://neotys.com*), the creator of a robust stress-testing product called NeoLoad that allows testers to emulate the workload of tens of thousands of users hitting a server via both the HTTP and AMF protocols.

This test was recorded, and you can watch a short screencast that emulates 5,000 users working with the Trader Desktop over a five-minute period. To view it, go to *http://myflex.org/demos/JettyBlazeDS/JettyBlazeDSloadTest.html*. One screen is shown in Figure 6-5.

The test starts with 200 users ramping up at the rate of 500 users per 10 seconds.

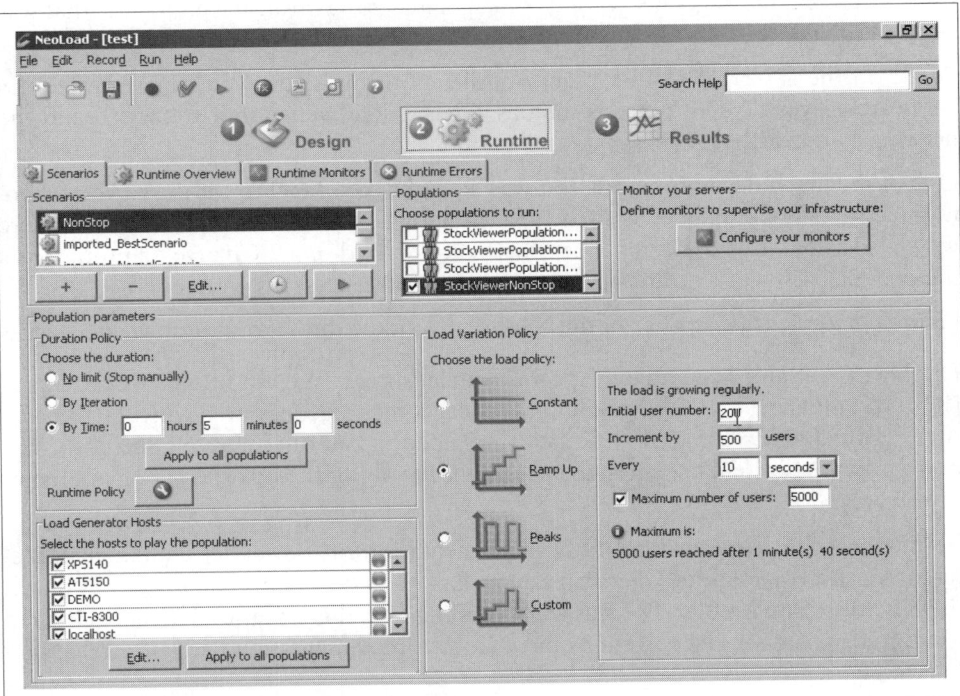

Figure 6-5. Configuring performance tests with NeoLoad

In this demo, the server-side feed sends the messages about the latest stock prices to the Flex subscribers. After that, you'll be monitoring this process using ds-console, which is yet another sample application that comes with BlazeDS.

First, the monitor will show just one client with a small number of messages, and the number of maximum streaming clients is set to 65,535.

Next, NeoLoad creates a large number of users. This test uses five machines to emulate the load. The push count is the number of messages sent by the server. The server runs on an eight-CPU machine. Watch the number of allocated threads and the number of users—the number of threads is several times lower than the number of users at any given time. Please note that even when the number of users grows, the number of threads doesn't. These processes are not expensive from the perspective of either the memory or the CPU utilization.

In this test, the system was purposely restricted by introducing throttling in the *Feed.java* file. During this 5-minute test, the server pushed about 2.1 million messages. Because during the first 3 minutes (180 seconds) of the test NeoLoad was ramping up the number of users until it reached 5,000, you should count this time as half of this amount, or 90 seconds. Adding another 2 minutes (after the first 3) brings the adjusted test time to 210 seconds, or 10,000 messages per second. This means that each of 5,000 users received 2 messages per second, which matches the throttling parameter that was set in *Feed.java* (400 ms of sleep time between messages broadcast).

Based on the server CPU and memory utilization this setup won't have difficulties supporting over 12,000 users, as long as external load generators are added and the network bandwidth is increased.

One of the machines used in this test was an eight-core MacPro for the server, where four of the cores were shared with the VM emulating one of the client's machines. There were also two 3 Ghz desktops, one MacBook Pro, and one 2 Ghz Dell laptop; that's the one that will work really hard trying to parse 300 messages per second.

Figure 6-6 depicts a snapshot of the NeoLoad window during our performance test.

Farata ran the same test with an Apache Tomcat server using traditional thread-based I/O and standard BlazeDS long polling. Tomcat comes preconfigured with 250 threads. After gradually increasing this number, the same test can run for about 800 users, but pretty soon the system becomes unstable, running out of threads and giving out memory errors.

Tomcat also has experimental NIO implementation of the servlet container implementing Comet techniques. Farata Systems has created an endpoint adapter to utilize the NIO of Jetty with BlazeDS. But while holding high the promises of a more efficient full-duplex protocol, the current Tomcat Comet implementation had some reliability issues.

The screencast should be treated as a feasibility study and technical comment, and not as a benchmark of any sort, as the implementation still has a lot of room for improvement. More tests are required for a proper scalability benchmark.

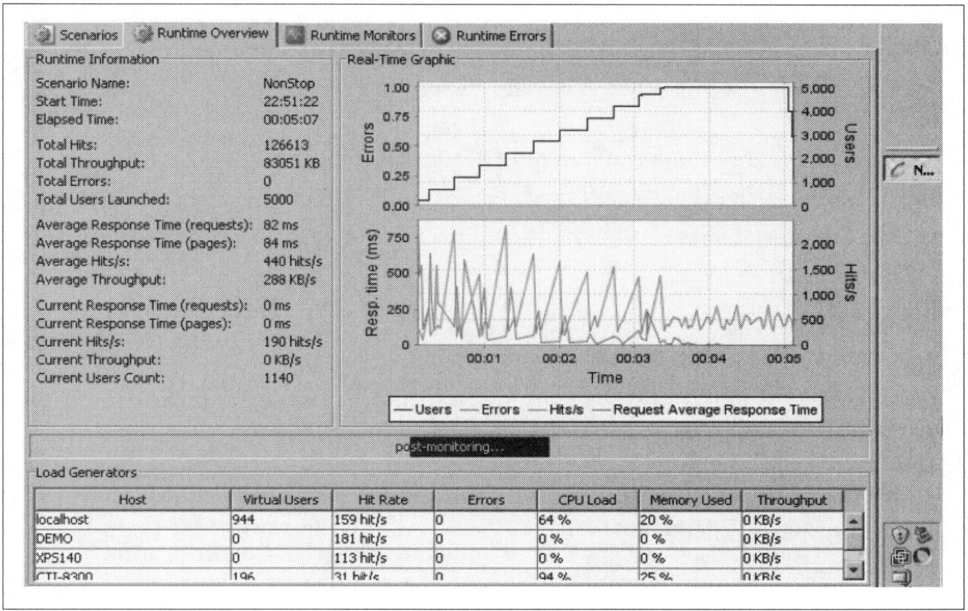

Figure 6-6. Monitoring performance tests with NeoLoad

Based on these results, you may consider using open source BlazeDS in the most demanding enterprise Flex applications. If you are looking for a no-cost extensible solution that works in a standard web environment with corporate firewalls and requires session management, properly tuned BlazeDS under a Jetty server becomes a good scalable solution for your next RIA.

In the summer of 2009, Jetty started offering its own asynchronous implementation of BlazeDS that utilizes Jetty 7 continuations. You can read about it at a blog post titled, "Asynchronous BlazeDS Polling with Jetty 7 Continuations (*http://blogs.webtide.com/athena/entry/asynchronous_blazeds_polling_with_jetty*)."

Both LCDS and BlazeDS can be treated as a very good transport solution between Flash Player on the client side and Java application server on the server side. But the main focus of RIA architects should remain the same—how to minimize the amount of coding of application programmers that need to communicate with the server, which will be the subject of the next section.

Data Access Automation

Once the transport technology has been selected, you need to try to remove the complexity of the data access and persistence layer. The Data Management Services that come with LCDS provide an excellent model for automation of this task. But you can develop your own framework based on the open source products, and in the following sections, you'll learn how to re-create all the necessary components for a data persistence framework.

To offer functionality similar to that of LCDS in our framework, we need to create the following data management components:

- Data transfer objects
- `ChangeObject`
- `Assembler`
- A change-tracking collection
- A destination-aware collection

In the following sections, we'll offer you Farata Systems' version of such components. If you like them, get their source code in the CVS repository at SourceForge (*http://cleartoolkit.cvs.sourceforge.net/cleartoolkit/*) and use them as you see fit. We also encourage you to enhance them and make them available for others in the same code repository.

Data Transfer Objects

Using data transfer objects (DTOs) is very important for architecting automated updates and synchronization. In Flex/Java RIA, there are at least two parties that need to have an "exchange currency": ActionScript and Java. Each of these parties has their own contracts on how to support the data persistence. Let's concentrate on the ActionScript part first.

In the Café Townsend sample, the data objects responsible for the exchange between Java and ActionScript are *EmployeDTO.java* and *EmployeeDTO.as* (see a fragment of *EmployeeDTO.as* in Example 6-2). The Java side sends instances of `EmployeDTO` objects, which are automatically re-created as their ActionScript peers on the frontend.

Example 6-2. Employee.DTO.as

```
/* Generated by Clear Data Builder (ActionScriptDTO_IManaged.xsl) */
package com.farata.datasource.dto
{
    import flash.events.EventDispatcher;
    import flash.utils.Dictionary;
    import flash.utils.ByteArray;
    import mx.events.PropertyChangeEvent;
    import mx.core.IUID;
    import mx.utils.UIDUtil;

    [RemoteClass(alias="com.farata.datasource.dto.EmployeeDTO")]
    [Bindable(event="propertyChange")]
    public dynamic class EmployeeDTO extends EventDispatcher //implements IManaged
```

```
{
        // Internals
        public var _nulls:String;

        // Properties
    private var _EMP_ID : Number;
    private var _MANAGER_ID : Number;
    ...
        public function get EMP_ID() : Number{
                return _EMP_ID;
        }
        public function set EMP_ID( value : Number ):void{
                var oldValue:Object = this._EMP_ID;
                if (oldValue !== value)   {
                        this._EMP_ID = value;
                        dispatchUpdateEvent("EMP_ID", oldValue, value);
                }
        }

        public function get MANAGER_ID() : Number{
                return _MANAGER_ID;
        }
        public function set MANAGER_ID( value : Number ):void{
                var oldValue:Object = this._MANAGER_ID;
                if (oldValue !== value)   {
                        this._MANAGER_ID = value;
                        dispatchUpdateEvent("MANAGER_ID", oldValue, value);
                }
        }


        public function get properties():Dictionary {
                var properties:Dictionary = new Dictionary();
                properties["EMP_ID"] = _EMP_ID;
                properties["MANAGER_ID"] = _MANAGER_ID;

                    return properties;
            }

        public function set properties(properties:Dictionary):void {

         _EMP_ID = properties["EMP_ID"];
         _MANAGER_ID = properties["MANAGER_ID"];
         ...
        }

        private var _uid:String;
        public function get uid():String
        {
                return _uid;
        }
        public function set uid(value:String):void
        {
                _uid = value;
        }
```

```
        public function EmployeeDTO() {
                _uid = UIDUtil.createUID();
        }

        public function newInstance() : * { return new EmployeeDTO();}

        private function dispatchUpdateEvent(propertyName:String,
                                      oldValue:Object, value:Object):void {
            dispatchEvent(
                PropertyChangeEvent.createUpdateEvent(this, propertyName,
                                               oldValue, value)
            );
        }

        public function clone(): EmployeeDTO {
            var x:EmployeeDTO = new com.farata.datasource.dto.EmployeeDTO();
            x.properties = this.properties;
            return x;
        }
    }
}
```

The class starts with a [RemoteClass] metadata tag that instructs the compiler that this class should be marshaled and re-created as its peer **com.farata.datasource.dto.EmployeeDTO** on the server side.

This class is an event dispatcher and any changes to its members will result in the update event, which allows you to perform easy tracking of its properties' changes by dispatching appropriate events. This feature is also important for the UI updates if the DTOs are bound to UI controls, such as a DataGrid.

Note that all the properties in this class are getter/setter pairs: they can't remain public variables, because we want the dispatchUpdateEvent() method to be called every time the variable's value is being changed.

In addition to the functional properties like EMP_ID and EMP_FNAME, the class also contains a setter and getter for the uid property; this qualifies the class as an implementer of the IUID interface. Existence of a uid property allows easy indexing and searching of records on the client.

However, implementing uid as a primary key on the server side is crucial in order to ensure synchronization and uniqueness of updates. Usually uid represents the primary key from a database table. The other function often required by automatic persistence algorithms is getChangedPropertyNames(), in order to teach DTO to mark updated properties (Example 6-3).

Example 6-3. EmployeeDTO.java

```
package com.farata.datasource.dto;
import java.io.Serializable;
import com.farata.remoting.ChangeSupport;
```

```
import java.util.*;
import flex.messaging.util.UUIDUtils;

public class EmployeeDTO implements Serializable, ChangeSupport {

 private static final long serialVersionUID = 1L;
 public String _nulls; // internals
 public long EMP_ID;
 public long MANAGER_ID;
 ...
 public Map getProperties() {
 HashMap map =  new HashMap();
 map.put("EMP_ID", new Long(EMP_ID));
 map.put("MANAGER_ID", new Long(MANAGER_ID));
...
 return map;
}

// Alias names is used by code generator of CDB in the situations
// if select with aliases is used, i.e.
// SELECT from A,B  a.customer cust1, b.customer cust2

// In this case plain names on the result set would be cust1 and cust2,
// which would complicate generation of the UPDATE statement.
// If you don't use code generators, there is no need to add aliasMap
// to your DTOs
public static HashMap aliasMap =  new HashMap();

public String getUnaliasedName(String name) {
 String result = (String) aliasMap.get(name);
 if (result==null)
  result = name;

return result;
}

public String[] getChangedPropertyNames(Object o) {
 Vector  v =  new Vector();
 EmployeeDTO old = (EmployeeDTO)o;
 if (EMP_ID != old.EMP_ID)
     v.add(getUnaliasedName("EMP_ID"));

 if (MANAGER_ID != old.MANAGER_ID)
     v.add(getUnaliasedName("MANAGER_ID"));
 ...
 String [] _sa = new String[v.size()];
 return (String[])v.toArray(_sa);
}
}
```

To better understand how changes are kept, take a look at the internals of the `ChangeObject` class, which stores all modifications performed on the DTO. It travels between the client and the server.

ChangeObject

ChangeObject is a special DTO that is used to propagate the changes between the server and the client. The ChangeObject class exists in the Data Management Services of LCDS, and is shown in Example 6-4. On the client side, it is just a simple storage container for original and new versions of a record that is undergoing some changes. For example, if the user changes some data in a DataGrid row, the instance of the ChangeObject will be created, and the previous version of the DTO that represents this row will be stored along with the new one.

Example 6-4. ChangeObject.as

```
package  com.farata.remoting {
   [RemoteClass(alias="com.farata.remoting.ChangeObjectImpl")]
   public class ChangeObject {

      public var state:int;
      public var newVersion:Object = null;
      public var previousVersion:Object = null;
      public var error:String = "";
      public var changedPropertyNames:Array= null;

      public static const UPDATE:int=2;
      public static const DELETE:int=3;
      public static const CREATE:int=1;

       public function ChangeObject(state:int=0,
             newVersion:Object=null, previousVersion:Object = null) {
          this.state = state;
          this.newVersion = newVersion;
          this.previousVersion = previousVersion;
       }

       public function isCreate():Boolean {
          return state==ChangeObject.CREATE;
       }
       public function isUpdate():Boolean {
          return state==ChangeObject.UPDATE;
       }
       public function isDelete():Boolean {
          return state==ChangeObject.DELETE;
       }
   }
}
```

As you can see, every changed record can be in a DELETE, UPDATE, or CREATE state. The original version of the object is stored in the previousVersion property and the current one is in the newVersion. That turns the ChangeObject into a lightweight implementation of the Assembler pattern, which offers a simple API to process all the data changes in a standard way, similar to what's done in the Data Management Services that come with LCDS.

The Java counterpart of the ChangeObject (Example 6-5) should have few extra convenience generic methods. All specifics are implemented in a standard way in the EmployeeDTO.

Example 6-5. ChangeObjectImpl.java

```
Package com.theriabook.remoting;
import java.util.*;
public class ChangeObjectImpl {
   public void fail() {
      state = 100;
   }
   public void fail(String desc) {
      // TODO Auto-generated method stub
      fail();
        error = desc;
   }
   public String[] getChangedPropertyNames() {
      // TODO Auto-generated method stub
      changedNames = newVersion.getChangedPropertyNames(previousVersion);
      return changedNames;
   }
    public Map getChangedValues()
    {
       if ((newVersion==null) || (previousVersion==null)) return null;
        if(changedValues == null)
        {
            if(changedNames == null)
               changedNames = getChangedPropertyNames();
            if (newMap == null)
               newMap = newVersion.getProperties();
            changedValues = new HashMap();
            for(int i = 0; i < changedNames.length; i++)
            {
                String field = changedNames[i];
                changedValues.put(field, newMap.get( field));
            }
      }
         return Collections.unmodifiableMap(changedValues);
    }
   public Object getPreviousValue(String field) {
      if (previousMap == null)
         previousMap = previousVersion.getProperties();
      return previousMap.get( field );
   }
   public boolean isCreate() {
      return state == 1;
   }
   public boolean isDelete() {
      return state == 3;
   }
   public boolean isUpdate() {
      return state == 2;
   }
 public void setChangedPropertyNames(String [] columns)
```

```
    {
       changedNames = columns;
       changedValues = null;
    }
public void setError(String s) {
       error = s;
    }
   public void setNewVersion(Object nv) {
      newVersion = (ChangeSupport)nv;
        changedValues = null;
   }
   public void setPreviousVersion(Object o) {
      previousVersion = (ChangeSupport)o;
   }
   public void setState(int s) {
      state = s;
   }

//---------------------- E X T E N S I O N S-------------------------
   public int state = 0;
   public ChangeSupport newVersion = null;
   public ChangeSupport previousVersion = null;
   public String error ="";

   protected Map newMap = null;
   protected Map previousMap = null;
   protected String[] changedNames = null;
   protected Map changedValues = null;
}
```

Assembler and DAO Classes

In Core J2EE Patterns, the Transfer Object Assembler means a class that can build DTOs from different data sources (see *http://java.sun.com/blueprints/corej2eepatterns/Patterns/TransferObjectAssembler.html*). In Flex/Java RIA, the `Assembler` class would hide from the Flex client actual data sources used for data retrieval. For example, it can expose the method `getEmployees()` for retrieval of the `EmployeeDTO` objects that are actually retrieved from more than one data source.

For simplicity, the method `getEmployees()` shown in Example 6-6 delegates the processing to a single Data Access Object (DAO), but this does not have to be the case, and the data required for population of the list of `EmployeeDTOs` can be coming from several data sources.

Similarly, for data updates the client calls the `sync()` method without knowing the specifics; the DAO class or classes take care of the data persistence.

In the example framework, you'll build an `Assembler` class similar to what Adobe recommends creating in the case of using LCDS. The instances of `ChangeObject` are used for communication between Flex and the Java `Assembler` class, which in turn will use them for communication with DAO classes.

The Assembler pattern cleanly separates the generic `Assembler`'s APIs from specifics of the DAO implementation.

Example 6-6. EmployeeAssembler.java

```
package com.farata.datasource;

import java.util.*;

public final class EmployeeAssembler{
        public EmployeeAssembler(){
        }

        public  List getEmployees() throws Exception{
                return new EmployeeDAO().getEmployees();
        }

        public final List getEmployees_sync(List items){
                return new EmployeeDAO().getEmployees_sync(items);
        }
}
```

The two main entry points (data retrieval and updates) will show you how easy it is to build a DAO adapter.

First, you need to separate the task into the DAO and Assembler layers by introducing methods with *fill* (retrieve) and *sync* (update) functionality. The complete source code of the `EmployeeDAO` class is included in the code samples accompanying this book, and the relevant fragments from this class follow in Example 6-7.

Example 6-7. Fill and sync fragment from EmployeeDAO.java

```
package com.farata.datasource;
import java.sql.*;
import java.util.*;
import flex.data.*;
import javax.naming.Context;
import javax.naming.InitialContext;
import javax.transaction.*;
import com.farata.daoflex.*;

public final class EmployeeDAO extends Employee {

   public final List getEmployees_sync(List items)    {
      Coonection conn = null;
      try  {
         conn = JDBCConnection.getConnection("jdbc/test");
         ChangeObject co = null;
         for (int state=3;  state > 0; state--) { //DELETE, UPDATE, CREATE
              Iterator iterator = items.iterator();
                 while (iterator.hasNext()) {   // Proceed to all updates next
                      co = (ChangeObject)iterator.next();
                      if(co.state == state && co.isUpdate())
                          doUpdate_getEmployees(conn, co);
```

```
                if(co.state == state && co.isDelete())
                           doDelete_getEmployees(conn, co);
                if(co.state == state && co.isCreate())
                           doCreate_getEmployees(conn, co);
             }
          }
      } catch(DataSyncException dse) {
               dse.printStackTrace();
               throw dse;
      } catch(Throwable te) {
             te.printStackTrace();
             throw new DAOException(te.getMessage(), te);
      } finally {
         JDBCConnection.releaseConnection(conn);
      }
         return items;
   }
  public final List /*com.farata.datasource.dto.EmployeeDTO[]*/
                                               getEmployees_fill() {

        String sql = "select * from employee    where dept_id=100";
        ArrayList list = new ArrayList();
        ResultSet rs = null;
        PreparedStatement stmt = null;
        Connection conn = null;
        try   {
            conn = JDBCConnection.getConnection("jdbc/test");
            stmt = conn.prepareStatement(sql);
            rs = stmt.executeQuery();
            StringBuffer nulls = new StringBuffer(256);
            while( rs.next() )    {
              EmployeeDTO dto = new dto.EmployeeDTO();
              dto.EMP_ID = rs.getLong("EMP_ID");
              if( rs.wasNull() ) { nulls.append("EMP_ID|"); }
              dto.MANAGER_ID = rs.getLong("MANAGER_ID");
              if( rs.wasNull() ) { nulls.append("MANAGER_ID|"); }
              ...
              dto.uid = "|" +   dto.EMP_ID;
              list.add(dto);
            }
            return list;
        } catch(Throwable te) {
            te.printStackTrace();
            throw new DAOException(te);
        } finally {
            try {rs.close(); rs = null;} catch (Exception e){}
            try {stmt.close(); stmt = null;} catch (Exception e){}
            JDBCConnection.releaseConnection(conn);
    }   }
```

As you can see in Example 6-7, the implementation of the `fill` method is really straightforward. Review the code of the `sync` method, and you'll see that it iterates through the collection of `ChangeObjects`; calls their methods `isCreate()`, `isUpdate()`, and isDelete(); and calls the corresponding function in the DAO class. These functions are shown in the example.

Implementation of the insert and delete statements is based on new or old versions wrapped inside ChangeObject. Example 6-8 calls the method getNewVersion() to get the data for insertion in the database and getPreviousVersion() for delete.

Example 6-8. Create and delete fragment from EmployeeDAO.java

```
private ChangeObject doCreate_getEmployees(Connection conn,
         ChangeObject co) throws SQLException{

      PreparedStatement stmt = null;
      try {
          String sql = "INSERT INTO EMPLOYEE " +
            "(EMP_ID,MANAGER_ID,EMP_FNAME,EMP_LNAME,
            DEPT_ID,STREET,CITY,STATE,ZIP_CODE,PHONE,
            STATUS,SS_NUMBER,SALARY,START_DATE,TERMINATION_DATE,
            BIRTH_DATE,BENE_HEALTH_INS,BENE_LIFE_INS,
            BENE_DAY_CARE,SEX)"+
            " values (?,?,?,?,?,?,?,?,?,?,?,?,?,?,?,?,?,?,?,?)";

          stmt = conn.prepareStatement(sql);
          EmployeeDTO item = (EmployeeDTO) co.getNewVersion();
          stmt.setLong(1, item.EMP_ID);
          stmt.setLong(2, item.MANAGER_ID);
          ...
          if (stmt.executeUpdate()==0)
             throw new DAOException("Failed inserting.");
          co.setNewVersion(item);
          return co;
      } finally {
          try { if( stmt!=null) stmt.close(); stmt = null;}
          catch (Exception e){// exception processing goes here}
  }   }

  private void doDelete_getEmployees(Connection conn, ChangeObject co)
                                           throws SQLException{
      PreparedStatement stmt = null;
      try {
          StringBuffer sql = new StringBuffer
                      ("DELETE FROM EMPLOYEE WHERE (EMP_ID=?)");
          EmployeeDTO item = (EmployeeDTO) co.getPreviousVersion();
          stmt = conn.prepareStatement(sql.toString());
          stmt.setLong(1, item.EMP_ID);

          if (stmt.executeUpdate()==0)
              throw new DataSyncException(co, null,
                 Arrays.asList(new String[]{"EMP_ID"}));
          } finally {
          try { if( stmt!=null) stmt.close(); stmt = null;
          } catch (Exception e){}
  }   }
```

To form the update statement, you need both the previous and the new versions of the data available inside `ChangeObject` instances (Example 6-9).

Example 6-9. Update fragment from EmployeeDAO.java

```
private void doUpdate_getEmployees(Connection conn, ChangeObject co)
                                                 throws SQLException{

      String updatableColumns ",EMP_ID,MANAGER_ID,EMP_FNAME,EMP_LNAME,
             DEPT_ID,STREET,CITY,STATE,ZIP_CODE,
             PHONE,STATUS,SS_NUMBER,SALARY,START_DATE,
             TERMINATION_DATE,BIRTH_DATE,BENE_HEALTH_INS,
             BENE_LIFE_INS,BENE_DAY_CARE,SEX,";

        PreparedStatement stmt = null;

        try {
            StringBuffer sql = new StringBuffer("UPDATE EMPLOYEE SET ");
            EmployeeDTO oldItem =
                      (EmployeeDTO) co.getPreviousVersion();
            String [] names = co.getChangedPropertyNames();
            if (names.length==0) return;

            for (int ii=0; ii < names.length; ii++) {
               if (updatableColumns.indexOf("," + names[ii] +",")>=0)
                    sql.append((ii!=0?", ":"") + names[ii] +" = ? ");
            }

            sql.append( " WHERE (EMP_ID=?)" );
            stmt = conn.prepareStatement(sql.toString());

            Map values = co.getChangedValues();
            int ii, _jj;
            Object o;
            _jj = 0;

            for (ii=0; ii <    names.length; ii++) {
               if (updatableColumns.indexOf("," + names[ii] +",")>=0) {
                  _jj++;
                  o =  values.get(names[ii]);
                    if ( o instanceof java.util.Date)
                       stmt.setObject(
             _jj,DateTimeConversion.toSqlTimestamp((java.util.Date)o) );
                    else
                        stmt.setObject( _jj, o );
               }
            }

            _jj++;
            stmt.setLong(_jj++, oldItem.EMP_ID);

            if (stmt.executeUpdate()==0)
                throw new DataSyncException(co, null,
                        Arrays.asList(new String[]{"EMP_ID"}));
        } finally {
```

```
            try { if( stmt!=null) stmt.close(); stmt = null;
            } catch (Exception e){}
        }     }

}
```

You can either manually write the code shown in Examples 6-2 to 6-9, or use the Clear Data Builder for automated code generation.

The code in the examples is generic and can be either generated for the best performance or parameterized for Java frameworks such as Spring or Hibernate.

DataCollection Class

It's time to establish an ActionScript collection that will have two important features:

- It will know how to keep track of changes to its data.
- It will be destination-aware.

Such a collection would keep track of the data changes made from the UI. For example, a user modifies the data in a `DataGrid` that has a collection of some objects used as a data provider. You want to make a standard Flex `ArrayCollection` a little smarter so that it'll automatically create and maintain a collection of `ChangeObject` instances for every modified, new, and deleted row.

We've developed a class `DataCollection` that will do exactly this seamlessly for the application developer. This collection also encapsulates all communications with the server side via `RemoteObject`, and it knows how to notify other users about the changes made by you if they are working with the same data at the same time.

Shown in Example 6-10, this collection stores its data in the property `source`, the array of `ChangeObjects` in `modified`, and the name of the remote destination in `destination`. Every time the data in the underlying collection changes, this collection catches the `COLLECTION_CHANGE` event, and based on the event's property `kind` (`remove`, `update`, `add`) removes or modifies the data in the collection. To support undo functionality, all modified objects are stored in the properties `deleted` and `modified`.

Example 6-10. DataCollection.as—take 1

```
package com.farata.collections {
   [Event(name="propertyChange", type="mx.events.PropertyChangeEvent")]
   [Bindable(event="propertyChange")]

   public class DataCollection extends ArrayCollection {

  public var destination:String=null;
      protected var ro:RemoteObject = null;
      public var deleted:Array = new Array();
      public var modified:Dictionary = new Dictionary();
      public var alertOnFault:Boolean=true;
      private var trackChanges:Boolean=true;
```

```
    // The underlying data of the ArrayCollection
    override public function set source(s:Array):void {
    super.source = s;
     list.addEventListener(CollectionEvent.COLLECTION_CHANGE,
                                               onCollectionEvent);
        resetState();
        refresh();
  }
     // collection's data changed
 private function onCollectionEvent(event:CollectionEvent) :void {
       if (!trackChanges) return;
       switch(event.kind) {
       case "remove":
          for (var i:int = 0; i < event.items.length; i++) {
           var item:Object = event.items[i];
              var evt:DynamicEvent = new DynamicEvent("itemTracking");
              evt.item = item;
              dispatchEvent(evt);
              if (evt.isDefaultPrevented()) break;
              var co:ChangeObject = ChangeObject(modified[item]);
              var originalItem:Object=null;
          if (co == null) {
             // NotModified
                 originalItem = item;
             } else if (!co.isCreate()) {
                // Modified
                 originalItem = co.previousVersion;
                 delete modified[item];
                 modifiedCount--;
              } else {
                 // NewModified
                 delete modified[item];
                 modifiedCount--;
              }
              if (originalItem!=null) {
             deleted.push(originalItem);
             deletedCount = deleted.length;
              };
           }
        break;
        case "add":
           for ( i = 0; i < event.items.length; i++) {
              item = event.items[i];
              evt = new DynamicEvent("itemTracking");
              evt.item = item;
              dispatchEvent(evt);
              if (evt.isDefaultPrevented()) break;
              modified[item] = new ChangeObject
                       (ChangeObject.CREATE, cloneItem(item), null);
          modifiedCount++;
           }
           break;
        case "update":
           for (i = 0; i < event.items.length; i++) {
```

```
            item = null;
        var pce:PropertyChangeEvent =
                   event.items[i] as PropertyChangeEvent;
            if ( pce != null) {
               item = pce.currentTarget; //as DTO;
               if( item==null )
                  item = pce.source;
               evt = new DynamicEvent("itemTracking");
               evt.item = item;
               dispatchEvent(evt);
               if (evt.isDefaultPrevented()) break;
            }
            if (item != null) {
               if(modified[item] == null) {
                  if (item.hasOwnProperty("properties")) {
                     var oldProperties:Dictionary =
                                          item["properties"];
                     oldProperties[pce.property] = pce.oldValue;
                 var previousVersion:Object = cloneItem(item,
                                                  oldProperties)
                  } else {
                     previousVersion = ObjectUtil.copy(item);
                     previousVersion[pce.property] = pce.oldValue;
                  }
                  modified[item] = new ChangeObject(ChangeObject.UPDATE,
                                       item, previousVersion);
                 modifiedCount++;
                  }
                  co = ChangeObject(modified[item]);
                  if (co.changedPropertyNames == null) {
                     co.changedPropertyNames = [];
                  }
                  for (  i = 0; i < co.changedPropertyNames.length; i++ )
                     if (  co.changedPropertyNames[i] == pce.property)
                        break;
                  if ( i >= co.changedPropertyNames.length)
                     co.changedPropertyNames.push(pce.property);
               }
            }

            break;

       }
         // to be continued
    }
```

For our `DataCollection` to really be useful for developers, it has to offer an API for querying and manipulating its state. Developers should be able to query the collection to find out whether this particular object is new, updated, or removed. The `modified` variable of `DataCollection` is a reference to `ChangeObject`'s, and each `ChangeObject` instance can "introduce" itself as new, updated, or removed. Hence we are adding the methods listed in Example 6-11 to the `DataCollection`.

Example 6-11. Adding more methods to DataCollection

```
public function isItemNew(item:Object):Boolean {
   var co: ChangeObject = modified[item] as ChangeObject;
   return (co!=null && co.isCreate());
}
public function setItemNew(item:Object):void {
   var co: ChangeObject = modified[item] as ChangeObject;
   if (co!=null){
      co.state = ChangeObject.CREATE;
   }
}
public function isItemModified(item:Object):Boolean {
   var co: ChangeObject = modified[item] as ChangeObject;
   return (co!=null && !co.isCreate());
}
public function setItemNotModified(item:Object):void {
   var co: ChangeObject = modified[item] as ChangeObject;
   if (co!=null) {
      delete modified[item];
         modifiedCount--;
   }
}

private var _deletedCount : int = 0;
 public function get deletedCount():uint {
   return _deletedCount;
}

 public function set deletedCount(val:uint):void {
   var oldValue :uint = _deletedCount ;
   _deletedCount = val;
   commitRequired = (_modifiedCount>0 || deletedCount>0);
   dispatchEvent(PropertyChangeEvent.createUpdateEvent(this, "deletedCount",
                                               oldValue, _deletedCount));
}

private var _modifiedCount : int = 0;
public function get modifiedCount():uint {
   return _modifiedCount;
}
public function set modifiedCount(val:uint ) : void{
   var oldValue :uint = _modifiedCount ;
   _modifiedCount = val;
   commitRequired = (_modifiedCount>0 || deletedCount>0);
   dispatchEvent(PropertyChangeEvent.createUpdateEvent(this, "modifiedCount",
                                               oldValue, _modifiedCount));
   }

  private var _commitRequired:Boolean = false;
  public function set commitRequired(val :Boolean) :void {
     if (val!==_commitRequired) {
      _commitRequired = val;
      dispatchEvent(PropertyChangeEvent.createUpdateEvent(this,
                 "commitRequired", !_commitRequired, _commitRequired));
     }
```

```
    }
    public function get commitRequired() :Boolean {
       return _commitRequired;
    }

  public function resetState():void {
     deleted = new Array();
     modified = new Dictionary();
     modifiedCount = 0;
     deletedCount = 0;
  }
```

The `DataCollection` can "tell" if any of its objects are new, removed, or updated; keeps the counts of modified and deleted objects; and knows if a commit (saving changes) is required.

All the changes are accessible as the properties **`deletes`**, **`inserts`**, and **`updates`**. The property **`changes`** will get you the entire collection of the **`ChangeObjects`** (Example 6-12).

Example 6-12. Adding more properties to DataCollection

```
public function get changes():Array {
   var args:Array = deletes;
   for ( var item:Object in modified) {
      var co: ChangeObject =
         ChangeObject(modified[item]);
      co.newVersion = cloneItem(item);
      args.push(co);
   }
     return args;
  }

  public function get deletes():Array {
   var args:Array = [];
   for ( var i :int = 0; i < deleted.length; i++) {
      args.push(
         new ChangeObject(
            ChangeObject.DELETE, null,
               ObjectUtils.cloneItem(deleted[i])
         )
      );
   }
   return args;
  }
  public function get inserts():Array {
   var args:Array = [];
   for ( var item:Object in modified) {
      var co: ChangeObject = ChangeObject(modified[item]);
      if (co.isCreate()) {
         co.newVersion = ObjectUtils.cloneItem(item);
         args.push( co );
      }
   }
   return args;
  }
```

```
public function get updates():Array {
 var args:Array = [];
 for ( var item:Object in modified) {
    var co: ChangeObject = ChangeObject(modified[item]);
    if (!co.isCreate()) {
          // make up to date clone of the item
       co.newVersion = ObjectUtils.cloneItem(item);
       args.push( co );
    }
 }
   return args;
}
```

This collection should also take care of the communication with the server and call the `fill()` and `sync()` methods. Because the `DataCollection` internally uses Flex remoting, it'll create the instance of the `RemoteObject` with result and fault handlers.

The application developer will just need to create an instance of `DataCollection`, then specify the name of the remote destination and the remote method to call for data retrieval and update.

As you saw in Example 1-27:

```
collection = new DataCollection();
collection.destination="com.farata.Employee";
collection.method="getEmployees";
...
collection.fill();
```

The `fill()` method here invokes the remote method `getEmployees()`. If the `sync()` method is not specified, its default name will be `getEmployees_sync()`. After the code fragment in Example 6-13 is added to `DataCollection`, it'll be able to invoke a remote object on the server after creating the instance of `RemoteObject` in the method `createRemoteobject()`. The method `fill()` calls `invoke()`, which in turn creates an instance of the remote method using `getOperation()` on the remote object.

Example 6-13. Adding destination awareness to DataCollection

```
public var _method : String = null;
public var syncMethod : String = null;

public function set method (newMethod:String):void {
   _method = newMethod;
   if (syncMethod==null)
      syncMethod = newMethod + "_sync";
}
public function get method():String {   return _method;      }

protected function createRemoteObject():RemoteObject {
   var ro:RemoteObject = null;
   if( destination==null || destination.length==0 )
      throw new Error("No destination specified");

   ro = new RemoteObject();
```

```
        ro.destination    = destination;
        ro.concurrency    = "last";
        ro.addEventListener(ResultEvent.RESULT, ro_onResult);
        ro.addEventListener(FaultEvent.FAULT,   ro_onFault);
        return ro;
    }

    public function fill(... args): AsyncToken {
        var act:AsyncToken = invoke(method, args);
        act.method = "fill";
        return act;
    }

    protected function invoke(method:String, args:Array):AsyncToken {
        if( ro==null ) ro = createRemoteObject();
        ro.showBusyCursor = true;
        var operation:AbstractOperation = ro.getOperation(method);
        operation.arguments = args;
        var act:AsyncToken = operation.send();
        return act;
    }

    protected function ro_onFault(evt:FaultEvent):void {
            CursorManager.removeBusyCursor();
        if (evt.token.method == "sync") {
            modified = evt.token.modified;
            modifiedCount = evt.token.modifiedCount;
            deleted = evt.token.deleted;
        }
        dispatchEvent(evt);
        if( alertOnFault && !evt.isDefaultPrevented() ) {
            var dst:String = evt.message.destination;
            if( dst==null || (dst!=null && dst.length==0) )
            try{ dst = evt.target.destination; } catch(e:*){};

            var ue:UnhandledError = UnhandledError.create(null, evt,
                    DataCollection, this, evt.fault.faultString,
                      "Error on destination: " + dst);
            ue.report();
        }
    }


    public function sync():AsyncToken {
        var act:AsyncToken = invoke(syncMethod, [changes]);
        act.method = "sync";
        act.modified = modified;
        act.deleted = deleted;
        act.modifiedCount=modifiedCount;
        return act;
    }

    }
}
```

Let's recap what you've done. You subclassed `ArrayCollection` and created the `DataCollection` class that remembers all the changes to the underlying collection in the form of `ChangeObject` instances. Each `ChangeObject` "knows" if it's there because the user modified, removed, or added a new object to the collection. The `DataCollection` internally creates a `RemoteObject` based on the name of the destination and calls the `sync()` method, passing the collection of `ChangeObjects` to it for persistence on the server. Data retrieval is performed by calling `DataCollection.fill()`.

Deep Data Synchronization with BlazeDS

Due to space constraints, you've been presented with the simplified fragments of the `DataCollection` code to highlight its main features and give you a push in the right direction, should you want to create your own version of such a collection. Here are a few more possible approaches that may prove useful.

You can find the complete and up-to-date source code of the `DataCollection` class (900+ lines of code) in the SourceForge repository (*http://tinyurl.com/cqnw8x*).

Nested DataCollections

Previously, you learned about data synchronization between `DataCollection` and remote Java objects via the method `sync()`. But what if you have a situation with nested `DataCollection` objects that can be modified on the client side? How do you synchronize the changes in this case? Here's the magic line of code that will perform deep synchronization of the `DataCollection` and all its nested children:

```
collection.sync(true);
```

If you don't like manual coding, Clear Data Builder will perform deep synchronization of hierarchical `DataCollections` with the server, so that if an item of the collection contains child collections (Example 6-16, shown later), the entire tree of changes gets synchronized with the Java backend in one transaction.

Consider a sample order-processing application (Figure 6-7) that allows the user to navigate from order to order, editing the master information (order) as well as its details (order items).

The user can modify either of the data grids. All interactive changes are accumulated in the underlying `DataCollection` until the button labeled Commit is clicked. That's exactly when deep sync happens in one transaction—it's all or nothing, the commit of all changes or complete rollback.

Each of the data grids is supported by a subclass of `DataCollection`: `OrderCollection` and `OrderItemCollection`, respectively (Example 6-14).

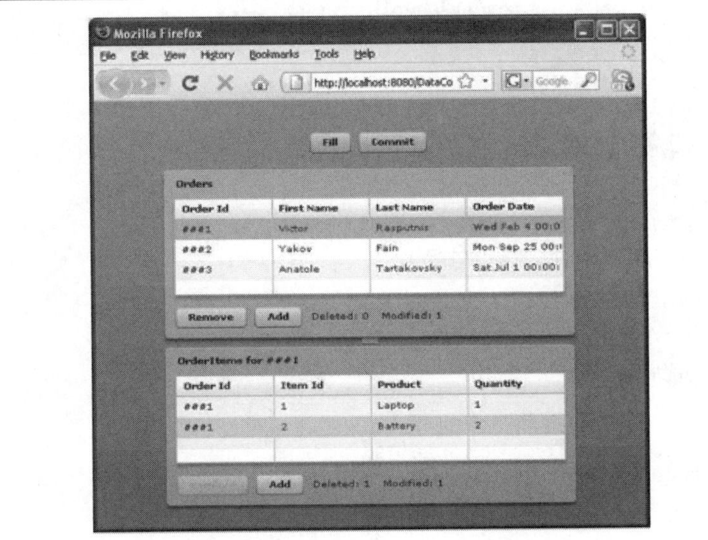

Figure 6-7. The order-processing application

Example 6-14. OrderCollection and OrderItemCollection

```
package collections {
import com.farata.collections.DataCollection;
public class OrderCollection extends DataCollection {
   public function OrderCollection(source:Array=null) {
      super(source);
      destination="com.farata.test.Order";
      method="getOrders";
   }
}
}

package collections {
import com.farata.collections.DataCollection;
public class OrderItemCollection extends DataCollection {
   public function OrderItemCollection(source:Array=null) {
      super(source);
      destination="com.farata.test.Order";
      method="getOrderItems";
   }
}
}
```

The source code of the application shown in Figure 6-7 is listed in Example 6-15.

Example 6-15. The code of the order-processing application object

```
<?xml version="1.0" encoding="UTF-8"?>
<!--OrderEntryDemo.mxml -->
<mx:Application
```

```
    xmlns:mx="http://www.adobe.com/2006/mxml"
    xmlns="*" xmlns:collections="collections.*">
    <collections:OrderCollection id="orders"/>
    <mx:ControlBar>
       <mx:Button label="Fill"  click="selectedOrder=null;orders.fill()"  />
       <mx:Button label="Commit"  click="orders.sync(true)"
          enabled="{orders.commitRequired}" />
    </mx:ControlBar>
    <mx:VDividedBox  >
       <OrdersPanel id="master" orders="{orders}"
          orderSelectionChange="selectedOrder = event.order"
       />
       <OrderItemsPanel id="detail" width="100%"
          selectedOrder="{selectedOrder}"
       />
    </mx:VDividedBox>
    <mx:Script>
       <![CDATA[
          import com.farata.test.dto.OrderDTO;
          [Bindable] private var selectedOrder:OrderDTO;
       ]]>
    </mx:Script>
</mx:Application>
```

The example application contains two custom objects: `OrdersPanel` and `OrderItemsPanel`. The `OrdersPanel` object uses `OrderCollection` as a data provider for its data grid. Each item of the `OrderCollection` carries `orderItems` referring to the child collection of line items of this order. At the application level, you need to expose only the master collection orders, which hold the entire master/detail data hierarchy.

The Commit button is enabled automatically when there are changes to commit (the collection's array of `ChangeObjects` is not empty). On click, the `sync(true)` is called, requesting deep synchronization, or persistence of all nested `DataCollections`:

```
<mx:Button label="Commit"  click="orders.sync(true)"
   enabled="{orders.commitRequired}" />
```

As mentioned earlier, you can substantially reduce the amount of manual coding in DTOs: Clear Data Builder will do it for you. In particular, it takes the Java class `Order` written by you (Example 6-17, shown later) and generates the ActionScript class `_OrderDTO` and its subclass `OrderDTO` (Example 6-16).

Example 6-16. A DTO with nested collection orderItems

```
package com.farata.test.dto{
import collections.OrderItemCollection;
import com.farata.collections.dto.HierarchicalDTOAdapter;
import com.farata.collections.dto.IHierarchicalDTO;

[RemoteClass(alias="com.farata.test.dto.OrderDTO")]
public class OrderDTO extends _OrderDTO implements IHierarchicalDTO{
[Transient] [Bindable] public var orderItems:OrderItemCollection;
[Transient] public var adapter:HierarchicalDTOAdapter;
```

```
public function OrderDTO() {
    super();
    adapter = new HierarchicalDTOAdapter(this);
    orderItems = new OrderItemCollection();
    adapter.addCollection(orderItems);
}

public function get childCollections():Array {
    return adapter.childCollections;
}

public override function set order_id(orderId:String):void {
    if (orderId !== super.order_id) {
         super.order_id = orderId;
         orderItems.fill(order_id);
    }
}
}//OrderDTO
}
```

Note the [Transient] metadata tags that ensure that these objects won't be serialized and sent to the server.

Though the properties of the _OrderDTO will match the fields returned by the SQL select specified in the doclet section of getOrders() in Example 6-17, the subclass OrderDTO is your playground. You can add any code there, and it won't be overwritten by the next CDB code generation.

In particular, the secret sauce here is that OrderDTO implements the IHierarchicalDTO interface, which you have to add manually to the generated OrderDTO if you want your collection to include nested collections. You'll also need to add code that uses HierarchicalDTOAdapter, the getter childCollections, and the setter order_id as it's done in the example.

Example 6-17 is the abstract Java class that is used with CDB to generate an ActionScript DTO from Example 6-16.

Example 6-17. Order.java

```
package com.farata.test;
import java.util.List;
/**
* @daoflex:webservice
* pool=jdbc/test
*/
public abstract class Order
{
/**
* @daoflex:sql
* sql=:: select order_id, customer_first_name,
* customer_last_name, order_date from simple_order
* ::
* transferType=OrderDTO[]
* keyColumns=order_id
```

```
* updateTable=simple_order
* autoSyncEnabled=true
*/
public abstract List getOrders();
/**
* @daoflex:sql
* sql=select * from simple_order_item WHERE ORDER_ID=:orderId
* transferType=OrderItemDTO[]
* updateTable=simple_order_item
* keyColumns=order_id,item_id,product_name
* autoSyncEnabled=true
*/
public abstract List getOrderItems(String orderId);
}
```

CDB doesn't force you to use SQL for the generation of ActionScript DTOs and automating the work with `fill()` and `sync()` methods. CDB allows your `DataCollections` to remote to any Java class implementing the `com.farata.daoflex.IJavaDAO` interface that returns an arbitrary Java DTO. See the CDB documentation (*http://sourceforge.net/projects/cleartoolkit/files/*) for more details.

The `autoSyncEnabled` attribute in Example 6-17 comes in handy when more than one user works with the same application and the same piece of data; Clear Data Builder offers an autonotification mechanism for data modifications. Changing the value of the `autoSyncEnabled` attribute allows you to turn on or off the sending of such notifications. For details, see the post at *http://www.tinyurl.com/autosync*.

Batching Remote Calls

In Example 6-7, you saw that the `sync()` method performed three steps (delete, update, and insert items) to maintain the referential integrity of data changes. If you want to perform updates of more than one `DataCollection` in one transaction, you can batch them. In the order-processing application, you have a case of nested collections, children have to be deleted prior to parents, and parents need to be inserted prior to children. But you may have another business reason to run multiple updates as one transaction.

That's where the `BatchService` class from *clear.swc* comes into play. It treats a sequence of several remote method calls as a batch, or simply as an array of `BatchMember` objects containing such elements as destination name, method name, and array of arguments.

Instead of making multiple remote calls, `BatchService` sends the entire batch as an argument of one remote call. On the server side, this call is performed by a Java class, `com.farata.remoting.BatchGateway`, located in *daoflex-runtime.jar*, which comes with CDB. In turn, `BatchGateway`'s method `execute(List<BatchMember>)` invokes the required remote calls sequentially, wrapping the entire sequence begin/commit/rollback as prescribed by the Java Transaction API (Figure 6-8).

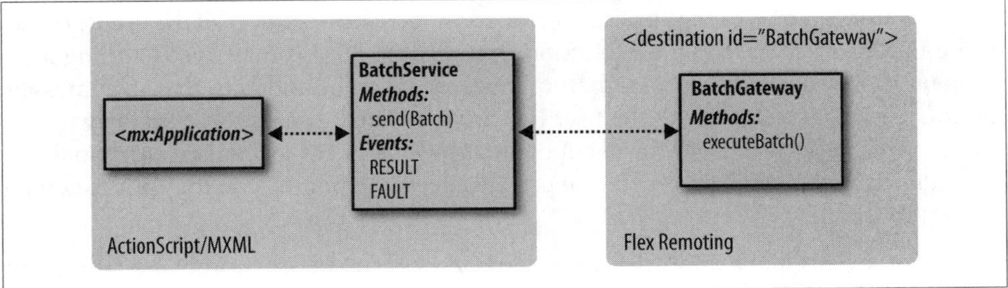

Figure 6-8. Batching remote calls

The following code snippet illustrates how you can add two collections from the order-processing example to one batch and send it for processing to the server:

```
var bs: com.farata.remoting.BatchService;
  ...
  bs = new BatchService();
  bs.addEventListener(FaultEvent.FAULT, onFault);
  bs.registerCollection(orders, 0); //0 - default (top) priority, parent
  bs.registerCollection(orderItems,1); //1 - priority, child of "0"
  ...
  var batch:Array = bs.batchRegisteredCollections();
  bs.send(batch);
```

You can use the `BatchService` not only with `DataCollections`, but also with regular Flex collections. It allows you to batch the execution of any sequence of remote calls.

Users of the SQL-based branch of CDB benefit from automatic generation of the required Java functions. Otherwise, your Java DAO has to implement the interface `IBatchTransactionServiceSupport`.

If your transaction includes only a data collection, consider using `DataCollection.sync(true)`, which further reduces the amount of manually written code required to perform transactional persistence of associated collections.

By now, you should have a good understanding of how to approach data automation in Flex and BlazeDS, and the next section will show you how to use the headers of the AMF messages that travel with your data in the protocol layer.

Using AMF Message Headers

The data access is automated, and the data gets transferred over the AMF protocol, which, as you may remember, is built on top of HTTP. The next goal is to continue minimizing the amount of coding that application programmers need to do in the client/server communication. For this, we'll try to modify the existing communications layer by adding to it application-specific information.

Sometimes, certain information needs to be passed from the client without introducing additional arguments to the application function calls. For example, if the user ID needs to be passed to the server-side function `getEmployee()`, you may avoid adding a parameter `userId` to the function signature. Instead, it can be added to the AMF message on the protocol level. Besides the user ID, you may need to pass some security restrictions, application tokens, or the client context—think of HTTP cookies. Although you might need to add these parameters at certain execution points, you may not pass them as part of the API.

Though the AMF payload is located in the bodies of the messages that are being sent, you can still add headers to these messages. Here is a quick five-step process:

1. Define a class to store the data you want to be passed in the message headers—sort of like your own cookies—for example, some operation context (Example 6-18).

   Example 6-18. OperationContext.as

   ```
   package com.farata.rpc.remoting {
      import flash.utils.Dictionary;
      import mx.messaging.messages.IMessage;

      public final class OperationContext extends Object
      {
         public static var globalHeaders   : Dictionary = new Dictionary();
         public var headers                : Dictionary = new Dictionary();

         public function _onBeforeInvoke(msg:IMessage):void {
            var fld:Object = null;
            for(fld in globalHeaders)
               msg.headers[fld] = globalHeaders[fld];

            for(fld in headers)
               msg.headers[fld] = headers[fld];
         }
      }
   }
   ```

2. Extend the Flex `Operation` class from the communication layer to append the previous headers on the Remote Method Invocation. Our `Operation` class will instantiate `OperationContext` and will call its method `_onBeforeInvoke()` every time its `invoke()` method is being called (Example 6-19).

   Example 6-19. Customized Operation.as

   ```
   package com.farata.rpc.remoting.mxml
   {
      import mx.core.mx_internal;
      use namespace mx_internal;
   ```

```
    import mx.rpc.remoting.mxml.Operation;
    import mx.rpc.remoting.RemoteObject;
    import mx.rpc.AsyncToken;
    import mx.messaging.messages.IMessage;
    import com.farata.rpc.remoting.OperationContext;

    public class Operation extends mx.rpc.remoting.mxml.Operation
    {
        public function Operation
            (remoteObject : RemoteObject = null,
             name : String = null) {

           super(remoteObject, name);
        }

       public var context:OperationContext = new OperationContext();

       mx_internal override function invoke(msg:IMessage,
                                  token:AsyncToken=null):AsyncToken
       {
          context._onBeforeInvoke(msg);
          return super.invoke(msg, token);
       }
    }
}
```

3. To complete the client-side extensions, extend Flex `RemoteObject` and make sure that it uses the extended `Operation` instead of its original one (Example 6-20).

Example 6-20. Customized RemoteObject.as

```
package com.farata.rpc.remoting.mxml
{
   import mx.rpc.remoting.mxml.RemoteObject;
   import mx.rpc.AbstractOperation;
   import mx.core.mx_internal;
   use namespace mx_internal;

   public class RemoteObject extends mx.rpc.remoting.mxml.RemoteObject   {

      public function RemoteObject(destination:String=null):void {
         super(destination);
      }

       override public function getOperation(name:String):AbstractOperation   {
           var o:Object = _operations[name];
           var op:AbstractOperation = o as AbstractOperation;
           if (op == null)
           {
               op = new Operation(this, name); // extended Operation
               _operations[name] = op;
               op.asyncRequest = asyncRequest;
           }
           return op;
       }
```

```
    }
}
```

4. To intercept the additional headers and make them available to the server-side Java programs, create a placeholder for the headers on the Java side and keep the data located in this placeholder in the Java `ThreadLocal` object to avoid a mix-up between different client requests (Example 6-21).

   Example 6-21. MessageContext.java

```
package  com.farata.remoting;

import java.util.Hashtable;
public class MessageContext {
    public static void setParams(Hashtable session)
    {
        sessions.set(session);
    }
    public static Hashtable getParams()
    {
        return (Hashtable)sessions.get();
    }
    private static ThreadLocal sessions = new ThreadLocal();
   }
```

5. As shown in Example 6-22, modify the AMF endpoint to load the `MessageContext` object upon servicing the client's requests (don't forget to specify this endpoint on the AMF channel in the *services-config.xml* configuration file).

   Example 6-22. CustomAMFEndpoint.java

```
package com.farata.remoting;
import java.util.Hashtable;

import flex.messaging.endpoints.*;

import flex.messaging.MessageBroker;
import flex.messaging.config.ChannelSettings;
import flex.messaging.messages.Message;

public class CustomAMFEndpoint extends AMFEndpoint {
   public CustomAMFEndpoint()  {
      super();
   }

    public CustomAMFEndpoint( boolean enableManagement)    {
        super( enableManagement);

    }
    public Message serviceMessage(Message message)    {
       Hashtable ht = new Hashtable();
      ht.put("context", message.getHeaders());
      MessageContext.setParams(ht);
       return super.serviceMessage(message);
```

```
    }
}
```

Once the system part is done, you can set the properties on the `OperationContext` object in your application code, just like this:

```
OperationContext.globalHeaders["name"] = "john".
```

On the Java side, you can retrieve headers sent from the client by retrieving the corresponding parameter(s) from the `MessageContext` object:

```
public String helloUser() {
   Hashtable ht = MessageContext.getParams();
   String userId = (String)context.get("name");
   return "Hello, " + userId;
}
```

Data Push in Data Access

To give you an example of BlazeDS at work, we're going to revisit the Café Townsend application and bring it even closer to reality. It's great that the Café owner's wife can populate (and update) employee data from a database, but in the real world of enterprise applications, more than one user often must work with the same data.

Say that users A and B have populated the employees' data, and user B decides to update a record in the database. Will user A be notified about this change, or will she keep working with stale data?

You want multiple users to be able to update the table `Employee` *simultaneously* and to promote the data changes to other users *instantaneously*. Such data synchronization is available with LCDS Data Management Services, and with adjustments, you can achieve similar functionality using the open source implementation of AMF as well.

To start, examine the `Assembler` class that will be working closely with `EmployeeDAO`. As you can see in Example 6-23, the Java code takes all the changes submitted by any user and broadcasts them to all clients subscribed to the destination `com.farata.datasource.Employee.getEmployees`.

Example 6-23. Server-side push with the Assembler class

```
package com.farata.datasource;
import java.util.*;
import flex.messaging.MessageBroker;
import flex.messaging.messages.AsyncMessage;
import flex.messaging.util.UUIDUtils;

public final class EmployeeAssembler{

 public  List /*EmployeeDTO[]*/  getEmployees() throws Exception       {
  return new EmployeeDAO().getEmployees();
 }
```

```
 public final List getEmployees_sync(List items)        {

    List result = new EmployeeDAO().getEmployees_sync(items);

   MessageBroker msgBroker = MessageBroker.getMessageBroker(null);
   AsyncMessage msg = new AsyncMessage();
   msg.setDestination("com.farata.datasource.Employee.getEmployees");
   msg.setClientId(UUIDUtils.createUUID(true));
   msg.setMessageId(UUIDUtils.createUUID(true));
   msg.setTimestamp(System.currentTimeMillis());
   msg.setBody(result);
   msgBroker.routeMessageToService(msg, null);

    return result;
 }

 public  List /*DepartmentDTO[]*/  getDepartments() throws Exception{
  return new EmployeeDAO().getDepartments();
 }
}
```

Next, you need to receive these messages on the client and apply the changes. As you can see in Example 6-24, the Flex client receives the changes via subscription and applies them (the subscription name is a destination name).

Example 6-24. Receiving pushed data on the client

```
private var _subscription : Consumer ;
private var _subscriptionName : String ;

public function set feed( subscriptionName : String ) : void {
   _subscription = new  Consumer();
   _subscription.destination = subscriptionName;
   _subscription.addEventListener("message", messageHandler );
   _subscription.subscribe();
   _subscriptionName = subscriptionName;
}

public function get feed() : String {
   return _subscriptionName;
}

protected function messageHandler(ev:MessageEvent):void
{
   if ( ev.message.body is ChangeObject)
      processChange(ev.message.body as ChangeObject) ;
   if ( ev.message.body is ArrayCollection)
     for (var i:int = 0; i<ev.message.body.length; i++)
      processChange(ev.message.body[i] as ChangeObject) ;
   }

protected function processChange( co : ChangeObject) : void {

switch ( co.state) {
   case ChangeObject.CREATE:
```

```
      addItem(co.newVersion);
      break;
   case ChangeObject.DELETE:
      var uid:String = co.previousVersion.uid;
      for ( var j :int = 0; j < length; j++ ) {
         if(getItemAt(j).uid == uid) {
            removeItemAt(j);
            break;
         }
      }
      break;
   case ChangeObject.UPDATE:
      uid = co.newVersion.uid;
      for ( j  = 0; j < length; j++ ) {
        if(getItemAt(j).uid == uid ) {
        var item: EventDispatcher=getItemAt(j) as EventDispatcher;
              item["properties"] = co.newVersion["properties"];
                     // notify the UI of the change
              item.dispatchEvent(
                     PropertyChangeEvent.createUpdateEvent(item,"any","x","y"));
         break;
         }
      }
      break;
   }
}
```

Example 6-24 is a simplified code snippet of updating the client content based on the data pushed from the server. It assumes that the function `getItemAt()` works with the data collection that needs to be updated. It does not deal with conflicts or application of concurrent changes, because this part is application-specific and has to be enforced based on the best strategy to avoid conflicts rather than forcing the user to deal with them—either via record locking or multistage update.

The code of Example 6-24 depends upon the `uid` value of the DTO. You need to make sure that a unique, consistent ID is being used by every user. The simplest way to do it is by mapping `uid` to the database primary key on the server side.

You can also use a data push to implement the background retrieval of the large data sets. All you need to do is to push the retrieval results as `ChangeObjects` with the `CREATED` flag on.

A Server As a Command Center

Strange as it sounds, a clock is another excellent example of streaming. Using a streaming AMF channel to deliver the server time, you can create a clock that updates its display every second. As a bonus, the clock application demonstrates another useful concept: the reverse remote procedure call (RPC).

Reverse RPC

A *remote procedure call* is when a client invokes a function on the server-side object. For example, you can create an instance of the `RemoteObject` that points at a destination (a Java class) configured in the server-side BlazeDS. Then this Flex client calls a method on this destination.

The example clock application instructs a server to control the client when it wants, the way it wants. This is a *reverse RPC*: the server calls a client. Traditional server-side destinations are usually preconfigured in XML files, such as *remoting-config.xml*; however, you don't have this luxury on the client. Instead, during runtime you need to pass the name of the client destination, the method to call, and an array of parameters, if any. Here, the AMF protocol becomes quite handy once again. Remember, it offers an easy way to serialize a Java object on the server and deserialize it as an ActionScript object on the client.

If you understand the concept of DTO being an exchange currency between Java and ActionScript, the rest of this section won't be difficult. Just think outside the box and create a DTO that will carry not some application-specific data (e.g.,the current server time), but the metadata—the name of the destination, a method to call on the client, and its parameters.

Example 6-25 shows the server-side Java DTO that wraps up the data and metadata.

Example 6-25. RemoteCall.java

```
package com.farata.remoting ;
import java.util.*;

public class RemoteCall {
 public String destinationName; // destination configured on the server
 public String methodName;      // method to call on the client
 public List   parameters;      // method arguments

 public RemoteCall(String d, String m, List p) {
      destinationName = d;
      methodName = m;
      parameters = p;
 }
}
```

When instances of `RemoteCall` objects arrive at the client, they are represented as the ActionScript instances in Example 6-26.

Example 6-26. RemoteCall.as

```
package  com.farata.remoting {
   import mx.collections.ArrayCollection;
```

```
    [RemoteClass(alias="com.farata.remoting.RemoteCall")]
    public class RemoteCall {
       public var destinationName:String;
       public var methodName:String;
       public var parameters:ArrayCollection;

      public function RemoteCall(destinationName:String=null,
                           methodName:String=null,
                           parameters:ArrayCollection=null) {

       this.destinationName = destinationName;
       this.methodName = methodName;
       this.parameters = parameters;
        }
    }
}
```

BlazeDS, with the help of AMF, automatically turns any instance of *RemoteCall.java* into an instance of *RemoteCall.as*. The big idea is to have the server push this `RemoteCall` to the client, which should obediently call the requested method (the `methodName` property of the `RemoteCall` instance) on the specified object with the provided parameters.

Add the following destination in the *message-config.xml* file where BlazeDS is deployed:

```
<destination id="ControlCenter">
  <channels>
   <channel ref="my-streaming-amf"/>
  </channels>
</destination>
```

Please note that this destination is configured to use the streaming AMF channel. BlazeDS includes a class, `MessageBroker`, that knows how to push messages to destinations.

At this point, you know that the server will have to create instances of `RemoteCall` objects and send them to the destination called `ControlCenter`. To do this, simply write another Java class called `ControlCenter.java`, as shown in Example 6-27. Note once again that this code sends not just the data to the client, but also the information about the RPC.

Example 6-27. ControlCenter.java

```
package com.farata.remoting;
import java.util.*;
import flex.messaging.MessageBroker;
import flex.messaging.messages.AsyncMessage;
import flex.messaging.util.UUIDUtils;

public class ControlCenter {
   private static ControlCenterThread thread;

    //start a new thread to send RemoteCall instances
   public void start() {
```

```
        if (thread == null) {
            thread = new ControlCenterThread();
            thread.start();
        }
    }

    public void stop() {
        if (thread != null){
            thread.running = false;
            thread = null;
        }
    }

    public static class ControlCenterThread extends Thread {
        public boolean running = true;

        public void run() {

            MessageBroker msgBroker = MessageBroker.getMessageBroker(null);
            String clientID = UUIDUtils.createUUID();

            while (running) {

                    // create a message object set the destination and
                    // assign unique client and message IDs
                AsyncMessage msg = new AsyncMessage();
                msg.setDestination("ControlCenter");
                msg.setClientId(clientID);
                msg.setMessageId(UUIDUtils.createUUID());
                msg.setTimestamp(System.currentTimeMillis());

                    // Create an array of parameters to be used as
                    // arguments for the setTime() function call
                ArrayList params = new ArrayList();
                    // Add current system time
                params.add( new Date()); //

                    // Create RemoteCall wrapper an use it as the message body
                msg.setBody(new RemoteCall("clock", "setTime", params));
                msgBroker.routeMessageToService(msg, null);

                try {
                        // pause the loop for one second
                    Thread.sleep(1000);
                } catch (InterruptedException e) {      }
            }
        }
    }
}
```

The `CallCenter` program creates and starts a separate thread named `CallCenterThread` that every second creates a new instance of the `RemoteCall`, puts it into the message body of `AsyncMessage`, and using the `MessageBroker` publishes it to the destination called `ControlCenter`.

The Flex client shown in the following example creates a consumer object and subscribes it to the destination `ControlCenter`.

We borrowed the code for the alarm clock UI from Adobe's manual on programming ActionScript 3. This example was used there for explaining events (see *http://livedocs.adobe.com/flex/3/html/help.html?content=16_Event_handling_7.html*). For your convenience, we've included this code in Flash Builder's project *NetworkingSamples*, which contains all examples from this chapter.

In Example 6-28's Flex application you can find the consumer that is ready to consume messages from the destination `ControlCenter`. `RemoteObject` is used to start or stop the server-side feed.

Example 6-28. RemotingViaStreaming.mxml

```
<?xml version="1.0" encoding="utf-8"?>
<mx:Application xmlns:mx="http://www.adobe.com/2006/mxml"
   xmlns:remoting="com.farata.remoting.*"
   xmlns:example="com.example.programmingas3.clock.*"
   creationComplete="co.subscribe()" layout="vertical" horizontalAlign="left">

  <mx:Consumer destination="ControlCenter"  id="co"
     message="handleMessage(event.message)"/>

  <mx:RemoteObject destination="ControlCenterRO" id="ro"/>
   <mx:Button label="Start" click="ro.start()"/>
   <mx:Button label="Stop" click="ro.stop()"/>
   <mx:Label text="Time"/>   <mx:Label width="259" id="serverClock"/>
   <example:SimpleClock id="clock" creationComplete="clock.initClock()"/>

 <mx:Script>
 <![CDATA[
   import com.farata.remoting.RemoteCall;
   import mx.messaging.messages.IMessage;

   private function handleMessage(msg:IMessage) : void {
      if (msg.body is RemoteCall) {
         var rc:RemoteCall = msg.body as RemoteCall;
         this[rc.methodName].apply(this, rc.parameters.source);
      }
   }

   public function setTime( d:Date) : void {
      serverClock.text = d.toTimeString();
      clock.setTime( d);
   }
]]>
</mx:Script>
</mx:Application>
```

When the consumer receives the message, the function `handleMessage()` extracts the instance of `RemoteCall` from the message body and calls the method whose name is located in the property `RemoteCall.methodName`:

```
    var rc:RemoteCall = msg.body as RemoteCall;
    this[rc.methodName].apply(this, rc.parameters.source);
```

In Example 6-28, this [rc.methodName] gets the reference to the Function object based on the received name, which is setTime() here. Then the function apply() calls this method, passing parameters contained in the RemoteCall object.

This technique is yet another way to implement the Command design pattern, but here the server publishes a message that is a command to the client to call a function specified in methodName.

Extending the Protocol

Although this technique of making RPC calls from the server is pretty cool, you can make it even better by hiding the processing of the received messages at the protocol level, so that the application developers will use this enhanced consumer without needing to know how it works under the hood.

First, extend the AMF endpoint and move the consumer portion into the new class RemoteStreamingChannel, which extends the standard StreamingAMFChannel, which will be responsible for filtering and executing remote procedure calls.

Note the meta tag [Mixin] in Example 6-29. In Flex, it's used to ensure that a static initializer's code located in the method init() will be executed as soon as the SystemManager becomes available.

Example 6-29. RemoteStreamingChannel.as

```
package com.farata.messaging.channel{
   import com.farata.remoting.RemoteCall;

   import flash.utils.Dictionary;
   import mx.managers.ISystemManager;
   import mx.messaging.Consumer;
   import mx.messaging.channels.StreamingAMFChannel;
   import mx.messaging.events.MessageEvent;
   import mx.messaging.messages.IMessage;

   [Mixin]
   public class RemoteStreamingChannel extends StreamingAMFChannel{

      public static var destinations:Dictionary = new Dictionary();

      public function RemoteStreamingChannel(id:String=null, uri:String=null){
       super(id, uri);
       this.addEventListener(MessageEvent.MESSAGE, filterAndInvoke,false,1);
      }

         // if the receieved message is an instance of the RemoteCall,
         // get the destination and call the passed method on it
      protected function filterAndInvoke( evt:MessageEvent ) : void {
         var msg : IMessage = evt.message;
```

```
            if (msg.body is RemoteCall) {
               var rc:RemoteCall = msg.body as RemoteCall;
               var destination : Object = destinations[ rc.destinationName];
               if ( destination )
                  var result:* =
               destination[rc.methodName].apply(destination, rc.parameters.source);
               else
                           //log the error
                  trace( "missing destination " + rc.destinationName );
               evt.preventDefault();
            }
         }

         public static function init( systemManager:ISystemManager ) : void {
            //stub for static initializer
            var c:Consumer = new Consumer();
            c.destination = "ControlCenter";
            c.subscribe();
         }
      }
   }
```

If the code in Example 6-28 was calling the specified function on the `this` object, you can make it more generic by specifying the destination object on the client and calling the function on it:

```
destination[rc.methodName].apply(destination, rc.parameters.source);
```

To let BlazeDS know that you want to use this endpoint on the client instead of the original `StreamingAMFChannel`, change the channel configuration in *services-config.xml* (Example 6-30).

Example 6-30. Modified channel definition in services-config.xml

```
<channel-definitionid="my-streaming-amf"
      class="com.farata.messaging.channel.RemoteStreamingChannel">
<endpointurl="http://{server.name}:{server.port}/{context.root}/messagebroker/
            streamingamf"
class="com.farata.nioblaze.messaging.endpoints.NioAmfEndpoint"/>
</channel-definition>
```

The application in Example 6-31 uses the new channel.

Example 6-31. RemotingViaStreamingGeneric.mxml

```
<?xml version="1.0" encoding="utf-8"?>
<mx:Application xmlns:mx="http://www.adobe.com/2006/mxml"
   xmlns:remoting="com.farata.remoting.*"
   xmlns:example="com.example.programmingas3.clock.*"
   creationComplete="RemoteStreamingChannel.destinations['clock']=simpleClock;"
    layout="vertical" horizontalAlign="left">

    <mx:RemoteObject destination="ControlCenterRO" id="ro"/>
   <mx:Button label="Start" click="ro.start()"/>
   <mx:Button label="Stop" click="ro.stop()"/>
```

```
    <example:SimpleClock id="simpleClock" creationComplete="clock.initClock()"/>

 <mx:Script>
 <![CDATA[
   import com.farata.messaging.channel.RemoteStreamingChannel;
 ]]>
 </mx:Script>

</mx:Application>
```

Upon the `creationComplete` event, this application assigns the `SimpleClock` object as the client destination of all that goes under the name `clock`:

```
RemoteStreamingChannel.destinations['clock']=simpleClock;
```

The server-side sender from Example 6-27 is sending a command to call the function `setTime()` of the destination clock, which is now mapped to the instance of the `SimpleClock` component:

```
msg.setBody(new RemoteCall("clock", "setTime", params));
```

The destination clock was not used in the MXML application shown in Example 6-28, which was calling the function `setTime()` on the `this` object no matter what. But the more generic application shown in Example 6-31 explicitly routes the server calls to the destination `clock`.

And the clock (Figure 6-9) is ticking, driven by the reverse RPC calls from the server.

Now you *own* a communication channel on both the server and client sides and you're ready to program high-level protocols.

Custom Serialization and AMF

AMF is a very efficient protocol, and part of that efficiency is thanks to the strict rules for supporting a limited set of data types in an optimized way. One of the most frequent cases in which it needs to be customized is when you have to work with non-UTC `Date` and `Time`. UTC stands for Coordinated Universal Time.

First, you need to understand how Flex deals with transfer of the `Date` objects. Dates are always transferred to/from Flex clients as UTC `Date`, where no time zone information is available on the object. Translation to the UTC/local time happens automatically on the AMF protocol level, which adds the client time zone offset to the incoming dates and subtracts it from outgoing ones.

The server does not know about the client's time zone; it always operates in UTC time. This means that if a user from New York City entered 1:00 p.m. as the time, a user in Denver, Colorado, will see it as 11:00 a.m. In some applications, such behavior may be desirable, but this is not the case in a global application in which the users can be located around the world.

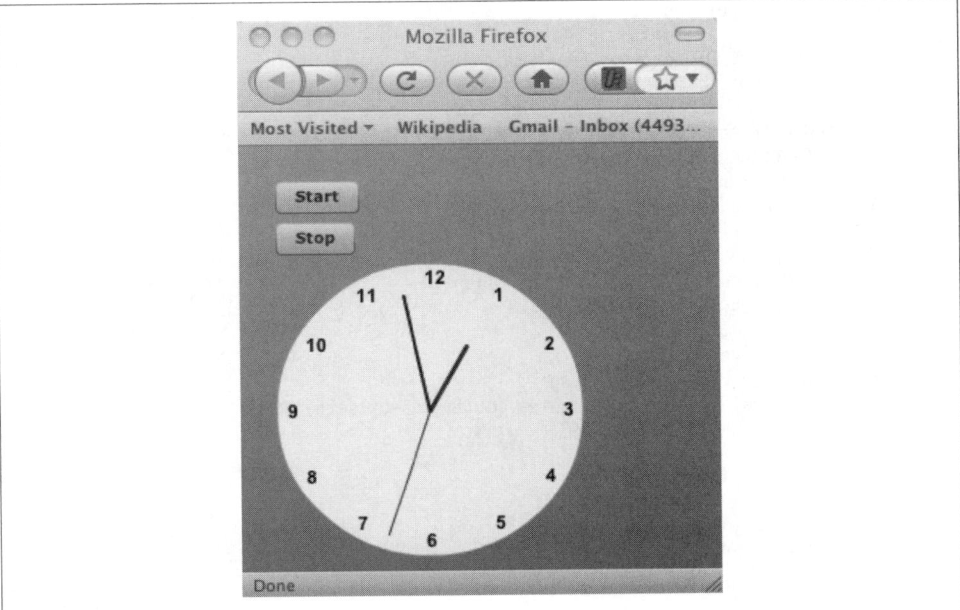

Figure 6-9. The clock controlled by the server

The user wants to enter the time in the client's local time; 1:00 p.m. will be 1:00 p.m. regardless of the time zone of the person who entered this time.

For example, requests for an appointment for the installation of the local TV cable service may be handled by a call center located on the other side of the globe. Ashish from the call center talks to you, and if you agreed to see the cable guy at 10:00 a.m., he enters 10:00 a.m. in the application. By the way, the server can be located in yet another time zone. This should be irrelevant for the distributed RIA.

Such an application has to operate without the use of time zones, or, for that matter, in one time zone. This can be done either on the server side by keeping the client time zone information in the session and adjusting the dates on each transfer or by communicating the date as a `String`. In either case, it requires additional application code that should be added in multiple places that deal with dates.

However, there is more elegant solution if, during data transfer, you'll be using the ActionScript metadata tag `transient`. Examine Example 6-32, which contains the code of an ActionScript DTO called `LineItemDTO`.

Example 6-32. LineItemDTO.as

```
package com.farata.datasource.dto{

import flash.events.EventDispatcher;

[RemoteClass(alias="com.farata.datasource.dto.LineItemDTO")]
```

```
[Bindable(event="propertyChange")]

 public class LineItemDTO extends EventDispatcher {
   private var _myDate : Date;

    // myDateUTC is not to be used on the client
   protected function get myDateUTC() : Date {
     return _myDate==null? null:
     new Date(_myDate.valueOf() - _myDate.getTimezoneOffset()*60000);
   }

    // myDateUTC is not to be used on the client
   protected function set myDateUTC( value : Date ):void {
   var oldValue:Object = _myDate;
   if (oldValue !== value) {
      this._myDate = value == null? null:
         new Date(value.valueOf() + value.getTimezoneOffset()*60000);
   }
 }

[Transient]
 public function get myDate() : Date {
   return _myDate;
 }

 public function set myDate( value : Date ):void {
   var oldValue:Object = this._myDate;
   if (oldValue !== value) {
      this._myDate = value;
    dispatchUpdateEvent("myDate", oldValue, value);
   }
 }
```

On the server, its Java twin may look like Example 6-33.

Example 6-33. LineItemDTO.java

```
package com.farata.datasource.dto;

import java.io.Serializable;
import java.util.*;

 public class LineItemDTO implements Serializable{
  transient public java.util.Date myDate;

  // This getter is serialized as a property myDateUTC
  public java.util.Date getMyDateUTC() {
     return myDate;
  }

  public void setMyDateUTC(java.util.Date value){
     this.myDate = value;
  }
}
```

Please note the use of the keyword `transient`, which server-side JVM interprets like this: "Don't serialize the value of this member variable when you'll be sending the `LineItemDTO` instances over the wire."

On the other hand, when JavaBean *LineItemDTO.java* gets serialized, the word *get* gets cut off from the `getMyDateUTC` and arrives as a `myDateUTC` property of the object *LineItemDTO.as*, where it's automatically converted into the UTC `Date`.

That's all there is to it. You have normal public variables on both sides, and AMF serialization works transparently, keeping the `Date` and `Time` values in the UTC zone on both sides (you also need to set the JVM time zone to UTC), and now you are always operating in the server's time zone.

This code will work in any implementation of the AMF protocol: BlazeDS, LCDS, OpenAMF, WebORB, GraniteDS, and so on.

Armed with this knowledge, reevaluate your needs for local versus global time to avoid the follow-up calls from the call center in India at 2:00 in the morning.

Even though this example uses custom AMF serialization for dates, you may use the same technique to provide custom serialization for any other application-specific objects.

Security Appliances

Once you've developed and tested your Flex application locally, and you're ready to share it with the rest of the world, you need to move it to a secured hosting environment. Usually, for simplicity and performance, enterprises deploy Java EE servers behind standalone SSL accelerators and load balancers. Sometimes it's just an Apache server or similar appliance.

This means that the client sends the data via an SSL channel to such an SSL appliance configured on the edge of a firewall. The appliance authenticates the user and maintains the session, and in turn calls the application server running on the intranet via unsecured HTTP to minimize the CPU load on the application server.

In this setup, you have to use a secured endpoint on the client side and an unsecured endpoint on application server. You can configure the channel to use such a pair of endpoints in the *services-config.xml* file of BlazeDS, but this would require separate builds and configuration files for external and internal deployments. As an alternative, you might want to switch the channels and endpoints dynamically during the runtime, based on which protocol is being used: HTTP or HTTPS.

During the `preInitialize` event of the Flex application, you can apply a regular expression and find out whether it was started via a secure or nonsecure protocol (Example 6-34).

Example 6-34. Switching channels and endpoints

```
import mx.messaging.config.ServerConfig;

private function preinitializeApplication() : void {

   const reUrl:RegExp= /(http|https):\/\/(([^:]+)(:([^@]+))?@)?([^:\/]+)(:([0-
   9]{2,5}))?(\/([\w#!:.?+=&%@!\-\/]+))?/;

   const appUrl:String = Application.application.url;

   const parts:Array = reUrl.exec(appUrl);

   if (parts!=null)
      if (parts[1] == "https" )
      {
         const channels:XMLList = ServerConfig.xml..channels.channel;
         for (var channel:String in channels) {
            if (channels[channel].@type=="mx.messaging.channels.AMFChannel")                      {

               channels[channel].@type="mx.messaging.channels.SecureAMFChannel";
               var endpoint : XML = channels[channel].endpoint[0];
               var uri:String = endpoint.@uri
               uri = uri.replace( /^http:/, "https:" );
               uri = uri.replace( /\{server.port\}/, "443" );
               endpoint.@uri = uri;
            }
         }
      }
}
```

This code checks to see whether the application is executed over the secure HTTPS protocol. If it is, the code goes through the `ServerConfig` singleton and updates the channel specifications to use a secured endpoint, the HTTPS protocol, and port number 443 on the web server. Because the client executes this code, you can have a single configuration point for a variety of deployment options.

Third-Party Networking Solutions

AMF is an open protocol, and various vendors offer their implementations. Your RIA may or may not use Java on the server side, and you may consider the following alternatives to BlazeDS, which are available as open source projects or offered by third-party vendors:

WebORB (http://www.themidnightcoders.com/weborb/)
: This family of products by the Midnight Coders includes implementations of AMF for Java, .NET, Ruby on Rails, and PHP. WebORB offers the best reliability and performance for these platforms, and it is free. Its .NET stack is the most impressive one, as it offers full-featured messaging, RTMP support, data push, and the

best .NET integration. The Java stack of WebORB is similar to the BlazeDS offering; it also uses Red5 for RTMP/multimedia integration.

RubyAMF (http://code.google.com/p/rubyamf/)
: RubyAMF is an open source implementation of Ruby.

AMFPHP (http://www.amfphp.org)
: AMFPHP is an open source implementation of PHP.

PyAMF (http://pyamf.org)
: PyAMF is an open source product for Python.

Granite Data Services (http://www.graniteds.org)
: Granite Data Services (GDS) is a free open source package that offers functionality similar to LCDS. It caters to developers who use Flex and AMF to communicate with server-side POJOs and such Java technologies and frameworks as Enterprise JavaBeans 3 (EJB3), Seam, Spring, and Guice. It also features Comet-like data communications with AMF, as well as Tide, a framework that positions itself as an alternative to Cairngorm, combined with the Data Management Services offered by LCDS.

Red5 (http://code.google.com/p/red5/)
: An open source Flash server, Red5 supports RTMP and AMF remoting and streaming of audio and video. Red5 is written in Java and can be installed on any platform that supports Java. Even though typically Red5 is considered to be an alternative to Flash Media Server, you may also start using it as an alternative to BlazeDS. You can use either a standalone version of Red5, or deploy it in the Java servlet container as a web application archive (WAR) file. (At the time of this writing, Red5 has not been officially released and is at version 0.9 Final.)

Summary

This chapter covered a lot of ground. Not only did you learn how data can travel between Flex and Java using the AMF protocol, but you also learned how to automate the coding of the objects that are being transported by AMF. You got familiar with the internals of the pretty powerful `DataCollection` object, and went through a set of code fragments that illustrate various techniques applicable to creating a data synchronization solution based on Flex remoting.

The authors of this book have created and made available a fully functional version of such a `DataCollection` object, and we've provided the reference to its complete code on SourceForge. You'll revisit `DataCollection` in Chapter 9, where its subclass, `OfflineDataCollection`, will do a good job synchronizing data between the local and remote databases in an AIR application. Finally, you've learned yet another advanced technique for pushing the data from the server to the client, via the AMF protocol implemented in BlazeDS and making reverse RPC calls.

And the most exciting part is that in this chapter we've been using only open source solutions!

CHAPTER 7

Modules, Libraries, Applications, and Portals

Before software can be reusable, it first has to be usable.

—Ralph Johnson

Flex Portals and Modularization

For many people, the word "portal" stands for content personalization, as in Yahoo! or iGoogle. In the enterprise world, portals are mainly about content *aggregation*. HTML portals consist of pieces wrapped into HTML tags; Flex portals aggregate Flex applications or modules into a bigger Flex application. Quite naturally, aggregation does not exist without *modularization*. After all, while developing any decent size application, we tend to break it into smaller, relatively independent parts.

Such intervening of aggregation and modularization determines the layout of this chapter. You'll start with image loading as the nucleus of Flex modularization, and then progress to Flex modules and subapplications. You'll learn how to use such classes as `Loader` and `URLLoader` and how they deal with style modules and code modules.

This chapter will suggest an approach of creating custom Flex portals that load and communicate with independently built and compiled subapplications: portlets. Finally, you will learn how to integrate existing Flex application as legacy portlets in a JSR 168 portal.

Basic Modularization: Image

The essence of Flex application modularization is dynamic loading of the byte code.

Consider the following two lines of code:

```
<mx:Image source="@Embed('assets/logo.png')"/>
<mx:Image source="assets/logo.png"/>
```

The first line illustrates *image embedding*. It increases the size of the application by the size of the image. As a result, the application carries the image as a part of the SWF file. The loading of such applications takes longer, but the actual rendering of the image will be faster, as there is no need to make a network call just to bring the image to the client.

The second line of code illustrates runtime loading of the image bytes. This time the application's *.swf* does not include the image *logo.png* and loads faster than the embedded one. The download of *logo.png* will need additional time, but that time will be deferred until the view that contains the image is displayed.

Now consider an alternative, explicit way of image embedding:

```
<mx:Script>
   <![CDATA[
      [Embed(source="assets/farata_logo.png")]
      [Bindable] private var logoClass:Class;
   ]]>
</mx:Script>

<mx:Image source="{logoClass}"/>
<mx:Button icon="{logoClass}"/>
```

This method explicitly exposes the variable `logoClass` of type `Class`. In fact, the Flex compiler generates an instance of `mx.core.BitmapAsset` that is a wrapper around the `ByteArray` of the actual image. The similar variable is generated when you use the `@Embed` meta tag, although explicit embedding lets you reuse it multiple times. The resource pointed to by the URL, in this case *assets/farata_logo.png*, gets copied across the network and displayed on the *stage*. In the case of embedding, copying is done during compilation of the SWF and the job of the `Image` component is reduced to merely displaying the content of a `ByteArray`. Importantly, the `source` property of the `Image` may outright point to an existing `ByteArray` representing an image.

You can get a reference to this `ByteArray` with the help of the class `flash.net.URLLoader`, as presented in Example 7-1.

Example 7-1. Separating transfer of byte code from loading into stage

```
<mx:Script>
   [Bindable] private var imageData:ByteArray;
   private function loadImage():void {
      var urlRequest:URLRequest =  new URLRequest(IMAGE_URL);
      var urlLoader:URLLoader = new URLLoader();
      urlLoader.dataFormat = URLLoaderDataFormat.BINARY;
      urlLoader.addEventListener(Event.COMPLETE, onComplete);
urlLoader.load(urlRequest);
   }
   private function onComplete(event:Event):void{
      var urlLoader:URLLoader = event.target as URLLoader;
      imageData = urlLoader.data as ByteArray;
   }
</mx:Script>
```

```
<mx:Button label="Load Image" click="loadImage()" />
<mx:Image id="image" source="{imageData}"/>
```

The code snippet in Example 7-1 emphasizes that transferring of the remote byte code over the network (by `URLLoader`) and adding it to the stage (by `Image`) are two independent actions.

Using this technique for image loading is a good demonstration of two important application modularization concepts:

- The ultimate subjects of the dynamic loading are class definitions, either definitions of assets or components.
- Transfer of the byte code and actual creation of class definitions are two separate actions.

Once you master loading a single image, you can move up to *style modules*, which enable you to load many images in one shot.

Runtime Style Modules

Say you have a set of images that collectively, via CSS, determine the skin of your application, as in Example 7-2.

Example 7-2. Sample CSS file

```
/* styles.css */
Application {
   background-image:Embed("assets/background.png") ;
   background-size:"100%" ;
}
.arrowLeft {
   skin: Embed("assets/arrow_right.png") ;
   over-skin: Embed("assets/arrow_right_rollover.png") ;
   down-skin: Embed("assets/arrow_right_down.png") ;
}

.arrowRight {
   skin: Embed("assets/arrow_left.png") ;
   over-skin: Embed("assets/arrow_left_rollover.png") ;
   down-skin: Embed("assets/arrow_left_down.png") ;
}

.tileStyle {
   skin: Embed("assets/tile.png") ;
   over-skin: Embed("assets/tile_rollover.png") ;
   down-skin: Embed("assets/tile_rollover.png") ;
}

.minimizeStyle{
   skin: Embed("assets/minimizeall.png") ;
   over-skin: Embed("assets/minimizeall_rollover.png") ;
```

```
    down-skin: Embed("assets/minimizeall_rollover.png") ;
}

.restoreStyle {
    skin: Embed("assets/restoreall.png") ;
    over-skin: Embed("assets/restoreall_rollover.png") ;
    down-skin: Embed("assets/restoreall_rollover.png") ;
}

.saveButtonStyle {
    skin: Embed("assets/save_gray.png") ;
    over-skin: Embed("assets/save_rollover.png") ;
    down-skin: Embed("assets/save_rollover.png") ;
}
.showPanelButtonDown {
    skin: Embed("assets/gray_down_small.png") ;
    over-skin: Embed("assets/rollover_down_small.png") ;
    down-skin: Embed("assets/rollover_down_small.png") ;
}
.hidePanels {
    skin: Embed("assets/hide_panels.png") ;
    over-skin: Embed("assets/hide_panels_rollover.png") ;
    down-skin: Embed("assets/hide_panels_rollover.png") ;
}
.showPanels {
    skin: Embed("assets/show_panels.png") ;
    over-skin: Embed("assets/show_panels_rollover.png") ;
    down-skin: Embed("assets/show_panels_rollover.png") ;
}

.controlBarPanelStyle {
    border-style: none ;
    fillColors: #4867a2, #4f75bf ;
    border-skin: ClassReference("border.SimpleGradientBorder");
}
```

A CSS file can be compiled to the corresponding *.swf*. To do so via Flash Builder, right-click the filename and select "Compile CSS to SWF." Now you can dynamically load all required byte code, define classes, create instances, and apply styles to objects that are already present in the display list—all with the single instruction `StyleManager.loadStyleDeclarations()`, as shown in Example 7-3.

Example 7-3. Dynamic style loading via StyleManager

```
<?xml version="1.0" encoding="utf-8"?>
<!-- RuntimeStyleDemo.mxml -->
<mx:Application
xmlns:mx="http://www.adobe.com/2006/mxml"
xmlns:navigation="com.farata.portal.navigation.*"
layout="absolute"
click="toggleStyles()"
>
<mx:Script>
<![CDATA[
```

```
import mx.modules.IModuleInfo;
import mx.modules.ModuleManager;
private function toggleStyles():void {
  var moduleInfo:IModuleInfo = ModuleManager.getModule('styles.swf');
  if (moduleInfo.loaded) {
     StyleManager.unloadStyleDeclarations('styles.swf');
  } else {
     StyleManager.loadStyleDeclarations('styles.swf');
  }
}
]]>
</mx:Script>
<navigation:ControlBar/>
</mx:Application>
```

The sample application presented in Example 7-3 allows you to load and unload the compiled stylesheet *styles.swf* when the user clicks anywhere in the application area. Figure 7-1 illustrates the striking difference before and after the styles were loaded.

When developing a portal, you can apply similar styling techniques. If every portlet is styled dynamically, making them conform to the required look and feel is simply a matter of adjusting and recompiling the relevant CSS files. Perhaps the portal owner may even rebuild the CSS module without bothering the creator of the portlet. The portlet itself will not have to be rebuilt to change its appearance.

Example 7-4 represents the top-level control bar of a sample portal desktop.

Example 7-4. ControlBar of a sample portal

```
<?xml version="1.0" encoding="utf-8"?>
<!-- com.farata.portal.navigation.ControlBar.mxml -->
<mx:HBox xmlns:mx="http://www.adobe.com/2006/mxml"
    width="100%" height="28"    verticalAlign="middle"
    styleName="controlBarPanelStyle">

   <mx:HBox verticalAlign="middle" horizontalGap="10" paddingLeft="10">
      <mx:Button id="saveButton" height="16" width="16"
         styleName="saveButtonStyle" toolTip="Save Portal"
         useHandCursor="true" buttonMode="true"/>
      <mx:Button id="showTopPanelButton" height="16" width="16"
         styleName="hidePanels" toolTip="Hide/Show Top Panel"
         useHandCursor="true" buttonMode="true"/>
      <mx:Button id="showPanelButton"   height="16" width="16"
         styleName="showPanelButtonDown" toolTip="Show Panel"
         useHandCursor="true" buttonMode="true"/>
   </mx:HBox>
   <mx:HBox width="100%" horizontalAlign="right" paddingRight="5">
      <mx:HBox borderStyle="solid" cornerRadius="13"
                    borderThickness="0" horizontalGap="0" >
         <mx:Button styleName="arrowRight"
            useHandCursor="true" buttonMode="true" />
         <mx:Button styleName="arrowLeft"
            useHandCursor="true" buttonMode="true" />
         <mx:filters>
```

```
            <mx:BevelFilter />
            <mx:GlowFilter color="#d3dffd"/>
         </mx:filters>
      </mx:HBox>
      <mx:Button
         styleName="tileStyle" toolTip="Arrange Windows"
      useHandCursor="true" buttonMode="true" />
      <mx:Button styleName="minimizeStyle" toolTip="Minimize All "
         useHandCursor="true" buttonMode="true" />
      <mx:Button styleName="restoreStyle" toolTip="Restore All
         useHandCursor="true" buttonMode="true" />
   </mx:HBox>
</mx:HBox>
```

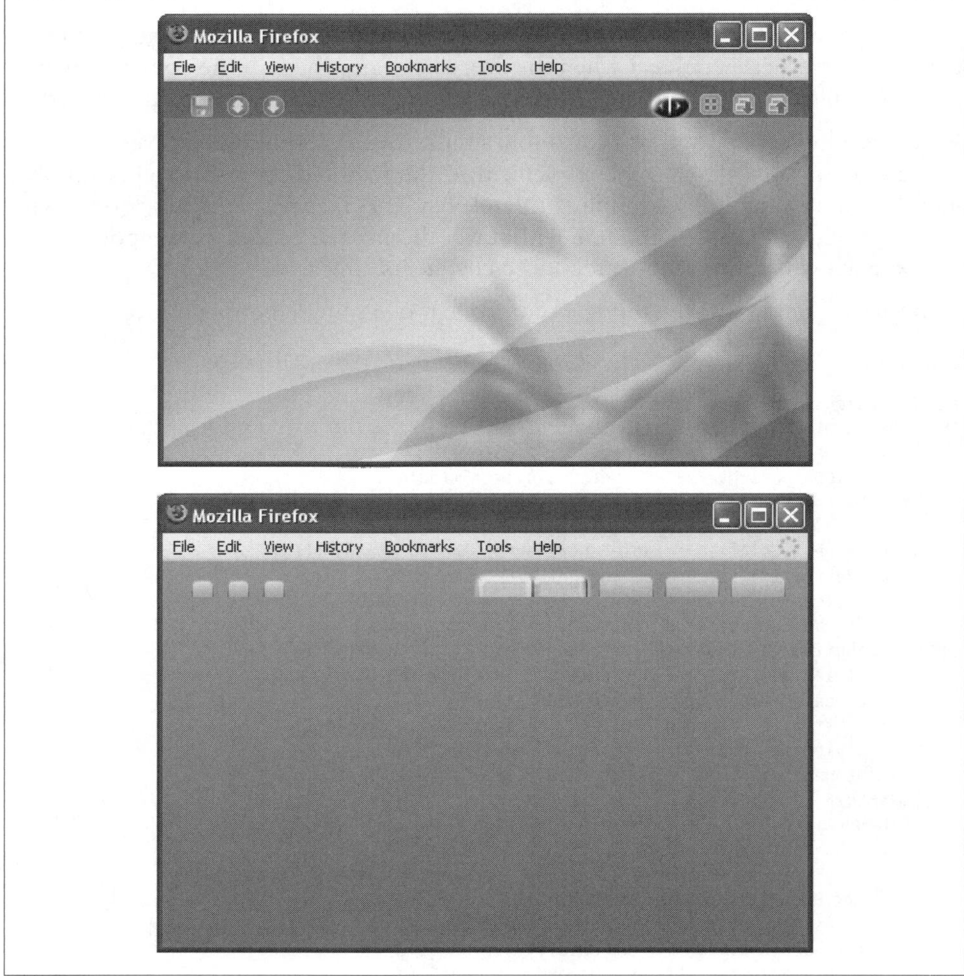

Figure 7-1. RuntimeStyleDemo with styles.swf loaded (top) and unloaded (bottom)

Now you are ready to investigate the most obvious part of the modularization API.

Real Actors: Loader and URLLoader

So far this chapter has touched briefly on the `Image`, `StyleManager`, and `ModuleManager` classes, and equally briefly used `ModuleManager`. To further your understanding of the modularization techniques, you need to be aware of two important connections:

- The `Image` class is a descendant of `SWFLoader`, the Flex component that facilitates loading of SWF files in addition to images, such as JPEG and GIF.
- Both `SWFLoader` and `ModuleManager` delegate the actual loading to `flash.display.Loader`.

As the saying goes, all roads lead to Rome, and for your purposes Rome is `flash.display.Loader`. Be it `SWFLoader`, `ModuleManager`, `StyleManager` (or the similar `ResourceManager`), modularization is all about loading and unloading classes via `flash.display.Loader`, the only Flash component that creates class definitions and class instances from the remote URL. In addition, `flash.display.Loader` can create classes from the existing byte code, for instance, the byte code obtained with the help of `flash.net.URLLoader` (as illustrated in Example 7-1).

Loading Modules with Module Loader

The simplest way you can modularize your application is by using Flex *modules*. The class `Module` is a `VBox` that, like `Application`, is a `Container` that also gets compiled, along with the dependent classes, to a separate *.swf* file. Example 7-5 illustrates a trivial module.

Example 7-5. Example of the module

```
<?xml version="1.0"?>
<!-SimpleModule.xml -->
<mx:Module xmlns:mx=http://www.adobe.com/2006/mxml layout="vertical">
    <mx:Text text="This is the simplest module" >
</mx:Module>
```

Any functional part of your application UI that can be developed and tested independently is a good candidate to become a module. The advantages are obvious: you can delegate the development and testing efforts to a different team or allocate a different time slot to it. Modularization will also improve memory utilization, because you can unload the module when the application does not need it anymore.

For Flash Builder to compile your module, it needs to be included into the *.actionScriptProperties* file of your project. You typically add the module via the project's properties, as shown in Figure 7-2, or by using the New Module wizard.

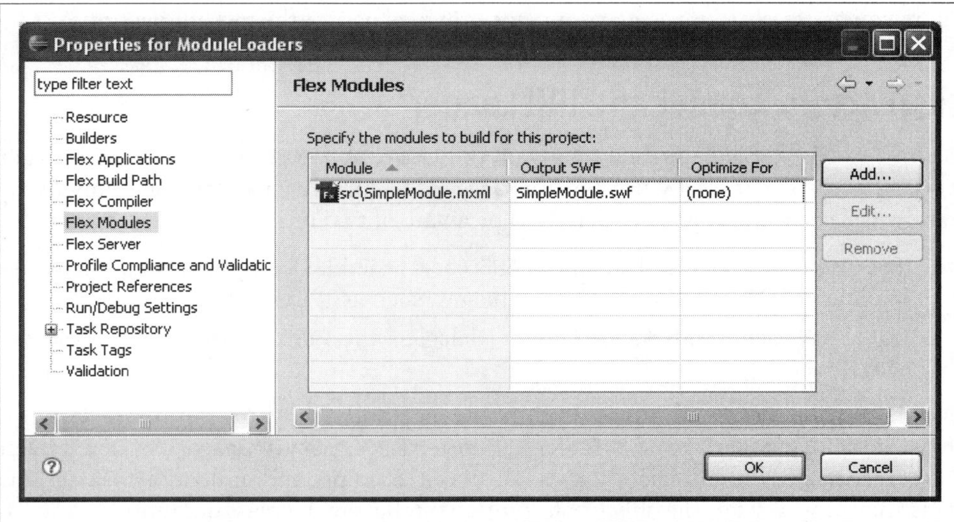

Figure 7-2. Registration of the module to be compiled by Flash Builder

The easiest way to load a module to your application during runtime is via `ModuleLoader`, a descendant of the `VBox` that has an extra API to load and unload module SWF files, as shown in Example 7-6.

Example 7-6. Loading a module via ModuleLoader

```
<?xml version="1.0"?>
<!-- ModuleLoaderDemo.mxml -->
<mx:Application xmlns:mx="http://www.adobe.com/2006/mxml">
   <mx:HBox>
      <mx:Button label="Load Module"
         click="moduleLoader.loadModule('SimpleModule.swf')" />
      <mx:Button label="Unload Module"
         click="moduleLoader.unloadModule()"
         enabled="{moduleLoader.loaderInfo.bytesTotal!=0}"/>
   </mx:HBox>
<mx:ModuleLoader id="moduleLoader"/>
</mx:Application>
```

As you could figure by now, the ultimate performer of the class loading in the case of the `ModuleLoader` is, again, `flash.display.Loader`. Being clear on the role of `flash.display.Loader` will help you understand other concepts in this chapter.

Preloading Modules with ModuleManager

In addition to `ModuleLoader`, which is a high-level module API, Flex offers `ModuleManager`. The prime benefit of using `ModuleManager` is that you can separate the transfer of the module byte code over the network, which is potentially a lengthy operation, from the actual creation of the module instance(s). Certainly, you could do it yourself with the `URLLoader` (as illustrated in Example 7-1), but you should take advantage of the nice abstraction layer provided by the `ModuleManager` class. In particular, the contract of the `ModuleManager` guarantees that you won't transfer the module bytes over the network more than once.

To load a module into a singleton registry of modules provided by `ModuleManager`, you use a *module proxy*, such as an implementation of the `IModuleInfo` interface, corresponding to the module URL. You then perform the `load()` via this module proxy, as shown in Example 7-7. The actual loading task will be delegated to `flash.display.Loader`.

Example 7-7. Module preloading technique

```
private var moduleInfoRef:Object = {};

private function loadModule(moduleUrl:String):void {
   var moduleInfo:IModuleInfo  = ModuleManager.getModule(moduleUrl);
   moduleInfo.addEventListener(ModuleEvent.READY, onModuleReady ) ;
   //You need to protect moduleInfo from being garbage-collected
   moduleInfoRef[moduleUrl] = moduleInfo;
   moduleInfo.load();
}

// Module is loaded. You may create modules via event.module.factory
private   function onModuleReady(event:ModuleEvent):void {
   // Remove 'protection' from moduleInfo
   moduleInfoRef[event.module.url]=null;
}
```

The code, similar to the function `loadModule()`, can be called well in advance of the immediate need of the module. Then, to create an instance of the module, you obtain another instance of the module proxy and use its `factory` property, as shown in Example 7-8.

Example 7-8. Creating an instance of the preloaded module

```
private function createModuleInstance(moduleUrl:String,
parent:UIComponent=null):Module {
   var module:Module;
   var moduleInfo:IModuleInfo  = ModuleManager.getModule(moduleUrl);
   var flexModuleFactory:IFlexModuleFactory = moduleInfo.factory;
   if (flexModuleFactory != null) {
      module = flexModuleFactory.create() as Module;
      if (parent) {
         parent.addChild(module); // in Flex 4 use addElement()
      }
   }
   return module;
}
```

If this code looks confusing and leaves you wondering what to think of IFlexModule Factory and where create() comes from, try this: from the Flash Builder project's Properties, navigate to Flex Compiler, and in the pop-up window add the compiler option -keep in the field Additional Compiler Arguments to see the generated ActionScript code. Then, in the *src/generated* folder, open the file *_SimpleModule_mx_core_FlexModuleFactory.as*. The Flex compiler adds an implementation of IFlexModuleFactory for each module, similar to the one shown in the Example 7-9.

Example 7-9. Compiler-generated descendant of FlexModuleFactory

```
package{
public class _SimpleModule_mx_core_FlexModuleFactory
    extends mx.core.FlexModuleFactory
    implements IFlexModuleFactory{
   . . .
    override public function create(... params):Object{
        if (params.length > 0 && !(params[0] is String))
            return super.create.apply(this, params);

        var mainClassName:String = params.length == 0 ? "SimpleModule" :
                                                        String(params[0]);
        var mainClass:Class = Class(getDefinitionByName(mainClassName));
        if (!mainClass) return null;

        var instance:Object = new mainClass();
        if (instance is IFlexModule)
            (IFlexModule(instance)).moduleFactory = this;
        return instance;
    }

    override public function info():Object {
        return {
            compiledLocales: [ "en_US" ],
            compiledResourceBundleNames: [ "containers", "core", "effects",
                                                     "skins", "styles" ],
            creationComplete: "onCreationComplete()",
            currentDomain: ApplicationDomain.currentDomain,
            mainClassName: "SimpleModule",
            mixins: [ "_SimpleModule_FlexInit",
"_richTextEditorTextAreaStyleStyle", "_ControlBarStyle",
. . .
"_SimpleModuleWatcherSetupUtil" ]
        }
    }
}
}
```

Finally, to enable the unloading of the module, you need to detach all module instances from their parents. To that end, the example application maintains a Dictionary of loaded modules instances, one per module URL:

```
[Bindable]private var modules:Dictionary = new Dictionary();
```

Although this example deals with only one module (*SimpleModule.swf*), you may upgrade this code to a reusable utility. Then the unloading of the module can be coded like in Example 7-10.

Example 7-10. Module unloading technique

```
private function unloadModule(moduleUrl:String):void {
   var moduleInfo:IModuleInfo  = ModuleManager.getModule(moduleUrl);
   if (moduleInfo.loaded) {
      var moduleList:Array = modules[moduleUrl];
      // If more then one module instance was loaded, unload each one
      for  each(var module:Module in  moduleList) {
          module.parent.removeChild(module);
      }
      delete modules[moduleUrl];
      moduleInfo.unload();
      moduleInfo.release();
   }
   isModuleLoaded = false;
}
```

Figure 7-3 illustrates the example application after the creation of one instance of *SimpleModule*. Example 7-11 lists the complete code of the *ModuleManagerDemo* application.

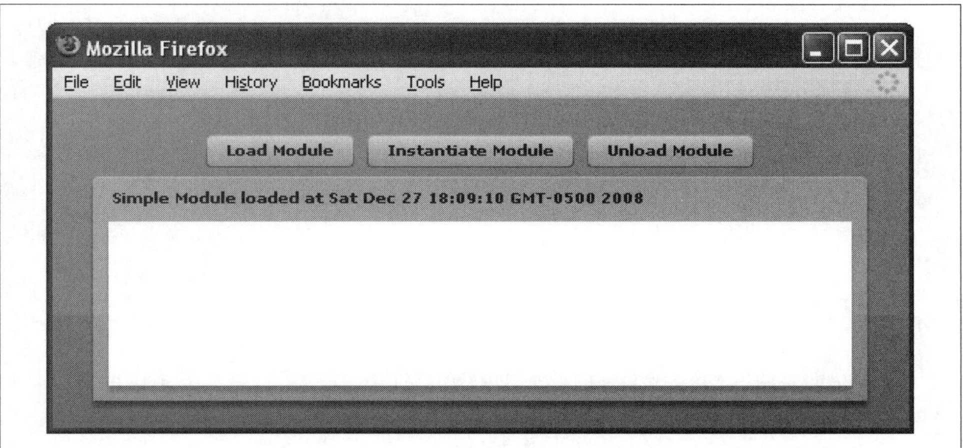

Figure 7-3. ModuleManagerDemo with one instance of the module

Example 7-11. Complete code of ModuleManagerDemo

```
<?xml version="1.0" encoding="utf-8"?>
<!-- ModuleManagerDemo.mxml -->
<mx:Application xmlns:mx="http://www.adobe.com/2006/mxml">
<mx:Script>
   <![CDATA[
   import mx.core.UIComponent;
```

```
import mx.controls.Alert;
import mx.modules.Module;
import mx.core.IFlexModuleFactory;
import mx.modules.IModuleInfo;
import mx.events.ModuleEvent;
import mx.modules.ModuleManager;

private const MODULE_URL:String='SimpleModule.swf';
private var moduleInfoRef:Object = {};
[Bindable]private var modules:Dictionary = new Dictionary();

private function loadModule(moduleUrl:String,
                   applicationDomain:ApplicationDomain=null):void {
   var moduleInfo:IModuleInfo  = ModuleManager.getModule(moduleUrl);
   moduleInfo.addEventListener(ModuleEvent.READY, onModuleReady ) ;
   moduleInfo.addEventListener(ModuleEvent.ERROR, onModuleError ) ;
   moduleInfoRef[moduleUrl] = moduleInfo;
   moduleInfo.load(
      applicationDomain?
          applicationDomain:ApplicationDomain.currentDomain
   );
}

private function createModuleInstance(moduleUrl:String,
                                   parent:UIComponent=null):Module {
   var module:Module;
   var moduleInfo:IModuleInfo  = ModuleManager.getModule(moduleUrl);
   var flexModuleFactory:IFlexModuleFactory = moduleInfo.factory;
   if (flexModuleFactory != null) {
      module = flexModuleFactory.create() as Module;
      var moduleList:Array = modules[moduleUrl] ?  modules[moduleUrl] :
                                                  new Array();
      moduleList.push(module);
      modules[moduleUrl] = moduleList;
      if (parent) {
         parent.addChild(module);
      }
   }
   return module;
}

[Bindable] private var isModuleLoaded:Boolean=false;
 private   function onModuleReady(event:ModuleEvent):void {
   // Module is loaded. You may create module instances
   //  via event.module.factory (moduleInfo)
   moduleInfoRef[event.module.url]=null;
   isModuleLoaded = true;
}

private function onModuleError (event:ModuleEvent):void {
   Alert.show( event.errorText );
}

private function unloadModule(moduleUrl:String):void {
   var moduleInfo:IModuleInfo  = ModuleManager.getModule(moduleUrl);
```

```
        if (moduleInfo.loaded) {
           var moduleList:Array = modules[moduleUrl];
           for  each(var module:Module in  moduleList) {
               module.parent.removeChild(module);
           }
           delete modules[moduleUrl];
           moduleInfo.unload();
           moduleInfo.release();
        }
        isModuleLoaded = false;
    }
]]>
</mx:Script>

    <mx:HBox>
        <mx:Button label="Load Module" click="loadModule(MODULE_URL)" />
        <mx:Button label="Instantiate Module"
           click="createModuleInstance(MODULE_URL, this)"
           enabled="{isModuleLoaded}"/>
        <mx:Button label="Unload Module"
           click="unloadModule(MODULE_URL)"
           enabled="{isModuleLoaded}"/>
    </mx:HBox>
</mx:Application>
```

Note that Example 7-11 applies the concept of *application domains*:

```
moduleInfo.load(
   applicationDomain?applicationDomain:ApplicationDomain.currentDomain
);
```

You'll learn about domains a bit later in this chapter. For now, suffice it to say that the code loads module classes into the same area (in memory) where the classes of the calling applications were loaded.

Whether via `ModuleLoader` or `ModuleManager`, you have loaded your module. How will the application communicate with it?

Communicating with Modules

You've designed your modules to be independent, but there should be provisions to allow external applications to communicate with them, pass them some information and receive response notifications. From the user's point of view, it may look like an innocent drag-and-drop action, but internally you must resort to one of the several available means of communication. We will start with direct references to the module variables and methods.

First, consider the method-based interfaces. We'll assume that you have the `IGreeting` interface, as shown in Example 7-12.

Example 7-12. IGreeting interface

```
//IGreeting.as
package
{
   public interface IGreeting {
      function getGreeting():String;
      function setGreeting( value:String ):void;
   }
}
```

Further, suppose that a module, such as `ModuleWithIGreeting` in Example 7-13, is *implementing* this interface. Please notice that calling `setGreeting()` will modify the bindable variable `greeting` that affects the title of the module's panel.

Example 7-13. Example of a module implementing the IGreeting interface

```
<?xml version="1.0"?>
<!- ModuleWithIGreeting.mxml -->
<mx:Module xmlns:mx="http://www.adobe.com/2006/mxml" xmlns="*"
   implements="IGreeting"
   creationComplete="onCreationComplete()"
>
 <mx:Script>
<![CDATA[
   [Bindable] private var greeting:String="";

   public function setGreeting(value:String):void {
      greeting = value;
   }
   public function getGreeting():String {
      return greeting;
   }
]]>
 </mx:Script>
   <mx:Panel id="panel" title="Module With Greeting{greeting}" width="400"
height="200">
   </mx:Panel>
</mx:Module>
```

How can your application take advantage of the fact that the loaded module implements a known interface? Assuming that it has used a `ModuleLoader`, as the following snippet shows, you can cast its `child` property to the `IGreeting` interface:

```
var greeting:IGreeting = moduleLoader.child as IGreeting;
greeting.setGreeting(" loaded by application");
```

Then again, no one prevents you from simply referencing the panel from *ModuleWithIGreeting* by name:

```
var module:Module = moduleLoader.child as Module;
var panel:Panel = module.getChildByName("panel") as Panel;
trace(panel.title); //Simple Module  loaded by application
```

The complete *ReferenceCommunicationDemo* application is presented in Example 7-14.

Example 7-14. ReferenceCommunicationDemo application

```
<?xml version="1.0"?>
<!-- ReferenceCommunicationDemo.mxml -->
<mx:Application xmlns:mx="http://www.adobe.com/2006/mxml">
<mx:Script>
<![CDATA[
   import mx.modules.Module;
   import mx.containers.Panel;

   private const MODULE_URL:String="ModuleWithIGreeting.swf";

   private function modifyLoadedContent():void {
      var greeting:IGreeting = moduleLoader.child as IGreeting;
      greeting.setGreeting(" loaded by application");

      var module:Module = moduleLoader.child as Module;
      var panel:Panel = module.getChildByName("panel") as Panel;
      trace(panel.title); //Simple Module  loaded by application
}
]]>
</mx:Script>
   <mx:HBox>
      <mx:Button label="Load Module"
         click="moduleLoader.loadModule(MODULE_URL)" />
      <mx:Button label="Modify Content"
         click="modifyLoadedContent()"/>
      <mx:Button label="Unload Module"
         click="moduleLoader.unloadModule()"
         enabled="{moduleLoader.loaderInfo.bytesTotal!=0}"/>
   </mx:HBox>

   <mx:ModuleLoader id="moduleLoader"/>
</mx:Application>
```

This application has three buttons labeled Load Module, Modify Content, and Unload Module (Figure 7-4), each associated with a similarly named function. This separation of functions enables you to profile the application and verify that there is no memory leak associated with module unloading.

Although this interface-based method of working with modules is appealing, use it with care: it uses direct references to the modules, and any unreleased direct reference will indefinitely lock your module in memory. Against this backdrop, the elegance of the interfaces does not matter much.

The best way to make sure you do not have unreleased references is to avoid them to begin with. Instead, use *events* to communicate with the loaded modules. To do so, you need an `EventDispatcher` that can be commonly accessed by the module and the loading application (here's yet another example of the Mediator design pattern from

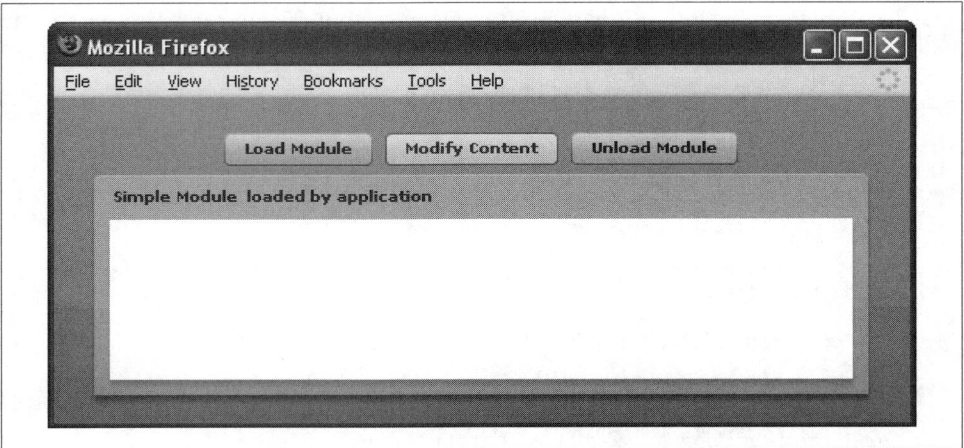

Figure 7-4. ReferenceCommunicationDemo

Chapter 2). One object that suits the task particularly well is `sharedEvents`, accessible as `loader.loaderInfo.sharedEvents` from the module and loading application as well.

The complete code of the sample application `EventCommunicationDemo` is presented in Example 7-15. Note that in the `loadModule()`, you subscribe to `Event.COMPLETE` to be sent by the modules upon loading and creating the module's display list. Then the `onComplete()` handler application itself sends an event to the module. The module, as you will see soon, interprets this event to modify a panel's header.

Example 7-15. EventCommunicationDemo application

```
<?xml version="1.0"?>
<!-- EventCommunicationDemo.mxml -->
<mx:Application xmlns:mx="http://www.adobe.com/2006/mxml">
<mx:Script>
<![CDATA[
   import mx.events.DynamicEvent;
   import mx.controls.Alert;
   import mx.events.ModuleEvent;
   import mx.modules.Module;

   private const MODULE_URL:String="ModuleWithEvents.swf";
   [Bindable] private var moduleLoaded:Boolean;

   private function loadModule():void {
      // Subscribe to notifications from the module
      var sharedEventDispatcher:IEventDispatcher =
         moduleLoader.loaderInfo.sharedEvents;
      sharedEventDispatcher.addEventListener(
         Event.COMPLETE, onModuleCreated
      );
      moduleLoader.loadModule(MODULE_URL);
      moduleLoaded = true;
   }
```

```
    // This event "comes" from the module
    private function onModuleCreated(event:Event):void {
       trace("Module CreateComplete happened");
       //Send commands to the module
       var sharedEventDispatcher:IEventDispatcher =
          moduleLoader.loaderInfo.sharedEvents;
       var dynamicEvent:DynamicEvent = new DynamicEvent("command");
       dynamicEvent.data = " Two-way talk works!";
       sharedEventDispatcher.dispatchEvent(dynamicEvent);
    }
    private function unloadModule():void {
       moduleLoader.unloadModule();
       moduleLoaded = false;
    }

]]>
</mx:Script>
   <mx:HBox>
      <mx:Button label="Load Module" click="loadModule()" />
      <mx:Button label="Unload Module"   click="unloadModule()"
         enabled="{moduleLoaded}"/>
     </mx:HBox>

   <mx:ModuleLoader id="moduleLoader"/>
</mx:Application>
```

Example 7-16 presents the corresponding module sample `ModuleWithEvents`. Notice the handler of the `creationComplete` event. It subscribes to the *command* events sent by the application and notifies the application that the module is ready for receiving such events by dispatching `Event.COMPLETE`.

The syntax of `addEventListener()` specifies *weak* reference, because strong reference to the `sharedEventDispatcher` would prevent the module from being garbage-collected. If you run the application and click on the button Load Module, you will see the screen shown in Figure 7-5.

The panel's header will read "Module With Events. Two-way talk works!" to emphasize the fact that the application and the module exchange events in both directions. You may want to actually profile the application and watch how referencing of the event listener (*weak* versus *strong*) dramatically affects the ability to unload the module.

Example 7-16. Counterpart module example to EventCommunicationDemo

```
<?xml version="1.0"?>
<!- ModuleWithEvents.mxml -->
<mx:Module xmlns:mx="http://www.adobe.com/2006/mxml"
   creationComplete="onCreationComplete()"
   >
 <mx:Script>
   <![CDATA[
   import mx.events.DynamicEvent;
```

```
    [Bindable] private var command:String="";
    private function onCreationComplete():void {
        var sharedEventDispatcher:IEventDispatcher =
            systemManager.loaderInfo.sharedEvents
        //Subscribe to command from the application
        sharedEventDispatcher.addEventListener(
            "command", onCommand,false,0,true
        ); //Strong reference would lock the module to application

        // Notify the applications that creation has completed
sharedEventDispatcher.dispatchEvent(new Event(Event.COMPLETE)
        );
    }

    private function onCommand(event:DynamicEvent):void {
         command = event.data as String;
    }
]]>
</mx:Script>
    <mx:Panel id="panel" title="Module With Events. {command}" width="400"
     height="200"/>
</mx:Module>
```

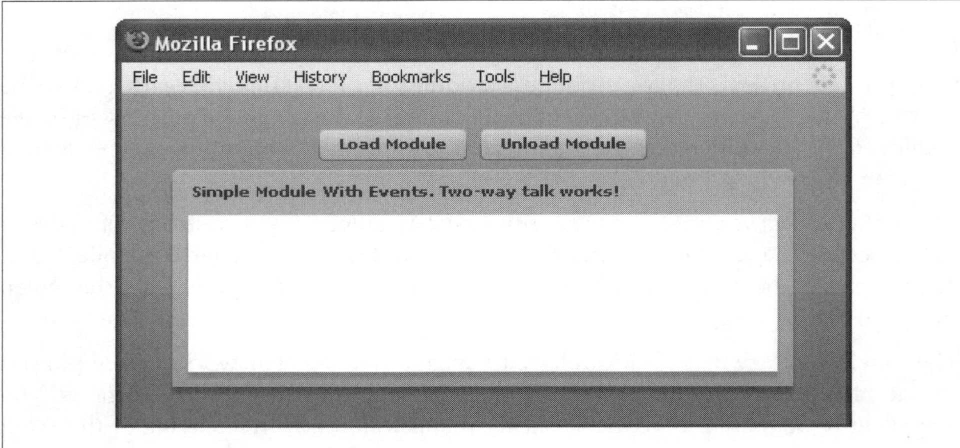

Figure 7-5. EventCommunicationDemo application

Introducing Application Domains

You're packing for the snorkeling trip with your kid. Into your travel bag you put the two new pairs of goggles you bought just yesterday. Meanwhile, your small one found two old pairs in the garage and placed them in his backpack. You arrive to the beach with two sets of goggles. Which ones are you going to use?

- You are a perfectionist. You want the spotless snorkeling, and use the new goggles.

- You are a good father. You want your kid to feel that his preparation for the trip was important and use the old goggles.
- You are a pedant. You use the new goggles. Your kid should have consulted with you instead of bringing old ones.

Now, if we replace the travel bag with a *parent application domain*, your kid's backpack with a *child application domain*, and start discussing class definitions instead of goggles, the only choice you are going to get is #3, or "delegate to your parent."

Classes get loaded into application domains, which form a tree. By default, a module's classes get loaded into the child domain (of the application or parental module). The child has access to all classes in the parental chain. This means that a module can create all the classes the application can (your kid can use your goggles).

On the contrary, the application does not get access to the classes carried by the module (you are not allowed to open your kid's backpack), and the child can't reload the class already known to the parent (your goggles are the *only* ones your kid gets to use).

The application *ModuleDomainDemo* illustrates this concept. Its `ModuleLoader` has an `applicationDomain` property set to a bindable expression that depends on the user-controlled radio button:

```
<mx:ModuleLoader id="moduleLoader"
    applicationDomain="{
       same_domain.selected?
       ApplicationDomain.currentDomain:
       new ApplicationDomain(ApplicationDomain.currentDomain)
   }"
/>
```

For the complete code of *ModuleDomainDemo*, see Example 7-19 (a bit later).

The subexpression `ApplicationDomain.currentDomain` refers to the domain that the very code containing this expression belongs to. In the example's case, it means the domain that keeps the class definitions of the application itself. At the same time, the expression `new ApplicationDomain(ApplicationDomain.currentDomain)` refers to the child of that domain. These are two alternative application domain settings when you are loading the modules: the same domain or a child domain (default). The module that you are going to load is a slightly modified version of the `SimpleModule` you used earlier: it explicitly links in the `CustomGrid` control, as shown in Examples 7-17 and 7-18.

Example 7-17. SimpleModule with linked-in CustomGrid component

```
<?xml version="1.0"?>
<!-- SimpleModule -->
<mx:Module xmlns:mx="http://www.adobe.com/2006/mxml"
```

```
><mx:Script>
   <![CDATA[
      CustomGrid; //Needed only for ModuleDomainDemo
   ]]>
</mx:Script>
  <mx:Panel id="panel" title="Simple Module" width="400" height="200">
 </mx:Panel>
</mx:Module>
```

Example 7-18. CustomGrid component

```
<?xml version="1.0" encoding="utf-8"?>
<!-- CustomGrid.mxml -->
<mx:DataGrid xmlns:mx="http://www.adobe.com/2006/mxml">
   <mx:columns>
      <mx:Array>
         <mx:DataGridColumn  dataField="name" headerText="Name" width="150"/>
         <mx:DataGridColumn  dataField="phone" headerText="Phone"/>
      </mx:Array>
   </mx:columns>
</mx:DataGrid>
```

The application attempts dynamic creation of the `CustomGrid`, purely by class name. To obtain the class definition from the current application domain, use the **`loaderInfo`** property shared by all display objects:

```
var clazz:Class =
   loaderInfo.applicationDomain.getDefinition("CustomGrid") as Class;
dg  = DataGrid(new clazz());
```

Run the application and make sure that the radio button Same Domain is selected. This means that classes will get loaded into the `ApplicationDomain.currentDomain`. In other words, you have allowed your kid to put his things into *your* bag (it's a "MiracleCompactPro" bag, all right, because it does not accept the same article twice). Click Load Module and then click Create Custom Grid. The application will look as shown in Figure 7-6. The application (not the module!) has created `DataGrid` using the class from the module's *.swf*.

Restart the application and load the module with the radio button Child Domain selected. The application won't be able to create the `CustomGrid`. It's out of the application's reach now, because you loaded modules classes in the isolated child application domain (Figure 7-7).

By no means are we suggesting the use of modules instead of the *libraries*, as far as reusable resources are concerned (we discuss libraries in the next section). Example 7-19, *ModuleDomainDemo.mxml*, merely illustrates the class isolation provided by the application domains. That said, if you find yourself loading your modules into the same domain—you've got company! Provided you use careful class naming, this is a viable alternative to child domains.

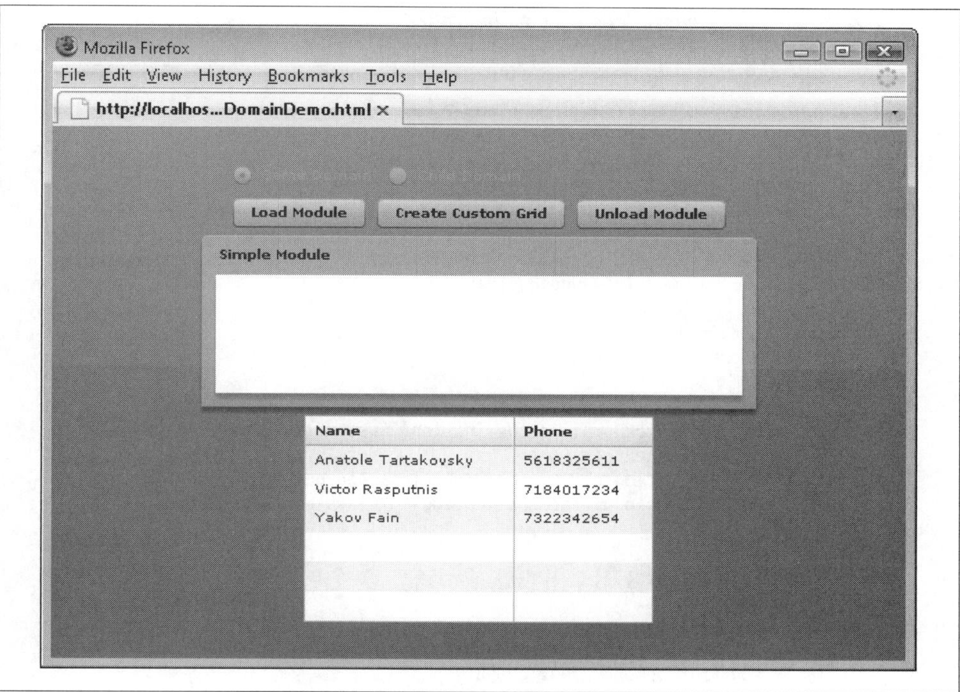

Figure 7-6. ModuleDomainDemo: loading the module to the same domain

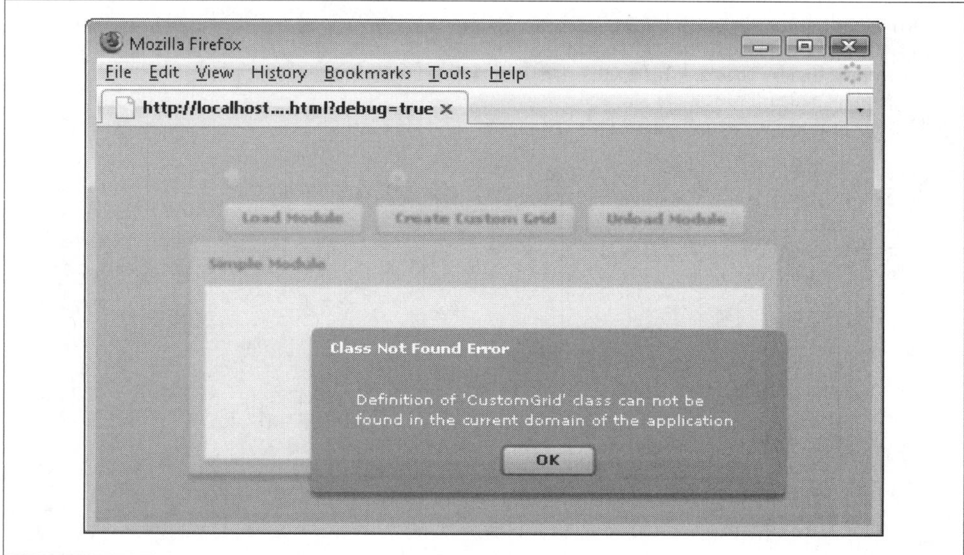

Figure 7-7. ModuleDomainDemo: loading the module to the child domain

Example 7-19. Complete code of ModuleDomainDemo

```
<?xml version="1.0"?>
<!-- ModuleDomainDemo.mxml -->
<mx:Application xmlns:mx="http://www.adobe.com/2006/mxml">
<mx:Script>
<![CDATA[
   import mx.controls.Alert;
   import mx.controls.DataGrid;

   private const  MODULE_URL:String = "SimpleModule.swf";
   [Bindable] private var moduleLoaded:Boolean;

   private var dg:DataGrid;
   private function createCustomGrid():void {
      try {
         var clazz:Class =
         loaderInfo.applicationDomain.getDefinition("CustomGrid") as Class;
      } catch (error:ReferenceError) {
         Alert.show ("Definition of 'CustomGrid' class can not be found
          in the current domain of the application ","Class Not Found Error");
         return;
      }
      dg  = DataGrid(new clazz());
      dg.dataProvider = [
         {name:"Anatole Tartakovsky", phone:"5618325611"},
         {name:"Victor Rasputnis", phone:"7184017234"},
         {name:"Yakov Fain",phone:"7322342654"}
      ];
      addChild(dg);
   }

   [Bindable] private var moduleLoaded:Boolean;
   private function loadModule():void {
      moduleLoader.loadModule(MODULE_URL);
      moduleLoaded=true;
   }

   private function unloadModule():void {
      removeChild(dg); // Remove references to the module
      dg = null;
      moduleLoader.unloadModule();
      moduleLoaded=false;
   }  ]]>
   </mx:Script>
   <mx:VBox>
      <mx:HBox>
         <mx:RadioButton groupName="domain" label="Same Domain"
         id="same_domain" selected="true" enabled="{!moduleLoaded}"/>
         <mx:RadioButton groupName="domain" label="Child Domain"
                       id="child_domain" enabled="{!moduleLoaded}"/>
      </mx:HBox>

      <mx:HBox>
         <mx:Button label="Load Module" click="loadModule(MODULE_URL) "  />
         <mx:Button label="Create Custom Grid" click="createCustomGrid()" />
```

```
        <mx:Button label="Unload Module" click="unloadModule()"
        enabled="{moduleLoaded}"/>
    </mx:HBox>
  </mx:VBox>

   <mx:ModuleLoader id="moduleLoader"
       applicationDomain="{
          same_domain.selected?
          ApplicationDomain.currentDomain:
          new ApplicationDomain(ApplicationDomain.currentDomain)
       }"
   />

</mx:Application>
```

Paying Tribute to Libraries

If you need to modularize reusable components, look no further than libraries: *Runtime Shared Libraries* (*RSL*), to be specific. Assuming that you are using Flash Builder, the basic procedure is:

1. Create a Flex Library project containing classes to be reused (call it, say, *ComponentLibrary*).
2. Add a mapping to this project to the Flex Build Path of the application(s) that makes use of the library classes.

If you do not have the source code, add a mapping to the SWC file of the library compiled by a third party instead of to the library project. Look in the Flex Build Path of your application: all Flex framework classes are added via several *.swc* files, similar to Figure 7-8.

At this configuration level, library projects merely separate development of the business application from building of the reusable components; however, your application is still built as monolithic *.swf*. Why? Because when you add mapping to the library project or *.swc* of the compiled library, the default *link type* is *"Merged into code."* This is static linking, where the application *.swf* contains only those classes it could determine as required at compile time. Recall the dynamic instantiation from Example 7-19:

```
var clazz:Class =
   loaderInfo.applicationDomain.getDefinition("CustomGrid") as Class;
dg  = DataGrid(new clazz());
```

Assuming the `CustomGrid` class belongs to *ComponentLibrary*, under "Merged into code," this dynamic instantiation will not work, because definition of the `CustomGrid` will not become a part of the application *.swf*.

If you want to reference `CustomGrid` explicitly, you may add the following line to your application:

```
import CustomGrid; CustomGrid;
```

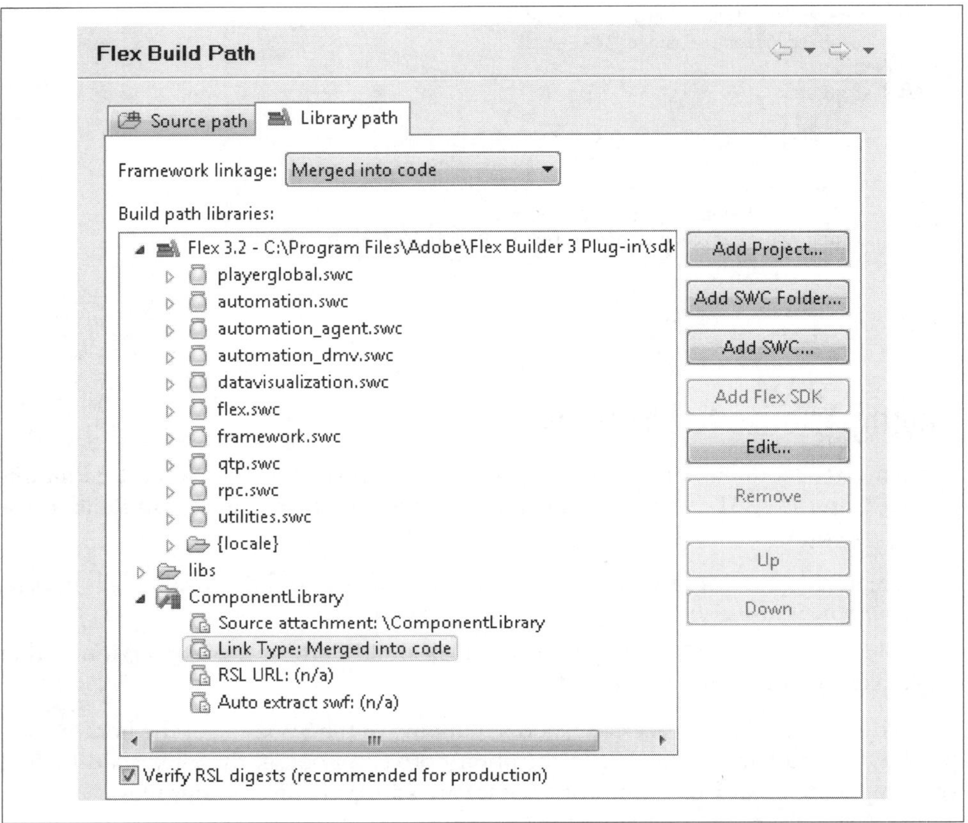

Figure 7-8. Default link type: merge into code

Alternatively, you may add `-includes CustomGrid` to the compiler options.

Either way, you are not using the library (RSL), you're only creating a monolithic SWF via a library project. To use the RSL, change the link type to "Runtime shared library." Figure 7-9 shows one way to do it, with the option "Automatically extract swf to deployment" turned on. What this really means is that the SWF of the library (RSL) will be created on each compile of the application. (You'll learn about the opposite setting of this option later in the chapter.)

According to Figure 7-9, after building an application that is mapped to the *ComponentLibrary* (Flex Library) project, you will find *ComponentLibrary.swf* in the output folder.

Now your application is using an RSL. To be precise, the compiler-generated code will have `flash.display.Loader` (what else?) preload the classes of the RSL *.swf* into `ApplicationDomain.currentDomain`. In other words, the default application domain setting for libraries is the *same domain* as the application (same bag for you and your kid).

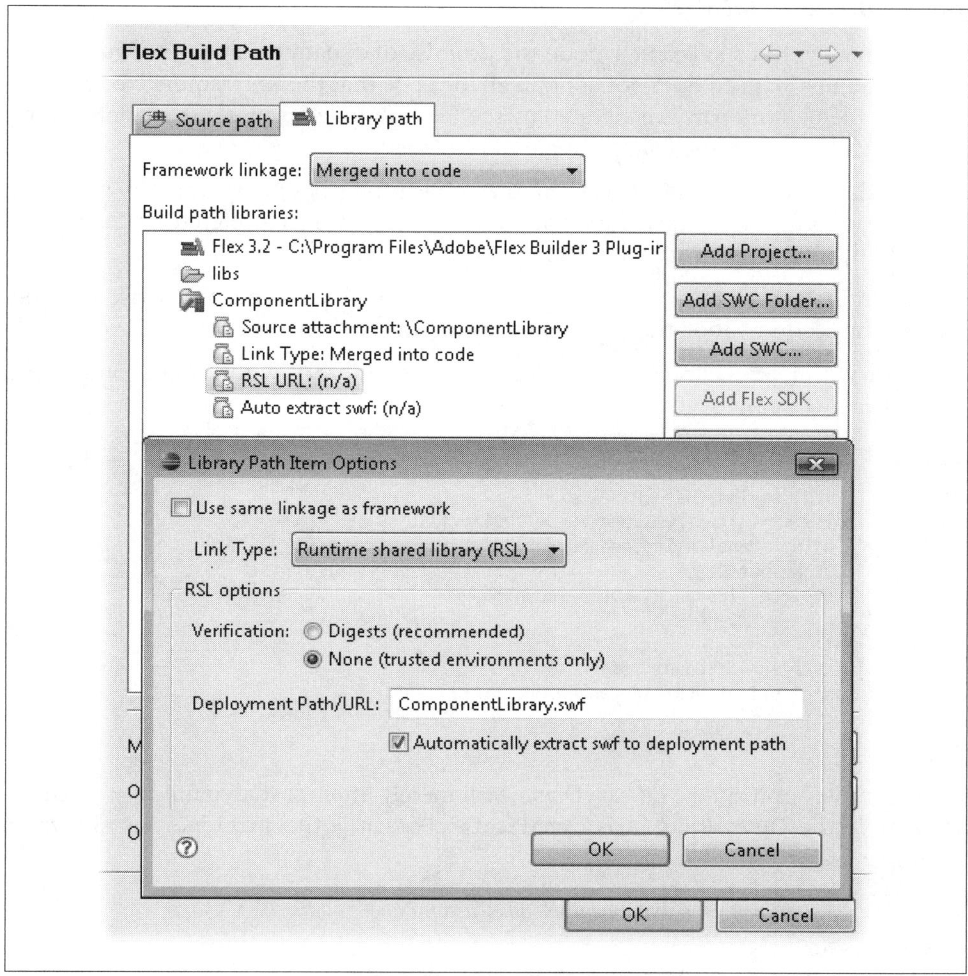

Figure 7-9. RSL link type defaults to autoextraction of the RSL SWF

The application *.swf* gets smaller, because it does not carry the footprint of any of the library classes, whether statically required or not. That said, you incurred extra *.swf* content: the library itself. If you are developing an intranet application, the size does not matter much. Additionally, if you are deploying for extranet use, recall that library *.swf* files get cached in the browser cache per domain.

On top of that, as far as Flex framework RSLs are concerned, the latest releases of Flash Player 9 and Flash Player 10 support Adobe-signed RSLs that get cached by Flash Player; these *.swf* files are cached across different server domains.

RSLs: "Under"-Libraries

Unfortunately, RSLs fail to deliver on the promise of dynamic linking. As it turns out, a SWF of the RSL itself does not contain all the code that the RSL requires to function. The complementary part is generated by the Flex compiler as part of the application's (or module's) bootstrap. That's not all.

Besides dependency of an RSL SWF on the application's bootstrap, the very bootstrap is totally ignoring any library class that the application does not reference statically. As a result, dynamic instantiation of RSL-based classes fails.

This section demonstrates the problem. If you are looking for the immediate solution, skip to the section "Bootstrapping Libraries As Applications" on page 357.

Here you will create a Flex library project, *ComponentLibrary*, with a single component, `CustomPanel` (Example 7-20).

Example 7-20. CustomPanel, to be dynamically loaded by LibraryDemo

```
<!-- com.farata.samples.CustomPanel.mxml -->
<mx:Panel xmlns:mx="http://www.adobe.com/2006/mxml"
   title="'Custom' Panel #{instanceNumber}"
   width="300" height="150"
   creationComplete="instanceNumber=++count;"
>
   <mx:Script>
      public static var count:int;
      [Bindable] private var instanceNumber:int;
   </mx:Script>
</mx:Panel>
```

The example application, *LibraryDemo*, will merely attempt to dynamically create instances of the `CustomPanel` using `applicationDomain.getDefinition()`, as shown in Example 7-21.

Example 7-21. LibraryDemo dynamically loads CustomPanel

```
<!-- LibraryDemo -->
<mx:Application xmlns:mx="http://www.adobe.com/2006/mxml"
   layout="vertical"
>
   <mx:Button label="CreatePanel"
click="createComponent('com.farata.samples.CustomPanel')"/>
   <mx:Script>
   <![CDATA[
      //import mx.containers.Panel;Panel; // Make sure this is commented out

      private var displayObject:DisplayObject;
      private function createComponent(componentName:String) : void {
         var clazz : Class =
loaderInfo.applicationDomain.getDefinition(componentName) as Class;
         displayObject = DisplayObject(new clazz() );
         addChild(displayObject);
```

```
        }
    ]]>
    </mx:Script>
</mx:Application>
```

To test the application, add the *ComponentLibrary* project to the Flex Build Path of the application project, as shown in Figure 7-9. Now, if you run the application and click Create Panel, the application will crash, as shown in Figure 7-10.

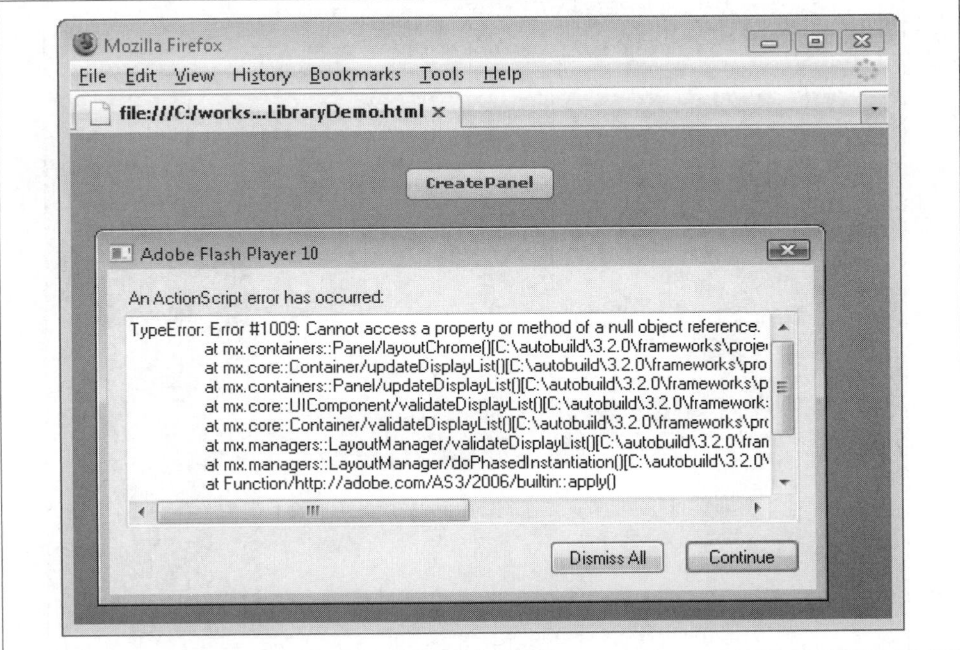

Figure 7-10. LibraryDemo fails to dynamically create CustomPanel

If, however, you uncomment this line:

```
//import mx.containers.Panel;Panel;
```

the application will run successfully, as shown in Figure 7-11.

Consider the problem. Debugging the application reveals that the null pointer error happens because of an uninitialized instance variable of the `Panel` class: `titleBarBackground`. The corresponding snippet of the *Panel.as* is presented in Example 7-22. At the time of the crash, the `titleBarBackground` class is null.

Example 7-22. First snippet of Panel.as

```
override protected function layoutChrome(unscaledWidth:Number,
                            unscaledHeight:Number):void
{
```

```
    super.layoutChrome(unscaledWidth, unscaledHeight);
    . . .
       titleBarBackground.move(0, 0);
       . . .
}
```

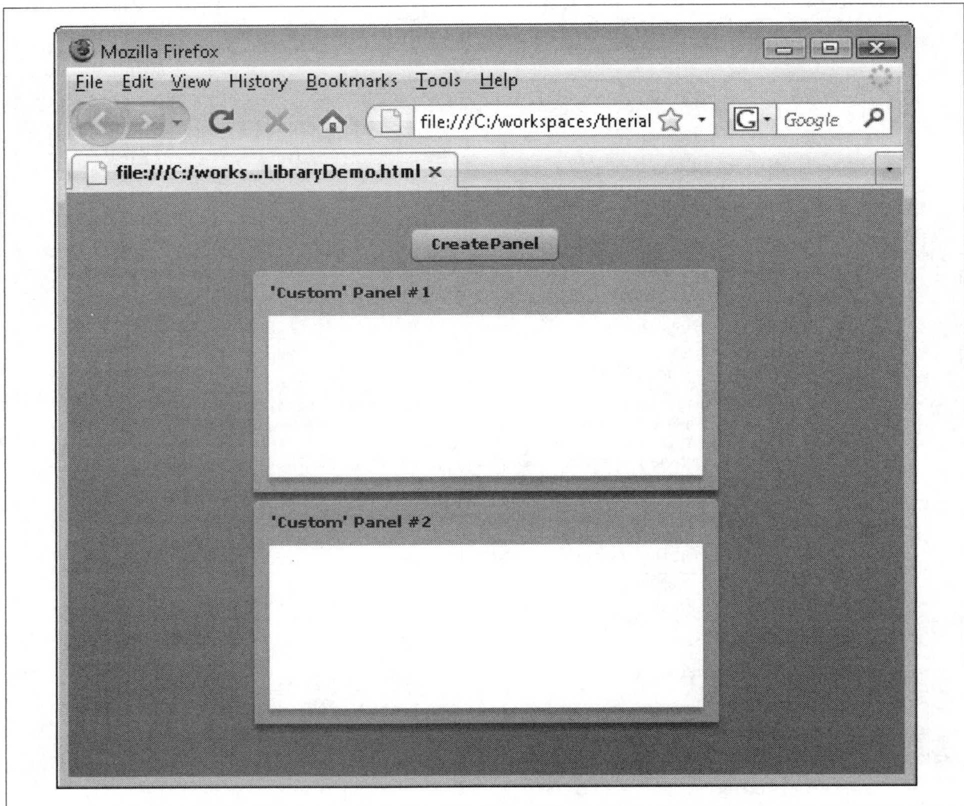

Figure 7-11. If you link in the Panel class, LibraryDemo works well

Following the lead, in the same *Panel.as* you will discover that the value of `titleBarBackground` is dependent on dynamic instantiation of `titleBackgroundSkin` (Example 7-23).

Example 7-23. Second snippet of Panel.as

```
var titleBackgroundSkinClass:Class = getStyle("titleBackgroundSkin");

if (titleBackgroundSkinClass){
     titleBarBackground = new titleBackgroundSkinClass();
. . .
```

Because you did not do anything beyond linking in the `Panel` to make the *LibraryDemo* application work, the difference between the working application and the buggy one must be in the generated code. Specifically, the difference is in the compiler-generated descendant of `SystemManager`, `_LibraryDemo_mx_managers_SystemManager`, which is the main application class.

The code of the nonworking application is presented in Example 7-24. Note that the class implements `IFlexModuleFactory` again. You came across this interface first during the discussion of loading modules with `ModuleManager`. At that time, you learned that modules get bootstrapped by classes implementing `IFlexModuleFactory` interface (see Example 7-9). As you see now, the same technique works with applications.

Also note the `currentDomain` and `rsls` properties of the object returned by the `info()` method. This `rsls` property contains the `url` of the *ComponentLibrary.swf* that will be loaded in the current domain of the application.

And last, compare the `mixins` array with Example 7-25, which presents the second version of the `mixins` array—this time taken from the *working* application (the one where you force linking in of the `Panel` class). This is the only place where two applications are different! And the only two *lines* that make this difference mention `_ControBarStyle` and `_Panel mixins` classes. FYI: the `mixins` class is a helper class with the method `initialize(baseObject)`.

Example 7-24. Compiler-generated SystemManager for the LibraryDemo (nonworking version)

```
// Compiler-generated SystemManager for the LibraryDemo
package
{

import . . .

[ResourceBundle("containers")]
[ResourceBundle("core")]
[ResourceBundle("effects")]
[ResourceBundle("skins")]
[ResourceBundle("styles")]
public class _LibraryDemo_mx_managers_SystemManager
    extends mx.managers.SystemManager
    implements IFlexModuleFactory
{
    public function _LibraryDemo_mx_managers_SystemManager() {
        super();
    }

    override     public function create(... params):Object {
        if (params.length > 0 && !(params[0] is String))
            return super.create.apply(this, params);

        var mainClassName:String = params.length == 0 ? "LibraryDemo" :
                                  String(params[0]);
        var mainClass:Class = Class(getDefinitionByName(mainClassName));
        if (!mainClass)
```

```
            return null;

        var instance:Object = new mainClass();
        if (instance is IFlexModule)
            (IFlexModule(instance)).moduleFactory = this;
        return instance;
    }

    override    public function info():Object {
        return {
            compiledLocales: [ "en_US" ],
            compiledResourceBundleNames: [ "containers", "core", "effects",
           "skins", "styles" ],
            currentDomain: ApplicationDomain.currentDomain,
            layout: "vertical",
            mainClassName: "LibraryDemo",
            mixins: [ "_LibraryDemo_FlexInit", "_richTextEditorTextAreaStyleStyle",
"_alertButtonStyleStyle", "_textAreaVScrollBarStyleStyle", "_headerDateTextStyle",
"_globalStyle", "_todayStyleStyle", "_windowStylesStyle", "_ApplicationStyle",
"_ToolTipStyle", "_CursorManagerStyle", "_opaquePanelStyle", "_errorTipStyle",
"_dateFieldPopupStyle", "_dataGridStylesStyle", "_popUpMenuStyle",
"_headerDragProxyStyleStyle", "_activeTabStyleStyle",
"_ContainerStyle", "_windowStatusStyle", "_ScrollBarStyle",
"_swatchPanelTextFieldStyle", "_textAreaHScrollBarStyleStyle", "_plainStyle",
"_activeButtonStyleStyle", "_advancedDataGridStylesStyle", "_comboDropdownStyle",
"_ButtonStyle", "_weekDayStyleStyle", "_linkButtonStyleStyle" ],
             rsls: [{url: "ComponentLibrary.swf", size: -1}]

        }
    }
}

}
```

Example 7-25. mixins array from the compiler-generated SystemManager for the working version of the LibraryDemo

```
mixins: [ "_LibraryDemo_FlexInit", "_richTextEditorTextAreaStyleStyle",
"_ControlBarStyle",
"_alertButtonStyleStyle", "_textAreaVScrollBarStyleStyle", "_headerDateTextStyle",
"_globalStyle", "_todayStyleStyle", "_windowStylesStyle", "_ApplicationStyle",
"_ToolTipStyle", "_CursorManagerStyle", "_opaquePanelStyle", "_errorTipStyle",
"_dateFieldPopupStyle", "_dataGridStylesStyle", "_popUpMenuStyle",
"_headerDragProxyStyleStyle", "_activeTabStyleStyle",
"_PanelStyle",
"_ContainerStyle", "_windowStatusStyle", "_ScrollBarStyle",
"_swatchPanelTextFieldStyle", "_textAreaHScrollBarStyleStyle", "_plainStyle",
"_activeButtonStyleStyle", "_advancedDataGridStylesStyle", "_comboDropdownStyle",
"_ButtonStyle", "_weekDayStyleStyle", "_linkButtonStyleStyle" ]
```

MXML applications are, by design, two-phased. The first phase is the bootstrap (the first frame of the Flex application or Flex module *.swf*). At this time, the application preloads the RSLs and manipulates support classes generated by the compiler, such as `mixins`. In this example's case, *not* knowing about `Panel` made the Flex compiler omit the creation and use of `_ControlBarStyle` and `_PanelStyle` `mixins`, which in turn lead to an uninitialized `titleBackgroundSkin` and, finally, a reference error in the panel's `layoutChrome()`. All in all, there are two problems:

- RSLs are not quite reusable libraries. They are "under"-libraries that require bootstrap support from the loading *.swf*.
- The bootstrap code generated by the Flex compiler fails to support classes that your application (or module) is referencing dynamically.

Now that we've admitted the problems, the rest is technicality.

Bootstrapping Libraries As Applications

Step back a little and consider Flex library projects, or more specifically, library *.swc* files. At the end of the day, when you link your application with the library, you link it with the *.swc*, whether made from sources in a library project or obtained from a third party.

If you recall, Figure 7-9 included the option "Automatically extract swf to deployment path." Being an option, it underscores the two missions of the SWC. The critical mission is to resolve the compile-time references for the application. The optional mission is to begin autoextracting the RSL SWF.

Here comes the big idea: do not rely on the automatically extracted library SWF, because it's incomplete, and do not trust the bootstrap from the application SWF, because the application does not necessarily know about all library classes. Instead, purposely create this *knowing* application yourself, merge it with the library classes, and give it the same name as the SWF of the library that otherwise would have been autoextracted. In other words, say "no" to autoextraction. Replace it with the custom compilation of the library as a fully bootstrapped application. Doing so changes nothing in how the main application gets compiled, but it no longer relies on bootstrap generation for the main application. Copy the custom-compiled library into the deployment folder, and when the main application loads the library (for instance, *ComponentLibrary.swf*), it will not know that it is loading a self-sufficient, custom-compiled SWF instead of the immature, autoextracted one.

Example 7-26 contains the example of the `ComponentLibrary_Application` class that is added to the library project to bootstrap the library. Notice the static reference to the `CustomPanel`: it is your responsibility to add such references as `import com.farata.samples.CustomPanel; CustomPanel;` to the body of the `ComponentLibrary_Application` class whenever you add new components to the library. Importantly, all these references stay encapsulated in the library itself. This library will not need outside help to guarantee the success of the dynamic calls.

Example 7-26. Example of bootstrapping the library as SimpleApplication to consolidate compiler-generated and manual code in one SWF

```
// ComponentLibrary_Application.as
// Example of Library bootstrapped as SimpleApplication
// Libraries created this way do not have problems with dynamic class references
package {
   import mx.core.SimpleApplication;

   public class ComponentLibrary_Application extends SimpleApplication {

      import com.farata.samples.CustomPanel; CustomPanel;

      public function ComponentLibrary_Application() {
         // Custom library initialization code should go here
         trace("ComponentLibrary_Application.swf has been loaded and initialized");
      }

   }
}
```

Example 7-27 contains the example of the *ComponentLibrary_Bootstrap.mxml* class derived from the `ComponentLibrary_Application`.

Example 7-27. MXML extension of the bootstrap to force MXML compiler into code generation

```
<?xml version="1.0" encoding="UTF-8"?>
<!-- ComponentLibrary_Bootstrap.mxml
   By wrapping ComponentLibrary_Application into MXML tag, we
   force Flex compiler to create all mixins required by the
   library  classes  (in the generated bootstrap class)
-->
<ComponentLibrary_Application xmlns="*" />
```

This extra step up to MXML is required to trick the Flex compiler into generating its own bootstrap class (the code of that class is shown in Example 7-30). Finally, Example 7-28 contains the example of the Ant script that can be used to compile the SWF of the self-initializing library.

Example 7-28. Ant script that compiles ComponentLibrary_Bootstrap.mxml

```
<project name="Library-Application" default="compile" basedir="." >
   <target name="compile">
      <property name="sdkdir" value="C:/Program Files/Adobe/Flash Builder 3 Plug-
       in/sdks/3.2.0" />
      <property name="swclibs" value="${sdkdir}/frameworks/libs"   />
      <property name="application.name" value="ComponentLibrary_Bootstrap" />
      <property name="library.name" value="ComponentLibrary" />
      <exec executable="${sdkdir}/bin/mxmlc.exe" dir="${basedir}">
            <arg line="-external-library-
             path='${swclibs}/player/9/playerglobal.swc'"/>
            <arg line="-keep-generated-actionscript=true "/>
            <arg line="src/${application.name}.mxml"/>
            <arg line="-output bin/${library.name}.swf"/>
      </exec>
```

```
  </target>
</project>
```

When you run this script in Flash Builder, you will see output similar to that of Example 7-29.

Example 7-29. Output of the Ant script compiling library-bootstrapped-as-application

```
Buildfile: C:\workspaces\farata.samples\ComponentLibrary\build.xml
compile:
     [exec] Loading configuration file C:\Program Files\Adobe\Flash Builder 3
            Plug-in\sdks\3.2.0\frameworks\flex-config.xml
     [exec] C:\workspaces\farata.samples\ComponentLibrary\bin\ComponentLibrary.swf
            (181812 bytes)
BUILD SUCCESSFUL
Total time: 5 seconds
```

Make sure you copy *ComponentLibrary.swf* into the output folder of your application project and do not forget to turn off the autoextraction of the SWF, as shown in Figure 7-12.

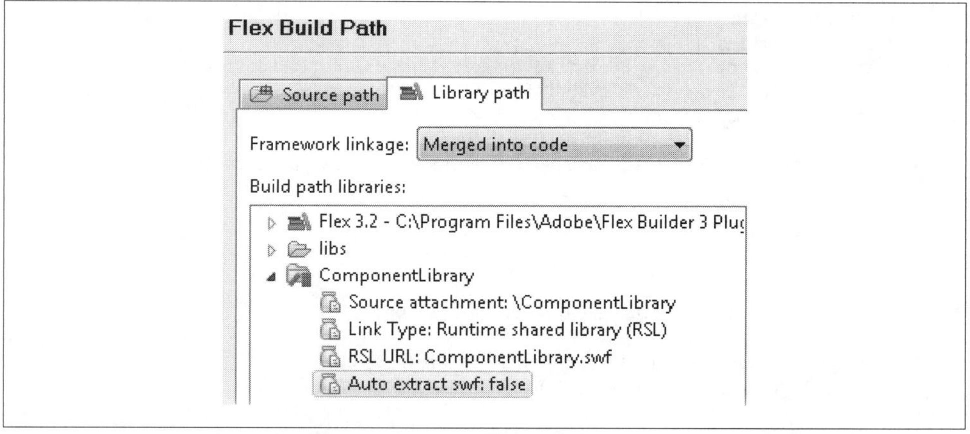

Figure 7-12. Autoextraction of the RSL SWF is turned off to avoid overwriting the custom-compiled library

Congratulations! You just created a bulletproof Flex RSL. If you are a practitioner, your job is complete. If you are a researcher, however, you may want to look at Example 7-30, which is the bootstrap class generated by the Flex compiler in response to this Ant-based compilation. Notice it contains yet another implementation of the `IFlexModuleFactory` interface. In response to the base class being `flex.core.SimpleApplication`, the compiler generates a descendant of `mx.core.FlexApplicationBootstrap` (as opposed to `mx.managers.SystemManager`, which is being generated in response to `mx.core.Application`). Upon the load of the library's SWF, Flash will instantiate the `ComponentLibrary_Bootstrap_mx_core_FlexApplicationBootstrap` class. The construction of the superclass results in calling the `create()` method, which consumes the return of the method `info()`. This way, the library bootstrap is completely owned and controlled by the library itself.

Example 7-30. Compiler-generated main class for the bootstrapped library

```
// Compiler-generated descendant of the FlexApplicationBootstrap
package
{

import flash.text.Font;
import flash.text.TextFormat;
import flash.system.ApplicationDomain;
import flash.utils.getDefinitionByName;
import mx.core.IFlexModule;
import mx.core.IFlexModuleFactory;

import mx.core.FlexApplicationBootstrap;

[ResourceBundle("containers")]
[ResourceBundle("core")]
[ResourceBundle("effects")]
[ResourceBundle("skins")]
[ResourceBundle("styles")]
public class _ComponentLibrary_Bootstrap_mx_core_FlexApplicationBootstrap
    extends mx.core.FlexApplicationBootstrap
    implements IFlexModuleFactory
{
    public function _ComponentLibrary_Bootstrap_mx_core_FlexApplicationBootstrap()
    {

        super();
    }

    override     public function create(... params):Object
    {
        if (params.length > 0 && !(params[0] is String))
            return super.create.apply(this, params);

        var mainClassName:String = params.length == 0 ?
                "ComponentLibrary_Bootstrap" : String(params[0]);
        var mainClass:Class = Class(getDefinitionByName(mainClassName));
        if (!mainClass)
            return null;

        var instance:Object = new mainClass();
        if (instance is IFlexModule)
            (IFlexModule(instance)).moduleFactory = this;
        return instance;
    }

    override    public function info():Object{
        return {
            compiledLocales: [ "en_US" ],
            compiledResourceBundleNames: [ "containers", "core", "effects",
```

```
                                            "skins", "styles" ],
            currentDomain: ApplicationDomain.currentDomain,
            mainClassName: "ComponentLibrary_Bootstrap",
            mixins: [ "_ComponentLibrary_Bootstrap_FlexInit",
"_richTextEditorTextAreaStyleStyle",
"_ControlBarStyle",
"_alertButtonStyleStyle", "_textAreaVScrollBarStyleStyle", "_headerDateTextStyle",
"_globalStyle", "_todayStyleStyle", "_windowStylesStyle", "_ApplicationStyle",
"_ToolTipStyle", "_CursorManagerStyle", "_opaquePanelStyle", "_errorTipStyle",
"_dateFieldPopupStyle", "_dataGridStylesStyle", "_popUpMenuStyle",
"_headerDragProxyStyleStyle", "_activeTabStyleStyle",
"_PanelStyle",
"_ContainerStyle", "_windowStatusStyle", "_ScrollBarStyle",
"_swatchPanelTextFieldStyle", "_textAreaHScrollBarStyleStyle", "_plainStyle",
"_activeButtonStyleStyle", "_advancedDataGridStylesStyle", "_comboDropdownStyle",
"_ButtonStyle", "_weekDayStyleStyle", "_linkButtonStyleStyle",
 "_CustomPanelWatcherSetupUtil" ]
        }
    }
}

}
```

Read the blog post "Avoiding pitfalls of Flex RSL with Self Initialized Libraries" (*http://flexblog.faratasystems.com/2010/01/27/taming-flex-rsl*) for more information.

Sibling Domains and Multiversioning

By now, it should be clear that applications, modules, and libraries (albeit bootstrapped as applications) are simply different forms of packaging *.swf* files. *Libraries* assume the tightest coupling with the loading code, and that's why they get preloaded (by the application's code generated by the Flex compiler). *Modules* get loaded and unloaded on demand, because they are needed only conditionally and only temporarily. *Applications* are similar to modules, in that they get loaded and unloaded on demand. The important advantage of applications over modules (as units of modularization) is that applications are self-sufficient, which allows you to mix multiple application *.swf*s compiled against different versions of the Flex framework (Flex 3.1, Flex 3.2, Flex 4.0, and so on).

Let's elaborate. As you already know, libraries get loaded into the same domain as the application: `ApplicationDomain.currentDomain`. Accordingly, to avoid conflicts, a library has to be compiled against the same version of the Flex framework as the enclosing application. With modules, you get to choose between the same domain or a child domain (`new ApplicationDomain(ApplicationDomain.currentDomain)`), but even in the latter case, the class search starts with the parent domain. Again, to avoid conflicts, modules have to be compiled against the same version of the Flex framework as the consuming application. When it comes to applications, you still may use same-domain or child-domain techniques, provided that the loading application and subapplication are compiled against the same version of the Flex framework. What if you can't recompile the Flex 3.2 subapplication and you want to load it from the Flex 4 main application? Then you need to load into the domain that is the sibling of the main application domain (`new ApplicationDomain(null)`).

Sibling domains allow ultimate separation of classes; you absolutely have to load the *sub* into the sibling domain to support multiversioning. That said, you may want to indiscriminately use sibling domains even when multiversioning is not an issue. A typical use case for this is portals, when you have to integrate portlets, perhaps developed by a third party. In brief:

- If you can compile from sources, make modules and load them into the same domain or a child domain.
- If you are integrating compiled applications, use sibling domains.

To simplify the discussion, the following sections will use the term "portlet" instead of the subapplication and "portal" instead of the loading application.

Four Scenarios of Loading Portlets

To load and unload a portlet, you have to use `SWFLoader` (unless you are into writing your own loader). As you remember, `SWFLoader` is a wrapper around `flash.display.Loader`. As such, `SWFLoader` exposes the `loaderContext` property that controls the application domain precisely, like it does it for `Loader`. For instance, Example 7-31's MXML illustrates the loading of the *RemoteApplication.swf* portlet using the default `loaderContext`.

Example 7-31. Using SWFLoader with default LoaderContext

```
<mx:SWFLoader id="swfLoader"
   source="http://localhost:8080/RemoteSite/RemoteApplication.swf"
/>
```

Identical results can be achieved by Example 7-32's script.

Example 7-32. Using SWFLoader with explicit LoaderContext

```
private function loadApplication():void {
   swfLoader.loaderContext = new LoaderContext(
      false,
      new ApplicationDomain(ApplicationDomain.currentDomain)
   );
   swfLoader.source = "http://localhost:8080/RemoteSite/RemoteApplication.swf";
}
```

In both cases, the portlet's classes get loaded in the child domain of the portal, according to the default `loaderContext` of a `flash.display.Loader`. However, there is more to `loaderContext` than controlling the application domain.

When a Flex application is loaded from a web domain, Flash Player, by default, assigns it a *security sandbox*. Applications coming from the different web domains get assigned different sandboxes. As an example, consider that the portal comes from *http://localhost* and loads the portlet from *http://127.0.0.1*. Unless you deviate from the default settings, these two applications will be assigned different sandboxes. Remember that class definitions get loaded into application domains and that application domains form a tree. There is one and only one tree per sandbox.

You can read more about sandboxes in the Flash documentation (Adobe often refers to them as security domains as well), but a few important points should be noted here:

- You can indicate the sandbox preference in the constructor of the `LoaderContext`. For instance, Example 7-33's code snippet results in loading classes into the current security sandbox.

  Example 7-33. Forced loading into the current sandbox

  ```
  swfLoader.loaderContext = new LoaderContext(
      false,
      new ApplicationDomain(
         ApplicationDomain.currentDomain
      )
      SecurityDomain.currentDomain
  )
  ```

- Although you can easily load portlets from other web domains into the current sandbox, there is no way you can programmatically load the portlet from the same web domain into the different sandbox. In other words, you can admit strangers into your family, but you can't expel your kin. And the only way to load a portlet into a different sandbox is to host it in a different web domain or subdomain.
- Assigning a different sandbox means a totally different tree of application domains.

To sum up, there are only four `loaderContext` combinations that you can arrange either programmatically or via hosting the portlet on the different subdomain:

- Different Sandbox Different Domain (DSDD)
- Same Sandbox Different (sibling) Domain (SSDD)
- Same Sandbox Child Domain (SSCD)
- Same Sandbox Same Domain (SSSD)

Table 7-1 illustrates how you can achieve a particular combination—DSDD, SSDD, SSCD, and SSSD (in this order)—provided that the portal and the portlet are hosted by the different web domains. You can explicitly use the `loaderContext` property or you can manipulate `loadForCompatibility` and `trustContent`.

Table 7-1. Loading portlets across web domains

loaderContext syntax	SWFLoader syntax
swfLoader.loaderContext=new LoaderContext(false, new ApplicationDomain(null), null);	<mx:SWFLoader id="swfLoader" />
swfLoader.loaderContext=new LoaderContext(false, new ApplicationDomain(null), SecurityDomain.currentDomain);	<mx:SWFLoader id="swfLoader" loadForCompatibility="true" trustContent="true" />
swfLoader.loaderContext=new LoaderContext(false, new ApplicationDomain(ApplicationDomain.currentDomain), SecurityDomain.currentDomain);	<mx:SWFLoader id="swfLoader" trustContent="true" />
swfLoader.loaderContext=new LoaderContext(false, ApplicationDomain.applicationDomain, SecurityDomain.currentDomain);	Not applicable

Table 7-2 illustrates how the combination SSDD, SSCD, and SSSD can be achieved, provided that the portal and the portlet are located on the same web domain.

Table 7-2. Loading portlets from the same web domain

loaderContext syntax	SWFLoader syntax
swfLoader.loaderContext=new LoaderContext(false, new ApplicationDomain(null));	<mx:SWFLoader id="swfLoader" loadForCompatibility="true" />
swfLoader.loaderContext=new LoaderContext(false, new ApplicationDomain(ApplicationDomain.currentDomain));	<mx:SWFLoader id="swfLoader" />
swfLoader.loaderContext=new LoaderContext(false, ApplicationDomain.currentDomain);	Not applicable

Some of these scenarios make more sense than the others. In particular, the Same Sandbox Same Domain scenario is the one most prone to class name clashing. To reiterate: duplicate loading of a class in the tree of application domains is not possible. At the same time, *sub*'s code can easily and perhaps inadvertently modify static variables of the classes hosted by the parent application. This relates to classes, such as mx.core.Application and mx.messaging.config.ServerConfig, for instance, and their properties application and xml, respectively.

On the opposite end is the Different Sandbox Different Domain scenario. Here you have the ultimate class isolation, which supports multiversioning plus ultimate security (more on this a bit later), at the price of a not-so-seamless user experience. For instance, the pop ups and alerts of the portlet will appear centered and clipped relative to the portlet rather than the entire portal, as shown in Figure 7-13.

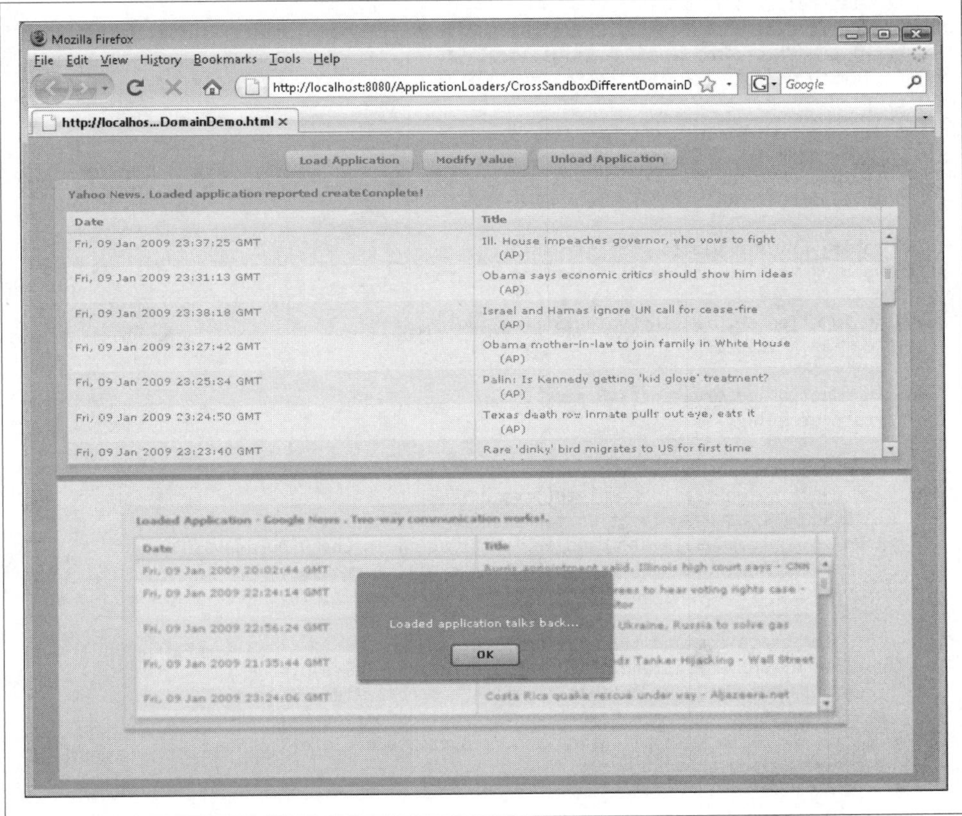

Figure 7-13. DifferentSandboxDifferentDomainDemo; pop up is centered relatively to the loaded portlet

The remaining two scenarios are Same Sandbox Child Domain and Same Sandbox Different Domain. The latter should be considered the top choice for enterprise portals, as it supports multiversioning and delivers a seamless user experience. The simpler scenario, Same Sandbox Child Domain, is the one you'll examine next. After that, you'll investigate scenarios that provide multiversioning support.

Default Portlet Loading: Same Sandbox Child Domain

Same Sandbox Child Domain is the default scenario when the application and the subapplication are located in a single web domain. Unless you tell `SWFLoader` otherwise, portlet classes get loaded into the child application domain. To see how this works, start with a sample portlet, such as *RegularApplication.mxml*, in Example 7-34.

Example 7-34. RegularApplication.mxml—sample portlet

```
<?xml version="1.0"?>
<!-- RegularApplication.mxml-->
<mx:Application xmlns:mx="http://www.adobe.com/2006/mxml" implements="IGreeting"
     backgroundColor="0xffeeff"   xmlns:local="*"
      creationComplete="onCreationComplete()">
<mx:Script>
<![CDATA[
   import mx.events.DynamicEvent;
   import mx.controls.Alert;
   import events.RemoteEvent;

   [Bindable] private var command:String="";
    [Bindable]  public var greeting:String = "";

   public function setGreeting(value:String):void {
      greeting = value;
   }
   public function getGreeting():String {
      return greeting;
   }

   private function onCreationComplete():void {
      Alert.show("Loaded application talks back...");
      // While you may use systemManager["swfBridge"] in the DSDD and SSDD,
      //   systemManager.loaderInfo.sharedEvents will work always
      var swfBridge:IEventDispatcher = systemManager.loaderInfo.sharedEvents;

      // Subscribe to command from the application
       swfBridge.addEventListener("command", onCommand,false,0,true );
       // Notify the application that creation has completed
      var evt:RemoteEvent = new RemoteEvent("creationComplete");
      evt.data = ". Loaded application reported createComplete!";
       swfBridge.dispatchEvent(evt);
   }

   private function onCommand(event:Event):void {
       command = event["data"] as String;
    }

]]>
</mx:Script>
    <mx:Panel title="Loaded Application - Google News {greeting}{command}."
                                width="90%" height="90%">
       <local:GoogleNews width="100%" height="100%"/>
```

```
    </mx:Panel>
</mx:Application>
```

RegularApplication.mxml implements the interface `IGreeting` from Example 7-12. Under the SSCD scenario, a portlet will see the definition of the `IGreeting` loaded by the portal. Accordingly, the portal will be able to cast the portlet to `IGreeting`, as shown in Example 7-35 (you may compare `swfLoader.content` with `moduleLoader.child`).

Example 7-35. Interface-based scripting of the portlet loaded into the child domain

```
public function modifyValue():void {
   var systemManager:SystemManager = SystemManager(swfLoader.content);
   var loadedApplication:IGreeting = systemManager.application as IGreeting;
   loadedApplication.setGreeting(" accessed from outside");
}
```

Similarly to the way you arranged event-based communication with the modules, this portlet listens to and communicates with the loading application via `loaderInfo.sharedEvents` (Example 7-36).

Example 7-36. Event-based portlet-portal communication via sharedEvents

```
private function onCreationComplete():void {
   var swfBridge:IEventDispatcher = systemManager.loaderInfo.sharedEvents;

   // Subscribe to command from the application
   swfBridge.addEventListener("command", onCommand,false,0,true );

   // Notify the application that creation has completed
   var evt:RemoteEvent = new RemoteEvent("creationComplete");
   evt.data = ". Loaded application reported createComplete!";
   swfBridge.dispatchEvent(evt);
}
```

Make sure to deploy *RegularApplication.mxml* into an entirely dedicated BlazeDS or LCDS context. This example creates a combined Flex/Java LCDS/Web Tools Platform (WTP) project called *RemoteSite*, as shown in Figure 7-14. (Please see the Adobe documentation on how to create a combined Flex/Java project with LiveCycle Data Services and WTP.) Having a dedicated Flex/JEE project enables you to define destinations of the portlet without affecting a portal or another portlet application.

To the *RemoteSite/WebContent/WEB-INF/flex/proxy-config.xml* file of this project, you need to add the destination `GoogleNews`, as shown in Example 7-37.

Example 7-37. GoogleNews proxy destination

```
<destination id="GoogleNews">
   <properties>
     <url>http://news.google.com/?output=rss</url>
   </properties>
</destination>
```

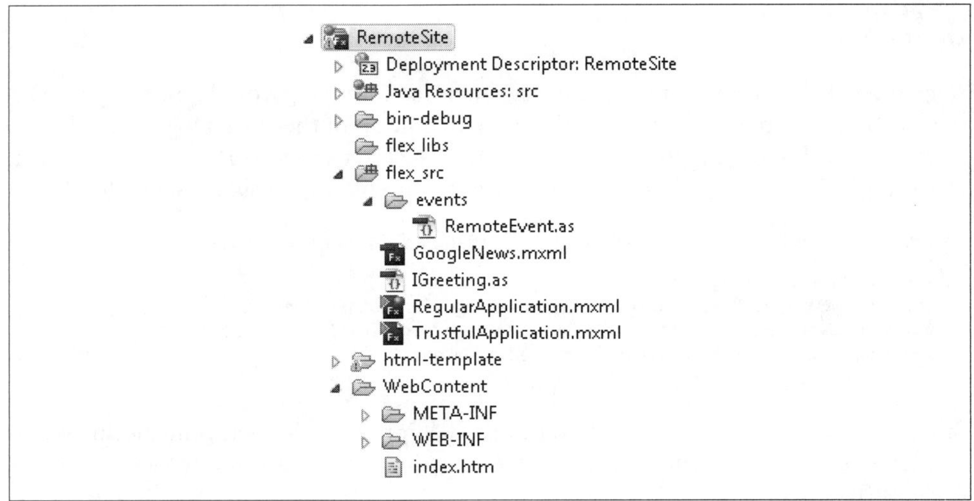

Figure 7-14. Applications from RemoteSite will be accessed via domain 127.0.0.1

Example 7-38 presents the class `GoogleNews`, a descendant of `DataGrid` that encapsulates `HTTPService` and displays Google News headlines to the user. When you run the portlet, it should look like Figure 7-15.

Example 7-38. GoogleNews DataGrid

```
<?xml version="1.0" encoding="utf-8"?>
<!-- GoogleNews.mxml -->
<mx:DataGrid  xmlns:mx="http://www.adobe.com/2006/mxml"
creationComplete="news.send()"
   dataProvider="{news.lastResult.channel.item}"
   variableRowHeight="true">
   <mx:columns>
     <mx:DataGridColumn headerText="Date"  dataField="pubDate" />
     <mx:DataGridColumn headerText="Title" dataField="title" wordWrap="true" />
   </mx:columns>


   <mx:HTTPService id="news" useProxy="true"  destination="GoogleNews"
resultFormat="e4x" fault="onFault(event)" />
<mx:Script>
<![CDATA[
   import mx.rpc.events.*;
   private function onFault(event:FaultEvent):void {
     mx.controls.Alert.show( "Destination:" + event.currentTarget.destination +
      "\n" + "Fault code:" + event.fault.faultCode + "\n" +
      "Detail:" + event.fault.faultDetail, "News feed failure"
      );
   }
]]>
</mx:Script>
</mx:DataGrid>
```

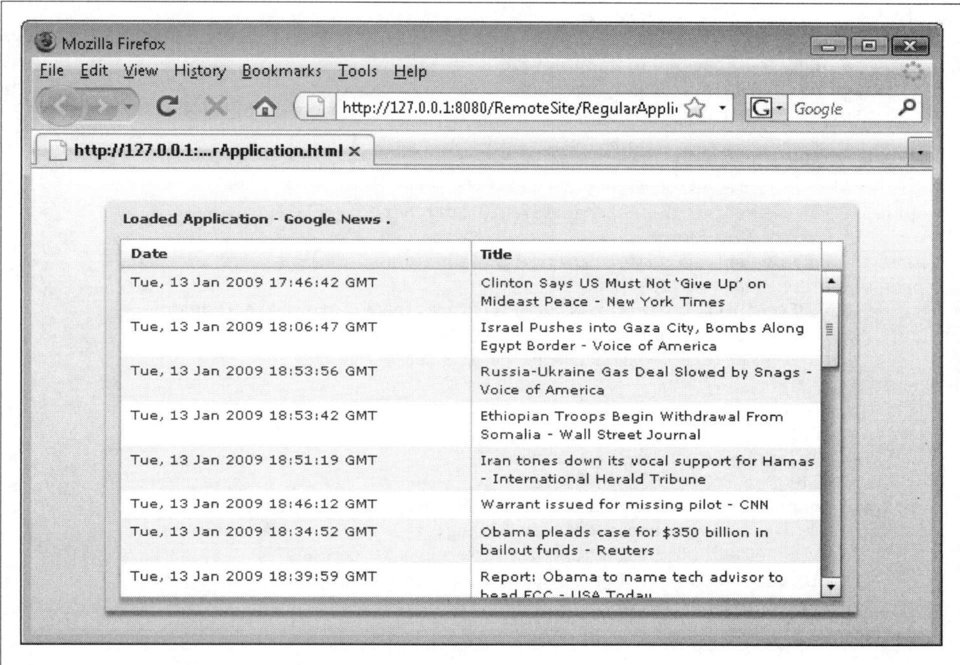

Figure 7-15. Sample portlet of RegularApplication

Finally, consider the sample portal, *SameSandboxChildDomainDemo.mxml*, in Example 7-39. We suggest you create a separate combined Flex/Java/WTP Eclipse project, as shown in Figure 7-16. To illustrate the cross-domain specifics, you can run the portal from *http://localhost* while loading the portlet from the different domain, *http://127.0.0.1*.

Example 7-39. SameSandboxChildDomainDemo application

```
<?xml version="1.0"?>
<!-- SameSandboxChildDomainDemo.mxml -->
<mx:Application xmlns:mx="http://www.adobe.com/2006/mxml" xmlns:local="*" >
<mx:Script>
<![CDATA[
   import events.RemoteEvent;
    import mx.managers.SystemManager;

   private const APP_URL:String =
"http://127.0.0.1:8080/RemoteSite/RegularApplication.swf";

   public function modifyValue():void {
      // Casting to SystemManager and IGreeting is possible
      var systemManager:SystemManager = SystemManager(swfLoader.content);
      var loadedApplication:IGreeting = systemManager.application as IGreeting;
      loadedApplication.setGreeting(" accessed from outside");
```

```
    }

    private function loadApplication():void {
      swfLoader.addEventListener("complete", onLoadComplete);
         swfLoader.source = APP_URL;
   }

    [Bindable] private var applicationLoaded:Boolean;
    private var sharedEventDispatcher:IEventDispatcher;

   private function onLoadComplete(event:Event):void {
      applicationLoaded = true;
         sharedEventDispatcher = swfLoader.content.loaderInfo.sharedEvents;
         sharedEventDispatcher.addEventListener(
         "creationComplete", onLoadedApplicationCreated
      );
    }

      [Bindable] private var reply:String="";
   // Casting to RemoteEvent is possible
    private function onLoadedApplicationCreated(event: RemoteEvent):void
                    reply = event.data as String;
         var remoteEvent:RemoteEvent = new RemoteEvent("command");
         remoteEvent.data = ". Two-way communication works!";
         sharedEventDispatcher.dispatchEvent(remoteEvent);
    }
    ]]>
    </mx:Script>
    <mx:HBox>
      <mx:Button label="Load Application" click="loadApplication()" />
          <mx:Button label="Modify Value" click="modifyValue();"
         enabled="{applicationLoaded}"/>
    </mx:HBox>

    <mx:Panel title="Yahoo News{reply}" width="100%" height="50%"
              id="panel">
       <local:YahooNews width="100%" height="100%"/>
    </mx:Panel>
    <mx:SWFLoader id="swfLoader" width="100%" height="50%"
                                                trustContent="true"/>
</mx:Application>
```

Notice the setting `trustContent="true"` of the `swfLoader`. This guarantees that despite different web domains of the portal and portlet, class loading happens into the same sandbox and, by default, to the child application domain.

That said, you should stick to the golden Flash security rule that the *.swf* (of the portal) can access a resource (portlet) on the different web domain only when such domain holds a cross-domain policy file that expresses trust to the domain of the *.swf*. So make sure your root web application contains the file shown in Example 7-40.

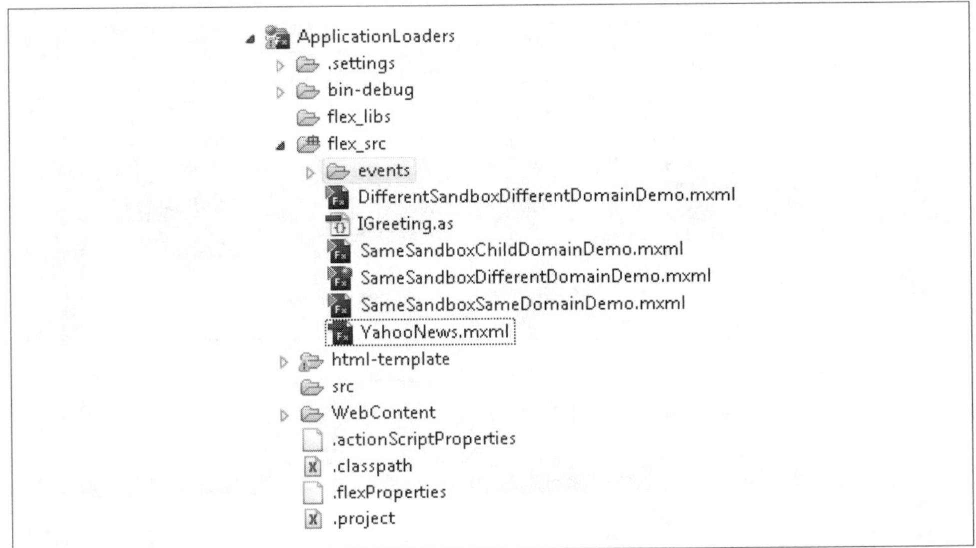

Figure 7-16. ApplicationLoaders project

Example 7-40. Policy file cross-domain.xml

```
<?xml version="1.0"?>
<!DOCTYPE cross-domain-policy
  SYSTEM "http://www.macromedia.com/xml/dtds/cross-domain-policy.dtd">
<cross-domain-policy>
 <allow-access-from domain="*"/>
</cross-domain-policy>
```

Make sure that you do not use this indiscriminating policy file in production. For more information on secure cross-domain communication in Flash Player, see *http://www.adobe.com/devnet/flashplayer/articles/secure_swf_apps.html*.

SameSandboxChildDomainDemo.mxml has its own news grid—it displays Yahoo! News. (The code of `YahooNews` is identical to `GoogleNews` from Example 7-37, except that it uses the different destination, as presented in Example 7-41. You should add this destination to *ApplicationLoaders/WebContent/WEB-INF/flex/proxy-config.xml*.)

Example 7-41. Proxy destination for Yahoo! News

```
<destination id="YahooNews">
   <properties>
     <url>http://rss.news.yahoo.com/rss/topstories</url>
   </properties>
</destination>
```

When you run the application and click OK on the pop up called "Loaded application talks back," it will look like Figure 7-17.

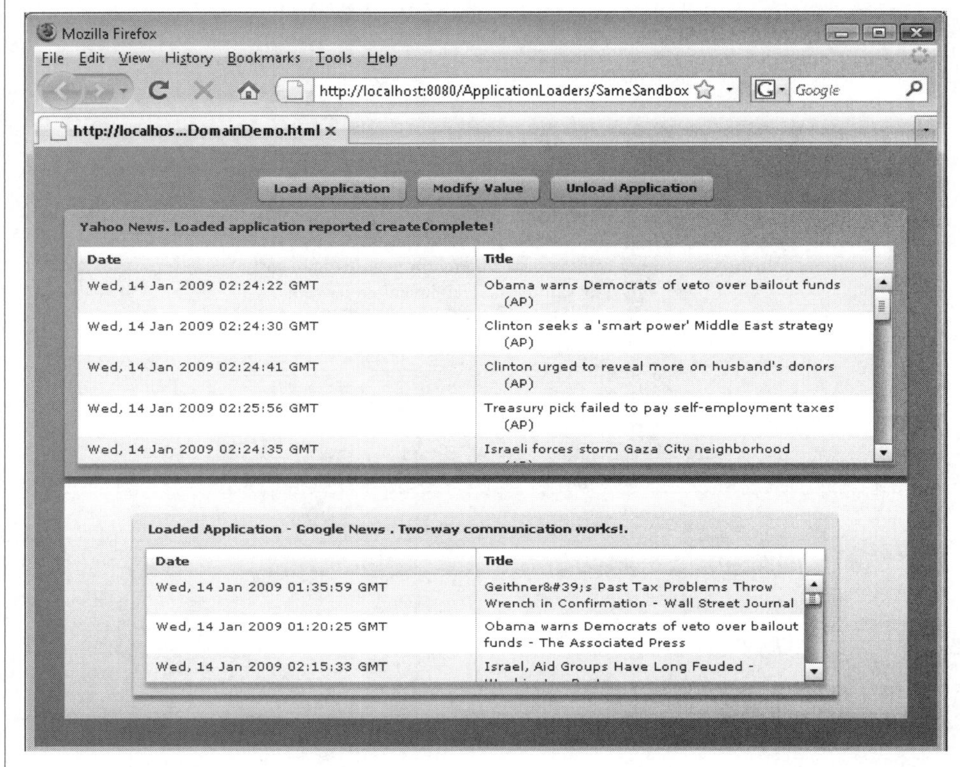

Figure 7-17. SameSandboxChildDomainDemo

Loading Portlets for Multiversioning

What about the scenarios that support multiversioning? The default loading scenario from different web domains is Different Sandbox Different Domain. Example 7-42's sample portal, *DifferentSandboxDifferentDomainDemo*, not only illustrates this scenario, it will also help you to understand the Same Sandbox Different Domain scenario.

When you examine the code, notice the seemingly redundant reference to the class `PopUpManager`. It's not accidental. You always have to link the `PopUpManager` class to your portal to allow pop-up controls in the portlets. That's how Adobe implemented it, and this requirement does not seem like too much to ask for.

Next, note that casting across sibling domains is out of reach. Look at the body of the `modifyValue()` method. You can't cast the `loadedApplication` either to `IGreeting` or to `mx.core.Application`. Instead, the example declares it as `flash.display.DisplayObject`. For similar reasons, the declaration of the `onLoadedApplicationCreated()` method downcasts the type of object to `flash.events.Event`. If you instead try to declare `loadedApplication` as `Application`, you will receive this runtime error:

```
TypeError: Error #1034: Type Coercion failed: cannot convert
TrustfulApplication@c8f20a1 to mx.core.Application.
```

Now, examine the function `onLoadComplete()`. To obtain the reference to the `sharedEventDispatcher`, the function uses the expression `swfLoader.swfBridge` instead of `swfLoader.content.loaderInfo.sharedEvents`.

Example 7-42. DifferentSandboxDifferentDomainDemo

```
<?xml version="1.0"?>
<!-- DifferentSandboxDifferentDomainDemo.mxml -->
<mx:Application xmlns:mx="http://www.adobe.com/2006/mxml" xmlns:local="*" >
<mx:Script>
<![CDATA[
   import events.RemoteEvent;
    import mx.managers.PopUpManager; PopUpManager;
    import mx.managers.SystemManager;

    private const APP_URL:String =
    "http://127.0.0.1:8080/RemoteSite/TrustfulApplication.swf";

   public function modifyValue():void {
      var loadedApplication:DisplayObject = swfLoader.content["application"];
loadedApplication["setGreeting"]("loaded from outside");
    }

    private function loadApplication():void {
         swfLoader.addEventListener("complete", onLoadComplete);
            swfLoader.source=APP_URL;
    }

    [Bindable] private var applicationLoaded:Boolean;
     private var sharedEventDispatcher:IEventDispatcher;
     private function onLoadComplete(event:Event):void {
            swfLoader.removeEventListener("complete", onLoadComplete);
            applicationLoaded = true;
           // Since swfLoader.content.loaderInfo.sharedEvents=null,
           // use swfLoader.swfBridge
            sharedEventDispatcher = swfLoader.swfBridge;
            sharedEventDispatcher.addEventListener("creationComplete",
                                          onLoadedApplicationCreated);
     }

      [Bindable] private var reply:String="";
      // We cannot cast RemoteEvent across Application Domains
    private function onLoadedApplicationCreated(event:/*RemoteEvent*/ Event):void {
         if (event.hasOwnProperty("data")) {
               reply = event["data"];
         }
         var remoteEvent:RemoteEvent = new RemoteEvent("command");
         remoteEvent.data = ". Two-way communication works!";
         sharedEventDispatcher.dispatchEvent(remoteEvent);
    }

]]>
```

```
</mx:Script>
    <mx:HBox>
      <mx:Button label="Load Application" click="loadApplication()" />
          <mx:Button label="Modify Value" click="modifyValue();"
        enabled="{applicationLoaded}"/>
    </mx:HBox>

    <mx:Panel title="Yahoo News{reply}" width="100%" height="50%" id="panel">
       <local:YahooNews width="100%" height="100%"/>
    </mx:Panel>
    <mx:SWFLoader id="swfLoader" width="100%" height="50%"/>
</mx:Application>
```

The same concepts hold true for the Same Sandbox Different Domain scenario as well. Specific to the cross-domain scenario, however, is that *DifferentSandBoxDifferentDomainDemo* loads *TrustfulApplication.swf* (Example 7-43), which extends the `RegularApplication` merely to express cross-scripting trust to the web domain of the portal via `Security.allowDomain("*")`.

Example 7-43. TrustfulApplication

```
<?xml version="1.0"?>
<!-- TrustfulApplication.mxml-->
<RegularApplication xmlns:mx="http://www.adobe.com/2006/mxml" xmlns="*"
preinitialize="onPreinitialize(event)">
   <mx:Script>
      <![CDATA[
         // Try to use without allowDomain and see the r.t. SecurityError
         private function onPreinitialize(event:Event):void {
            Security.allowDomain("*"); //localhost, wwww.adobe.com, etc.
         }
      ]]>
   </mx:Script>
</RegularApplication>
```

The body of the function `modifyValue()` takes advantage of these cross-scripting permissions, referring to `swfLoader.content`. Had you loaded the untrusted *RemoteApplication.swf*, you would have received the error shown in Example 7-44.

Example 7-44. Example of security error

```
SecurityError: Error #2121: Security sandbox violation: Loader.content:
http://localhost:8080/ApplicationLoaders/DifferentSandboxCommunicationDemo.swf
cannot access http://127.0.0.1:8080/RemoteSite/RegularApplication.swf.
This may be worked around by calling Security.allowDomain.
    at flash.display::Loader/get content()
    at mx.controls::SWFLoader/get content
```

This is the only coding specific to the DSDD scenario versus SSDD. Of course, in the case of SSDD, the `loadingForCompatibility` property of the `swfLoader` would be set to true, and you would specify `trustContent="true"` to offset the domain difference.

The successfully running DSDD application was previously presented in Figure 7-16, and Figure 7-18 illustrates a problem in the SSDD scenario: the Google News panel is showing up empty. As it turns out, in the case of SSDD, you need to change your architecture and preload Flex messaging, RPC, and Data Management Services–related classes in the application domain that will parent the domain of the portal.

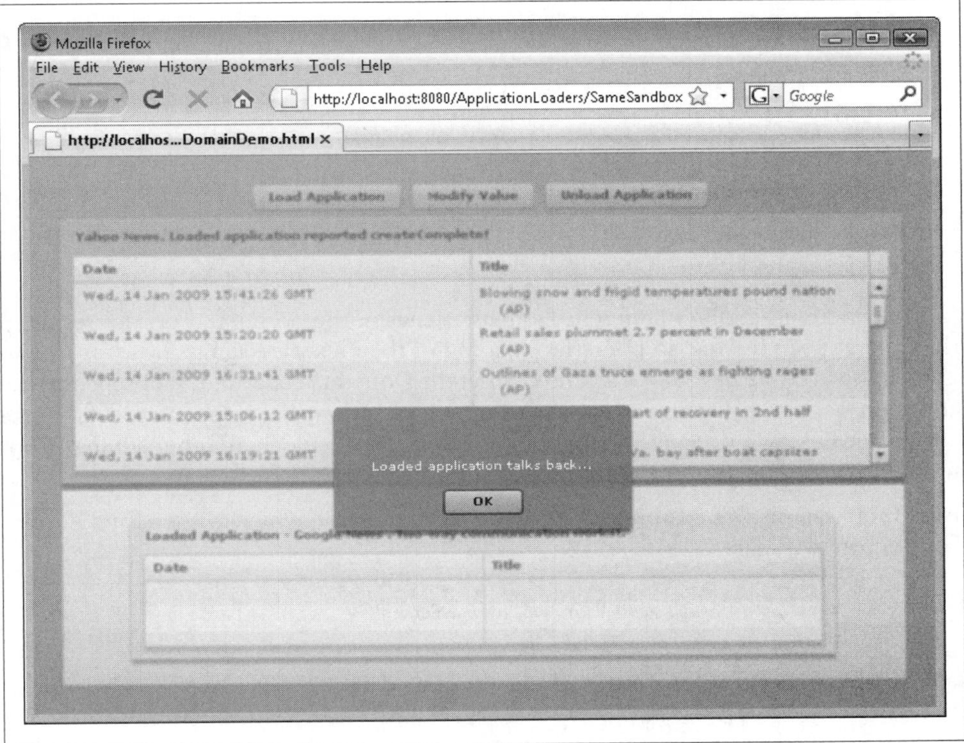

Figure 7-18. Same Sandbox Different Domain: Flex Messaging does not work without bootstrap loading of the messaging classes

Bootstrap Class Loading

The previous section mentioned that casting is out of reach across sibling domains. That constraint is not as tight, however, as you might think. Remember how you cast loaded modules and applications to the `IGreeting` interface earlier in the chapter? You did not cast the `IGreeting` *of the child* to the `IGreeting` *of the parent*, because the `IGreeting` of the child did not exist. A child is always reusing classes loaded in the parental chain. So, two sibling domains can cast classes if they share a common parent that preloads these classes. In particular, such *bootstrap class loading*, as Adobe calls it, is required to maintain a common definition of the following classes from the `mx.messaging.messages` package per security domain:

- `ConfigMap`
- `AcknowledgeMessage`
- `AcknowledgeMessageExt`
- `AsyncMessage`
- `AsyncMessageExt`
- `CommandMessage`
- `CommandMessageExt`
- `ErrorMessage`
- `HTTPRequestMessage`
- `MessagePerformanceInfo`
- `RemotingMessage`
- `SOAPMessage`

In the Different Sandbox Different Domain scenario, the portal and portlet reside in the different sandboxes, so bootstrap loading of the Flex messaging classes is not an issue. However, in the Same Sandbox Different Domain scenario, the absence of the common bootstrap loader results in the first application that happens to load these classes into its own domain (be that portal or portlet) to block all other siblings from receiving messages from the `MessageBroker`.

At Farata Systems, we customized *PortalBootstrapLoader*, which is a separate ActionScript project (Figure 7-19).

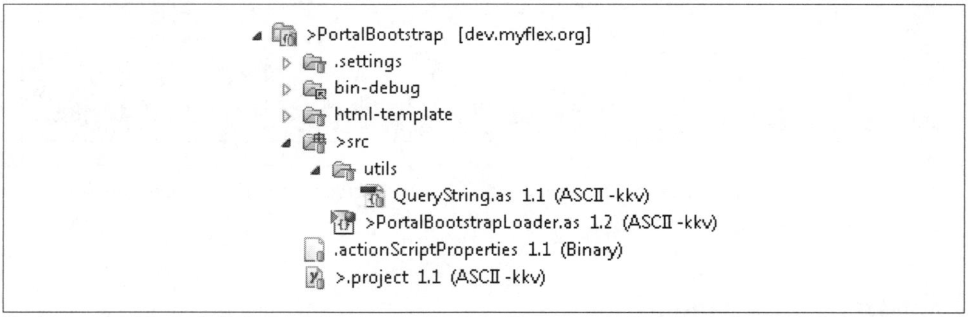

Figure 7-19. PortalBootstrapLoader project

As you study the code for *PortalBootstrapLoader* in Example 7-45, notice that in addition to linking in all classes required by Adobe, we also link in the class `com.farata.portal.Message`. Follow this pattern to link in any class that you want to make available for all portlets in your portal (and the portal itself).

Example 7-45. PortalBootstrapLoader.as

```
//PortalBootstrapLoader.as
package {
```

```
import flash.display.Loader;
import flash.display.Sprite;
import flash.display.StageAlign;
import flash.display.StageScaleMode;
import flash.events.Event;
import flash.net.URLRequest;
import flash.system.ApplicationDomain;
import flash.system.LoaderContext;
import flash.system.SecurityDomain;

import utils.QueryString;

import mx.messaging.config.ConfigMap; ConfigMap;
import mx.messaging.messages.AcknowledgeMessage; AcknowledgeMessage;
import mx.messaging.messages.AcknowledgeMessageExt; AcknowledgeMessageExt;
import mx.messaging.messages.AsyncMessage; AsyncMessage;
import mx.messaging.messages.AsyncMessageExt; AsyncMessageExt;
import mx.messaging.messages.CommandMessage; CommandMessage;
import mx.messaging.messages.CommandMessageExt; CommandMessageExt;
import mx.messaging.messages.ErrorMessage; ErrorMessage;
import mx.messaging.messages.HTTPRequestMessage; HTTPRequestMessage;
import mx.messaging.messages.MessagePerformanceInfo; MessagePerformanceInfo;
import mx.messaging.messages.RemotingMessage; RemotingMessage;
import mx.messaging.messages.SOAPMessage; SOAPMessage;

import com.farata.portal.Message;Message;

public class PortalBootstrapLoader extends Sprite {

public function PortalBootstrapLoader() {
   super();

 if (ApplicationDomain.currentDomain.hasDefinition("mx.core::UIComponent"))
    throw new Error("UIComponent should not be in the bootstrap loader.");
 if (ApplicationDomain.currentDomain.hasDefinition("mx.core::Singleton"))
    throw new Error("Singleton should not be in the bootstrap loader.");

 if (stage) {
      stage.scaleMode = StageScaleMode.NO_SCALE;
      stage.align = StageAlign.TOP_LEFT;
 } else
      isStageRoot = false;
   root.loaderInfo.addEventListener(Event.INIT, onInit);
}

/**
* The Loader that loads the main application's SWF file.
*/
private var loader:Loader;

/**
* Whether the bootstrap loader is at the stage root or not,
* it is the stage root only if it was the root
* of the first SWF file that was loaded by Flash Player.
* Otherwise, it could be a top-level application but not stage root
```

```
    * if it was loaded by some other non-Flex shell or is sandboxed.
    */
    private var isStageRoot:Boolean = true;

    /**
    * Called when the bootstrap loader's SWF file has been loaded.
    * Starts loading the application SWF specified by the applicationURL
    * property.
    */
    private function onInit(event:Event):void {
       loader = new Loader();

        var loaderContext:LoaderContext  = new LoaderContext(
          false,
          new ApplicationDomain(ApplicationDomain.currentDomain),
          SecurityDomain.currentDomain
        );

       addChild(loader);
       loader.load(new URLRequest(applicationUrl), loaderContext );

       loader.addEventListener(
          "mx.managers.SystemManager.isBootstrapRoot",
          bootstrapRootHandler
       );
       loader.addEventListener(
          "mx.managers.SystemManager.isStageRoot",
          stageRootHandler
       );

       loader.addEventListener(Event.ADDED, resizeHandler );
       stage.addEventListener(Event.RESIZE, resizeHandler);
    }

    private function get applicationUrl():String{
       var qs:QueryString = new QueryString();
       return qs.root + qs.parameters.app;
    }

    private function bootstrapRootHandler(event:Event):void {
       event.preventDefault();
    }

    private function stageRootHandler(event:Event):void {
       if (!isStageRoot)
          event.preventDefault();
    }

    private function resizeHandler(event:Event=null):void {
       if ( loader.content ){
          Object(loader.content).setActualSize(stage.stageWidth, stage.stageHeight);
       }
    }
  }
}
```

To use the bootstrap loader, we copy *PortalBootstrapLoader.html* and *PortalBootstrapLoader.swf* to the deployment folder of the portal and, in the browser, type the URL, similar to:

> *http://localhost:8080/ApplicationLoaders/PortalBootstrapLoader.html?app=ApplicationLoaders/SameSandboxDifferentDomain.swf*

As you can see from Figure 7-20, now the Google News panel of the portlet is filled by the data. Flex Messaging works because we made the definitions of the messaging classes visible to all application domains in the portal.

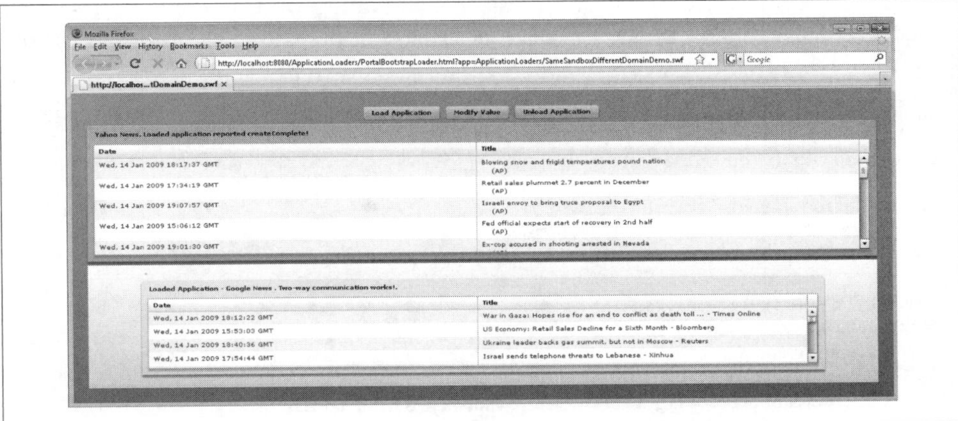

Figure 7-20. SameSandboxDifferentDomain with bootstrap class loading

Sample Flex Portal

To speed up your portal development, this section describes a sample Flex portal that you can download from the site accompanying this book. You'll need to download the following projects:

PortalLib
: Utility library referenced by all other projects

Feeds
: Combined Flex/Java Dynamic Web Project with *GoogleFinancialNews* and *YahooFinancialNews* applications

Charts
: Combined Flex/Java Dynamic Web Project with *Chart1* and *Chart2* applications

Portal
: Combined Flex/Java Dynamic Web Project with the *SamplePortal* application

PortalBootstrapLoader
: ActionScript project

Figure 7-21 illustrates running *SamplePortal*, which you should start via *PortalBootstrapLoader*:

> *http://localhost:8080/Portal/PortalBootstrapLoader.html?app=/Portal/SamplePortal.swf*

You can to create instances of portlets of different types by dragging and dropping on the portal canvas the navigational items located in the lower part of the screen, such as "Same Sandbox—Child Domain," "Same Sandbox—Sibling Domain," and "Different Sandbox—Different Domain."

Each portlet is contained by a custom resizable and draggable `Panel` and carries either the `GoogleFinancialNews` or the `YahooFinancialNews` application, according to the descriptor of the navigation items in *SamplePortal*, as shown in Example 7-46.

Example 7-46. SamplePortal

```
<?xml version="1.0" encoding="utf-8"?>
<!--  SamplePortal  -->
<mx:Application layout="absolute"
   xmlns:mx="http://www.adobe.com/2006/mxml"
   xmlns:fx="http://www.faratasystems.com/2009/portal" >

   <mx:Style source="styles.css"/>
   <fx:PortalCanvas  width="100%" height="100%">
      <fx:navItems>
         <fx:NavigationItem>
            <fx:PortletConfig title="Same Sandbox - Child Domain"
               preferredHeight="400" preferredWidth="850" >
               <fx:props>
                  <mx:Object trusted="true" multiversioned="false"
               url="http://127.0.0.1:8080/Feeds/YahooFinancialNews.swf"/>
               </fx:props>
            </fx:PortletConfig>
         </fx:NavigationItem>
         <fx:NavigationItem>
            <fx:PortletConfig title="Same Sandbox - Sibling Domain"
               preferredHeight="400" preferredWidth="850">
               <fx:props>
                  <mx:Object trusted="true" multiversioned="true"
               url="http://127.0.0.1:8080/Feeds/GoogleFinancialNews.swf"/>
               </fx:props>
            </fx:PortletConfig>
         </fx:NavigationItem>
         <fx:NavigationItem>
            <fx:PortletConfig title="DifferentSandbox - Different Domain"
               preferredHeight="400" preferredWidth="850" >
               <fx:props>
                  <mx:Object trusted="false" multiversioned="true"
               url="http://127.0.0.1:8080/Feeds/YahooFinancialNews.swf"/>
               </fx:props>
            </fx:PortletConfig>
         </fx:NavigationItem>
      </fx:navItems>
```

```
    </fx:PortalCanvas>

    <mx:Script>
        <![CDATA[
            import mx.managers.PopUpManager;PopUpManager;
            import PortletInfo;PortletInfo;
        ]]>
    </mx:Script>
</mx:Application>
```

A click on the Show Chart button loads *Chart1* or *Chart2* into a sibling domain and flips the portlet's content. Each portlet allows you to send messages to the portal, and from the portal itself you can broadcast a text message to all active portlets, shown in Figure 7-21.

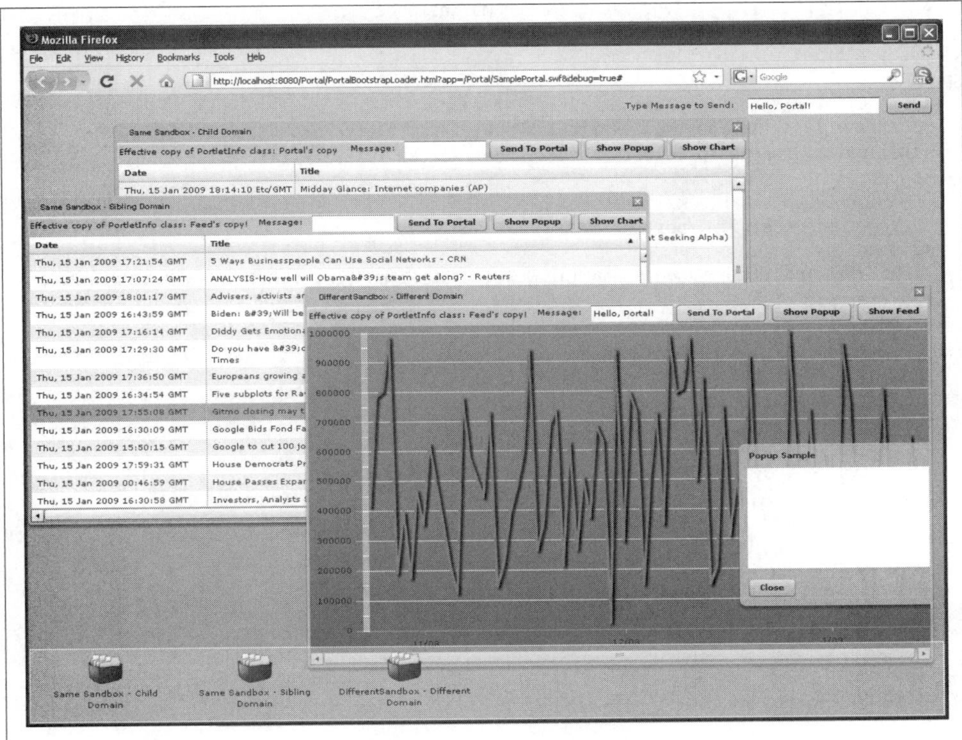

Figure 7-21. SamplePortal

Integrating Flex into Legacy JEE Portals

If you are the owner of a legacy Web 1.0 portal, you can consider integrating Flex applications into your portal space in an entirely different way.

The good news is that any Flex *.swf* file is valid content for a generic Flex portlet prewritten by Adobe. Open the *resources/wsrp/lib* folder from the root of the installed LiveCycle Data Services; you will find *flex-portal.jar* with *flex.portal.GenericFlexPortlet* inside. Add the *.jar* to the class path of your web application (*WebContent/lib*) and also copy the *resources/wsrp/wsrp-jsp* folder to the deployment root of your project (*WebContent*).

Now take the *portlet.xml* of your legacy portal, and inject Example 7-47's code to instantly add the `YahooFinancialNews` portlet.

Example 7-47. Registering a Flex application as a portlet via flex.portal.GenericFlexPortlet

```
<?xml version="1.0" encoding="UTF-8"?>
<portlet-app version="1.0"
   xmlns="http://java.sun.com/xml/ns/portlet/portlet-app_1_0.xsd"
   xmlns:xsi="http://www.w3.org/2001/XMLSchema-instance">
. . . .
<!-Descriptor of Flex portlet YahooFinancialNews -->
<portlet>
   <portlet-name>YahooFinancialNews</portlet-name>
   <portlet-class>flex.portal.GenericFlexPortlet</portlet-class>
   <init-param><name>wsrp_folder</name><value>/Portal</value></init-param>
   <supports>
      <mime-type>text/html</mime-type>
      <portlet-mode>view</portlet-mode>
   </supports>
   <portlet-info><title>Yahoo Financial News</title></portlet-info>
   <portlet-preferences>
      <preference>
         <name>app_uri</name>
         <value>/Portal/YahooFinancialNews</value>
      </preference>
      <preference>
          <name>norm_width</name>
         <value>400</value>
      </preference>
      <preference>
         <name>norm_height</name>
         <value>400</value>
      </preference>
   </portlet-preferences>
</portlet>
<portlet>
</portlet-app>
```

The preference `app_uri` points to the URL of the *YahooFinancialNews.swf*, stripped of the "*.swf*", and the parameter `wsrp_folder` points to the parent URL of the *wsrp-jsp*.

That's all it takes to have your Flex application running inside a Web 1.0 portal! Because `YahooFinancialNews` has been compiled to communicate with the `MessageBroker` of the Feeds web application, however, you do have to make sure that Feeds is deployed in the same domain.

But don't get carried away. First of all, you can't flexibly control the real estate dedicated to your portlet. Look at the rigid layout of Figure 7-22, which illustrates a BEA WebLogic portal with the mixture of two instances of `GenericFlexPortlet` (running `YahooFinancialNews` and `GoogleFinancialNews`), `SingleVideoPortlet`, and `ShowTimePortlet`; you can download the second two from Portlet Repository Downloads (*https://portlet-repository.dev.java.net/public/Download.html*). The Flex applications appear squeezed and cumbersome to use.

Second, and even more important, mixing Web 2.0 portlets based on Flash or AJAX with Web 1.0 ones (such as `ShowTimePortlet` in the example) is outright dangerous, if you consider that Flex applications and Web 2.0 portlets maintain state on the client, but rerendering of the Web 1.0 ones eliminates the entire HTML page.

As a result, the only way to integrate a Flex application in your legacy portal may be to run a single application per page.

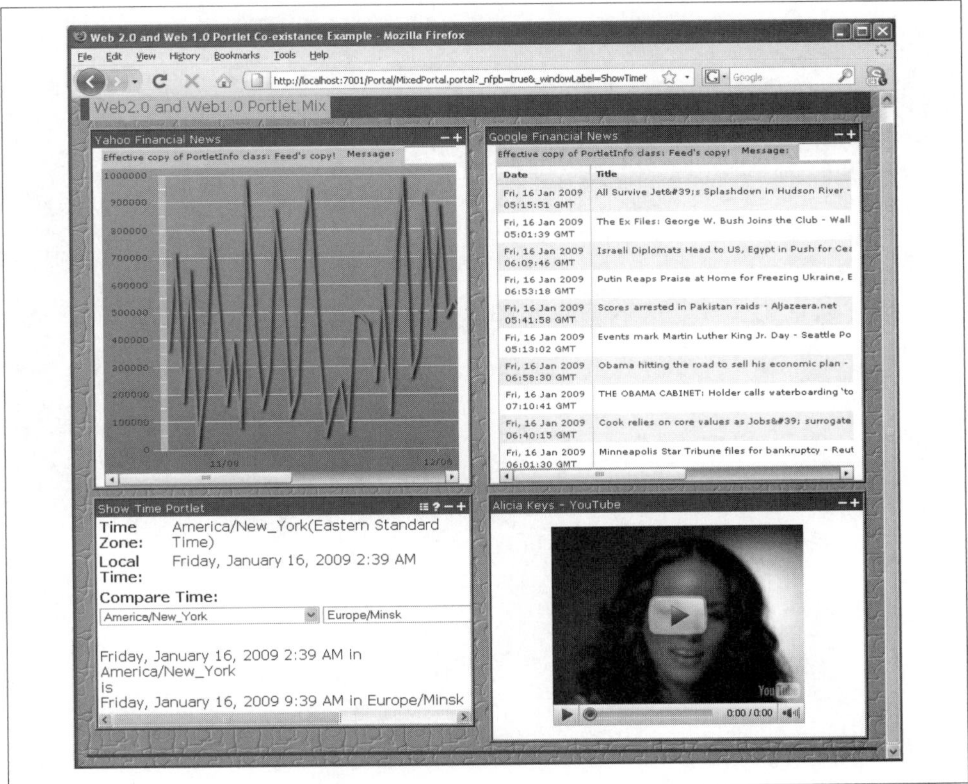

Figure 7-22. A Flex application's ad portlets in a WebLogic portal 10.2

Summary

Understanding how Flex loaders work, combined with the knowledge of different ways of linking modules and libraries to your main application, is crucial for the creation of Flex portals. Even if you are not concerned with portals, the chances are high that your application size will increase, and sooner or later you'll need to decide how to cut it into pieces. The sooner you start planning for modularizing your application, the better.

CHAPTER 8

Performance Improvement: Selected Topics

We have to stop optimizing for programmers and start optimizing for users.

—Jeff Atwood

The greatest performance improvement of all is when a system goes from not working to working.

—John Ousterhout

People consider your web application fast for one of two reasons: either it's actually fast or it gives an impression of being fast. Ideally, you should do your best to create an RIA that is very responsive, but if you hit the ceiling imposed by a technology you're using, at least try to improve the *perceived* performance of the system. To draw an analogy to the weather, the temperature may be cool, but it "feels like" freezing. No matter how slow your RIA is, it should never feel like freezing.

In this chapter, you'll learn how to use application *preloaders* to make the first page of your RIA appear on the display as soon as possible while loading the rest of the application in the background.

Once loaded on the user's machine, your application should use its memory efficiently. To help you identify trouble spots, we'll discuss possible drains on performance, such as memory leaks, garbage collectors, complex containers, event listeners, and closures. For example, if your application experiences memory leaks, Flash Builder's profiler may help. With it, you can monitor the number of object instances to ensure that you don't have memory leaks. The monitoring of your application performance must be done continuously from the start of your project.

In Chapter 7, you learned that cutting a monolithic application into modules, libraries, and subapplications can substantially minimize the initial download time of an RIA. In this chapter, we'll build on that technique. Specifically, you'll learn how you can use small Flash modules and link application libraries that are made with the same version of the Flex SDK. You'll also investigate the advantages of *resource-shared libraries*, including how to use them with modules and how to optimize them.

Planning for Modularization

After deciding to use the module and library approach, carefully review all resources besides the ActionScript or MXML code—namely images, sound, and movies (*.swf* files)—to decide whether you really need to embed them. The rule of thumb is that unless the image must be displayed on the first page, it should not be embedded. It is almost never worthwhile to embed any sizable sound or *.swf* in the Flex application, as they can use streaming and provide much better control of the execution by starting to play when just enough data is loaded.

Embedded images required in your RIA should be located in a separate Flash Builder project and loaded as RSLs.

The next part is to separate stylesheets and skins into modules. Doing so offers three advantages: first, it separates the work of the designers from the application developers. Second, removing stylesheets and skins from the compilation process significantly reduces rebuild time during development, because the cost of resource *transcoding* (compilation of fonts and styles) is high. Third, keeping skins and stylesheets outside of the modules simplifies initialization and eliminates unnecessary reloading and reapplying of CSS, thus making module initialization faster and safer.

Precompile CSS into a SWF file (right-click on the file to see this option) and then load it from the main application using the `StyleManager` class.

RSLs do introduce performance issues, however. They are loaded one by one and thus impose a "round-trip" effect. Breaking a monolithic application into 10 RSLs results in additional round-trip requests to the server and, as a result, slightly increases the initial load time. A solution to this problem is to use smarter loading of multiple RSLs by modifying the source code of the `RSLListLoader` class available in the SDK and placing it in your application (we'll cover this later in this chapter). Special care has to be taken in that case to ensure that framework libraries that other elements depend upon are loaded first.

Another rule of thumb for large applications is to make the first page as light and free of dependencies as possible. In other words, keep the first page super small. Once all of the system and CSS RSLs are loaded and the application enters the preinitialize event, you can start loading the rest of the application code. We recommend that you use the portal approach discussed in Chapter 7 as a starting point for any large application, as it provides a clean break between applications. We'll cover this topic in the section "Optimizing RSL Loading" on page 416.

It Takes Two to Perform

Fast applications are your goal, but how do you get there? On one hand, the RIA deployed on the server should consist of a number of relatively small *.swf*, *.swc*, and asset files. On the other, ideally, the end users should use fast and reliable network connections. First, let's define how fast your RIA should appear, and then we'll look at how quickly the data arrives to the user's machine.

The major difference between an internal enterprise and a consumer-facing RIA is that the former runs on fast and reliable networks with predictable speed and the latter runs in a Wild West with unknown bandwidth. You have to set the proper expectations of your RIA download speed from the very start. To do that you need an SLA.

SLA stands for *service level agreement*, and the stakeholders of your project should sign off on an agreement that states the acceptable delivery speed of your application and data. If your application will run on, say, a 15 Mbps intranet, the main page of the application should appear in less than about 7 seconds. If yours is a consumer-facing application, you can reasonably expect that the users have a network connection with 1 Mbps bandwidth. To put yourself into their shoes, run special tests emulating such a slow speed; for example, you could use the HTTP proxy and monitor Charles (see the sidebar "Troubleshooting with Charles" on page 202 in Chapter 4) or a hardware network emulator. To keep initial response time for the application, you need to make sure that the initially downloadable portion of your application is smaller than 1 MB.

After an enterprise application is downloaded, often it starts bringing some serious amounts of data from the server. The data should arrive quickly, and safe and sound. RIA applications are extremely susceptible to network problems. Even a small probability of lost or misdelivered packages becomes significant when multiplied by the sheer number of the small data packages involved. Lost, duplicate, and reordered packages, combined with high latency and low bandwidth, cause significant issues for applications fully tested *only* on reliable intranets and then released in the wild of unreliable WAN communications.

The authors of this book use several Linux boxes (both virtual and physical ones) to simulate WAN problems. The setup of a testing environment can be tedious, and you might want to consider using a simple portable appliance that will turn the simulation of a slow environment into a trivial task. One such portable, inexpensive, and easy-to-use network simulators is called Mini Maxwell.

Purposely increasing (with software or hardware) the simulated latency up to a realistic 200 ms and the package loss to an unrealistic 10 percent will quickly expose the problems in error-handling code. It will also give you a quick feel for the robustness of the code. Then you should check to see whether duplicate or out-of-sequence packages affect your application as described in Chapter 5.

While consulting one of our customers, a foreign exchange trading company, we had to enhance the endpoints in the RTMP protocols to ensure that out-of-sequence messages and network congestions were dealt with properly. But the remedies depend on the communication protocols used by RIA.

Obviously, with SOAP web services and similar high-level protocols, you have very loosely bound communications, making implementation of a QoS layer impossible. As the number of simultaneous `HTTPRequests` per domain is limited by the web browsers, the latency can cause performance slowdown and timeouts. Missing communication packages escalate the connection-starving issue even further.

LCDS 3.0 introduced QoS improvements at the protocol level. To learn more, get familiar with the new parameters in the Data Management configuration files.

If you use one of the AMF implementations for *data-intensive applications*, they will perform a lot faster (the *.swf* arrival time remains the same). With AMF, the latency is less of a problem, as Flex would automatically batch server requests together. Implementing symmetrical checkpoints on both client and server endpoints allows the processing of lost and duplicate packages. The lost packages remain a problem, as they cause request timeouts.

Robustness of an RIA improves if you move from HTTP/SOAP/REST to either RTMP or BlazeDS long-polling connected protocols. Keeping open connections and two-way sockets is ideal for high performance and reliable protocols. Comparing these to `HTTPRequests` is like comparing a highway with multiple lanes going in each direction to a single-lane dirt road.

More and more enterprise applications are built using always-connected protocols for tasks ranging from regular RPC to modules loading implementing streaming (the same thing as movie streaming). As these protocols evolve, you'll see more open source products that provide transparent implementations using a mixture of protocols. Meanwhile, we can mix protocols using such Flex techniques as configuring the fallback channels.

Application Startup and Preloaders

Perceived performance is as important as actual performance. While a large Flex application loads, users may experience unpleasant delays. Rather than frustrate them with inactivity, give the users something productive to work on. This can be a main window of your application or just a logon view. The point is that this very first view should be extremely lightweight and arrive on the user's machine even before the Flex frameworks and the rest of the application code starts downloading. Giving users the ability to start working quickly with partially loaded code gives a perception that your application loads faster.

In this section, you'll learn how to create and load a rapidly arriving logon screen to keep the user occupied immediately. Here are the four challenges you face:

- The logon screen has to be very lightweight. It must be under 50 KB, so using classes from the Flex framework is out of the question.
- The application shouldn't be able to remove the logon window upon load, as the user must log in first.
- If the user completes logging in before the application finishes its load, the standard progress bar has to appear.
- The application should be able to reuse the same lightweight logon window if the user decides to log out at any time during the session.

What Happens in Flash Player Before the Flex Application Is Loaded

The `SystemManager` is a main manager that controls the application window; creates and parents the `Application` instance, pop ups, and cursors; manages the classes in the `ApplicationDomain` container (see the Flex language reference at *http://livedocs.adobe.com/flex/gumbo/langref/*), and more. The `SystemManager` is the first class that is instantiated by Flash Player in the first frame of your application (modules and subapplications have their own `SystemManager` classes). `SystemManger` is responsible for loading all RSL libraries, which will be discussed later in this chapter.

Hanging off of a `stage` object, `SystemManger` stores the size and position of the main application window, and keeps track of its children, such as floating pop ups and modal windows. Using the `SystemManager`, you can access embedded fonts, styles, and the document object. `SystemManager` also controls application domains, which are used to partition classes by security domains.

If you're developing custom visual components (descendants of the `UIComponent` class), keep in mind that initially such components are not connected to any display list and the `SystemManager=null`. Only after the first call of `addChild()` is `SystemManager` assigned to them. You should not access `SystemManager` from the constructor of your component, because at this point in time it can still be `null`.

In general, when the `Application` object is created, the process is:

1. The `Application` object instantiates.
2. Its property `Application.systemManager` initializes.
3. The `Application` dispatches the `FlexEvent.PREINITIALIZE` event at the beginning of the initialization process.

4. Flash Player calls the method `createChildren()` on the `Application`. At this point, each of the `application`'s components is constructed, and each component's `createChildren()` is also called.
5. The `Application` dispatches the `FlexEvent.INITIALIZE` event, which indicates that all of the application's components have been initialized.
6. Flash Player dispatches `FlexEvent.CREATION_COMPLETE`.
7. Flash Player adds the `Application` object to the display list, and the `Preloader` object gets removed.
8. Flash Player dispatches the `FlexEvent.APPLICATION_COMPLETE` event.

In most cases, you should use the MXML tag `<mx:Application>` to create the `Application` object, but if you need to write it in ActionScript, do not create components in the constructor. Instead, override `createChildren()`, which is a bit more efficient.

As opposed to Flash movies that consist of multiple frames being displayed over a timeline, Flex *.swf* files utilize only two frames. The `SystemManager`, `Preloader`, `DownloadProgressBar`, and a handful of other helper classes live in the first frame. The rest of the Flex framework, your application code, and embedded assets like fonts and images reside in the second frame.

When Flash Player initially starts downloading your *.swf*, as soon as enough bytes come for the first frame, it instantiates a `SystemManager`, which creates an instance of the `Preloader`, which is monitoring the process of the application download and initialization and in turn creates a `DownloadProgressBar`.

At the point when all bytes for the first frame are in, `SystemManager` sends the `FlexEvent.ENTER_FRAME` for the second frame, and then renders other events.

Dissecting LightweightPreloader.swf

The sample application that will demonstrate how these challenges are resolved is located in the Eclipse Dynamic Web Project and is called *lightweight-preloader*. This application is deployed under the server. Note that the interactive login window (Figure 8-1) arrives from the server very fast, even though the large application *.swf* file continues downloading, and this process may or may not be complete by the time the user enters her credentials and clicks the Login button.

This view was created in Photoshop and then saved as an image. Figure 8-2 depicts the directory structure of the Flash Builder project *lightweight-preloader*. In particular, the assets directory has the image file *logon.psd* created in Photoshop and saved as a lighter *logon.png*. At this point, any Flash developer can open this file in Flash Professional IDE and add a couple of text fields and a button, saving it as a Flash movie. This window can be saved in binary formats (*.fla* and *.swf*), but we've exported this file into a program written in ActionScript.

Figure 8-1. Login view of lightweight preloader

This generated ActionScript code may not be pretty, and you might want to manually edit it, which we did. The final version of this code (class `LightweightPreloader`) is shown in Example 8-2.

The text elements shown in Figure 8-1 are not Flex components. Example 8-1 shows the ActionScript class that uses the *logon.png* file.

Example 8-1. The background of the login view

```
package com.farata.preloading{
    import flash.display.Bitmap;

    [Embed(source="assets/logon.png")]
    public class PanelBackground extends Bitmap
    {
        public function PanelBackground ()
        {
            smoothing = true;
        }
    }
}
```

The *logon.png* image is 21 KB, and you can reduce this size further by lowering the resolution of the image. The ActionScript class `LightweightPreloader` that uses the `PanelBackground` class adds another 6 KB, bringing the total size of the precompiled *LightweightPreloader.swf* to a mere 27 KB. This file will be loaded by the Flex `Preloader` in parallel with the larger *MainApplication.swf* file.

The fragment of the code of `LightweightPreloader` is shown in Example 8-2. The total size of this class is 326 lines of code. Most of this code was exported from Flash Pro, but some additional coding was needed. Even though it's tempting to use Flex and create such a simple view in a dozen of lines of code, you need to understand that keeping down the size of the very first preloaded *.swf* file is a lot more important than

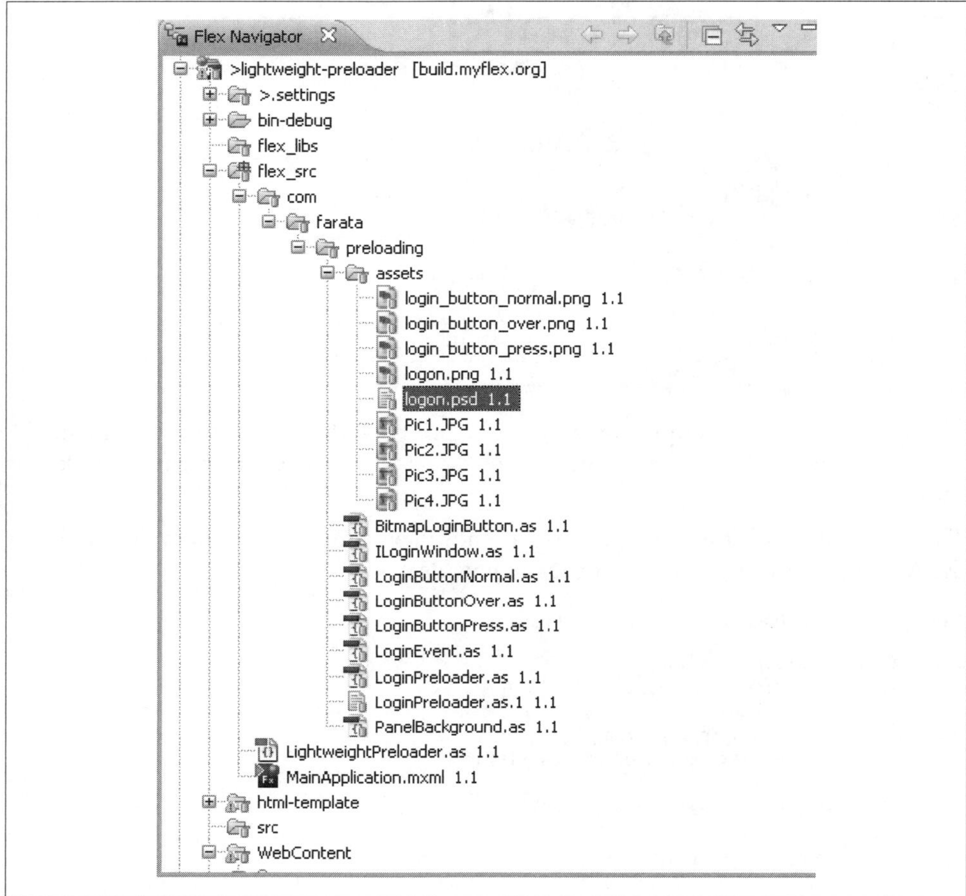

Figure 8-2. The Flash Builder project lightweight-preloader

minimizing the amount of manual coding. This is the only case where we are advocating manual coding versus the automation offered by Flex.

Using Flash Catalyst for generation of the code of `LightweightPreloader` from a Photoshop image is also not advisable in this case, because Flash Catalyst uses Flex framework objects, which would substantially increase the size of *LightweightPreloader.swf*. Note that the import section of Example 8-2 doesn't include any of the classes from the Flex framework.

Example 8-2. LightweightPreloader.as

```
package{
    import com.farata.preloading.BitmapLoginButton;
    import com.farata.preloading.ILoginWindow;
```

```
import com.farata.preloading.LoginButtonNormal;
import com.farata.preloading.LoginEvent;
import com.farata.preloading.PanelBackground;

import flash.display.DisplayObject;
import flash.display.InteractiveObject;
import flash.display.Sprite;
import flash.events.Event;
import flash.events.FocusEvent;
import flash.events.IOErrorEvent;
import flash.events.KeyboardEvent;
import flash.events.MouseEvent;
import flash.events.SecurityErrorEvent;
import flash.net.URLLoader;
import flash.net.URLLoaderDataFormat;
import flash.net.URLRequest;
import flash.net.URLVariables;
import flash.text.TextField;
import flash.text.TextFieldType;
import flash.text.TextFormat;
import flash.text.TextFormatAlign;
import flash.ui.Keyboard;
import flash.utils.Dictionary;
import flash.net.SharedObject;

public class LightweightPreloader extends Sprite
    implements ILoginWindow{
    public static const loginURL:String = "login";
    public static const LOGIN_INCORRECT_MESSAGE:String =
                        "Failed. Use your myflex.org credentials";
    public static const HTTP_ERROR_MESSAGE:String =
                        "Connection error. Please try again.";

    private var testMode:Boolean = true; //No server data available
    private var loginField:TextField;
    private var passwordField:TextField;
    private var messageField:TextField;
    private var loginButton:DisplayObject;
    public var background:PanelBackground;
    private var focuses:Array = new Array ();
    private var focuseMap:Dictionary = new Dictionary ();
.....

    private function doInit ():void{
        background = new PanelBackground ();
        addChild (background);

        loginField = new TextField ();
        addChild (loginField);
        configureTextField (loginField);

        passwordField = new TextField ();
        addChild (passwordField);
        configureTextField (passwordField);
        passwordField.displayAsPassword = true;
```

```
            messageField = new TextField ();
            addChild (messageField);
            messageField.type = TextFieldType.DYNAMIC;
            var format:TextFormat = new TextFormat ("_sans", 12, 0xFF0000);
            format.align = TextFormatAlign.CENTER;
            messageField.defaultTextFormat = format;
            messageField.selectable = false;
            messageField.width = 300;
            messageField.height = 20;

            loginButton = new BitmapLoginButton ();
            addChild (loginButton);
            loginButton.addEventListener (KeyboardEvent.KEY_DOWN,
                                          onButtonKeyboardPress);
            loginButton.addEventListener (MouseEvent.CLICK, onButtonClick);
            loginButton.addEventListener (FocusEvent.KEY_FOCUS_CHANGE,
                                             onFocusChange);
            loginButton.addEventListener (FocusEvent.FOCUS_OUT, onFocusOut);
            focuses.push (loginButton);
            focuseMap [loginButton] = true;

            var so:SharedObject = SharedObject.getLocal( "USER_INFO");
            if (so.size > 0) {
                try {
                    var arr:Array = so.data.now;
                    loginField.text = arr[0];
                    passwordField.text = arr[1];
                }
                catch(error:Error) {
                   //Error processing goes here
                   }
            }

            if (stage != null) {
                stage.stageFocusRect = false;
                stage.focus = loginField;
                focus = loginField;
            }
        }
...
        private function doLayout ():void{
            loginField.x = 230;
            loginField.y = 110;

            passwordField.x = 232;
            passwordField.y = 163;

            loginButton.y = 200;
            loginButton.x = (background.width - loginButton.width) / 2;

            messageField.y = 215;
            messageField.x = 65;
        }
```

```
        private function onEnterPress (event:KeyboardEvent):void{
            if (event.keyCode == Keyboard.ENTER){
                onLogin ();
            }
        }

        private function onButtonKeyboardPress (event:KeyboardEvent):void{
            if ((event.keyCode == Keyboard.ENTER) ||
                (event.keyCode == Keyboard.SPACE)) {
                onLogin ();
            }
        }

        private function onButtonClick (event:MouseEvent):void {
            onLogin ();
        }

        private function onLogin ():void{
            if (testMode) {
                onLoginResult ();
            }
            else {
                try{
                    var request:URLRequest = new URLRequest (loginURL);

                    var thisURL:String = loaderInfo.url;
                    if (thisURL.indexOf ("file") < 0) {
                        var variables:URLVariables = new URLVariables ();
                        variables.user = loginField.text;
                        variables.password = passwordField.text;
                        variables.application = "Client Reports";
                        request.data = variables;
                    }

                    var loader:URLLoader = new URLLoader (request);

                    loader.addEventListener (SecurityErrorEvent.SECURITY_ERROR,
                                                              onSecurityError);
                    loader.addEventListener (IOErrorEvent.IO_ERROR, onIOError);
                    loader.addEventListener (Event.COMPLETE, onLoginResult);
                    loader.load (request);
                }
                catch (e:Error) {
                    messageField.text = HTTP_ERROR_MESSAGE;
                }
            }
        }

...
        private function onLoginResult (event:Event = null):void{
            if (testMode) {
                dispatchEvent (new LoginEvent (LoginEvent.ON_LOGIN, "test",
                                               null));
            }
            else {
```

```
                var loader:URLLoader = URLLoader(event.target);
                if (loader.dataFormat == URLLoaderDataFormat.TEXT) {
                    var response:String = loader.data;
                    var responseXML:XML = new XML (response);
                    var status:String = responseXML.status [0];
                    if (status == "1"){
                        var so:SharedObject =
                                    SharedObject.getLocal("USER_INFO");
                        so.data.now = new Array (loginField.text,
                                                   passwordField.text);
                        so.flush();
                        dispatchEvent (new LoginEvent (LoginEvent.ON_LOGIN,
                               "no session available", // no sessionID for now
                          responseXML));
                    } else
                        messageField.text = LOGIN_INCORRECT_MESSAGE;
                }
                else{
                    messageField.text = HTTP_ERROR_MESSAGE;
                }
            }
        }
    }
}
```

This class extends `flash.display.Sprite`, a very light display node that can have children and display graphics. It adds the image displayed earlier in Figure 8-1 as a background (see the method `doInit()` in Example 8-2):

```
background = new PanelBackground ();
addChild (background);
```

On top of this background, `doInit()` adds a couple of `flash.text.TextField` controls and a subclass of the `flash.display.SimpleButton`, as shown in Example 8-3.

Example 8-3. BitmapLoginButton.as

```
package com.farata.preloading{
    import flash.display.DisplayObject;
    import flash.display.SimpleButton;

    public class BitmapLoginButton extends SimpleButton{

        public function BitmapLoginButton (){
            super(new LoginButtonNormal (),
                    new LoginButtonOver (),
                    new LoginButtonPress (),
                    new LoginButtonNormal ());
            useHandCursor = false;
        }
    }
}
```

The constructor of `SimpleButton` takes tiny wrapper classes with images representing different states of the button, as shown in Example 8-4.

Example 8-4. LoginButtonOver.as

```
package com.farata.preloading{
    import flash.display.Bitmap;

    [Embed(source="assets/login_button_over.png")]
    public class LoginButtonOver extends Bitmap{

        public function LoginButtonOver (){
            smoothing = true;
        }
    }
}
```

This is pretty much it; the graphic portion is taken care of.

The login functionality in a typical Flex application should be initiated from inside the Flex code and not from the HTML wrapper. This will allow you to minimize the vulnerability of the application as you eliminate the step in which the user's credentials have to be passed from JavaScript to the embedded *.swf* file.

The `LightweightPreloader` from Example 8-2 contains Example 8-5's code in its `onLogin()` method.

Example 8-5. Authenticating the user from ActionScript

```
var request:URLRequest = new URLRequest (loginURL);

        var thisURL:String = loaderInfo.url;
        if (thisURL.indexOf ("file") < 0) {
            var variables:URLVariables = new URLVariables ();
            variables.user = loginField.text;
            variables.password = passwordField.text;
            variables.application = "Client Reports";
            request.data = variables;
        }

        var loader:URLLoader = new URLLoader (request);

        loader.addEventListener (SecurityErrorEvent.SECURITY_ERROR,
                                                            onSecurityError);
        loader.addEventListener (IOErrorEvent.IO_ERROR, onIOError);
        loader.addEventListener (Event.COMPLETE, onLoginResult);
        loader.load (request);
```

The code in Example 8-5 creates a `URLRequest` object, wrapping the values entered in the Flex view. The `URLLoader` makes a request to the specified URL that authenticates the user and returns a piece of XML describing the user's role and any other business-specific authorization parameters provided by your web access management system, such as SiteMinder from CA. No sensitive data exchange between JavaScript and the *.swf* file is required.

The function `onLoginResult()` gets the user's data from the server, and saves this as an XML object on the local disk via a `SharedObject` API, providing functionality similar to cookies.

The Main SWF Talks to LightweightPreloader.swf

The main application (Example 8-6) was written with the use of the Flex framework, and it communicates with the external *LightweightPreloader.swf* via an additional class called `LoginPreloader`, shown in Example 8-7. We've embedded several images into the *MainApplication.mxml* file just to make the *.swf* file extremely heavy (10 MB) to illustrate that the login window appears quickly, and the main application may continue loading even after the user enters login credentials and presses the Login button.

Note the line `preloader="com.farata.preloading.LoginPreloader"` in the fourth line of *MainApplication.mxml* in the example.

Example 8-6. MainApplication.mxml

```
<?xml version="1.0" encoding="utf-8"?>
<mx:Application
    xmlns:mx="http://www.adobe.com/2006/mxml"
    preloader="com.farata.preloading.LoginPreloader"
    layout="vertical"
    horizontalAlign="center"
    backgroundColor="white"
    verticalAlign="top">
    <mx:Script>
        <![CDATA[
            import mx.containers.TitleWindow;
            import mx.containers.Panel;
            import com.farata.preloading.ILoginWindow;
            import mx.managers.PopUpManager;
            import mx.core.UIComponent;
            import com.farata.preloading.LoginEvent;

            public function set sessionID (value:String):void{
                // code to store app. specific session id goes here
              trace ("sessionID in Main: " + value);
            }

              public function set loginXML (value:String):void{
                // code to process authotization XML goes here
               trace ("loginXML in Main: " + value);
            }

            private var loginPanel:Panel;
            private var content:Sprite;

            // Embed several large images just to increase the size
            // of the main SWF to over 10 MB.
              // This is done to illustrate fast preloading
            // of the LightweightPreloader login window
```

```
[Embed(source="com/farata/preloading/assets/Pic1.JPG")]
public var pic1:Class;
[Embed(source="com/farata/preloading/assets/Pic2.JPG")]
public var pic2:Class;
[Embed(source="com/farata/preloading/assets/Pic3.JPG")]
public var pic3:Class;
[Embed(source="com/farata/preloading/assets/Pic4.JPG")]
public var pic4:Class;

private function onLogout ():void {
    var loader:Loader = new Loader ();
    var url:URLRequest = new URLRequest
                              ("LightweightPreloader.swf");
    var context:LoaderContext = new LoaderContext ();
    var applicationDomain:ApplicationDomain =
        ApplicationDomain.currentDomain;
    context.applicationDomain = applicationDomain;
    loader.load (url, context);
    loader.contentLoaderInfo.addEventListener
            (Event.COMPLETE,onLoginLoaded);
}

private function onLoginLoaded (event:Event):void {
    content = event.target.content as Sprite;
    var component:UIComponent = new UIComponent ();
    loginPanel = new TitleWindow ();
    loginPanel.title = "Log In";

    component.addChild (content);
    loginPanel.addChild(component);

    PopUpManager.addPopUp(loginPanel, this, true);

    (content as ILoginWindow).activate();

     component.width = content.width;
    component.height = content.height;
    PopUpManager.centerPopUp(loginPanel);

    content.addEventListener (LoginEvent.ON_LOGIN, onLogin);
}

private function onLogin (event:LoginEvent):void {
    (content as ILoginWindow).deactivate();
    PopUpManager.removePopUp (loginPanel);
    loginPanel = null;
    content = null;

    passParamsToApp(event);
       focusManager.activate();
}

private function passParamsToApp (event:LoginEvent):void {
    for (var i:String in event) {
        try{
```

```
                        this [i] = event [i];
                    }catch (e:Error) {
                        trace ("There is no parameter " + i +
                                "in " + this + " defined");
                    }
                }
            }
        ]]>
    </mx:Script>
    <mx:ApplicationControlBar width="100%"
        horizontalAlign="right">

        <mx:Button click="onLogout()" label="Log Out" />
    </mx:ApplicationControlBar>
    <mx:VBox
        verticalAlign="middle"
        horizontalAlign="center"
        width="100%"
        height="100%">
        <mx:Panel
            title="Hello"
            paddingLeft="20"
            paddingRight="20"
            paddingTop="10"
            paddingBottom="10">
            <mx:Label text="Application" />
        </mx:Panel>

    </mx:VBox>
</mx:Application>
```

The class `LoginPreloader` is a subclass of `DownloadProgressBar`. It cares about two things:

- That the loading of the main application is finished and it can be displayed.
- That the login request is complete.

If the user presses the Login button before the main application (which is 10 MB in this case) arrives, the `LoginPreloader` turns itself into a progress bar until the application is fully downloaded and displayed. The `LoginPreloader` (Example 8-7) acts as a liaison between the main application and the `LightweightPreloader`.

Example 8-7. Classes LoginPreloader and UnprotectedDownloadProgressBar

```
package com.farata.preloading{
    import flash.display.Loader;
    import flash.display.Sprite;
    import flash.events.Event;
    import flash.events.ProgressEvent;
    import flash.net.URLRequest;
    import flash.system.ApplicationDomain;
    import flash.system.LoaderContext;
    import flash.utils.getDefinitionByName;
```

```
import mx.events.FlexEvent;
import mx.managers.FocusManager;
import mx.managers.IFocusManager;
import mx.managers.IFocusManagerComponent;
import mx.managers.IFocusManagerContainer;
import mx.preloaders.DownloadProgressBar;
import flash.utils.getTimer;
import flash.utils.Timer;
import flash.events.TimerEvent;

public class LoginPreloader extends DownloadProgressBar {
    private var loginWindow:Sprite;
    private var event:LoginEvent;
    private var loggedIn:Boolean = false;
    private var isLoaded:Boolean = false;
    private var appInited:Boolean = false;
    private var aPreloader:Sprite;
    private var progress:UnprotectedDownloadProgressBar;
    private var _displayTime:int;

    public function LoginPreloader(){
        super();
        _displayTime = getTimer();
        MINIMUM_DISPLAY_TIME = 0;
        var loader:Loader = new Loader ();
        var url:URLRequest = new URLRequest ("LightweightPreloader.swf");
        var context:LoaderContext = new LoaderContext ();
        var applicationDomain:ApplicationDomain =
            ApplicationDomain.currentDomain;
        context.applicationDomain = applicationDomain;
        loader.load (url, context);
        loader.contentLoaderInfo.addEventListener (Event.COMPLETE,
                                    onLoginLoaded);
    }

    private function onLoginLoaded (event:Event):void{
        var content:Sprite = event.target.content as Sprite;
        addChild (content);
        loginWindow = content;
        (loginWindow as ILoginWindow).activate();
        content.x = (stage.stageWidth - content.width) / 2;
        content.y = (stage.stageHeight - content.height) / 2;
        content.addEventListener (LoginEvent.ON_LOGIN, onLogin);
    }

    override public function set preloader( preloader:Sprite ):void {
        preloader.addEventListener( FlexEvent.INIT_COMPLETE ,
                                            initCompleteHandler );
        aPreloader = preloader;
    }

    private function onLogin (event:LoginEvent):void
    {
        this.event = event;
        loggedIn = true;
```

```
    (loginWindow as ILoginWindow).deactivate();
    removeChild (loginWindow);
    if (isLoaded) {
        var anApp:Object = getApplication();
        passParamsToApp();
           (anApp as IFocusManagerContainer).focusManager.activate();
        dispatchEvent( new Event( Event.COMPLETE ) );
    }
    else{
        progress = new UnprotectedDownloadProgressBar ();
        progress.isLoaded = appInited;
        progress.minTime = MINIMUM_DISPLAY_TIME - getTimer() + _displayTime;
        addChild (progress);

        progress.preloader = aPreloader;
    var xOffset:Number = Math.floor((progress.width -
                       progress.publicBorderRect.width) / 2);
    var yOffset:Number = Math.floor((progress.height -
                       progress.publicBorderRect.height) / 2);
      progress.x = (stage.stageWidth - progress.width) / 2 + xOffset;
    progress.y = (stage.stageHeight - progress.height) / 2 + yOffset;
    progress.addEventListener (Event.COMPLETE, onProgressComplete);
    }
}

private function onProgressComplete (event:Event):void{
    progress.removeEventListener (Event.COMPLETE, onProgressComplete);
    dispatchEvent( new Event( Event.COMPLETE ) );
}

private function initCompleteHandler(event:Event):void{
    appInited = true;
    var elapsedTime:int = getTimer() - _displayTime;

    if (elapsedTime < MINIMUM_DISPLAY_TIME) {
      var timer:Timer = new Timer(MINIMUM_DISPLAY_TIME - elapsedTime, 1);
      timer.addEventListener(TimerEvent.TIMER, flexInitComplete);
    timer.start();
    } else{
        flexInitComplete();
    }
}

private function flexInitComplete( event:Event = null ):void {
    isLoaded = true;
    if (progress) {
       removeChild (progress);
    }
   var anApp:Object = getApplication();
    if (loggedIn) {
       passParamsToApp();
       dispatchEvent( new Event( Event.COMPLETE ) );
    }else{
     (anApp as IFocusManagerContainer).focusManager.deactivate();
    }
```

```
        }

        private function passParamsToApp ():void{
            var anApp:Object = getApplication();
            for (var i:String in event) {
                try{
                    anApp [i] = event [i];
                }
                catch (e:Error) {
                    trace ("There is no parameter " + i +
                                "in " + anApp + " defined");
                }
            }
        }

        private function getApplication ():Object{
            return getDefinitionByName
            ("mx.core.Application").application;
        }
    }
}

import mx.preloaders.DownloadProgressBar;
import mx.graphics.RoundedRectangle;
import flash.display.Sprite;

class UnprotectedDownloadProgressBar extends DownloadProgressBar{
    public var isLoaded:Boolean = false;

    public function set minTime (value:int):void{
        if (value > 0) {
            MINIMUM_DISPLAY_TIME = value;
        }
    }

    public function get publicBorderRect ():RoundedRectangle{
        this.backgroundColor = 0xffffff;
        return borderRect;
    }

    public override function set preloader(value:Sprite):void{
        super.preloader = value;
        visible = true;
        if (isLoaded) {
            setProgress (100, 100);
            label = downloadingLabel;
        }
    }
}
```

As soon as the loading of the login window is complete, the window centers itself on the screen and starts listening to the `LoginEvent.ON_LOGIN`, which is dispatched by `LightweightPreloader` when the XML with the user's credentials arrives from the server.

This XML is nicely packaged inside the `LoginEvent` and saved on the local disk cache under the name `USER_INFO` (see the method `onLoginResult()` in Example 8-2).

Because the `LightweightPreloader` was added as a child of `LoginPreloader` (see `onLoginLoaded()` in Example 8-8), the latter object will receive all events dispatched by the former.

Example 8-8. The method onLoginLoaded() of LoginPreloader

```
private function onLoginLoaded (event:Event):void
{
            var content:Sprite = event.target.content as Sprite;
            addChild (content);
            loginWindow = content;
            (loginWindow as ILoginWindow).activate();
            content.x = (stage.stageWidth - content.width) / 2;
            content.y = (stage.stageHeight - content.height) / 2;
            content.addEventListener (LoginEvent.ON_LOGIN, onLogin);
}
```

This code also stores in `loginWindow` the reference to the login window, which is a subclass of `Sprite`, for further reuse in case the user decides to log out, which should bring the login window back on the screen. The function `activate` just puts the focus there.

When the `ON_LOGIN` event arrives, the event handler `onLogin()` shown in Example 8-8 has to figure out whether the download of the main application has completed and whether it's ready for use. If it is ready, the application gets activated; otherwise, the instance of the regular progress bar `UnprotectedDownloadProgressBar` is created and displayed until the application is ready.

The `Timer` object checks for the downloading progress, and dispatches `Event.COMPLETE` to the application from the `flexInitComplete()` handler.

Supporting Logout Functionality

Besides supporting our custom preloader, the main application (Example 8-6) knows how to reuse the login component when the user decides to log out and relogin at any time during the session.

After successful login, the user will see a screen like Figure 8-3.

Even though `LightweightPreloader` (the login component) was intended to be used as the very first visible component of our application, we want to be able reuse its functionality later on, too.

Hence `LightweightPreloader` is used either by the preloader or by a `PopupManager`. The following fragment from the main application does this job when the user clicks the Log Out button:

```
private function onLogout ():void{
    var loader:Loader = new Loader ();
    var url:URLRequest = new URLRequest ("LightweightPreloader.swf");
    var context:LoaderContext = new LoaderContext ();
    var applicationDomain:ApplicationDomain =
            ApplicationDomain.currentDomain;
    context.applicationDomain = applicationDomain;
    loader.load (url, context);
    loader.contentLoaderInfo.addEventListener (Event.COMPLETE,
                                                        onLoginLoaded);
}

private function onLoginLoaded (event:Event):void{
    content = event.target.content as Sprite;
    var component:UIComponent = new UIComponent ();
    loginPanel = new TitleWindow ();
    loginPanel.title = "Log In";

    component.addChild (content);
    loginPanel.addChild(component);

    PopUpManager.addPopUp(loginPanel, this, true);

     (content as ILoginWindow).activate();

    component.width = content.width;
    component.height = content.height;
    PopUpManager.centerPopUp(loginPanel);

    content.addEventListener (LoginEvent.ON_LOGIN, onLogin);
}
```

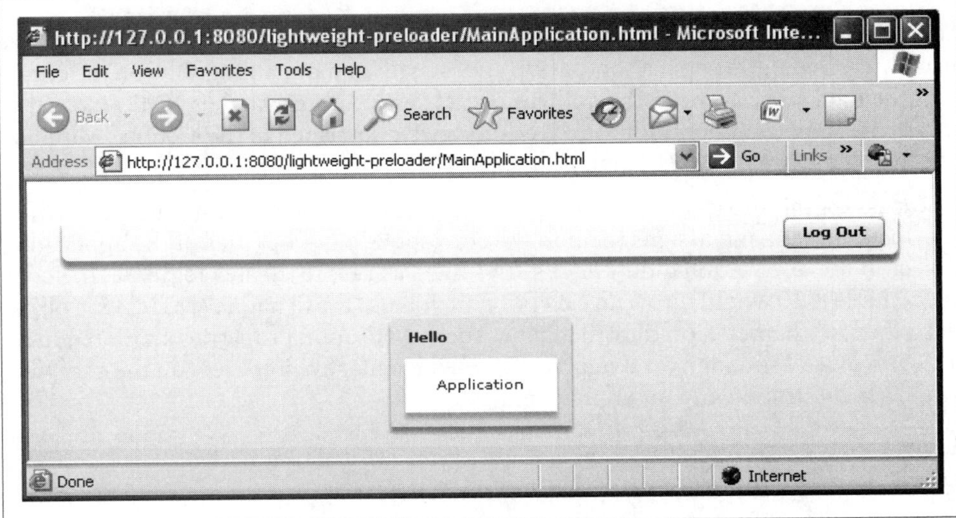

Figure 8-3. After the user is logged in

The call to `PopupManager.addPopup()` from the fragment is an example of how a Flex application can work with a Flash component.

If you have Flash programmers in your team, you can use Flash for creating lightweight components when appropriate. Not only can you create lightweight login windows in Flash, but the entire main application view can be coded in this way. As a matter of fact, all static views from your application that mostly contain the artwork and don't pull the data from the server can be made a lot slimmer if programmed as Flash components.

All communications between `LightweightPreloader`, `LoginPreloader`, and *MainApplication.mxml* are handled by dispatching and listening to the custom event `LoginEvent`, shown in Example 8-9.

Example 8-9. LoginEvent

```
package com.farata.preloading{
    import flash.events.Event;

    public dynamic class LoginEvent extends Event{
        public static const ON_LOGIN:String = "onLogin";

        public function LoginEvent(type:String, sessionID:String, xml:XML){
            super(type);
            this.sessionID = sessionID;
            this.loginXML = xml;
        }
    }
}
```

`LoginEvent` encapsulates the user's session ID (an application-specific session ID that's usually created upon application startup and is used for maintaining state on the client) and the data received from the authentication server represented as XML. Note that this is the somewhat nontraditional dynamic event described in the section "Minimizing the Number of Custom Events" on page 169.

The class `LoginPreloader` has a function that extracts the values of the parameters from the custom event and assigns them to the corresponding properties of the application object. If the application didn't have such setters as `sessionID` and `loginXML`, the code in Example 8-10 would throw an exception. If you use the dynamic `Application` object described in Chapter 2, on the other hand, such application properties aren't required. This is a typical situation for dynamically typed languages: don't rely on the compiler, and do better testing of your application.

Example 8-10. Non-object-oriented way of data exchange between components

```
private function passParamsToApp (event:LoginEvent):void{
            var anApp:Object = getApplication();
            for (var i:String in event) {
```

```
            try{
                anApp [i] = event [i];
            }
            catch (e:Error) {
                trace ("There is no parameter " + i +
                            "in " + anApp + " defined");
            }
        }
    }
```

Examples 8-9 and 8-10 use dynamic typing because of a special situation: when a Flash *.swf* file may have a bunch of properties in the event, it dispatches. The `Application` object, however, may not need all these properties. The `for in` loop shown assigns only those dynamic properties that exist in the `Application` object.

Objects that use strongly typed properties perform better than dynamic ones. For a typical Flex way of exchanging data between components, implement the Mediator design pattern described in Chapter 2.

The sample application with `Preloader` not only demonstrates how to use pure Flash components in a Flex application for improving perceived performance, but also illustrates techniques for mixing and matching Flex and native Flash components.

Just to recap: the main application is written in Flex; the `LightweightPreloader` is a Flash component created in Flash Professional IDE with some manual modifications of the generated ActionScript code; and the `LoginPreloader` is a manually written reusable ActionScript class that loads the *.swf* file with the Flash login component and removes it when the functionality of this *.swf* is no longer needed.

Using Resource-Shared Libraries

Tricks with a tiny preloader *.swf* can give users the feeling that your application loads quickly, but you should also endeavor to make the main application load as quickly as possible. A typical enterprise Flex RIA consists of several *.swf* files (the main application, fonts and styles, and modules) as well as several *.swc* libraries (both yours and the Flex framework's). Your goal with these remains the same: ensure that only a minimum portion of the code travels over the network to the end user's machine.

How to Link Flex Libraries

Right-click on a project name in Flash Builder, select the Flex Build Path option, and you'll see a "Library path" panel similar to the one in Figure 8-4. This panel lists only the libraries from the Flex framework (AIR applications have some additional libraries). Both the framework and the necessary libraries must be linked to your project. You set the linkage method for the Flex framework via the "Framework linkage" drop-down menu (more on this in the next section). For now, however, just concentrate on linking the Flex libraries that your project needs for successful compilation and execution. To do this, click on the plus sign by the library name (see Figure 8-4) and double-click on the link method. You can choose one of three methods:

- RSLs
- Merged into code
- External

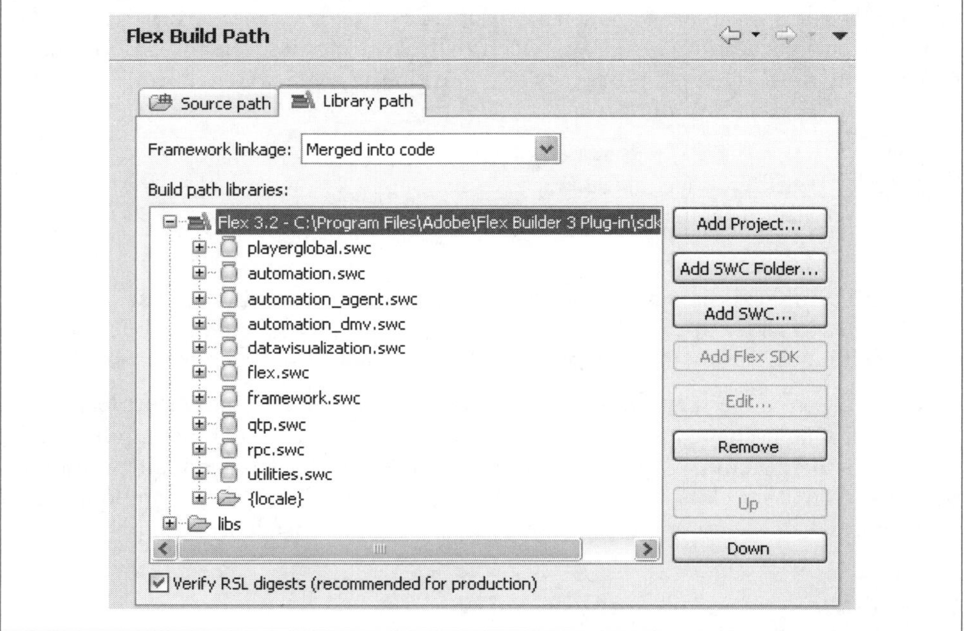

Figure 8-4. The library path of a simple Flex project

A typical enterprise application is the product of several Flash Builder projects. The main application must link the libraries that are absolutely necessary to support the first screen. Optionally, it also can include some common libraries for multiple modules that might be downloaded as a result of a user's interactions with your RIA. Loading common *RSL* libraries during the application startup is not such a good idea, however, if you load modules in the application security domain and not their own subdomains (see Chapter 7). You need to manage RSLs and ensure that the RSL is loaded only once, and this can be done by the singleton `ModuleManager`. You'll learn how to do this a bit later, in the section "Optimizing RSL Loading" on page 416.

Selecting *merge-in* linkage for an application or a module increases the *.swf* size only by the size of the classes from the library that were actually mentioned in the *.swf* file. This requirement has a negative side effect for dynamically created (and, therefore, not referenced in advance) objects. To have all objects available, you must declare a number of variables of each type that exists in the *.swc* file to ensure that all the classes that are needed (even for code that's loaded later) are included in the *.swf* file.

The section "Bootstrapping Libraries As Applications" on page 357 described the process that happens once libraries are loaded. If the linker does not find explicit references to some classes from the linkage tree originated by the `Application` or `Module` class, it might omit both necessary supporting classes and not perform some parts of the necessary initialization process. If you are developing large data-driven dynamic applications, using bootstrapping libraries instead of modules is the safer and more reusable solution.

For example, if the code in your application never uses *`SomeGreatClass`* from a library *xyz.swc*, its code will not be included in the *.swf* file during compilation. Hence if your business code "weighs" 300 KB and the *xyz.swc* is 100 KB, the compiled *.swf* file's size won't reach 400 KB unless each and every class from *xyz.swc* has been used. Merge-in linkage is justifiable only for small applications, which are not going to use most of the framework classes anyway.

Consider a RIA that consists of two Flash Builder projects: the main application (*proj1* at 250 KB) and a Flex module (*proj2* at 50 KB). Both of these projects use classes from the library *xyz.swc*. The chances are good that *proj1* and *proj2* need some of the same and some different classes from *xyz.swc*. What are your options here?

Of course, you can link *xyz.swc* using the merge-in option, in which case each project will include into its *.swf* file only those classes that are needed from *xyz.swc*. As you can guess, some amount of code duplication is unavoidable here. Classes that are needed in both projects will be traveling to the user's machine twice.

But in an enterprise application with multiple *.swf* files, you should consider a different approach. In *proj1*, specify that *xyz.swc* should be linked as an RSL; hence none of its classes will be included into the *.swf*, but the entire library (100 KB) will be downloaded even before the `applicationComplete` event is triggered. In this case, you can safely specify in the *proj2* "external" as a linkage type for *xyz.swc*, which means that by the time this project's *.swf* file is downloaded, *xyz.swf* will already be there. Even though the library is created as a file with a *.swc* extension, its content will be deployed as a *.swf* file (in our case *xyz.swf*).

Now assume that the module from *proj2* is not immediately needed at application startup. In the RSL approach, the total size of the compiled code that has to exist on the user's machine is 250 KB +100 KB + the size of the Flex framework (500 KB or more). If the user initiates an action that requires the module from *proj2*, yet another 50 KB will be downloaded. (In the next section, you'll learn a way to avoid repeatedly downloading the 500 KB of the Flex framework.)

Both RSL and external linkage imply that libraries will be available in the browser by the time an application or module needs them. The difference between the methods is that when you link a library as an RSL, the compiled *.swf* file contains a list of these libraries and Flash Player loads them. When you use external linkage, the compiled *.swf* doesn't contain a mention of external *.swf* library files, because it expects that another *.swf* has already loaded them. For more details, refer to the section "Bootstrapping Libraries As Applications" on page 357 in Chapter 7 or search for "IFlexModuleFactory interface" online.

As soon as a project is created, you should remove the default libraries that it doesn't need. For example, all libraries with the Automation API in general and *qtp.swc* (support of the QTP testing tool from HP) are not needed unless you are planning to run automated functional tests that record and replay user interactions with your RIA. Even if you are using the automation libraries during development, don't forget to remove them from the production build. Don't be tempted to rely on the libraries' merge-in linking option to limit the included classes. Although the merge-in option includes only objects that are used in the code when Flash Builder builds your project, its linker must still sift through all the libraries just to determine which are needed and which are not. (The linkage options will be discussed in detail a bit later.)

You can read more about using automation tools in Flex applications at the site *http://livedocs.adobe.com/flex/3/html/help.html?content=functest_components2_10.html*.

Remove *datavisualization.swc* from the main application. In general, this library has to be linked on the module level. Your enterprise application should consist of a small shell that will be loading modules on an as-needed basis. This shell definitely doesn't need to link *datavisualization.swc*. (Later in this chapter you'll see an example of the optimized library loader.) Consider an example when a shell application loads 10 modules and 3 of them use Flex charting classes located in *datavisualization.swc*. In this scenario, you should link *datavisualization.swc* as an RSL. But you may argue that if you do so and at some point all three charting modules need to be loaded, the data visualization RSL will be loaded three times! This would be correct unless you use an optimized way of loading modules, as described in the section "Optimizing RSL Loading" on page 416.

Flex Framework RSL

Before your application starts, `SystemManager` downloads (or loads from the local cache) all required RSL libraries and resource bundles (localization support) required by your application.

Choosing "Runtime shared library" from the "Library path" panel's "Framework linkage" drop-down (see Figure 8-4) is simple and smart at the same time: deploy the Flex framework separately from the application *.swf* libraries, and on the user's first download of the RIA, Flash Player (version 9.0.115 or later) will save the framework library in its own disk cache. It gets even better: this library is designed to work across different domains, which means that users might get this library *not necessarily from your website*, but from any other site that was built in Flex and deployed with the Flex framework as an RSL.

Starting from Flash Builder 4, Flex Framework RSLs are linked as RSLs by default. If you want to change this option, use the "Library path" panel of your project. Adobe will also offer hosting of these RSLs at its sites, which might be useful for the applications that have limited bandwidth and want to minimize the amount of bytes going over the wire from their servers.

These libraries are signed RSLs; their filenames end with *.swz* and only Adobe can sign them. If you open the *rsls* directory in your Flex or Flash Builder installation directory, you will find these signed libraries there. For example, the path to the *rsls* directory may look like:

C:\Program Files\Adobe\Flex Builder 3 Plug-in\sdks\3.2.0\frameworks\rsls

At the time of this writing, the following RSLs are located there:

- *framework_3.2.0.3958.swz*
- *datavisualization_3.2.0.3958.swz*
- *rpc_3.2.0.3958.swz*

As you see, the filename includes the number of the Flex SDK version (3.2.0) and the number of the build (3958).

We recommend that you build Flex applications on the assumption that users already have or will be forced to install Flash Player, a version not older than 9.0.115. If you can't do this for any reason, include pairs of libraries (*.swz* and corresponding *.swf*) in the build path, such as *rpc_3.2.0.3958.swz* and *rpc_3.2.0.3958.swf*. If the user has the player supporting signed libraries, the *.swz* file will be engaged. Otherwise, the unsigned fallback *.swf* library will be downloaded.

For a detailed description of how to use Flex framework RSLs, read the Adobe documentation (*http://livedocs.adobe.com/flex/3/html/help.html?content=rsl_09.html*).

At Farata we were involved with creating a website for an American branch of Mercedes-Benz (*http://www.mbusa.com*). By examining this site with the web monitoring tool Charles, you can see which objects are downloaded to the user's machine.

While measuring performance of a web application, you should use tools that clearly show you what's being downloaded by the application in question. Charles does a great job monitoring AMF, and we also like the Web Developer toolbar for the Mozilla Firefox browser, available at *http://chrispederick.com/work/web-developer/*. This excellent toolbar allows you with a click of a button to enable/disable the browser's cache, cookies, and pop-up blockers; validate CSS; inspect the DOM, images, etc.; and more.

In Figure 8-5 you can see that a number of *.swf* files are being downloaded to the user's machine. We took this Charles screenshot (see Chapter 4) on a PC with a freshly installed operating system, just to ensure that no Flex applications that might have been deployed with a signed framework RSL were run from this computer. This website is a large and well-modularized RIA, and the initial download includes *.swf* files of approximately 162 KB, 95 KB, 52 KB, 165 KB, and 250 KB, which is the main window of this RIA plus the required shareable libraries for the rest of the application. It totals around 730 KB, which is an excellent result for such a sophisticated RIA.

But there is one more library that is coming down the pipe: *framework_3.0.0.477.swz*, which is highlighted in Figure 8-5.

This Flex framework RSL is pretty heavy—525 KB—but the good news is that it's going to be downloaded only once, whenever the user of this PC runs into a Flex application deployed with a signed RSL.

Figure 8-6 depicts the second time we hit *http://www.mbusa.com* after clearing the web browser's cache. As you can see, the *.swf* files are still arriving, but the *.swz* file is not there any longer, as it was saved in the local Flash Player's cache on disk.

Clearing the web browser's cache removes the cached RSLs (*.swf* files), but doesn't affect the signed ones (*.swz*). This cache is not affected by clearing the web browser's cache.

Isn't it a substantial reduction of the initial size of a large RIA: from 1.3 MB down to 730 KB?

For large applications, we recommend that you *always use signed framework RSLs*. Flex became a popular platform for development RIA, driving adoption of the latest versions of Flash Player. The probability is high that cross-domain signed RSLs will exist on client computers within the first year after release of those libraries.

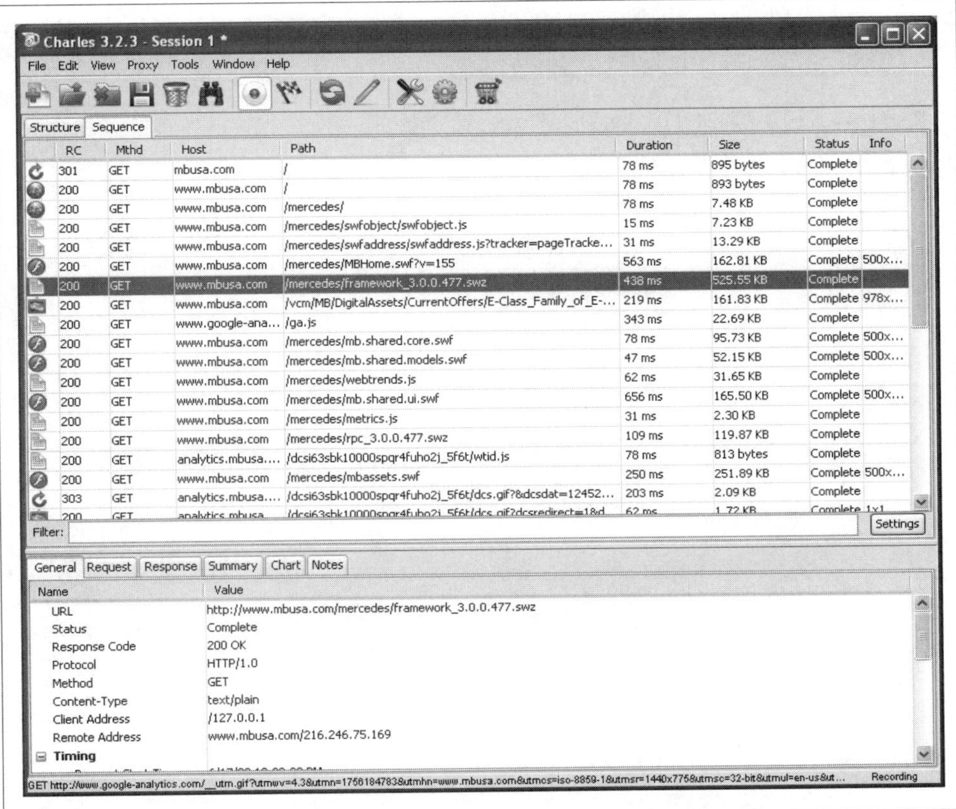

Figure 8-5. Visiting http://www.mbusa.com from a new PC

Starting from Flex 4, Adobe will officially host signed RSLs on their servers, which is an extra help for websites with limited network bandwidth. If you prefer, don't even deploy the *.swz* files on your server. Unofficially, this feature exists even now: select and expand any library with the RSL linkage type, go to the edit mode, and select the button Add (see Figure 8-7). You'll be able to specify the URL where your *.swz* libraries are located.

If the benefits of cached RSLs are so obvious, why not deploy each and every project with signed libraries? We see three reasons for this:

- There is a remote chance that the user has a version of Flash Player older than release 9.0.115, the version where signed RSLs were introduced.
- The initial downloadable size of the Flex application is a bit larger if it's deployed with RSLs versus the merge-in option. At the time of this writing, no statistics are published regarding the penetration of the signed Flex RSLs, and if someone makes a wrong assumption that no users have cached RSLs, the RIA with a merge-in

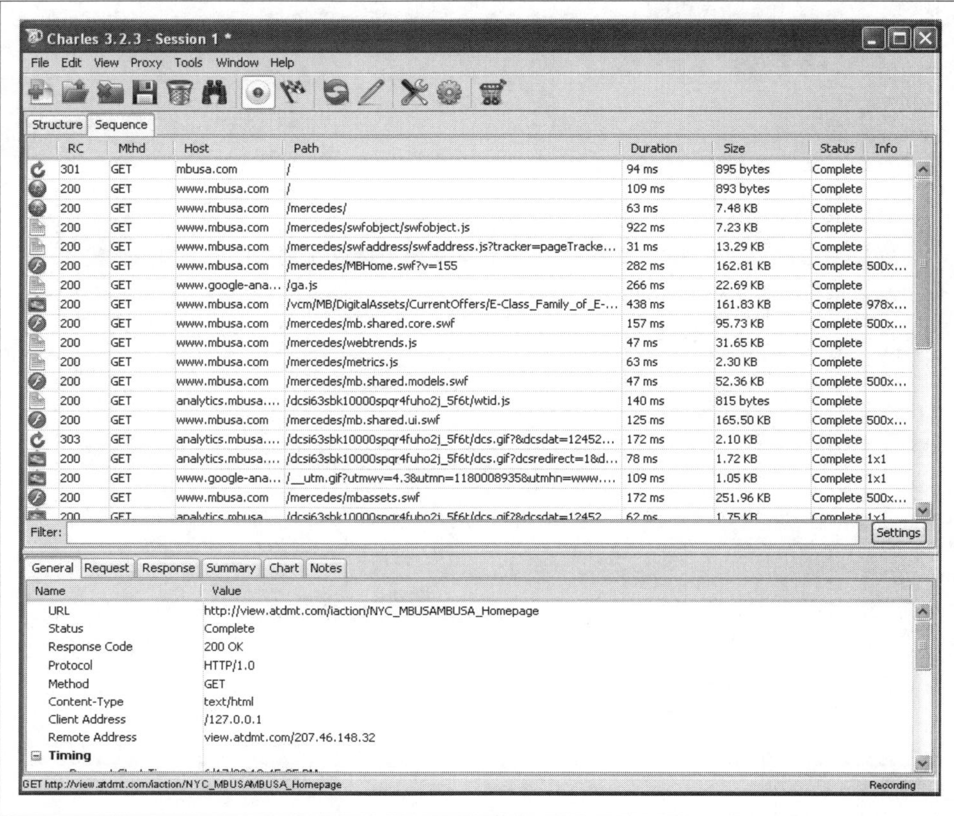

Figure 8-6. Visiting http://www.mbusa.com after the framework RSL has been cached

option would produce, say, one *.swf* of 1.1 MB as opposed to two files totaling 1.3 MB for virgin machines. In consumer applications, any reduction of a hundred kilobytes matters.

- In case of the merge-in option, the client's web browser wouldn't need to make this extra network call to load the *.swz*; the entire code would be located in one *.swf*.

To address these valid concerns, you can:

- Force users to upgrade to the later version of the player, if you're working in a controlled environment. For users who can't upgrade the player, provide fall-back *.swf* files.
- Repackage RSLs for distribution that would include only the classes your application needs. This technique is described on James Ward's blog (*http://www.jamesward.com/blog/2007/02/19/faster-flex-applications-shrink-your-rsls/*).

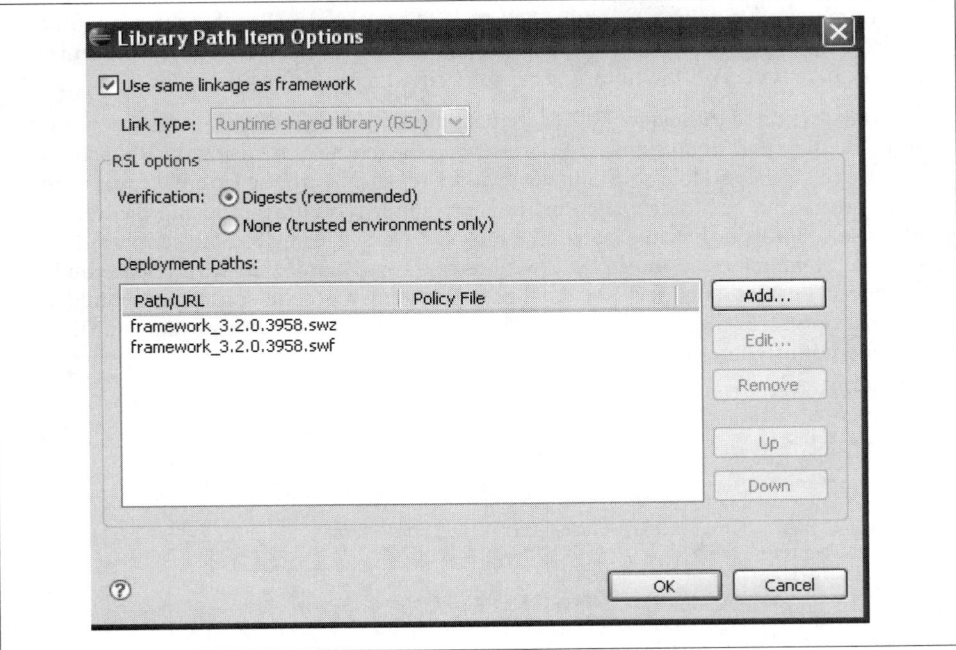

Figure 8-7. Specifying location of RSL libraries

- Intervene in the load process (keep in mind that the Flex framework is open source and all initialization routines can be studied and modified to your liking).

If you have the luxury of starting a new enterprise RIA from scratch rather than trying to fit a *.swf* file here and there in the existing HTML/JavaScript website, we recommend that you get into a "portal state of mind." In no time, your RIA will grow and demand more and more new features, modules, and functionality. Why not expect this from the get-go?

Assume that the application you are about to develop will grow into a portal in a couple of years. Create a lightweight, shell-like Flex application that loads the rest of the modules dynamically. If you start with such a premise, you'll naturally think of the shared resources that have to be placed into RSLs, and the rest of the business functionality will be developed as modules and reusable components.

Optimization of Library Linkage with Fx2Ant

Deploying a multiproject Flex RIA is yet another step that should be optimized for performance. Flash Builder's Export Release Build option, however, is not applicable for enterprise applications, which are deployed into production by running a set of scripts from a command line.

Farata's Fx2Ant utility (see Chapter 4) is known in the Flex community as a tool for the automation of writing Ant build scripts for Flex projects. But there is yet another added benefit of using Fx2Ant compared to manually writing build scripts: it optimizes linkage parameters of RSL libraries for multiproject applications.

Another section of the generated Ant scripts removes debug and metadata information from the *.swf*: Fx2Ant optimizes the cases when the modules are using the RSLs. In the build scripts, the module's RSL linkage will be replaced with the external type, as the RSLs are guaranteed to be loaded by the main application, thus reducing the number of server calls during module load procedure. On average, using Fx2Ant scripts reduces the size of generated modules by 10–25 percent, even compared with release builds produced by Flash Builder. For example, the following code snippet generated by Fx2Ant optimizes the size of *all* resources and removes unnecessary metadata (those that are not listed in the `--keep-as3-metadata` option):

```
<unzip src="${DOCUMENTS}/PortalLib/bin/PortalLib.swc"
dest="${build.dir}">
<patternset>
<include name="library.swf"/>
</patternset>
</unzip>
<java jar="${flex.sdk.dir}/lib/optimizer.jar" fork="true"
failonerror="true">
<jvmarg line="-ea -DAS3 -DAVMPLUS -
Dflexlib='${flex.sdk.dir}/frameworks' -Xms32m -Xmx384m -
Dsun.io.useCanonCaches=false"/>
<arg line="'${build.dir}/library.swf' --output
'${build.dir}/PortalLib.swf' --keep-as3-
metadata='Bindable,Managed,ChangeEvent,NonCommittingChangeEvent,Transient' "/>
</java>
<delete file="${build.dir}/library.swf"/>
```

Consider an example in which an RIA consists of two Flash Builder projects, and in each project the developer specified the library *xyz.swc* with a link type RSL. The script generated by Fx2Ant will keep the RSL as a linkage type for the *xyz.swc* in the main project and replace the linkage for this library with "external" in the second one.

You might try shaving off another 10–20 percent of the unused framework code by repackaging framework *.swc* files to keep only those used in your application and modules, but for large applications it is seldom worth the effort.

Optimizing RSL Loading

Optimizing the loading of the RSLs is an important step in optimizing your project. Think of an application with 10 modules, 3 of which use *datavisualization.swc* as an RSL. To avoid redundant loading, we want to insert a singleton's behavior in the holy grail of any Flex application, `SystemManager`, which gets engaged by the end of the very first application frame and starts loading RSLs.

The sample application that you'll be studying in this section is an improved version of the projects from Chapter 7's section "Sample Flex Portal" on page 379. This section's source code includes the following Flash Builder projects: *OptimizedPortal*, *FeedModule*, *ChartsModule*, and *PortalLib*.

Creating Modules with Test Harness

Once again, here's our main principle of building enterprise Flex applications: a lightweight shell application that loads modules when necessary. This approach leads to the creation of modularized and better-performing RIAs. But when a developer works on a particular module, to be productive, he needs to be able to quickly perform unit and functional tests on his modules without depending too much on the modules his teammates are working on.

The project *FeedsModule* is an Eclipse Dynamic Web Project with its own "server-side" *WebContent* directory. This project also includes a very simple application, *TestHarness.mxml*, that includes just two modules: `GoogleFinancialNews` and `YahooFinancialNews`. Let's say Mary is responsible for the development of these two modules that later will become part of a larger *OptimizedPortal*. But if in Chapter 7 the portal was created for integrating various applications, here we are building it as a shell for hosting multiple modules.

To avoid having issues caused by merging module and application stylesheets, we recommend having only one CSS file on the application level. This may also save you some grief trying to figure out why modules are not being fully unloaded as the description of the `unload()` function promises; merged CSS may create strong references that won't allow a garbage collector to reclaim the memory upon module unloads.

You also want to avoid linking into the module's byte code the information from the *services-config.xml* file that comes with BlazeDS/LCDS. If you specify a separate *services-config.xml* in the compiler's option of the module's project, the content of such *services-config.xml* (configured destinations and channels) gets sucked into the compiled *.swf*.

On our team, all developers must submit their modules fully tested and in the minimal configuration. Example 8-11 lists the application that Mary uses for testing, and Figure 8-8 shows the results.

Example 8-11. TestHarness.mxml

```
<?xml version="1.0" encoding="utf-8"?>
<mx:Application xmlns:mx="http://www.adobe.com/2006/mxml" layout="vertical" >
    <mx:Label text="google"/>
    <mx:ModuleLoader id="mod1"
        creationComplete="mod1.loadModule('GoogleFinancialNews.swf')"
        width="800" height="300"
        applicationDomain="{ApplicationDomain.currentDomain}"
        ready="mod2.loadModule('YahooFinancialNews.swf')"/>
    <mx:Label text="yahoo"/>
    <mx:ModuleLoader  id="mod2" width="800" height="300"
```

```
        applicationDomain="{ApplicationDomain.currentDomain}"/>
</mx:Application>
```

Figure 8-8. Running TestHarness.mxml

Each of the modules in `TestHarness` has the ability to load yet another module: `ChartModule`. This is done by switching to the view state `ChartState` and calling the function `loadChartSWF()`. Example 8-12 shows the code of the module `YahooFinancialNews`.

Example 8-12. The module YahooFinancialNews

```
<?xml version="1.0" encoding="utf-8"?>
<mx:Module xmlns:mx="http://www.adobe.com/2006/mxml" layout="vertical"
    horizontalGap="0" verticalGap="0"  width="100%" height="100%"
    paddingBottom="0" paddingLeft="0" paddingRight="0" paddingTop="0"
    backgroundColor="white"
    >

    <mx:states>
      <mx:State name="ChartState">
        <mx:RemoveChild target="{newsGrid}"/>
        <mx:AddChild relativeTo="{header}" position="after">
         <mx:ModuleLoader id="chart_swf"
```

```
        applicationDomain="{ApplicationDomain.currentDomain}"
       creationComplete="loadChartSWF()" width="100%" height="100%"/>
     </mx:AddChild>
   </mx:State>
 </mx:states>

 <mx:HBox id="header"
   width="100%" height="25"
   backgroundColor="#ffffff" backgroundAlpha="0.8"
   verticalAlign="middle" color="black">

   <mx:Label htmlText="Yahoo: Effective copy of PortletInfo class:
                    {PortletInfo.INFO}"/>
     <mx:HBox width="100%" horizontalAlign="right" horizontalGap="3"
                                                 verticalGap="0">
      <mx:Label text="Message: "/>
      <mx:TextInput id="textInput" text="{_messageText}" width="100"/>
      <mx:VRule height="20"/>
      <mx:Button label="{currentState == 'ChartState' ? 'Show Feed' :
            'Show Chart'}" click="currentState = (currentState == 'ChartState' ?
                             '' : 'ChartState')"/>
     </mx:HBox>
     <mx:filters>
         <mx:DropShadowFilter angle="90" distance="2"/>
     </mx:filters>
 </mx:HBox>

 <mx:DataGrid id="newsGrid" width="100%" height="100%"
     dataProvider="{newsFeed.lastResult.channel.item}"
      variableRowHeight="true"
     dragEnabled="true"     creationComplete="onCreationComplete()">
   <mx:columns>
    <mx:Array>
     <mx:DataGridColumn headerText="Date" dataField="pubDate" width="80"/>
     <mx:DataGridColumn headerText="Title" dataField="title" wordWrap="true"
                                       width="200"/>
     </mx:Array>
   </mx:columns>
 </mx:DataGrid>

 <mx:HTTPService id="newsFeed" useProxy="true"
      destination="YahooFinancialNews"  concurrency="last"
     resultFormat="e4x" fault="onFault(event)"/>

 <mx:Script>
     <![CDATA[
     import mx.managers.PopUpManager;
     import com.farata.portal.Message;
     import com.farata.portal.events.BroadcastMessageEvent;
     import mx.controls.Alert;
     import mx.rpc.events.*;

     [Bindable]
     private var _messageText:String;
```

```
        private function onCreationComplete():void {
            var bridge:IEventDispatcher = systemManager.loaderInfo.sharedEvents;
                bridge.addEventListener(
         BroadcastMessageEvent.BROADCAST_MESSAGE_TO_PORTLETS, messageBroadcasted );

          newsFeed.send({s:"YAHOO"});
        }

        private function loadChartSWF():void{
                chart_swf.loadModule("/ChartsModule/ChartModule.swf");
        }

        private function messageBroadcasted( event:Event ):void{
            var newEvent:BroadcastMessageEvent =
                          BroadcastMessageEvent.unmarshal( event );
            var message:Message = newEvent.message;
            _messageText = message.messageBody;
        }


        private function onFault(event:FaultEvent):void {
            Alert.show( event.toString() );
            mx.controls.Alert.show(
               "Destination:" + event.currentTarget.destination + "\n" +
               "Fault code:" + event.fault.faultCode + "\n" +
               "Detail:" + event.fault.faultDetail, "News feed failure"
            );
        }
        ]]>
    </mx:Script>
</mx:Module>
```

Click the application's Show Chart button to make sure that loading one module from the other works fine and that they properly pick the destination from the main application's *services-config.xml* file. Figure 8-9 shows the expected result.

Because you want to have a test harness that will allow you to run and test these modules outside of the main portal, we'll do a trick that will link the *TestHarness* application with the one and only *services-config.xml* of the main portal project. Example 8-13 lists the file named *TestHarness-config.xml* located in the *FeedsModule* project.

Example 8-13. TestHarness-config.xml

```
<flex-config>
 <compiler>
  <services>
    c:/farata/oreilly/OptimizedPortal/WebContent/WEB-INF/flex/services-config.xml
   </services>
 </compiler>
</flex-config>
```

The very fact that a project has a file with the same name as the main application but with the suffix *-config* will make the Flex compiler use it as configuration file that

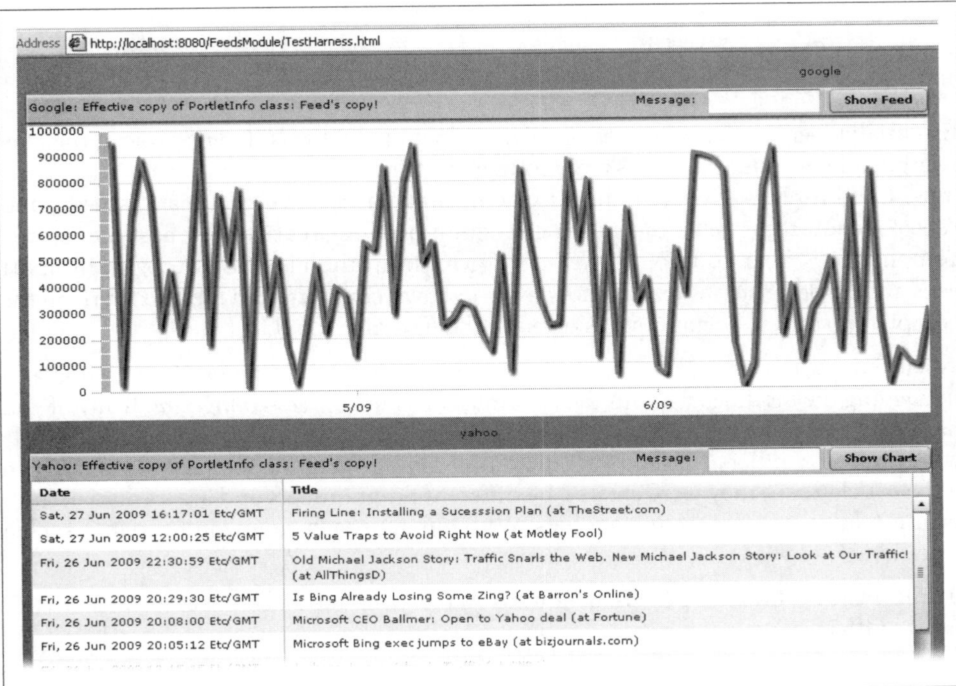

Figure 8-9. Switching to chart view

redirects to the real *services-config.xml*. (Remember, you need to replace *c:/farata/oreilly* with the actual location of the workspace of the *OptimizedPortal* project.)

Open the class *TestHarness_FlexInit_generated.as* in the generated folder of the *FeedModule* project, and you'll see a section taken from the portal project. A fragment of this section is shown here:

```
ServerConfig.xml =
<services>
    <service id="remoting-service">
        <destination id="AnnualGenerator">
            <channels>
                <channel ref="my-amf"/>
            </channels>
        </destination>
        <destination id="QuoterDataGenerator">
            <channels>
                <channel ref="my-amf"/>
            </channels>
        </destination>
    </service>
    ...
    <channels>
        <channel id="my-rtmp" type="mx.messaging.channels.RTMPChannel">
            <endpoint uri="rtmp://{server.name}:58010"/>
```

```
            <properties>
            </properties>
        </channel>
</services>;
```

Essentially, here's what's happening: while building the *FeedsModule* project, the Flex compiler determines that it has two modules and one application and that it, therefore, must build three *.swf* files. It checks whether `TestHarness`, `GoogleFinancialNews`, and `YahooFinancialNews` have their own configuration files. `TestHarness` has one, so the compiler uses it in addition to *flex-config.xml* from the Flex SDK. `GoogleFinancialNews` and `YahooFinancialNews` do not have their own configuration files, so for them the compiler just uses the parameters listed in the *flex-config.xml*.

What did we achieve? We've created a small project that can be used for testing and debugging the modules without the information from *services-config.xml*. If any of you have worked on a large modularized Flex application, chances are that once in a while you ran into conflicts caused by destinations having the same names but pointing to different classes—they were created by different programmers and are located in multiple modules' *services-config.xml* files. With our approach, you won't run into such a situation.

In the next section, you'll learn how to make your modules go easy on network bandwidth.

Creating a Shell Application with a Custom RSL Loader

Mary, the application developer, knows how to test her modules, and she'd really appreciate it if she didn't have to coordinate with other developers who might link the same RSLs to their modules. Is it possible to have a slightly smarter application that won't load a particular RSL with the second module if it already downloaded it with the first one?

To avoid duplication in modules, the Flex framework offers a singleton class, `ModuleManager` (see Chapter 7), but it falls short when it comes to RSLs. Luckily, the Flex framework is open sourced, and we'll show you how to fix this shortcoming. Take a closer look at the problem first.

As you remember, the singleton `SystemManager` is the starting class that controls loading of the rest of the application's objects. Our sample application is a portal located in the Flash Builder project *OptimizedPortal*. Adding the compiler's `-keep` option allows you to see the generated ActionScript code for the project. The main point of interest is the class declaration in the file *_OptimizedPortal_mx_managers_SystemManager-generated.as*, located in the *generated* folder (Example 8-14).

Example 8-14. Generated SystemManager for OptimizedPortal

```
package{

import flash.text.Font;
import flash.text.TextFormat;
import flash.system.ApplicationDomain;
import flash.utils.getDefinitionByName;
import mx.core.IFlexModule;
import mx.core.IFlexModuleFactory;

import mx.managers.SystemManager;

[ResourceBundle("collections")]
[ResourceBundle("containers")]
[ResourceBundle("controls")]
[ResourceBundle("core")]
[ResourceBundle("effects")]
[ResourceBundle("logging")]
[ResourceBundle("messaging")]
[ResourceBundle("skins")]
[ResourceBundle("styles")]
public class _OptimizedPortal_mx_managers_SystemManager
    extends mx.managers.SystemManager
    implements IFlexModuleFactory{
    // Cause the CrossDomainRSLItem class to be linked into this application.
    import mx.core.CrossDomainRSLItem; CrossDomainRSLItem;

    public function _OptimizedPortal_mx_managers_SystemManager(){
        super();
    }

    override   public function create(... params):Object{
        if (params.length > 0 && !(params[0] is String))
            return super.create.apply(this, params);

        var mainClassName:String = params.length == 0 ?
                       "OptimizedPortal" : String(params[0]);
        var mainClass:Class = Class(getDefinitionByName(mainClassName));
        if (!mainClass)
            return null;

        var instance:Object = new mainClass();
        if (instance is IFlexModule)
            (IFlexModule(instance)).moduleFactory = this;
        return instance;
    }

    override public function info():Object{
        return {
            cdRsls: [{"rsls":["datavisualization_3.3.0.4852.swz"],
 "policyFiles":[""]
 ,"digests":["6557145de8b1b668bc50fd0350f191ac33e0c33d9402db900159c51a02c62ed6"],
 "types":["SHA-256"],
 "isSigned":[true]
 },
```

```
{"rsls":["framework_3.2.0.3958.swz","framework_3.2.0.3958.swf"],
"policyFiles":["",""]
,"digests":["1c04c61346a1fa3139a37d860ed92632aa13decf4c17903367141677aac966f4","1c04
c61346a1fa3139a37d860ed92632aa13decf4c17903367141677aac966f4"],
"types":["SHA-256","SHA-256"],
"isSigned":[true,false]
},
{"rsls":["rpc_3.3.0.4852.swz"],
"policyFiles":[""]
,"digests":["f7536ef0d78a77b889eebe98bf96ba5321a1fde00fa0fd8cd6ee099befb1b159"],
"types":["SHA-256"],
"isSigned":[true]
}]
,
            compiledLocales: [ "en_US" ],
            compiledResourceBundleNames: [ "collections", "containers", "controls",
"core", "effects", "logging", "messaging", "skins", "styles" ],
            currentDomain: ApplicationDomain.currentDomain,
            layout: "vertical",
            mainClassName: "OptimizedPortal",
            mixins: [ "_OptimizedPortal_FlexInit",
"_richTextEditorTextAreaStyleStyle", "_ControlBarStyle", "_alertButtonStyleStyle",
"_SWFLoaderStyle", "_textAreaVScrollBarStyleStyle", "_headerDateTextStyle",
"_globalStyle", "_ListBaseStyle", "_HorizontalListStyle", "_todayStyleStyle",
"_windowStylesStyle", "_ApplicationStyle", "_ToolTipStyle", "_CursorManagerStyle",
"_opaquePanelStyle", "_TextInputStyle", "_errorTipStyle", "_dateFieldPopupStyle",
"_dataGridStylesStyle", "_popUpMenuStyle", "_headerDragProxyStyleStyle",
"_activeTabStyleStyle", "_PanelStyle", "_DragManagerStyle", "_ContainerStyle",
"_windowStatusStyle", "_ScrollBarStyle", "_swatchPanelTextFieldStyle",
"_textAreaHScrollBarStyleStyle", "_plainStyle", "_activeButtonStyleStyle",
"_advancedDataGridStylesStyle", "_comboDropdownStyle", "_ButtonStyle",
"_weekDayStyleStyle", "_linkButtonStyleStyle",
"_com_farata_portal_PortalCanvasWatcherSetupUtil",
"_com_farata_portal_controls_SendMessageWatcherSetupUtil" ],
            rsls: [{url: "flex.swf", size: -1}, {url: "utilities.swf", size: -1},
{url: "fds.swf", size: -1}, {url: "PortalLib.swf", size: -1}]

        }
    }
}

}
```

Skim through this code, and you'll see that all the information required by the linker is there. The Flex code generator created a system manager for the *OptimizedPortal* application that's directly inherited from `mx.managers.SystemManager`, which doesn't give us any hooks for injecting the new functionality in a kosher way. Whatever you put in the class above will be removed by code generators during the next compilation. The good news is that the Flex SDK is open sourced and you are allowed to do any surgeries to its code and even submit the changes to be considered for inclusion in upcoming releases of Flex.

The goal is to change the behavior of the SystemManager so that it won't load duplicate instances of the same RSL if more than one module links them. (Remember the *datavisualization.swc* used in 3 out of 10 modules?)

Scalpel, please!

The *flex_src* directory of the project *OptimizedPortal* includes a package *mx.core*, which includes two classes: RSLItem and RSLListLoader. These are the classes from the Adobe Flex SDK that underwent the surgery. The class RSLListLoader sequentially loads all required libraries. The relevant fragment of this class is shown in Example 8-15.

Example 8-15. Modified Flex SDK class RSLListLoader

```
////////////////////////////////////////////////////////////////////////////////
//                                                                            //
//  ADOBE SYSTEMS INCORPORATED                                                //
//  Copyright 2007 Adobe Systems Incorporated                                  //
//  All Rights Reserved.                                                      //
//                                                                            //
//  NOTICE: Adobe permits you to use, modify, and distribute this file        //
//  in accordance with the terms of the license agreement accompanying it.    //
//                                                                            //
////////////////////////////////////////////////////////////////////////////////

package mx.core{

import flash.events.IEventDispatcher;
import flash.events.Event;
import flash.utils.Dictionary;

[ExcludeClass]

/**
 *  @private
 *  Utility class for loading a list of RSLs.
 *
 *  A list of cross-domain RSLs and a list of regular RSLs
 *  can be loaded using this utility.
 */

public class RSLListLoader{
/**
     *  Constructor.
     *
     *  @param rslList Array of RSLs to load.
     *  Each entry in the array is of type RSLItem or CdRSLItem.
     *  The RSLs will be loaded from index 0 to the end of the array.
     */
    public function RSLListLoader(rslList:Array)
    {
        super();
        this.rslList = rslList;
    }
```

```
    /**
     *  @private
     *  The index of the RSL being loaded.
     */
    private var currentIndex:int = 0;

     public static var  loadedRSLs:Dictionary = new Dictionary();
    /**
     *  @private
     *  The list of RSLs to load.
     *  Each entry is of type RSLNode or CdRSLNode.
     */
    private var rslList:Array = [];

  ...
    /**
     *  Increments the current index and loads the next RSL.
     */
    private function loadNext():void{
        if (!isDone()){
            currentIndex++;

            // Load the current RSL.
            if (currentIndex < rslList.length){
                // Load RSL and have the RSL loader chain the
                // events our internal events handler or the chained
                // events handler if we don't care about them.
                if (loadedRSLs[(rslList[currentIndex] as RSLItem).url] == null){
                       rslList[currentIndex].load(chainedProgressHandler,
                            listCompleteHandler, listIOErrorHandler,
                            listSecurityErrorHandler, chainedRSLErrorHandler);
                        loadedRSLs[(rslList[currentIndex] as RSLItem).url] = true;
                } else {
                    loadNext();// skip already loaded rsls
                }
            }
        }
    }
     ...
 }
}
```

Example 8-15 adds only a few lines to the class:

```
public static var  loadedRSLs:Dictionary = new Dictionary();
...
if (loadedRSLs[(rslList[currentIndex] as RSLItem).url] == null){
...
loadedRSLs[(rslList[currentIndex] as RSLItem).url] = true;
...
loadNext();// skip already loaded rsls
```

but these had a dramatic effect on the RSL loading process.

The `static` dictionary `loadedRSL` keeps track of already loaded RSLs (the `url` property of the `RSLItem`), and if a particular RSL that's about to be loaded already exists there, it doesn't bother loading it. This will prevent the loading of duplicate RSLs and will substantially reduce the download time of some enterprise Flex applications.

In the class `RSLItem`, we've changed the access level of the property `url` from `protected` to `public`:

```
public var url:String;//PATCHED - was protected
```

Because the source code of our versions of `RSLItem` and `RSLListLoader` is included in the project, these classes will be merged into the *.swf* file and have precedence over the original classes with the same names provided in Flex SDK libraries.

As a side note, we recommend not using the keyword `protected`. For more details, read the blog post at *http://tinyurl.com/m6sp32*.

"Flex open sourcing in action!" would have made a nice subtitle for this section. The very fact that the Flex SDK was open sourced gives us a chance to improve its functionality in any enterprise application and possibly even submit some of the changes to Adobe.

Now let's run the *OptimizedPortal* application, which uses modified `RSLLoader`. Example 8-16 depicts the code of this application, but we aren't going to give a detailed explanation of this code, because in the context of this chapter, it's more important to understand what's happening under the hood when the modules are being loaded.

Example 8-16. OptimizedPortal.mxml

```
<?xml version="1.0" encoding="utf-8"?>
<mx:Application layout="vertical"
    xmlns:mx="http://www.adobe.com/2006/mxml"
    xmlns:fx="http://www.faratasystems.com/2009/portal" >

    <mx:Style source="styles.css"/>
    <mx:Button id="b" label="Add module" click="addModule()"/>
    <mx:Script>
        <![CDATA[
    import mx.core.UIComponent;
    import mx.modules.Module;
    import mx.events.ModuleEvent;
    import mx.modules.ModuleManager;
    import mx.modules.IModuleInfo;

    private var _moduleInfo:IModuleInfo;

    private function addModule() : void {
    // create the module - note, we're not loading it yet
    moduleInfo =
    ModuleManager.getModule("/FeedsModule/YahooFinancialNews.swf");
    // add some listeners
    _moduleInfo.addEventListener(ModuleEvent.READY, onModuleReady, false, 0, true);
    _moduleInfo.addEventListener(ModuleEvent.SETUP, onModuleSetup, false, 0, true);
```

```
    _moduleInfo.addEventListener(ModuleEvent.UNLOAD,onModuleUnload,false, 0, true);
    _moduleInfo.addEventListener(ModuleEvent.PROGRESS,onModuleProgress,false,0,
                                                                         true);
    // load the module
    _moduleInfo.load();
    }

/**
* The handlers for the module loading events
**/
  private function onModuleProgress (e:ModuleEvent) : void {
          trace("ModuleEvent.PROGRESS received: " + e.bytesLoaded + " of " +
           e.bytesTotal + " loaded.");
  }

  private function onModuleSetup (e:ModuleEvent) : void {
          trace("ModuleEvent.SETUP received");
          // cast the currentTarget
                var moduleInfo:IModuleInfo = e.currentTarget as IModuleInfo;
          trace("Calling IModuleInfo.factory.info ()");
          // grab the info and display information about it
          var info:Object = moduleInfo.factory.info();
          for (var each:String in info) {
             trace("      " + each + " = " + info[each]);
          }
   }

      private function onModuleReady (e:ModuleEvent):void {
            trace("ModuleEvent.READY received");
            // cast the currentTarget
            var moduleInfo:IModuleInfo = e.currentTarget as IModuleInfo;
            // Add an instance of the module's class to the
            // display list.
            trace("Calling IModuleInfo.factory.create ()");
            this.addChild( moduleInfo.factory.create () as UIComponent);
            trace("module instance created and added to Display List");
  }
    private function onModuleUnload (e:ModuleEvent) : void {
           trace("ModuleEvent.UNLOAD received");
    }
        ]]>

</mx:Script>
    <fx:PortalCanvas  width="100%" height="100%">
        <fx:navItems>
            <fx:NavigationItem>
                <fx:PortletConfig title="Complete Application" isModule="true"
                    preferredHeight="400" preferredWidth="850">
                    <fx:props>
                      <mx:Object
                        url="/FeedsModule/GoogleFinancialNews.swf"/>
                    </fx:props>
                </fx:PortletConfig>
            </fx:NavigationItem>
            <fx:NavigationItem>
```

```
            <fx:PortletConfig title="Just a Module" isModule="true"
                preferredHeight="400" preferredWidth="850">
                <fx:props>
                    <mx:Object
                        url="/FeedsModule/YahooFinancialNews.swf"/>
                </fx:props>
            </fx:PortletConfig>
        </fx:NavigationItem>
    </fx:navItems>
</fx:PortalCanvas>
</mx:Application>
```

Example 8-16 uses a number of tags from our library *PortalLib*, which is linked to the *OptimizedPortal* project; its source code comes with the sample code for this chapter (see the Preface). Following are very brief descriptions of these components:

`PortletConfig`
: A bunch of public variables: `portletId`, `title`, `preferredWidth`, `showMaximized`, `isSingleton`, `props`, and `content`, which is a `DisplayObject`

`NavItem`
: A component with a getter and setter for a label, a tooltip, an icon, and an associated portlet of type `PortletConfig`

`PortletConfig`
: Describes the future portlet window

`NavigationItem`
: Describes an icon on the portal desktop that can be clicked to create an instance of that window

For the next experiment, we'll clear the browser's cache and start Charles to monitor the loading process.

Flash Builder has a known issue: it sorts the libraries in the project's build path in alphabetical order, which may produce hard-to-explain runtime errors in some cases. In particular, before running the *OptimizedPortal* application, Flash Builder opens its project build path. Ensure that *datavisualization.swc* is listed after *utilities.swc*; otherwise, you may see an error about `TweenEffect`.

Running the *OptimizedPortal* application displays the main view shown in Figure 8-10 *really quickly*, which is one of the most important goals of any RIA.

In Figure 8-11, Charles shows what *.swf* files have been loaded so far: *OptimizedPortal.swf*, *flex.swf*, *utilities.swf*, *fds.swf*, and *PortalLib.swf*.

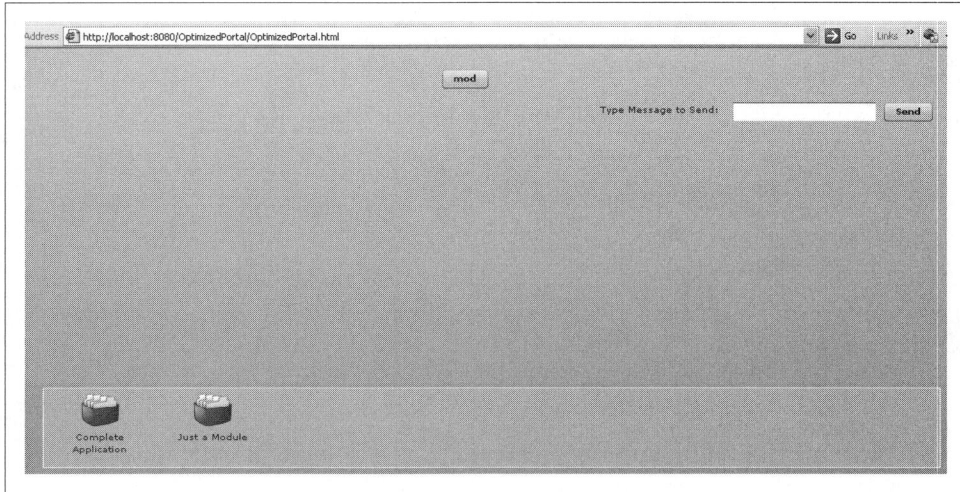

Figure 8-10. The main view of the application OptimizedPortal

Charles 3.2.3 - Session 1 *

File Edit View Proxy Tools Window Help

Structure | Sequence

RC	Mthd	Host	Path	Duration	Size	Status	Info
200	GET	localhost:8080	/OptimizedPortal/OptimizedPortal.html	15 ms	4.63 KB	Complete	
200	GET	localhost:8080	/OptimizedPortal/AC_OETags.js	15 ms	8.92 KB	Complete	
200	GET	localhost:8080	/OptimizedPortal/history/history.css	15 ms	863 bytes	Complete	
200	GET	localhost:8080	/OptimizedPortal/history/history.js	16 ms	24.46 KB	Complete	
200	GET	localhost:8080	/OptimizedPortal/OptimizedPortal.swf	188 ms	118.02 KB	Complete	500x...
200	GET	localhost:8080	/OptimizedPortal/flex.swf	15 ms	47.28 KB	Complete	500x...
200	GET	localhost:8080	/OptimizedPortal/utilities.swf	0 ms	26.82 KB	Complete	500x...
200	GET	localhost:8080	/OptimizedPortal/fds.swf	47 ms	195.25 KB	Complete	500x...
200	GET	localhost:8080	/OptimizedPortal/PortalLib.swf	15 ms	19.26 KB	Complete	500x...

Figure 8-11. Charles shows initial downloads

Dragging the "Just a Module" icon from the bottom bar to the empty area of the application loads the module and populates it with the data, as you can see in Figure 8-12.

In Figure 8-13, Charles shows that two more *.swf* files were loaded: the modules *YahooFinancialNews.swf* and *datavisualization_3.3.0.4852.swf*.

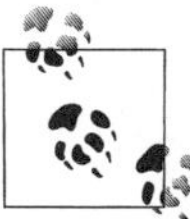

For this experiment, we didn't use a signed *datavisualization.swz*, because the goal here was to demonstrate the fact that even though the *datavisualization* library is linked as RSL to more than one module, it'll get loaded only once.

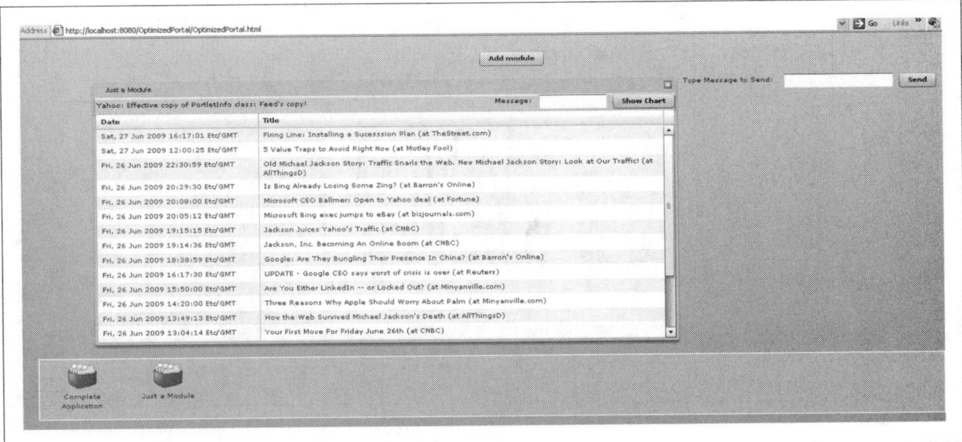

Figure 8-12. Loading the YahooFinancialNews module

Charles 3.2.3 - Session 1 *

	RC	Mthd	Host	Path	Duration	Size	Status	Info
	200	GET	localhost:8080	/OptimizedPortal/OptimizedPortal.html	15 ms	4.63 KB	Complete	
	200	GET	localhost:8080	/OptimizedPortal/AC_OETags.js	15 ms	8.92 KB	Complete	
	200	GET	localhost:8080	/OptimizedPortal/history/history.css	15 ms	863 bytes	Complete	
	200	GET	localhost:8080	/OptimizedPortal/history/history.js	16 ms	24.46 KB	Complete	
	200	GET	localhost:8080	/OptimizedPortal/OptimizedPortal.swf	188 ms	118.02 KB	Complete	500x...
	200	GET	localhost:8080	/OptimizedPortal/flex.swf	15 ms	47.28 KB	Complete	500x...
	200	GET	localhost:8080	/OptimizedPortal/utilities.swf	0 ms	26.82 KB	Complete	500x...
	200	GET	localhost:8080	/OptimizedPortal/fds.swf	47 ms	195.25 KB	Complete	500x...
	200	GET	localhost:8080	/OptimizedPortal/PortalLib.swf	15 ms	19.26 KB	Complete	500x...
	200	GET	localhost:8080	/FeedsModule/YahooFinancialNews.swf	125 ms	52.75 KB	Complete	500x...
	200	GET	localhost:8080	/OptimizedPortal/datavisualization_3.3.0.4852.swf	93 ms	275.82 KB	Complete	500x...
	200	POST	localhost:8080	/OptimizedPortal/messagebroker/http	16 ms	2.14 KB	Complete	
	200	POST	localhost:8080	/OptimizedPortal/messagebroker/http;jsessionid=849A94E...	328 ms	13.35 KB	Complete	

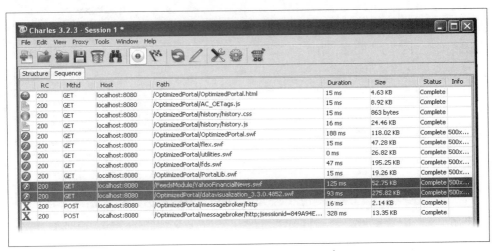

Figure 8-13. YahooFinancialNews came with datavisualization.swf

After clicking the Show Chart (Figure 8-9) button, yet another module, *ChartModule*, will be loaded, which also has the *datavisualization* RSL in its build path. The *OptimizedPortal* view looks like Figure 8-14.

Charles then shows the results in Figure 8-15.

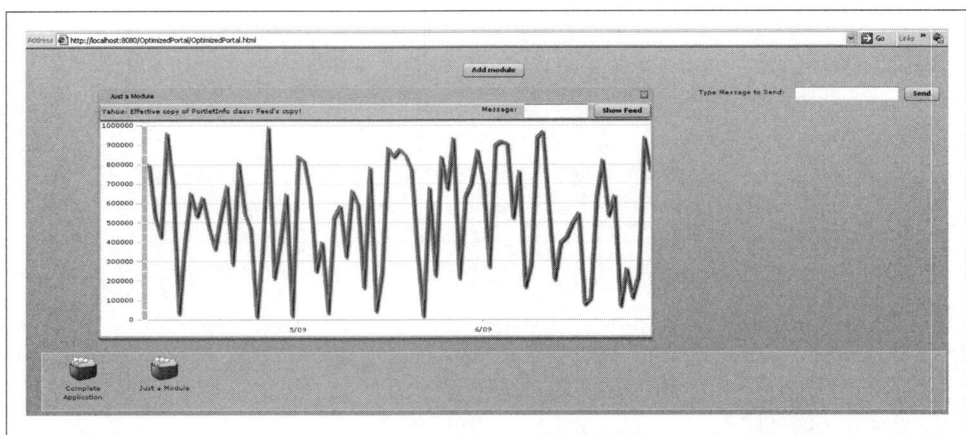

Figure 8-14. ChartModule is loaded

Charles 3.2.3 - Session 1 *

File Edit View Proxy Tools Window Help

Structure Sequence

RC	Mthd	Host	Path	Duration	Size	Status	Info
200	GET	localhost:8080	/OptimizedPortal/OptimizedPortal.html	15 ms	4.63 KB	Complete	
200	GET	localhost:8080	/OptimizedPortal/AC_OETags.js	15 ms	8.92 KB	Complete	
200	GET	localhost:8080	/OptimizedPortal/history/history.css	15 ms	863 bytes	Complete	
200	GET	localhost:8080	/OptimizedPortal/history/history.js	16 ms	24.46 KB	Complete	
200	GET	localhost:8080	/OptimizedPortal/OptimizedPortal.swf	188 ms	118.02 KB	Complete	500x...
200	GET	localhost:8080	/OptimizedPortal/flex.swf	15 ms	47.28 KB	Complete	500x...
200	GET	localhost:8080	/OptimizedPortal/utilities.swf	0 ms	26.82 KB	Complete	500x...
200	GET	localhost:8080	/OptimizedPortal/fds.swf	47 ms	195.25 KB	Complete	500x...
200	GET	localhost:8080	/OptimizedPortal/PortalLib.swf	15 ms	19.26 KB	Complete	500x...
200	GET	localhost:8080	/FeedsModule/YahooFinancialNews.swf	125 ms	52.75 KB	Complete	500x...
200	GET	localhost:8080	/OptimizedPortal/datavisualization_3.3.0.4852.swf	93 ms	275.82 KB	Complete	500x...
200	POST	localhost:8080	/OptimizedPortal/messagebroker/http	16 ms	2.14 KB	Complete	
200	POST	localhost:8080	/OptimizedPortal/messagebroker/http;jsessionid=849A94E...	328 ms	13.35 KB	Complete	
200	GET	localhost:8080	/ChartsModule/ChartModule.swf	62 ms	48.98 KB	Complete	500x...
200	POST	localhost:8080	/OptimizedPortal/messagebroker/amf	31 ms	1.33 KB	Complete	null
200	POST	localhost:8080	/OptimizedPortal/messagebroker/amf	15 ms	3.24 KB	Complete	null

Figure 8-15. ChartModule came without datavisualization

As you can see, *ChartModule.swf* has been downloaded, but its *datavisualization* RSL has not, because it was already downloaded by the module `YahooFinancialNews`—proof that you can do a smarter RSL loading to improve your portal's performance.

In this experiment, we've been using *datavisualization.swc* as a guinea pig RSL, but you can and should apply the same technique for any business-specific RSL that your application might use.

A Grab Bag of Useful Habits

This section discusses three areas that may seriously affect performance of your application: memory leaks, Flash Builder's Profiler, and the just-in-time compiler. At the end of this section, you'll find a checklist of items that can help you in planning performance-tuning tasks.

Dealing with Memory Leaks

Wikipedia defines a memory leak as "a particular type of unintentional memory consumption by a computer program where the program fails to release memory when no longer needed. This condition is normally the result of a bug in a program that prevents it from freeing up memory that it no longer needs" (*http://en.wikipedia.org/wiki/Memory_leak*).

Flash Player offers help in dealing with memory leaks. A special process called *Garbage Collector* (GC) periodically runs and removes objects from memory that the Flex application no longer uses. It counts all references to each object in memory, and when it gets down to zero, the object is removed from memory.

In some cases, two objects have references to each other, but neither of them is referred to anywhere else. In this case, the reference count never becomes zero, but Flash Player tries to identify such situations by running a slower method called *mark and sweep*.

Sure enough, you need to write code that nullifies reference variables that point to objects that are not needed (`myGreatObj=null;`): if you call `addChild()`, be sure not to forget about `removeChild()`; if you call `addEventListener()`, keep in mind `removeEventListener()`.

The function `addEventListener()` has three more optional arguments, and if the last one is set to `true`, it'll use so-called weak references with this listener, meaning that if this object has only weak references pointing to it, GC can remove it from memory.

Of course, if you ignore these recommendations, that'll lead to littering RAM with unneeded objects, but your main target in optimization of memory consumption should be the unloading of unneeded data.

Closures

In some cases, there is not much you can do about memory leaks, and some instances of the objects get stuck in memory, gradually degrading the performance of your application.

A closure—or rather, an object representing an anonymous function—will never be garbage-collected. Here's an example:

```
myButton.addEventListener("click",
        function (evt:MouseEvent){//do something});
```

With such syntax, the object that represents the handler function gets attached to the stage as a global object. You can't use syntax like `removeEventListener("click", myHandlerFunction)` here, because the closure used as an event handler didn't have a name. Things get even worse because all objects created inside this closure won't be garbage-collected, either.

Be careful with closures. Don't use them just because it's faster to create an anonymous in-place function than declaring a named one. Unless you need to have an independent function that remembers some variables' values from its surrounding context, don't use closures, as they may result in memory leaks.

You can't use weak references with the listeners that use closures, as they won't have references to the function object and will be garbage-collected.

If you add a listener to the `Timer` object, use a weak reference; otherwise, Flash Player will keep the reference to it as long as the timer is running.

Opportunistic garbage collector

The GC will work differently depending on the web browser your Flex application runs in. The mechanism of allocating and deallocating the memory by Flash Player can be browser-specific.

How do you determine that you have memory leaks? If you can measure available heap memory before and after GC runs, you can make a conclusion about the memory leaks. But this brings the next question: "How can you force GC?"

There is a trick with the `LocalConnection` object that can be used to request immediate garbage collection. If your program creates two instances of the `LocalConnection` object using the same name in the `connect()` call, Flash Player will initiate the process of GC.

```
var conn1:LocalConnection = new localConnection();
var conn2:LocalConnection = new localConnection();
conn1.connect("MyConnection");
conn2.connect("MyConnection");
```

It's not typical, but you can use the `LocalConnection` object to send and receive data in a single *.swf*, for example to communicate between modules of the same Flex application.

Some web browsers force GC on their own. For example, in Internet Explorer minimizing the browser's window causes garbage collection.

If you can force all your users to use Flash Player version 9.0.115 or later, you may use the following API to cause GC: `flash.system.System.gc()`.

Just-in-Time Benefits and Implications

Flex compiler is actually a set of subcompilers converting your ActionScript and MXML code into different formats. For example, besides *mxmlc* and *compc*, there is a precompiler that extracts the information from the precompiled *ActionScript Byte Code (ABC)*. You can read more about compilers at *http://opensource.adobe.com/wiki/display/flexsdk/Flex+3+Compiler+Design*. The ABC is the format that Flash Player runs. But the story doesn't end here.

Most of the performance advances in the current version of AS3 as compared to AS2 are based on its *just-in-time* (*JIT*) compiler, which is built into Flash Player. During the *.swf* load process, a special *byte code verifier* performs a lot of code analysis to ensure that code is valid for execution: validation of code branches, type verification/linkage, early binding, constants validation.

The results of the analysis are used to produce *machine-independent representation* (*MIR*) of the code that can be used by the JIT compiler to efficiently produce machine-dependent code optimized for performance. Unlike Flash VM code, which is a classic *stack machine*, MIR is more like a parsed execution path prepared for easy register optimization. The MIR compiler does not process the entire class, though; it rather takes an opportunistic approach and optimizes one function at a time, which is a much simpler and faster task. For example, the following is how the source code of an ActionScript function is transformed into the assembly code of the x86 Intel processor.

In ActionScript 3:

```
function (x:int):int {
return x+10
}
```

In ABC:

```
getlocal 1
pushint 10
add
returnvalue
```

In MIR:

```
@1 arg +8// argv
@2 load [@1+4]
@3 imm 10
@4 add (@2,@3)
@5 ret @4 // @4:eax
```

In x86:

```
mov eax,(eap+8)
mov eax,(eax+4)
```

```
add eax,10
ret
```

The difference in time for execution of the ABC code and x86 can be on the order of 10 to 100 times and easily justifies having an extra step such as the JIT process. In addition, the JIT process does dead code elimination, common expressions optimization, and constants folding. On the machine-code generation side, it adds optimized use of registers for local variables and instruction selection.

You need to help realize these benefits by carefully coding *critical* (as opposed to overoptimized) loops. For example, consider the following loop:

```
for (var i:int =0; I < array.length; i++) {
    if( array[i] == SomeClass.SOMECONSTANT)...
```

It can be optimized to produce very efficient machine code by removing calculations and references to other classes, thus keeping all references local and optimized:

```
var someConstant:String = SomeClass.SOMECONSTANT;
var len:int = array.length;

for (var i :int = 0; I < len; i++) {
    if (array[i] == someConstant)
```

JIT is great at providing machine code performance for heavy calculations, but it has to work with data types that the CPU is handling natively. At the very least, in order to make JIT effective, you should typecast to strong data types whenever possible. The cost of typecasting and fixed property access is lower than the cost of lookup, even for a single property.

JIT works only on class methods. As a result, all other class constructs—variable initialization on the class level and constructors—are processed in interpreter mode. You have to make a conscious effort to defer initialization from constructors to a later time so that JIT has a chance to perform.

Using the Flash Builder Profiler

The Flash Builder Profiler monitors memory consumption and the execution time. However, it monitors very specific execution aspects based on information available inside the Virtual Machine and currently is incomplete. For example, memory reported by the Profiler and memory reported by the OS will differ greatly, because the Profiler fails to account for the following:

- Flash Player's memory for code and system areas: hidden areas of properties associated with display objects
- Memory used by JIT
- The unfilled area of the 4 KB memory pages as a result of deallocated objects

More importantly, when showing memory used by object instances the Profiler will report the size used by object itself and not by subobjects. For example, if you are looking at 1,000 employee records, the Profiler will report the records to be of the same size, regardless of the sizes of last and first names. Only the size of the property pointing to the string values is going to be reported within the object. Actual memory used by strings will be reported separately, and it's impossible to quantify it as belonging to employee records.

The second problem is that with deferred garbage collection there are a lot of issues with comparing memory snapshots of any sizable application. Finding holding references as opposed to circular ones is a tedious task and hopefully will be simplified in the next version of the tool.

As a result, it is usually impractical to check for memory leaks on the large application level. Most applications incorporate memory usage statistics like `System.totalMemory` into their logging facility to give developers an idea of possible memory issues during the development process. A much more interesting approach is to use the Profiler as a monitoring tool while developing individual modules. You also need to invoke `System.gc()` prior to taking memory snapshots so that irrelevant objects won't sneak into your performance analysis.

As far as using the Profiler for performance analysis, it offers a lot more information. It will reveal the execution times of every function and cumulative times. Most importantly, it will provide insights into the true cost of excessive binding, initialization and rendering costs, and computational times. You would not be able to see the time spent in handling communications, loading code, and doing JIT and data parsing, but at least you can measure direct costs not related to the design issues but to the coding techniques.

Read about new Flash Builder 4 profiler features in the article by Jun Heider at *http://www.adobe.com/devnet/flex/articles/flashbuilder4_debugging_profiling.html?devcon=f7*.

Performance Checklist

While planning for performance improvement of your RIA, consider the following five categories.

Startup time

To reduce startup time:

- Use preloaders to quickly display either functional elements (logon, etc.) or some business-related news.
- Design with modularization and optimization of *.swf* files (remove debug and metadata information).
- Use RSLs, signed framework libraries.

- Minimize initially displayed UI.
- Externalize (don't embed) large images and unnecessary resources.
- Process large images to make them smaller for the Web.

UI performance

To improve user interface performance at startup:

- Minimize usage of containers within containers (especially inside data grids). Most of the UI performance issues are derived from container measurement and layout code.
- Defer object creation and initialization (don't do it in constructors). If you postpone creation of UI controls up to the moment they become visible, you'll have better performance. If you do not update the UI every time one of the properties changes but instead process them together (`commitProperties()`), you are most likely to execute common code sections responsible for rendering once instead of multiple times.
- For some containers, use `creationPolicy` in queues for perceived initialization performance.
- Provide adaptive user-controlled duration of effects. Although nice cinematographic effects are fine during application introduction, their timing and enablement should be controlled by users.
- Minimize update of CSS during runtime. If you need to set a style based on data, do it early, preferably in the initialization stage of the control and not in the `creationComplete` event, as this minimizes the number of lookups.
- Validate performance of data-bound controls (such as `List`-based controls) for scrolling and manipulation (sorting, filtering, etc.) early in development and with maximum data sets. Do not use the Flex `Repeater` component with sizable data sets.
- Use the `cacheAsBitmap` property for fixed-size objects, but not on resizable and changeable objects.

I/O performance

To speed up I/O operations:

- Use AMF rather than web services and XML-based protocols, especially for large (over 1 KB) result sets.
- Use strong data types with AMF on both sides for the best performance and memory usage.
- Use streaming for real-time information. If you have a choice, select the protocols in the following order: RTMP, AMF streaming, long polling.
- Use lazy loading of data, especially with hierarchical data sets.

- Try to optimize a legacy data feed; compress it on a proxy server at least, and provide an AMF wrapper at best.

Memory utilization

To use memory more efficiently:

- Use strongly typed variables whenever possible, especially when you have a large number of instances.
- Avoid using the XML format.
- Provide usage-based classes for nonembedded resources. For example, when you build a photo album application, you do want to cache more than a screenful of images, so that scrolling becomes faster without reloading already scrolled images. The amount of utilized memory and common sense, however, should prevent you from keeping all images loaded.
- Avoid unnecessary bindings (like binding used for initialization), as they produce tons of generated code and live objects. Provide initialization through your code when it is needed and has minimal performance impact.
- Identify and minimize memory leaks using the Flash Builder Profiler.

Code execution performance

For better performance, you can make your code JIT-compliant by:

- Minimizing references to other classes
- Using strong data types
- Using local variables to optimize data access
- Keeping code out of initialization routines and constructors

Additional code performance tips are:

- For applications working with a large amount of data, consider using the `Vector` data type (Flash Player 10 and later) over `Array`.
- Bindings slow startup, as they require initialization of supporting classes; keep it minimal.

Summary

In this chapter, you learned how to create a small no-Flex logon (or any other) window that gets downloaded very quickly to the user's computer, while the rest of the Flex code is still in transit.

You know how to create any application as a miniportal with a light main application that loads light modules that:

- Don't have the information from *services-config.xml* engraved into their bodies
- Can be tested by a developer with no dependency on the work of other members of the team

You won't think twice when it comes to modifying the code of even such a sacred cow as `SystemManager` to feed your needs. Well, you *should* think twice, but don't get too scared if the source code of the Flex framework requires some surgery. If your version of the modified Flex SDK looks better than the original, submit it as a patch to be considered for inclusion in the future Flex build; the website is *http://opensource.adobe.com/wiki/display/flexsdk/Submitting+a+Patch*.

While developing your enterprise RIA, keep a copy of the "Performance Checklist" on page 437 handy and refer to it from the very beginning of the project.

If you've tried all the techniques that you know to minimize the size of a particular *.swf* file and you are still not satisfied with its size, as a last resort, create an ActionScript project in Flash Builder and rewrite this module without using MXML. This might help.

CHAPTER 9

Working with Adobe AIR

First axiom of user interface design: Don't make the user look stupid.

—Alan Cooper

In this chapter, you'll investigate Adobe Integrated Runtime (AIR), which is a valuable addition to the arsenal of Flex developers for many reasons:

- AIR allows you to perform all I/O operation with the filesystem on the user's desktop.
- AIR allows you to sign applications and allows versioning of applications.
- AIR offers an updater that make it easy to ensure proper upgrades of the applications on the user's desktop computer.
- AIR comes with a local database, SQLite, which is a great way to arrange a repository of the application data (in clear or encrypted mode) right on the user's computer.
- AIR applications can easily monitor and report the status of the network connection.
- The user can start and run an AIR application even when there is no network connection available.
- AIR has better support for HTML content.

At the time of this writing, AIR 1.5 has been officially released and AIR 2.0 is in beta. As you can see, AIR 1.5 is a significant step toward providing a platform for desktop application development. However, AIR 1.5 is not a full-featured desktop development environment because of the following limitations:

- It can't make calls to the user's native operating system.
- It can't launch non-AIR applications on the desktop (except the default browser).
- It can't instantiate a dynamic link library (DLL).
- It can't directly access the ports (i.e., USB or serial) of the user's computer.

AIR 2.0 introduces significant improvements that have received a warm welcome in the developer community, such as:

- It can launch and communicate with native (non-AIR) applications.
- It lowers CPU and memory consumption.
- It supports the detection of mass storage devices (e.g., when a USB device or a camera is connected or disconnected).
- It knows how to open files with default programs (e.g., PDF files are opened by Acrobat Reader).
- It gives you access to uncompressed microphone data via the Microsoft Access API.
- It introduces multitouch functionality.
- It introduces UDP sockets, which are a great improvement for such real-time applications as online games or Voice over IP.
- It includes global error handling, which is guaranteed to catch all unhandled errors.
- It supports screen readers (Windows OS only) for visually impaired users.
- The sizes of the runtime installers are smaller than those in AIR 1.5.
- It can create applications for the iPhone.

In addition to the technical improvements of AIR, Adobe has created a central resource that collects a growing set of AIR applications developed by third parties. It's called Adobe AIR Marketplace (*http://www.adobe.com/go/marketplace*).

If you want to create, publish, and sell your own applications, get familiar with a service code-named Shibuya (*http://labs.adobe.com/technologies/shibuya/*), which is a monetization service for AIR developers (it's currently in beta).

Our message is simple: we highly recommend using AIR for development of desktop applications.

To help you get started with AIR, this chapter provides a fast-paced review of the basics of the AIR APIs that are not available in Flex. You'll then move on to the more advanced topic of data synchronization between the client and a BlazeDS-powered server. As an alternative to using LCDS and its Data Management Services, this chapter offers a synchronization solution with a subclass of `DataCollection` (see Chapter 6) and BlazeDS.

Finally, you'll use AIR to build a small application for a salesperson at a pharmaceutical firm who visits doctors' offices, offering the company's latest drug, *Xyzin*. During these visits, the salesperson's laptop is disconnected from the Internet, but the application allows note-taking about the visit and saves the information in the local SQLite database bundled into the AIR runtime. When the Internet connection becomes available, the application automatically synchronizes the local data with a central database.

All code samples in this chapter were developed in AIR 1.5.

How AIR Is Different from Flex

You can think of AIR as a superset or a shell for the Flex, Flash, and AJAX programs. First of all, AIR includes the API for working with files on the user's computer; Flex has very limited access to the disk (only file uploading and local shared objects via advanced cookies). The user can run an AIR application installed on his desktop if it has the AIR runtime. This runtime is installed pretty seamlessly with minimal user interaction.

On the other hand, the very fact that AIR applications have to be installed on the user's computer forces us developers to take care of things that just don't exist in Flex applications. For example, to release a new version of a Flex application, you need to update the SWFs and some other files on a single server location. With AIR, each user has to install a new version of your application on his computer, which may already have an old version installed. The installer should take precautions to ensure that versioning of the application is done properly and that the application being installed is not some malicious program that may damage the user's computer.

In the Flex world, if the user's computer is not connected to the Internet, he can't work with your RIA. This is not the case with AIR applications, which can work in disconnected mode, too. Although Flex does not have language elements or libraries that can work with a relational DBMS, AIR comes bundled with a version of SQLite that is installed on the client and is used to create a local database (a.k.a. local cache) to store application data in the disconnected mode. If needed, AIR can encrypt the data stored in this local database. Consider the salesperson visiting customers with a laptop. Although no Internet connection is available, she can still use the AIR application and save the data in the local database. As soon as the Internet connection becomes available, the AIR application then synchronizes the local and remote databases.

Rendering of HTML is yet another area where AIR beats Flex hands down. AIR does it by leveraging the open source web-browsing engine called WebKit (*http://webkit.org*). Loading a web page into your AIR application is a simple matter of adding a few lines of code; you'll learn how to do it later in this chapter.

The inclusion of WebKit makes AIR an attractive environment not only for Flex, but also for HTML/AJAX developers as well. If you are an AJAX developer and your application works with WebKit, it'll work inside AIR, which opens a plethora of additional functionalities in any AJAX program.

Hello World in AIR

The AIR SDK is free, so if you are willing to write code in Notepad (or your favorite text editor) and compile and build your applications using command-line tools either directly or hooked up to an IDE of your choice, you can certainly create AIR applications without having to purchase any additional software. In particular, AIR comes with the following tools:

ADL
: The AIR Debug Launcher that you can use from a command line

ADT
: The AIR Developer Tool with which you create deployable *.air* files

Most likely, you'll work in the Flash Builder IDE, which includes the AIR project creation wizard. To get familiar with this method, try developing a *HelloWorld* application.

1. Create a new Flex project called *HelloWorld* in Flash Builder.
2. In the same window where you enter the project name, select the radio button titled "Desktop application (runs in Adobe AIR)." Click the Finish button to see a window similar to Figure 9-1.
3. Instead of the familiar <mx:Application> tag, the root tag of an AIR application is <mx:WindowedApplication>. Add a line <mx:Label text="Hello World"> to the code and run this application. Figure 9-2 shows the results.

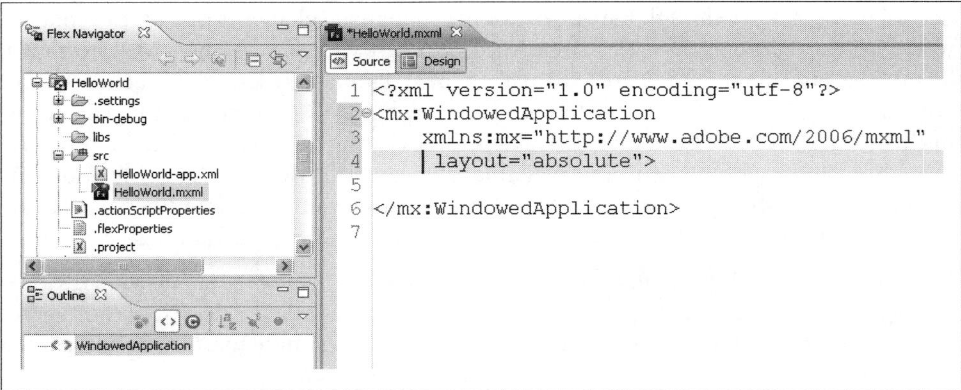

Figure 9-1. An empty template of the AIR application

The *src* folder of your Flash Builder project now contains an application descriptor file called *HelloWorld-app.xml*. Example 9-1 shows a fragment of this file. (If you don't use Flash Builder, you'll have to write the file manually.)

Figure 9-2. Running the HelloWorld application

Example 9-1. Partial application descriptor file for HelloWorld

```
<application xmlns="http://ns.adobe.com/air/application/1.5.1">

<!-- The application identifier string, unique to this application. Required. -->

   <id>HelloWorld</id>

<!-- Used as the filename for the application. Required. -->

   <filename>HelloWorld</filename>

<!-- The name that is displayed in the AIR application installer.
     May have multiple values for each language. See samples or xsd schema file.
     Optional. -->

   <name>HelloWorld</name>

<!-- An application version designator (such as "v1", "2.5", or "Alpha 1").
     Required. -->

   <version>v1</version>
```

The namespace that ends with 1.5.1 indicates the minimum required version of the AIR runtime. AIR is forward compatible, however, so an application built in, say, AIR 1.0 can be installed on the machines that have any runtime with a version greater than 1.0.

You may run into an issue while trying to run an AIR application from Flash Builder: it won't start but doesn't report any errors either. To fix this issue, make sure that the namespace ends with 1.5.1 or whatever the current version of AIR is that you use.

The application ID must be unique for each installed AIR application signed by the same code-signing certificate. Hence using reverse domain notation, like `com.farata.HelloWorld`, is recommended.

To prepare a package for deploying your application:

1. Choose Project→Export Release Build, just as you would for deploying Flex applications. Flash Builder will offer to create an installer for the application, an AIR file named *HelloWorld.air*. There is no need to create an HTML wrapper here as with Flex applications.
2. Press the Next button. Flash Builder displays a window that asks for you to sign this application using a precreated digital certificate or to export to an intermediate file (with the *.air* name extension) that you can sign later. This second option is useful if, for example, your firm enforces a special secure way of signing applications.
3. If you don't have a real digital certificate, click on the Create button to create a self-signed certificate, which is good enough for the development stage of your AIR application.
4. Fill out the creation form in Figure 9-3 and name the file *testCertificate.p12*.

You can purchase a digital certificate from ChosenSecurity (*http://chosensecurity.com*), GlobalSign (*http://globalsign.com*), Thawte (*http://www.thawte.com*), or VeriSign (*http://www.verisign.com*).

5. Click OK to save the file.

   You'll now see a window that specifies what to include in the *HelloWorld.air* file. This simple example requires only two files: the application descriptor *HelloWorld-app.xml* and the application file *HelloWorld.swf*.

Congratulations—you've created your first AIR application. Now what? How do users run *HelloWorld.air* if their computers don't have Flash Builder? They must download and install the latest version of the AIR runtime (about 15 MB) from *http://get.adobe.com/air/*.

When this is complete, they double-click on *HelloWorld.air* to start the installation of the *HelloWorld* application and see the scary message in Figure 9-4.

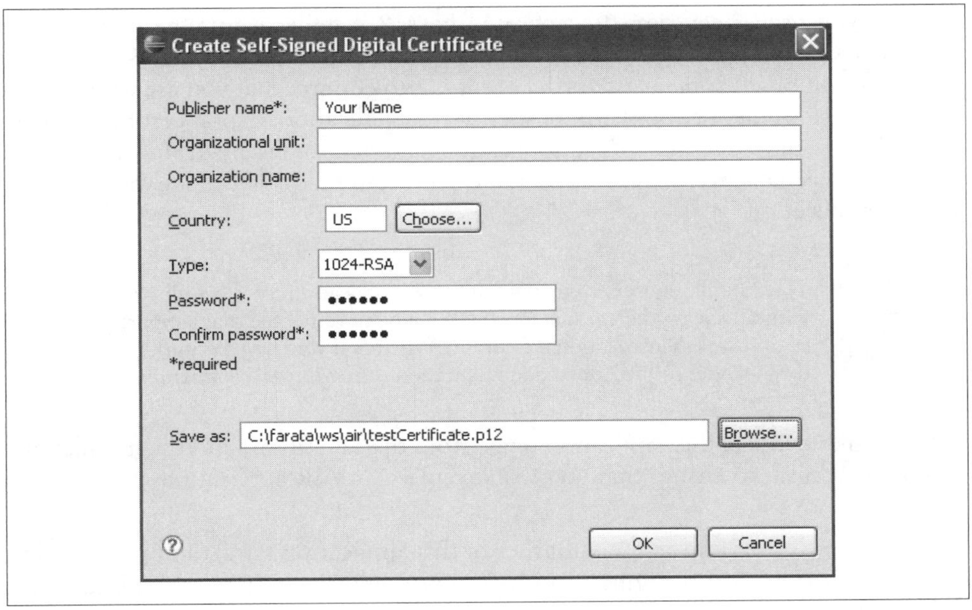

Figure 9-3. Creating a self-signed certificate

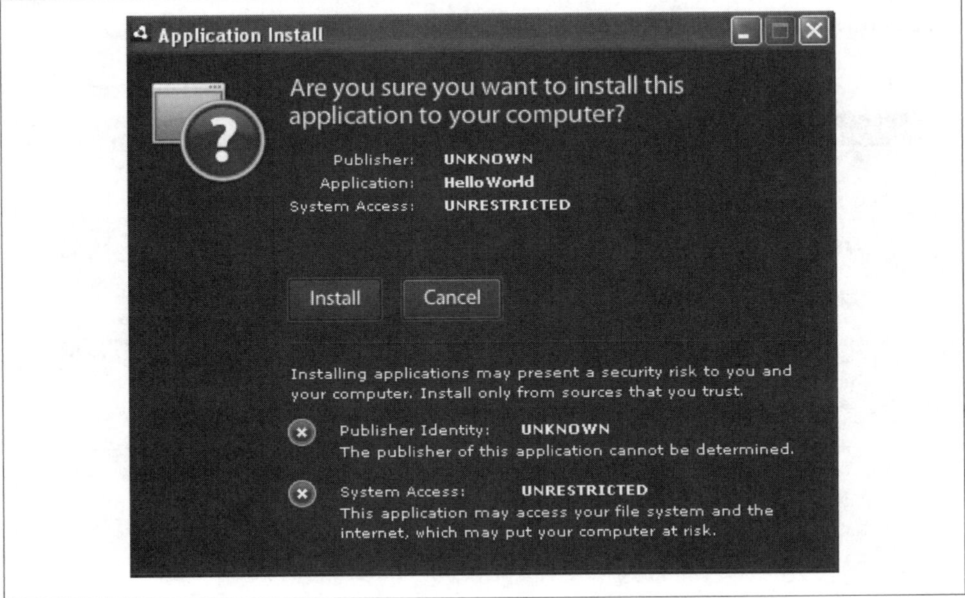

Figure 9-4. Installing the AIR application

Because you used a self-signed certificate, the AIR installer warns the user that the publisher's identity is unknown. The fact that you've entered your name as a publisher is not good enough; some trustworthy agent has to confirm that you are who you say you are. Besides identifying the publisher of the application, digital certificates guarantee that the binary content of the application has not been modified after signing (the checksum mechanism is being used there). Using the *.air* file is one of the ways to install an AIR application.

> You can allow users to install your AIR application from a web page without saving the *.air* file. Flex SDK has a *badge.swf* file that supports such seamless installation (of both AIR itself and your application). For details, refer to the Adobe documentation (*http://tinyurl.com/akntmc*).

The installer extracts the application name from the descriptor, and the installer also has a mechanism to ensure that you won't replace an AIR application with its older version.

Assuming your user knows the publisher of this application (you), and clicks Install, the installation process continues, and *HelloWorld* will take its honorable place among other applications installed on the user's computer. For example, if no settings are changed, on Windows a new *HelloWorld.exe* application will be installed in the folder *C:\Program Files\HelloWorld*, as shown in Figure 9-5. Double-click on the *.air* file after this application was installed (the ID and the version were compared), and you'll see a screen offering to either uninstall the application or run it.

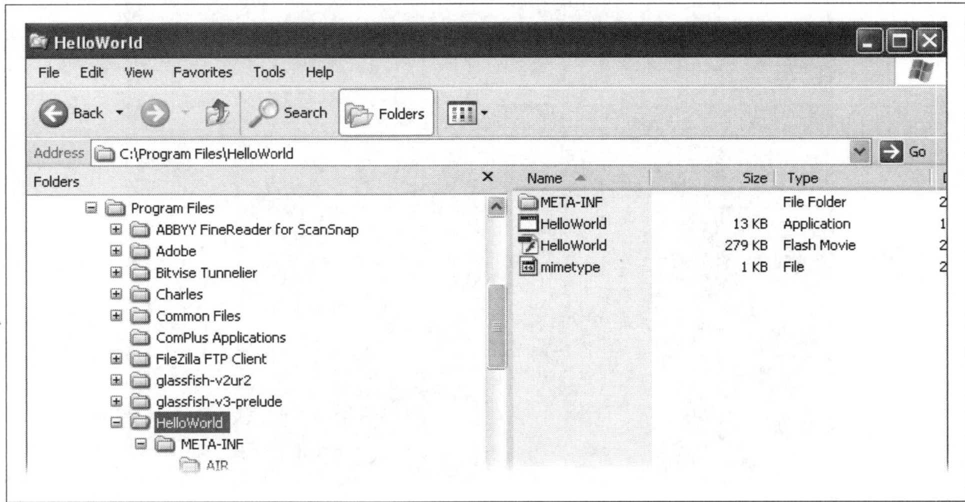

Figure 9-5. AIR application folders

Native Windows

The root tag of any AIR application is `<mx:WindowedApplication>`, which is all it takes to make the application look like a native window of the OS where it runs. For example, install and run the same *HelloWorld.air* application on Mac OS, and, instead of looking like Figure 9-2, the window looks like Figure 9-6.

You can have only one `<mx:WindowedApplication>` tag per application, however. If you need to instantiate other windows, you need to use the `<mx:Window>` component. With it, you can specify multiple windows that may or may not look like a native window based on the *chrome* you specify. The `Window` class contains an important property called `nativeWindow` of type `flash.display.NativeWindow`, which is the class you would use to create new windows if you were developing a plain Flash (no Flex) application.

Figure 9-6. HelloWorld on MAC OS

If you need to open a new native window, create a custom component called *HelloWindow* with `<mx:Window>` as the root tag:

```
<?xml version="1.0" encoding="utf-8"?>
<mx:Window xmlns:mx="http://www.adobe.com/2006/mxml"
              layout="absolute" width="400" height="300">
   <mx:Button label="Close me" click="close()"/>
</mx:Window>
```

The following application instantiates and opens this native window:

```
<?xml version="1.0" encoding="utf-8"?>
<mx:WindowedApplication xmlns:mx="http://www.adobe.com/2006/mxml"
   layout="vertical">
   <mx:Label text="Hello World" />
```

```
    <mx:Button  label="Open Native Window" click="openMyWindow()" />

    <mx:Script>
       <![CDATA[
       import mx.core.Window;
          private function openMyWindow():void{
             var helloNativeWindow:Window=new HelloWindow();
             helloNativeWindow.open();
          }
       ]]>
    </mx:Script>
 </mx:WindowedApplication>
```

You can change the chrome and transparency of the `<mx:Window>` component by using its properties `systemChrome` and `transparent`, respectively.

> You can't set the `systemChrome` and `transparent` properties of `<mx:WindowedApplication>` programmatically, but you can do it in the application descriptor file.

Working with Files

The class `flash.filesystem.File` is a means of getting access to the files and directories on the user's computer. This class enables you to create, move, copy, or delete files. It also comes with generic constants that resolve the path to the user, desktop, or document directories and offer a unified cross-platform way to access application resource files. For read/write operations, use the class `FileStream` from the package `flash.filesystem`.

AIR supports working with files in two modes: synchronous and asynchronous. *Synchronous* mode forces the application to block (wait) until this I/O operation is complete. In *asynchronous* mode, the user can continue working with the application while it works with files, and an event notification mechanism monitors the progress of the I/O. Those methods that work asynchronously have the suffix *Async* in their names—for example, `File.copyToAsync()` or `FileStream.openAsync()`. Using the asynchronous versions of I/O requires a bit more coding, but it should be your first choice when you need to process files of substantial sizes.

Commonly Used Directories

Because AIR is a cross-platform runtime, it shields the user from knowing specifics of the structure of the native filesystem by introducing predefined alias names for certain directories.

The `app:/` alias refers to your application's root read-only directory, where all files (both code and assets) that you packaged with your application are located. For example, if your application includes an *images* directory, which holds the file *cafeLogo.jpg*, you would create an instance of a File pointing to this image (regardless of where this application is installed) as follows:

```
var cafeLogo: File= new File("app:/images/cafeLogo.jpg");
```

Similar to Java, in AIR the fact that you've created an instance of a File providing a path to a specific file or directory doesn't mean that it exists and is in good health. By instantiating a File object, you are just preparing a utility object capable of working with a file at a given location. Don't forget to provide error processing while performing I/O operations on this file.

Alternatively, you could use a static property File.applicationDirectory:

```
var cafeLogo: File=
        File.applicationDirectory.resolvePath("images/cafeLogo.jpg")
```

The resolvePath() method enables you to write the file access code without worrying about differences of native file path notation in Windows, Mac OS, and Linux. On the other hand, you are still allowed to reference a file by its absolute path, as in this code:

```
 var cafeLogo: File= new File(
"c:\Documents and Settings\mary\MyApplicationDir\images/cafeLogo.jpg");
```

This notation has an obvious disadvantage: it works only on Windows machines. If you want to specify the path starting from a root directory of the user's hard disk but in a cross-platform fashion, use the alias file:/.

The application shown in Example 9-2 will allow the user to enter the filename and any text in the left text box. When the user clicks the "Write" button, the entered text will be asynchronously written into the file with the specified name. When the user clicks the "Read" button, the content of this file will be read in synchronous mode.

The app-storage:/ alias is used to work with an automatically created directory for persisting offline data. Each AIR application has its own storage directory, and the sample application shown in Example 9-2 will save the files there.

Alternatively, you can use the applicationStorageDirectory property of the class File.

The class File has some more static constants for commonly used directories: desktopDirectory, documentsDirectory, and userDirectory. The following code fragment, for example, creates a directory *testDir* specifically for the application *WorkingWithFiles*:

```
var myDir:File=new File("app-storage:/testDir")
if (!myDir.exists){
    myDir.createDirectory();
}
```

The actual location of this directory depends on the OS, and in Windows XP you can find it here (make sure that Windows Explorer is set to show hidden files):

C:\Documents and Settings\Administrator\Application Data\WorkingWithFiles\LocalStore\testDir

In Mac OS X, the same code will create the directory:

/Users/yourUserID/Library/Preferences/WorkingWithFiles/Local Store/testDir

Reading and Writing to Files

After finding a file, you may want to work with it. Example 9-2, which lists the source code of the application *WorkingWithFiles*, illustrates the reading, writing, and deleting of the file with the hardcoded name *MyTextFile.txt*. Figure 9-7 shows the results. The user can type any text in the box on the left, click the button "Write asynchronously," and the file *myTextFile.txt* will be saved in the directory *testDir*. Clicking the button "Read synchronously" will read this file into the text box on the right.

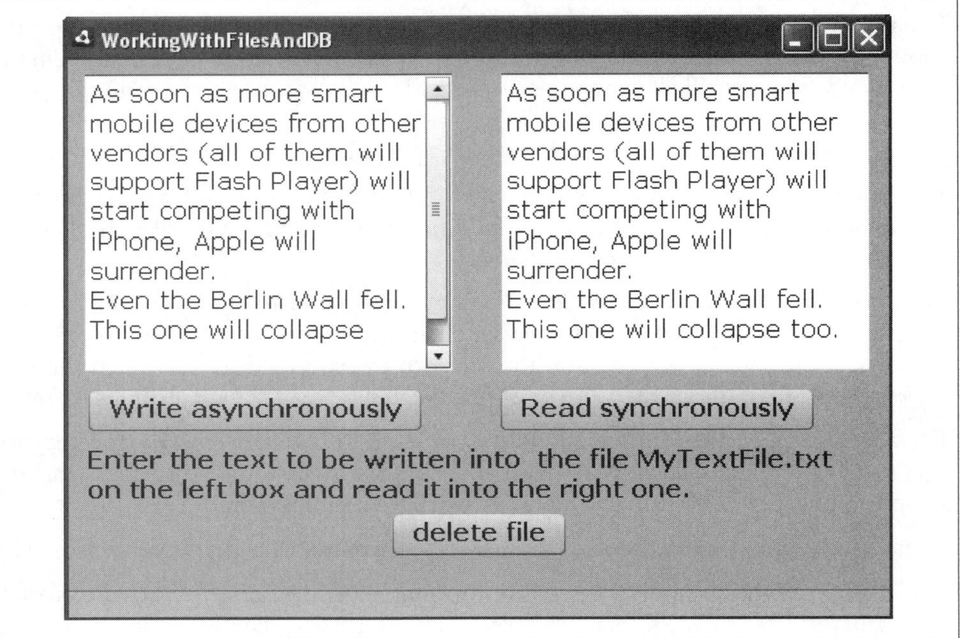

Figure 9-7. Reading/writing into files

If the user clicks the "delete file" button and then clicks "Read synchronously," the application will try to read *MyTextFile.txt* and display the error message shown in Figure 9-8.

Example 9-2 contains the source code of the *WorkingWithFiles* application. For illustration purposes, it includes both asynchronous and synchronous modes for file I/O operations performed by the methods of the class `FileStream`; the stream is opened either by openAsync() or open(), respectively. The functions writeFile(), readFile(), and deleteFile() use try/catch blocks to report I/O errors, if there are any. Don't forget to close opened streams as is done in the finally clause.

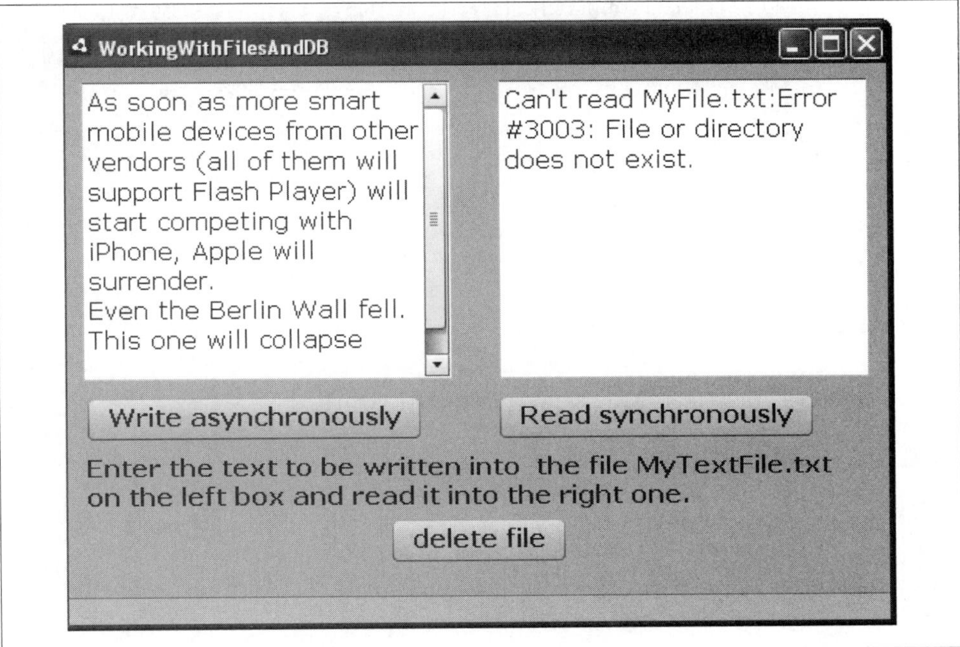

Figure 9-8. I/O Error message

Example 9-2. WorkingWithFiles.mxml

```
<?xml version="1.0" encoding="utf-8"?>
<mx:WindowedApplication xmlns:mx="http://www.adobe.com/2006/mxml"
   layout="absolute" width="530"  fontSize="16">

<mx:Script>
   <![CDATA[
       import mx.controls.Alert;
       import flash.filesystem.File;
        import flash.filesystem.FileStream;

        var myDir:File=new File("app-storage:/testDir")
        var myFile:File = myDir.resolvePath("MyTextFile.txt");
        var myFileStream4Write: FileStream = new FileStream();
        var myFileStream4Read: FileStream = new FileStream();

      private function writeFile():void{
         if (!myDir.exists){
             myDir.createDirectory();
         }
```

```
            myFileStream4Write.addEventListener(Event.CLOSE,completeHandler);

            try {
              myFileStream4Write.openAsync(myFile,FileMode.WRITE);

              myFileStream4Write.writeMultiByte(textToWrite.text, "iso-8859-1");

            } catch(error:IOError){
               Alert.show("Writing to file failed:" + error.message);
            } finally {
              myFileStream4Write.close();
            }
      }

      private function completeHandler (event:Event):void{
          Alert.show("File MyFile.txt has been written successfully");
      }

        private function  readFile():void{

            try {
              myFileStream4Read.open(myFile,FileMode.READ);

              textRead.text=
                myFileStream4Read.readMultiByte(
                        myFileStream4Read.bytesAvailable, "iso-8859-1");

            } catch(error:IOError){
               textRead.text="Can't read MyFile.txt:" + error.message;
            } finally {
              myFileStream4Read.close();
            }
        }

        private function deleteFile():void{
           try{
            myFile.deleteFile();
           } catch(error:IOError){
               textRead.text="Can't delete file MyFile.txt:" + error.message;
            }
        }
   ]]>
</mx:Script>

   <mx:Text x="10" y="259" text="Enter the text to be written into  the file
            MyTextFile.txt on the left box and read it into the right one."
            fontWeight="bold" width="508" height="48" />
   <mx:TextArea id="textToWrite" x="10" y="10" height="201" width="239"
                                                   borderStyle="inset"/>
   <mx:TextArea id="textRead" x="279" y="10" height="201" width="239"
                                                   borderStyle="inset"/>
   <mx:Button x="13"  y="223" label="Write asynchronously" click="writeFile()"/>
   <mx:Button x="279" y="223" label="Read synchronously" click="readFile()"/>
   <mx:Button x="209" y="306" label="delete file" click="deleteFile()"/>
</mx:WindowedApplication>
```

Working with Local Databases

Flex applications can save data on local filesystems using the class `SharedObject`. This is a useful feature for storing user preferences or serializing other memory objects on the disk. The API for working with `SharedObject` allows the application to write an instance of the object to disk and re-create the instance afterward, on the next run.

AIR offers a more sophisticated API, as it comes with an embedded relational DBMS called SQLite. The application can create and work with the data using SQL syntax on the user's machine. Such data is often referred as a *local cache*. The data stored in the local cache can be encrypted, if needed. You can see it in action in a sample *Salesbuilder* application at *http://tinyurl.com/bbq4dj*.

There are three main uses of the local cache:

- Create an independent desktop application with its own local database.
- Allow the AIR application to remain operational even when there is no network connection. In this case, a local database may have a number of tables (i.e., Customers and Orders) that will be synchronized with the central database as soon as the network connection becomes available.
- Offload large chunks of intermediate application data to lower memory utilization.

A SQLite database is stored in a single file, and an understanding of the basics of the *File* API covered in the previous section is helpful.

Creating a database file

To create a new SQLite database, you need to pass an instance of the `File` object to the class `flash.data.SQLConnection`. The latter can open the connection to the given `File` instance in either synchronous or asynchronous modes (similar to performing I/O with files). If the physical file does not exist, it'll be created; otherwise, the `SQLConnection` object will just open the database file.

If you open the connection in synchronous mode, do it inside the `try/catch` block to perform error processing if something goes wrong (Example 9-3).

Example 9-3. Connecting to the local database

```
var connection:SQLConnection = new SQLConnection();
var dbFile:File = File.applicationStorageDirectory.resolvePath("myLocal.db");
try{
     connection.open(dbFile);
   } catch(err:SQLError){
         Alert.show(err.details,
                "Can't connect to the local database");
}
```

The function open() can be used with a number of arguments, and one of them can specify an encryption key, which will be used for encrypting data in the specified database file.

In the case of an asynchronous connection, you'll add SQLEvent.OPEN and SQLEvent.ERROR listeners and write the success and error processing code in separate event handlers.

Although using a synchronous connection prevents the user from working with the UI until the database operation completes, this mode allows you to program several operations as one transaction that can be either committed or rolled back in its entirety:

```
try{
    connection.begin();
    // several SQL statements can go here
    connection.commit();
} catch(err:SQLError){
    connection.rollback()
    ...
}  finally  {
    connection.close()
}
```

To create a table or execute any other SQL statements, you need to create an instance of the SQLStatement object, assign a SQL statement to its property text, pass it an instance of an opened SQLConnection, and call the function execute. For instance, Example 9-4 creates a table called *visit_schedule*; for illustration purposes, the code uses an asynchronous mode with event listeners.

Example 9-4. Creating a table in the local database

```
var ddl: SQLStatement = new SQLStatement();
     ddl.sqlConnection=connection;
     ddl.text="CREATE  TABLE IF NOT EXISTS visit_schedule (" +
           "id INTEGER PRIMARY KEY AUTOINCREMENT,"+
           "salesman_id INTEGER,"+
           "address_id INTEGER,"+
           "scheduled_date DATE ) ";
   ddl.addEventListener(SQLEvent.RESULT, onTableCreated);
    ddl.addEventListener(SQLErrorEvent.ERROR, onSQLFault);

    try{
       ddl.execute();
    } catch(err:SQLError){
       Alert.show(err.details,"Can't create table visit_schedule");
    }

  private function onTableCreated(event:SQLEvent):void{
          Alert.show("Table visits created", "Success");
  }

  private function onSQLFault(event:SQLEvent):void{
          Alert.show("SQL failed: ");
  }
```

Now add a new row to the table *visit_schedule* (Example 9-5).

Example 9-5. Inserting into a table in the local database

```
var ddl: SQLStatement = new SQLStatement();
     ddl.sqlConnection=connection;
     ddl.text="INSERT INTO visit_schedule (salesman_id,address_id,scheduled_date)"
+
        "VALUES (401, 2, '2009-01-09')";
       try{
    ddl.execute();
       Alert.show("Table visit_schedule populated", "Success");
  } catch(err:SQLError){
    Alert.show(err.details,"Can't insert into table visit_schedule");
  }
```

Note that we didn't include the value for the ID column, as it has been declared with the attribute AUTOINCREMENT.

It's a good idea to have some kind of database administrator tool that will allow you to work with the SQLite objects. Several different tools can give you a view into the database; we use a simple Mozilla Firefox add-on called SQLite Manager, which you can download from *https://addons.mozilla.org/en-US/firefox/addon/5817*. After you install SQLite Manager, it becomes a menu item under the Tools menu of the Firefox browser. Figure 9-9 shows what SQLite Manager displays after executing the code in Examples 9-4 and 9-5.

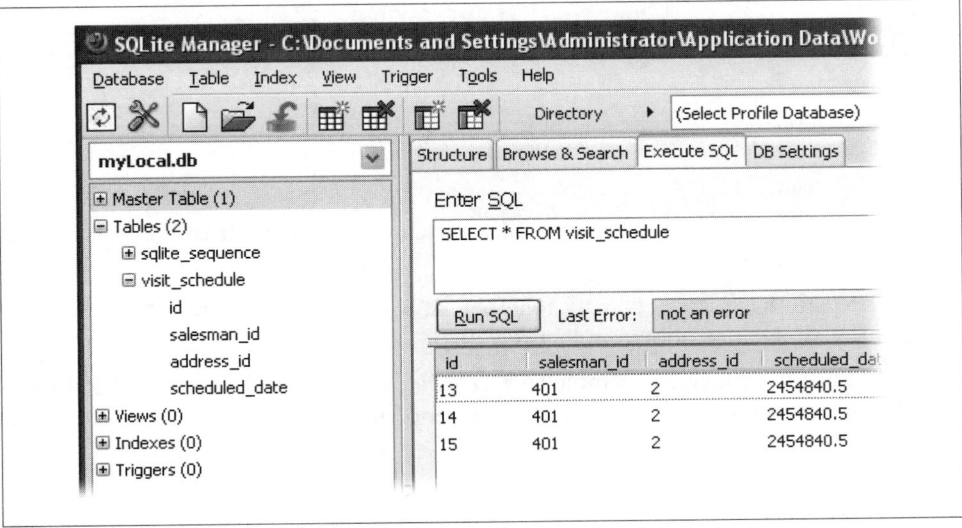

Figure 9-9. Viewing data with SQLite Manager

To finish up this mini tutorial on working with local databases from AIR, review Example 9-6, which demonstrates how to select the data previously saved in the local database.

You'll be using the class `SQLStatement` as in Example 9-4, but this time for running SQL `SELECT`. When the result of your query arrives, it can be extracted from `SQLStatement` using the method `getResult()`, which returns an instance of the `SQLResult` object. The latter stores the result as an array of `Object` instances in the variable `data`.

At this point, you can either write a loop accessing the key/value pairs (table columns) from the `data` array, or just wrap the entire array into an `ArrayCollection` and use it as a data provider for a UI component such as `DataGrid`, `List`, or the like.

Example 9-6. Querying the local database

```
var sql: SQLStatement = new SQLStatement();
sql.sqlConnection=connection;
sql.text="select salesman_id,address_id,
                        scheduled_date from visit_schedule";
try{
  sql.execute();
  var result:SQLResult = sql.getResult();
  var numRows:int = result.data.length;

  for (var i:int = 0; i < numRows; i++) {
     var output:String = "";
     for (var columnName:String in result.data[i]) {
       output += columnName + ": " + result.data[i][columnName] + "; ";
    }
    trace("row[" + i.toString() + "]\t", output);
  }

} catch(err:SQLError){
   Alert.show(err.details,"Can't retrieve data from visit_schedule");
}
```

Example 9-6 demonstrates data retrieval in synchronous mode. It will output column names and their values.

To see how all these snippets work together, review Example 9-7, which contains the code of the application shown in Figure 9-10.

The first button-click creates a table *visit_schedule* in the local database. Click the second button to insert one row in this table, and the third to retrieve the data from *visit_schedule* and populate the data grid.

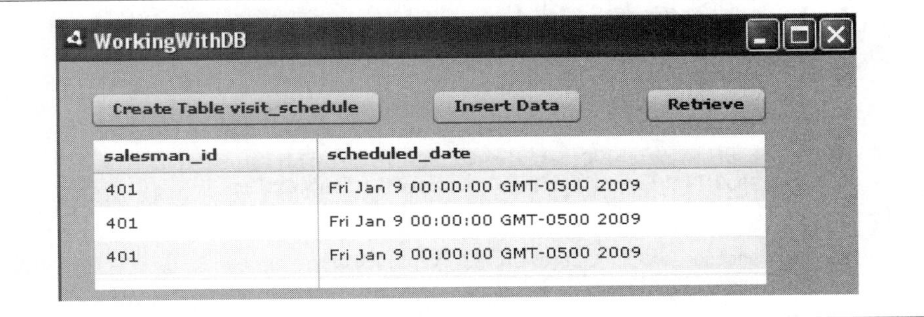

Figure 9-10. Running the WorkingWithDB application

Example 9-7. WorkingWithDB.mxml

```
<?xml version="1.0" encoding="utf-8"?>
<mx:WindowedApplication xmlns:mx="http://www.adobe.com/2006/mxml"
    layout="absolute" creationComplete="openConnection()">

<mx:Script>
   <![CDATA[
      import mx.collections.ArrayCollection;
          import flash.data.SQLConnection;
          import flash.filesystem.File;
          import mx.controls.Alert;
          import flash.errors.SQLError;

          var connection: SQLConnection;

          [Bindable]
          var theData:ArrayCollection;

          // Open connection to local DB
        private function openConnection():SQLConnection {
          connection = new SQLConnection();
          var dbFile:File =
              File.applicationStorageDirectory.resolvePath("myLocal.db");
          try{
                 connection.open(dbFile);
           } catch(err:SQLError){
             Alert.show(err.details,"Can't connect to the local database");
           }
           return connection;
       }

       // populate the table in asynchronous mode
         private function createTable():void{
            var ddl: SQLStatement = new SQLStatement();
            ddl.sqlConnection=connection;
            ddl.text="CREATE  TABLE IF NOT EXISTS visit_schedule (" +
                   "id INTEGER PRIMARY KEY AUTOINCREMENT," +
                   "salesman_id INTEGER,"+
                   "address_id INTEGER,"+
```

```
                "scheduled_date DATE ) ";
        ddl.addEventListener(SQLEvent.RESULT, onTableCreated);
           ddl.addEventListener(SQLErrorEvent.ERROR, onSQLFault);
           ddl.execute();
        }

        private function onTableCreated(event:SQLEvent):void{
           Alert.show("Table visit_schedule created", "Success");
        }

        private function onSQLFault(event:SQLEvent):void{
           Alert.show("SQL failed: ");
        }

          // populate the table in synchronous mode
        private function populateTable():void{
           var ddl: SQLStatement = new SQLStatement();
           ddl.sqlConnection=connection;
           ddl.text="INSERT INTO visit_schedule " +
                 "  (salesman_id,address_id,scheduled_date)" +
            " VALUES (401, 2, '2009-01-09')";
            try{
             ddl.execute();
                 Alert.show("Table visit_schedule populated", "Success");
            } catch(err:SQLError){
              Alert.show(err.details,"Can't insert into table visit_schedule");
          }
        }

        // retrieve the data from the table visit_schedule
        // into an ArrayCollection
          private function retrieveVisitSchedule():void{
            var sql: SQLStatement = new SQLStatement();
           sql.sqlConnection=connection;
           sql.text="select salesman_id, address_id,scheduled_date from " +
                       "visit_schedule";
            try{
             sql.execute();
             var result:SQLResult = sql.getResult();
             theData=new ArrayCollection(result.data);
            } catch(err:SQLError){
            Alert.show(err.details,"Can't retrieve data from  visit_schedule");
          }
          }
   ]]>
</mx:Script>
   <mx:Button x="368" y="21" label="Retrieve" click="retrieveVisitSchedule()"/>
   <mx:Button x="20" y="21" label="Create Table visit_schedule"
click="createTable();"/>
   <mx:Button x="234" y="21" label="Insert Data" click="populateTable();"/>
   <mx:DataGrid dataProvider="{theData}" x="20" y="51" width="423" height="140">
      <mx:columns>
         <mx:DataGridColumn dataField="salesman_id" width="100"/>
         <mx:DataGridColumn dataField="scheduled_date" width="200"/>
      </mx:columns>
```

```
    </mx:DataGrid>
</mx:WindowedApplication>
```

This example should give you an idea of how you can work with SQLite from AIR. This was not a comprehensive tutorial, though, and we encourage you to read the AIR product documentation to get a better understanding of how to work with a local database in AIR.

To learn more about the SQL syntax of the SQLite DBMS, refer to its product documentation at *http://www.sqlite.org*.

In the next sections, you'll automate working with a SQLite database to create a data synchronization solution for an example application called *PharmaSales*. This application will offer you a solution for data synchronization of AIR/BlazeDS and will illustrate how to monitor the network status and use the Google Maps API.

PharmaSales Application

Adobe AIR offers a data synchronization solution based on Data Management Services for those who own licenses of LiveCycle Data Service ES 2.6. This solution is described at the InsideRIA blog at *http://tinyurl.com/6fa254*.

But application developers who use an open source BlazeDS don't have any generic way of setting such data synchronization process. This section offers a smart component called `OfflineDataCollection` that's based on the `DataCollection` object described in Chapter 6. This component will take care of the data synchronization for you.

`OfflineDataCollection` is part of the Clear Toolkit's component library *clear.swc*. You'll see how to use it while reviewing a sample *PharmaSales* application that supports the sales force of a fictitious pharmaceutical company called Acme Pharm.

This application will have two types of users:

- A salesperson visiting doctors' offices trying to persuade doctors to use Acme Pharm's latest drug, Xyzin
- The Acme Pharm dispatcher who schedules daily routes for each salesperson

The corporate database schema supporting *PharmaSales* will look like Figure 9-11 (for simplicity, there are no relationships between tables).

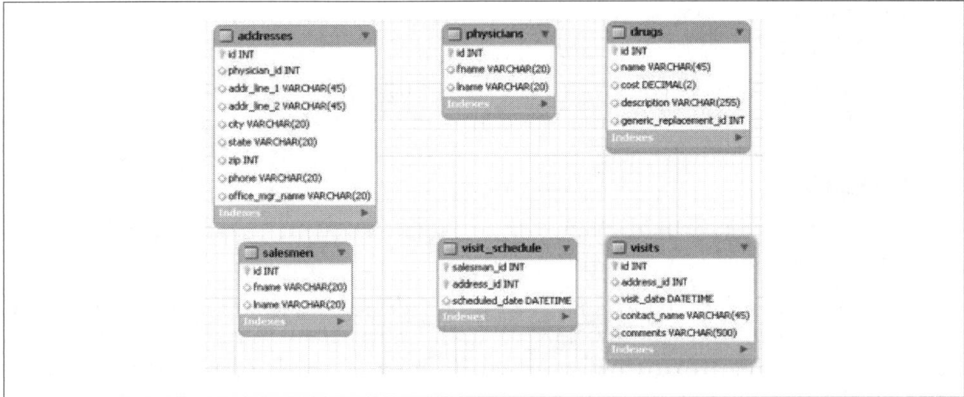

Figure 9-11. The PharmaSales database model

Every morning a salesman starts the *PharmaSales* application, which connects to the corporate database (MySQL) and automatically loads his visit schedule for the day from the table *visit_schedule*. At this point, the data is being loaded into a local database (SQLite) that exists on the salesman's laptop. The database will be automatically created on the first run of the application. The salesman's laptop has to be connected to the Internet.

While visiting a particular doctor's office, the salesman uses the *PharmaSales* application to take notes about the visit. In this case, the salesman's laptop is disconnected from the Internet and all the records about visitations are saved in the local database only. As soon as Sal, the salesman, starts this application in connected mode, the local data with the latest visit information should be automatically synchronized with the corporate database.

To help Sal in finding doctors' offices on the road, the application can be integrated with Google Maps.

Installing PharmaSales

For testing the *PharmaSales* application, you'll need the following software installed:

- Java development kit version 1.5 or higher
- Eclipse JEE 3.3 or higher with the Flash Builder 3 plug-in
- Apache Tomcat Servlet container
- MySQL Server 5 DBMS

In Eclipse, import the *PharmaSales* application; it comes as two projects: *air.offline.demo*, which can be used in connected or disconnected mode by a salesperson, and *air.offline.demo.web*, which is used by the Acme Pharm dispatcher in connected mode only.

If, after importing the project, you see an *Unbound JDK* error, go to the properties of the *air.offline.demo.web* project, select the option Java Build Path → Libraries, remove the unbound JDK, select Add Library, and point at the directory where your JDK is installed—for example, *C:\Program Files\Java\jdk1.6.0_12*.

To simplify the installation, create a *C:\workspace* soft link pointing at your Eclipse workspace directory as described in the section "Preparing for Teamwork" on page 181 in Chapter 4. For example, if your workspace is located at *D:\myworkspace*, the junction utility command will look like this:

```
junction c:\workspace d:\myworkspace
```

The PharmaSales Application for Dispatchers

The *air.offline.demo.web* project has a folder *db* that contains the file *database.sql*, which is a DDL script for creation of sample *pharma* database in MySQL Server. Download the MySQL GUI tools and create the database and the user *dba* with the password *sql*. Run these scripts and grant all the privileges to the *dba* user.

The easiest way to create this sample database is to open a command window and run the *mysql* utility, entering the right user ID and password for the user *root*. The following line is written for the user *root* with the password *root*, assuming that the file *database.sql* is located in the same directory as MySQL:

```
mysql -u root -p root < database.sql
```

The *air.offline.demo.web* project also has the file *pharma.properties* in the *.settings* directory with the database connectivity parameters. If you created the *pharma* database under a different user ID than *dba*, modify the user and the password there accordingly.

If you didn't run the Café Townsend (the CDB version) example from Chapter 1, create a new server in the Eclipse JEE IDE by selecting File → New Server and point it to your Tomcat installation. Add the project to the Tomcat server in Eclipse IDE and start the server.

If you are not willing to install and run this application on your computer, you can instead watch a screencast that shows the process of configuring and running the *PharmaSales* application, which is available at *http://www.myflex.org/demos/PharmaAir/PharmaAir.html*.

The Acme Pharm's dispatcher is the only user of the application *VisitSchedules.mxml* (the Flash Builder's project *air.offline.demo.web*). Its main window allows scheduling new visits and viewing existing visits for each salesperson (Figure 9-12).

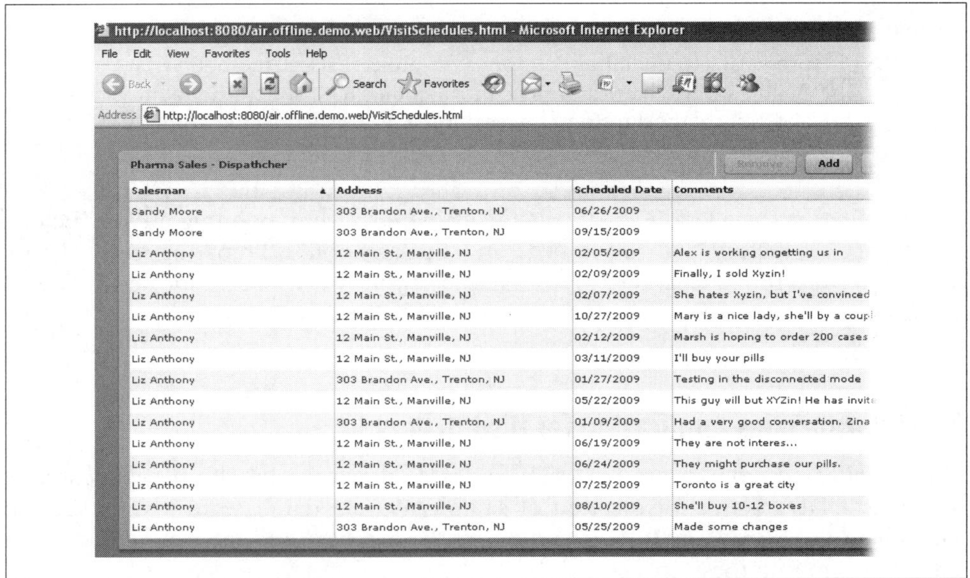

Figure 9-12. Viewing visit schedules

Click the Add button to open another view and schedule a new visit for any salesperson (Figure 9-13).

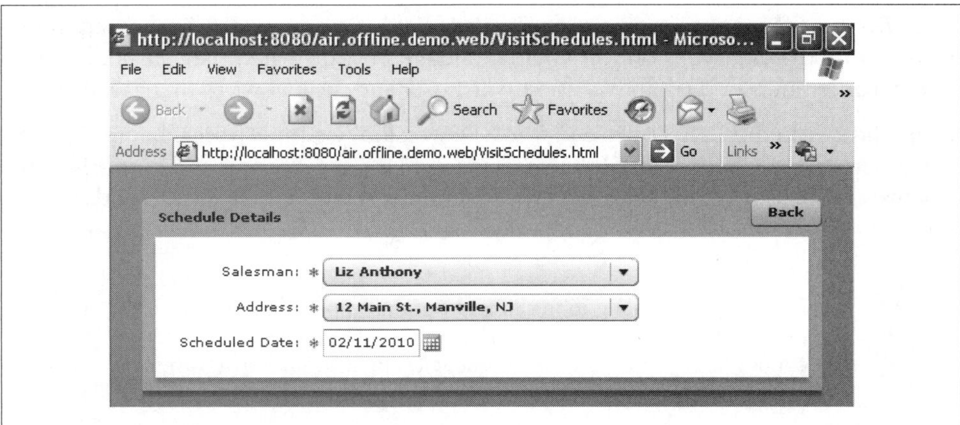

Figure 9-13. Scheduling a new visit

Scheduled visits are saved in the central MySQL Server database in the table *visit_schedule*, and each time the salesperson logs on to the system from her laptop, her visits are automatically downloaded to the local SQLite DBMS.

We won't review all the code of this application; it was generated by Clear Data Builder similarly to Café Townsend, as described in Chapter 1. CDB has generated this application based on the abstract Java class `VisitSchedule` shown in Example 9-8.

Example 9-8. VisitSchedule.java

```
package com.farata.demo.pharmasales;

import java.util.List;

/**
 * @daoflex:webservice
 *   pool=jdbc/pharma
 */
public abstract class VisitSchedule {
    /**
     * @daoflex:sql
     *  pool=jdbc/pharma
     *  sql=::  SELECT
     *   visit_schedule.id as id,
     *   visit_schedule.salesman_id as salesman_id,
     *   visit_schedule.address_id as address_id,
     *   visit_schedule.scheduled_date as scheduled_date,
     *   CONCAT(salesmen.fname, " ", salesmen.lname) as fullname,
     *   CONCAT(addresses.addr_line_1, ", ", addresses.city, ", ",
                                 addresses.state) as fulladdress,
     *   visits.comments as comments
     *   FROM (visit_schedule LEFT JOIN visits ON visit_schedule.id =
                     visits.visit_schedule_id), salesmen, addresses
     *   WHERE
     *   visit_schedule.salesman_id = salesmen.id AND
     *   visit_schedule.address_id = addresses.id
     *
     *  ::
     *  transferType=VisitScheduleDTO[]
     *  keyColumns=id, salesman_id, address_id, scheduled_date
     *  updateTable=visit_schedule
     */
     public abstract List getVisitSchedules();

     /**
      * @daoflex:sql
      *  pool=jdbc/pharma
      *  sql=::  SELECT
      *   visit_schedule.id as id,
      *   visit_schedule.salesman_id as salesman_id,
      *   visit_schedule.address_id as address_id,
      *   visit_schedule.scheduled_date as scheduled_date,
      *   CONCAT(salesmen.fname, " ", salesmen.lname) as fullname,
      *   CONCAT(addresses.addr_line_1, ", ", addresses.city, ", ",
              addresses.state) as fulladdress,
      *   visits.comments as comments
      *   FROM (visit_schedule LEFT JOIN visits ON visit_schedule.id =
                     visits.visit_schedule_id), salesmen, addresses
      *   WHERE
```

```
     *   visit_schedule.salesman_id = salesmen.id AND
     *   visit_schedule.address_id = addresses.id AND
     *   CONCAT(salesmen.fname, " ", salesmen.lname)=:fullName
     *  ::
     *  transferType=VisitScheduleDTO[]
     *  keyColumns=salesman_id, address_id, scheduled_date
     *  updateTable=visit_schedule
     */
     public abstract List getVisitSchedulesBySalesman(String fullName);

}
```

The generated Java code that implements the methods declared in the abstract class in the example is located in the project *air.offline.demo.web* in the Java file *Resources \Libraries\Web App Libraries\services-generated.jar*. You need to open the Eclipse Java perspective to see this file.

The salesman and address drop-downs were populated using resources described in Chapter 6. *AddressComboResource.mxml* (Example 9-9) populates the address drop-down.

Example 9-9. ComboBoxResource.mxml

```
<?xml version="1.0" encoding="utf-8"?>
<resources:ComboBoxResource
   xmlns:resources="com.farata.resources.*"
   width="240"
   dropdownWidth="240"
   destination="com.farata.demo.pharmasales.Address"
   keyField="id"
   labelField="fulladdress"
   autoFill="true"
   method="getAddressesCombo"
   >
</resources:ComboBoxResource>
```

The component *SalesmanComboResource.mxml* (Example 9-10) takes care of the salesman drop-down.

Example 9-10. SalesmanComboBoxResource.mxml

```
<?xml version="1.0" encoding="utf-8"?>
<resources:ComboBoxResource
   xmlns:resources="com.farata.resources.*"
   width="240"
   dropdownWidth="240"
   destination="com.farata.demo.pharmasales.Salesman"
   keyField="id"
   labelField="fullname"
   autoFill="true"
   method="getSalesmenCombo"
   >
</resources:ComboBoxResource>
```

Now you're ready to get into the nitty-gritty details of the project *air.offline.demo*, which is used by salespeople and contains the code for monitoring network connectivity, data synchronization, and integration with Google Maps.

The PharmaSales Application for Salespeople

The *PharmaSales* application starts with a logon screen (Figure 9-14) that requires the user to enter a valid full name to retrieve the schedule for that person (the password is irrelevant here).

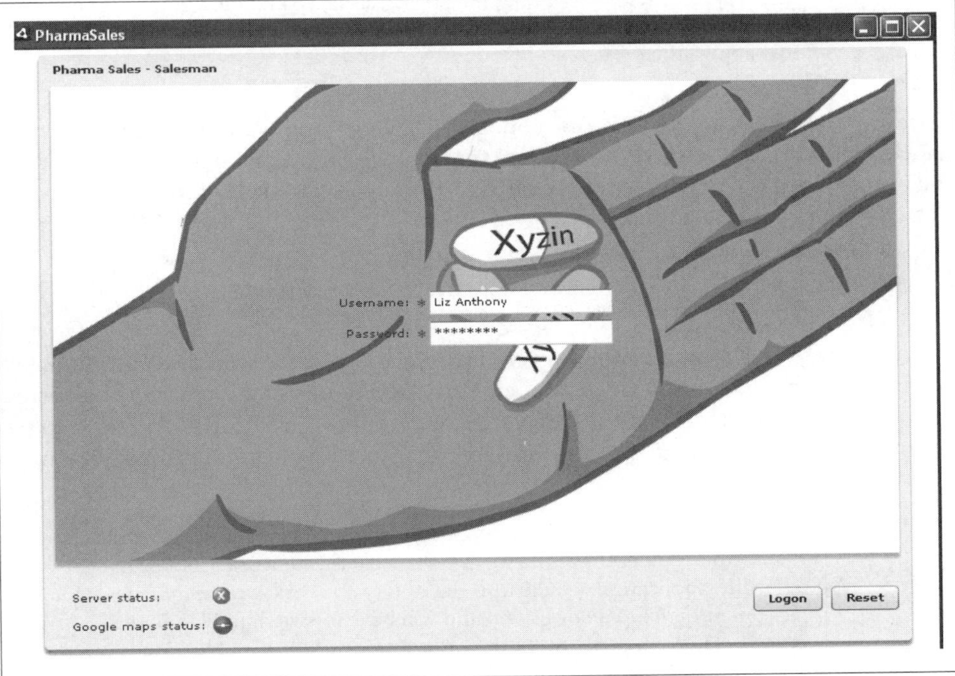

Figure 9-14. The PharmaSales logon screen

Just to double-check that the newly inserted schedule gets downloaded to the client's computer, log on as a salesperson who has scheduled visits.

Detecting Network Availability

Note the two round indicators at the bottom of the logon screen that show both the network and the application server statuses. There are two reasons why an AIR application might not be able to connect to its server-side components: either there is no connection to the network or the application server doesn't respond. Take a look at how an AIR application can detect whether the network and a URL resource are available.

Any AIR application automatically has access to a global object called `flash.desktop.NativeApplication`. This object has a number of useful properties and methods that can give you runtime access to the application descriptor, provide information about the number of the opened windows, and also provide other application-wide information.

You may want to get familiar with yet another useful class called `flash.system.System`. For one thing, this class has a method `gc()` that forces the garbage collector to kick in to avoid memory leaks in your AIR application.

To catch a change in the network connectivity, your application should check the `NativeApplication`'s property `nativeApplication`, which points to an object dispatching events when the network status changes. Your application can almost immediately detect a change in the connectivity by listening to the `Event.NETWORK_CHANGE` event as shown here:

```
flash.desktop.NativeApplication.nativeApplication.addEventListener(
                Event.NETWORK_CHANGE, onNetworkChange);
```

Unfortunately, this event may be triggered with a 10- to 15-second delay after the network status changes, and it does not bear any specific information about the current status of the network. This means that after receiving this event, you still need to test the availability of a specific network resource that your application is interested in.

The *PharmaSales* application uses Google Maps to help salespeople find the doctors' offices they need to visit. Hence if the network is not available, the application would lose the ability to work with *maps.google.com (http://maps.google.com)* and will have to switch to Plan B, discussed later in the section "Integrating with Google Maps" on page 487.

If you check the library path of a Flash Builder AIR project, you'll find there a library *servicemonitor.swc*, which includes `SocketMonitor` and `URLMonitor` classes. These classes can monitor the availability of a specific socket or URL resource.

You can start monitoring the status of a specific HTTP-based resource by calling `URLMonitor.start()` and periodically checking the property `URLMonitor.available`.

Example 9-11 is the complete code of the *NetworkStatus.mxml* component, which monitors both the status of the network (*http://maps.google.com*) and the *PharmaSales* application server and displays either a red or green light depending on the health of the corresponding resource.

Example 9-11. Monitoring network status: NetworkStatus.mxml

```
<?xml version="1.0" encoding="utf-8"?>
<mx:ControlBar xmlns:mx="http://www.adobe.com/2006/mxml" horizontalAlign="left"
width="100%" creationComplete="onCreationComplete()" height="55">
   <mx:Canvas width="200" height="55">
      <mx:Label text="Server status:"/>
      <mx:Image id="serverStatusIcon" x="125" source="{serverConnected ?
                  'assets/connected.gif' : 'assets/disconnected.gif'}"/>
      <mx:Label text="Google maps status: " y="26"/>
      <mx:Image id="googleMapsStatusIcon" x="125" y="26"
            source="{googleMapsConnected ? 'assets/connected.gif' :
                                          'assets/disconnected.gif'}"/>
   </mx:Canvas>
   <mx:Script>
      <![CDATA[
         import air.net.URLMonitor;
         import mx.messaging.config.ServerConfig;

         //Monitor connection status every second
         private static const TIMER_INTERVAL:int=1000;
         private static var _googleMapsURLMonitor:URLMonitor;
         private static var _serverURLMonitor:URLMonitor;

         public function get googleMapsConnected():Boolean{
            return _googleMapsURLMonitor && _googleMapsURLMonitor.available;
         }

         public function get serverConnected():Boolean{
            return _serverURLMonitor && _serverURLMonitor.available;
         }

         public function onCreationComplete():void{

            if (_googleMapsURLMonitor == null){
               initGoogleMapsURLMonitor();
            }
            _googleMapsURLMonitor.addEventListener(StatusEvent.STATUS,
                                                  showGoogleMapsStatus);

            if (_serverURLMonitor == null){
               initServerURLMonitor();
            }
            _serverURLMonitor.addEventListener(StatusEvent.STATUS,
                                                  showServerStatus);
         }

         private function initGoogleMapsURLMonitor():void{
            var request:URLRequest=new
                           URLRequest("http://maps.google.com/");
            request.method="HEAD";
            _googleMapsURLMonitor=new URLMonitor(request);
            _googleMapsURLMonitor.pollInterval=TIMER_INTERVAL;
            _googleMapsURLMonitor.start();
         }
```

```
        private function initServerURLMonitor():void{
           var xml:XML=ServerConfig.serverConfigData;
           var channels:XMLList=xml.channels.channel.(@id == "my-amf");
           var channelConfig:XML=channels[0];
           var uri:String=
        channelConfig.endpoint[0].attribute(ServerConfig.URI_ATTR).toString();
           _serverURLMonitor=new URLMonitor(new URLRequest(uri));
           _serverURLMonitor.pollInterval=TIMER_INTERVAL;
           _serverURLMonitor.start();
        }

        private function showServerStatus(evt:StatusEvent):void{
           serverStatusIcon.source=_serverURLMonitor.available ?
                        "assets/connected.gif" : "assets/disconnected.gif"
        }

        private function showGoogleMapsStatus(evt:StatusEvent):void {
           googleMapsStatusIcon.source=_googleMapsURLMonitor.available ?
                         "assets/connected.gif" : "assets/disconnected.gif"
        }
     ]]>
   </mx:Script>
</mx:ControlBar>
```

In Example 9-11, the network status is being checked as often as specified in the polling interval:

```
_googleMapsURLMonitor.pollInterval=TIMER_INTERVAL;
```

The `NetworkStatus` component checks the health of an HTTP resource using the `URLMonitor` object that listens to `StatusEvent` in the function `initNetworkURLMonitor()`. Based on our experience, the `pollInterval` does not guarantee that notifications of connectivity changes will arrive at the intervals specified in the `TIMER_INTERVAL` constant.

As an alternative, you can create a `Timer` object and check the value of `URLMonitor.available` in the timer's event handler function. If you decide to go this route, keep in mind that it has additional overhead, which comes with any timer object.

Example 9-11 demonstrates yet another useful technique to specify the URI of the network resource without the need to hardcode it in the program as is done in the method `initNetworkURIMonitor()`:

```
new URLRequest('http://maps.google.com/')
```

The chances that the URL of Google Maps will change are rather slim. But the URL of the *PharmaSales* server will definitely be different, say, in development, QA, and production environments. The function `initServerURIMonitor()` extracts the URI of the server based on the information about the location of the AMF channel in the *server-config.xml* of the JEE server that was specified during the creation of the Flex project.

This information is available inside the SWF file, and if your *PharmaSales* server runs locally, the value of the `uri` variable from the method `initServerURIMonitor()` may look as follows:

http://localhost:8080/air.offline.demo.web/messagebroker/amf

To test this component, you can emulate the network outage by physically unplugging the network wire. To test whether the monitoring of the *PharmaSales* server works properly, just stop the server where the Java portion of the *air.offline.demo.web* application has been deployed (in our case, we were stopping the Apache Tomcat server configured in Eclipse IDE).

After the Salesperson Logs On

The *PharmaSales* application is used by salespeople. After a successful logon, the following code is invoked:

```
private function initCollections():void{

 visitCollection=new OfflineDataCollection("com.farata.demo.pharmasales.Visit",
                                    "getVisitsBySalesman", VisitDTO);
 visitCollection.addEventListener(PropertyChangeEvent.PROPERTY_CHANGE, showStatus);

 visitDataCollection=new OfflineDataCollection(
   "com.farata.demo.pharmasales.VisitData", "getVisitDataBySalesman",VisitDataDTO);

 fill_onClick();
}

...
private function fill_onClick():void {
   visitDataCollection.fill(username.text);
   visitCollection.fill(username.text);
}
```

This code populates two collections (`visitCollection` and `visitDataCollection`) by bringing the salesperson's (*username.text*) data from the server. For example, after logon, Liz Anthony will see only her schedule of visits.

The `visitCollection` object will participate in data synchronization with a remote database server, as it has to keep the table *visits* up-to-date.

The `visitDataCollection` object brings the data from `visit_schedule` plus the comments field from the table *visits*. This collection doesn't need to be synchronized, as the *visit_schedule* table is being taken care of by a dispatcher of the corporation Acme Pharm.

You'll get familiar with the code of the class `OfflineDataCollection` later in this chapter, but for now suffice it to say that its function `fill()` will retrieve all the data from a Java class that is configured in the *remoting-config.xml* file of BlazeDS (or LCDS).

For example, the following code creates an instance of OfflineDataCollection that's ready to work with the server-side destination com.faratasystems.demo.pharmasales:

```
visitCollection = new
         OfflineDataCollection("com.farata.demo.pharmasales.Visit",
                              "getVisitsBySalesman", VisitDTO)
```

In general, an application developer needs to decide which DTOs are to be saved in the local storage and should specify them while instantiating one or more OfflineDataCollection objects.

The function initCollection() assigns an event listener to the visitCollection just to display the current status of the data on the UI (e.g., the data is saved in the local database).

The call of the method fill() on OfflineDataCollection gets converted by BlazeDS to a server-side call to Java's method getVisitBySalesman(), which returns instances of the VisitDTO objects with the information about the visits of the salesperson. The first argument of the OfflineDataCollection constructor is the name of the remote destination, the second one is the name of the method to call, and the third one is the type of the ActionScript DTOs arriving to the client.

When the user logs on to the *PharmaSales* application, his computer doesn't have any local databases. The local database is being created during the first call to the method fill(), described in the section on OfflineDataCollection.

Open your application storage directory after running the application for the very first time, and you'll find there a file called *local.db* (in Windows, it's *C:\Documents and Settings\Administrator\Application Data\PharmaSales\Local Store*). This database is not a copy of all the tables of the remote database—it stores only the data arrived in the form of DTOs from the server.

As you continue using the application, you'll find yet another file in the same directory. The file *local.db.bak* is a backup copy of the *local.db* file created when you modified the data in a disconnected mode.

You'll better understand when, how, and why these databases are created after reading the next section of this chapter, which describes the class OfflineDataCollection. At this point, just remember that after the method fill() is complete, you have two databases that store application-specific DTOs on your local computer.

When the user starts working with the application, he needs to be able to save and sync the data with the remote server, which is done in the *PharmaSales* application in the function onSave():

```
visitCollection.sync();
visitDataCollection.updateLocalDB(); // update visit comments
visitDataCollection.backUp();
visitDataCollection.resetState();
```

You sync only the data from the `visitCollection` here, as it represents the data from the remote table `visits`.

The `visitDataCollection` object represents the remote table *visit_schedule*, which is not being changed by the salesperson and hence doesn't need to be synchronized. You call the function `backup()` here just to make the database tables supporting `visitDataCollection` identical in the main and backup databases.

Example 9-12 contains the complete code of the file *PharmaSales.mxml*. This application was initially generated by Clear Data Builder, as explained in Chapter 1. In addition to generating all the code for Flex and Java, it includes such functionality as master/detail relationships.

When the user clicks on the visit row in the `DataGrid`, the detail screen where the salesperson enters visit details opens up. This application uses the `DataForm` and `DataFormItem` components described in Chapter 3.

The UI portion of the *PharmaSales* application contains a `ViewStack` component that wraps the following views:

- Logon
- Grid with visits
- Visit details
- Google Maps

Example 9-12. PharmaSales.mxml

```
<?xml version="1.0" encoding="UTF-8"?>
<mx:WindowedApplication xmlns:mx="http://www.adobe.com/2006/mxml"
xmlns:fx="http://www.faratasystems.com/2008/components" width="800" height="600"
xmlns:controls="com.farata.controls.*" backgroundColor="white" xmlns:ns1="*">
   <mx:ViewStack id="vs" height="100%" width="100%">

      <!--   Logon view   -->
         <mx:Canvas height="100%" width="100%">
       <mx:Panel title="Pharma Sales - Salesman" width="100%"
                 verticalAlign="middle" horizontalAlign="center" height="100%"
                  backgroundImage="assets/PillHand.png">
        <mx:Form>
          <mx:FormItem label="Username:" required="true">
           <mx:TextInput id="username" text="Liz Anthony" maxChars="16"/>
          </mx:FormItem>
          <mx:FormItem label="Password:" required="true">
           <mx:TextInput id="password" text="p455w0rd" maxChars="16"
                                       displayAsPassword="true"/>
          </mx:FormItem>
        </mx:Form>
        <mx:ControlBar horizontalAlign="right">
       <ns1:NetworkStatus/>
       <mx:Button id="logon" label="Logon" click="onLogon()"/>
           <mx:Button id="reset" label="Reset" click="onReset()"/>
        </mx:ControlBar>
```

```
    </mx:Panel>
  </mx:Canvas>

    <!--   Data grid view with visits  -->
  <mx:Canvas height="100%" width="100%">
    <mx:Panel title="Pharma Sales - Salesman" width="100%" height="100%">
     <fx:DataGrid toolTip="Double click for details"
            doubleClick="onDoubleClick()" doubleClickEnabled="true"
            horizontalScrollPolicy="auto" width="100%" id="dg"
            dataProvider="{visitDataCollection}" editable="true" height="100%">
      <fx:columns>
        <fx:DataGridColumn dataField="fullname" editable="false"
                   headerText="Salesman"/>
        <fx:DataGridColumn dataField="fulladdress"
                  editable="false" headerText="Address" width="150"/>
        <fx:DataGridColumn dataField="scheduled_date" editable="false"
                 headerText="Scheduled Date" itemEditor="mx.controls.DateField"
                 editorDataField="selectedDate" formatString="shortDate"/>
        <fx:DataGridColumn dataField="comments" editable="false"
                                           headerText="Comments"/>
        </fx:columns>
        </fx:DataGrid>
       <mx:ControlBar horizontalAlign="right">
        <ns1:NetworkStatus id="network"/>
        <mx:Button enabled="{dg.selectedIndex != -1 &&
                   (network.googleMapsConnected || hasMapImage())}"
                   click="googleMap_onClick()" label="Google Map"/>
        <mx:Button enabled="{!visitCollection.commitRequired &&
                             !visitCollection.syncRequired}"
                            click="fill_onClick()" label="Retrieve"/>
        <mx:Button enabled="{ visitCollection.commitRequired ||
                       visitCollection.syncRequired}" click="onSave()"
                 label="{visitCollection.commitRequired?'Save':'Sync'}"/>
        <mx:Button click="vs.selectedIndex=0;" label="Log out"/>
       </mx:ControlBar>
     </mx:Panel>
  </mx:Canvas>

    <!--   Visit detail view -- >
  <mx:Canvas>
     <mx:Panel width="100%" height="100%" title="Visit Details">
        <fx:DataForm dataProvider="{dg.selectedItem}">
        <fx:DataFormItem dataField="fullname" label="Salesman:"
                                                  enabled="false"/>
        <fx:DataFormItem dataField="fulladdress" label="Address:"
                                                  enabled="false"/>
        <fx:DataFormItem dataField="scheduled_date" label="Scheduled
                      Date:" formatString="shortDate" enabled="false"/>
        </fx:DataForm>
        <fx:DataForm dataProvider="{visit}" width="100%">
        <fx:DataFormItem dataField="visit_date" label="Visit Date:"
                                           formatString="shortDate"/>
        <fx:DataFormItem dataField="contact_name"
                                   label="Contact   Name:" width="100%"/>
        <fx:DataFormItem dataField="comments" label="Comments:"
```

```
                                                         width="100%">
         <mx:TextArea width="100%" height="100"/>
      </fx:DataFormItem>
      </fx:DataForm>
     <mx:ControlBar horizontalAlign="right">
      <ns1:NetworkStatus/>
      <mx:Button label="Back" click=
               "vs.selectedIndex=1;updateVisitSchedule(dg.selectedItem)"/>
     </mx:ControlBar>
    </mx:Panel>
 </mx:Canvas>

    <!--   Google Maps integration view-->
 <mx:Canvas>
   <mx:Panel width="100%" height="100%" title="Google Map">
   <maps:Map xmlns:maps="com.google.maps.*" id="map"
          mapevent_mapready="onMapReady(event)" width="100%" height="100%"
          key="ABQIAAAAthGneZS6I6ekX8SgzwL2HxSVN_sXTad_Y..."
          url="http://code.google.com/apis/maps/"/>
     <mx:ControlBar horizontalAlign="right">
     <ns1:NetworkStatus/>
     <mx:Button click="saveMap()" label="Save"/>
     <mx:Button click="vs.selectedIndex=1;" label="Back"/>
     </mx:ControlBar>
   </mx:Panel>
 </mx:Canvas>

    <!--   Saved Google map view-->
 <mx:Canvas>
    <mx:Panel id="map_image" width="100%" height="100%"
                                         title="Google Map">
    <mx:Image id="saved_map" width="100%" height="100%"
                              creationComplete="openMapImage()"/>
    <mx:ControlBar horizontalAlign="right">
       <ns1:NetworkStatus/>
       <mx:Button click="vs.selectedIndex=1;" label="Back"/>
    </mx:ControlBar>
    </mx:Panel>
 </mx:Canvas>
</mx:ViewStack>

<mx:Script>
   <![CDATA[
      import com.google.maps.overlays.Marker;
      import com.google.maps.InfoWindowOptions;
      import com.google.maps.LatLng;
      import com.google.maps.services.ClientGeocoder;
      import mx.graphics.codec.PNGEncoder;
      import com.google.maps.controls.ZoomControl;
      import com.farata.demo.pharmasales.dto.VisitDataDTO;
      import com.farata.demo.pharmasales.dto.VisitDTO;
      import com.farata.collections.OfflineDataCollection;
      import com.google.maps.services.GeocodingEvent;
      import mx.events.PropertyChangeEvent;
```

```
[Bindable]
public var visitDataCollection:OfflineDataCollection;
[Bindable]
public var visitCollection:OfflineDataCollection;
[Bindable]
public var visit:VisitDTO;

private function onSave():void {
   visitCollection.sync();
   visitDataCollection.updateLocalDB();
   visitDataCollection.backUp();
   visitDataCollection.resetState();
}

private function onDoubleClick():void {
   if (dg.selectedItem){
      vs.selectedIndex=2;
      calculateVisit(dg.selectedItem);
   }
}

private function updateVisitSchedule(obj:Object):void {
   var dto:VisitDataDTO=obj as VisitDataDTO;
   dto.comments=visit.comments;
}

private function calculateVisit(obj:Object):void {
   var dto:VisitDataDTO=obj as VisitDataDTO;
   for(var i:int=0; i < visitCollection.length; i++){
      var visitDto:VisitDTO=visitCollection[i]as VisitDTO;
      if (dto.id == visitDto.visit_schedule_id) {
         visit=visitDto;
         return ;
      }
   }
   visit=new VisitDTO();
   visit.visit_schedule_id=dto.id;
   visitCollection.addItem(visit);
}

private function initCollections():void {
    visitCollection=new OfflineDataCollection(
             "com.farata.demo.pharmasales.Visit",
                       "getVisitsBySalesman", VisitDTO);
   visitCollection.addEventListener(
             PropertyChangeEvent.PROPERTY_CHANGE, showStatus);
   visitDataCollection=new OfflineDataCollection(
             "com.farata.demo.pharmasales.VisitData",
             "getVisitDataBySalesman", VisitDataDTO);
   fill_onClick();
}

private function showStatus(evt:PropertyChangeEvent):void {
   if (evt.property == "statusMessage"){
      status=evt.newValue as String;
```

```
        }
    }

    private function fill_onClick():void {
        visitDataCollection.fill(username.text);
        visitCollection.fill(username.text);
    }

    private function googleMap_onClick():void {
        if (network.googleMapsConnected) {
            cursorManager.setBusyCursor();
            vs.selectedIndex=3;
            showAddress();
        }
        else {
            vs.selectedIndex=4;
            openMapImage();
        }
    }

    private function onLogon():void {
        initCollections();
        vs.selectedIndex=1;
    }

    private function onReset():void {
        username.text="Liz Anthony";
    }

    private function onMapReady(event:Event):void {
        map.setZoom(20);
        showAddress();
    }

    private function deleteMap():void {
        var dto:VisitDataDTO=dg.selectedItem as VisitDataDTO;
        var file:File= File.applicationStorageDirectory.resolvePath(
                                        dto.fulladdress + ".png");
        if (file.exists){
            file.deleteFile();
        }
    }

    private function saveMap():void {
        deleteMap();
        var bd:BitmapData=new BitmapData(map.width, map.height);
        bd.draw(map);
        var pngEncoder:PNGEncoder=new PNGEncoder();
        var ba:ByteArray=pngEncoder.encode(bd);
        var dto:VisitDataDTO=dg.selectedItem as VisitDataDTO;
        var file:File=
                File.applicationStorageDirectory.resolvePath(
                                        dto.fulladdress + ".png");
        var fileStream:FileStream=new FileStream();
        fileStream.open(file, FileMode.WRITE);
```

```
            fileStream.writeBytes(ba);
            fileStream.close();
            status="Google map image is saved to '" + file.nativePath + "'";
        }

        private function openMapImage():void {
            if (saved_map && saved_map.initialized){
                var dto:VisitDataDTO=dg.selectedItem as VisitDataDTO;
                var file:File=
                        File.applicationStorageDirectory.resolvePath(
                                                dto.fulladdress + ".png");
                saved_map.source=file.nativePath;
                map_image.title="Displaying '" + file.name + "'";
            }
        }

        private function hasMapImage():Boolean
        {
            var dto:VisitDataDTO=dg.selectedItem as VisitDataDTO;
            var file:File= File.applicationStorageDirectory.resolvePath(
                                                dto.fulladdress + ".png");
            return file.exists;
        }

        private function showAddress():void {
            if (map && map.initialized){
                var cg:ClientGeocoder=new ClientGeocoder();
                cg.addEventListener(
                        GeocodingEvent.GEOCODING_SUCCESS, onGeocodeSuccess);
                var dto:VisitDataDTO=dg.selectedItem as VisitDataDTO;
                cg.geocode(dto.fulladdress);
            }
        }

        private function onGeocodeSuccess(event:GeocodingEvent):void{
            cursorManager.removeBusyCursor();
            var point:LatLng=event.response.placemarks[0].point as LatLng;
            var marker:Marker=new Marker(point);
            map.addOverlay(marker);
            map.setCenter(point);
            var dto:VisitDataDTO=dg.selectedItem as VisitDataDTO;
            var opt:InfoWindowOptions=new InfoWindowOptions();
            opt.drawDefaultFrame=true;
            opt.contentHTML=dto.fulladdress;
            marker.openInfoWindow(opt);
        }
    ]]>
  </mx:Script>
</mx:WindowedApplication>
```

OfflineDataCollection

The Clear component library includes a descendant of `DataCollection` (described in Chapter 3), the `com.farata.collections.OfflineDataCollection` class. The class

`OfflineDataCollection` is responsible for performing data synchronization between the local and remote databases.

If the network connection is available, the method `fill()` gets the data from the server and the application creates the backup copy of the existing local database and creates a fresh one:

```
public override function fill(... args):AsyncToken {
      var changes:Array=getChangesFromLocalDB();
      syncRequired=changes.length > 0;
      if (!commitRequired && !syncRequired) {
         var act:AsyncToken=invoke(method, args);
         act.method="fill";
         return act;
      }else{
         fillFromLocalDB();
      }
   return null;
}
```

This function starts with getting the data from the local database. If this is the very first invocation, the array `changes` will be empty and no other function calls will be made.

If no modifications were made in the data grid with visit information and no unsynchronized changes exist in the local database, this function will just retrieve the data from the remote destination using `DataCollection`'s `invoke()` method.

How does `OfflineDataCollection` know that there are local changes to be synchronized? Each instance of `OfflineDataCollection` persists its data in a database table. When the application calls the function `OfflineDataCollection.backup()`, it copies this table to a backup database.

Comparing the content of the corresponding tables in the main and backup databases allows the application to find out whether the data is different, or in other words, whether data synchronization is required.

If the network connection is not available, the method `fill()` will get the visits data from the local database.

The class `OfflineDataCollection` uses the `com.farata.collections.LocalDBHelper` helper class for all database operations. You can find the source code of this class in the Clear Toolkit project *com.farata.components* at the SourceForge code repository (*http://sourceforge.net/projects/cleartoolkit/*).

When the connection is restored, the `OfflineDataCollection` object can synchronize the data in both directions: from the local storage to the server and back.

The property `commitRequired` specifies whether the local data were modified and should be synchronized with the server.

Example 9-13 contains the complete code of *OfflineDataCollection.as*. (Note that comments and import statements were removed in the interest of space.)

Example 9-13. OfflineDataCollection.as

```
package com.farata.collections {

   [Event(name="result", type="mx.rpc.events.ResultEvent")]
   [Event(name="fault", type="mx.rpc.events.FaultEvent")]
   [Event(name="propertyChange", type="mx.events.PropertyChangeEvent")]

   [Bindable(event="propertyChange")]
   public class OfflineDataCollection extends DataCollection
   {
      private var _dtoClass:Class;
      private var _syncRequired:Boolean;

      public function OfflineDataCollection(destination:String=null,
                              method:String=null, dtoClass:Class=null){

         this.destination=destination;
         this.method=method;
         this.dtoClass=dtoClass;
      }

      public function get syncRequired():Boolean
      {
         return _syncRequired;
      }

      public function set syncRequired(value:Boolean):void{
         var oldValue:Boolean=_syncRequired;
         if (oldValue != value){
           _syncRequired=value;
           dispatchEvent(PropertyChangeEvent.createUpdateEvent(this,
                              "syncRequired", oldValue, value));
         }
      }

      public function get dtoClass():Class{
         return _dtoClass;
      }

      public function set dtoClass(dtoClass:Class):void{
         _dtoClass=dtoClass;
      }

      public function set doFill(bFill:Boolean):void{
         if (bFill){
            fill();
         }
      }

      public override function fill(... args):AsyncToken{
         var changes:Array=getChangesFromLocalDB();
         syncRequired=changes.length > 0;

         if (!commitRequired && !syncRequired){
            var act:AsyncToken=invoke(method, args);
```

```
            act.method="fill";
            return act;
        }
        else {
            fillFromLocalDB();
        }
        return null;
    }

    public override function sync():AsyncToken {
        updateLocalDB();
        commitRequired = false;
        var act:AsyncToken=syncOfflineChanges();
        return act;
    }

    public function updateLocalDB():void {
        var conn:SQLConnection=LocalDBHelper.openDBConnection();
        try {
            for(var i:int=0; i < deletes.length; i++) {
                LocalDBHelper.deleteDTO(conn, destination, method,
                                        deletes[i].previousVersion);
            }
            for(i=0; i < inserts.length; i++){
                LocalDBHelper.insertDTO(conn, destination, method,
                                            inserts[i].newVersion);
            }
            for(i=0; i < updates.length; i++) {
                LocalDBHelper.updateDTO(conn, destination, method,
                        updates[i].previousVersion, updates[i].newVersion);
            }
            dispatchEvent(PropertyChangeEvent.createUpdateEvent(this,
                    "statusMessage", "", "Local database is updated"));
        }
        finally {
            if (conn != null) {
                conn.close();
            }
        }
    }

    public function fillFromLocalDB():void {
        var conn:SQLConnection=LocalDBHelper.openDBConnection();
        source=LocalDBHelper.readDTOs(conn, destination, method, dtoClass);
        dispatchEvent(PropertyChangeEvent.createUpdateEvent(this,
                    "statusMessage", "", "Retrieved from local database"));
    }

    public function backUp():void {
        LocalDBHelper.backUp(destination, method, dtoClass);
        syncRequired=false;
    }

    public override function resetState():void {
        super.resetState();
```

```
    commitRequired=false;
}

protected override function createRemoteObject():RemoteObject {
    var ro:RemoteObject=super.createRemoteObject();
    ro.addEventListener(ResultEvent.RESULT, onResult);
    return ro;
}

private function onResult(evt:ResultEvent):void {
    if (evt.token.method == "fill") {
        var dtos:Array=evt.result.source;
        if (dtos.length > 0) {
            var conn:SQLConnection=LocalDBHelper.openDBConnection();
            try {
                LocalDBHelper.createTable(conn, destination, method,
                                                                dtos[0]);
                LocalDBHelper.clearTable(conn, destination, method,
                                                                dtos[0]);
                for(var i:int=0; i < dtos.length; i++) {
                    LocalDBHelper.insertDTO(conn, destination,
                                                   method, dtos[i]);
                }
            }
            finally {
                if (conn != null) {
                    conn.close();
                    backUp();
                }
            }
        }
        dispatchEvent(PropertyChangeEvent.createUpdateEvent(this,
                "statusMessage", "", "Retrieved from remote server"));
    }
}

protected override function ro_onFault(evt:FaultEvent):void {
    if (evt.token.method == "fill"){
        fillFromLocalDB();
    }
}

private function syncOfflineChanges():AsyncToken {
    var changeObjects:Array=getChangesFromLocalDB();
    if (changeObjects.length > 0) {
        var ro:RemoteObject=null;
        if (destination == null || destination.length == 0)
            throw new Error("No destination specified");

        ro=new RemoteObject();
        ro.destination=destination;
        ro.concurrency="last";
        ro.addEventListener(ResultEvent.RESULT,
                                   syncOfflineChanges_onResult);
        ro.addEventListener(FaultEvent.FAULT,
```

```
                                    syncOfflineChanges_onFault);
        ro.showBusyCursor=true;
        var operation:AbstractOperation=ro.getOperation(syncMethod);
        operation.arguments=[changeObjects];
        if ((operation is IContextOperation) && headers != null){
           var co:IContextOperation=IContextOperation(operation);
           co.context.headers=headers;
        }
        var act:AsyncToken=operation.send();
        return act;
     }
     return null;
  }

  private function syncOfflineChanges_onResult(event:ResultEvent):void{
     backUp();
     resetState();
     dispatchEvent(PropertyChangeEvent.createUpdateEvent(this,
                        "statusMessage", "", "Saved on remote server"));
  }

  private function syncOfflineChanges_onFault(event:FaultEvent):void{
     var changes:Array=getChangesFromLocalDB();
     syncRequired=changes.length > 0;
  }


  private function getChangesFromLocalDB():Array{
     var changeObjects:Array=new Array();
     var conn:SQLConnection=LocalDBHelper.openDBConnection();
     var newDtos:Array=LocalDBHelper.readDTOs(conn, destination,
                                                   method, dtoClass);
     conn.close();
     conn=LocalDBHelper.openBackupDBConnection();
     var oldDtos:Array=LocalDBHelper.readDTOs(conn, destination,
                                                   method, dtoClass);
     conn.close();
     var names:Array=null;
     if (oldDtos.length > 0){
        names=LocalDBHelper.getPropertyNames(oldDtos[0]);
     }
     else if (newDtos.length > 0){
        names=LocalDBHelper.getPropertyNames(newDtos[0]);
     }
     else{
        return changeObjects;
     }
     for(var i:int=0; i < oldDtos.length; i++) {
        var found:Boolean=false;
        for(j=0; j < newDtos.length; j++){
           if (oldDtos[i].uid == newDtos[j].uid){
              found=true;
              var changedProperties:Array=new Array();
              for(var k:int=0; k < names.length; k++){
                 if (!compareObject(oldDtos[i][names[k]],
```

```
                                        newDtos[j][names[k]])){
                        changedProperties.push(names[k]);
                    }
                }
                if (changedProperties.length > 0){
                    var changeObject:ChangeObject=new
                ChangeObject(ChangeObject.UPDATE, newDtos[j], oldDtos[i]);

                    changeObject.changedPropertyNames=changedProperties;
              changeObjects.push(changeObject);
                   }
                break;
            }
        }
        if (!found){
            changeObject=new ChangeObject(ChangeObject.DELETE,
                      null, oldDtos[i]);
            changeObject.changedPropertyNames=names;
            changeObjects.push(changeObject);
        }
    }

    for(var j:int=0; j < newDtos.length; j++) {
        found=false;
        for(i=0; i < oldDtos.length; i++){
            if (oldDtos[i].uid == newDtos[j].uid){
                found=true;
                break;
            }
        }
        if (!found){
            changeObject=new ChangeObject(ChangeObject.CREATE,
                                          newDtos[j], null);
            changeObject.changedPropertyNames=names;
            changeObjects.push(changeObject);
        }
    }
    return changeObjects;
}

private static function compareObject(obj1:Object,obj2:Object):Boolean{
    var buffer1:ByteArray=new ByteArray();
    buffer1.writeObject(obj1);
    var buffer2:ByteArray=new ByteArray();
    buffer2.writeObject(obj2);

    var size:uint=buffer1.length;
    if (buffer1.length == buffer2.length){
        buffer1.position=0;
        buffer2.position=0;

        while(buffer1.position < size){
            var v1:int=buffer1.readByte();
            if (v1 != buffer2.readByte()){
                return false;
```

```
                }
            }
            return true;
        }
        return false;
    }
}
}
```

The function `fillFromLocalDB()` asks the `LocalDBHelper` to read the DTOs that were saved in the local database:

```
source=LocalDBHelper.readDTOs(conn, destination, method, dtoClass);
```

The local database stores the DTOs' data in tables. The names of the tables are formed automatically by `LocalDBHelper`. It glues together the name of the destination, the method, and the DTO. For example, if you look at the content of the local database using SQLite Manager, you'll see there the following tables (one table per instance of `OfflineDataCollection`), as shown in Figure 9-15:

```
com_demo_pharmasales__Visit__getVisitBySalesman__VisitDTO

com_demo_pharmasales__VisitData_getVisitDataBSaleseman_VisitDatDTO
```

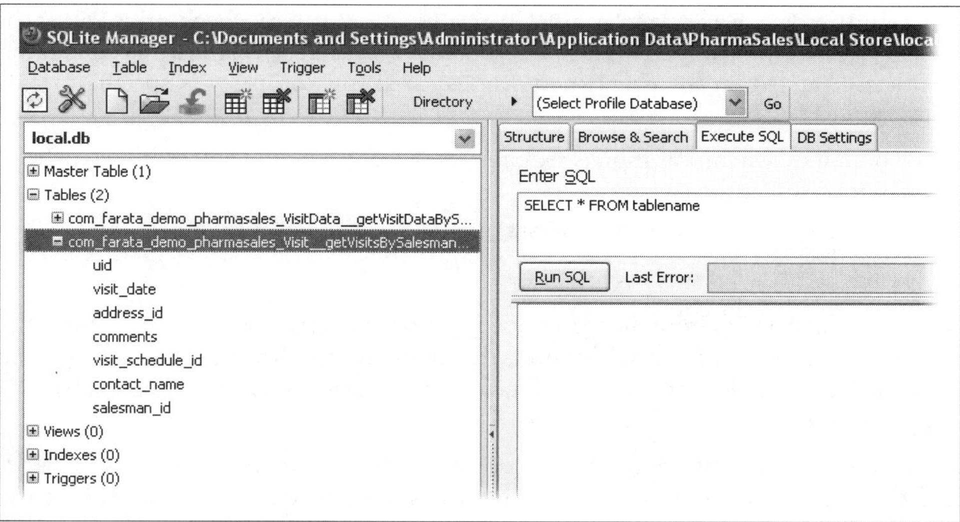

Figure 9-15. DTOs in the local cache

The function `getChangesFromLocalDB()` connects to both main and backup databases and reads the DTOs that store the data for this `OfflineDataCollection` (table names are the same in both databases). Then it finds the names of the DTOs' properties and compares their values. The `uid` value of DTOs in the main and backup databases never changes, but the values of regular properties might differ if the user were working with the application in the disconnected mode. If some property values are not the same, data synchronization with the remote database is required.

The names of the local databases are hardcoded in the `LocalDBHelper`: *local.db* and *local.db.bak*. This doesn't cause any conflicts, as each AIR application has its own storage directory with a unique name, and these two databases are stored there.

The function creates a collection of `ChangeObject` instances, and each of them contains the old and new values of the modified DTO. Collection of these `ChangeObjects` will be sent to the server, and the rest of the processing will be handled in Java code, the same way as was done in the CDB version of Café Townsend.

If the object exists only in the backup database, this means that the user deleted this record, and this particular instance of `ChangeObject` will be marked as deleted and will contain only the old DTO instance.

If the object exists only in the main database, this means that the user has inserted a new record, and this particular instance of `ChangeObject` will be marked as created and will contain only the new DTO instance.

On return from `changesFromLocalDB()`, the function `fill()` checks the values of `commitRequired` (this property is derived from `DataCollection`; it signals that something has been changed on the client) and `syncRequired` (this property is specific to AIR applications).

If no commit or synchronization is required, the `fill()` function will get the data from the remote destination:

```
var act:AsyncToken=invoke(method, args);
act.method="fill";
return act;
```

When the data arrives from the server, the function `onResult()` is invoked. If this is the very first invocation of the application, the main and the backup databases will be created, and the table that stores the data for this DTO is populated. Then the backup copy of this table is created in the backup database.

If commit or synchronization is required, the function `fillFromLocalDB()` is invoked, and the property `source` of `DataCollection` will get all the data. The user will see the data if `source` is bound to a UI component:

```
source=LocalDBHelper.readDTOs(conn, destination, method, dtoClass);
```

The function `sync()` in `OfflineDataCollection` updates the local database and calls a function to synchronize the local changes with the remote server:

```
updateLocalDB();
commitRequired = false;  //we already saved the data locally
var act:AsyncToken=syncOfflineChanges();
```

The function syncOfflineChanges() creates an array of ChangeObject instances based on the data from the *local.db* and sends it to the remote destination using Flex RemoteObject. If remote data were successfully updated, the function syncOffline Changes_onResult() will copy the data from *local.db* to *local.db.bak* to make them identical again.

Integrating with Google Maps

The *PharmaSales* application offers an additional convenience to the salespeople from Acme Pharm: they can find the address of the medical office to visit without leaving *PharmaSales*. The Google Maps API for Flash has proven to be pretty simple to use with Flex and AIR.

You can find the detailed tutorial to this API at *http://tinyurl.com/65ne8j*, and there's no need to repeat it here. But it's worth highlighting some important concepts required to understand how such AIR/Maps mashups can be created.

To integrate your application with Google Maps, you have to get a special Maps API key from Google. Look for the following fragment in the source code of *PharmaSales.mxml* to see how we used our key (obtain yours to run the *PharmaSales* application):

```
<maps:Map xmlns:maps="com.google.maps.*" id="map"
mapevent_mapready="onMapReady(event)" width="100%" height="100%" key=
"ABQIAAAAthGneZS6I6ekX8SgzwL2HxSVN_sXTad_Y81zCJbFz..."
url="http://code.google.com/apis/maps/"/>
```

The url property here is the one that's used during the registration at Google for obtaining the API key.

Check the library path of the project *air.offline.demo*; it includes a file *map_flex_1_8c.swc*, which supports communication between Flex/AIR applications and Google Maps.

When the Map component is initialized, it dispatches the mapevent_mapready event, and the application calls the function showAddress(), which gets the selected address from the data grid, or to be more specific from its data provider, and asks the ClientGeo coder to find the map of this address:

```
cg.geocode(dto.fulladdress);
```

When the map is found, the ClientGeocoder object receives the event GeocodingEvent.GEOCODING_SUCCESS, and the function onGeocodeSuccess() displays the map with a marker at the address location in the center:

```
private function onGeocodeSuccess(event:GeocodingEvent):void{
   cursorManager.removeBusyCursor();
   var point:LatLng=event.response.placemarks[0].point as LatLng;
   var marker:Marker=new Marker(point);
   map.addOverlay(marker);
   map.setCenter(point);
```

```
        var dto:VisitDataDTO=dg.selectedItem as VisitDataDTO;
        var opt:InfoWindowOptions=new InfoWindowOptions();
        opt.drawDefaultFrame=true;
        opt.contentHTML=dto.fulladdress;
        marker.openInfoWindow(opt);
    }
```

The function `onGeocodeSuccess()` uses a helper class, `InfoWindowOptions`, from the Google Maps API to display the address on the marker, as shown in Figure 9-16.

Even though the *PharmaSales* application may not always be connected to the Internet, the salespeople need at least a static map of the area. Before hitting the road, a salesperson can find the required map online, press the Save button, and save the map in a local file as an image. The code of the function `saveMap()` is what enables this:

```
    private function saveMap():void {
        deleteMap();
        var bd:BitmapData=new BitmapData(map.width, map.height);
        bd.draw(map);
        var pngEncoder:PNGEncoder=new PNGEncoder();
        var ba:ByteArray=pngEncoder.encode(bd);
        var dto:VisitDataDTO=dg.selectedItem as VisitDataDTO;
        var file:File=
                File.applicationStorageDirectory.resolvePath(
                                     dto.fulladdress + ".png");
        var fileStream:FileStream=new FileStream();
        fileStream.open(file, FileMode.WRITE);
        fileStream.writeBytes(ba);
        fileStream.close();
        status="Google map image is saved to '" + file.nativePath + "'";
    }
```

If a salesperson selects a row in the visits data grid (`dg.selectedItem`) and clicks the Google Maps button in disconnected mode, the `openMapImage()` function will display the previously saved image of the map for the selected address (`dto.fulladdress`):

```
    private function openMapImage():void {
        if (saved_map && saved_map.initialized){
            var dto:VisitDataDTO=dg.selectedItem as VisitDataDTO;
            var file:File=
                 File.applicationStorageDirectory.resolvePath(
                                        dto.fulladdress + ".png");
            saved_map.source=file.nativePath;
            map_image.title="Displaying '" + file.name + "'";
        }
    }
```

The title of the map will prompt the user that she is watching an image, not a live map. Figure 9-17's screenshot was taken in disconnected mode (the server status indicator is green because we ran the Tomcat server on the local computer). The title of the view now reads, "Displaying '12 Main St., Manville, NJ.png,'" which is the name of the local file when the image of the map has been saved.

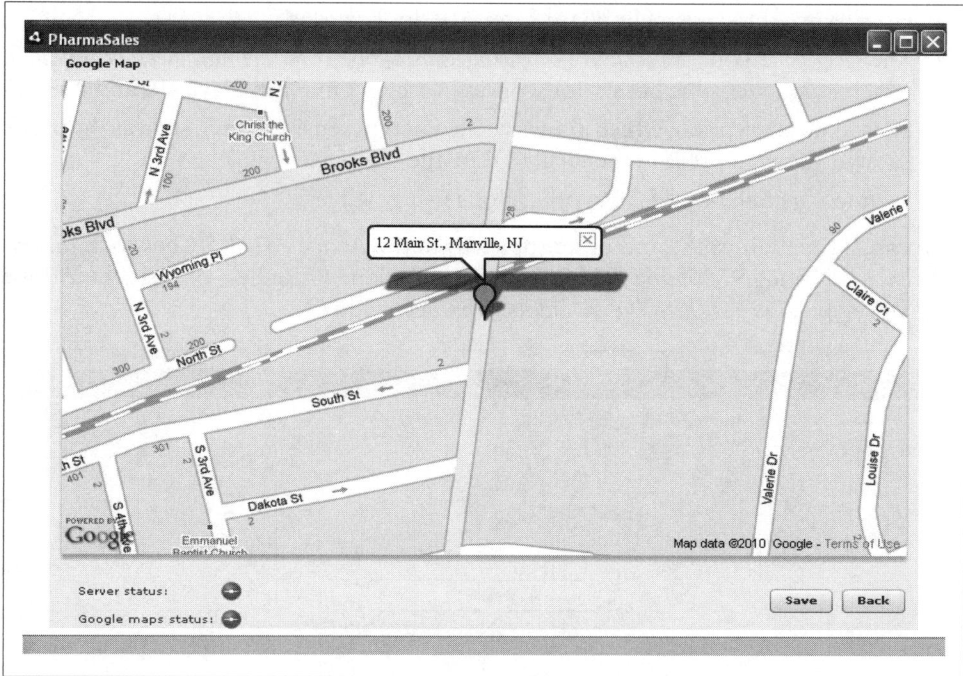

Figure 9-16. Real Google Maps view

If the connection is available, the salesperson can enjoy working with the real Google Maps website without leaving *PharmaSales*.

Summary

The main deliverable of this chapter is a solution for data synchronization of AIR/BlazeDS applications. To better understand this solution, you reviewed the basics of AIR 1.5 development. Now you have a reference implementation of the application that may help you in building AIR-based systems—even if your users are not working as salespeople for a pharmaceutical company. By the time this book is printed, AIR 2.0 will be released and we are sure that you'll enjoy working with it.

In no way should you treat this chapter as a complete tutorial; your education in the AIR development field has just begun.

Following is a laundry list of topics that you should get familiar with on your own:

- `<mx:HTML>`, which is a component that allows you to build an AIR web browser in several minutes
- AIR Updater; the class `flash.desktop.Updater` controls the updating of the application installed on the client's computer

- How to use the system clipboard from AIR applications
- The Text Layout Framework (*http://labs.adobe.com/technologies/textlayout/*), which is an extensible library for working with text in Flash Player 10 and AIR 1.5
- Local data encryption, which allows you to encrypt sensitive data, such as the user's password, and store it in the local SQLite file
- Seamless installation of AIR applications using badges

You can learn about these and other topics from the *Adobe AIR 1.5 Cookbook (http://oreilly.com/catalog/9780596522513)* by David Tucker (O'Reilly), or visit the Adobe AIR Developer Center (*http://www.adobe.com/devnet/air/*).

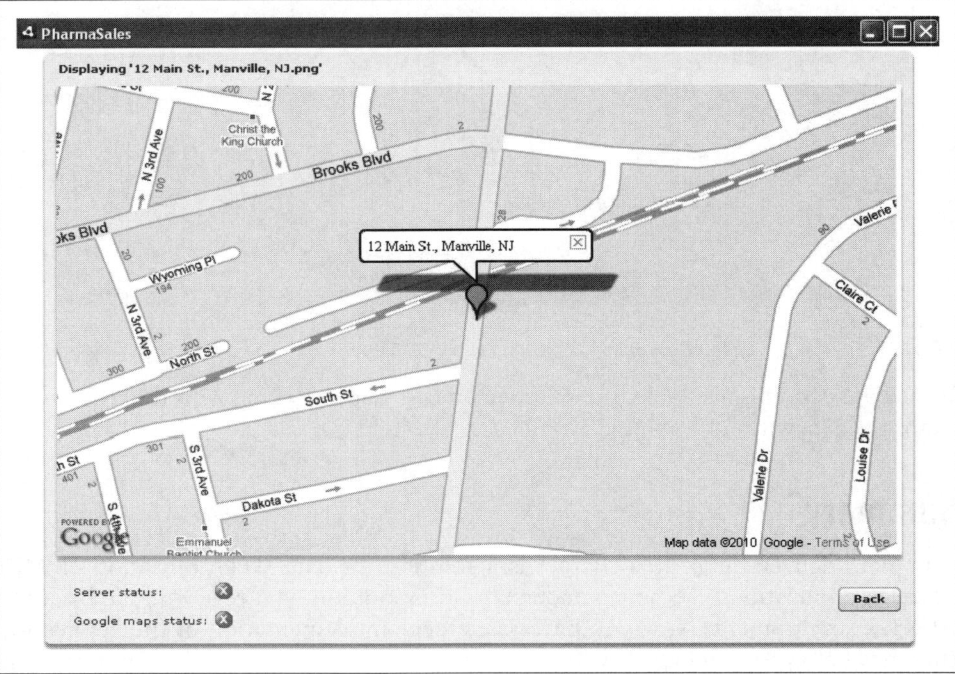

Figure 9-17. Saved map image

CHAPTER 10
Developing Flex Applications for LiveCycle Enterprise Suite

Good design can't fix a broken business model.

—Jeffrey Veen

Adobe LiveCycle Enterprise Suite (ES) as an enterprise server platform is targeted at automation of business processes. One example of a business process is a hardware retail store that sells nails and hammers. The retailer orders the goods online from one of the known suppliers. Assume that an explicit approval of the *supplier* is required for each ordered item. Because the supplier wants to be able to fulfill all the orders, the supplier attempts to predict the demand.

To that end, the supplier monitors the inventory and, when the level is beyond a certain threshold, reorders the items from a *manufacturer*. The supplier's orders also need to be approved by the manufacturer. The *activities* between the companies occur in a predefined sequence: order-approval-reorder-approval. On a more granular level, within each company there is a certain business process as well: receiving orders, ordering materials and parts, production, quality assurance, invoicing, shipping, and so forth.

Business process automation assumes software-based modeling of the process as well as software-based enforcement of the model that ensures that the process activities are consistently handled by the process *participants*: retailer, supplier, manufacturer, and so forth. Often, such software is called *workflow* or *business process management* (*BPM*) software.

Unlike other workflow products, LiveCycle ES features unparalleled integration with PDF processing and Adobe Flex. Accordingly, the combination of Flex and LiveCycle technologies becomes a natural choice for many enterprises that require productive workflow solutions featuring a rich user experience.

This chapter focuses on how to use Flex to support human-centric business processes in LiveCycle ES and on the most essential enterprise process management topics. After a brief introduction of LiveCycle ES, the chapter illustrates two scenarios:

- How to build Flex applications that work in concert with a LiveCycle ES frontend—LiveCycle Workspace. This scenario requires minimal development effort, but it locks you into the capabilities of the Workspace.
- How to embed LiveCycle ES functionality into your own Flex application. This scenario assumes deeper involvement in the LiveCycle API and more coding, but it opens unlimited integration opportunities.

By the end of this chapter, you will understand:

- How to extend LiveCycle ES with custom components
- How to support user and group management from the external enterprise repository
- How to use LiveCycle ES *events* to synchronize the processes in the publisher/subscriber style

This chapter was written about LiveCycle ES 8.2, because the version branded as LiveCycle ES2 was not available at the time of this writing. LiveCycle ES2 improves the productivity of developers in various workflows, substantially reducing the number of steps needed to populate a form, design a parallel approval process, get attachments from an initial task, and more. The Eclipse-based Workspace introduces a new concept: the *Application Model*, which eliminates the need to separately manage forms, processes, and assets. You now can deploy applications without the need to leave the Workbench. Please refer to the latest LiveCycle ES2 documentation (*http://www.adobe.com/products/livecycle*).

Business Process Example: Vacation Request

In this simple scenario, a company employee requests a vacation. The manager must approve or reject the request, and the employee must acknowledge the decision, completing the process. In business process management lingo, the *process assigns tasks*: to the manager (to review the incoming vacation request) and to the employee (to review and acknowledge the manager's decision). See Figure 10-1.

The diagram of the corresponding *SimpleVacationRequest* is presented in Figure 10-1. It has two user activities: *Manager's Review* and *Employee's Review*, each requiring a custom UI (user interface) application to communicate the data between the user and the process management software.

Figure 10-2 illustrates a sample UI that could be used for the manager's review: name, email, department, vacation type, and date range are all completed automatically

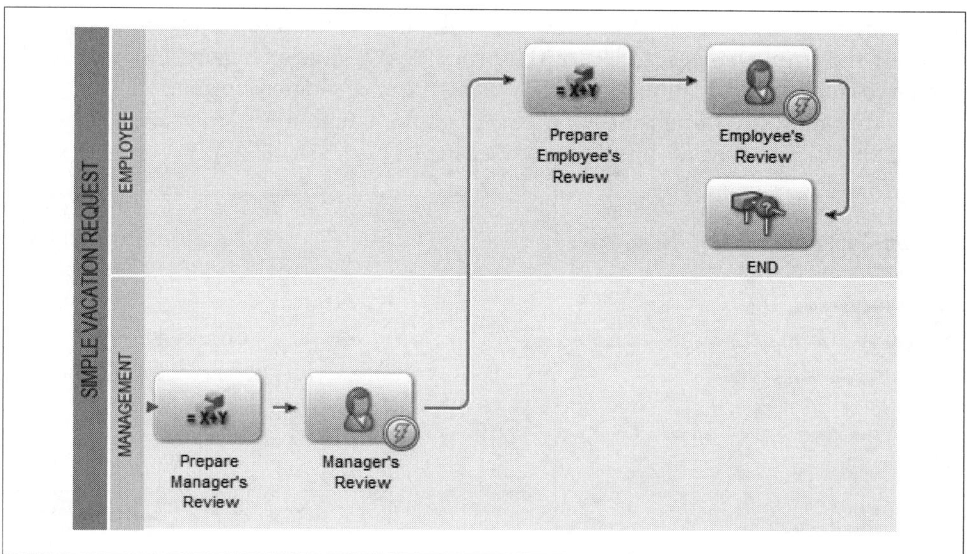

Figure 10-1. Diagram of the SimpleVacationRequest

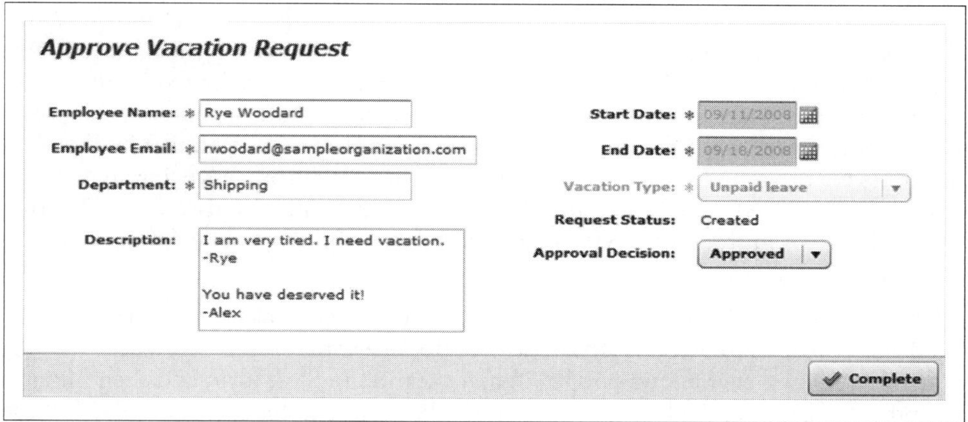

Figure 10-2. The UI of the vacation request approval

beforehand. The manager can append comments to the optional description field and pick either "approved" or "rejected" as the approval decision. Finally, the manager clicks the Complete button to send the decision to the system.

The employee review/acknowledgment screen might look almost identical to Figure 10-2, except that the Approval Decision combo box would be disabled and the title word "Approve" would yield to the humble "Review". To communicate acknowledgment, the employee would click Complete, indicating his awareness of the manager's decision.

But wait: how does the vacation request make it into the system in the first place? Doesn't the employee need a UI for that, too? Yes, of course. Figure 10-3 shows the screen to submit the vacation request. By using the user's login information, the system might automatically initialize the employee name, email, and department. The employee specifies the vacation type and date range.

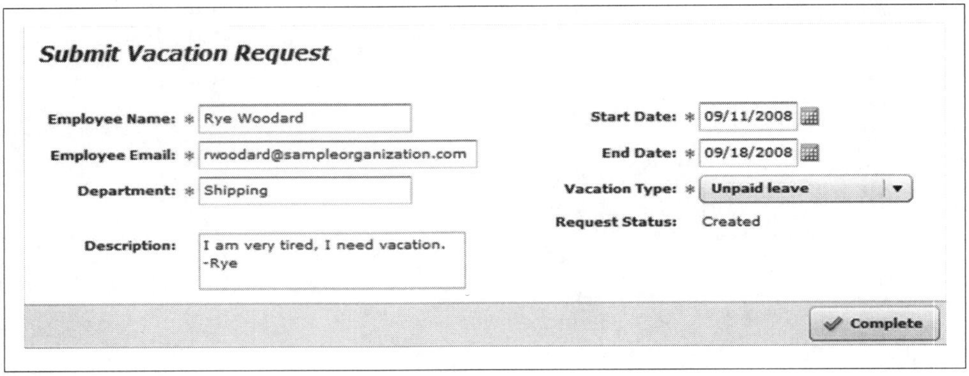

Figure 10-3. The UI of the vacation request submission

All three use cases are supported by a single Flex application, *VacationRequest.swf*, discussed in detail later in this chapter. Make no mistake, however: the initial submission of the request is *not* a part of the process diagram. That's right, from the process management engine's point of view, the process instance (for this specific request) starts only *after* the request is submitted. Does it sound confusing? Well, think of it this way: a process is a program with input parameters. If you start the process using an API, you can pass hardcoded values, read them from the external files, and so forth. Alternatively, the program can pop up a dialog box in front of the employee, forcing him to enter the values.

Think of a web service with a method `startProcess(vacationRequestData)`. The web service is oblivious to preparation of the `vacationRequestData`. Imagine a user-friendly software program that allows you to fill in a vacation request form and then initiates the process instance by calling the web service. What might this software be in the case of the LiveCycle ES? One option is to write a custom program from scratch; another is to use LiveCycle Workspace ES, as explained in the next section.

Meet LiveCycle Workspace ES

Using the LiveCycle ES API, you can start the process instance, pull all tasks assigned for a particular user, complete a task, forward it to another user, and so on. But APIs do not help the end user. That is why almost any workflow product comes with an off-the-shelf generic frontend that allows participants to use the workflow engine without paying a dime to an API-savvy geek.

Recognizing the universal need for such software, Adobe created a generic process management frontend program called *LiveCycle Workspace ES*. It is written entirely in Flex and its sources are part of the LiveCycle ES installation (later in the chapter, you will learn how to rebuild the Workspace from scratch). Figure 10-4 illustrates the default look of the LiveCycle Workspace.

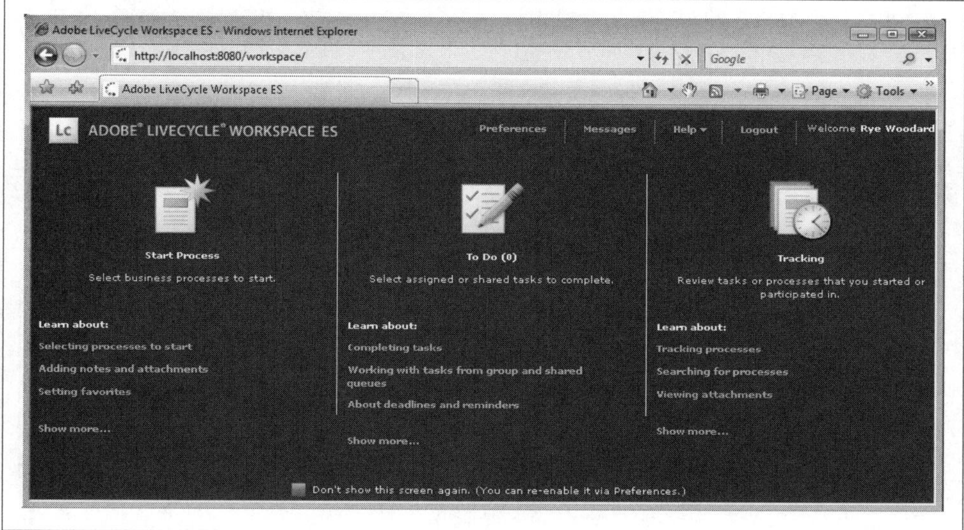

Figure 10-4. Default screen of the LiveCycle Workspace ES

Importantly, LiveCycle ES allows you, during the process design, to nominate a Flex subapplication that the Workspace loads and activates whenever a user picks a particular task from the To Do list (otherwise called a queue), as shown in Figure 10-4.

At Farata Systems, we call these applications *Flexlets*. Once the Flexlet is loaded, Workspace initializes it with the relevant process data. When the user is satisfied with the data entered, she clicks Complete, and Workspace transmits the data captured by the Flexlet back to the process.

Figure 10-5 illustrates the task queue of Alex Pink, one of the example users automatically configured by the turnkey installation of LiveCycle ES. Double-click the task line to initiate the underlying Flexlet and review the vacation request issued by Rye Woodard, another user, also shown in Figure 10-5.

Meet the Flexlet: Vacation Request

Take a look at Figure 10-6. It illustrates the state of the Workspace screen when Workspace has loaded the *SimpleVacationRequest* Flexlet and added it to the Workspace's Display List under the Form tab. Notice two buttons added by the Workspace to the

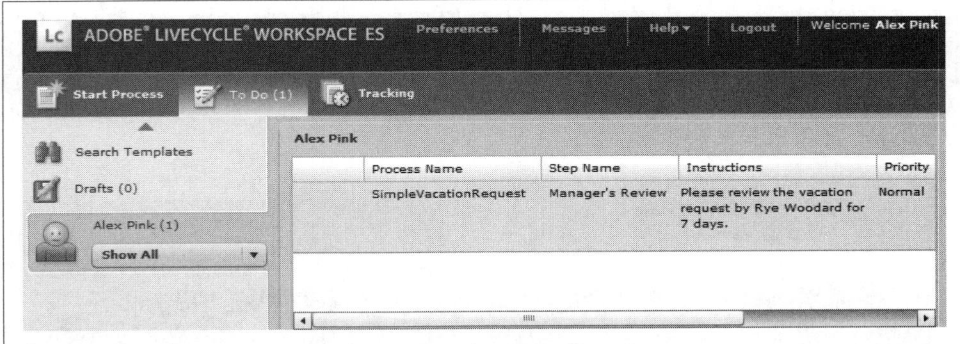

Figure 10-5. Task queue of a manager (Alex Pink)

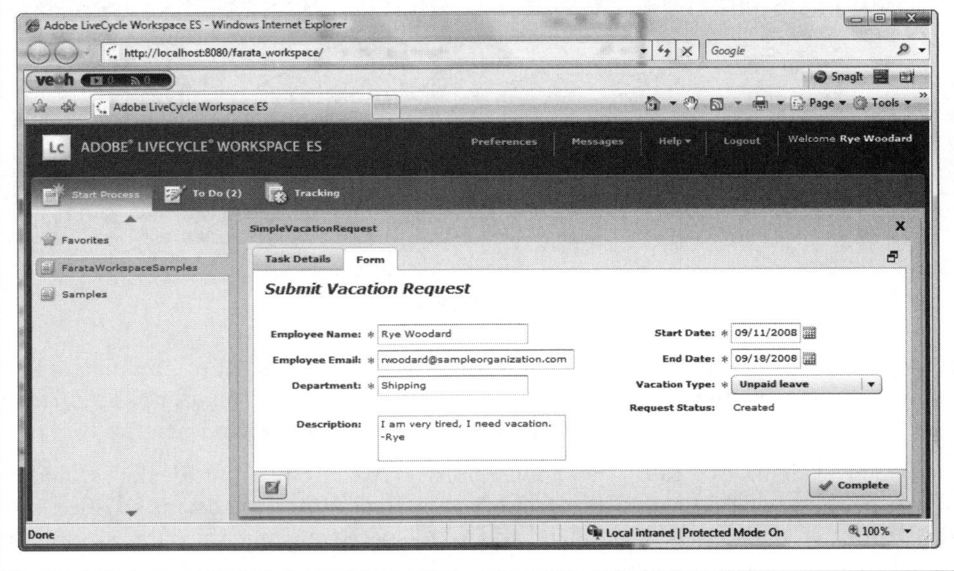

Figure 10-6. Workspace with the activated Flexlet (SimpleVacationRequest.swf, employee's view)

control bar of the *SimpleVacationRequest* panel: a small Save button on the left, and the Complete button on the right. The Save button preserves the draft of the incomplete request for further use (accumulating under the user's To Do list), and the Complete button passes the request data to the process.

Also, notice the title of the form: Submit Vacation Request. It corresponds to the visual state of the Workspace when the employee, Rye Woodard, enters the initial request (to start the process). In particular, date fields appear enabled so that an employee can enter the vacation period.

Compare this screen with the one presenting the manager's view, Figure 10-7, where the manager, Alex Pink, makes the approval decision. The date fields are disabled, and one extra control—the Approval Decision combo box—is on the form. Notice the similarity between the screens to emphasize the reuse of the single Flexlet for different users' activities within the process.

In the earlier releases of LiveCycle, PDF forms were the main mode for capturing data from the user. Flexlets are a step up from PDF forms, because they offer the user a rich experience. However, despite the word "form," a Flexlet may have nothing to do with the form at all. All that a Flexlet is required to do is to accept an XML document from the Workspace upon initialization and send it back when a user clicks Complete or Save.

Again, note the most important difference between the two appearances of the Flexlet. Figure 10-6 represents the collection of data from the employee that *precedes* the start of the process. On the contrary, Figure 10-7 corresponds to the *Manager's Review* activity of the process (instance), which has already started.

Now that you are acquainted with Workspace and Flexlets, let's look at the broader landscape of LiveCycle ES. After that, we'll return to discussing the design of the *SimpleVacationRequest* process and the matching Flexlet.

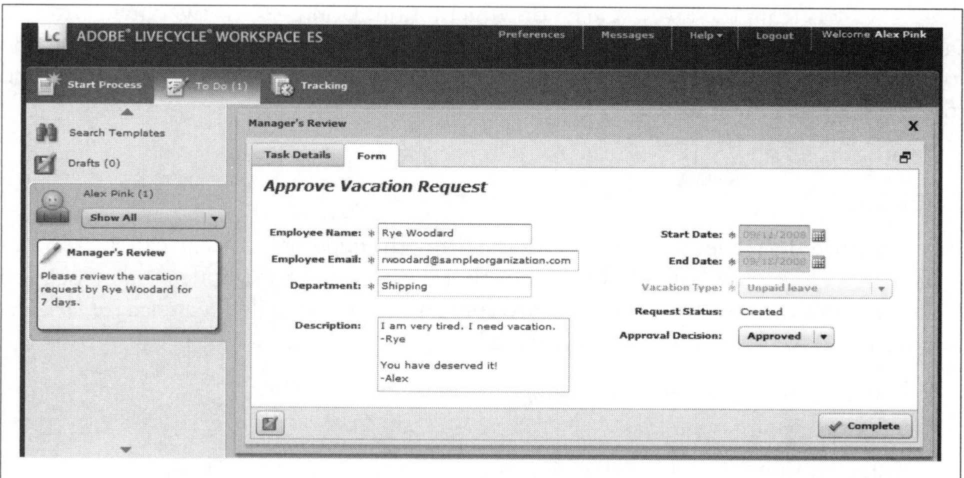

Figure 10-7. Workspace with the activated Flexlet (SimpleVacationRequest.swf, manager's view)

LiveCycle ES Architecture in a Nutshell

Architecturally, LiveCycle ES is an extendable service container and a set of tools to use these services. From the functional point of view, LiveCycle ES services can be grouped as *foundation services* and *solution services*.

Foundation services provide basic functionality such as querying or modifying a database, reading and writing to the filesystem, sending and receiving messages from a Java Message Service (JMS) queue, or sending and receiving emails.

Solution services relevant to this chapter are further grouped by LiveCycle ES as two *components*:

- Process Management ES
- Data Services ES

Data Services is software that enables messaging between a Flex frontend and a Java application server. It was known as Flex Data Services in the previous releases of Flex. The services of the former component, Process Management ES, allow you to programmatically start an instance of the process, query tasks available for a given user, complete the tasks, retry the stalled tasks or terminate them, and more. Importantly, any business process that you design automatically becomes a new service, with a single operation, `invoke()`.

All current implementations of LiveCycle ES are built on top of JEE server technology and require an EJB container. For the full list of LiveCycle ES 8.2 services, you can view online references at *http://help.adobe.com/en_US/livecycle/8.2/services.pdf*.

The ecosystem of LiveCycle ES service components, tools, and technologies shown in Figure 10-8 is from the LiveCycle ES documentation. Don't get overwhelmed with the number of the diagram blocks, such as those for Forms ES, Digital Signatures ES, and other *solution components* that deal exclusively with PDF technology; these are beyond the scope of this book.

Endpoints

Services hosted by LiveCycle ES get invoked through *endpoints*. You can call the services using the Java API and SOAP. On top of that, LiveCycle ES facilitates the invocation of services by sending an email or by dropping a file in a so-called *watched folder*. The service can have many different endpoints:

- EJB endpoint (otherwise called the Java endpoint)
- SOAP endpoint
- Email endpoint
- Watched folder endpoint

Notice the unfortunate terminology conflict between Flex and LiveCycle developers. Flex developers know endpoints as channel-specific artifacts, such as the AMF endpoint or the HTTP endpoint. Meanwhile, LiveCycle ES folks think of the endpoints *per service*. From the Flex perspective, LiveCycle ES endpoints look more like a Flex *destination*, which in the Flex world is an order of magnitude smaller than an endpoint.

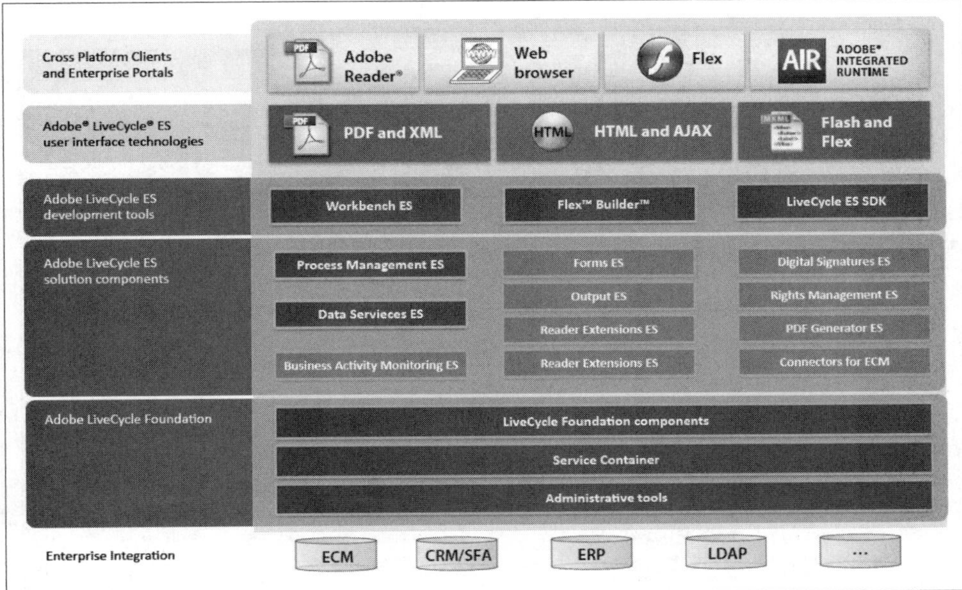

Figure 10-8. LiveCycle ES ecosystem

For further convenience, LiveCycle ES supports a universal Flex remoting destination, so you can invoke the service's methods via the `RemoteObject` tag. This destination is serviced by the `MessageBroker` of the web application *remoting*, deployed as a part of LiveCycle ES installation with the following URL:

> *//`<server>`:`<port>`/remoting/messagebroker/amf*

The previously mentioned (LiveCycle ES) endpoints are applicable to any service. As mentioned already, any LiveCycle ES *process* is also a service, albeit with a single operation—`invoke()`. To start a LiveCycle ES *process* through the LiveCycle Workspace ES, you must add an additional `TaskManager` *endpoint*. Figure 10-9 shows a snapshot of the LiveCycle administration UI after adding the `TaskManager` endpoint. The rest of the endpoints get created for you automatically.

Custom Services

You are not limited to existing LiveCycle ES services. The component model of LiveCycle ES is easy to extend with custom services. Custom services are packaged and deployed as JAR files. These JAR files are also known as *data service components*, each carrying one or more services. Using Java you can write your own services, jar them along with a component descriptor, and deploy them into LiveCycle ES.

For instance, if you need to query the status of the purchase order, you may use the foundational Java Database Connectivity (JDBC) service. Alternatively, you can write

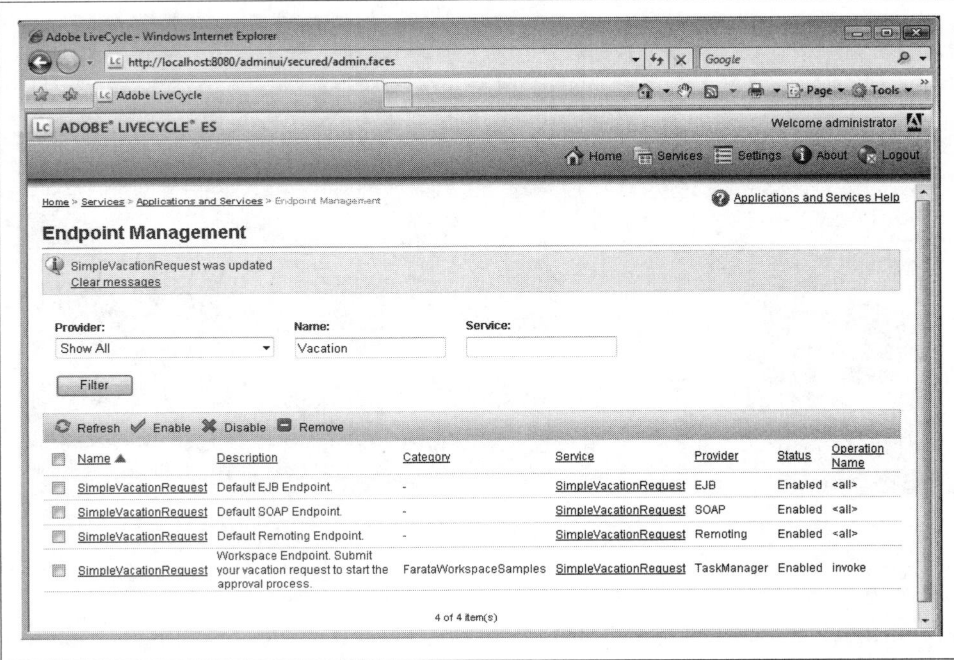

Figure 10-9. Endpoints of the SimpleVacationRequest process (service)

your own Java class with JDBC code and expose its public methods as operations of your custom service. Then, while modeling the business process, you can seamlessly mix the services provided by LiveCycle ES with your own. Every business process is a service of itself, so processes can invoke other processes.

Figure 10-10 illustrates the tree of LiveCycle ES components after *FarataSampleComponent.jar* has been deployed and its services have been activated.

Tools

The important part of the LiveCycle ES ecosystem is its toolset. The Eclipse-based *Workbench* gives you features such as visual design, deployment, and debugging of the business processes as flow chart–type diagrams, in which operations of the LiveCycle ES services appear as flow-chart building blocks (see Figure 10-11).

Your old pal Adobe Flash Builder, which is also based on Eclipse, is yet another LiveCycle ES tool. A custom Flex application can enable a user to start instances of a business process; investigate tasks assigned for a particular user; and facilitate task completion, forwarding to another user, locking, and so on.

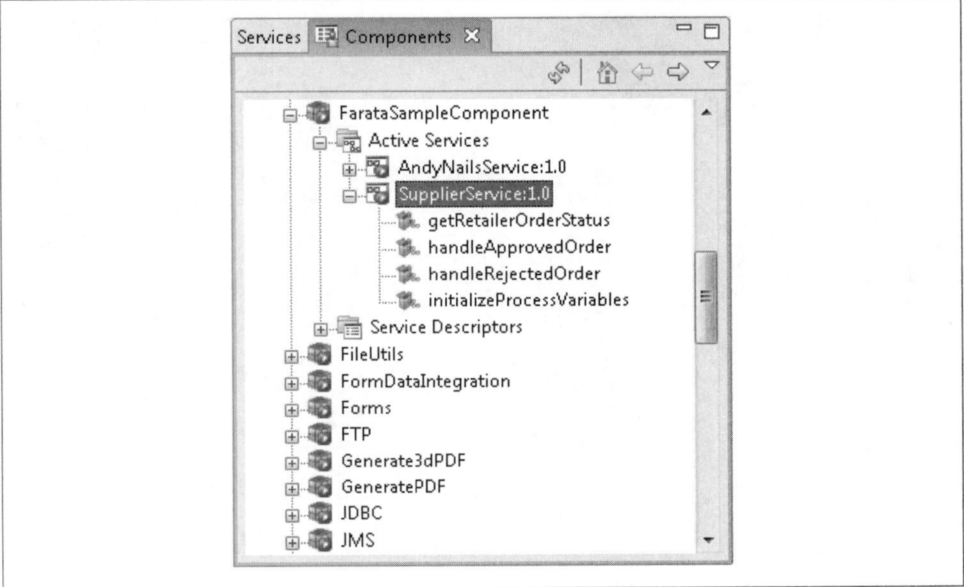

Figure 10-10. The Components panel of the LiveCycle ES Workbench, with the installed FarataSampleComponent

You also get a LiveCycle ES Administration Console (partially shown earlier in Figure 10-2). The current version of the Console is an upgrade of the previous HTML-based one, with a few minor patches coded in Flex. This chapter explains relevant parts of the Administration Console with regards to importing the sample processes, custom components, and advanced user management.

Creating Flex Applications Enabled for LiveCycle Workspace ES

This section explains how to develop Flex subapplications compliant with LiveCycle Workspace ES. As mentioned, we call these applications Flexlets. The Workspace activates Flexlets only when required to do so by the *human-centric process* conditions, which is why this chapter starts with describing the design of a sample process. For information about configuring human-centric processes, see the LiveCycle Workbench Help section (*http://www.adobe.com/go/learn_lc_workbench*) and navigate to Creating Processes → Designing Human-Centric Processes. Further reading on creating the Flexlets is available at *http://help.adobe.com/en_US/livecycle/es/createflexapps.pdf*.

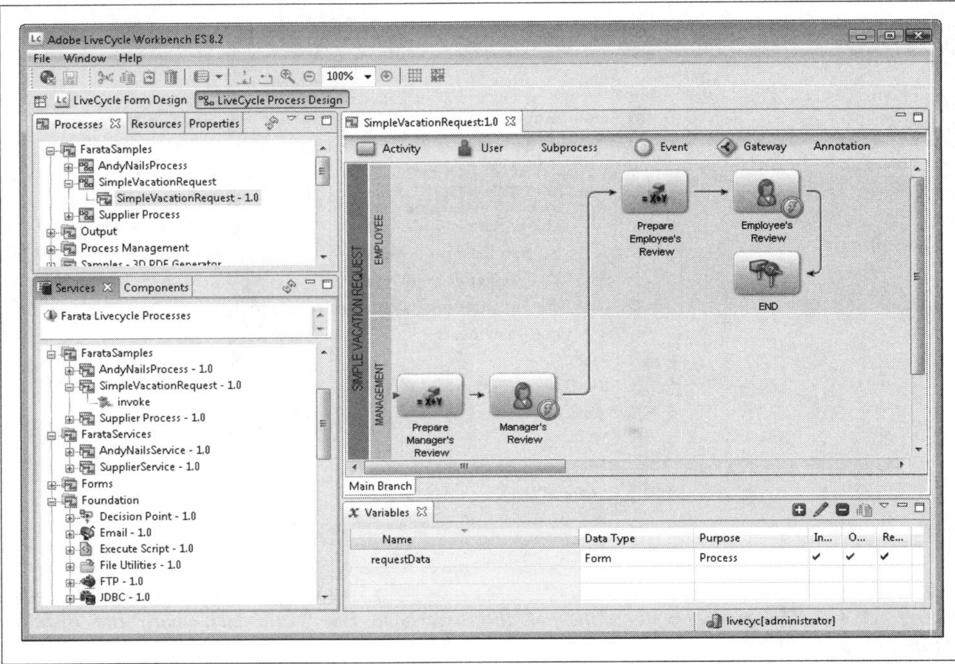

Figure 10-11. LiveCycle ES Workbench with the SimpleVacationRequest process diagram

Form Variable Declaration and Process Instantiation

When a human-centric process requires data entry from the participant, the workflow software pops up a dialog window. In the case of LiveCycle ES, the dialog is a PDF form or a Flexlet. From the programmer's perspective, the outcome of the data entry is a variable of the XML-based type `Form`. A `Form` variable carries the data and can, optionally, reference the SWF of the Flexlet that enables end users to pass the form data to the Workspace. Do not forget that the Workspace passes similar form data to the Flexlet to initialize it. In other words, the form data travels back and forth between the Flexlet and the LiveCycle ES process, using the Workspace as a middleman. The Workspace loads the Flexlet in two use cases:

As part of interactive process instantiation
: When a `Form` variable pointing to the SWF file has been declared in the LiveCycle Workbench as the input variable of the entire process

As part of the task execution
: When a `Form` variable pointing to the SWF file has been mapped as input to the user activity (for example, the `assignTask()` operation of the `UserService` service)

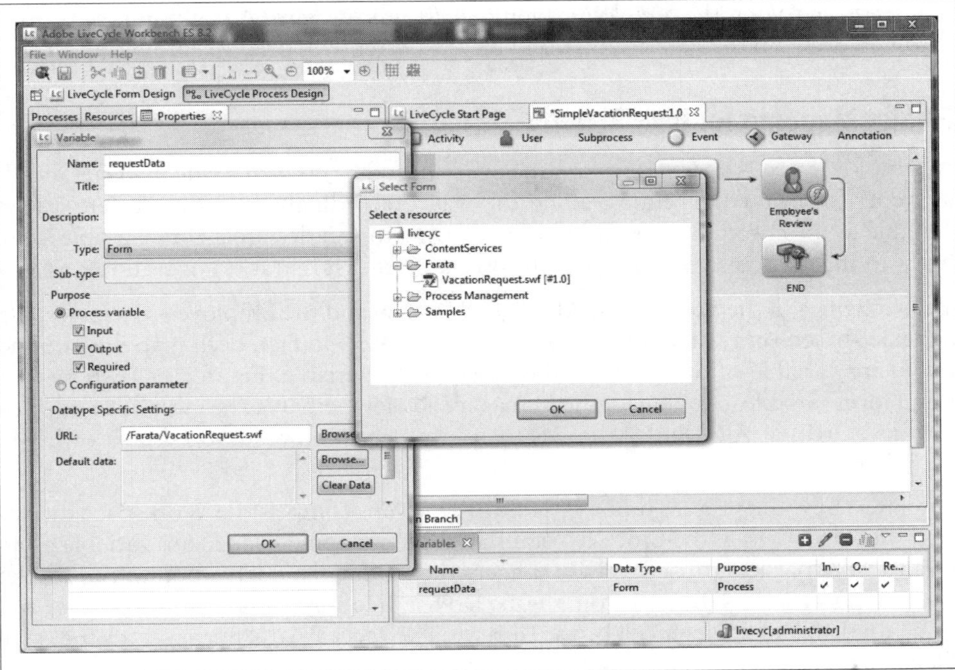

Figure 10-12. Input Form variable requestData gets declared to force Workspace to interact with the VacationRequest.swf Flexlet

When you assign a SWF URL to the `Form` variable in the Workbench, the default setting keeps the SWF file in the LiveCycle resources repository. Figure 10-12 shows the `requestData Form` variable declared within the LiveCycle Workbench. The variable is defined as the input variable of the process, and its URL property points to the *VacationRequest.swf* file, located under the *Farata* folder of the repository. Stepping ahead, the data that this `Form` variable carries through the process looks similar to the following XML document:

```
<vacationRequest>
  <requestId>8CE28354-E831-11E8-76EB-4DE38A29F087</requestId>
  <decision>approved</decision>
  <duration>7</duration>
  <isEmployee>true</isEmployee>
  <employeeName>Rye Woodard</employeeName>
</vacationRequest>
```

Once you declare a Flexlet-pointing `Form` variable as a process input, you should also add a `TaskManager` endpoint, using the Administration Console. This enlists the process for the end users of the Workspace. It also mandates the Workspace to pop up the Flexlet prior to invoking the actual process instance. In this scenario, the Workspace will start displaying the *SimpleVacationRequest process card*. A click on that process card will bring up the Flexlet initialized for the currently logged-in employee.

Flexlet Mapping for User Activity

An employee needs a Flexlet to start the process, and he, as well as the manager, needs a Flexlet to review the request along the way. Accordingly, you can declare a `Form` variable as input to the entire process, and you also can declare a `Form` variable as an input to the particular user activity (the `UserService.assignTask()` operation).

Two activities in the process, the Manager's Review and the Employee's Review, map a Flexlet-based `Form` variable as an input form variable. In fact, both map the one and only `Form` variable of our process, the `requestData` variable. Figure 10-13 shows the input form variable mapping for the Manager's Review activity. The initial user selected for this activity is Alex Pink, who has to approve vacation requests (shown earlier in Figure 10-9).

Similar to how the process input variable of type `Form` compels the Workspace to activate the Flexlet when the process instantiates, the mapping of the `Form` variable as an input to the particular user activity triggers the loading and activation of the Flexlet when the user selects the task from the To Do list. In our scenario, the Workspace will bring up the Flexlet referenced by the `Form` variable `requestData`. Surprise: it's the same Flexlet assigned to start the process.

Controlling the View State of the Reusable Flexlet from the Process

Whether you base your process on many different Flexlets or reuse one *.swf* file is up to you. We find the latter to be a convenient approach, because you can develop Flex applications to accommodate different process participant roles through different view states.

The process diagram has two `SetValue.execute()` activities:

- Prepare a Manager's Review
- Prepare an Employee's Review

The value of the `isEmployee` node of `requestData` is set to a value of `false` in Prepare a Manager's Review and to `true` in Prepare an Employee's Review. Internally, the code of the Flexlet displays different views based on the value of the node. Figure 10-14 shows the assignment of the `isEmployee` node to Prepare a Manager's Review.

Workspace: Flexlet Conversation Basics

The conversation between the Flexlet and the Workspace that loaded it is entirely event-based. The Workspace dispatches the following events.

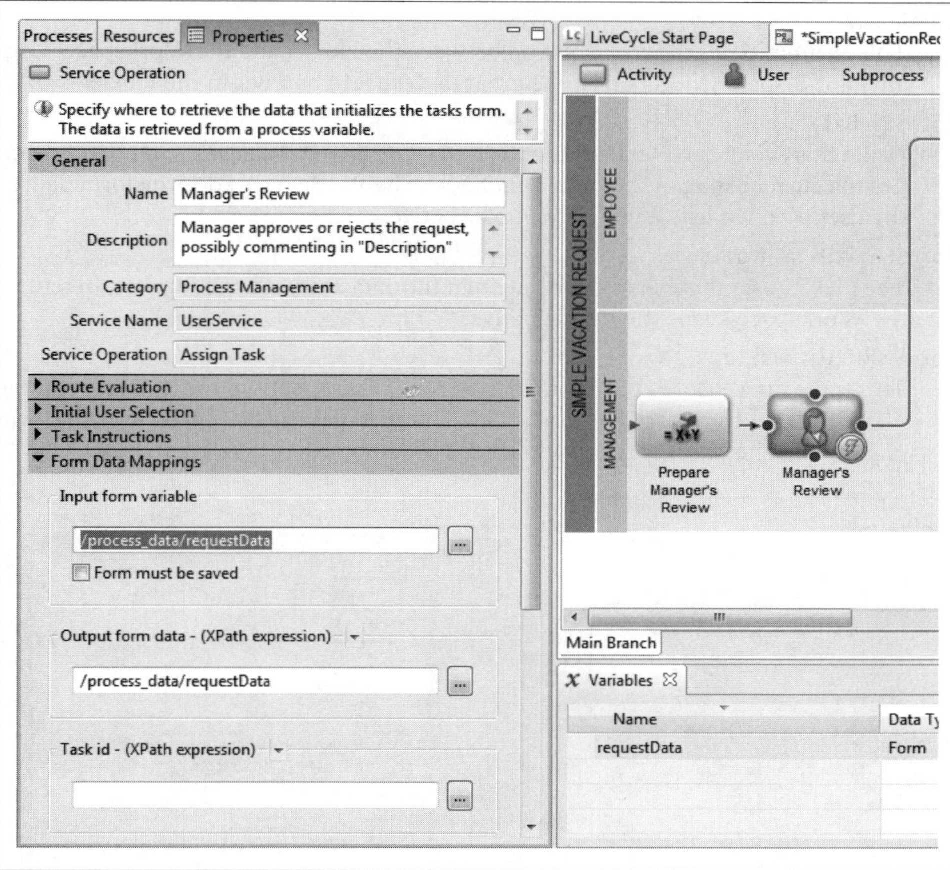

Figure 10-13. The variable requestData gets mapped as the input Form variable for the Manager's Review

`formInitialData`
: This event is being sent in response to the Flexlet signaling to the Workspace that it has finished loading (see the `formReady` event in the next list).

`formSaveDataRequest`
: This event is sent when the user clicks Save.

`formSubmitDataRequest`
: This event is sent when the user clicks Complete.

It is mandatory for the Flexlet to handle these events and dispatch the following ones back to the Workspace:

`formReady`
: This event initiates the conversation between the Flexlet and the Workspace. Usually, it is dispatched as part of the `creationComplete` handler in the Flexlet.

`formSaveData`
: Using this event, the Flexlet responds to the `formSaveDataRequest` event and specifies the current state of the form data XML. The Workspace adds the form data to the user's To Do list, leaving the Flexlet active.

`formSubmitDataInvalid`
: The Flexlet uses this event to indicate that the data entry is not complete. In return, the Workspace keeps the Flexlet active.

`formSubmitDataValid`
: This is the final event in the Workspace–Flexlet conversation. Using this event, the Flexlet responds to `formSaveDataRequest` and specifies the current state of the form data XML. The Workspace unloads the Flexlet.

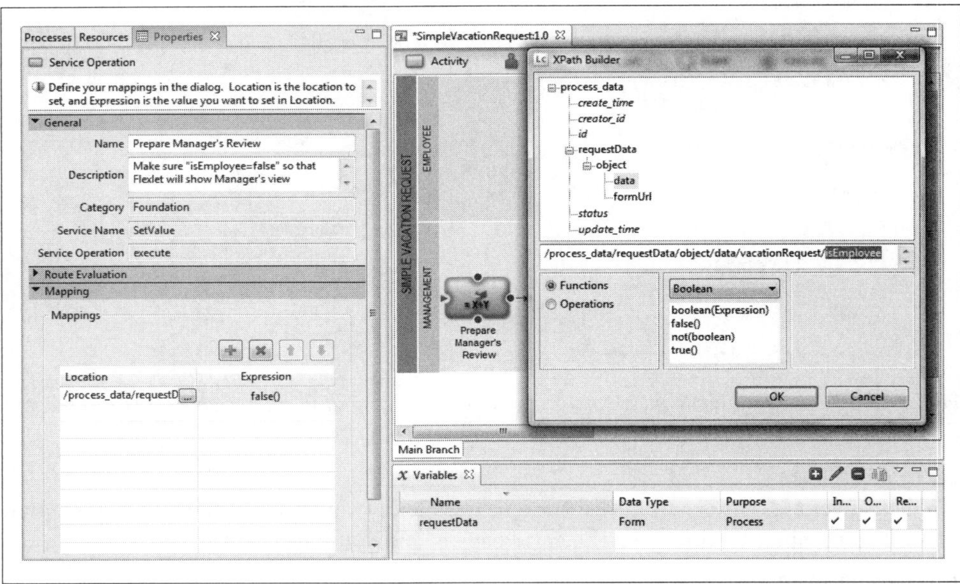

Figure 10-14. Value of isEmployee gets set to false before entering the Manager's Review

Additionally, a Flexlet may dispatch optional events:

`formClean` *and* `formDirty`
: These events specify to the Workspace whether it should prompt the user to save the form data if the user tries to close the Flexlet.

All of the event types listed are defined in the `lc.core.events.FormEvents` class, which is part of the *workspace-runtime.swc* library. Upon installing LiveCycle ES, you can find this class in your *LiveCycle8.2* installation directory at *...\LiveCycle_ES_SDK\misc \Process_Management\Workspace*.

LiveCycle FormConnector

The conversation between a Flexlet and the Workspace happens through a Flash `sharedEvents` object. As a reminder, `sharedEvents` is an `EventDispatcher` that is accessible both by the loading and the loaded SWFs. The loaded application accesses it as `systemManager.loaderInfo.sharedEvents`.

The loading application gets access to the very same `EventDispatcher` object either as `swfLoader.swfBridge` if the two *.swf* files belong to the different security sandboxes, or as `swfLoader.content.loaderInfo.sharedEvents` if both SWFs are hosted by the same security sandbox.

Accordingly, the Workspace dispatches its events, such as `formInitialData` and `formSubmitDataRequest`, to the `sharedEvents` and listens, on the same object, for the events `formReady` and `formSubmitData` coming from the Flexlet.

Sending and receiving `FormEvents` is greatly simplified by a helper class, `lc.core.FormConnector`. This class, an instance of `EventDispatcher`, is provided by the same *workspace-runtime.swc* library that contains the definition of the Workspace–Flexlet conversation events. In particular, in the `creationComplete()` event handler, `FormConnector` translates events intercepted on `sharedEvents` into ones dispatched on itself (see Example 10-1).

Example 10-1. FormConnector intercepts events on sharedEvents and redispatches them to itself

```
public function creationComplete(event:Event):void {
  dispatcher = UIComponent(event.target).systemManager.loaderInfo.sharedEvents;
  dispatcher.addEventListener(FormEvents.FORM_INITIAL_DATA, dispatchEvent);
  dispatcher.addEventListener(FormEvents.FORM_SAVE_DATA_REQUEST, dispatchEvent);
  dispatcher.addEventListener(FormEvents.FORM_SUBMIT_DATA_REQUEST, dispatchEvent);
}
```

As a result, your Flexlet code does not have to listen directly to `sharedEvents`. As long as the Flexlet keeps an instance of the `FormConnector`, it may instead listen to the `FormConnector`'s events. Example 10-2 shows how you can do it.

Example 10-2. A Flexlet can utilize the FormConnector to listen to events dispatched by the Workspace

```
 <?xml version="1.0" encoding="utf-8"?>
<mx:Application xmlns:mx="http://www.adobe.com/2006/mxml"
   xmlns:lc="http://www.adobe.com/2006/livecycle">

   <lc:FormConnector id="formConnector"
         formInitialData="onFormInitialData(event)"
         formSaveDataRequest="onFormSaveDataRequest(event)"
         formSubmitDataRequest="onFormSubmitDataRequest(event)"/>

. . .
</mx:Application>
```

To facilitate sending events to the Workspace, FormConnector offers methods like setSubmitData(), which alleviates the need to explicitly dispatch the formSubmitData event (Example 10-3).

Example 10-3. FormConnector wraps the data-sending event logic into a set of convenient methods

```
public function setSubmitData(data:XML):void {
  trace("form: " + FormEvents.FORM_SUBMIT_DATA + " event dispatched to Workspace");
  dispatcher.dispatchEvent(
   new DataEvent(FormEvents.FORM_SUBMIT_DATA, false, false, data.toXMLString())
  );
}
```

This allows a Flexlet to use calls such as formConnector.setSubmitData(data) or formConnector.setSubmitDataInvalid() instead of dispatching the corresponding events to loaderInfo.sharedEvents (Example 10-4).

Example 10-4. A Flexlet can use the FormConnector API to simplify sending data events to the Workspace

```
private function onFormSubmitDataRequest(event:Event):void   {
   if (isDataValid()) {
      . . .
      formConnector.setSubmitData(xml);
   } else {
      formConnector.setSubmitDataInvalid();
   }
}
```

Which data should you trust more: Enterprise data or LiveCycle internal data?

All human-centric processes in LiveCycle are created as long-lived processes. From the persistence point of view, this means that LiveCycle stores all intermediate data that needs to be passed between the operations of the process in its internal database (see the documentation in *LiveCycle Workbench Help, Creating Processes → Process concepts → Process execution*).

The question is, "How much data really needs to touch the LiveCycle database?" Or rather, "How much of it should never leave your business database in the first place?"

Let's look at the *SimpleVacationRequest* process. Clearly, the start and end dates of the approved vacation need to be stored in the business database. Example 10-5 presents the CREATE TABLE statement that describes the structure of the corresponding *vacation-request* table from the *farata_livecycle_sampledb* database.

Example 10-5. Definition of the vacationrequest table from farata_livecycle_sampledb (MySQL)

```
CREATE TABLE  vacationrequest (
  Request_ID varchar(60) NOT NULL,
  Description varchar(500) NULL,
  Status varchar(30) NOT NULL,
  Start_Date datetime NULL,
```

```
  End_Date datetime NULL,
  Employee_ID varchar(100) default NOT NULL,
  Employee_Name varchar(120) default NOT NULL,
  Vacation_Type varchar(30) NOT NULL,
  Decision tinyint(1) default NULL,
  Decision_Made_At datetime default NULL,
  Employee_Email varchar(100) default NULL,
  Department varchar(100) default NULL,
  PRIMARY KEY  (Request_ID)
)
```

Given the `requestId`, all the table data can be accessed by the Flexlet, through, for instance, remote calls to Java methods that access the database through a JDBC layer. Seemingly, the only data that needs to be passed between the process and the Flexlet is the following:

```
<vacationRequest>
  <requestId>8CE28354-E831-11E8-76EB-4DE38A29F087</requestId>
  <isEmployee>true</isEmployee>
</vacationRequest>
```

In this snippet, `requestId` is the key to the database record and `isEmployee` is a view selector the Flexlet uses to present different UIs to the employee and the approving manager.

The `requestData` node has extra nodes: `decision`, `employeeName`, and `duration`, because it's not only about a Flexlet, it's also about the process (see Example 10-6).

For instance, while creating the Task Instructions Template of the Manager's Review task, it was *convenient* to use all these nodes in the template expression.

The bottom line is this: although you should avoid carrying business data in your process variables, exercise your own judgment.

Example 10-6. Form data XML of the requestData form variable

```
<vacationRequest>
  <requestId>8CE28354-E831-11E8-76EB-4DE38A29F087</requestId>
  <decision>approved</decision>
  <duration>7</duration>
  <isEmployee>true</isEmployee>
  <employeeName>Rye Woodard</employeeName>
</vacationRequest>
```

Flexlet Code Walkthrough

Let's examine the Flexlet's namespaces and variables. After doing so, you will learn how the Flexlet gets the incoming process data that it uses to read more data from the enterprise data store. Finally, you will learn how the Flexlet writes the data to the enterprise data store and follows up with submitting the output data back to the process.

Namespaces and variables

In addition to the traditional *http://www.adobe.com/2006/mxml*, the Flexlet application declares two extra namespaces (Example 10-7):

http://www.adobe.com/2006/livecycle
: To allow reference of the `FormConnector` helper from *workspace-runtime.swc*.

http://www.faratasystems.com/2008/components
: To allow references to controls from the *clear.swc* component library made by Farata Systems. Components such as `DataCollection`, `DataForm`, and `DataFormItem` were described in Chapter 3.

Example 10-7. Namespaces of the SimpleVacationRequest.swf Flexlet

```
<mx:Application width="100%" height="100%" layout="absolute"
   xmlns:mx="http://www.adobe.com/2006/mxml"
   xmlns:lc="http://www.adobe.com/2006/livecycle"
   xmlns:fx="http://www.faratasystems.com/2008/components"
   creationComplete="onCreationComplete()"
>
```

As explained earlier, `FormConnector` facilitates exchange of the data events with the Workspace. In addition, our Flexlet conducts independent data exchange with the *farata_livecycle_sampledb* database. This is done using the `requestsCollection` variable, which is a `DataCollection` object (see Chapter 3) capable of talking to the database through its `fill()` and `sync()` methods, as shown in Example 10-8.

Example 10-8. DataCollection variable: requestsCollection encapsulates data exchange between the Flexlet and the database

```
import com.theriabook.collections.DataCollection;
private var requestsCollection:DataCollection = new DataCollection();
. . .
// Invoke remote method to retrieve the existing vacation request record
var token:AsyncToken = requestsCollection.fill(requestId);

. . .
// Invoke remote method to the database with the current state of
// the vacation request
var token:AsyncToken = requestsCollection.sync();
```

The Flexlet also declares a bindable variable, `vacationRequestDTO`, that is used as the `dataProvider` for the `DataForm` (see Chapter 3). As a reminder, `DataForm` provides the same convenience in regards to binding as `DataGrid`. As soon as the user modifies a property of the `vacationRequestDTO`, the corresponding input control is updated and vice versa (Example 10-9).

Example 10-9. Use of DataForm provides automatic two-way binding between the bindable properties of vacationRequestDTO and form items

```
import com.farata.datasource.dto.VacationRequestDTO;
[Bindable] private var vacationRequestDTO:VacationRequestDTO ;
. . .
<fx:DataForm id="left" width="100%" dataProvider="{vacationRequestDTO}">
     <fx:DataFormItem label="Employee Name: " fontWeight="bold"
                 dataField="EMPLOYEE_NAME" required="true"
                 validators="{[nameValidator]}">
         <mx:TextInput  fontWeight="normal" editable="{isEmployee}" />
     </fx:DataFormItem>
. . .
</fx:DataForm>
```

Finally, the Flexlet declares another bindable variable `isEmployee` that is used to alternate between the two view states of the form: the Employee's View and Manager's View. This property is managed exclusively by the process. The Flexlet obtains it as part of the `onFormInitialData()` event handler, as Example 10-10 demonstrates.

Example 10-10. Boolean variable isEmployee is used to alternate between two "views" of the Flexlet: Manager's View and Employee's View

```
[Bindable] private var isEmployee:Boolean = false ;
. . .
private function onFormInitialData(event: DataEvent): void   {
      if ((event.data != null) || (event.data != " ")) {
      var requestData:XML = new XML(event.data);
      var xmlList:XMLList = requestData.isEmployee;
      isEmployee = (xmlList.toString()!="false");
      . . .
}
```

Reading data from the process and enterprise data store

The Flexlet has to ask the Workspace to feed it with the process data. It makes sense to do it in the `onCreationComplete()` handler, shown in part in Example 10-11. The `formConnector.setReady()` serves precisely this purpose. The rest of the `oncreationComplete()` handler is initializing `requestsCollection` to communicate with the remote destination `com.farata.datasource.VacationRequest`.

Example 10-11. Snippet of the onCreationComplete() event handler

```
requestsCollection.destination = "com.farata.datasource.VacationRequest";
requestsCollection.method = "getVacationRequest";
requestsCollection.addEventListener(
   ResultEvent.RESULT,
   function(event:ResultEvent):void {
      if (event.token.method == "fill") {
         onRequestsCollectionFill(event);
      } else {
         onRequestsCollectionSync(event);
      }
```

```
    }
);
requestsCollection.addEventListener(FaultEvent.FAULT, onFault);
```

The Java code for this destination has been generated by the Clear Data Builder (see Chapters 1 and 6) based on the abstract class in Example 10-12.

Example 10-12. Abstract Java class used by Clear Data Builder to generate all Java artifacts required to remotely access and modify the VacationRequest table of the farata_livecycle_sampledb database

```
package com.farata.datasource;

import java.util.List;

/**
 * @daoflex:webservice
 *   pool=jdbc/farata
 */
@SuppressWarnings("unchecked")
public abstract class VacationRequest
{
      /**
      * @daoflex:sql
      *  sql=::  select * from VacationRequest
      *  ::
      *  transferType=VacationRequestDTO[]
      *  keyColumns=Request_ID
      *  updateTable=VacationRequest
      */
      public abstract List getAllRequests();

      /**
      * @daoflex:sql
      *  sql=::  select * from VacationRequest where Request_ID=:reqId
      *  ::
      *  transferType=VacationRequestDTO[]
      *  keyColumns=Request_ID
      *  updateTable=VacationRequest
      */
      public abstract List getVacationRequest(String reqId);
}
```

The actual feed of the process data into the Flexlet happens within the `onFormInitialData()` handler. Remember, the Workspace sends a `formInitialData` event in response to the `setReady` event. `event.data` should bring the XML corresponding to the process variable `requestData` (in other words, `process_data/requestData`).

If this XML contains `requestId`, the Flexlet issues the asynchronous `fill()` call; otherwise, it creates the brand-new vacation request record. The latter case corresponds to the use case where the process `Form` variable and, accordingly, the Flexlet start the process. Either way, the Flexlet populates the value of `vacationRequestDTO` with the vacation request record (Example 10-13).

Example 10-13. For existing requests the Flexlet brings all data from the database

```
private function onFormInitialData(event: DataEvent): void   {
   if ((event.data != null) || (event.data != " ")) {
   var requestData:XML = new XML(event.data);
   var xmlList:XMLList = requestData.isEmployee;
   isEmployee = (xmlList.toString()!="false");

   var requestId:String = requestData.requestId;
   if ( requestId && requestId != "") {
      var token:AsyncToken = requestsCollection.fill(requestId);
      token.requestId = requestId;
   } else {
      // create a new request
      vacationRequestDTO = new VacationRequestDTO;
      vacationRequestDTO.REQUEST_ID = UIDUtil.createUID();
      vacationRequestDTO.STATUS = "Created";
      vacationRequestDTO.START_DATE = new Date(
         new Date().time + 1000 * 3600 * 24
      );

      var authenticatedUser:User = WorkspaceSession.getSessionManager(
         Application.application.session).authenticatedUser;
      vacationRequestDTO.EMPLOYEE_NAME = authenticatedUser.displayName;
      vacationRequestDTO.EMPLOYEE_EMAIL = authenticatedUser.email;
      vacationRequestDTO.VACATION_TYPE = "L"; //Unpaid leave - default
      requestsCollection.addItem(vacationRequestDTO);

      isEmployee = true;
   }
   formConnector.setClean();
  }
}
private function onRequestsCollectionFill( event:ResultEvent ):void {
   var requestId:String = event.token.requestId;
   if ( requestsCollection.length > 0 ){
      vacationRequestDTO = requestsCollection[0];
   } else {
      Alert.show("Vacation Request was not found: " + requestId);
   }
}
```

Writing data to the enterprise data store and the process

Remember the persistence motto: *keep the enterprise data in the enterprise data store*. For the Flexlet, this means: save the data to the enterprise store first and then let the process know only the bare minimum. Accordingly, the event sending the call `formConnector.setSubmitData()` is not being issued directly from the `onFormSubmitDataRequest()` handler. Instead, the handler just initiates the remote update of the data store by calling the `sync()` method of the `requestsCollection`, as you can see in Example 10-14.

Example 10-14. Event handler onFormSubmitDataRequest() updates the database instead of sending the event to the Workspace

```
private function onFormSubmitDataRequest(event:Event):void   {
   if (isDataValid()) {
      applyDecision();
      vacationRequestDTO.DECISION_MADE_AT = new Date();
      var token:AsyncToken = requestsCollection.sync();
      token.submit = true;
   } else {
      formConnector.setSubmitDataInvalid();
   }
}
```

Once the update of the enterprise data store is complete within the `onRequestsCollectionSync()` body, the Flexlet can confidently return to process the new value of the form data and cease to exist (Example 10-15). Please note that `onFormSaveDataRequest()` is organized in a similar way, with one exception: it does not have `token.submit=true`, which affects the logic of the `onRequestsCollectionSync()` method.

Example 10-15. Flexlet submits the data to the process only after the database has been updated

```
private function onRequestsCollectionSync( event:ResultEvent ):void {
   var duration:Number = 0;
       if ((vacationRequestDTO.START_DATE != null) &&
         (vacationRequestDTO.END_DATE!=null)) {
      duration = Math.ceil((vacationRequestDTO.END_DATE.time -
                 vacationRequestDTO.START_DATE.time)/(1000 * 3600 * 24));
   }
   var requestData:XML = <vacationRequest>
      <requestId> {vacationRequestDTO.REQUEST_ID}</requestId>
      <decision>{decision.selectedItem.data}</decision>
      <duration>{duration}</duration>
      <isEmployee>{isEmployee}</isEmployee>
      <employeeName>{vacationRequestDTO.EMPLOYEE_NAME}</employeeName>
   </vacationRequest>;

   if ( event.token.submit ){
      formConnector.setSubmitData(requestData);
   } else {
      formConnector.setSaveData(requestData);
      formConnector.setClean();
   }
}
```

Example 10-16 presents the complete code of the Flexlet *SimpleVacationRequest*.

Example 10-16. Complete code of the SimpleVacationRequest Flexlet

```
<?xml version="1.0" encoding="utf-8"?>
<mx:Application width="100%" height="100%" layout="absolute"
   xmlns:mx="http://www.adobe.com/2006/mxml"
   xmlns:lc="http://www.adobe.com/2006/livecycle"
```

```
xmlns:fx="http://www.faratasystems.com/2008/components"
creationComplete="onCreationComplete()"
>

<lc:FormConnector id="formConnector"
   formInitialData="onFormInitialData(event)"
   formSaveDataRequest="onFormSaveDataRequest(event)"
   formSubmitDataRequest="onFormSubmitDataRequest(event)"/>

<mx:VBox width="100%" height="100%" backgroundColor="white">
   <mx:Label text="{isEmployee ? 'Submit' : 'Approve'} Vacation Request"
      fontWeight="bold"
      fontSize="16"
      fontStyle="italic"
      paddingTop="10"
      paddingBottom="5"
      paddingLeft="10"
      />
   <mx:HBox width="100%" height="100%" >
   <fx:DataForm id="left" width="100%"
      dataProvider="{vacationRequestDTO}">
     <fx:DataFormItem label="Employee Name: " fontWeight="bold"
              dataField="EMPLOYEE_NAME" required="true"
              validators="{[nameValidator]}">
      <mx:TextInput  fontWeight="normal" editable="{isEmployee}" />
     </fx:DataFormItem>
     <fx:DataFormItem label="Employee Email: " fontWeight="bold"
          dataField="EMPLOYEE_EMAIL" required="true"
          validators="{[emailValidator]}">
      <mx:TextInput   fontWeight="normal" editable="{isEmployee}"/>
     </fx:DataFormItem>
         <fx:DataFormItem label="Department: " fontWeight="bold"
          dataField="DEPARTMENT" required="true"
          validators="{[departmentValidator]}">
      <fx:TextInput fontWeight="normal" editable="{isEmployee}"/>
     </fx:DataFormItem>
     <mx:Spacer height="10"/>
     <fx:DataFormItem label="Description: " fontWeight="bold"
      dataField="DESCRIPTION">
      <mx:TextArea width="200"  height="80" fontWeight="normal" />
     </fx:DataFormItem>
   </fx:DataForm>
   <fx:DataForm id="right" width="100%"
      dataProvider="{vacationRequestDTO}">
     <fx:DataFormItem label="Start Date: " fontWeight="bold"
      dataField="START_DATE"  valueName="selectedDate" required="true">
      <mx:DateField fontWeight="normal"  enabled="{isEmployee}"/>
     </fx:DataFormItem>
     <fx:DataFormItem label="End Date: " fontWeight="bold"
      dataField="END_DATE" valueName="selectedDate" required="true">
       <mx:DateField  fontWeight="normal" enabled="{isEmployee}"/>
       <fx:validators>
      <mx:Array>
        <fx:ValidationRule
         rule="{
```

```
            function(data:Object):Boolean {
             return data.START_DATE >= data.END_DATE;
            }
          }"
          errorMessage="End Date must be later than Start Date">
         </fx:ValidationRule>
       </mx:Array>
        </fx:validators>
      </fx:DataFormItem>
      <fx:DataFormItem label="Vacation Type: " fontWeight="bold"
       dataField="VACATION_TYPE"
       resource="{com.farata.resources.VacationTypeComboResource}"
       enabled="{isEmployee}" required="true">
      </fx:DataFormItem>
          <fx:DataFormItem label="Request Status: " fontWeight="bold"
           dataField="STATUS">
             <mx:Label  fontWeight="normal"/>
          </fx:DataFormItem>
          <mx:FormItem id="approvalDecision" label="Approval Decision: "
           fontWeight="bold"  visible="{!isEmployee}">
             <mx:ComboBox id="decision">
                <mx:Array>
                   <mx:Object label="Approved" data="approved"/>
                   <mx:Object label="Rejected" data="rejected"/>
                </mx:Array>
             </mx:ComboBox>
          </mx:FormItem>
       </fx:DataForm>
    </mx:HBox>
 </mx:VBox>

 <mx:Script>
 <![CDATA[
 import com.farata.datasource.dto.VacationRequestDTO;
 import com.farata.resources.VacationTypeComboResource;
 import com.theriabook.collections.DataCollection;
 import com.farata.datasource.dto.VacationRequestDTO;
 import lc.core.WorkspaceDataService;
 import lc.domain.User;
 import lc.domain.workspace.WorkspaceSession;
 import mx.rpc.events.FaultEvent;
 import mx.rpc.AsyncToken;
 import mx.controls.Alert;
 import mx.rpc.events.ResultEvent;
 import mx.utils.UIDUtil;

 [Bindable] private var vacationRequestDTO:VacationRequestDTO ;
 [Bindable] private var isEmployee:Boolean = false ;

 private var requestsCollection:DataCollection = new DataCollection();

 private function onCreationComplete():void {
    formConnector.setReady();

    requestsCollection.destination = "com.farata.datasource.VacationRequest";
```

```
    requestsCollection.method = "getVacationRequest";
    requestsCollection.addEventListener(
        ResultEvent.RESULT,
        function(event:ResultEvent):void {
            if (event.token.method == "fill") {
                onRequestsCollectionFill(event);
            } else {
                onRequestsCollectionSync(event);
            }
        }
    );
    requestsCollection.addEventListener(FaultEvent.FAULT, onFault);
}

private function onFormInitialData(event: DataEvent): void   {
    if ((event.data != null) || (event.data != " ")) {
    var requestData:XML = new XML(event.data);
    var xmlList:XMLList = requestData.isEmployee;
    isEmployee = (xmlList.toString()!="false");

    var requestId:String = requestData.requestId;
    if ( requestId && requestId != "") {
        var token:AsyncToken = requestsCollection.fill(requestId);
        token.requestId = requestId;
    } else {
        // create a new request
        vacationRequestDTO = new VacationRequestDTO;
        vacationRequestDTO.REQUEST_ID = UIDUtil.createUID();
        vacationRequestDTO.STATUS = "Created";
        vacationRequestDTO.START_DATE = new Date(
            new Date().time + 1000 * 3600 * 24
        );

        var authenticatedUser:User = WorkspaceSession.getSessionManager(
                Application.application.session).authenticatedUser;
        vacationRequestDTO.EMPLOYEE_NAME = authenticatedUser.displayName;
        vacationRequestDTO.EMPLOYEE_EMAIL = authenticatedUser.email;
        vacationRequestDTO.VACATION_TYPE = "L"; //Unpaid leave - default
        requestsCollection.addItem(vacationRequestDTO);

        isEmployee = true;
    }
    formConnector.setClean();
  }
}

private function onFormSaveDataRequest (event:Event):void{
    applyDecision();
    var token:AsyncToken = requestsCollection.sync();
    token.submit=false;
}

private function onFormSubmitDataRequest(event:Event):void   {
    if (isDataValid()) {
        applyDecision();
```

```
            vacationRequestDTO.DECISION_MADE_AT = new Date();
            var token:AsyncToken = requestsCollection.sync();
            token.submit = true;
        } else {
            formConnector.setSubmitDataInvalid();
        }
    }

    private function onFault( event:FaultEvent ):void   {
        Alert.show( event.fault.faultString);
    }

    private function applyDecision():void {
        if ( !isEmployee )   {
            vacationRequestDTO.DECISION = decision.selectedItem.data ;
            vacationRequestDTO.STATUS = decision.selectedItem.label;
        }
    }


    private function onRequestsCollectionFill( event:ResultEvent ):void {
        var requestId:String = event.token.requestId;
        if ( requestsCollection.length > 0 ){
            vacationRequestDTO = requestsCollection[0];
        } else {
            Alert.show("Vacation Request was not found: " + requestId);
        }
    }

    private function onRequestsCollectionSync( event:ResultEvent ):void {
        var duration:Number = 0;
             if ((vacationRequestDTO.START_DATE != null) &&
                (vacationRequestDTO.END_DATE!=null)) {
            duration = Math.ceil((vacationRequestDTO.END_DATE.time -
                       vacationRequestDTO.START_DATE.time)/(1000 * 3600 * 24));
        }
        var requestData:XML = <vacationRequest>
            <requestId> {vacationRequestDTO.REQUEST_ID}</requestId>
            <decision>{decision.selectedItem.data}</decision>
            <duration>{duration}</duration>
            <isEmployee>{isEmployee}</isEmployee>
            <employeeName>{vacationRequestDTO.EMPLOYEE_NAME}</employeeName>
        </vacationRequest>;

        if ( event.token.submit ){
            formConnector.setSubmitData(requestData);
        } else {
            formConnector.setSaveData(requestData);
            formConnector.setClean();
        }
    }

    private function isDataValid():Boolean {
        var failedLeft:Array = left.validateAll();
        var failedRight:Array = right.validateAll();
```

```
        return ((failedLeft.length == 0)&&(failedRight.length == 0));
    }

    ]]>
    </mx:Script>

    <mx:StringValidator id="nameValidator" minLength="6"
        requiredFieldError="Provide your name, more than 5 symbols" />
    <mx:EmailValidator id="emailValidator"
        requiredFieldError="Provide correct email" />
    <mx:StringValidator id="departmentValidator"
        requiredFieldError="Provide department" />
</mx:Application>
```

Running Workspace from Adobe Sources

As we have already mentioned, LiveCycle Workspace is a Flex application. Assuming that your default install root is at *C:\Adobe\LiveCycle8.2*, you can find its Flex project archive, *adobe-workspace-src.zip*, at the following location:

> *[root]\LiveCycle_ES_SDK\misc\Process_Management\Workspace*

You can benefit greatly from these source files. First, it's the best way to acquire knowledge of how Flex applications work with the LiveCycle API. Second, you can customize the look and feel of the Workspace, or you can completely cannibalize it, borrowing certain pieces for your business application.

In any case, the first step is to rebuild the Workspace from sources and ensure that you can run and debug it. This is also the best scenario for debugging your Flexlets as well.

To rebuild and run the Workspace from sources, you must first prepare the enterprise application archive, or EAR (this example uses JBoss). To accomplish this, you must follow these steps:

1. Find *adobe-workspace-client.ear* under *[root]\jboss\server\all\deploy*.
2. Expand (unzip) the file *farata-workspace-client.ear* as *farata-workspace-client.ear* into a working directory on your hard drive.
3. Find the file *application.xml* inside the *adobe-workspace-client.ear* folder.
4. Replace the reference to *adobe-workspace-client.war* with a reference to *farata-workspace-client.war*: `<web-uri>farata-workspace-client.war</web-uri>`.
5. Replace the context root workspace with *farata_workspace* `<context-root>farata_workspace</context-root>`.
6. Find the *adobe-workspace-client.war* file in the *farata-workspace-client.ear* folder.
7. Unzip it as folder *farata-workspace-client.war* on your hard drive.
8. Replace the *farata-workspace-client.war* file with the *farata-workspace-client.war* folder (inside *adobe-workspace-client.ear*).

The remaining steps in the process are:

9. Deploy the EAR: copy the entire *farata-workspace-client.ear* into `[root]`*\jboss\server\all\deploy*.
10. Import the Flash Builder/Flex Project archive—*adobe-workspace-src.zip*—into the Eclipse workspace. It will create the new project, called Workspace.
11. Navigate to the project's *Properties/Flex Build Path* and change the *Main source folder* to *src_workspace* (originally, this was *src*).
12. Add the following three SWC files to the Flex library path. The paths to all three are relative to *C:\Adobe\LiveCycle8.2\LiveCycle_ES_SDK\misc*:

    \Process_Management\Workspace\workspace-runtime.swc

    \DataServices\Client-Libraries\fds.swc

    \DataServices\Client-Libraries\fds-rb.swc
13. Set the *Output folder* to `[root]`*\jboss\server\all\deploy\farata-workspace-client.ear\farata-workspace-client.war*. By the time you complete this step, your project configuration should resemble Figure 10-15.

The setup is complete.

Business Example: Warehouse Processes

The remaining part of this chapter refers to a more complex business scenario. Instead of creating Flexlets to complement the design of the Workspace, here you are in charge of the entire application. This scenario has a much wider applicability scope: in particular, it illustrates how you can add workflow capabilities to an existing Flex application.

The participants of the scenario are a *Retailer*, a *Supplier*, and a *Manufacturer*. First consider the *Retailer–Supplier* interaction. The Retailer places orders of nails and hammers. The Supplier may approve or reject the Retailer's order. The Retailer acknowledges the decision. Omitting the complexity of the real world, assume that approval instantly increases the Retailer's inventory.

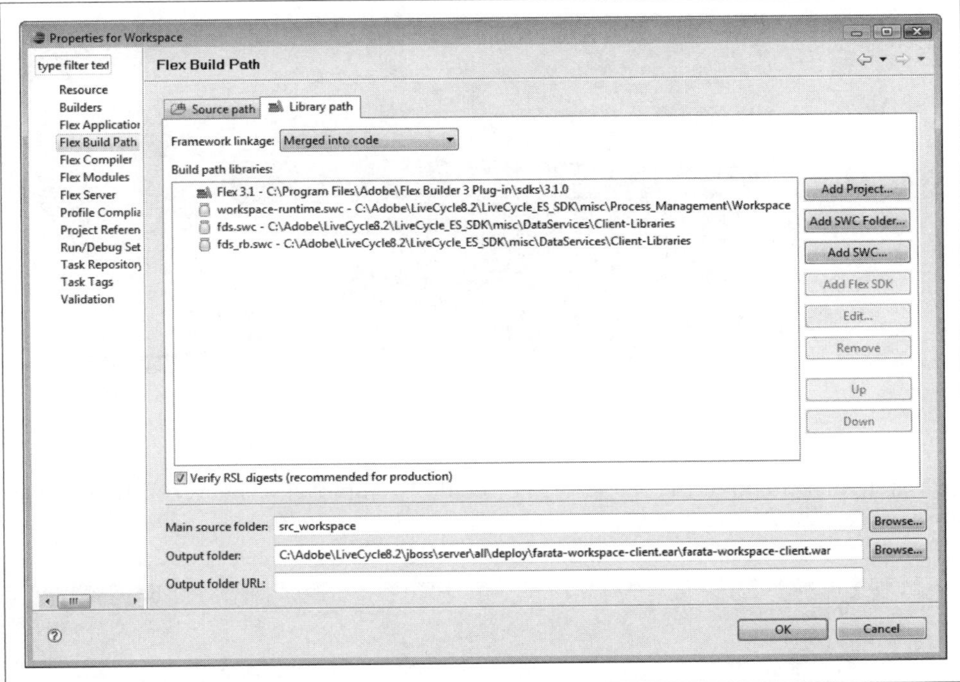

Figure 10-15. Workspace project configuration

Now look at the *Supplier–Manufacturer* interaction. The Supplier attempts to fulfill the order from its own storage and reorders the inventory based on a certain threshold. These orders have to be approved or rejected by the Manufacturer. Approval of the order instantly increases the Supplier's inventory.

Instead of designing one complex process with three participants, however, you can design and coordinate two simple processes with two participants each. The first process is a Retailer–Supplier workflow; the second one is a Supplier–Manufacturer workflow. In fact, our business scenario supports many different Supplier–Manufacturer processes, which differ from manufacturer to manufacturer. First, though, take a look at the UI for all three participants.

User Interface for the Retailer

The Retailer logs in to the system, as shown in Figure 10-16.

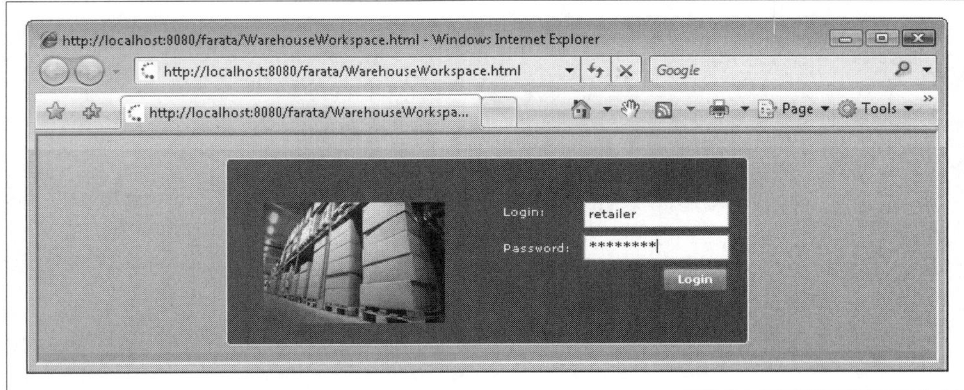

Figure 10-16. The Retailer's login screen

The system recognizes the name of the retailer's employee. The Work Inbox, Figure 10-17, is initially empty.

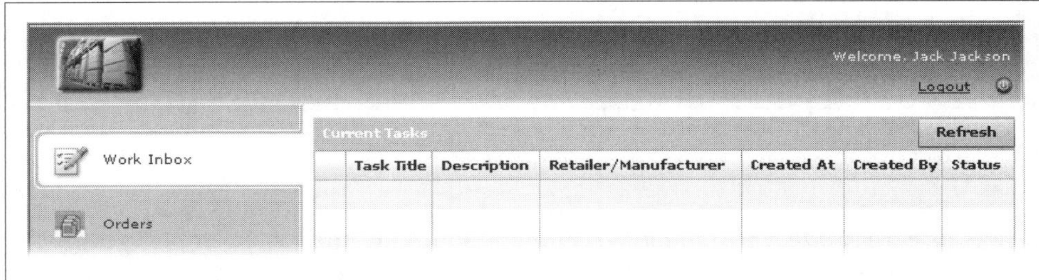

Figure 10-17. The Retailer's Work Inbox screen

The list of the placed orders, Figure 10-18, is initially empty as well.

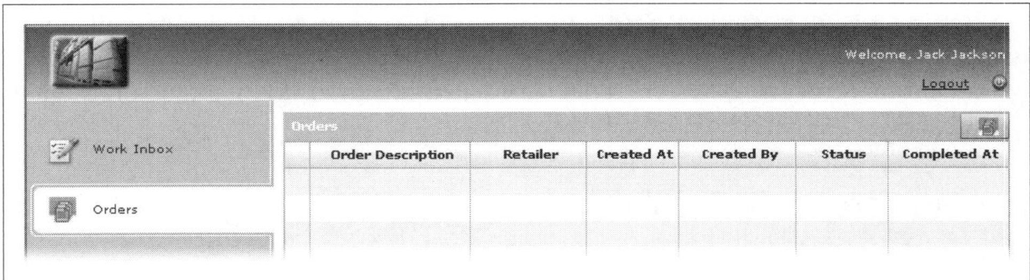

Figure 10-18. The empty list of the Retailer's orders

Say that the Retailer enters an order of 25 packs of nails from Andy's Nails, as shown in Figure 10-19.

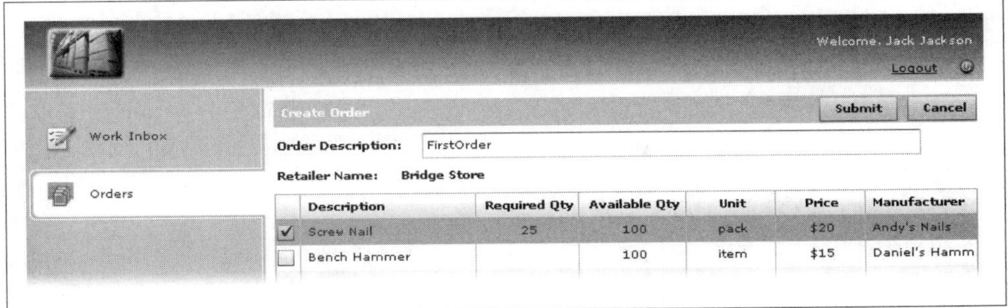

Figure 10-19. Details of the particular Retailer's order at submission

Once the Retailer submits the order, its list of orders shows an In Progress status, as shown in Figure 10-20. At this point, the decision passes to the Supplier.

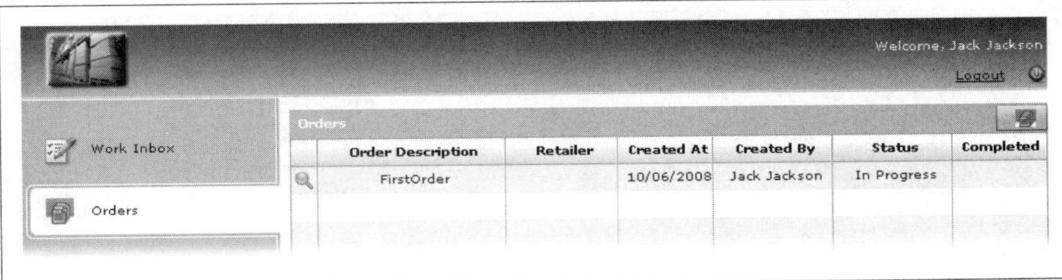

Figure 10-20. The Retailer's order is pending the Supplier's reply

If the Supplier approves the order, both the Orders and Work Inbox panels update the order status as Approved, shown in Figure 10-21.

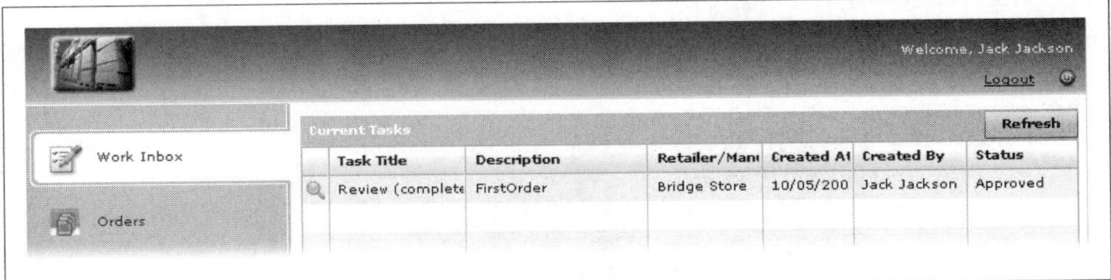

Figure 10-21. The Retailer's order shown as approved by a Supplier

The process returns to the Retailer, who must confirm the decision, as shown in Figure 10-22.

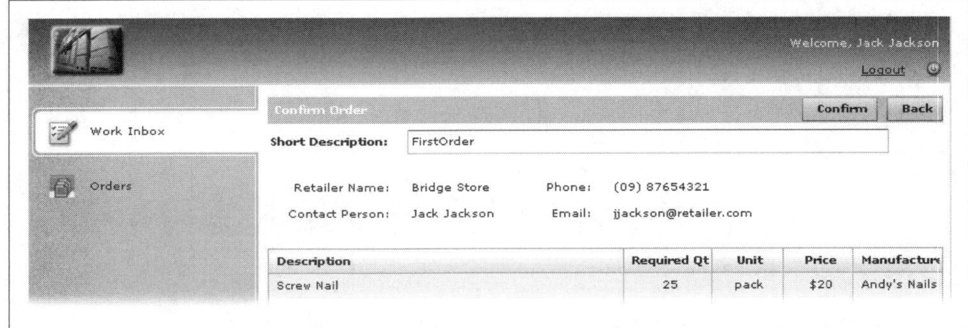

Figure 10-22. Details of the Retailer's order confirmed by the Retailer

Upon confirmation, the Work Inbox is empty; the Orders box shows the complete order, as displayed in Figure 10-23.

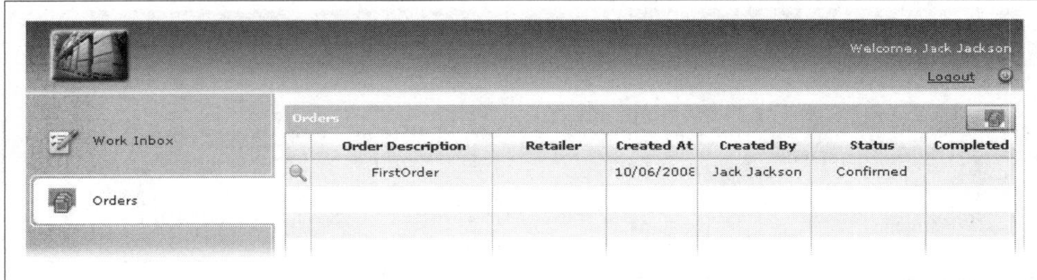

Figure 10-23. The Retailer's order list showing the completed, confirmed order

This concludes the Retailer's work cycle.

User Interface for the Supplier

The Supplier logs in to the same system, as shown in Figure 10-24.

Figure 10-24. The Supplier's login screen

The Supplier's Work Inbox shows the list of retailer orders to be approved. Figure 10-25 shows an earlier order from Jack Jackson.

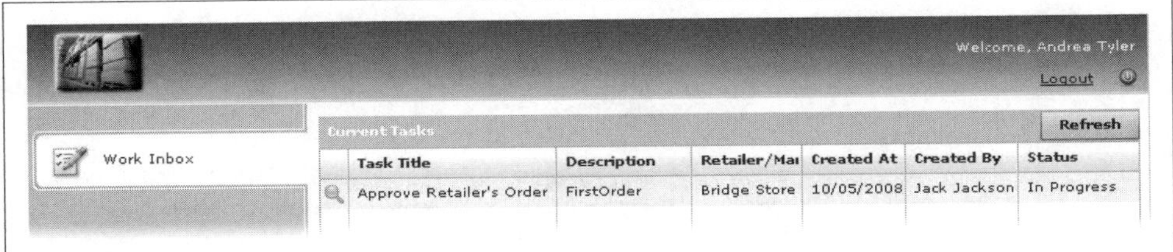

Figure 10-25. The Supplier's list of orders

The Supplier approves or rejects the order (Figure 10-26).

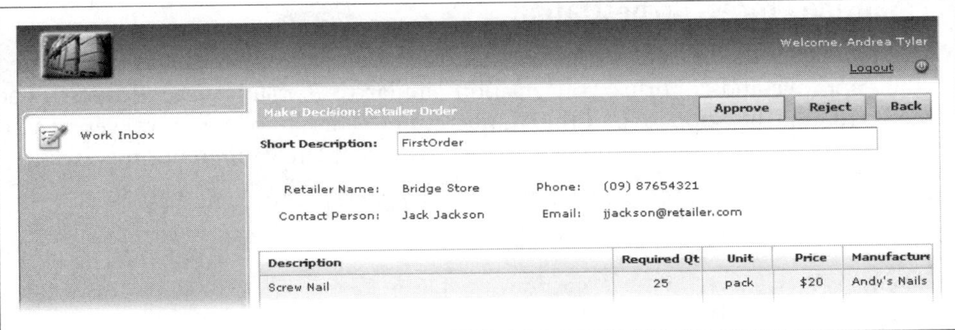

Figure 10-26. The Supplier's approval or rejection of orders

That concludes the Supplier's work cycle.

User Interface for the Manufacturer

In the Manufacturer's workflow, upon login, the employee of the Manufacturer will see the Work Inbox, as shown in Figure 10-27.

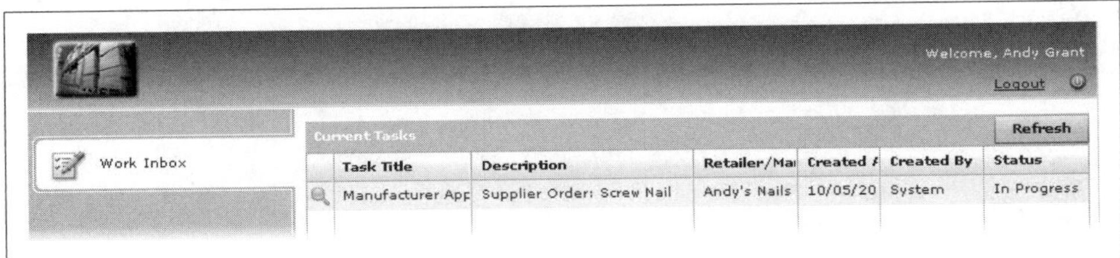

Figure 10-27. The Manufacturer's Work Inbox

The Manufacturer's employee will be able to approve or reject the order in a way similar to that of the Supplier and then, in the case of approval, his Work Inbox will look like Figure 10-28.

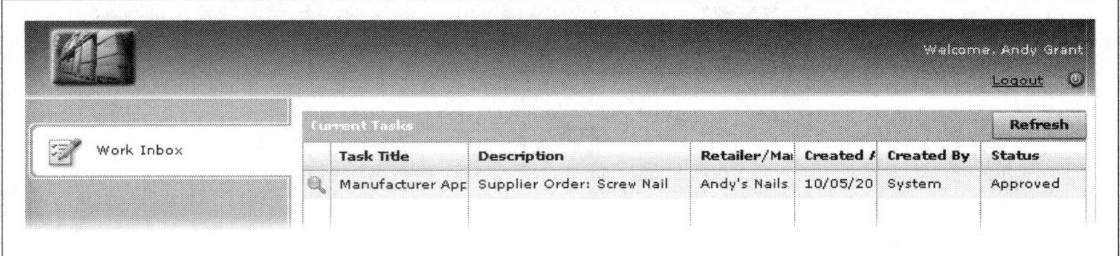

Figure 10-28. The Manufacturer's Work Inbox after order approval

Introducing Process Orchestration

While looking at the UI, did you realize that the Retailer and the Supplier are engaged in the "approve-and-confirm" conversation similar to *SimpleVacationRequest*? The same is true for the Supplier and the Manufacturer. This simplicity, however, is achieved by premeditated separation of activities into completely different processes.

Take a first look at the process diagram of the *SupplierProcess*, Figure 10-29.

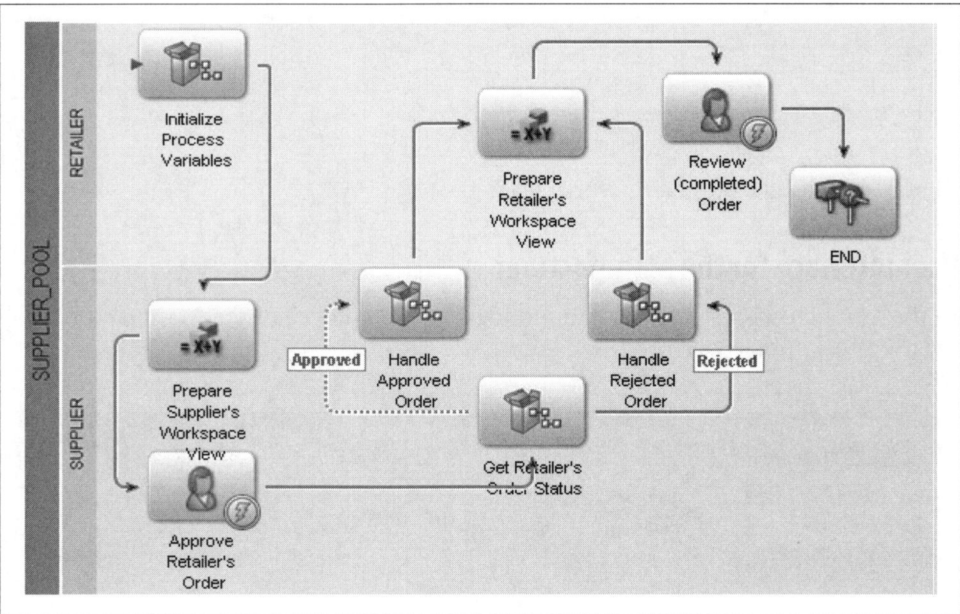

Figure 10-29. SupplierProcess describes the workflow between the Retailer and a Supplier

Not only does it not have the reordering logic for the Supplier, but it actually does not mention a Manufacturer at all. Instead, the Handle Approved Order activity is jump-starting (see the section "Orchestrating Processes with Asynchronous Events" on page 551 later in this chapter) a set of entirely different processes between the Supplier and its Manufacturers, such as *AndyNailsProcess*, presented in Figure 10-30.

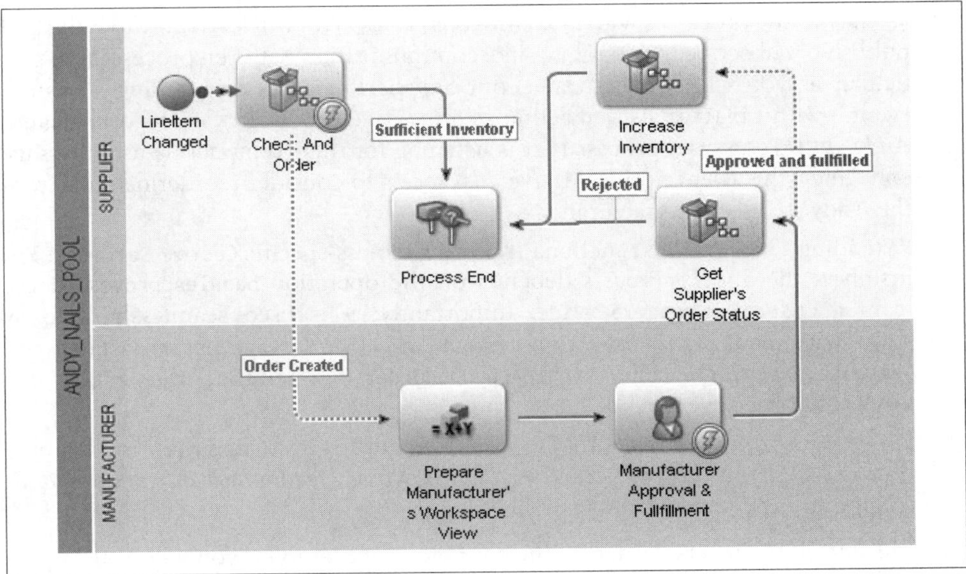

Figure 10-30. AndyNailsProcess describes the workflow between a Supplier and Andy's Nails, our sample nails manufacturer

As a reminder, the Supplier maintains local storage to fulfill the orders without delays. For instance, in the case of products made by Andy's Nails, the Supplier keeps as much as has been ordered over the last week (the duration varies from Manufacturer to Manufacturer based on their production cycle). And, in case of the *AndyNailsProcess*, it is the activity *CheckAndOrder* that either starts actual (re)ordering from a Manufacturer or returns immediately, if the order can be fulfilled from the local storage.

As you can see, the workflow between the three parties gets decomposed into two separate processes, each of which is relatively simple. This approach scales to an unlimited number of Suppliers and Manufacturers. Notice that ultimately, we are not talking about two processes. Each Manufacturer may have a different process with the Supplier, similar to the *AndyNailsProcess* only in how it gets started and in the outcome.

The following sections illustrate details of the process orchestration.

The Warehouse Processes Under the Hood

Now that you know the business use case, let's look at the implementation side. We are going to discuss four topics:

- Using the LiveCycle API from the custom Flex application, which absolves us from the confines of the prebuilt Adobe Workspace. We will be illustrating snippets of the *WarehouseWorkspace* application that accompanies this chapter.
- Orchestrating processes with *asynchronous events*. You will learn how to build and publish or subscribe to messaging-like communication between processes. In particular, as you will see a bit later, our *SupplierProcess* is dispatching a custom event—with `LineItemChanged` acting as a message producer. On the other hand, *AndyNailsProcess* is a process that is listening for this event, acting as a message consumer; this event notifies *AndyNailsProcess* to consider reordering nails from the Andy's Nails manufacturer.
- Extending LiveCycle ES functionality with business-specific `Custom Services`. For instance, the *SupplierProcess* depends on the operation `handleApprovedOrder()` from a custom `SupplierService`. Importantly, it is used seamlessly, side by side with standard operations such as `UserService.assignTask()` and `SetValue.execute()`. The `handleApprovedOrder()` operation dispatched the `LineItemChanged` event.
- Plugging in your own repository of users and groups from an enterprise database through a custom infrastructure service known as *custom authentication and directory service providers*.

We will start in the reverse order. In the course of the examples, you will be using the *farata_livecycle_sampledb* presented in Figure 10-31.

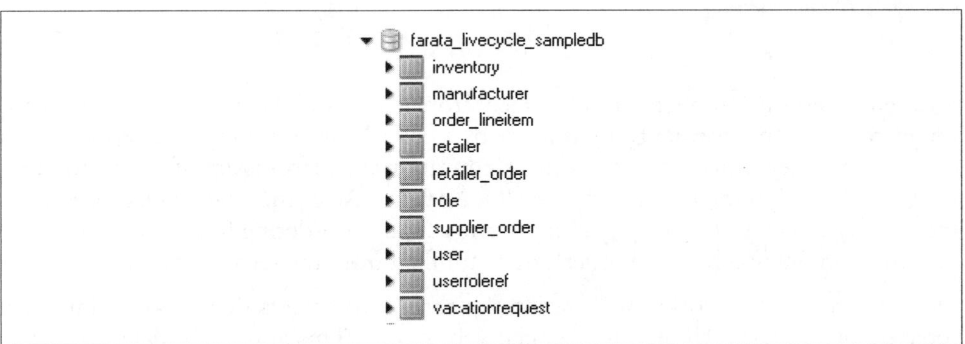

Figure 10-31. Sample database farata_livecycle_sampledb

Extending LiveCycle with Custom Services

You can create your own custom services and add them to the LiveCycle ES repository. No, we are not talking about processes here. As a reminder, any process is ultimately a service, too, with one and only one method: `invoke()`. In contrast, this section is about multifunctional, multimethod services. How do you create those? In a nutshell, you start with a Java POJO class. Once you have a POJO, you may drop it into the LiveCycle service container and use the public methods of the class as service operations within a LiveCycle ES workflow. The simplicity of POJO gets augmented by the packaging: along with the class, you have to JAR the *component.xml* descriptor file plus the JARs of the support classes your POJO depends on. The devil, as usual, is in the details; see the Adobe LiveCycle ES SDK Help, under "Developing Components."

The following sections illustrate two types of custom services: infrastructure services that make LiveCycle ES read users and groups from an enterprise data store instead of its own internal repository, and functional services that will be directly embedded in the Retailer and Supplier processes.

Custom Providers for the User and Group Repository

Imagine that the users of the enterprise are maintained in the database table. How do you tell LiveCycle ES to recognize the custom user and group repository? This is the topic of this section.

Out of the box, LiveCycle ES allows you to plug in an enterprise user repository kept in LDAP. For all other cases, you need to create a customization of the User Management ES component that will enable you to create your own *enterprise domain*. In our example, this will result in the synchronization of LiveCycle's repository of users and groups with the one kept in *farata_livecycle_sampledb*. Figure 10-32 presents the view of the LiveCycle ES Administration Console after such a `FarataDomain` has been configured. Sparing you the configuration steps (see the LiveCycle Administration Console Help, "Configuring Enterprise Domain"), you will jump straight to building the custom services that enable this functionality.

User Management ES provides authentication, authorization, and user management for LiveCycle ES services. By default, it supports Java Authentication and Authorization Service (JAAS) and Lightweight Directory Access Protocol (LDAP) authentication. However, the part of the LiveCycle API known as the User Management SPI (SPI stands for Service Provider Interface) supports creation of custom providers:

- Authentication provider
- User provider
- Group provider

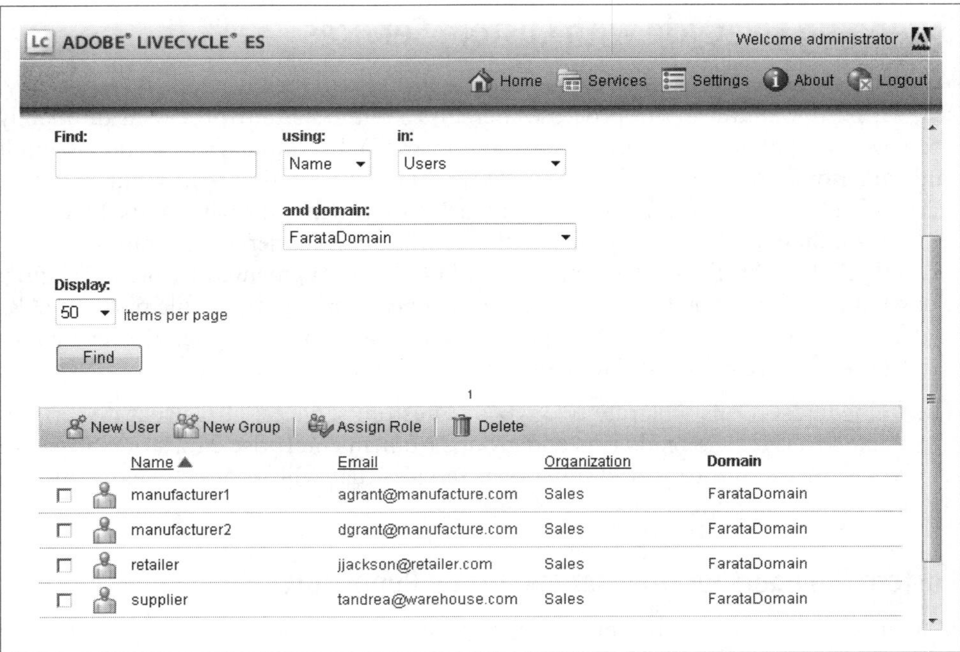

Figure 10-32. The LiveCycle Administration Console is seeing users from farata_livecycle_sampledb after FarataDomain has been configured via a custom authentication provider and custom directory service

The last two are often jointly referred to as the *directory service provider*. More information is available in the online reference "Programming LiveCycle 8.2: Developing SPIs for LiveCycle ES" (*http://tinyurl.com/y92r4p9*).

Creating custom authentication providers

The *authentication provider* is being used by LiveCycle ES far beyond authorization and the interactive logon to the Workspace. In fact, any API-based invocation of a LiveCycle ES service requires a username and password credentials pair, as shown in Example 10-17, which samples the Java code that completes a certain task. Notice the username and password credentials that are required to create the instance of the `ServiceClientFactory`.

Example 10-17. Snippet of the Java code required to complete a task

```
import com.adobe.idp.dsc.clientsdk.ServiceClientFactory;
import com.adobe.idp.taskmanager.dsc.client.TaskManagerClientFactory;

final Properties props = new Properties();
props.setProperty("DSC_DEFAULT_EJB_ENDPOINT", "jnp://localhost:1099");
props.setProperty("DSC_TRANSPORT_PROTOCOL","EJB");
props.setProperty("DSC_SERVER_TYPE", "JBoss");
```

```
props.setProperty("DSC_CREDENTIAL_USERNAME", username);
props.setProperty("DSC_CREDENTIAL_PASSWORD", password);

ServiceClientFactory factory = ServiceClientFactory.createInstance(props);
final TaskManager taskManager = TaskManagerClientFactory.getTaskManager(factory) ;
taskManager.completeTask( taskId ) ;
```

Conversely, User Management ES has to recognize the user with these credentials in one of the registered domains. To do that, User Management is invoking the `authenticate()` method of the domain's authentication provider. To write the custom authentication provider, you have to implement `com.adobe.idp.um.spi.authentication.AuthProvider` with the `authenticate()` and `getConfigName()` methods.

Suppose the enterprise users are registered in the `user` table of *farata_livecycle_sampledb* (Example 10-18).

Example 10-18. User table from farata_livecycle_sampledb

```
CREATE TABLE  user (
  User_ID varchar(36) NOT NULL,
  Description varchar(255) default NULL,
  Last_Name varchar(100) NOT NULL,
  First_Name varchar(100) NOT NULL,
  Email varchar(100) NOT NULL,
  Phone varchar(30) default NULL,
  Department varchar(100) NOT NULL,
  Locked bit(1) NOT NULL,
  LoginName varchar(60) NOT NULL,
  Pass_Code varchar(32) NOT NULL,
  PRIMARY KEY  (User_ID)
)
```

At the end of the day, you have to confirm that the user/password combination is valid, so you again resort to the Clear Data Builder approach; the snippet of the `UMRepository` class in the Example 10-19 shows how to annotate the method `checkPassword()` to access our database.

Example 10-19. Definition of annotated checkPassword() method; the concrete class UMRepositoryDAO gets generated by Clear Data Builder as part of the Ant build script

```
package com.farata.datasource;

import java.util.List;

/**
 * @daoflex:webservice
 *   pool=jdbc/farata
 */
@SuppressWarnings("unchecked")
public abstract class UMRepository {
   . . .
   /**
   * @daoflex:sql
```

```
   *  sql=::  select count(*) matchCount from User where LoginName=:loginName and
   *  Pass_Code=:passCode
   *  ::
   *  transferType=UMPasswordValidationDTO[]
   */
   public abstract List checkPassword(String loginName, String passCode);
}
```

As a part of the project build, Clear Data Builder generates two JAR files: one with the original abstract classes and another with the DAO extensions, called *services-original.jar* and *services-generated.jar* by default. The latter contains the generated `UMRepositoryDAO` class, which implements the `checkPassword()` method.

Example 10-20 shows the complete code of the custom authentication provider. See how this method is used to validate the `loginName/password` combination.

Example 10-20. Complete code of the example custom authentication provider

```
package com.farata.lc.spi;

import java.util.List;
import java.util.Map;
import java.util.logging.Level;
import java.util.logging.Logger;

import com.adobe.idp.um.spi.authentication.AuthProvider;
import com.adobe.idp.um.spi.authentication.AuthResponse;
import com.adobe.idp.um.spi.authentication.AuthResponseImpl;
import com.adobe.idp.um.spi.authentication.AuthScheme;
import com.farata.datasource.UMRepositoryDAO;
import com.farata.datasource.dto.UMPasswordValidationDTO;
import com.farata.lc.spi.impl.UsersProvider;

@SuppressWarnings("unchecked")
public class AuthenticationManager implements AuthProvider {
  public static final Logger logger = Logger.getLogger(
   AuthenticationManager.class.getName()
  );

  public AuthResponse authenticate(Map credential, List authConfigs) {

    String authType = (String)credential.get(AuthProvider.AUTH_TYPE);
     if ( authType == null || !AuthScheme.AUTHTYPE_USERNAME_PWD.equals(authType) ){
      String message = "Farata auth provider does not support " + authType + "
             authentication type";
      logger.severe(message);
      throw new PrincipalProviderException(message) ;
    }

    String userName = (String) credential.get(AuthProvider.USER_NAME);
    String password = (String) credential.get(AuthProvider.PASSWORD);

    AuthResponse response = new AuthResponseImpl();
    response.setAuthStatus(
      checkPassword(userName, password) ?
```

```
        AuthResponse.AUTH_SUCCESS :
        AuthResponse.AUTH_FAILED
    );
    response.setDomain(UsersProvider.FARATA_DOMAIN);
        response.setAuthType(AuthScheme.AUTHTYPE_USERNAME_PWD);
        response.setUsername(userName);
        return response ;
    }

     private boolean checkPassword(String loginName, String password){
      if ( loginName == null || password == null )
          return false;
      try{
       UMRepositoryDAO umRepository = new UMRepositoryDAO();
       List<UMPasswordValidationDTO> checkResult = umRepository.checkPassword(
          loginName, password
       );
       return checkResult.size() > 0 && checkResult.get(0).MATCHCOUNT > 0;
      }catch(Exception e){
       logger.log(Level.WARNING, "Error occured during user authentication.", e);
       return false;
      }
   }

   public String getConfigName() {
    return "FarataAuthenticationProvider";
   }
}
```

Finally, Example 10-21 presents a snippet of the *component.xml* descriptor relevant to our custom authentication provider.

Example 10-21. Registration of the custom authentication provider in component.xml

```
<service name="FarataAuthenticationService">
  <implementation-class>com.farata.lc.spi.AuthenticationManager</implementation-
class>
  <specifications>
   <specification spec-id="com.adobe.idp.um.spi.authentication.AuthProvider"/>
  </specifications>
  <operations>
      <operation name="authenticate" method="authenticate" >
         <input-parameter name="credential" type="java.util.Map" />
         <input-parameter name="authConfigs" type="java.util.List" />
         <output-parameter name="echoed-value"
type="com.adobe.idp.um.spi.authentication.AuthResponse"/>
      </operation>
      <operation name="getConfigName" method="getConfigName" >
         <output-parameter name="echoed-value" type="java.lang.String"/>
      </operation>
  </operations>
</service>
```

Creating a custom directory service provider

As a reminder, according to User Management SPI, in addition to a custom authentication provider, we have to implement a user provider and group provider. These two are jointly called a *directory service provider*.

This means that your Java class has to implement two interfaces: `DirectoryUserProvider` and `DirectoryGroupProvider`. Each of these interfaces extends the `DirectoryPrincipalProvider` interface with its two methods:

```
DSPrincipalCollection getPrincipals(DirectoryProviderConfig config, Object state)
boolean testConfiguration(DirectoryProviderConfig config)
```

The `DirectoryUserProvider` does not have any other methods. The single remaining method of the custom directory service provider comes from the `DirectoryGroupProvider` interface:

```
public DSGroupContainmentRecord getGroupMembers (
      DirectoryProviderConfig config,
      DSPrincipalIdRecord principalID
)throws IDPException;
```

The `config` parameter of `getGroupMembers()` allows it to recognize whether `getPrincipals()` is called on the `DirectoryGroupProvider` or the `DirectoryUserProvider` interface. The following snippet illustrates how this can be done by calling one of the `getUserConfig()` or `getGroupConfig()` methods:

```
if  config.getUserConfig() == null )?
      new GroupsProvider():
      new UsersProvider();
```

The most interesting part is that `getPrincipals()` is designed to be called many times, in sequence, to support the piecemeal retrieval of the user and group records in batches until it returns `null`, indicating that all records have been retrieved. From the performance point of view, it would be undesirable to fetch all users' database records in one chunk, and to that end, the second parameter—`state`—enables the developer to pass some data between the two sequential calls. This provision is obviously of high value for large enterprises with thousands of users.

The actual implementation of `state` is entirely open. In particular, you will be using the partial retrieval from the database based on the `LIMIT` clause, as supported by MySQL Server DBMS. Accordingly, our `state` object will carry the sequential offset to the number of the record to start the next batch, initially zero.

When `getPrincipals()` gets called first (in the sequence), `state` is `null`. Otherwise, `state` is what it was assigned to during the previous invocation. Accordingly, if—like it is in our case—`State`'s constructor does not require arguments, the following logic will apply:

```
State state = (obj==null)? new State(): (State) obj;
```

Example 10-22 is the high-level view of our implementation. We will define a custom `DSPrincipalCollectionProvider` interface that deals only with `state`, and not related to `config`.

Example 10-22. Definition of the DSPrincipalCollectionProvider interface

```
package com.farata.lc.spi;

import com.adobe.idp.um.spi.directoryservices.DSPrincipalCollection;
import com.farata.lc.spi.impl.State;

public interface DSPrincipalCollectionProvider {
   DSPrincipalCollection getPrincipalCollection(State state);
}
```

With both `GroupsProvider` and `UserProvider` implementing the method `getPrincipalCollection()`, the logic of the `getPrincipals()` method gets reduced to the following snippet:

```
DSPrincipalCollectionProvider provider =
     ( config.getUserConfig() == null )?
      new GroupsProvider():
      new UsersProvider();

State state = (obj==null)? new State(): (State) obj;
return provider.getPrincipalCollection( state );
```

And, with `UserProvider` encapsulating the inner workings of the `getGroupMembers()` method, the complete code of the corresponding `DirectoryManager` class looks like Example 10-23.

Example 10-23. Complete code of DirectoryManager.java

```
package com.farata.lc.spi;

import java.util.logging.Level;
import java.util.logging.Logger;

import com.adobe.idp.common.errors.exception.IDPException;
import com.adobe.idp.um.spi.directoryservices.DSGroupContainmentRecord;
import com.adobe.idp.um.spi.directoryservices.DSPrincipalCollection;
import com.adobe.idp.um.spi.directoryservices.DSPrincipalIdRecord;
import com.adobe.idp.um.spi.directoryservices.DirectoryGroupProvider;
import com.adobe.idp.um.spi.directoryservices.DirectoryProviderConfig;
import com.adobe.idp.um.spi.directoryservices.DirectoryUserProvider;
import com.farata.lc.spi.impl.GroupsProvider;
import com.farata.lc.spi.impl.State;
import com.farata.lc.spi.impl.UsersProvider;

public class DirectoryManager implements DirectoryUserProvider,
DirectoryGroupProvider
{
   public static final Logger logger = Logger.getLogger(
      DirectoryManager.class.getName()
```

```
    );

    public DSGroupContainmentRecord getGroupMembers (
       DirectoryProviderConfig config,
       DSPrincipalIdRecord principalID
    )throws IDPException{
       return UsersProvider.getGroupMembers(config, principalID);
    }

    public DSPrincipalCollection getPrincipals   (
       DirectoryProviderConfig config,
       Object obj
    ) throws IDPException{
       try   {
          DSPrincipalCollectionProvider provider =
            ( config.getUserConfig() == null )?
             new GroupsProvider():
             new UsersProvider();

          State state = (obj==null)? new State(): (State) obj;

          return provider.getPrincipalCollection( state );
       } catch (PrincipalProviderException e) {
          logger.log(Level.SEVERE, e.getMessage(), e);
          throw e;
       } catch(Exception e){
          String message = "Farata principal provider: error occurred during
          principals retrieval.";
          logger.log(Level.SEVERE, message, e);
          throw new PrincipalProviderException(message, e);
       }
    }

    public boolean testConfiguration(DirectoryProviderConfig config){
       if ( !UsersProvider.FARATA_DOMAIN.equals(config.getDomain()) )
          return false;
       return true;
    }
}
```

Creating a custom groups provider

Now that the task is delegated to two different classes, you will start with the simplest—the *groups provider*. It implements only one method, `getPrincipalCollection()`, which returns a partial collection, that is, a batch of groups. Example 10-25 shows the definition of the tables where these groups are, based on the **role** table of the *farata_livecycle_sampledb*, shown in Example 10-24.

Example 10-24. Role (group) database repository from farata_livecycle_sampledb

```
CREATE TABLE  role (
  Role_ID varchar(36) NOT NULL,
  Role_Name varchar(100) NOT NULL,
```

```
  PRIMARY KEY  (Role_ID)
)
```

Piggybacking on the Clear Data Builder methodology, you add one more annotated method to the abstract class `UMRepository–getGroupsBatch()`; see Example 10-25. Please note the use of the `limit` clause, which allows elegant data pagination in MySQL (the mechanisms of data pagination are very database-specific and are beyond the scope of this book).

Here you select only `batchSize` (or fewer) number of records from the `role` table starting at the given `offset`. The result of the method is an `ArrayList` of `UMGroupDTO` records, each having `ROLE_ID` and `ROLE_NAME` properties of type `String`.

Example 10-25. Annotated method getGroupsBatch

```
public abstract class UMRepository {
. . .
/**
* @daoflex:sql
*  sql=::  select * from Role order by Role_ID limit :offset, :batchSize
*  ::
*  transferType=UMGroupDTO[]
*/
public abstract List getGroupsBatch(long offset, int batchSize);
}
```

Finally, Example 10-26 defines the `State` object. It will carry the `offset` at which you should be starting the retrieval of the next record batch plus the `completed` flag, initially set to `false`.

Example 10-26. The State object

```
package com.farata.lc.spi.impl;

public class State {
   public long offset = 0;
   public boolean completed = false;
}
```

And now you are ready to outline the code of the `getPrincipalCollection(State state)` method. It should start with checking the `completed` property of `state`. As a reminder, the incoming `state` has been set during the previous invocation of the method. If the value is `true`, you should return `null`:

```
if ( state.completed )
      return null;
```

Otherwise, you obtain the current batch of groups from the database using the `UMRepositoryDAO` class (generated for us by Clear Data Builder). If the batch is empty we, again, return `null`:

```
UMRepositoryDAO umRepository = new UMRepositoryDAO();
List<UMGroupDTO> groups = umRepository.getGroupsBatch(
```

```
        state.offset, GROUPS_BATCH_COUNT
    );
    if ( groups.size() == 0 )
        return null;
```

It is also possible that the size of the retrieved data is simply less than you asked for. In this case, you have reached the end of the data and should raise the `state.completed` flag to `true`, so that the next invocation of the method will return `null`. Alternatively, if you retrieved the full batch, you can increase `state.offset` one batch more:

```
    if ( groups.size() < GROUPS_BATCH_COUNT)
        state.completed = true;
    else
        state.offset = state.offset + GROUPS_BATCH_COUNT;
```

Now you should create the empty `DSPrincipalCollection` and set its `state` property to carry the `offset` and `complete` into the next time's sequential call:

```
    DSPrincipalCollection principalCollection = new DSPrincipalCollection();
    principalCollection.setState( state );
```

The rest is technicality: looping through the list of groups, you will add records to the `principalCollection` one at a time:

```
        for ( UMGroupDTO group: groups ){
            DSPrincipalRecord principalRecord = new DSPrincipalRecord();
            . . .
            principalRecord.setOid( group.ROLE_ID );
            principalRecord.setOriginalName( group.ROLE_NAME );
            . . .
            principalCollection.addDSPrincipalRecord( principalRecord );
        }
        return principalCollection;
    }
```

The complete code of the `GroupsProvider` class is presented in Example 10-27.

Example 10-27. Complete code of the GroupsProvider class

```
package com.farata.lc.spi.impl;

import java.util.List;
import java.util.logging.Level;
import java.util.logging.Logger;


import com.adobe.idp.um.spi.directoryservices.DSPrincipalCollection;
import com.adobe.idp.um.spi.directoryservices.DSPrincipalRecord;
import com.farata.datasource.UMRepositoryDAO;
import com.farata.datasource.dto.UMGroupDTO;
import com.farata.lc.spi.DSPrincipalCollectionProvider;
import com.farata.lc.spi.PrincipalProviderException;

@SuppressWarnings("unchecked")
public class GroupsProvider implements DSPrincipalCollectionProvider{
    public static final Logger logger = Logger.getLogger(
```

```
        GroupsProvider.class.getName());

    private static final String CANONICAL_NAME_SEPARATOR = ":";
    private static final String CANONICAL_GROUPNAME_PREFIX = "GROUP" +
                                                          CANONICAL_NAME_SEPARATOR;
    private static final int GROUPS_BATCH_COUNT = 2000;

    public DSPrincipalCollection getPrincipalCollection(State state){
        try{
            if (state.completed )
                return null;
            UMRepositoryDAO umRepository = new UMRepositoryDAO();
            List<UMGroupDTO> groups = umRepository.getGroupsBatch(
                state.offset, GROUPS_BATCH_COUNT
            );
            if ( groups.size() == 0 )
                return null;
            else if ( groups.size() < GROUPS_BATCH_COUNT)
                state.completed = true;
            else
                state.offset = state.offset + GROUPS_BATCH_COUNT;

            DSPrincipalCollection principalCollection = new DSPrincipalCollection();
            for ( UMGroupDTO group: groups ){
                DSPrincipalRecord principalRecord = new DSPrincipalRecord();
                principalRecord.setOid( group.ROLE_ID );
                principalRecord.setCanonicalName(composeGroupCanonicalName(
                                        group.ROLE_ID, group.ROLE_NAME ));
                principalRecord.setDomainName( UsersProvider.FARATA_DOMAIN );
                principalRecord.setCommonName( group.ROLE_NAME );
                principalRecord.setOriginalName( group.ROLE_NAME );
                principalRecord.setFamilyName( group.ROLE_NAME );
                principalRecord.setGivenName( group.ROLE_NAME );
                principalRecord.setDescription( group.ROLE_NAME );
                principalRecord.setIsSystem(false);
                principalRecord.setDisabled(false);
                principalRecord.setPrincipalType( DSPrincipalRecord.PRINCIPALTYPE_GROUP );
                principalCollection.addDSPrincipalRecord( principalRecord );
            }
            principalCollection.setState( state );
            return principalCollection;
        }catch(Exception e){
            String message = "Farata groups provider: error occured during
                            groups retrieval.";
            logger.log(Level.SEVERE, message, e);
            throw new PrincipalProviderException(message, e);
        }
    }

    private static String composeGroupCanonicalName(String userId, String groupName){
        return CANONICAL_GROUPNAME_PREFIX + userId + CANONICAL_NAME_SEPARATOR + groupName;
    }
}
```

Creating a custom users provider

Implementation of the custom users provider is, to a large degree, very similar to that of the custom groups provider. After all, both classes implement the `DSPrincipalCollectionProvider` interface with the single method `getPrincipalCollection()`. In this respect, the difference between groups and users providers is that instead of batches of groups, you have to deliver batches of users. To that end, you are relying on the `getUserBatch()` method of the generated `UMRepositoryDAO` class:

```
/**
* @daoflex:sql
*  sql=::  select * from User order by User_ID limit :offset, :batchSize
*  ::
*  transferType=UMUserDTO[]
*/
public abstract List getUsersBatch(long offset, int batchSize);
```

Also, properties of each `DSPrincipalRecord` returned in the collection of users are slightly different from those of the groups' records:

```
principalRecord.setEmail( user.getEMAIL() ) ;
principalRecord.setFamilyName( user.getLAST_NAME() ) ;
principalRecord.setGivenName( user.getFIRST_NAME() ) ;
principalRecord.setTelephoneNumber( user.getPHONE() ) ;
principalRecord.setUserid( user.getLOGINNAME() ) ;
```

Besides implementing `getPrincipalCollection()`, a custom user provider should implement the static `getGroupMembers()` method, returning members of the group in the so-called `DSGroupContainmentRecord`. The definition of the relevant *userroleref* table from *farata_livecycle_sampledb* is shown in Example 10-28.

Example 10-28. table from farata_livecycle_sampledb

```
CREATE TABLE  userroleref (
  ID varchar(36) NOT NULL,
  Role_ID varchar(36) NOT NULL,
  User_ID varchar(36) NOT NULL,
  PRIMARY KEY  (ID)
)
```

Example 10-29 depicts the implementation of this method from our `UsersProvider` class.

Example 10-29. Implementation of the getGroupMembers() method for the custom users provider

```
public static DSGroupContainmentRecord getGroupMembers
(
   DirectoryProviderConfig config,
   DSPrincipalIdRecord principalID
)
throws IDPException{
   DSGroupContainmentRecord groupRecord = new DSGroupContainmentRecord() ;
   groupRecord.setCanonicalName( principalID.getCanonicalName() ) ;
   groupRecord.setDomainName( principalID.getDomainName() ) ;
```

```
    String groupId = getPrincipalId(principalID.getCanonicalName()) ;
    UMRepositoryDAO dao = new UMRepositoryDAO();
    List<UMRoleUsersDTO> users = dao.getUsersByRole( groupId );
    for ( UMRoleUsersDTO user: users ){
       DSPrincipalIdRecord member = new DSPrincipalIdRecord();
       member.setDomainName( groupRecord.getDomainName() ) ;
       member.setCanonicalName( composeUserCanonicalName(user.getUSER_ID(),
                                                   user.getLOGINNAME())) ;
       groupRecord.addPrincipalMember( member ) ;
    }
    return groupRecord;
 }
```

The example code relies on the `getUsersByRole()` method of the generated `UMRepositoryDAO` class:

```
/**
* @daoflex:sql
*  sql=::  select us.User_ID, us.LoginName from User us inner join UserRoleRef
*  ref on us.User_ID=ref.User_ID where ref.Role_ID=:roleId
*  ::
*  transferType=UMRoleUsersDTO[]
*/
public abstract List getUsersByRole(String roleId);
```

The complete code of our custom users provider is shown in Example 10-30.

Example 10-30. Complete code of UsersProvider.java

```
package com.farata.lc.spi.impl;

import java.util.List;
import java.util.logging.Level;
import java.util.logging.Logger;

import com.adobe.idp.common.errors.exception.IDPException;
import com.adobe.idp.um.spi.directoryservices.DSGroupContainmentRecord;
import com.adobe.idp.um.spi.directoryservices.DSPrincipalCollection;
import com.adobe.idp.um.spi.directoryservices.DSPrincipalIdRecord;
import com.adobe.idp.um.spi.directoryservices.DSPrincipalRecord;
import com.adobe.idp.um.spi.directoryservices.DirectoryProviderConfig;
import com.farata.datasource.UMRepositoryDAO;
import com.farata.datasource.dto.UMRoleUsersDTO;
import com.farata.datasource.dto.UMUserDTO;
import com.farata.lc.spi.DSPrincipalCollectionProvider;
import com.farata.lc.spi.PrincipalProviderException;

@SuppressWarnings("unchecked")
public class UsersProvider implements DSPrincipalCollectionProvider{

    public static final Logger logger = Logger.getLogger(UsersProvider.class.getName());

   public static final String FARATA_DOMAIN = "FarataDomain";
   private static final String CANONICAL_NAME_SEPARATOR = ":" ;
   private static final String CANONICAL_USERNAME_PREFIX = "USER" +
```

```
                                                        CANONICAL_NAME_SEPARATOR ;
private static final int USERS_BATCH_COUNT = 2000 ;

public DSPrincipalCollection getPrincipalCollection(State state){
   try{
      if ( state.completed )
         return null;

      UMRepositoryDAO umRepository = new UMRepositoryDAO();
      List<UMUserDTO> users = umRepository.getUsersBatch(state.offset,
                                                        USERS_BATCH_COUNT);
      if ( users.size() < USERS_BATCH_COUNT && users.size() > 0 )
         state.completed = true;
      else if ( users.size() == 0 )
         return null;
      else
         state.offset=state.offset + USERS_BATCH_COUNT;

      DSPrincipalCollection principalCollection = new DSPrincipalCollection() ;
      principalCollection.setState( state );
      for ( UMUserDTO user: users ){
         DSPrincipalRecord principalRecord = new DSPrincipalRecord() ;
         principalRecord.setOid( user.getUSER_ID() ) ;
         principalRecord.setDescription( user.getDESCRIPTION() ) ;
         principalRecord.setEmail( user.getEMAIL() ) ;
         principalRecord.setFamilyName( user.getLAST_NAME() ) ;
         principalRecord.setGivenName( user.getFIRST_NAME() ) ;
         principalRecord.setTelephoneNumber( user.getPHONE() ) ;
         principalRecord.setUserid( user.getLOGINNAME() ) ;

         principalRecord.setCanonicalName(composeUserCanonicalName(
                                 user.getUSER_ID(), user.getLOGINNAME() )) ;
         principalRecord.setCommonName( user.getLOGINNAME() ) ;
         principalRecord.setDomainName(UsersProvider.FARATA_DOMAIN) ;
         principalRecord.setOrg( user.getDEPARTMENT() ) ;
         principalRecord.setPrincipalType( DSPrincipalRecord.PRINCIPALTYPE_USER ) ;
         principalRecord.setLocale( "en" ) ;
         principalRecord.setDisabled( user.getLOCKED() ) ;
         principalRecord.setIsSystem(false) ;
         principalCollection.addDSPrincipalRecord(principalRecord) ;
      }
      return principalCollection;
   }
   catch(Exception e){
      String message = "Farata users provider: error occured during users retrieval.";
      logger.log(Level.SEVERE, message, e);
      throw new PrincipalProviderException(message, e) ;
   }
}

public static DSGroupContainmentRecord getGroupMembers
(
   DirectoryProviderConfig config,
   DSPrincipalIdRecord principalID
)
```

```
    throws IDPException{
        DSGroupContainmentRecord groupRecord = new DSGroupContainmentRecord() ;
        groupRecord.setCanonicalName( principalID.getCanonicalName() ) ;
        groupRecord.setDomainName( principalID.getDomainName() ) ;

        String groupId = getPrincipalId(principalID.getCanonicalName()) ;
        UMRepositoryDAO dao = new UMRepositoryDAO();
        List<UMRoleUsersDTO> users = dao.getUsersByRole( groupId );
        for ( UMRoleUsersDTO user: users ){
            DSPrincipalIdRecord member = new DSPrincipalIdRecord();
            member.setDomainName( groupRecord.getDomainName() ) ;
            member.setCanonicalName( composeUserCanonicalName(user.getUSER_ID(),
                                                    user.getLOGINNAME())) ;

            groupRecord.addPrincipalMember( member ) ;
        }
        return groupRecord;
    }

    private static String composeUserCanonicalName(String userId, String loginName){
        return CANONICAL_USERNAME_PREFIX + userId + CANONICAL_NAME_SEPARATOR + loginName ;
    }

    private static String getPrincipalId(String canonicalName){
        if ( canonicalName != null && canonicalName.length() > 0 ){
            final int startIndex = canonicalName.indexOf(CANONICAL_NAME_SEPARATOR) ;
            final int endIndex = canonicalName.indexOf(CANONICAL_NAME_SEPARATOR,
                                                        startIndex + 1) ;
            if ( startIndex != -1 && endIndex != -1 )
                return canonicalName.substring( startIndex + 1, endIndex ) ;
        }

        return null ;
    }
}
```

Custom Solution Components

The custom authentication, users, and groups providers described in the previous sections illustrate the creation of custom services that extend the infrastructure of LiveCycle ES. On top of that, you can create functional custom services that directly participate in the logic of the processes that you design. In LiveCycle ES, these services are referred to as *custom solution components*. (This name can be quite confusing. The fact is that for the purposes of deployment, one or more services can get JARed together in one file along with *component.xml*. So, strictly speaking, there are custom services deployed through component JARs.)

Custom solution components are direct extensions of the services provided by LiveCycle ES and you may use them side by side with each other. For instance, *SupplierProcess* from Figure 10-33 is using four operations of the custom *SupplierService* that has been deployed into LiveCycle ES as part of the custom component *FarataSampleComponent.jar*:

- `initializeProcess`
- `handleApprovedOrder`
- `handleRejectedOrder`
- `getRetailerOrderStatus`

The complete *SupplierService.java* application is presented in Example 10-33; next, we will walk you through two methods: `initializeProcessVariables()` and `handleApprovedOrder()`.

Implementation of initializeProcessVariables()

The method `initializeProcessVariables()` computes the variables of `orderStatus` and `supplierUserName` given the `orderId`, where `orderId` is a key to locate the order in the *farata_livecycle_sampledb* database. Figure 10-33 presents the partial diagram of the process, highlighting the properties of the activity based on this method.

The service that carries the `initializeProcessVariables()` method—`SupplierService`—is listed in the *component.xml* descriptor of the *FarataComponent-Sample.jar* file along with the JARs required to resolve references to the dependent classes (these classes are required by the Clear Data Builder methodology), as in Example 10-31.

Example 10-31. Component descriptor for FarataComponentSample.jar

```
<component xmlns="http://adobe.com/idp/dsc/component/document">
   <component-id>com.farata.livecycle.FarataSampleComponent</component-id>
   <version>4.0</version>
    <class-path>log4j.jar services-generated.jar services-original.jar daofle10-
runtime.jar</class-path>
   <bootstrap-class>com.farata.lc.ComponentBootstrap</bootstrap-class>
   <lifecycle-class>com.farata.lc.ComponentLifeCycle</lifecycle-class>
   <descriptor-
class>com.adobe.idp.dsc.component.impl.DefaultPOJODescriptorImpl</descriptor-class>
   <search-order>PARENT_FIRST</search-order>
   <dynamic-import-packages>
      <package version="1.0" isOptional="true">*</package>
   </dynamic-import-packages>
   <services>
      <service name="SupplierService">
           <implementation-
class>com.farata.lc.warehouse.SupplierService</implementation-class>
         <operations> . . .
. . .
       </service>
  </services>
</component>
```

All operations of `SupplierService` are registered in *component.xml* along with both the input and output parameters. Please notice the `binding-type="Bean"` in the definition of the `Supplier` and `Status` parameters. It indicates that particular public properties of

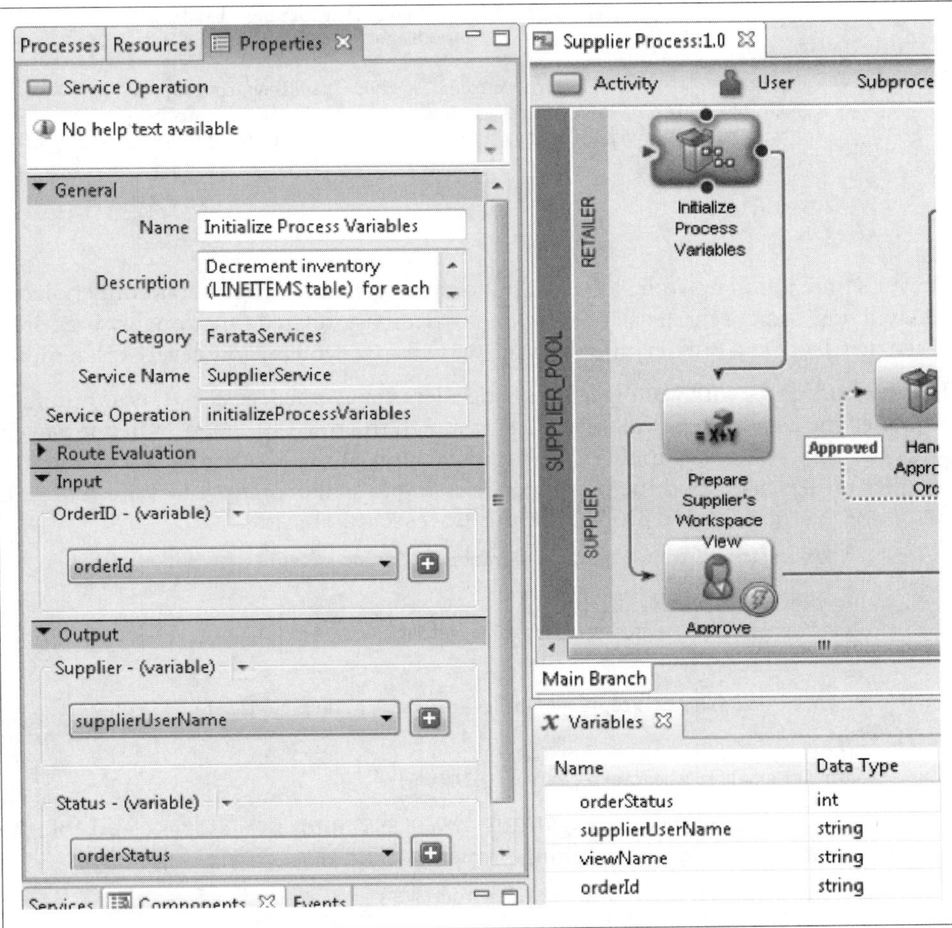

Figure 10-33. Initialization of the SupplierProcess's variables by the custom service method

a class returned by the Java method should be interpreted as "independent" output variables of the service method. In comparison, parameters of `handleApprovedOrder()` use the default binding type (Example 10-32).

Example 10-32. Fragment of SupplierService related to registering operations

```
<service name="SupplierService">
    <implementation-class>com.farata.lc.warehouse.SupplierService
    </implementation-class>
  <operations>
    <operation name="initializeProcessVariables"
             method="initializeProcessVariables" >
    <input-parameter name="OrderID" type="java.lang.String" />
    <output-parameter name="Supplier" type="java.lang.String" binding-
                                type="Bean" property="supplier"/>
```

```
        <output-parameter name="Status" type="java.lang.String" binding-
                                        type="Bean" property="status"/>
        </operation>
        <operation name="handleApprovedOrder" method="handleApprovedOrder" >
        <input-parameter name="OrderID" type="java.lang.String" />
        <output-parameter name="Status" type="java.lang.Integer" />
        </operation>
  . . .
      </operations>
   </service>
```

Now it's time to roll up your sleeves or put on your glasses—whatever is your choice—you will now look at the Java code. Again, all database-related functionality is entirely based on Clear Data Builder, and this time we will spare you the low-level explanations.

The method starts with pulling a list of suppliers via `userDao.getSuppliers()`. In fact, it queries the `user` table for all records that match the role "supplier." Then it naïvely picks the first available supplier (the sophistication of the geographical location and supplier ratings is beyond the point we are trying to make) and prepares to return its `LOGINNAME` via the `supplier` property of the `ProcessData` object:

```
public ProcessData initializeProcessVariables( String orderId ){

    UserDAO userDao = new UserDAO();
    List<SupplierDTO> suppliers = userDao.getSuppliers();

    if ( suppliers.size() == 0 ){
       throw new RuntimeException("There are no suppliers available.");
    }
    ProcessData data = new ProcessData();
    data.setSupplier(suppliers.get(0).LOGINNAME);
```

Then, the method writes `ORDER_STATUS_INPROCESS` into the `status` field of the `retailer_order` table and the matching property of the `ProcessData` object:

```
RetailerOrderDAO orderDao = new RetailerOrderDAO();
orderDao.updateOrderStatus(orderId, ORDER_STATUS_INPROCESS);


data.setStatus(ORDER_STATUS_INPROCESS);
```

Finally, it decreases the inventory, effectively prebooking the order:

```
   decreaseInventory( orderId );

   return data;
}
```

Implementation of handleApprovedOrder()

Now let's look at the `handleApprovedOrder()` method. It deserves our attention: after all, this is where the event dispatching is being done. Figure 10-34 illustrates how the method is plugged into *SupplierProcess*.

The method takes single argument `orderId`. It pulls down the list of the order line items and for each item dispatches a custom event, `LineItemChanged` (more on defining events, using them as a process start point, and dispatching them in the following sections of the chapter):

```
for ( int i = 0; i < orderLineItems.size(); i++ ){
   OrderLineItemDTO lineItem = orderLineItems.get(i);
   EventsHelper.dispatchLineItemEvent(
      lineItem.LINEITEM_ID, lineItem.MNF_CODE, "quantity");
}
```

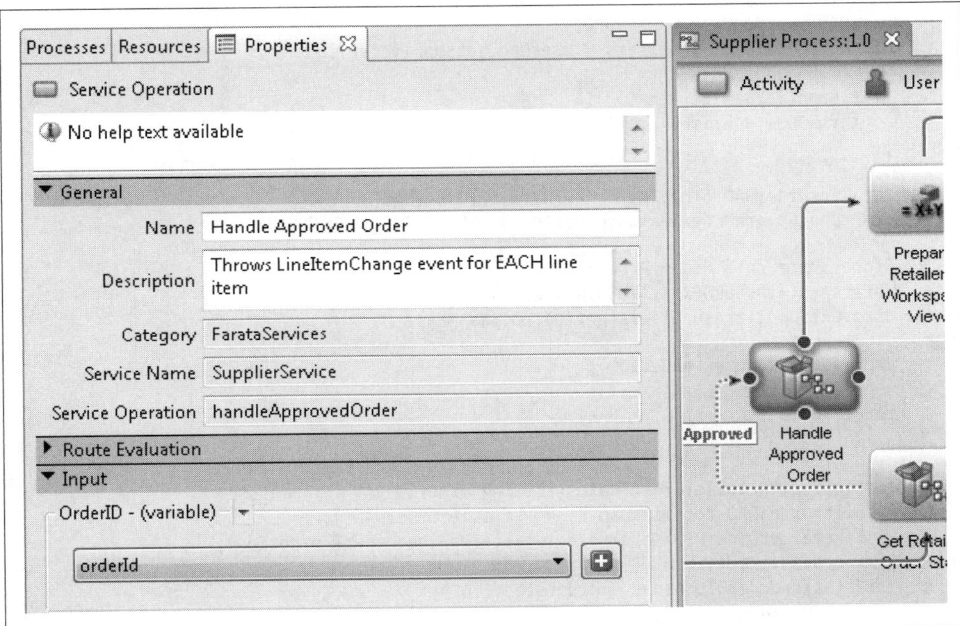

Figure 10-34. Operation handleApprovedOrder encapsulates dispatching of the LineItemChanged events

This concludes our limited walkthrough of *SupplierService.java*. The complete code is available in Example 10-33.

Example 10-33. Complete code of the custom file SupplierService.java

```
package com.farata.lc.warehouse;

import java.util.*;
import com.farata.datasource.*;
import com.farata.datasource.dto.*;
import com.farata.lc.events.EventsHelper;
import com.theriabook.remoting.ChangeObjectImpl;

@SuppressWarnings("unchecked")
```

```
public class SupplierService{

   public static final int ORDER_STATUS_UNDEFINED = -1;
   public static final int ORDER_STATUS_CREATED = 1;
   public static final int ORDER_STATUS_INPROCESS = 2;
   public static final int ORDER_STATUS_APPROVED = 3;
   public static final int ORDER_STATUS_REJECTED = 4;
   public static final int ORDER_STATUS_COMPLETED = 5;
   public static final int ORDER_STATUS_CONFIRMED = 6;

   public ProcessData initializeProcessVariables( String orderId ){

      UserDAO userDao = new UserDAO();
      List<SupplierDTO> suppliers = userDao.getSuppliers();

      if ( suppliers.size() == 0 ){
         throw new RuntimeException("There are no suppliers available.");
      }

      RetailerOrderDAO orderDao = new RetailerOrderDAO();
      orderDao.updateOrderStatus(orderId, ORDER_STATUS_INPROCESS);

      ProcessData data = new ProcessData();
      data.setStatus(ORDER_STATUS_INPROCESS);
      data.setSupplier(suppliers.get(0).LOGINNAME);

      decreaseInventory( orderId );

      return data;
   }

   public long getRetailerOrderStatus( String orderId ){
      RetailerOrderDAO retailerDao = new RetailerOrderDAO();
      List<RetailerOrderDTO> orders = retailerDao.getOrder( orderId );
      if ( orders.size() > 0 ){
         RetailerOrderDTO order = orders.get( 0 );
         return order.STATUS;
      }
      return ORDER_STATUS_UNDEFINED;
   }

   public int handleApprovedOrder( String orderId ){
      OrderLineItemDAO orderLineItemDao = new OrderLineItemDAO();
      List<OrderLineItemDTO> orderLineItems = orderLineItemDao.getLineItems(
         orderId
      );
      for ( int i = 0; i < orderLineItems.size(); i++ ){
         OrderLineItemDTO lineItem = orderLineItems.get(i);
         EventsHelper.dispatchLineItemEvent(
            lineItem.LINEITEM_ID, lineItem.MNF_CODE);
      }
      return ORDER_STATUS_APPROVED;
   }

   public int handleRejectedOrder( String orderId ){
```

```
    OrderLineItemDAO orderLineItemDao = new OrderLineItemDAO();
    List<OrderLineItemDTO> orderLineItems = orderLineItemDao.getLineItems(
       orderId
    );
    Map<String, OrderLineItemDTO> orderLIMappings =
          new HashMap<String, OrderLineItemDTO>( orderLineItems.size() );
    Map params = getOrderLineItemsParam( orderLineItems, orderLIMappings );

    InventoryDAO inventoryDao = new InventoryDAO();
    List<UpdatableInventoryItemDTO> lineItems =
       inventoryDao.getLineItemsByGuids(
          params
       );

    List changeObjects = new ArrayList( lineItems.size() );
    for ( int i = 0; i < lineItems.size(); i++ ){
       UpdatableInventoryItemDTO lineItem = lineItems.get(i);
       String lineItemId = lineItem.LINEITEM_ID;
       OrderLineItemDTO orderItem = orderLIMappings.get( lineItemId );
       long quantityAvailable = lineItem.QUANTITY;
       long quantityRequired = orderItem.QUANTITY;
       quantityAvailable += quantityRequired;
       ChangeObjectImpl co = new ChangeObjectImpl();
       co.setPreviousVersion(lineItem);
       UpdatableInventoryItemDTO newLineItem = clone( lineItem );
       newLineItem.setQUANTITY( quantityAvailable );
       co.setNewVersion(newLineItem);
       co.setState(2);
       changeObjects.add( co );
    }

    try {
       inventoryDao.getLineItemsByGuids_updateItems( changeObjects );
    } catch(Exception e){
       // TODO: add logging
       throw new RuntimeException(e);
    }
    return ORDER_STATUS_REJECTED;
}

private void decreaseInventory (String orderId){
    OrderLineItemDAO orderLineItemDao = new OrderLineItemDAO();
    List<OrderLineItemDTO> orderLineItems = orderLineItemDao.getLineItems(
        orderId
    );
    Map<String, OrderLineItemDTO> orderLIMappings =
          new HashMap<String, OrderLineItemDTO>( orderLineItems.size() );
    Map params = getOrderLineItemsParam( orderLineItems, orderLIMappings );

    InventoryDAO inventoryDao = new InventoryDAO();
    List<UpdatableInventoryItemDTO> lineItems = inventoryDao.getLineItemsByGuids(
        params
    );

    List changeObjects = new ArrayList( lineItems.size() );
```

```
        for ( int i = 0; i < lineItems.size(); i++ ){
            UpdatableInventoryItemDTO lineItem = lineItems.get(i);
            String lineItemId = lineItem.LINEITEM_ID;
            OrderLineItemDTO orderItem = orderLIMappings.get( lineItemId );
            long quantityAvailable = lineItem.QUANTITY;
            long quantityRequired = orderItem.REQUIRED_QUANTITY;
            quantityAvailable -= quantityRequired;
            quantityAvailable = quantityAvailable < 0 ? 0 : quantityAvailable;

            ChangeObjectImpl co = new ChangeObjectImpl();
            co.setPreviousVersion(lineItem);
            UpdatableInventoryItemDTO newLineItem = clone( lineItem );
            newLineItem.QUANTITY = quantityAvailable ;
            co.setNewVersion(newLineItem);
            co.setState(2);
            changeObjects.add( co );
        }

         try{
            inventoryDao.getLineItemsByGuids_updateItems( changeObjects );
        } catch(Exception e){
            // TODO: add logging
            throw new RuntimeException(e);
        }
    }

    private Map getOrderLineItemsParam( List<OrderLineItemDTO> orderLineItems,
                  Map<String, OrderLineItemDTO> orderLIMappings ){
       int lineItemsSize = orderLineItems.size();
       List<String> keys = new ArrayList<String>( lineItemsSize );

       for ( int i = 0; i < lineItemsSize; i++ ){
          OrderLineItemDTO orderLineItem = orderLineItems.get(i);
          keys.add( "'" + orderLineItem.LINEITEM_ID + "'" );
          orderLIMappings.put( orderLineItem.LINEITEM_ID, orderLineItem );
       }

       String keyString = keys.toString();
       keyString = keyString.substring(1, keyString.length() - 1);
       keyString = "( " + keyString + " )";
       return Collections.singletonMap("values", keyString);
    }

    private UpdatableInventoryItemDTO clone( UpdatableInventoryItemDTO source){
       UpdatableInventoryItemDTO target = new UpdatableInventoryItemDTO();
       target.DESCRIPTION = source.DESCRIPTION;
       target.LINEITEM_CODE = source.LINEITEM_CODE;
       target.LINEITEM_ID = source.LINEITEM_ID;
       target.MANUFACTURER_ID = source.MANUFACTURER_ID;
       target.PRICE = source.PRICE;
       target.QUANTITY = source.QUANTITY;
       target.UNIT = source.UNIT;
       return target;
    }
}
```

Orchestrating Processes with Asynchronous Events

While describing our business scenario, we mentioned that the `handleApprovedOrder` method of the *SupplierProcess* activity is initiating an entirely different process between the Supplier and a specific Manufacturer, *AndyNailsProcess* (see Figures 10-28 and 10-29). In fact, this was both an over- and an understatement at the same time.

It is an overstatement because *SupplierProcess* does not directly initiate any other processes. It is an understatement because indirectly it may initiate an arbitrary number of the processes—as many as will be willing to listen to the event.

Meet asynchronous events: *SupplierProcess* simply broadcasts an event per each line of the approved retailer order, as shown in Example 10-34.

Example 10-34. Fragment of SupplierProcess related to dispatching events

```
public int handleApprovedOrder( String orderId ){
   OrderLineItemDAO orderLineItemDao = new OrderLineItemDAO();
   List<OrderLineItemDTO> orderLineItems = orderLineItemDao.getLineItems(
      orderId
   );
   for ( int i = 0; i < orderLineItems.size(); i++ ){
      OrderLineItemDTO lineItem = orderLineItems.get(i);
      EventsHelper.dispatchLineItemEvent(
         lineItem.LINEITEM_ID, lineItem.MNF_CODE);
   }
   return ORDER_STATUS_APPROVED;
}
```

How are the processes are being set up to "wake up" based on the broadcast event, and what does it take to actually dispatch these events? These are the topics of the next section.

Defining Events

Asynchronous events look and act much like network messages. They have two sections that you may relate to the *headers* and *payload*, in messaging lingo. Example 10-35 represents the schema defining a record with two fields: `string LineItemId` and `string ManufacturerCode`. In Example 10-35, we call this record *LineItemEventTemplate* to hint at what we will do with it just a bit later.

Example 10-35. The XML schema used to define our custom LineItemChanged event

```
<?xml version="1.0" encoding="UTF-8"?>
<xs:schema xmlns:xs="http://www.w3.org/2001/XMLSchema"
elementFormDefault="qualified" attributeFormDefault="unqualified">
   <xs:element name="LineItemEventTemplate">
      <xs:complexType>
         <xs:sequence>
            <xs:element name="LineItemId">
               <xs:simpleType>
```

```
                <xs:restriction base="xs:string">
                    <xs:minLength value="1"/>
                    <xs:maxLength value="36"/>
                </xs:restriction>
            </xs:simpleType>
        </xs:element>
        <xs:element name="ManufacturerCode">
            <xs:simpleType>
                <xs:restriction base="xs:string">
                    <xs:minLength value="1"/>
                    <xs:maxLength value="100"/>
                </xs:restriction>
            </xs:simpleType>
        </xs:element>
    </xs:sequence>
  </xs:complexType>
 </xs:element>
</xs:schema>
```

The event gets defined in the Workbench (and, of course, you can import it, either separately or as a part of the LiveCycle archive). Figure 10-35 shows the screenshot of the Workbench dialog defining the `LineItemChanged` event. Notice that Event Data Template contains the XML schema we have just discussed. It corresponds to the headers if you switch to messaging lingo again. The event is ready to be thrown.

Dispatching Events

To dispatch this event, you should first obtain an instance of `EventServiceClient`:

```
ServiceClientFactory factory = ServiceClientFactory.createInstance(
   UMLocalUtils.getSystemContext()
);

EventServiceClient client = EventServiceClient.getInstance( factory );
```

Once you have `EventServiceClient`, you create the event, populate its **`properties`** (headers) and/or `data` (payload) properties:

```
CreateAsynchronousEventInfo info = client.newCreateAsynchronousEventInfo(
   "LineItemChanged"
);
Map props = new HashMap(2);
props.put("LineItemId", lineItemId );
props.put("Manufacturer_Code", mnfCode );
info.setEventProperties( props );
client.createEvent(info, null);
```

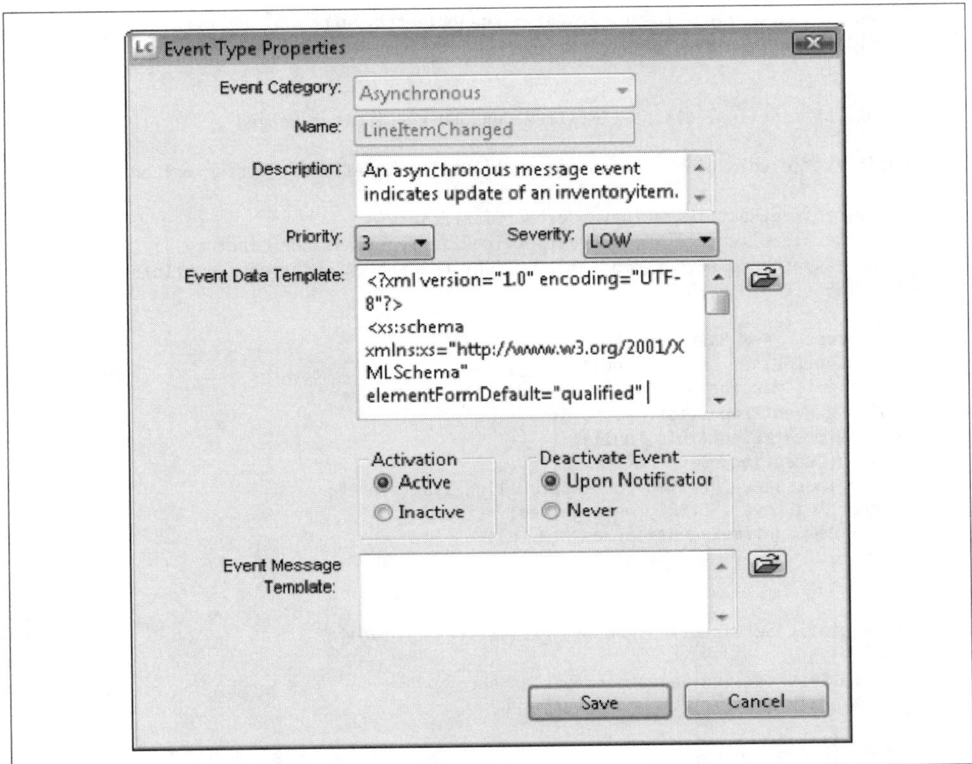

Figure 10-35. The Workbench dialog defining the event

Example 10-36 contains the complete code of the `EventsHelper` class illustrating this technique.

Example 10-36. The complete code of EventsHelper.java

```
package com.farata.lc.events;

import java.io.InputStream;
import java.util.HashMap;
import java.util.Map;
import java.util.logging.Level;
import java.util.logging.Logger;

import com.adobe.idp.dsc.clientsdk.ServiceClientFactory;
import com.adobe.idp.event.client.EventServiceClient;
import com.adobe.idp.event.command.CreateAsynchronousEventInfo;
import com.adobe.idp.event.exception.EventTypeDoesNotExistException;
import com.adobe.idp.um.api.UMLocalUtils;

@SuppressWarnings("unchecked")
public class EventsHelper {
```

```
    protected static final Logger logger = Logger.getLogger(
      EventsHelper.class.getName()
    );

    private static final String LINE_ITEM_CHANGED = "LineItemChanged";

    public static void dispatchLineItemEvent( String lineItemId, String mnfCode ){
     try{
      ServiceClientFactory factory = getServiceFactory();
      EventServiceClient client = EventServiceClient.getInstance( factory );
      CreateAsynchronousEventInfo info = client.newCreateAsynchronousEventInfo(
         LINE_ITEM_CHANGED
      );
      Map props = new HashMap(2);
      props.put("LineItemId", lineItemId );
      props.put("ManufacturerCode", mnfCode );
      info.setEventProperties( props );
      client.createEvent(info, null);
     } catch(Exception e){
      String message = "Failed to dispatch line item event";
      logger.log(Level.SEVERE, message, e);
      throw new RuntimeException(message, e);
     }
    }

    private static ServiceClientFactory getServiceFactory(){
     try{
      return ServiceClientFactory.createInstance(
         UMLocalUtils.getSystemContext()
      );
     } catch(Exception e){
      String message = "Error occured getting system service factory";
      logger.log(Level.SEVERE, message, e);
      throw new RuntimeException(message, e);
     }
    }
}
```

Starting the Process on an Asynchronous Event

To start the process on an event, you should, well, begin with the process. In our "nails and hammers" example, there are two Manufacturers' processes awaiting an asynchronous event to start. They are *AndyNailsProcess* and *DanielHammersProcess*. Let's have a close look at the diagram of the *AndyNailsProcess* in Figure 10-36.

The circle in the upper-left corner is the event that LiveCycle ES will monitor to instantiate the process: `LineItemChanged`. Meanwhile, the process-starting activity is *CheckAndOrder* (Figure 10-37).

Behind this activity is the Java method `checkAndOrder()` of the custom class *AndyNailsService*. It conditionally orders boxes of nails if the quantity on hand is less than was ordered by retailers over the last week. As shown in Example 10-37, `checkAndOrder()` returns the `SupplierOrderProcessData` (whose code is in Example 10-38) even when no order is necessary, as in one of the programmers' jokes—when a programmer goes to bed, she prepares two glasses: a glass of water, in case she will get thirsty, and an empty glass, in case she won't.

Example 10-37. Fragment of checkAndOrder()

```
public SupplierOrderProcessData checkAndOrder( String lineItemId )  throws
LineItemNotFoundException{
. . . .
if ( currentQuantity - lastWeekDemand < 0 ){
   return createSupplierOrder (
      lineItemDTO.LINEITEM_ID,
      (new Double(lastWeekDemand)).longValue()
   );
} else {
   SupplierOrderProcessData data = new SupplierOrderProcessData();
   data.setOrderCreated( false );
   return data;
}
```

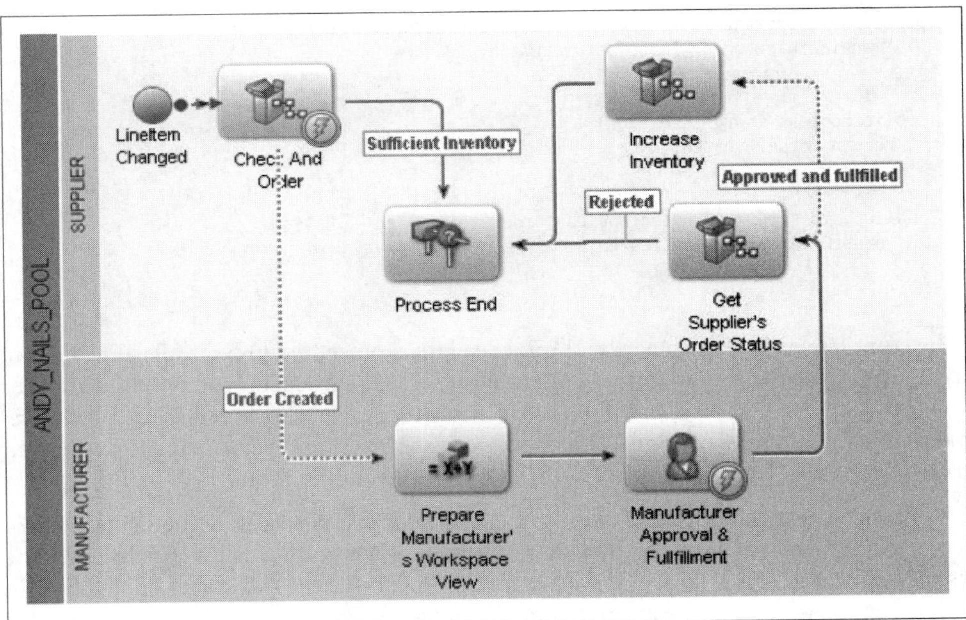

Figure 10-36. AndyNailsProcess starts dispatching the LineItemChanged event (if the event filter condition is met)

Example 10-38. The complete code of SupplierOrderProcessData

```
package com.farata.lc.warehouse;

public class SupplierOrderProcessData {
   private String _orderId;
   private String _manufacturerLogin;
   private boolean _orderCreated;

   public String getOrderId() {
      return _orderId;
   }

   public void setOrderId(String orderId) {
      _orderId = orderId;
   }

   public String getManufacturerLogin() {
      return _manufacturerLogin;
   }

   public void setManufacturerLogin(String manufacturerLogin) {
      _manufacturerLogin = manufacturerLogin;
   }

   public boolean isOrderCreated() {
      return _orderCreated;
   }

   public void setOrderCreated(boolean orderCreated) {
      _orderCreated = orderCreated;
   }
}
```

The complete code of the `AndyNailsService` class is presented in Example 10-39. Note that among the files accompanying this chapter (see the Preface), you will find another custom service class example—`DanielHammerService`. Both classes, `DanielHammerService` and `AndyNailsService`, extend `AbstractManufacturerService`; however, in the case of `DanielHammerService`, reordering is based on the monthly demand.

Importantly, both *AndyNailsProcess* and *DanielHammersProcess* define the asynchronous event `LineItemChanged` as their start point. In other words, the LiveCycle ES engine is monitoring the dispatching of the events and delivers these "messages" to "subscribers" such as *AndyNailsProcess* and *DanielHammersProcess*.

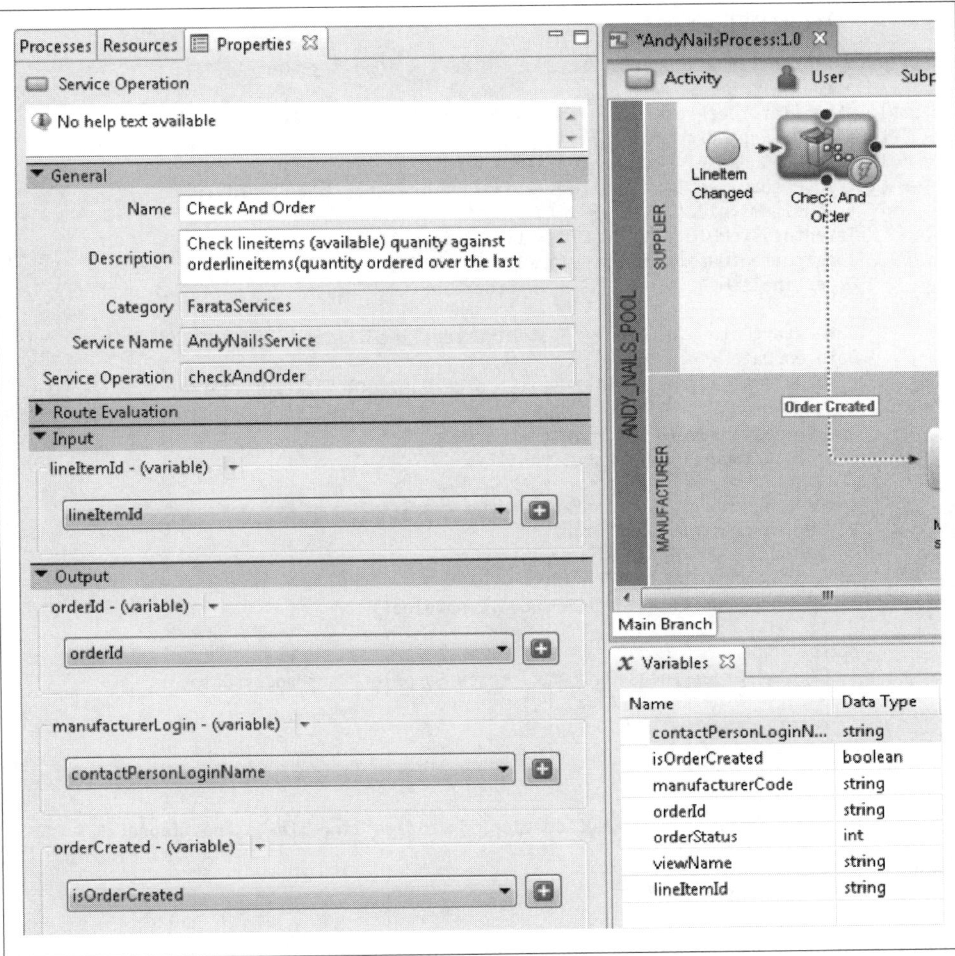

Figure 10-37. CheckAndOrder: the starting activity of AndyNailsProcess

Example 10-39. The complete code of custom class AndyNailsService

```
package com.farata.lc.warehouse;

import java.util.Date;
import java.util.List;

import com.farata.datasource.InventoryDAO;
import com.farata.datasource.OrderLineItemDAO;
import com.farata.datasource.dto.InventoryItemDTO;
import com.farata.datasource.dto.OrderLineItemSumDTO;

@SuppressWarnings("unchecked")
public class AndyNailsService extends AbstractManufacturerService implements
```

```
IManufacturerService{

   private static final long MILLISECONDS_IN_WEEK = 1000 * 3600 * 24 * 7;

   public SupplierOrderProcessData checkAndOrder( String lineItemId )  throws
      LineItemNotFoundException{
      InventoryDAO dao = new InventoryDAO();
      List<InventoryItemDTO> lineItems = dao.getLineItem( lineItemId );
      if ( lineItems.size() > 0 ){
         InventoryItemDTO lineItemDTO = lineItems.get(0);
         long currentQuantity = lineItemDTO.QUANTITY;
         OrderLineItemDAO orderDao = new OrderLineItemDAO();

         Date startDate = new Date( System.currentTimeMillis() - MILLISECONDS_IN_WEEK );
         Date endDate = new Date();
         List<OrderLineItemSumDTO> result = orderDao.getRetailerOrderSum(
                                            lineItemId, startDate, endDate );
         OrderLineItemSumDTO sum = result.get(0);
         double lastWeekDemand = sum.QUANTITY;

         if ( currentQuantity - lastWeekDemand < 0 ){
            return createSupplierOrder
            (
               lineItemDTO.LINEITEM_ID,
               (new Double(lastWeekDemand)).longValue()
            );
         }else{
            SupplierOrderProcessData data = new SupplierOrderProcessData();
            data.setOrderCreated( false );
            return data;
         }
      }
      else
         throw new LineItemNotFoundException("Specified line item is not found: " +
                                                                      lineItemId);
   }
}
```

While configuring the event (-based) start point, you can set the *filter*, similar to the message selector. Remember the line:

```
props.put("ManufacturerCode", mnfCode );
```

from the `EventsHelper` class from Example 10-36? Now look at Figure 10-38, which illustrates the start point filter for *AndyNailsProcess*. The filter is being set to `Manufacturer_Code=nail` and, accordingly, events that do not contain `"nail"` as the value of the `Manufacturer_Code` will not start the process instance.

Besides specifying a filter, you need to tell the LiveCycle engine how to map the incoming event data into variables of the process. Figure 10-39 illustrates how the process variable `LineItemId` is prescribed to take, upon the event's arrival, the value of `lineItemId`, which was set by the `props.put("LineItemId", lineItemId)` line of `EventHelper`.

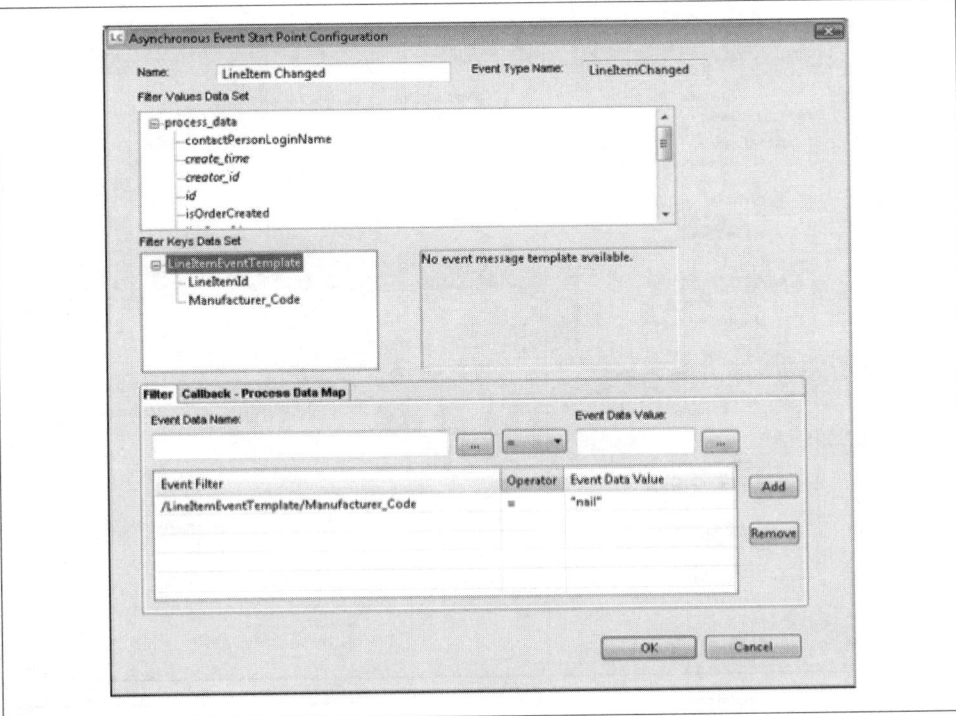

Figure 10-38. Setup of the event filter

And so you have decomposed a complex process into a set of the simple ones: *SupplierProcess*, *AndyNailsProcess*, *DanielHammersProcess*, and, for that matter, any other process that will react to the `LineItemChanged` event.

Here is the rest of the *AndyNailsProcess* logic. Upon return from the `AndyNailsProcess.checkAndOrder()` operation, the database might already contain a new record in the `supplier_order` table. In this case, the process will expect an approval by a representative of Andy's Nails. For the sake of simplicity, naïvely assume that such approval is enough for the palettes with boxes of nails to magically *appear* in a warehouse. The `SupplierService.getSupplierOrderStatus()` process might need to increase values in the `inventory` table using `SupplierService.increaseInventory()`. Otherwise—if the inventory did not need to be replenished, or if the manufacturer did not approve the order—the `inventory` will not get changed.

Now that you know how to create custom services, plug them into processes, and coordinate these processes with events, let's see how to ignite it all with LiveCycle API calls from inside your Flex application.

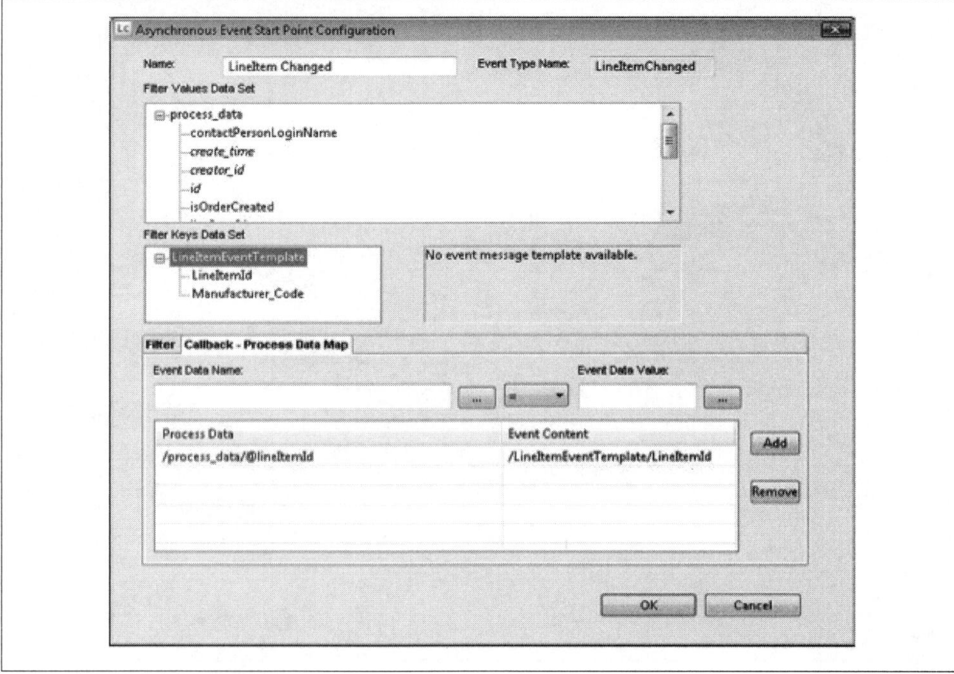

Figure 10-39. Mapping the event data to the process variables

Blending the LiveCycle API with Custom Flex Applications

We have armed ourselves with customer services. We have completed the *SupplierProcess* and modeled a Manufacturer's process with *AndyNailsProcess*. We coordinated all processes via an asynchronous event. Now, it's time to tie it all to the end-user UI.

We will limit the explanation to a single use case: how to start the process from the custom Flex application. Figure 10-40 represents the screen as it is seen by the retailer when placing an order.

The snippet of the `Create Order VBox` from this screen is shown in Example 10-40 (see Example 10-44 for the complete code of the corresponding *CreateRequest.mxml*).

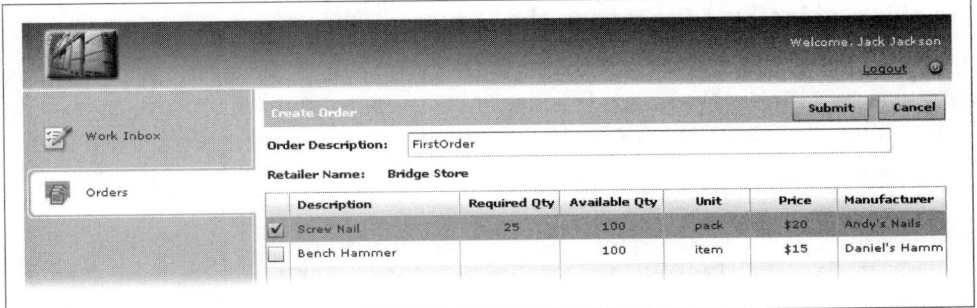

Figure 10-40. Retailer starts the SupplierProcess by clicking Submit

Example 10-40. The fragment of the CreateOrder VBox

```
<?xml version="1.0" encoding="UTF-8"?>
<mx:VBox xmlns:mx="http://www.adobe.com/2006/mxml"
   creationComplete="onCreationComplete()"
   >.  .  .

   <mx:HBox id="controlBar" width="100%" height="24" styleName="controlsStyle" >
      <mx:Label text="Create Order" width="100%" color="white" />
      <mx:Button label="Submit" click="submitRequest()"/>
      <mx:Button label="Cancel" click="cancelRequest()"/>
   </mx:HBox>

   <mx:Form width="100%">
      <mx:FormItem label="Order Description: " width="100%" fontWeight="bold">
         <mx:TextInput id="descriptionText" width="90%" fontWeight="normal"/>
      </mx:FormItem>
      <mx:FormItem label="Retailer Name: ">
         <mx:Label text="{retailers.getItemAt(0).RETAILER_NAME}"/>
      </mx:FormItem>
   </mx:Form>

   <mx:DataGrid id="dg_inventory" dataProvider="{inventoryItems}" height="100%"
width="100%" editable="true">
      </mx:columns>
   </mx:DataGrid>
.  .  .  .
</mx:VBox>
```

Remember now you want LiveCycle to store as little data as possible in its internal database? Here is the two-step algorithm:

- The function `submitRequest()` will remote (asynchronously) to the Java method that persists the order to the business database.
- Upon success, the "result" event handler will remote to yet another Java method to actually start the LiveCycle process instance, passing **`orderId`** as the only parameter.

Let's make it happen, unraveling the steps in the reverse order.

Invoking a LiveCycle Process on the Server

Short of DAO methods, we will concentrate all Java methods to remote to a single Java `facade` class, `WorkflowAssembler`. It will span methods to start the process, get a list of tasks, complete a task, and so on:

```
package com.farata.warehouse.wf;

. . .

public class WorkflowAssembler
{
   public String startProcess(   String orderId ){
      . . .
   }
   public void completeTask ( long taskId ){
      . . .
   }
}
```

To remote to this class, create the following destination in *remoting-config.xml*:

```
<destination id="WorkflowAssembler">
    <properties>
        <source>com.farata.warehouse.wf.WorkflowAssembler</source>
   </properties>
</destination>
```

Now look at the implementation of the `startProcess()` method. All roads lead to Rome. All Java API calls require an instance of `ServiceClientFactory` from the `com.adobe.idp.dsc.clientsdk.ServiceClientFactory` package. Example 10-41 presents the helper method `getServiceClientFactory()`, a part of the `WorkflowAssembler` that builds such a factory.

Example 10-41. A fragment of WorkflowAssember: building the ServiceClientFactory

```
public static ServiceClientFactory getServiceClientFactory() throws UMException {
   // Obtain user login name from the FlexSession
   . . .
   String loginName = . . .

   // Obtain password via loginName from the user table

   String password = . . .

   final Properties properties = new Properties();
   properties.setProperty("DSC_DEFAULT_EJB_ENDPOINT", "jnp://localhost:1099");
   properties.setProperty("DSC_TRANSPORT_PROTOCOL","EJB");
   properties.setProperty("DSC_SERVER_TYPE", "JBoss");
   properties.setProperty("DSC_CREDENTIAL_USERNAME", loginName);
   properties.setProperty("DSC_CREDENTIAL_PASSWORD", password);
   ServiceClientFactory clientFactory = ServiceClientFactory.createInstance(
      properties
   );
```

```
    return serviceClientFactory;
}
```

Now that you have the factory, you can invoke *SupplierProcess* as shown in Example 10-42. (Here, assume that an administrator has granted the authority to `invoke()` the process to the user authenticated with LiveCycle via `loginName` and `password`. In our case, that should be a retailer, although during the setup of the samples, we recommend granting the *invoke* right to all principals from the Farata enterprise domain.)

Example 10-42. A fragment of WorkflowAssember: starting the SupplierProcess

```
package com.farata.warehouse.wf;

. . .

public class WorkflowAssembler
{
   public String startProcess(   String orderId ){
      try   {
         final ServiceClientFactory factory = getServiceClientFactory();
         final ServiceClient serviceClient = factory.getServiceClient() ;
         Map<String, String> params = new HashMap<String, String>();
         params.put("orderId", orderId ) ;
         InvocationRequest request =  factory.createInvocationRequest
         (
            "Supplier Process",
            "invoke",
            params,
            false
         ) ;
         InvocationResponse response = serviceClient.invoke(request);
         JobId jobId = new JobId(response.getInvocationId());
         return jobId.getId() ;
      }
      catch(Exception e){
         throw new WorkflowAssemblerException("Failed to start SupplierService
                                                                   process", e);
      }
   }

   public static ServiceClientFactory getServiceClientFactory() throws UMException
 {
   . . .
 }
 }
```

Starting a Process Instance from the Flex Application

Once you have the Java code to instantiate the *SupplierProcess*, the sky's the limit. The following snippet shows the remoting destination that you add to our Flex application's *remoting-config.xml* file to reach the `WorkflowAssembler` class from ActionScript:

```
<destination id="WorkflowAssembler">
    <properties>
        <source>com.farata.warehouse.wf.WorkflowAssembler</source>
  </properties>
</destination>
```

In Chapter 6, we explained how to update several database tables from ActionScript in a single database (and JEE) transaction without writing a custom Java code. Piggybacking on this technique, you can include one more destination in the *remoting-config.xml* file:

```
<destination id="batchGateway">
    <properties>
        <source>com.theriabook.remoting.BatchGateway</source>
  </properties>
</destination>
```

And now you can send changes to collections of orders and order items (see Example 10-45) in a single transaction by calling `batchService.sendBatch()`. Associating the `ResultEvent.RESULT` with the `orderSubmitted()` method, you can ensure that the actual start of the process is executed only if the retailer's order has been saved in the database, as shown in Example 10-43. The complete code of *CreateRequest.mxml* is shown in Example 10-44.

Example 10-43. The fragment of WorkflowAssember: starting the SupplierProcess

```
private function submitRequest():void{

   if ( ! isValid() )
      return;
   . . .
   if ( selectedItems.length > 0 && order ){

      . . .
      // Update tables supplier_order and order_lineitem tables with
      // in a single JEE transaction, passing changes in
      // orderCollection and orderItemsCollection via Farata BatchService

      var batchService:BatchService = new BatchService();
      batchService.registerCollection( orderItems,1 );
      batchService.registerCollection( ordersCollection,0);
      var batch:Array = batchService.batchRegisteredCollections();
      batchService.addEventListener(ResultEvent.RESULT, orderSubmitted);
      var token:AsyncToken = batchService.sendBatch( batch );
      token.orderId = order.ORDER_ID;
   }
}

private function orderSubmitted( event:ResultEvent ):void{
   var orderId:String = event.token.orderId;
   const workflowAssembler:RemoteObject = new RemoteObject();
   workflowAssembler.destination = "WorkflowAssembler";
   workflowAssembler.addEventListener(
      FaultEvent.FAULT,
```

```
        function error( event:FaultEvent ):void{
            Alert.show( event.message.toString() );
        }
    );
    workflowAssembler.addEventListener(ResultEvent.RESULT, processInvoked);

    const token:AsyncToken = workflowAssembler.startProcess( orderId );
}
```

Example 10-44. Complete code of CreateRequest.mxml

```
<?xml version="1.0" encoding="UTF-8"?>
<mx:VBox xmlns:mx="http://www.adobe.com/2006/mxml"
    creationComplete="onCreationComplete()"
    >
     <mx:Metadata>
        [Event(name="back", type="mx.events.FlexEvent")]
    </mx:Metadata>

    <mx:HBox id="controlBar" width="100%" height="24" styleName="controlsStyle" >
        <mx:Label text="Create Order" fontSize="10" width="100%" fontWeight="bold"
                  color="white" paddingLeft="4"/>
        <mx:Button label="Submit" cornerRadius="0" click="submitRequest()"/>
        <mx:Button label="Cancel" cornerRadius="0" paddingRight="5"
                   click="cancelRequest()"/>
    </mx:HBox>

    <mx:Form width="100%">
        <mx:FormItem label="Order Description: " width="100%" fontWeight="bold">
            <mx:TextInput id="descriptionText" width="90%" maxChars="249"
                          fontWeight="normal"/>
        </mx:FormItem>
        <mx:FormItem label="Retailer Name: ">
            <mx:Label text="{retailers.getItemAt(0).RETAILER_NAME}"/>
        </mx:FormItem>
    </mx:Form>

    <mx:DataGrid id="dg_inventory" dataProvider="{inventoryItems}" height="100%"
                 width="100%" editable="true">
        <mx:columns>
            <mx:DataGridColumn width="5" editable="false">
                <mx:itemRenderer>
                    <mx:Component>
                        <mx:Canvas width="100%" height="100%">
                            <mx:CheckBox click="outerDocument.itemSelected(event)"
                                width="18"
                                horizontalCenter="0" verticalCenter="0"
                                />
                        </mx:Canvas>
                    </mx:Component>
                </mx:itemRenderer>
            </mx:DataGridColumn>
            <mx:DataGridColumn dataField="DESCRIPTION" headerText="Description"
                               width="100" editable="false"/>
            <mx:DataGridColumn dataField="REQUIRED_QUANTITY" headerText="Required Qty"
                               width="25" editable="true" textAlign="center"/>
```

```
            <mx:DataGridColumn dataField="QUANTITY" headerText="Available Qty"
                               width="25" editable="false" textAlign="center"/>
            <mx:DataGridColumn dataField="UNIT" headerText="Unit" width="20"
                               editable="false" textAlign="center"/>
            <mx:DataGridColumn dataField="PRICE" headerText="Price"
                               labelFunction="priceFunction" width="20"
                               editable="false" textAlign="center" />
            <mx:DataGridColumn dataField="MNF_NAME" headerText="Manufacturer"
                               width="25" editable="false"/>
        </mx:columns>
    </mx:DataGrid>
    <mx:Script>
        <![CDATA[
import warehouse.collections.OrdersCollection;
import warehouse.collections.OrderLineItemsCollection;
import com.farata.datasource.dto.UpdatableRetailerOrderDTO;
import warehouse.collections.RetailersCollection;
import warehouse.collections.InventoryItemsCollection;
import com.farata.datasource.dto.UpdatableOrderLineItemDTO;
import com.farata.datasource.dto.OrderLineItemDTO;
import com.farata.datasource.dto.InventoryItemDTO;
import warehouse.orderClasses.OrderStatus;
import mx.rpc.AsyncToken;
import mx.formatters.CurrencyFormatter;
import mx.formatters.NumberBase;
import mx.formatters.NumberFormatter;
import mx.rpc.events.ResultEvent;
import com.farata.datasource.dto.RetailerDTO;
import warehouse.security.ISecurityContext;
import warehouse.security.SecurityContext;
import com.theriabook.remoting.BatchService;
import mx.utils.UIDUtil;
import com.farata.datasource.dto.RetailerOrderDTO;
import mx.controls.CheckBox;
import mx.events.FlexEvent;
import mx.controls.Alert;
import mx.rpc.events.FaultEvent;
import mx.logging.Log;
import mx.logging.ILogger;
import com.theriabook.rpc.remoting.*;
import com.theriabook.collections.DataCollection;
import mx.collections.ArrayCollection;
import mx.controls.dataGridClasses.DataGridColumn;
import mx.events.CollectionEvent;
import mx.formatters.DateFormatter;

private var logger:ILogger = Log.getLogger("com.farata.datasource.CreateRequest.mxml");

 [Bindable]private var inventoryItems:DataCollection;
 [Bindable]private var retailers:DataCollection;
 [Bindable]private var ordersCollection:DataCollection;

 [Bindable]private var log : ArrayCollection;

private function onCreationComplete() : void {
```

```
    inventoryItems = new InventoryItemsCollection();
    inventoryItems.fill();

    var context:ISecurityContext = SecurityContext.instance();
    var userId:String = context.user.USER_ID;

    retailers = new RetailersCollection();
    retailers.fill( userId );
}

internal function itemSelected( event:Event ):void{
    var checkBox:CheckBox = event.target as CheckBox;
    var selected:Boolean = checkBox.selected;
    var selectedItem:InventoryItemDTO = dg_inventory.selectedItem as InventoryItemDTO;
    if ( !selectedItem )
        return;

    selectedItem.selected = selected;
}

private function isValid():Boolean{

    if ( !descriptionText.text ){
        Alert.show( "Description is empty" );
        return false;
    }

    if ( retailers.length == 0 ){
        Alert.show( "Retailer not found. Unable to submit this request." );
        return false;
    } else if ( retailers.length > 1 ){
        Alert.show( "Retailer is not selected. Please select it before submitting
this request." );
        return false;
    }

    var isSelected:Boolean = false;
    for ( var i:int = 0; i < inventoryItems.length; i++ ){
        var lineItem:InventoryItemDTO = inventoryItems[i] as InventoryItemDTO;
        if ( lineItem.selected ){
            isSelected = true;
            var quantity:Number = Number(lineItem.REQUIRED_QUANTITY);
            var quantityAvailable:Number = lineItem.QUANTITY;
            if ( isNaN(quantity) || quantity <= 0 ){
                Alert.show("Required quantity is not specified.");
                return false;
            }

            if ( quantity > quantityAvailable ){
                Alert.show("Available quantity can not be less than Required.");
                return false;
            }
        }
    }
```

```
    if (!isSelected){
        Alert.show("No items selected.");
    }

    return true;
}

private function submitRequest():void{

    if ( ! isValid() )
        return;

    var selectedItems:ArrayCollection = new ArrayCollection;

    var orderId:String = UIDUtil.createUID();
    for (var i:int = 0; i < inventoryItems.length; i++ ){
        var inventoryItem:InventoryItemDTO = inventoryItems.getItemAt(i) as InventoryItemDTO;
        var selected:Boolean = inventoryItem.selected;
        if ( selected ){
            var orderLineItem:UpdatableOrderLineItemDTO = new UpdatableOrderLineItemDTO ();
            orderLineItem.LINEITEM_ID = inventoryItem.LINEITEM_ID;
            orderLineItem.ORDER_ID = orderId;
            orderLineItem.QUANTITY = inventoryItem.REQUIRED_QUANTITY;
            orderLineItem.ORDER_TYPE = "retailer";
            selectedItems.addItem( orderLineItem );
        }
    }

    if ( selectedItems.length > 0 ){
        var context:ISecurityContext = SecurityContext.instance();
        var user:Object = context.user;

        var order:UpdatableRetailerOrderDTO = new UpdatableRetailerOrderDTO;
        order.CREATED_AT = new Date;
        order.CREATED_BY = user.USER_ID;
        order.ORDER_ID = orderId;
        order.STATUS = OrderStatus.STATUS_CREATED;
        order.DESCRIPTION = descriptionText.text;
        order.RETAILER_ID = retailers.getItemAt(0).RETAILER_ID;
    }

    if ( selectedItems.length > 0 && order ){

        ordersCollection = new OrdersCollection();
        ordersCollection.addItem( order );
        var orderItems:DataCollection = new OrderLineItemsCollection();
        for ( i = 0; i < selectedItems.length; i++ ) {
            orderItems.addItem( selectedItems[i] );
        }

        var batchService:BatchService = new BatchService();
        batchService.registerCollection( orderItems,1 );
        batchService.registerCollection( ordersCollection,0);
        var batch:Array = batchService.batchRegisteredCollections();
        batchService.addEventListener(ResultEvent.RESULT, orderSubmitted);
```

```
        var token:AsyncToken = batchService.sendBatch( batch );
        batchService.sendBatch( batch );
    }
}

private function orderSubmitted( event:ResultEvent ):void{
    var orderId:String = event.token.orderId;
    const workflowAssembler:RemoteObject = new RemoteObject();
    workflowAssembler.destination = "WorkflowAssembler";
    workflowAssembler.addEventListener(
        FaultEvent.FAULT,
        function error( event:FaultEvent ):void{
            Alert.show( event.message.toString() );
        }
    );
    workflowAssembler.addEventListener(ResultEvent.RESULT, processInvoked);

    const token:AsyncToken = workflowAssembler.startProcess( orderId );
}

private function processInvoked( event:ResultEvent ):void{
    dispatchEvent( new FlexEvent("back") );
}

private function cancelRequest():void{
    dispatchEvent( new FlexEvent("back") );
}


private function priceFunction( value:Object, column:DataGridColumn ):String{
    var formatter:CurrencyFormatter = new CurrencyFormatter;
    return formatter.format( value.PRICE );
}

public function refresh():void{
    onCreationComplete();
}
]]>
</mx:Script>
 </mx:VBox>
```

Example 10-45. Collection classes used by submitRequest() of CreateRequest.mxml

```
package warehouse.collections {
    import com.theriabook.collections.DataCollection;
    public class OrdersCollection extends DataCollection {
        public function OrdersCollection(source:Array=null)    {
            destination = "com.farata.datasource.RetailerOrder";
            method = "getUpdatableOrders";
        }
    }
}

package warehouse.collections {
    import com.theriabook.collections.DataCollection;
    public class OrderLineItemsCollection extends DataCollection {
```

```
        public function OrderLineItemsCollection(){
            destination = "com.farata.datasource.OrderLineItem";
            method = "getUpdatableLineItems";
        }
    }
}
```

This completes our study of blending the LiveCycle API into a custom Flex application.

Summary

Let's look back at what have you seen in this chapter. We started with small Flexlets, complementing the LiveCycle Workspace ES, and ended up with the completely independent Flex applications that treat LiveCycle ES as yet another service container.

We started with the sample set of users provided by the LiveCycle ES sample installation and arrived at an enterprise repository of users and groups from our own database.

We have benefited from LiveCycle ES services, but did not stop there, and extended them with our own. That, in particular, allowed us to perform a decomposition of the complex business process into a scalable set of simpler processes via events.

We have used a lot of Java. For instance, we used Java to dispatch events. You may take our example further by building a reusable event dispatching service and then invoking it, say, from a Flex application. It's just another service container!

CHAPTER 11
Printing with Flex

Measuring programming progress by lines of code is like measuring aircraft building progress by weight.

—Bill Gates

In general, the process of printing from web applications works a little differently compared to printing from the desktop. Web applications have good reason for not allowing direct access to a user's printer: malicious websites could immediately start printing their fliers on your home or corporate printer, offering you anything from pizza delivery to adult entertainment. That's why you can't write a program in JavaScript that would automatically detect all available printers and send them print jobs. That's why the user is forced to manually select the printer via the web browser's pop-up dialog window.

Existing Flash Player bugs add more issues for Flex developers; for example, the Print dialog might not report all features of the available printer, and setting such parameters as tray selection or paper size might not be possible. To put it simply, you may not have complete control over the user's printer from an application running in Flash Player. You may need to adjust your reports to standard printer settings.

Adobe had a product called FlashPaper that tried to mitigate these limitations by adding ActionScript 2 objects to a special control with complete access to the printer. In 2008, however, Adobe discontinued FlashPaper (*http://www.adobe.com/products/flashpaper/eod_faq/*), apparently promoting printing PDF documents using Acrobat instead.

The process of printing from Flash Player consists of starting a single-threaded print job and adding dynamically created pages to it (i.e., the data that comes from a database). Unfortunately, Flash Player's virtual machine AVM2 ActionScript timeout is 15 seconds. Accordingly, for both Flex and AIR, the interval between the following commands shouldn't be more than 15 seconds:

- `PrintJob.start()` and the first `PrintJob.addPage()`

- PrintJob.addPage() and the next PrintJob.addPage()
- PrintJob.addPage() and PrintJob.send()

If, at each of these commands, printing the specified page always completed in 15 seconds or less, your application will be able to print a multipage document, although somewhat slowly. If any of the intervals spans more than 15 seconds, however, your print job will receive a runtime exception, which turns direct printing from Flash Player into an unpleasant experience, if application developers don't handle exceptions properly. Plus, if the internal thread that started the print job failed, it may be automatically closed and unable to be recovered properly.

You can read more about handling printing errors in the Adobe document "Flash Player and Air tasks and system printing" (*http://tinyurl.com/p76s5p*).

You may think that setTimeout() can help break the 15-second barrier for printing, but it can't. Printing has to be handled by the same internal AVM2 thread (apparently a bug), and with setTimeout(), you are in fact spawning a new one. The issue with printing long documents is demonstrated in Example 11-1. The PrintJob starts and the method finishPrinting() is called in the same thread and works fine. If you instead comment out the call to finishPrinting() and uncomment the method setTimeout(), this printing job will fail: the addPage() will throw an exception, because it runs in a thread different than PrintJob.

Imagine that a timeout was initiated not by calling the function setTimeout(), but rather by Flash Player during printing of a multipage document because one of the addPage() calls took longer than 15 seconds. In this case, addPage() would be called on a different internal thread than PrintJob.start() and the addPage() operation would fail, even though Flash Player should've known how to process a such situation properly.

Example 11-1. PrintTimeout.mxml—an illustration of printing failure

```
<?xml version="1.0" encoding="utf-8"?>
<mx:WindowedApplication xmlns:mx="http://www.adobe.com/2006/mxml"
layout="vertical">
   <mx:Button label="Print Me" click="printMe()"/>
   <mx:Script>
      <![CDATA[

         private function printMe() :void {
            var pj:PrintJob = new PrintJob();
            pj.start();

   //           setTimeout(function() :void { finishPrinting(pj);}, 1);

                finishPrinting(pj);
         }
```

```
        private function finishPrinting(pj:PrintJob): void {
            pj.addPage(this);
            pj.send();
        }
    ]]>
  </mx:Script>
</mx:WindowedApplication>
```

Example 11-1 just prints itself, `addPage(this)`, but if it had to print, say, a slow-rendered `DataGrid` with a couple of thousand rows, the chances are high that such a program would time out before the printing job was finished.

There is a bigger problem than the technical restrictions mentioned so far, and it is in the very approach to printing via the `PrintJob` API. The process of programming reports in ActionScript comes down to creating snapshots of components displayed on the users' monitors and sending them to the printer. Because screen resolution differs from printer resolution, however, application developers pursing this method need to create separate layouts just for printing, which is time-consuming and challenging.

That's why you should consider creating and printing your reports as PDF files. Besides, it neatly reinforces this book's philosophy: minimize the amount of code that business application developers have to write. In this chapter, you'll learn how to create XDP-enabled Flex components that will allow application developers to generate PDF documents on the client side with minimal coding.

PDF and XDP

PDF stands for Portable Document Format. It was originally created by Adobe but in July 2008 became an open standard, ISO 32000-1:2008 (*http://www.iso.org/iso/catalogue_detail?csnumber=51502*).

The PDF format is device-independent, but—as opposed to PostScript—it's not a programming language. ISO 32000-1:2008 defines it as:

> a digital form for representing electronic documents to enable users to exchange and view electronic documents independent of the environment in which they were created or the environment in which they are viewed or printed. It is intended for the developer of software that creates PDF files (conforming writers), software that reads existing PDF files and interprets their contents for display and interaction (conforming readers) and PDF products that read and/or write PDF files for a variety of other purposes (conforming products).

PDF is a hierarchical structure that represents a collection of pages to be displayed or printed. Each page contains content objects and resources.

PDF documents can be used for both printing and data-entry purposes. For example, a bank or insurance company may offer applications for opening new accounts as PDF form documents to be filled out by the customers.

XDP (*XML Data Package*) enables storage of PDF content, forms, and data inside the forms and, of course, processes it as XML. On the downside, XDP format is not supported by older versions of Acrobat Reader. The XDP specification is available at *http://partners.adobe.com/public/developer/en/xml/xdp_2.0.pdf*.

PDF Generation on the Server

PDF generation is supported by Adobe LiveCycle and LCDS, as well as other server-side products. Suppose that you have a Flex or AIR window with a number of UI controls, and you want to create a PDF out of it. One option is to create a snapshot of the Flex component or container using the class `mx.graphics.ImageSnapshot` and its function `captureImage()`, which can scale the image to a specific resolution and encode it into a specified image format. You can send an instance of this class via `RemoteObject` to the server with LCDS installed. LCDS then creates a PDF document (or merges it with a PDF form) and includes the new image received from the client.

The problem with this approach is that the resulting PDF will not be searchable. For instance, if a Flex `Panel` has text fields, you won't be able to find the text of these fields in Acrobat Reader if the `Panel` is embedded as a bitmap.

Such PDFs have limitations on resolution as well (to create a PDF with resolution 300 dpi, you'd need to create a multimegabyte image). Also, printed materials often use different CSS and metrics from the screen ones. You don't want to print, say, a background gradient that looks fine on the monitor, but bad on paper.

To embed forms into PDF documents, Adobe uses the XDP format. If you purchase an LCDS license, you'll have the option to use it. You can design forms in Acrobat Designer and export the data from your Flex view, and LCDS will merge the data and the form on the server. On the Java side, LCDS adds several JARs in the *lib* directory of your web application, which makes the `XFAHelper` Java class available for your server-side PDF generation.

After generating the PDF, the server-side program can be:

- Placed as a `ByteArray` in `HTTPSession` object
- Saved as a file on the server for future use
- Streamed back to the client marked as a MIME type `application/pdf`
- Saved in a DBMS field as a binary large object (BLOB)

Depending on the business requirements, the server-side PDF generation might not be feasible. You might have just disconnected the AIR application, or the server software may not have any of the technologies supporting PDF creation installed. If the Flex UI is truly dynamic, that might change the number of displayed components based on some business criteria; developing an additional UI in Acrobat Designer just for printing can in these ways become either impossible or time-consuming. The LCDS Developer Guide describes this process in the document called "Using the PDF Generation Feature" (*http://tinyurl.com/mrjycr*).

Adobe has published an article (*http://www.adobe.com/devnet/flex/articles/portable_ria.html*) describing the process of creating PDF documents using templates.

In general, for server-side PDF generation from Adobe Flex applications, you have to do the following:

- Use Adobe LiveCycle Designer ES, which provides tools for creating interactive forms and personalized documents (see *http://www.adobe.com/products/livecycle/designer/*). This software comes with Acrobat Professional or can be purchased separately, and is well documented, but it requires someone to create the XDP form and the data model and establish a process of synchronizing the Flex application with the server-side LiveCycle.
- Initiate the server-side PDF generation from your Flex application seamlessly.

Although this process provides guaranteed quality and predictable results, it also requires the double effort of developing XDP forms for printing and Flex forms for displaying. Besides, LiveCycle Designer is another piece of software that application developers in your organization may not be familiar with.

LCDS generation with merging data and forms produces good printing quality with LCDS. The Flex client sends data as XML to the server along with the name of the form file (template) to be used for merging, as shown in Example 11-2. In this case, the LCDS layer just needs to process it with the `XDPXFAHelper` class and return it as a PDF stream to the browser for displaying.

Only commercial licenses of LCDS support PDF generation.

The ActionScript class `FormRenderer` sends generated XDP to the server and opens a web browser's window to display the PDF when it arrives from the server.

Example 11-2. Class FormRenderer.as

```
import flash.net.*;
import flash.utils.ByteArray;

public class FormRenderer {
 public static function openPdf(xdp:String, target:String="_blank"):void{
   var req:URLRequest = new URLRequest("/createPDF.jsp");
   req.method = URLRequestMethod.POST;

   var ba :ByteArray = new ByteArray();;
   ba.writeMultiByte(xdp, "iso-8859-1");
   ba.compress();
```

```
    ba.position = 0;
    req.data = ba;
    navigateToURL(req, target);
  }
}
```

You also need an XDP file with the data and presentation. If you don't have LiveCycle Designer, you can make the XDP file programmatically, ensuring that it matches the printer's paper size and corporate stationery. XDP documents are XML objects, which are easily processed in Flex using E4X syntax, for example:

1. Declare a variable of type XML, and initialize it with the required XDP template deployed on the server. A fragment of the XDP template may look like this:

```
<?xml version="1.0" encoding="UTF-8"?>
<?xfa generator="AdobeLiveCycleDesigner_V8.0" APIVersion="2.5.6290.0"?>
 <xdp:xdp xmlns:xdp="http://ns.adobe.com/xdp/" timeStamp="2007-01-25T10:40:38Z"
  uuid="784f469b-2fd0-4555-a905-6a2d173d0ee1">

  <template xmlns="http://www.xfa.org/schema/xfa-template/2.5/">
   <subform name="form1" layout="tb" restoreState="auto" locale="en_US">
    <pageSet>
     <pageArea name="Page1" id="Page1">
      <contentArea x="0.25in" y="0.25in" w="8in" h="10.5in"/>
      <medium stock="letter" short="8.5in" long="11in"/>
      <?templateDesigner expand 1?></pageArea>
      <?templateDesigner expand 1?></pageSet>

      <subform w="8in" h="10.5in" name="YourPageAttachedHere"/>
      <proto/>
      <desc>
        <text name="version">8.0.1291.1.339988.308172</text>
      </desc>
   </subform>
  </template>
```

2. Select a Flex UI container or component that you are going to print (a `Panel`, a `DataGrid`, and so on).
3. Query the object from step 2, get its XDP attributes and children, and create the XML preparing this object for printing. Attach the XML to the template as a page.

Because original Flex components don't know how to represent themselves in the XDP format, you'll need to teach them to do so. This becomes the next task in enhancing Flex components.

For example, each UI component can implement some interface (e.g., `IXdpObject` with the only getter, `xmlContent()`) that allows it to return its own XDP content or, in the case of containers, to traverse the list of its child components for their XDP content. For example, a new panel component (`PanelXdp`) may have the following structure:

```
public class PanelXdp extends Panel implements IXdpObject{
    public function get xmlContent():Object{
       // The code to return representation of the panel
```

```
            // in the XDP format goes here
        }
    }
```

Repeat the process of attaching XML to the XDP template using E4X until all print pages are ready. This method of printing from Flex requires less effort for reporting and creation of dynamic layouts. It might also provide better printing quality and searchability within the printed document.

Example 11-3 is the server-side part written as a Java ServerSide Page. It uncompresses the XDP stream received from the client, creates the PDF using `XDPXFAHelper`, turns it into an array of bytes, and sends it back to the client as the MIME type `"application/pdf"`.

Example 11-3. Render.jsp

```
<%@ page language="java"
   import="java.io.*,
   java.util.*,
   javax.xml.parsers.*,
   org.w3c.dom.Document,
   flex.messaging.*,
   flex.acrobat.pdf.XDPXFAHelper,
   flex.messaging.util.UUIDUtils,
   org.w3c.dom.Document
   "
%><%!
private static void _log(Object o){
   System.out.println(""+o);
}
private String getParam(HttpServletRequest request, String name, String defVal)
throws Exception{
       String val = request.getParameter(name);
     return (val!=null && val.length()>0)?val:defVal;
}
private String getParam(HttpServletRequest request, String name) throws Exception{
   return getParam(request, name, null);
}
private void processRenderRequest(HttpServletRequest request,
                        HttpServletResponse response) throws Exception{

   String data     = getParam(request, "document");
   String template = getParam(request, "template"); // Security hole, check path
   _log("template="+template);
   _log("data="+data);
   template = FlexContext.getServletContext().getRealPath(template);
   _log("template real="+template);

       // You must have LCDS license to use XDPXFAHelper
   XDPXFAHelper helper = new XDPXFAHelper();
   helper.open(template);
   // Import XFA dataset
   if( data!=null ){
      _log("data.length="+data.length());
```

```
        ByteArrayInputStream bais = new
                         ByteArrayInputStream(data.getBytes("UTF-8"));
        DocumentBuilderFactory builderFactory =
                                     DocumentBuilderFactory.newInstance();
        DocumentBuilder builder =
                                     builderFactory.newDocumentBuilder();
        Document dataset = builder.parse(bais);
        helper.importDataset(dataset);
    } else
        _log("data="+null);

    byte[] content = helper.saveToByteArray();
    _log("content="+content);
    helper.close();
    ServletOutputStream out3 = response.getOutputStream();
    response.setContentType("application/pdf");
    response.setContentLength(content.length);
    out3.write(content);
}
%><%
_log("");
_log("------------------------------------------");
_log("render.jsp");
processRenderRequest(request, response);
%>
```

The WebORB PDF Generator from Midnight Coders allows you to either create XML printing templates on the server or generate them in Flex clients. To use this solution, you have to install the WebORB Server. For more details, visit *http://www.themidnightcoders.com/products/pdf-generator/overview.html*.

Now we'll take a look at how to generate a PDF on the Flex side.

PDF Generation on the Client

AlivePDF is an open source library for generating PDFs in ActionScript on the client side. It's offered under the MIT license at *http://alivepdf.org*; download *AlivePDF.swc* and link it to your Flex Builder project. One of the classes included in *AlivePDF.swc* is called `PDF`.

Unless you are developing an AIR application or deploying it for Flash Player 10 (see the next note), even client-generated PDF content has to be sent to a server that will just bounce it back (see Example 11-20) to have the web browser open the Acrobat Reader plug-in.

Basic Printing with AlivePDF

The process of generating PDFs in AlivePDF starts with instantiation of the `PDF` class, specifying the print orientation, units of measurement, and the paper size. Then you create and add pages to the instance of the `PDF` object, and finally you call the function `savePdf()` to turn these pages into a `ByteArray` and save them to the PDF file on your filesystem if you use Adobe AIR. If this is a web application written in Flex, the same `savePdf()` function sends the `ByteArray` to the server with the deployed script *create.php* (supplied by alivepdf.org (*http://alivepdf.org*)), which will return this array of bytes to your web browser as a PDF document.

Starting from Flash Player 10, the `FileReference` class allows you to save files locally. Its function `save()` opens the pop-up window, allowing the user to specify the filename for saving the data. In our example, this eliminates the need for a round trip to the server that does nothing but bounce this array of bytes. Keep in mind, though, that after saving the PDF this way, the user will need to complete an extra step to open the file with Acrobat Reader or any other program.

Example 11-4 shows the process of preparing and saving a PDF file with AlivePDF.

Example 11-4. Basic printing with AlivePDF: test1.mxml

```
<?xml version="1.0" encoding="utf-8"?>
    <mx:WindowedApplication xmlns:mx="http://www.adobe.com/2006/mxml"
   layout="vertical" horizontalAlign="center" verticalAlign="middle">

   <mx:Button label="Hello World!!!" click="hw()"/>

 <mx:Script><![CDATA[

   import org.alivepdf.fonts.Style;
   import org.alivepdf.fonts.FontFamily;
    import org.alivepdf.saving.Method;
    import org.alivepdf.layout.Size;
    import org.alivepdf.layout.Unit;
        import org.alivepdf.layout.Orientation;
    import org.alivepdf.pdf.PDF;

  private function hw():void{

   var p:PDF = new PDF(Orientation.PORTRAIT, Unit.MM, Size.A4);
   p.addPage();
   p.setFont(FontFamily.ARIAL, Style.NORMAL, 12);
   p.addText("10x10", 10, 10);
   p.addText("100x100", 100, 100);
   p.addMultiCell(50, 8, "Hello World2");

   savePdf(p, "hw.pdf");
 }
```

```
 private function savePdf(p:PDF, fileName:String):void{

   var ba:ByteArray = p.save(Method.LOCAL);
   var fs:FileStream = new FileStream();
   var f:File = File.desktopDirectory.resolvePath(fileName);
   fs.open(f, FileMode.WRITE);

   try{
      fs.writeBytes(ba);
   } catch (e:*){}

     fs.close();
 }
]]></mx:Script>

</mx:WindowedApplication>
```

After you click the button Hello World!!! (see the example code), a file called *hw.pdf* is created in the AIR desktop directory (see Chapter 9 for details). For example, Figure 11-1 shows our *hw.pdf* file, which was saved in the directory *C:\Documents and Settings\Administrator\Desktop*.

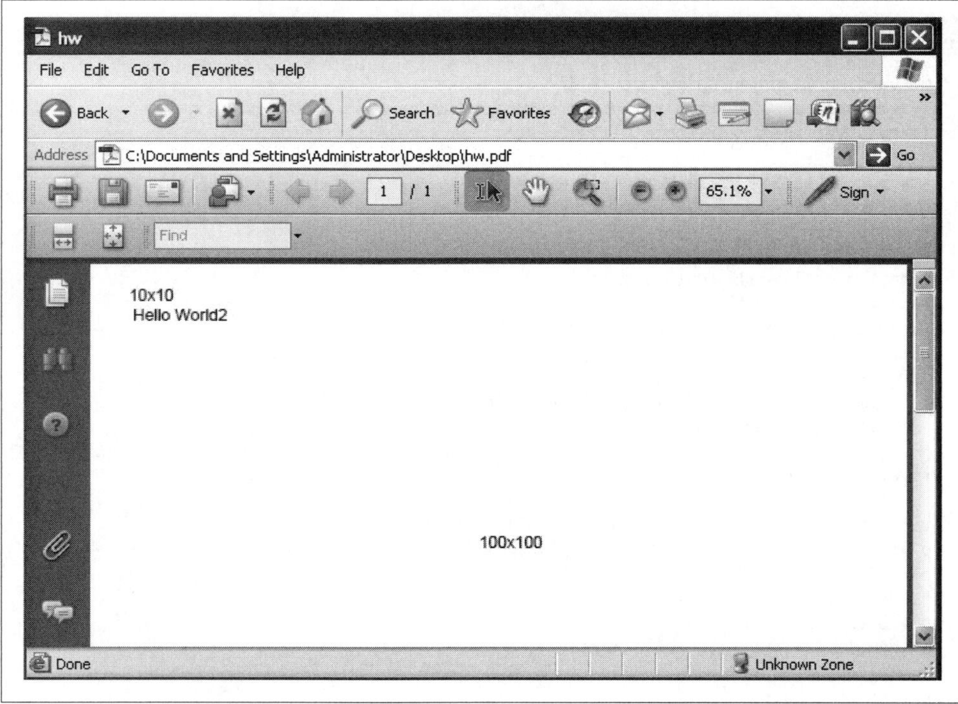

Figure 11-1. Sample output of the AlivePDF program

The goal here was to give you a taste of the process of preparing the document with AlivePDF. To investigate the complete set of AlivePDF's APIs, visit *http://AlivePDF.org*.

AlivePDF does a good job of creating objects and assembling them into pages, which are then converted into a PDF format. But it still requires you to prepare (in addition to the screen version) a second copy of the UI to be printed. It's not what-you-see-is-what-you-get (WYSIWYG) programming. This process requires manual allocation and measurements of each object in the PDF-to-be.

The blog *http://alivepdf.bytearray.org* is yet another good source of up-to-date information regarding AlivePDF.

Enhancing AlivePDF

What can be done to improve this process? We still want to use AlivePDF's printing engine, but we don't want to manually write the code specifying styles and measurements as we did in Example 11-4. In this section, you'll see how to create components and containers that are smart enough to present themselves as PDF or XDP objects.

All examples from this section are located in the Flex Builder project called *clientPdfAir* (which comes with this chapter; see the Preface for information on obtaining the sample code) and are self-contained AIR applications. *alivePDF.swc* has to be present in the build path of the project.

The program *test2.mxml* in Example 11-5 illustrates Flex-to-PDF-object conversion, a big difference compared to *test1.mxml*. It uses the ActionScript class `AlivePdfPrinter`, which is included with the code samples of this chapter. Its `addObject()` method converts a given Flex object to corresponding PDF snippets, one at a time. You don't need to worry about the sizes, locations, fonts, or styles of these objects. This is WYSIWYG. Flash Player is a rendering engine here.

Example 11-5. Printing with AlivePDF from an AIR application

```
<?xml version="1.0" encoding="utf-8"?>
    <mx:WindowedApplication xmlns:mx="http://www.adobe.com/2006/mxml"
     xmlns:printer="com.farata.printing.pdf.client.*"
   layout="vertical" >
   <mx:Style source="main.css"/>
   <mx:Canvas width="100%" height="100%" backgroundColor="white">
     <mx:Label id="lbl1" text="Hello" x="10" y="10"/>
     <mx:Label id="lbl2" text="World" x="50" y="30" fontWeight="bold"/>
          <mx:Label id="lbl3" text="And" x="150" y="60" fontStyle="italic"
                                                     enabled="false"/>
     <mx:Label id="lbl4" text="Happy" x="70" y="90" fontSize="16"
```

```
                                            textDecoration="underline"/>
        <mx:Label id="lbl5" text="New Year" x="50" y="140" fontSize="24"
                                            fontWeight="bold" color="green"/>
     <mx:Button id="btn1" label="Button1" x="70" y="240"/>
   </mx:Canvas>

 <mx:ApplicationControlBar width="100%">
   <mx:Label text="File name:"/>
   <mx:TextInput id="txtFileName" text="hw2.pdf"/>
   <mx:Button label="Save PDF" click="printPdf()"/>
     </mx:ApplicationControlBar>

   <printer:AlivePdfPrinter id="prn" printComplete="viewPdf()"/>
<mx:Script><![CDATA[

  import flash.net.URLRequest;

  private var file:File;

  private function printPDF():void{

   prn.addObject(lbl1);
   prn.addObject(lbl2);
   prn.addObject(lbl3);
   prn.addObject(lbl4);
   prn.addObject(lbl5);
   prn.addObject(btn1);

   file = prn.printToFile (txtFileName.text);
 }

 private function viewPdf():void{
   var req:URLRequest = new URLRequest(file.url);
   navigateToURL(req, "_blank");
}

]]></mx:Script>

</mx:WindowedApplication>
```

The code in Example 11-5 produces the screen as it's shown in the AIR runtime, on the left in Figure 11-2. On the right side, you can see the *hw2.swf* file produced by this program and shown in Adobe Acrobat. The fonts in the Acrobat Reader image look smaller because of the small zoom percentage.

The listings that follow do not include the entire source code of the class `AlivePdfPrinter`; that comes with the source code of this chapter's samples. The idea is to have a set of components that can expose their information in a form suitable for printing. The method `AlivePdfPrinter.addObject(o)` calls `locateExtension()`, which instantiates the appropriate object that can present itself in a form suitable for AlivePDF (Example 11-6).

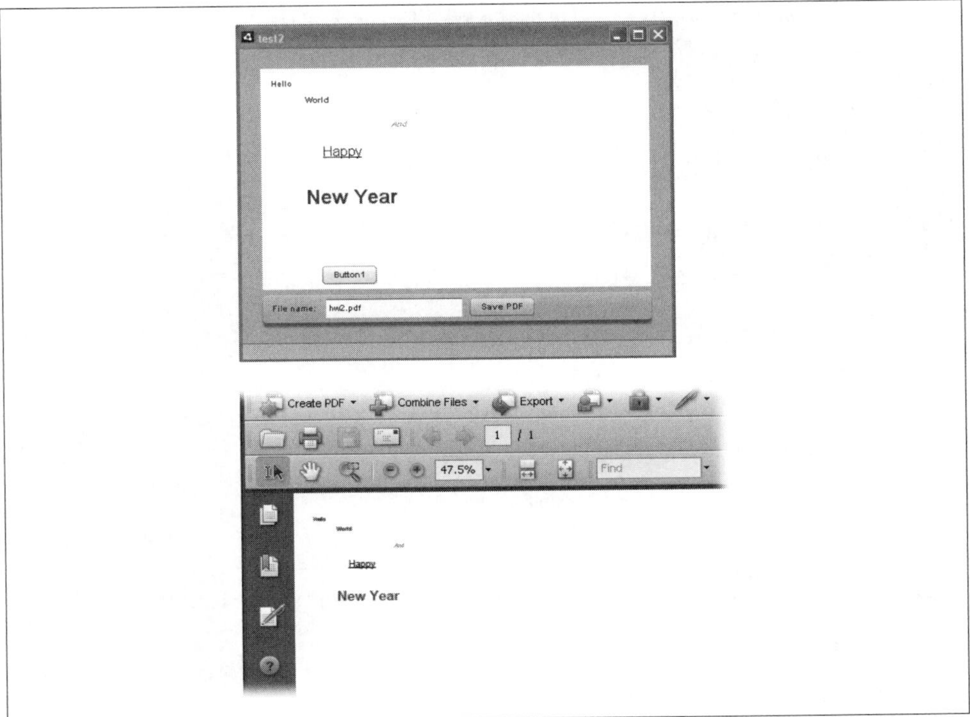

Figure 11-2. The results of printing with enhanced AlivePDF

Example 11-6. The method AlivePdfPrinter.locateExtension()

```
private static function locateExtension(o:*):IPdfPrinterExtension{
  if( o is Label )
   return new LabelPdfExtension(/*o*/);
  if( o is PdfPrintDataGrid )
   return new PdfPrintDataGridPdfExtension(/*o*/);
  if( o is DataGrid )
   return new DataGridPdfExtension(/*o*/);
  if( o is Container )
   return new ContainerPdfExtension(/*o*/);
  if( o is UIComponent )
   return new UIComponentPdfExtension(/*o*/);
 return null;
}
```

After identifying the type of the object to be printed, the object exposes its font and style information that's being passed to the AlivePDF's `PDF` object for printing. Example 11-7 shows the function `addObject()` from the ActionScript class `com.farata.printing.pdf.client.extensions.LabelPdfExtension`.

Example 11-7. The addObject() method in the LabelPdfExtension class

```
public function addObject(o:*, printer:IAlivePdfPrinter):void{
 var pdf:PDF = printer.pdf;
   var c:Label = Label(o);
   if( c==null ) return;
   if( !c.visible )
      return;

   var fontFamily:String = c.getStyle("fontFamily");
   if( fontFamily==null )
      fontFamily = FontFamily.ARIAL;

   var style:String = "";

   if( c.getStyle("fontWeight")=="bold" )
       style += "B";

   if( c.getStyle("fontStyle")=="italic" )
      style += "I";
   if( c.getStyle("textDecoration")=="underline" )
        style += "U";

   var size:int = c.getStyle("fontSize");
   var color:Color = new RGBColor(c.getStyle(c.enabled?"color":"disabledColor"));

   allocateSpace(c, printer);

   pdf.textStyle(color/*, alpha*/);
   pdf.setFont(fontFamily, style, pxToPt(size));

   var ptText:PPoint = mapPoint(c, printer);
   ptText.y.px += c.height;

   pdf.addText(c.text, ptText.x.pt, ptText.y.pt);

 }
```

Example 11-7's code gets the styles, font, and text from the Flex `Label` object and initializes appropriate properties of the `PDF` object per the requirements of the AlivePDF library.

The sample code of this chapter as well as the *clear.swc* library has several similar extensions for a number of Flex components (see `com.farata.printing.swc`), and you can keep adding more objects to your own business framework of PDF-ready components.

These extensions are not subclasses of corresponding Flex components, but rather utility classes that know how to present the content of components to AlivePDF.

While writing the method `addObjects()` for your components, keep in mind that measurements in Flash Player are in pixels and you may need to convert them into other units required by the AlivePDF API.

If you'd like to see what's inside the generated *hw2.pdf* file, just open it with any text editor; you'll see something like Example 11-8 (which is just a fragment of the file).

Example 11-8. A fragment of the h2.pdf content

```
%PDF-1.4
1 0 obj
<</Type /Pages
/Kids [3 0 R
]
/Count 1
>>
endobj
3 0 obj
<</Type /Page
/Parent 1 0 R
/MediaBox [0 0 595.28 841.89]
/Resources 2 0 R
/Rotate 0
/Dur 3
/Contents 4 0 R>>
endobj
4 0 obj
<</Length 780>>
stream
2 J
0.57 w
0 Tr
/GS0 gs
0 Tw 0 Tc 100 Tz 0 TL
BT /F1 7.00 Tf ET
q 0.043137254901960784 0.2 0.23529411764705882 rg BT 25.50 802.14 Td (Hello) Tj ET
Q
0 Tr
/GS1 gs
0 Tw 0 Tc 100 Tz 0 TL
BT /F2 7.00 Tf ET
q 0.043137254901960784 0.2 0.23529411764705882 rg BT 55.50 787.89 Td (World) Tj ET
Q
0 Tr
/GS2 gs
0 Tw 0 Tc 100 Tz 0 TL
BT /F3 7.00 Tf ET
q 0.6666666666666666 0.7019607843137254 0.7019607843137254 rg BT 130.50 764.64 Td
(And) Tj ET Q
0 Tr
/GS3 gs
0 Tw 0 Tc 100 Tz 0 TL
BT /F1 12.00 Tf ET
```

```
q 0.043137254901960784 0.2 0.23529411764705882 rg BT 70.50 738.39 Td (Happy) Tj ET
70.50 737.19 34.68 0.60 re f Q
0 Tr
/GS4 gs
0 Tw 0 Tc 100 Tz 0 TL
BT /F2 18.00 Tf ET
q 0 0.5019607843137255 0 rg BT 55.50 692.64 Td (New Year) Tj ET Q
/GS5 gs
q 47.25 0 0 16.50 52.50 645.39 cm
/I1 Do Q
endstream
endobj
5 0 obj
<</Type /ExtGState
/SA true
/CA 1
/n 5
/BM /Normal
/ca 1
>>
endobj
...
15 0 obj
<<
/Producer (Alive PDF 0.1.4.6)
/CreationDate (D:200905152226)
>>
endobj
16 0 obj
<<
/Type /Catalog
/Pages 1 0 R
/OpenAction [3 0 R /FitH null]
/PageLayout /SinglePage
>>
endobj
xref
...
trailer
<<
/Size 17
/Root 16 0 R
/Info 15 0 R
>>
startxref
2467
%%EOF
```

After this chapter was written, a new open source library called purePDF became available. It's an ActionScript port of a popular Java library called iText. You can download purePDF at *http://code.google.com/p/purepdf/*.

Printing Flex Containers

All these extensions for Flex controls are great, but there is another issue to tackle: Flex views often use containers. For example, you need to be able to generate a PDF for a `DataGrid` in two formats. This object should be similar to `mx.printing.PrintDataGrid`, but it should support PDF printing rather than working with `PrintJob`. It should support pagination, headers, and footers; this is a must for printing multipage documents.

Or imagine a `TabNavigator` container from which you need to print the content of each tab as a separate multipage PDF. The goal is to have a container that can iterate its children and tell each of them, "Hey, kiddo, print yourself." When this mission is accomplished, just implement the same behavior to allow containers (and components) to expose themselves in the XDP format, too.

Sample extensions for the most complex Flex components, such as `DataGrid`, `DataGridItemRenderer`, and `Canvas`, are supplied as code samples for this chapter. Use them as a guide for the creation of your own printing extensions.

For example, the application *test4.mxml* includes the `PdfPrintDataGrid` component from *clear.swc* and outputs the data grid to the file *hw4.pdf*, as shown in Figure 11-3 and Example 11-9.

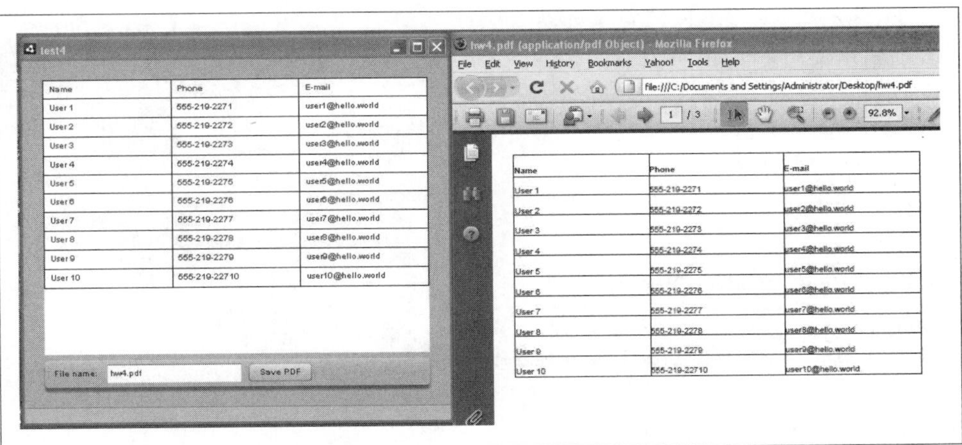

Figure 11-3. Running test4.mxml (left) generates PDF hw4 (right)

Example 11-9. An AIR application to print a data grid to a PDF file

```
<?xml version="1.0" encoding="utf-8"?>
<mx:WindowedApplication xmlns:mx="http://www.adobe.com/2006/mxml"
  xmlns:printer="com.farata.printing.pdf.client.*"
  layout="vertical"
  creationComplete="onCreationComplete(event)" >

   <mx:DataGrid id="dg" x="0" y="0"
```

```
   width="100%" height="100%" >

    <mx:columns>
      <mx:DataGridColumn dataField="name" headerText="Name"/>
      <mx:DataGridColumn dataField="phone" headerText="Phone"/>
      <mx:DataGridColumn dataField="email" headerText="E-mail"/>
    </mx:columns>
   </mx:DataGrid>

   <mx:ApplicationControlBar width="100%">
    <mx:Label text="File name:"/>
    <mx:TextInput id="txtFileName" text="hw4.pdf"/>
     <mx:Button label="Save PDF" click="doSavePdf()"/>
   </mx:ApplicationControlBar>

   <printer:AlivePdfPrinter id="prn" printComplete="viewPdf()"/>

<mx:Script><![CDATA[

import flash.net.URLRequest;
private var file:File;

private function onCreationComplete(evt:*):void{

   var array:Array = [];

   for(var i:int=1; i<=30; i++){
       var obj:Object = new Object();
      obj.name   = "User " +i;
      obj.phone  = "555-219-227"+i;
      obj.email  = "user"+i+"@hello.world";
      obj.active = (i % 2 ) == 1;
      array.push(obj);

   }
   dg.dataProvider = array;
}
private function printPdf():void{

   prn.addObject(dg);
   file = prn.printToFile(txtFileName.text);
}

private function viewPdf():void{
   var req:URLRequest = new URLRequest(file.url);
   navigateToURL(req, "_blank");
}

]]></mx:Script>
</mx:WindowedApplication>
```

The line:

```
prn.addObject(dg);
```

results in invoking the code from Example 11-6, and the DataGridPdfExtension class shown in Example 11-10 is engaged.

Example 11-10. Class DataGridPdfExtension

```
package com.farata.printing.pdf.client.extensions{

   import com.farata.printing.PdfPrintDataGrid;

   import com.farata.printing.pdf.client.IAlivePdfPrinter;
   import mx.controls.DataGrid;

   public class DataGridPdfExtension extends BasePdfExtension{

    override public function addObject(o:*, printer:IAlivePdfPrinter):void{

     var c:DataGrid = o as DataGrid;
      var p:PdfPrintDataGrid = new PdfPrintDataGrid();
      p.x = c.x;
       p.y = c.y;
     p.width = c.width;
     p.height = c.height;
     p.columns = c.columns;
     p.dataProvider = c.dataProvider;

      c.parent.addChild(p);
     printer.addObject(p);
     c.parent.removeChild(p);
   }

 }
}
```

If in Example 11-6 all components were located inside, say, Canvas, and the printing extensions for this container were ready, this code sample would become even shorter—something like this:

```
prn.addObject(myCanvas);
```

The myCanvas component would've taken care of its kids.

The good news is that you don't have to write printing extensions to all components. The code in Example 11-6 checks to see whether the component is an instance of Label, DataGrid, or Container.

Part of the sample code in the *test3.mxml* application has a canvas:

```
<mx:Canvas id="canvas" width="100%" height="100%"
      backgroundColor="white">

   <mx:Label id="lbl1" text="Hello" x="100" y="10"/>
    <mx:Label id="lbl2" text="World" x="50" y="30" fontWeight="bold"/>
    <mx:Label id="lbl3" text="And" x="150" y="60" fontStyle="italic"
          enabled="false"/>
    <mx:Label id="lbl4" text="Happy" x="90" y="90" fontSize="16"
```

```
                                          textDecoration="underline"/>
      <mx:Label id="lbl5" text="New Year" x="80" y="140" fontSize="24"
        fontWeight="bold" color="green"/>
      <mx:Button id="btn1" label="Button1" x="1" y="1"/>
       <mx:Button id="btn2" label="Button2" x="10" y="100"/>

       <mx:HBox x="250" y="130" borderThickness="3" borderColor="blue"
          borderStyle="solid"   backgroundColor="yellow">
         <mx:Label text="Inside HBox" color="gray"/>
      </mx:HBox>
   </mx:Canvas>
```

The code to print this `Canvas` is pretty simple: just pass a reference to the class `AlivePdfPrinter`, and it'll figure out how to print its child components:

```
   private function printPdf():void{
      prn.addObject(canvas);
      file = prn.printToFile(txtFileName.text);
   }
```

The function `addObject()` tries to locate an extension class for `Canvas` as shown in Example 11-6, and will use the `ContainerPdfExtension`, because `Canvas` is a `Container`. Should you want to provide some functionality specific to `Canvas`, you need to create `CanvasPdfExtension` and modify the code in Example 11-6 accordingly.

A fragment of `ContainerPdfExtension` is shown in Example 11-11.

Example 11-11. The main part of ContainerPdfExtension

```
package com.farata.printing.pdf.client.extensions{
 public class ContainerPdfExtension extends BasePdfExtension{

   private static var s_offsetLock:int = 0;

   override public function addObject(o:*, printer:IAlivePdfPrinter):void{

    s_offsetLock++;
    var c:Container = Container(o);
    setOffset(c, printer);
    allocateSpace(c, printer);
    drawBackgroundAndBorder(c, printer);

     var len:int = c.numChildren;
    for(var i:int=0; i<len; i++){
      var ch:DisplayObject = c.getChildAt(i);
      printer.addObject(ch);
    }

    s_offsetLock--;
    }

   private  function setOffset(o:Container, printer:IAlivePdfPrinter):void{
     if( s_offsetLock==1 ) {
      var ptLocal:Point = new Point(o.x, o.y);
        var ptGlobal:Point = o.parent.localToGlobal(ptLocal);
```

```
            printer.lastOffset.x.px = ptGlobal.x;
            printer.lastOffset.y.px = ptGlobal.y;
        }
      }
  }

}
```

All other components that the code in Example 11-6 won't recognize will be printed as prescribed in the `UIComponentPdfExtension` as a snapshot of an image (Example 11-12).

Example 11-12. Printing a Flex object as an image

```
public function addObject(o:*, printer:IAlivePdfPrinter):void{

   if( !o.visible ) return;
   var c:UIComponent = o;
   var pdf:PDF = printer.pdf;
   var rc:PRectangle = new PRectangle();
   rc.left.px = c.x;

   rc.top.px = c.y;
   rc.right.px = rc.left.px+c.width;
   rc.bottom.px = rc.top.px+c.height;

   printer.allocateSpace(rc);
   pdf.addImage(c, rc.left.pt, rc.top.pt, rc.right.pt-rc.left.pt,
   rc.bottom.pt-rc.top.pt);
}
```

Of course, it's better not to use a bitmap but instead a PDF representation specific to a component, which will allow Acrobat Reader to recognize its text content and generate searchable documents rather than bitmaps.

Extending Flex Components for PDF Generation in XDP Format

In this section, you'll learn how to enhance standard Flex UI components so that they can properly present themselves for rendering as PDF-friendly objects in the XML-based XDP format.

The ActionScript code snippet in Example 11-13 shows how you can present a checkbox as an element of the PDF form in XDP format (in XDP, a checkbox is called `checkButton`).

We'll introduce a new interface, `IXdpObject`, and each of our enhanced UI components will implement it to return properly prepared XML to represent itself. This will allow you to turn the entire Flex view into a searchable PDF.

Example 11-13 is an example of implementing the getter `xdpContent()` defined in the `IXdpObject` interface to produce a `CheckBox` in the XDP format.

Example 11-13. Representing a CheckBox as an XDP checkButton

```
// IXdpObject interface implementation
public  function get xdpContent():Object {
 var o:XML =
      <field  x={convert(x)} w={convert(width)} h={convert(height)}>
   <ui>
     <checkButton  allowNeutral="1">
       <border>
         <edge stroke="lowered"/>
         <fill/>
       </border>
      </checkButton>
   </ui>
   <value>
     <text>{value}</text>
   </value>
   <para vAlign="middle" hAlign="center"/>

   <items>
     <text>{onValue}</text>
     <text>{offValue}</text>
     <text></text>
   </items>
   <caption placement="bottom"/>
   </field>;

 return o;
}

private function convert(value:Number) : String {
   return  XdpUtil.px2pt(value) + "pt";
}
```

This code snippet includes a getter, `xdpContent`, that returns the representation of our `CheckBox` in XDP format. It uses a helper function, `convert()`, to convert the value from pixels to points.

Note that this code uses binding to insert the `onValue` and `offValue` variables that were introduced in Chapter 3 in Example 3-1.

To generate a PDF for a particular Flex view, you need to loop through its children (every UI control of each container) and get each one's `xdpContent`. If it's not null, add its value (XDP) to the output file. If it does not have `xdpConent`, just get an image snapshot of this child and add it to the output file.

At the end of this process, you'll get a mix of images and XDP content. If this is a Flex application, send this content to the server-side Java Servlet, which will sandwich it between the PDF header and footer. Voilà! Your PDF file is ready.

Obsessed with the mantra "Developers must write less code," we at Farata have already created a number of classes in the package *com.farata.printing* that allows Flex components to expose themselves in a form of XDP.

The sample application shown in Example 11-14 is a rewrite of Example 11-5. It'll produce the same output as in Figure 11-2, but this time the document will be encoded in the XDP format.

Example 11-14. Saving data in XDP format: test_xdp2.mxml

```
<?xml version="1.0" encoding="utf-8"?>

<mx:WindowedApplication xmlns:mx="http://www.adobe.com/2006/mxml"
 xmlns:local="*"
 xmlns:printer="com.farata.printing.pdf.client.*" layout="vertical">

   <mx:Style source="main.css"/>
   <mx:Canvas id="canvas" width="100%" height="100%"
      backgroundColor="white">
      <mx:Label id="lbl1" text="Hello" x="10" y="10"/>
      <mx:Label id="lbl2" text="World" x="50" y="30"
         fontWeight="bold"/>
           <mx:Label id="lbl3" text="And" x="150" y="60"
          fontStyle="italic" enabled="false"/>

      <mx:Label id="lbl4" text="Happy" x="70" y="90" fontSize="16"
              textDecoration="underline"/>
      <mx:Label id="lbl5" text="New Year" x="50" y="140" fontSize="24"
              fontWeight="bold" color="green"/>
      <mx:Button id="btn1" label="Button1" x="70" y="240"/>
   </mx:Canvas>

    <mx:ApplicationControlBar width="100%">
    <mx:Label text="File name:"/>
     <mx:TextInput id="txtFileName" text="hw2.pdf"/>
    <mx:Button label="Save PDF" click="savePdf()"/>
   </mx:ApplicationControlBar>

   <mx:Script>
      <![CDATA[
      import com.farata.printing.PrintOptions;
        import com.farata.printing.pdf.xdp.XdpDocument;
        import com.farata.printing.pdf.buffered.PDFHelper;

     private function savePdf():void{
      saveToFile(txtFileName.text, createXdpContent());
      }

     private function createXdpContent ():ByteArray{

      var xdpDocument:XdpDocument=new XdpDocument();
      xdpDocument.init(new PrintOptions());
      var pdf:PDFHelper=new PDFHelper(xdpDocument);
```

```
    pdf.createPDFPrologue();
    pdf.createPage(canvas, PDFHelper.TYPE_PAGE);
    pdf.createPDFEpilogue();

      return pdf.pdfContent;
  }

  private function saveToFile (file:String, ba:ByteArray):void{

    var fs:FileStream=new FileStream();
    var f:File=File.desktopDirectory.resolvePath(file);
    fs.open(f, FileMode.WRITE);

    try {
      fs.writeBytes(ba);
    } catch(e:*){
           // Process I/O errors here
     }
      fs.close();
  }

    ]]>
  </mx:Script>
</mx:WindowedApplication>
```

When you open the generated file *h2.pdf* in a text editor, notice that it looks different than the file shown in Example 11-8. The small PDF header and the trailer are there, but the main content of this file is in XDP format, as shown in Example 11-15.

Example 11-15. A fragment of the h2.pdf content in XDP format

```
 %PDF-1.7
1 0 obj
<</Type /Catalog /StructTreeRoot 9 0 R /MarkInfo <</Marked true>> /Pages 15 0 R
/AcroForm 16 0 R /NeedsRendering true>>
endobj
2 0 obj
<</Type /Page /MediaBox [0 0 612 792] /Resources 5 0 R /Contents 4 0 R
/StructParent 0 /StructParents 0 /Parent 15 0 R>>
endobj
4 0 obj
<</Length 298>>
stream
BT
/Content <</MCID 0>> BDC
0.0 0.0 0.0 rg
/RelativeColorimetric ri
/T1_0 1.0 Tf
10.0 0.0 0.0 10.0 72.0 720.0 Tm
(Warning: This form is not supported at all with the current version of Acrobat or
Adobe Reader.) Tj
0.0 -1.8 Td
(Upgrade to the latest version for full support.) Tj
0.0 -1.8 Td
EMC
```

```
ET
endstream
endobj
5 0 obj
<</Font 8 0 R /ProcSet [/PDF /Text]>>
endobj
6 0 obj
<</Type /Encoding /BaseEncoding /WinAnsiEncoding>>
endobj
7 0 obj
<</Type /Font /Subtype /Type1 /BaseFont /Helvetica /Encoding 6 0 R>>
endobj
8 0 obj
<</T1_0 7 0 R>>
endobj
9 0 obj
<</Type /StructTreeRoot /K 10 0 R /ParentTree 13 0 R /ParentTreeNextKey 1 /RoleMap
14 0 R>>
endobj
10 0 obj
<</S /Document /P 9 0 R /K 11 0 R>>
endobj
11 0 obj
<</S /Div /P 10 0 R /K 12 0 R>>
endobj
12 0 obj
<</S /P /P 11 0 R /Pg 2 0 R /K 0>>
endobj
13 0 obj
<</Nums [0 [12 0 R]]>>
endobj
14 0 obj
<</Field /Div /Subform /Sect /Page /Part /Draw /Div>>
endobj
15 0 obj
<</Type /Pages /Kids [2 0 R] /Count 1>>
endobj
16 0 obj
<</Fields [] /XFA 17 0 R>>
endobj
17 0 obj
<< /Length 18 0 R >>
stream
<xdp:xdp xmlns:xdp="http://ns.adobe.com/xdp/">
  <template xmlns="http://www.xfa.org/schema/xfa-template/2.5/">
    <subform name="doc1" layout="tb" restoreState="auto" locale="en_US">
      <proto/>
      <desc>
        <text name="version">8.0.1291.1.339988.308172</text>
      </desc>
      <pageSet>
        <pageArea name="Page1" id="Page1">
          <contentArea x="8.47mm" y="8.47mm" w="262.43mm" h="198.94mm"/>
          <medium stock="custom" short="215.87mm" long="279.37mm"
                                              orientation="landscape"/>
```

```
      </pageArea>
    </pageSet>
  <subform layout="tb" name="Subform1">
<subform name="Container1" x="6.35mm" y="6.35mm" w="119.58mm" h="70.9mm">
  <draw x="7.5pt" y="7.5pt" w="22.5pt" h="14.25pt">
    <ui>
      <textEdit hScrollPolicy="off" multiLine="0" vScrollPolicy="off"/>
    </ui>
    <value>
      <text>Hello</text>
    </value>
    <para hAlign="left"/>
    <font typeface="Arial" size="7.5pt" weight="normal" posture="normal"
              underline="0">
      <fill>
        <color value="11,51,60"/>
      </fill>
    </font>
    <border>
      <edge presence="hidden"/>
      <edge presence="hidden"/>
      <edge presence="hidden"/>
      <edge presence="hidden"/>
    </border>
  </draw>
  <draw x="37.5pt" y="22.5pt" w="24.75pt" h="13.5pt">
    <ui>
      <textEdit hScrollPolicy="off" multiLine="0" vScrollPolicy="off"/>
    </ui>
    <value>
      <text>World</text>
    </value>
    <para hAlign="left"/>
    <font typeface="Arial" size="7.5pt" weight="bold" posture="normal"
                                                   underline="0">
      <fill>
        <color value="11,51,60"/>
      </fill>
    </font>
    <border>
      <edge presence="hidden"/>
      <edge presence="hidden"/>
      <edge presence="hidden"/>
      <edge presence="hidden"/>
    </border>
  </draw>
  <draw x="112.5pt" y="45pt" w="18pt" h="14.25pt">
    <ui>
      <textEdit hScrollPolicy="off" multiLine="0" vScrollPolicy="off"/>
    </ui>
    <value>
      <text>And</text>
    </value>
    <para hAlign="left"/>
    <font typeface="Arial" size="7.5pt" weight="normal" posture="italic"
```

```
                                                              underline="0">
        <fill>
          <color value="11,51,60"/>
        </fill>
      </font>
      <border>
        <edge presence="hidden"/>
        <edge presence="hidden"/>
        <edge presence="hidden"/>
        <edge presence="hidden"/>
      </border>
    </draw>
    <draw x="52.5pt" y="67.5pt" w="37.5pt" h="18pt">
      <ui>
        <textEdit hScrollPolicy="off" multiLine="0" vScrollPolicy="off"/>
      </ui>
      <value>
        <text>Happy</text>
      </value>
      <para hAlign="left"/>
      <font typeface="Arial" size="12pt" weight="normal" posture="normal"
                                                    underline="1">
        <fill>
          <color value="11,51,60"/>
        </fill>
      </font>
      <border>
        <edge presence="hidden"/>
        <edge presence="hidden"/>
        <edge presence="hidden"/>
        <edge presence="hidden"/>
      </border>
    </draw>
    <draw x="37.5pt" y="105pt" w="83.25pt" h="26.25pt">
      <ui>
        <textEdit hScrollPolicy="off" multiLine="0" vScrollPolicy="off"/>
      </ui>
      <value>
        <text>New Year</text>
      </value>
      <para hAlign="left"/>
      <font typeface="Arial" size="18pt" weight="bold" posture="normal"
underline="0">
        <fill>
          <color value="0,128,0"/>
        </fill>
      </font>
      <border>
        <edge presence="hidden"/>
        <edge presence="hidden"/>
        <edge presence="hidden"/>
        <edge presence="hidden"/>
      </border>
    </draw>
    <draw x="18.52mm" y="63.49mm" w="16.67mm" h="5.82mm">
```

```
      <ui>
        <imageEdit/>
      </ui>
      <value>
        <image
contentType="image/png">iVBORw0KGgoAAAANSUhEUgAAAD8AAAAWCAYAAAB3/EQhAAABqElE
QVR42uWYTUsCURSGz76f07bfEtS2UkioqAgJKaMPERISQkJCqIggF2VItAsRi/5AhS11/BpH8YuT
rysb7jj35m7uhQfuOXPmnPvALGaGeLgaDZNz+cKIh6esZ4Ff4f1j5ItFvV6Ps88v/Pn1zeWywV5e
8IMnfOFNr7k85wtvPBgMtAG+8Kbr2zvu9/vaAW9KXd2MHgHdgDclL1Pc7Xa1A96UuEhyp9PRDnhT
/DzB7XZbmZnZuT/I1Iv2OzBNH3hT7CzOlmUpg8GT4kn1brWy86fpA2+Knsa42Wwqg8GiWJR3QlTj
dJ/MLBXgTceRKJumqYz9cON5e5O9r1ovip1yssCbwodHw9e9hjIYLIpl8k57mT5uOVngTaH9MNfr
dWUwWBTL5J32Mn3ccrLAm4K7Ia7VasrYH3u3a057e/14zt5TdIb/nB3Am7Z3glytVrUD3rSxucWV
SkU74E2BtXUt5eFN/tUAG4ahHfCmpRXf8CO/rB3wpuOTCN+nO1qJwxfeVCz+8LLPz4+ZDJdKJc8D
T/jCm/Bvy2q1eC98wPMLi54HnvDF+gUhlFFaqhacWgAAAABJRU5ErkJggg==</image>
      </value>
    </draw>
  </subform>
</subform></subform>
</template>

...

</xdp:xdp>
endstream
endobj
18 0 obj

endobj
xref
0 19
0000000000 65535 f
0000000016 00000 n
0000000151 00000 n
0000000000 65535 f
0000000287 00000 n
0000000635 00000 n
0000000688 00000 n
0000000754 00000 n
0000000838 00000 n
0000000869 00000 n
0000000976 00000 n
0000001028 00000 n
0000001076 00000 n
0000001127 00000 n
0000001166 00000 n
0000001236 00000 n
0000001292 00000 n
0000001335 00000 n
trailer
<</Root 1 0 R  /Size 19>>
startxref
%%EOF
```

The file *templates/generic.xdp* in *com.farata.printing* contains the generic template for XDP generation used for generation of *h2.pdf* and all other XDP samples from this chapter.

As you can see from Example 11-15, the values of the text fields (Hello, World, etc.) are represented as XML text fields, which makes this PDF searchable. Note that the binary image is also presented in the encoded form as one of the XML elements.

If you are developing not AIR but Flex applications, the client-side code can generate the entire XML portion of the Flex view components and send this XML to the server, where, say, Java Servlet puts it between the required PDF header and trailer and returns the entire document back to the web browser for printing.

The entire process of generation of this PDF in the XDP format is done by the following code from Example 11-14:

```
var xdpDocument:XdpDocument=new XdpDocument();
xdpDocument.init(new PrintOptions());
var pdf:PDFHelper=new PDFHelper(xdpDocument);

pdf.createPDFPrologue();

pdf.createPage(canvas, PDFHelper.TYPE_PAGE);

pdf.createPDFEpilogue();
```

This code uses the helper components `XdpDocument`, `PrintOptions`, and `PDFHelper`, which are located in `com.farata.printing.swc`. The class `PrintOptions` is just a holder of such page parameters as orientation, margins, page size, and the like.

The MXML component `XdpDocument` implements a generic getter `xdpContent`, introduced in the beginning of this section. The source code of *XDPDocument.mxml* and a fragment of *PDFHelper.as* are shown in Examples 11-16 and 11-17, respectively. But these constitute just the tip of the iceberg, as they use uses dozens of supporting classes in the process of creation of the XDP content.

The good news is that unless the XDP format changes, you don't need to learn all the nitty-gritty details, as we already did that tedious work of ensuring that the document is generated as required by the XDP specifications.

Example 11-16. Component XDPDocument.mxml

```
<?xml version="1.0" encoding="utf-8"?>

<xdp:XdpBaseObject
     xmlns:mx="http://www.adobe.com/2006/mxml"
     xmlns:xdp="com.farata.printing.pdf.xdp.*">
```

```
    <mx:XML id="xmlGen" source="/templates/generic.xdp"/>

<mx:Script><![CDATA[

import mx.core.UIComponent;

import com.farata.printing.pdf.buffered.PDFHelper;
    import com.farata.printing.geom.PNumber;
import mx.core.Container;
import com.farata.printing.geom.PSize;
import com.farata.printing.PrintOptions;
import com.farata.printing.geom.PRectangle;
import com.farata.printing.PaperSize;

public static var ns_xdp     : Namespace = new
Namespace("http://ns.adobe.com/xdp/");

public static var ns_xfat25  : Namespace = new Namespace(
                                          "http://www.xfa.org/schema/xfa-template/2.5/");

public static var ns_xci10   : Namespace = new
Namespace("http://www.xfa.org/schema/xci/1.0/");

public static var ns_xfals21 : Namespace = new
Namespace("http://www.xfa.org/schema/xfa-locale-set/2.1/");

public var paperSize   : PaperSize;
    public var margins     : PRectangle;
public var pageSize    : PSize;
public var orientation : String;
public var header:UIComponent;
public var footer:UIComponent;

public function get pages():Array{
   return children;
}

public override function get xdpContent():Object{

   var x:Object = xmlGen.copy();
   var f:Object = x..ns_xfat25::subform.(@name=="doc1")[0];
   var p:XML = <pageSet>
       <pageArea name="Page1" id="Page1">
     </pageArea>
   </pageSet>;

   var contentAreaX:Number = margins.left.px;
   var contentAreaY:Number = margins.top.px;
   var contentAreaH:Number = pageSize.height.px;
   var contentAreaW:Number = pageSize.width.px;

   if (header){
      var xdpHeader:XdpPage = new XdpPage();
      PDFHelper.createXdpPage(xdpHeader, header);
```

```
        xdpHeader.x = margins.left;
        xdpHeader.y = margins.top;
        contentAreaY = contentAreaY + header.height;
        contentAreaH = contentAreaH - header.height;

        p.pageArea.appendChild(xdpHeader.xdpContent);
    }



    if (footer){
        var xdpFooter:XdpContainer = new XdpContainer();
        PDFHelper.createXdpPage(xdpFooter, footer);
        xdpFooter.x = margins.left;
        var y:Number = pageSize.height.px + margins.top.px - footer.height;
        xdpFooter.y = new PNumber(y, PNumber.UNIT_PX);
        contentAreaH = contentAreaH - footer.height;

        p.pageArea.appendChild(xdpFooter.xdpContent);
    }

    p.pageArea.contentArea.@x = _pos(new PNumber(contentAreaX, PNumber.UNIT_PX));
    p.pageArea.contentArea.@y = _pos(new PNumber(contentAreaY, PNumber.UNIT_PX));
    p.pageArea.contentArea.@w = _pos(new PNumber(contentAreaW, PNumber.UNIT_PX));
    p.pageArea.contentArea.@h = _pos(new PNumber(contentAreaH, PNumber.UNIT_PX));

    p.pageArea.medium.@stock = "custom";
    p.pageArea.medium.@short = _pos(paperSize.width);
    p.pageArea.medium.@long  = _pos(paperSize.height);

    if( orientation==PrintOptions.ORIENTATION_LANDSCAPE )
        p.pageArea.medium.@orientation = "landscape";

    p.setNamespace(ns_xfat25);
    f.appendChild(p);
    f = applyStdData(f);

    return x;
}

public function addPage(p:XdpPage):void{

    addChild(p);
    p.pageNumber = pages.length;
    p.w = pageSize.width;
    p.h = pageSize.height;
}

public function init(opt:PrintOptions):void{

    paperSize = opt.paperSize.copy();
    margins = opt.margins.copy();

    pageSize = opt.pageSize;
```

```
   orientation = opt.orientation;
}
]]></mx:Script>

</xdp:XdpBaseObject>
```

The ActionScript class `PDFHelper` has about 300 lines of code; you can see some fragments of it in Example 11-17. We don't provide code explanations here, as teaching the internals of the XDP protocol is not the goal of this chapter.

Example 11-17. Fragments of PDFHelper.as

```
package com.farata.printing.pdf.buffered{

   public class PDFHelper{


       private static var prefix : Array =[["\%PDF-1.7"+ "\n"," 65535 f"],
         ["1 0 obj"+"\n"+
         "<</Type /Catalog /StructTreeRoot 9 0 R /MarkInfo <</Marked true>> /Pages
15 0 R /AcroForm 16 0 R /NeedsRendering true>>"+"\n"+
         "endobj"+"\n", " 00000 n"],
         ["2 0 obj"+"\n"+
         "<</Type /Page /MediaBox [0 0 612 792] /Resources 5 0 R /Contents 4 0 R
/StructParent 0 /StructParents 0 /Parent 15 0 R>>"+"\n"+
         "endobj"+"\n", " 00000 n"],
         [""," 65535 f"],
         ["4 0 obj"+"\n"+
         "<</Length 298>>"+"\n"+
         "stream"+"\n"+
         "BT"+"\n"+
         "/Content <</MCID 0>> BDC"+"\n"+
         "0.0 0.0 0.0 rg"+"\n"+
         "/RelativeColorimetric ri"+"\n"+
         "/T1_0 1.0 Tf"+"\n"+
         "10.0 0.0 0.0 10.0 72.0 720.0 Tm"+"\n"+
         "(Warning: This form is not supported at all with the current version of
Acrobat or Adobe Reader.) Tj"+"\n"+
         "0.0 -1.8 Td"+"\n"+
         "(Upgrade to the latest version for full support.) Tj"+"\n"+
         "0.0 -1.8 Td"+"\n"+
         "EMC"+"\n"+
         "ET"+"\n"+
         "endstream"+"\n"+
         "endobj"+"\n", " 00000 n"],
         ["5 0 obj"+"\n"+
         "<</Font 8 0 R /ProcSet [/PDF /Text]>>"+"\n"+
         "endobj"+"\n", " 00000 n"],
         ["6 0 obj"+"\n"+
         "<</Type /Encoding /BaseEncoding /WinAnsiEncoding>>"+"\n"+
         "endobj"+"\n"," 00000 n"],
         ["7 0 obj"+"\n"+
         "<</Type /Font /Subtype /Type1 /BaseFont /Helvetica /Encoding 6 0
R>>"+"\n"+
         "endobj"+"\n"," 00000 n"],
```

```
...
      private var ba:ByteArray = new ByteArray();
      public var xdpDocument:XdpDocument;

      public function PDFHelper(xdpDocument:XdpDocument) {
         this.xdpDocument = xdpDocument;
      }

      public function get pdfContent():ByteArray{
          return ba;
       }

      public function createPDFPrologue():void{
         //write pdf document prefix
         var xref:String ="";

         for (var i:int = 0; i < prefix.length; i++) {
            ba.writeMultiByte( prefix[i][0], "iso-8859-1");
            var str:String = padZeroes(ba.length, 10);
            xref = xref.concat(str + prefix[i][1] + " \n");
         }

         var s:String = xdpDocument.xdpContent.toString();
         s = s.substr(0, s.lastIndexOf("</subform>"));
         ba.writeMultiByte( s, "iso-8859-1");
       }
      public function createPage(obj:Object, type:int):void{
         var page:XdpPage = new XdpPage();
         createXdpPage(page, obj, type);
         ba.writeMultiByte(String(page.xdpContent), "iso-8859-1");
      }

     public function createPDFEpilogue():void{
         var xx:XML = xdpDocument.xdpContent as XML;
         ba.writeMultiByte( "</subform>"+"\r"+"</template>"+"\r", "iso-8859-1");
         ba.writeMultiByte( xx..ns_xci10::config[0].toString().replace("
xmlns:xdp=\"http://ns.adobe.com/xdp/\"", "")+"\r", "iso-8859-1");
         ba.writeMultiByte( xx..ns_xfals21::localeSet[0].toString().replace("
xmlns:xdp=\"http://ns.adobe.com/xdp/\"", "")+"\r", "iso-8859-1");
         ba.writeMultiByte( "</xdp:xdp>"+"\r", "iso-8859-1");
         ba.writeMultiByte( "endstream"+"\r", "iso-8859-1");
         ba.writeMultiByte( "endobj"+"\r", "iso-8859-1");
         ba.writeMultiByte("18 0 obj " +"\n" + /*streamLength + */"\n" +
"endobj"+"\n",  "iso-8859-1");

         //the footer for the pdf document
          var end:String = "xref"+"\n"+ "0 " + 19 +"\n";
         var closing:String = end +
               "0000000000 65535 f"+"\r"+
               "0000000016 00000 n"+"\r"+
...
              "trailer"+"\n"+
               "<</Root 1 0 R  /Size " + 19 +">>"+"\n"+
               "startxref"+"\n"+
```

```
            "%%EOF"+"\n";
      ba.writeMultiByte(closing , "iso-8859-1");
   }

   public static function createXdpPage(root:XdpPage, obj:Object,
            type:int = 1):void{

      obj = resolveXdp(obj);
      if (obj is Container){

         var c:Container=obj as Container;
         var count:int=c.numChildren;
         if (type == TYPE_LIST) {
            var page:XdpPage = new XdpPage();
         } else {
            page = new XdpContainer();
         }

         page.x = new PNumber(c.x, PNumber.UNIT_PX);
         page.y = new PNumber(c.y, PNumber.UNIT_PX);
         page.h = new PNumber(c.height, PNumber.UNIT_PX);
         page.w = new PNumber(c.width, PNumber.UNIT_PX);

         root.addChild(page);

         if (obj is FormItem){
            var formItemLabel:Label = (obj as FormItem).itemLabel;
            createXdpPage(page, formItemLabel);
         }

         for(var i:int=0; i < count; i++){

            createXdpPage(page, c.getChildAt(i));
         }
      } else if (obj is IXdpObject){

         root.addChild(obj as IXdpObject);
      } else if (obj is UIComponent){

         var uiComp:UIComponent = obj as UIComponent;
         var xdp:XdpBaseObject = XdpImage.grab(uiComp);
         xdp.x = new PNumber(uiComp.x, PNumber.UNIT_PX);
         xdp.y = new PNumber(uiComp.y, PNumber.UNIT_PX);

         // set the width and hight of UIComponent (i.e. image)
         // for proper image scaling and conversion of pixels
         xdp.w = new PNumber(uiComp.width, PNumber.UNIT_PX);
         xdp.h = new PNumber(uiComp.height, PNumber.UNIT_PX);
         root.addChild(xdp);
      }
   }

}
```

The code in Examples 11-16 and 11-17 is for illustration purposes only, because detailed coverage of the XDP generation is out of the scope of this book. Complete source code of *com.farata.printing.swc*, however, is available in the CVS repository of the Clear Toolkit project at SourceForge.

Example 11-18 shows the source code of *test4_xdp.mxml*, the modified version of *text4.mxml*, but this code generates a PDF in XDP format. The Flex window and PDF look the same as in Figure 11-3.

Example 11-18. AIR application test4_xdp.mxml

```
<?xml version="1.0" encoding="utf-8"?>

<mx:WindowedApplication xmlns:mx="http://www.adobe.com/2006/mxml" layout="vertical"
creationComplete="onCreationComplete(event)">

   <mx:Style source="main.css"/>

   <mx:DataGrid id="dg" x="0" y="0" width="100%" height="100%">
       <mx:columns>
      <mx:DataGridColumn dataField="name" headerText="Name"/>
      <mx:DataGridColumn dataField="phone" headerText="Phone"/>
      <mx:DataGridColumn dataField="email" headerText="E-mail"/>
      </mx:columns>

        </mx:DataGrid>
   <mx:ApplicationControlBar width="100%">
     <mx:Label text="File name:"/>
     <mx:TextInput id="txtFileName" text="hw4.pdf"/>
     <mx:Button label="Save PDF" click="savePdf()"/>
   </mx:ApplicationControlBar>

   <mx:Script>
      <![CDATA[
      import com.farata.printing.PrintOptions;
      import com.farata.printing.pdf.xdp.XdpDocument;
      import com.farata.printing.pdf.buffered.PDFHelper;

      private function doSavePdf():void{
         saveToFile(txtFileName.text , createXdpContent());
      }
      private function createXdpContent():ByteArray {

         var xdpDocument:XdpDocument=new XdpDocument();
         xdpDocument.init(new PrintOptions());
         var pdf:PDFHelper=new PDFHelper(xdpDocument);

         pdf.createPDFPrologue();
         pdf.createPage(canvas, PDFHelper.TYPE_LIST);
         pdf.createPDFEpilogue();

         return  pdf.pdfContent;
```

```
    }

    private function saveToFile(file:String, ba:ByteArray):void{

       var fs:FileStream=new FileStream();
       var f:File=File.desktopDirectory.resolvePath(file);

       fs.open(f, FileMode.WRITE);
       try{
          fs.writeBytes(ba);
       }catch(e:*){
                   // Error processing goes here
       }

       fs.close();
    }

    private function onCreationComplete(evt:*):void{

    var array:Array=[];
    for(var i:int=1; i <= 300; i++){

       var obj:Object=new Object();
       obj.name="User " + i;
       obj.phone="555-219-227" + i;
         obj.email="user" + i + "@hello.world";
         obj.active=(i % 2) == 1;

       array.push(obj);
         }

    dg.dataProvider=arrat;
   }

 ]]>
 </mx:Script>
</mx:WindowedApplication>
```

We decided to keep the name of the code sample as *test4_xdp.mxml*, and you can find all other samples (*test1* to *test5*) in the Flash Builder project *clientPdfAir*.

The previous example illustrates the printing of 300 rows of data to demonstrate that the pagination works properly and each page in the PDF file shows the header of the `DataGrid` (Figure 11-4).

Embed Your SWF in a PDF

Starting in version 9, Adobe Acrobat Professional includes Flash Player and allows you to easily drop a *.swf* or *.fla* file inside a PDF.

Now you can develop Flash content and embed it into a PDF sales brochure or any other document. To view this content, users just need the freely available Acrobat Reader version 9 or later. Visit *http://www.adobe.com/products/acrobat/* for details.

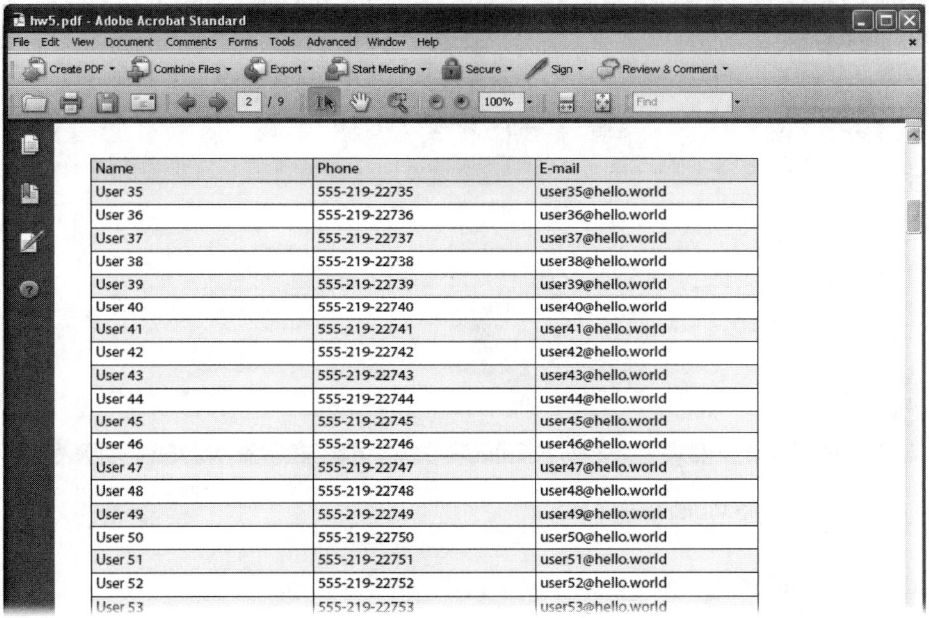

Name	Phone	E-mail
User 35	555-219-22735	user35@hello.world
User 36	555-219-22736	user36@hello.world
User 37	555-219-22737	user37@hello.world
User 38	555-219-22738	user38@hello.world
User 39	555-219-22739	user39@hello.world
User 40	555-219-22740	user40@hello.world
User 41	555-219-22741	user41@hello.world
User 42	555-219-22742	user42@hello.world
User 43	555-219-22743	user43@hello.world
User 44	555-219-22744	user44@hello.world
User 45	555-219-22745	user45@hello.world
User 46	555-219-22746	user46@hello.world
User 47	555-219-22747	user47@hello.world
User 48	555-219-22748	user48@hello.world
User 49	555-219-22749	user49@hello.world
User 50	555-219-22750	user50@hello.world
User 51	555-219-22751	user51@hello.world
User 52	555-219-22752	user52@hello.world
User 53	555-219-22753	user53@hello.world

Figure 11-4. The second page of the generated PDF hw5.pdf

Adding Printing to the PharmaSales Application

In Chapter 9, you learned how to create an occasionally connected AIR application. In this section, you'll modify it a little bit, armed with new knowledge and printing components. That's right, the Acme Pharm dispatcher should be able to print visitation data for all salespeople.

On the other hand, each salesperson will be able to print the data about his visits to medical offices without the need to be connected to the server.

Printing for Acme Pharm Dispatchers

You'll take care of the dispatcher's needs first. As you might remember from Chapter 9, *VisitSchedules.mxml* is a web application written in Flex. This means that you won't be able to save a generated PDF file on the client's filesystem and will need to send it to the server, which will just bounce it back so that the web browser will recognize it as a PDF and do the rest.

The source code of this version of *PharmaSales* is located in two Flex Builder projects, *air.offline.demo.print* and *air.offline.demo.web.print*. You'll need to start with the latter (don't forget to start MySQL Server and the servlet container first; the example uses Apache Tomcat). Your web browser should show you the view, similar to that shown in Figure 11-5.

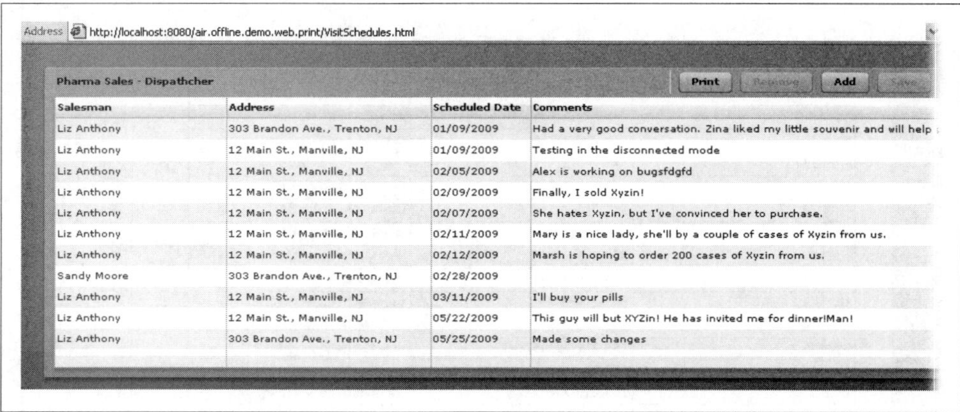

Salesman	Address	Scheduled Date	Comments
Liz Anthony	303 Brandon Ave., Trenton, NJ	01/09/2009	Had a very good conversation. Zina liked my little souvenir and will help
Liz Anthony	12 Main St., Manville, NJ	01/09/2009	Testing in the disconnected mode
Liz Anthony	12 Main St., Manville, NJ	02/05/2009	Alex is working on bugsfdgfd
Liz Anthony	12 Main St., Manville, NJ	02/09/2009	Finally, I sold Xyzin!
Liz Anthony	12 Main St., Manville, NJ	02/07/2009	She hates Xyzin, but I've convinced her to purchase.
Liz Anthony	12 Main St., Manville, NJ	02/11/2009	Mary is a nice lady, she'll by a couple of cases of Xyzin from us.
Liz Anthony	12 Main St., Manville, NJ	02/12/2009	Marsh is hoping to order 200 cases of Xyzin from us.
Sandy Moore	303 Brandon Ave., Trenton, NJ	02/28/2009	
Liz Anthony	12 Main St., Manville, NJ	03/11/2009	I'll buy your pills
Liz Anthony	12 Main St., Manville, NJ	05/22/2009	This guy will but XYZin! He has invited me for dinner!Man!
Liz Anthony	303 Brandon Ave., Trenton, NJ	05/25/2009	Made some changes

Figure 11-5. Running VisitSchedules.mxml

Click the Print button and Figure 11-6's PDF will show up.

Address http://localhost:8080/air.offline.demo.web.print/PDFServlet/dg.pdf

Salesman	Address	Scheduled Date	Comments
Liz Anthony	303 Brandon Ave., Trenton, NJ	01/09/2009	Had a very good conversation. Zina
Liz Anthony	12 Main St., Manville, NJ	01/09/2009	Testing in the disconnected mode
Liz Anthony	12 Main St., Manville, NJ	02/05/2009	Alex is working on bugsfdgfd
Liz Anthony	12 Main St., Manville, NJ	02/09/2009	Finally, I sold Xyzin!
Liz Anthony	12 Main St., Manville, NJ	02/07/2009	She hates Xyzin, but I've convinced
Liz Anthony	12 Main St., Manville, NJ	02/11/2009	Mary is a nice lady, she'll by a coupl
Liz Anthony	12 Main St., Manville, NJ	02/12/2009	Marsh is hoping to order 200 cases
Sandy Moore	303 Brandon Ave., Trenton, NJ	02/28/2009	
Liz Anthony	12 Main St., Manville, NJ	03/11/2009	I'll buy your pills
Liz Anthony	12 Main St., Manville, NJ	05/22/2009	This guy will but XYZin! He has invit
Liz Anthony	303 Brandon Ave., Trenton, NJ	05/25/2009	Made some changes

11.69 x 8.26 in

Figure 11-6. Generated PDF from VisitSchedules.mxml

The PDF has been generated, and for illustration purposes, we performed a search for the word "Sandy," which was successfully found.

The web browser reports that the PDF came from the following URL:

> *http://localhost:8080/air.offline.demo.web.print/PDFServlet/dg.pdf*

You'll see the code of this Java servlet, `PDFServlet`, in a little bit, but in the meantime, take a peek at the Flex code fragment in *VisitSchedules.mxml* (Example 11-19), which is invoked by clicking the Print button.

Example 11-19. Flex code fragment for PDF generation

```
<mx:Button click="openPDF(dg)" label="Print"/>
[Bindable]


   public var collection:DataCollection;

   private function openPDF(uiObject:Object):void{

      var xdpDocument:XdpDocument=new XdpDocument();
      var options:PrintOptions=new PrintOptions();
      options.paperSize=PaperSize.A4;
      options.orientation=PrintOptions.ORIENTATION_LANDSCAPE;

      xdpDocument.init(options);
      var pdf:PDFHelper=new PDFHelper(xdpDocument);

      pdf.createPDFPrologue();
      pdf.createPage(uiObject, PDFHelper.TYPE_LIST);
      pdf.createPDFEpilogue();

      sendToServer(uiObject.id + ".pdf", pdf.pdfContent);
   }


   private function sendToServer(file:String, ba:ByteArray):void{

      var req:URLRequest = new URLRequest("PDFServlet/"+file);
      req.method = URLRequestMethod.POST;

      ba.compress();

      req.data = ba;

      navigateToURL(req, "_blank");
   }
```

The function `openPDF()` looks similar to `savePdf()` from Example 11-18. It'll generate a PDF in the XDP format for the `DataGrid` container. At this point, the generated PDF is located in memory in the `ByteArray` object in `pdf.pdfContent`.

Next, the function `sendToServer()` compresses this `ByteArray` and sends it to the Java servlet,`PDFServlet`, deployed on the server. The source code of `PDFServlet` (Example 11-20) is located in the folder *src/com/Farata/demo/pdf* in the Flex Builder project *air.offline.demo.web.print*.

Example 11-20. PDFServlet.java

```
package com.farata.demo.pdf;

import java.io.IOException;
import java.io.InputStream;
import java.nio.ByteBuffer;
import java.nio.channels.Channels;
import java.nio.channels.ReadableByteChannel;
import java.util.zip.InflaterInputStream;
import javax.servlet.ServletException;
import javax.servlet.ServletInputStream;
import javax.servlet.http.HttpServletRequest;
import javax.servlet.http.HttpServletResponse;

public class PDFServlet extends javax.servlet.http.HttpServlet
                              implements javax.servlet.Servlet {

   static final long serialVersionUID = 1L;

   // The size of the reading block
   private static final int READ_BLOCK = 8192;

    public PDFServlet() {
      super();
   }

   protected void doPost(HttpServletRequest req, HttpServletResponse resp)
         throws ServletException, IOException {

      ServletInputStream in = req.getInputStream();
      InflaterInputStream iin = new InflaterInputStream(in);

      byte[] content = readAllFromInputStream(iin);

      resp.setContentType("application/pdf");
      resp.flushBuffer();

      resp.getOutputStream().write(content);
      resp.getOutputStream().close();
   }

   private byte[] readAllFromInputStream(InputStream is) throws IOException {

      // create channel for input stream
      ReadableByteChannel bc = Channels.newChannel(is);

      ByteBuffer bb = ByteBuffer.allocate(READ_BLOCK);

      while (bc.read(bb) != -1) {
         // get new buffer for read
         bb = resizeBuffer(bb);
      }

      bb.flip();
```

```
        return bb.array();
    }

    private ByteBuffer resizeBuffer(ByteBuffer in) {
        ByteBuffer result = in;

        if (in.remaining() < READ_BLOCK) {
            // create new buffer
            result = ByteBuffer.allocate(in.capacity() * 2);

            // set limit to current position in buffer and set position to zero.
            in.flip();

            // store the content of original buffer to new buffer
            result.put(in);
        }

        return result;

    }
}
```

In short, this Java servlet echoes received PDF content from the client, assigns to it the MIME type `"application/pdf"`, and sends it right back without doing any other processing.

Start reading this code from the method `doPost()`, which opens an input stream pointing at the request object (`HTTPRequest`) that arrived from the browser. Because the arrived content has been compressed by the client, the servlet inflates it first and writes it right back to the response object (`HTTPResponse`).

All manipulations with buffering in the code above are done for I/O efficiency.

The main takeaway here is that the server-side code didn't modify the received PDF object, but just sent it back as PDF content. Now it's the web browser's responsibility to engage its Acrobat Reader plug-in to display the document.

Printing for Acme Pharm Salespeople

Now consider the AIR application that salespeople use on a daily basis, either in connected or in disconnected mode. In this case, the generated PDF won't even go to the server side, but it will be saved in the file on the local disk.

You still want to print the list of visits for a particular salesperson as a grid, but to make this report a little fancier, the program should add the name of the salesperson as a header and the logo of Acme Pharm in the footer's area of the report.

After running the application *PharmaSales.mxml* from the *air.offline.demo.print* project filtering the data for visits done by Liz Anthony from February 5 to June 7 in 2009, click the Print button. The filtered data will be saved in the file *dg.pdf* at the local storage directory. Exact file location is displayed in the status bar, as shown in Figure 11-7.

After the PDF file is created, this AIR application automatically starts the web browser and opens *dg.pdf*. Figure 11-8 shows how it looks for the sample data.

The header of *dg.pdf* shows the date range and the footer—the logo of the company and some arbitrary text. The header and the footer will be repeated on each page in case of multipage printing.

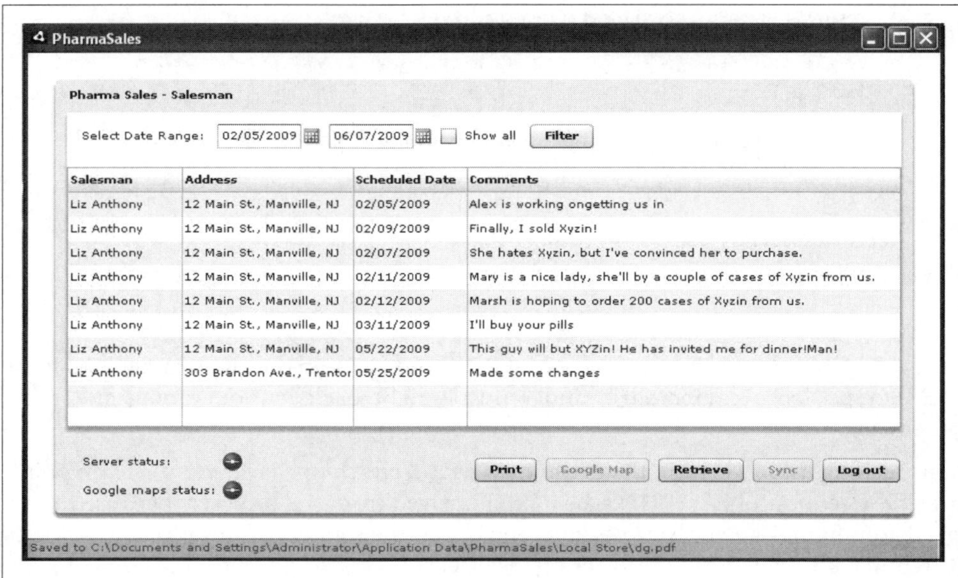

Figure 11-7. After clicking the buttons Filter and Print

The header component looks like Example 11-21.

Example 11-21. Header.mxml

```
<?xml version="1.0" encoding="utf-8"?>

 <mx:Canvas xmlns:mx="http://www.adobe.com/2006/mxml" width="594" height="56">

  <mx:Label id="headerLabel" x="10" y="13" text="Visits by Liz Anthony for the
   period from 02/05/09 to 06/07/09" width="565" height="27" fontSize="16"
   fontFamily="Arial" fontWeight="bold"/>

 </mx:Canvas>
```

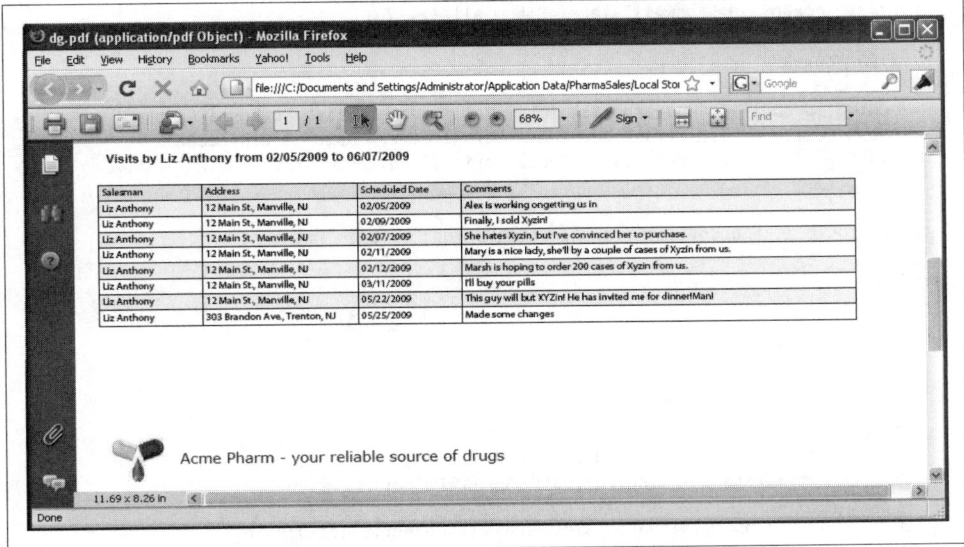

Figure 11-8. A generated local file with header and footer: dg.pdf

The footer components are shown in Example 11-22.

Example 11-22. Footer.mxml

```
<?xml version="1.0" encoding="utf-8"?>

<mx:Canvas xmlns:mx="http://www.adobe.com/2006/mxml" width="556" height="78"
   xmlns:ns1="com.farata.controls.*">

 <ns1:Image source="@Embed(source='assets/pharma_small.jpg')" x="10" y="10"
  width="75" height="57"/>

 <ns1:Label x="100" y="27" width="446" height="34" text="Acme Pharma - your
  reliable source of drugs" fontSize="19"/>

</mx:Canvas>
```

Example 11-23 is a code fragment from the *PharmaSales.mxml* application. It illustrates what's happening when the user clicks on the Print button.

Example 11-23. Code fragment for printing a data grid with visits from PharmaSales.mxml

```
<mx:Canvas height="100%" width="100%">
   <mx:Panel title="Pharma Sales - Salesman" width="100%" height="100%">
     <mx:ControlBar>
      <mx:Label text="Select Date Range:"/>
         <mx:DateField id="dateRangeFrom"
                enabled="{!showAll.selected}"/>
       <mx:DateField id="dateRangeTo"
                enabled="{!showAll.selected}"/>
```

```
        <mx:CheckBox id="showAll" label="Show all"/>
        <mx:Button label="Filter" click="doFilter()"/>
    </mx:ControlBar>

    <fx:DataGrid toolTip="Double click for details" doubleClick="onDoubleClick()"
        doubleClickEnabled="true" horizontalScrollPolicy="auto" width="100%"
        id="dg" dataProvider="{visitDataCollection}" editable="true" height="100%">
...

    <mx:Button click="openVisitDataCollectionPDF(dg)" label="Print"/>

</mx:Canvas>

    <mx:Script>
       <![CDATA[

       import com.farata.printing.PaperSize;
       import com.farata.printing.PrintOptions;
       import com.farata.printing.pdf.xdp.XdpDocument;
       import com.farata.printing.pdf.buffered.PDFHelper;

    private function openVisitDataCollectionPDF(uiObject:Object):void{

             var xdpDocument:XdpDocument=new XdpDocument();
             var options:PrintOptions=new PrintOptions();
             options.paperSize=PaperSize.A4;
             options.orientation=PrintOptions.ORIENTATION_LANDSCAPE;
             xdpDocument.init(options);

             //Create header text dynamically

       var text:String="";

       var df:DateFormatter=new DateFormatter();
       if (showAll.selected || (!dateRangeFrom.selectedDate &&
                                 !dateRangeTo.selectedDate)){
          text="All visits by " + username.text;
       } else if (!dateRangeFrom.selectedDate && dateRangeTo.selectedDate){
          text="Visits by " + username.text + " to " +
                    df.format(dateRangeTo.selectedDate);
       } else if (dateRangeFrom.selectedDate && !dateRangeTo.selectedDate){
              text="Visits by " + username.text + " from " +
                    df.format(dateRangeFrom.selectedDate);
       } else {
            text="Visits by " + username.text + " from " +
                    df.format(dateRangeFrom.selectedDate) + " to " +
                    df.format(dateRangeTo.selectedDate);
          }

         var header:Header=new Header();
       header.initialize();
         header.headerLabel.text=text;

       xdpDocument.header=header;
       xdpDocument.footer=new Footer();
```

```
    xdpDocument.footer.initialize();

    var pdf:PDFHelper=new PDFHelper(xdpDocument);

    pdf.createPDFPrologue();

    pdf.createPage(uiObject, PDFHelper.TYPE_LIST);

    pdf.createPDFEpilogue();

    savePDF(uiObject.id + ".pdf", pdf.pdfContent);
 }

 private function savePDF(file:String, ba:ByteArray):void {

    var fs:FileStream=new FileStream();
    var f:File=File.applicationStorageDirectory.resolvePath(file);

      try{
      fs.open(f, FileMode.WRITE);
      fs.writeBytes(ba);

         var req:URLRequest=new URLRequest(f.url);
      navigateToURL(req, "_blank");
      status="Saved to " + f.nativePath;

    } catch(e:*){
       status=e.message;
      } finally {
       fs.close();
     }

 }
 ]]>

 </mx:Script>

</mx:WindowedApplication>
```

The Visit Details window now has the Print button, too, as you can see in Figure 11-9. The produced PDF file looks like Figure 11-10.

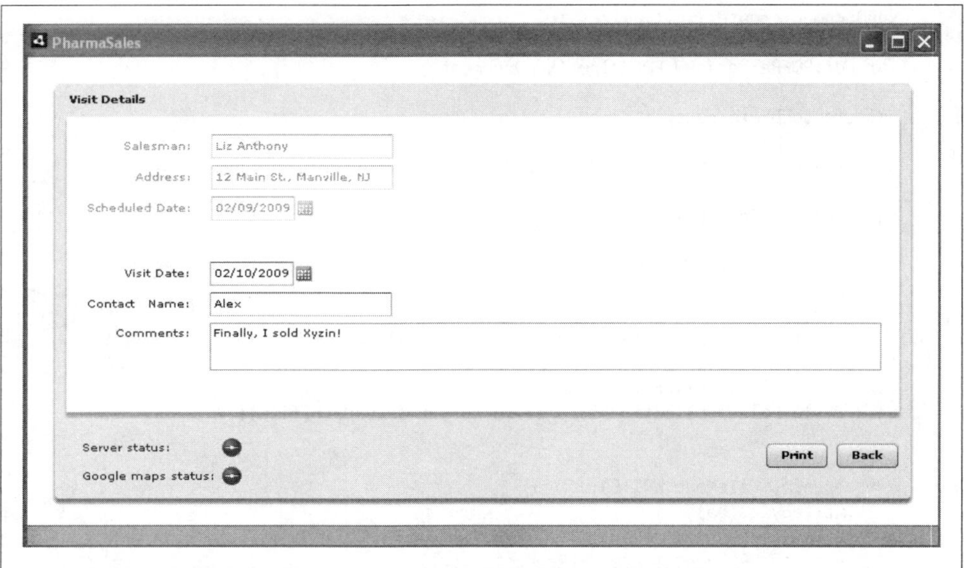

Figure 11-9. Visit Details with the Print button

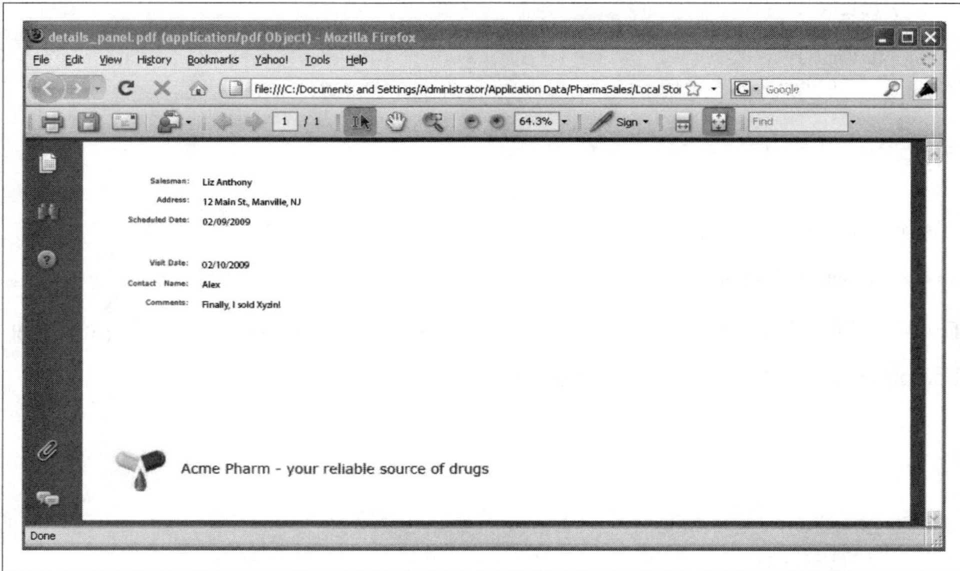

Figure 11-10. The generated PDF file details_panel.pdf

There is no reason why a Flex window with Google Maps can't have the Print button, as shown in Figure 11-11.

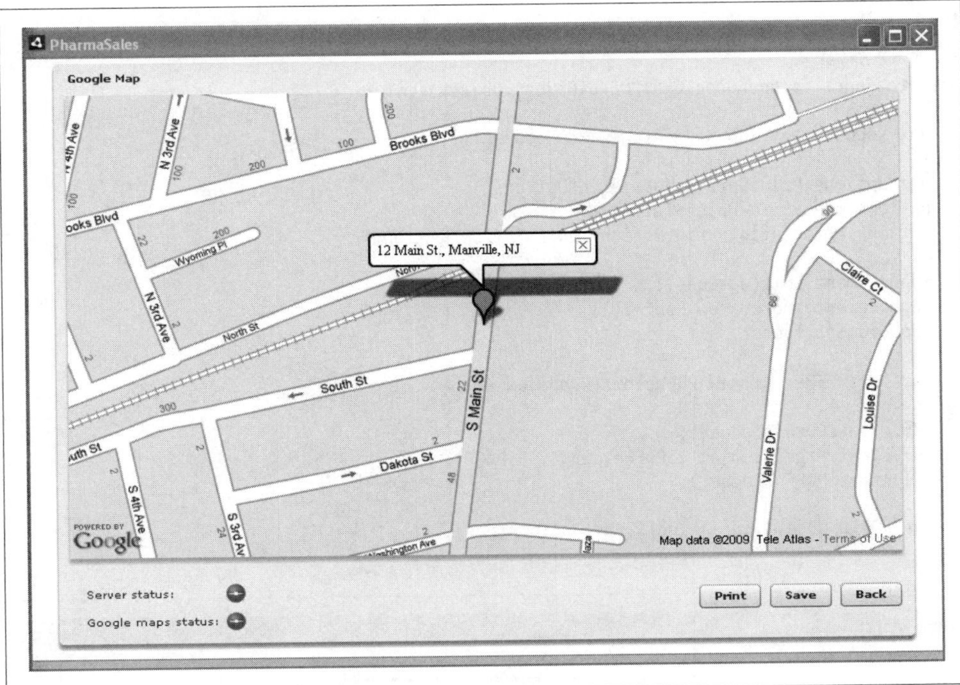

Figure 11-11. A Google Maps window with the Print button

The generated PDF with the map is shown in Figure 11-12.

The PDF files for both the Visit Details and map windows are generated by similar functions, as shown in Example 11-24.

Example 11-24. Functions for generation of Visit Details and map PDFs

```
private function openVisitPDF(uiObject:Object):void{

   var xdpDocument:XdpDocument=new XdpDocument();

     var options:PrintOptions=new PrintOptions();
   options.paperSize=PaperSize.A4;
   options.orientation=PrintOptions.ORIENTATION_LANDSCAPE;

   xdpDocument.init(options);
   xdpDocument.footer=new Footer();
   xdpDocument.footer.initialize();

   var pdf:PDFHelper=new PDFHelper(xdpDocument);
   pdf.createPDFPrologue();
   pdf.createPage(uiObject, PDFHelper.TYPE_PAGE);
   pdf.createPDFEpilogue();

   savePDF(uiObject.id + ".pdf", pdf.pdfContent);
```

```
}

private function openGoogleMapPDF(uiObject:Object):void{

   var xdpDocument:XdpDocument=new XdpDocument();

   var options:PrintOptions=new PrintOptions();
   options.paperSize=PaperSize.A4;
   options.orientation=PrintOptions.ORIENTATION_LANDSCAPE;

   xdpDocument.init(options);
   xdpDocument.footer=new Footer();
   xdpDocument.footer.initialize();

   var pdf:PDFHelper=new PDFHelper(xdpDocument);

   pdf.createPDFPrologue();
   pdf.createPage(uiObject, PDFHelper.TYPE_PAGE);
   pdf.createPDFEpilogue();

   savePDF(uiObject.id + ".pdf", pdf.pdfContent);
}
```

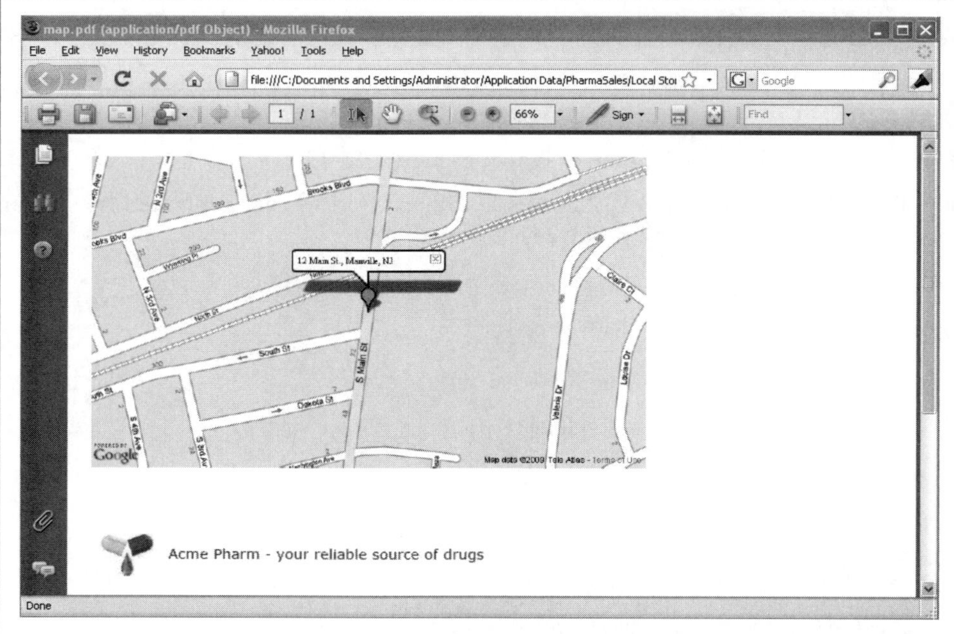

Figure 11-12. A Google map in a generated PDF

ClearBI: A Web Reporter for Flex

If you want to make more professional-looking reports with such features as adding formulas, creating totals and subtotals, exporting to Microsoft Excel, and charting, consider using the ClearBI reporter that will be included in a future version of the Clear Toolkit framework. To run these reports, end users don't need anything but Flash Player–enabled web browsers.

Flex developers use ClearBI's Designer (an AIR application) to create custom reports that can either be saved on the local drives or published in a DBMS.

More advanced business users can customize their reports right inside the web browser. For example, Figure 11-13 depicts a report with grouping by state, and departments with calculated totals and subtotals.

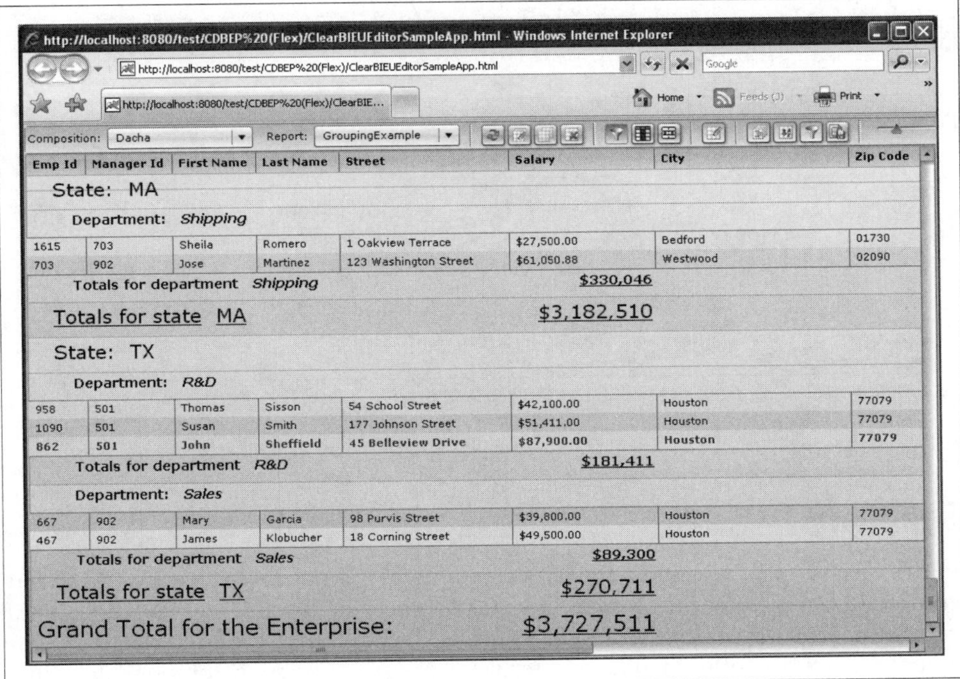

Figure 11-13. A sample report with grouping

When the user directs a web browser to a deployed ClearBI report player application (a SWF file; it'll arrive with an extra toolbar—see the toolbar below the address bar in Figure 11-13) that allows users to zoom in, export to Microsoft Excel, generate PDFs, and open a Designer view that allows you to create charts, grouping, filters, sorting, and format masks; compute fields; and introduce formulas. Figure 11-14 depicts a Designer view with a formula, converting department codes into titles.

ClearBI Designer can be invoked either by the user inside the web browser, or by any junior developer as a standalone AIR application (no knowledge of Flex is required).

ClearBI supports user roles and hierarchies to specify who can access specific reports.

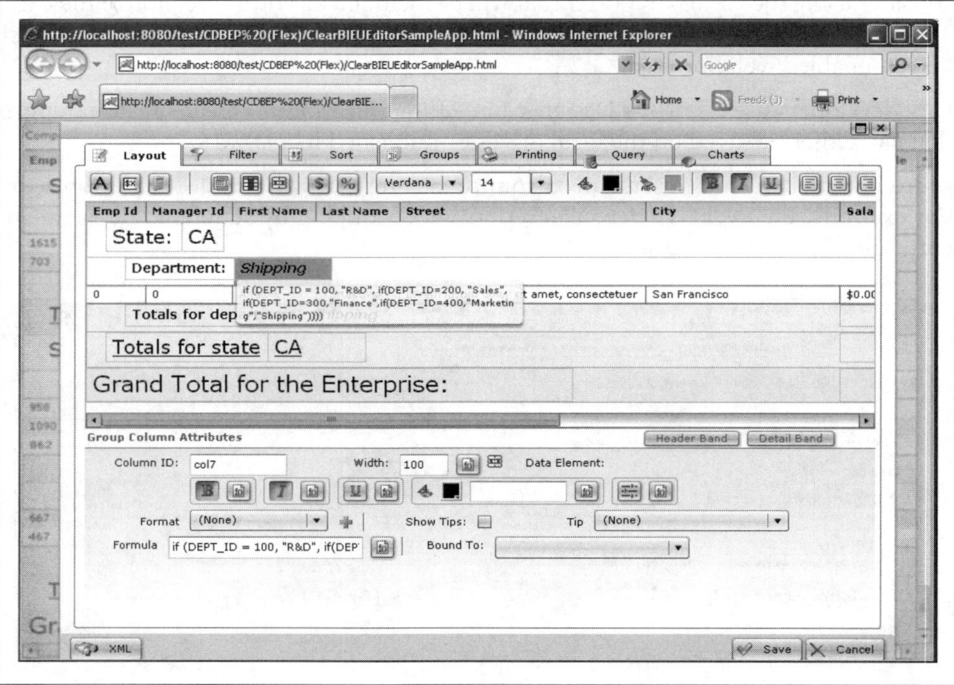

Figure 11-14. ClearBI Designer

Summary

In this chapter, you've learned how to extend Flex components to give them PDF generation capabilities. We encourage you to experiment in this area so you can be in full control of your own set of printable controls that reflect all printing needs of your enterprise. On the other hand, we offer you our version of such components, which are included in Clear Toolkit components—ready to use.

The principle of PDF generation on the client described in this chapter has several advantages:

- You don't have to create separate templates for further merging with data—everything is happening at the component level.
- Pagination of the long documents is also taken care of by the client-side code.
- Produced documents are fully searchable.

- If you sent editable components from Flex (e.g., a `DataGrid`), they will remain editable in the PDF document, too.

All source code for the examples used in this chapter is located under the Flex Builder projects *air.offline.demo.print*, *air.offline.demo.web.print*, *PrintingSamples*, and *clientPdfAir*. We've also included for your convenience the source code of the package *com.farata.printing*, which is a part of *clear.swc*. But to get the up-to-date version of the code of all components included in this library, visit the SourceForge repository of the Clear Toolkit framework at *https://sourceforge.net/projects/cleartoolkit/*.

Wouldn't you agree that with our smart Flex components, the task of printing becomes almost trivial?

CHAPTER 12

Model-Driven Development with LCDS ES2

A computer is a stupid machine with the ability to do incredibly smart things, while computer programmers are smart people with the ability to do incredibly stupid things. They are, in short, a perfect match.

—Bill Bryson

This chapter introduces you to the model-driven development workflow of LiveCycle Data Services ES2 (a.k.a. LCDS 3). The authors of this book are huge proponents of automated code generation wherever possible, and we applaud Adobe for moving in this direction. We believe that if this "stupid machine" is given the right instructions in the first place, it can generate smart code over and over again and free "smart programmers" to make their mistakes elsewhere.

This chapter is not intended to be a detailed tutorial on building a sample application. Instead, we'll highlight the key points and provide some sample configuration files that are important to understanding the process of model-driven development with LCDS 3.

If this leaves you hungry for more detail, you can consult several sources online. For example, at Adobe MAX 2009, Christophe Coenraets demonstrates the entire step-by-step process of model-driven development with Flash Builder 4 and LCDS 3. You can watch a recording of it at *http://2009.max.adobe.com/online/session/277*. A nicely written tutorial by Justin Shacklette, "Getting Real with LCDS 3," was published at O'Reilly's InsideRIA (*http://www.insideria.com/2009/12/getting-real-with-lcds-3-beta.html* and *http://www.insideria.com/2009/12/getting-real-with-lcds-3-part.html*).

Two major features that come with LCDS (but not BlazeDS) are support of RTMP and Data Management Services (DMS). Until LCDS version 2.6, however, DMS automated most of the work of Flex developers, but the server-side code had to be written manually. LCDS 3 introduces model-driven development in which not only is the entire CRUD application creation process automated, but Flash Builder 4 also includes a Modeler, which enables you to generate such applications just by working with a UML-like diagram. This chapter provides a high-level overview of this new workflow. In addition, you can easily find a number of articles and video tutorials online that contain step-by-step instructions on how to build an application using the LCDS 3 modeling tools and code generators.

The graphical Modeler tool is used not only in Flash Builder, but also in Adobe LiveCycle Workbench ES2.

Besides the model-driven workflow, LCDS ES2 offers many other welcome features for enterprise developers, including:

- *Reliable messaging* (implemented via `AdvancedChannelSet`), which guarantees that no messages are lost in case of network failures. This mode also guarantees that the messages arrive properly ordered.
- *Throttling*, which restricts the number of messages that are being sent between the server and client per second. This is important in network congestion situations to prevent servers from flooding the clients with messages (the same is true for the client-to-server data flows).
- An *EDGE server*, which can be deployed in the enterprise DMZ and can forward the messages of authenticated clients to other LCDS servers located in the secure zone behind the DMZ.
- A *load-test Java NIO testing tool*, which allows Flex developers to emulate heavy server-side hits by multiple clients.

In this chapter, we'll talk about model-driven development with LCDS. All features of LCDS 3 are described in the product documentation, available at *http://www.adobe.com/products/livecycle/dataservices/*.

Introduction to Model-Driven Development

LCDS ES2 eliminates the situation in which the client and server code don't know much about each other (LCDS 2.6 and earlier) and lots of code has to be written manually by software developers on both the client and the server sides.

For example, this version of LCDS doesn't require the manual creation of the same DTO on both the ActionScript and Java sides. You don't need to manually create similar validators in Flex and Java. You don't need to implement security in both in the Flex and Java classes. Now all this can be done at the Model level, abiding by the DRY principle of software engineering: Don't Repeat Yourself.

The DRY principle was introduced by Dave Thomas and Andy Hunt in their book *The Pragmatic Programmer* (Addison-Wesley Professional). It suggests that every piece of knowledge must have a single, unambiguous, authoritative representation within a system.

If the code generator and the tool know everything about the data, let them take care of the mundane task of writing tons of the boilerplate code and free yourself for implementing application-specific functionality.

Starting Model-Driven Development with Flash Builder 4

In the Flash Builder 4/LCDS 3 environment, the process of model-driven development starts with creating and saving a model. The model file gets deployed and code generators generate both client and server code, technically creating a CRUD application. In the next several pages, we'll highlight some of the milestones of this process.

You start by creating a new Flash Builder 4 project, selecting J2EE as a server-side technology, and pointing Flash Builder to the Java servlet container (that is, Apache Tomcat) where LCDS 3 is installed.

While highlighting the major steps of a model-driven workflow, we'll assume that you want to populate a `DataGrid` with the data coming from the server applying the model-driven workflow. You can do this with Flash Builder's new Data Services view. Remember, by "data service" we mean anything that can return the data.

As long as you know the API from which to get the data—that is, `getEmployees()`—it falls into a data service category. We're going to touch on modeling a new data service, rather than working with an existing data service (such as SQL or WebService). This way, you can start the model in the new Data Model perspective, which allows you to create a model in both Design and Source Code modes.

There is a new XML-based modeling language, which allows you to define the model for your application, save underlying XML in the file with the extension *.fml*, and deploy it on your LCDS 3 server. Typically, you'll be creating the model in the Design view of Flash Builder, and the XML code supporting the model will be generated automatically. But the Source Code view will let you see and manually modify, if need be, the model's XML. You can find a detailed explanation of all elements of this XML-based language at *http://help.adobe.com/en_US/LiveCycleDataServicesES/3.0/Modeling/index.html*.

Data Sources and RDS

You can open the Modeler by clicking the Model icon in Flash Builder's Package Explorer and selecting the Data Model view. Any data modeling tool needs to know where the data resides, and you have two options here. You can create a model and automatically generate database tables in an empty database, if you have configured the data source. Alternatively, if you already have a database with tables, the Modeler will introspect the data and build the entities required for the model.

In either case, to work with a relational DBMS using Java, you need to configure JDBC data sources. We've tested this workflow using Apache Tomcat and MySQLServer DBMS, and our data source configuration to the database *test* for the user *dba* with the password *sql* looked as shown in Example 12-1.

Example 12-1. Configuring MySQL Server database connection in Tomcat's file context.xml

```
<Context priviledged="true" antiResourceLocking="false"
   reloadable="true">
 <!-JOTM -->
 <Transaction factory="org.objectweb.jotm.UserTransactionFactory"
    jotm.timeout="60" />
 <Resource name="jdbc/test" type="javax.sql.DataSource"
     driverClassName="com.mysql.jdbc.Driver"
     url="jdbc:mysql:localhost:3306/test?autoReconnect=true"
     username="dba" password="sql" maxActive="20" maxIdle="10"
     maxWait="-1"
 />
</Context>
```

Flash Builder's Modeler will be able to access such data sources with the help of the server called *Remote Development Services* (*RDS*). After installing LCDS 3 in the Java Servlet container, you'll need to uncomment the RDS section shown in Example 12-2 in *web.xml*.

Example 12-2. RDSDispatchServlet is your RDS server

```
<servlet>
<servlet-name>RDSDispatchServlet</servlet-name>
<display-name>RDSDispatchServlet</display-name>
<servlet-class>
   flex.rds.server.servlet.FrontEndServlet
</servlet-class>
<init-param>
   <param-name>useAppserverSecurity</param-name>
   <param-value>false</param-value>
</init-param>
<load-on-startup>10</load-on-startup>
</servlet>
<servlet-mapping id="RDS_DISPATCH_MAPPING">
  <servlet-name>RDSDispatchServlet</servlet-name>
  <url-pattern>/CFIDE/main/ide.cfm</url-pattern>
</servlet-mapping>
```

Now, when the servlet container with LCDS starts, it'll launch the `RDSDispatchServlet`, which serves as a means of communication with Flash Builder Modeler. This `RDSDispatchServlet` tells the Modeler about its configured data sources; in the case of Apache Tomcat, this is in *context.xml*. Refer to the documentation for your Java Servlet container to learn how to configure data sources there.

The RDS server has to be configured in the Preferences panel of Flash Builder, as shown in Figure 12-1.

Figure 12-2 shows the RDS Data view of the Modeler that successfully connected to the test database configuration shown in Example 12-1.

If you drag one or more tables from the RDS view onto the Design perspective of the Modeler, you'll get the entity model of your data source with all relationships between them. Figure 12-3 shows how the Employee entity was generated based on the employee database table.

If you drag one more table department, all primary/foreign key relations defined in DBMS will turn into associations—lines connecting model entities. An *association* has properties (e.g., cardinality), and you can specify whether the association is uni- or bidirectional.

To assign validation rules to any of the Employee's properties, right-click on the property and enter the validation expression in the Styles panel.

You can also add to an entity so-called *variants*, which in other software tools are often called *computed fields*. Writing expressions for variants requires familiarity with the syntax of the expression language described in the product documentation. You can also use the graphical Expression Builder of Flash Builder 4.

If an entity has a unique `id` property, it's considered a persistent entity. In other words, you can save the changes to the entity's data on some media on the server side. Find the section `<annotation>` in the source code of the generated model; you'll see that by default, the entity will be manipulated using Java's JDBC notation with the help of the Hibernate dialect (`HSQLDialect`). To change the defaults and use custom classes as server-side assemblers, refer to the annotations section (*http://bit.ly/6zXkxd*) in the Adobe Application Modeling Technology Reference.

If you want to create a new table in DBMS, right-click somewhere in the blank area of the Model view and select New Entity.

Now you can save and deploy this model (the *.fml* file) in the LCDS server (this *.fml* file will be physically copied to the server). Because the plan is to display the data in a Flex view that will consist of the `DataGrid` and a `Form`, call it `masterDetailForm` as in Figure 12-4.

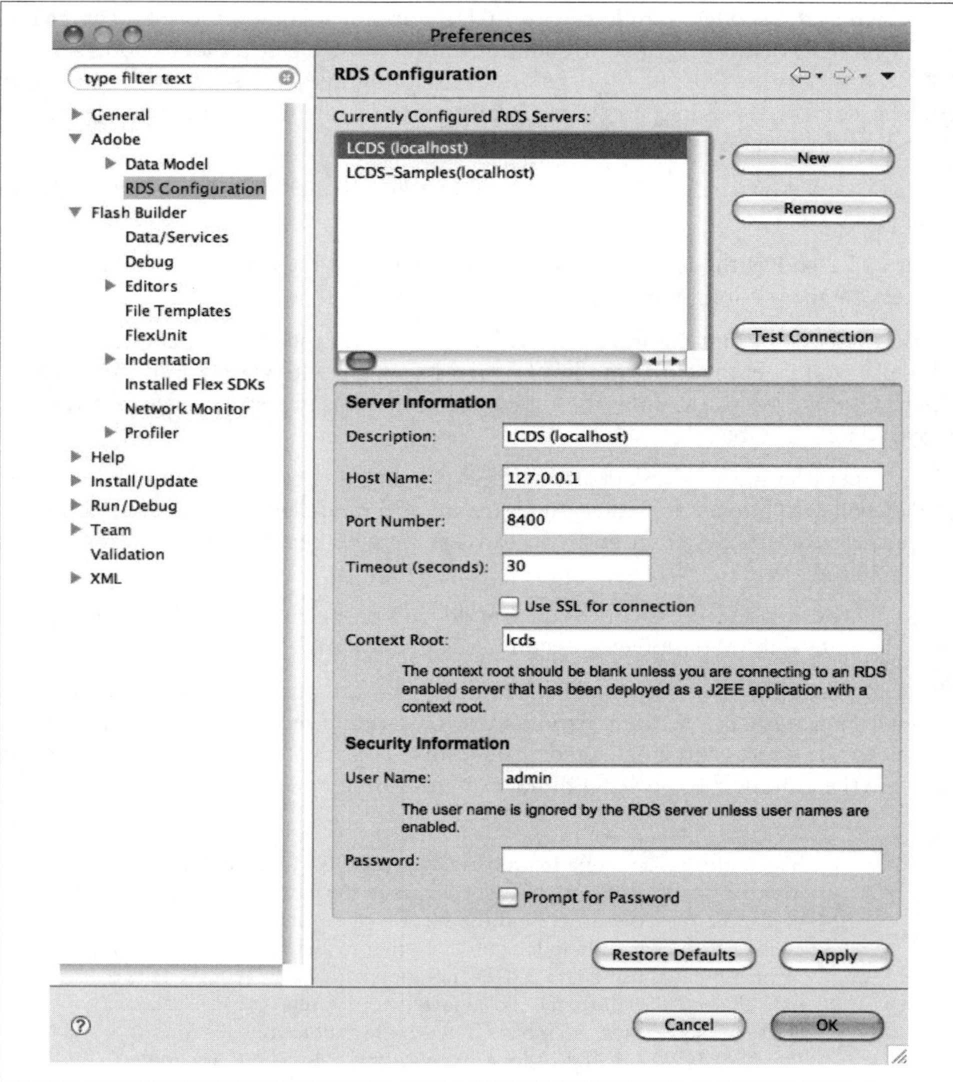

Figure 12-1. RDS configuration in Flash Builder 4

Note the group of radio buttons in Figure 12-4. If you are building the model from an existing database, the Unchanged option is selected. When you need to modify existing database entities, choose Update; to create new ones, choose Create/Recreate.

After deploying the model, Flash Builder, with help of Fiber, generates code on both the server and the client sides. On the server side, it generates a service with a number of methods based on the properties of the deployed entities. It also generates destinations, assemblers, endpoints, and whatever else you wrote manually in earlier versions

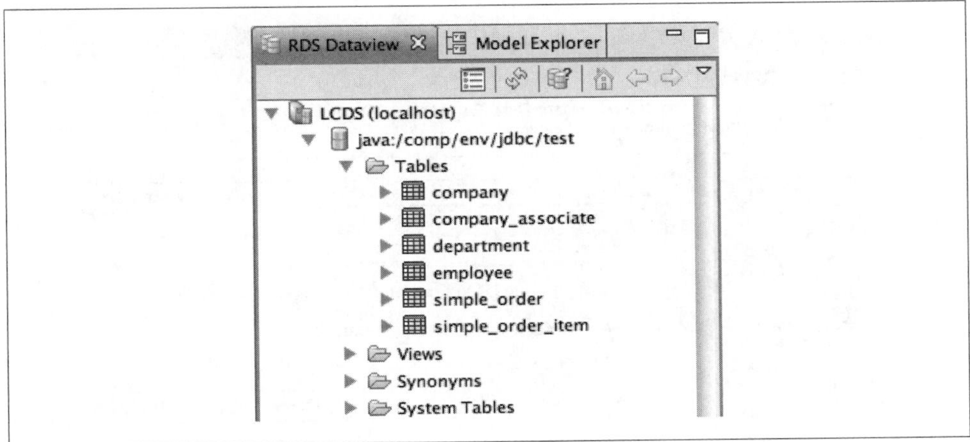

Figure 12-2. RDS view in Flash Builder Modeler

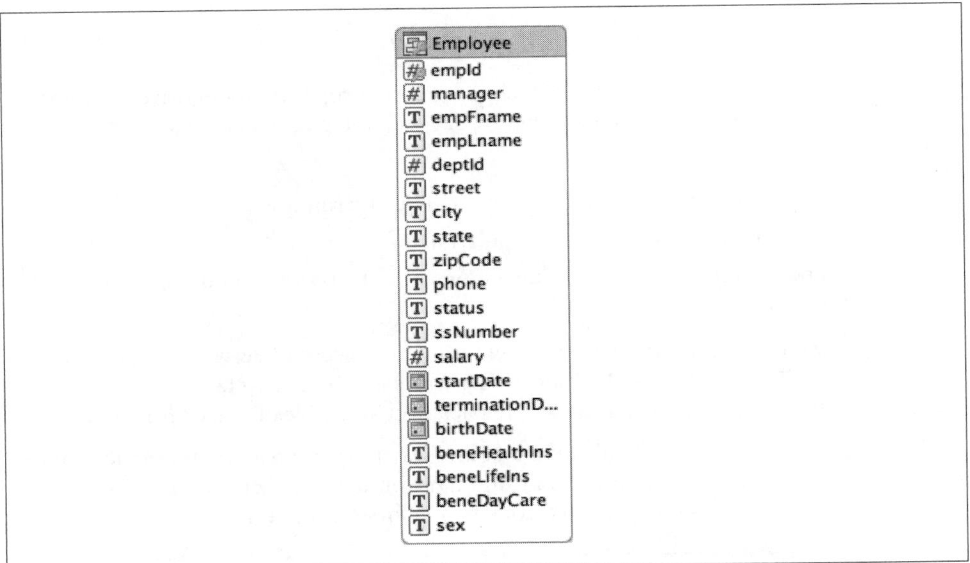

Figure 12-3. A one-entity data model: Employee

of LCDS; the difference is that Flash Builder does not create any custom Java classes on the disk. On the client side, Flash Builder deploys the model in the *.model* directory of your Flash Builder project and generates ActionScript classes acting as proxies for the service operations.

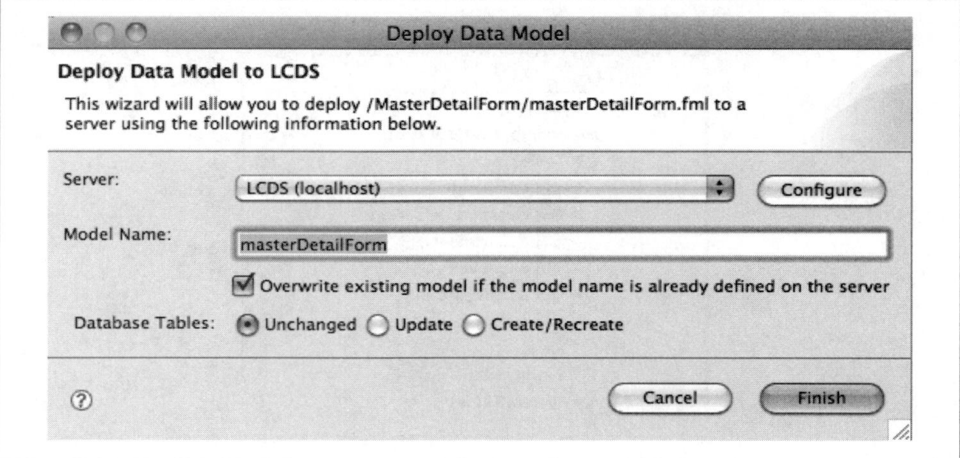

Figure 12-4. Deploying the data model

What Is Fiber?

Fiber is a code name for a number of technologies that support model-driven development. Used in Flash Builder 4 and other Adobe technologies. Fiber consists of:

- A modeling language
- The generator of the code to be interpreted during runtime
- Tools for model creation and manipulation
- A runtime (built into LCDS) that knows how to process model behavior and persistence

Fiber allows Flex applications to work with different types of services (`DataService`, `WebService`, `HTTPService`, `RemoteObject`). The wrapper classes that support these services as well as their supporting classes are packaged in the Flex library *fiber.swc*.

Based on the deployed model (a *.fml* file), Fiber generates in-memory destinations and assemblers for the services. You won't find *.java* or *.class* files created by Fiber. The LCDS server interprets the generated code in memory during runtime.

Figure 12-5 depicts the service `EmployeeService` with a number of generated methods. It's easy to guess that the method `getAll()` is for retrieval of all employees from the database table `Employee`.

Drag the `getAll()` method from the Data Services view onto the `DataGrid` in the Design view, and you'll see that the `DataGrid` will display the right-column names as defined in the entity `Employee`. Run the application, and the `DataGrid` will be populated with data from the database. No coding has been required.

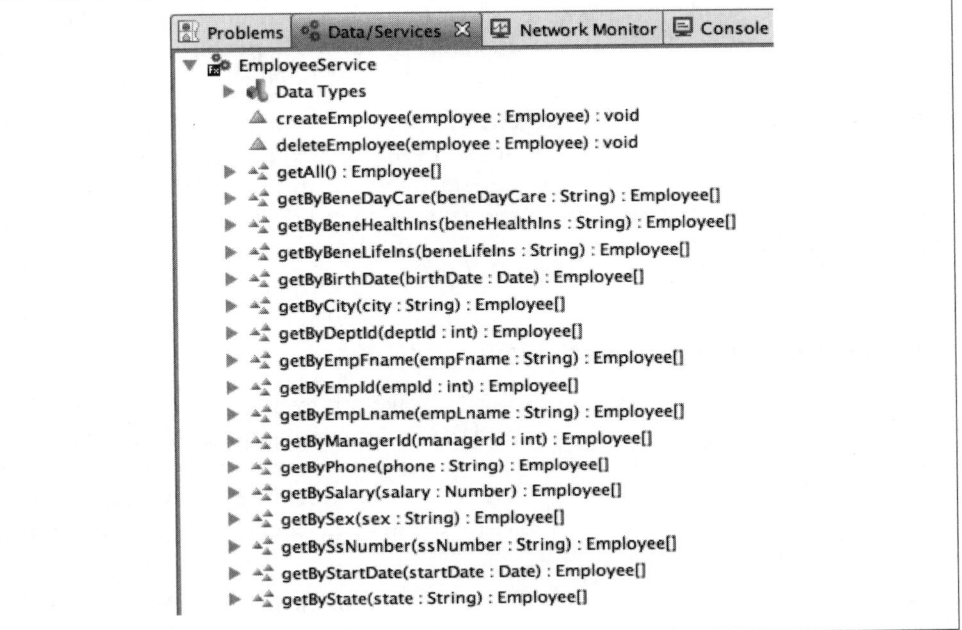

Figure 12-5. Generated data service: EmployeeService

Another way of binding the data service to the grid is the menu option Bind to Data in the right-click menu of the `DataGrid`.

What Has Been Generated?

What would you do after seeing the view shown in Figure 12-5? Chances are good that a Java developer would immediately try to find the generated Java class `EmployeeService`. But she wouldn't find it, because the Modeler generated Java access code in memory. So how does the whole thing work? This data service has been generated from your deployed model in the server's memory.

LCDS 3 includes a popular object-relational mapping framework called *Hibernate*, which is responsible for the data retrieval and persistence, but the code for the `EmployeeService` itself is generated and interpreted during the runtime in memory only.

On one hand, it's great: now even people who don't know Java can use LCDS. On the other hand, you are now completely dependent on the quality of this generated code. If the Java sources of the data service existed and something went wrong, you (as the Java developer) could debug and fix it. Because LCDS 3 was architected differently, you are at the mercy of the software engineers who created these code generators.

In the 1990s, the authors of this book had a very positive experience with the client/server tool PowerBuilder from Sybase, which was architected similarly. We didn't see the generated code, but everything worked fine there. We hope that the quality of the generated LCDS code will be as good as it was in PowerBuilder.

On the client side, although the Flex code has been generated, you'll be able to find classes for the DTOs and the ActionScript stubs that are required to support all CRUD operation communicating with the server-side methods from the data service. Generated DTOs are split into a superclass and its descendant; the superclass can be regenerated by the Modeler as often as needed, while the subclass, the descendant, is a placeholder for the custom code of an application developer.

Creating Master/Detail/Search View

The function `getAll()` populated the grid. To make this exercise a bit more complicated, you can add a Master/Detail view and search functionality to this view. When an employee is selected (say, Kristen Coe in Figure 12-6), you want to populate the form with detailed information on this person. This form should be editable and support data persistence (for example, the ability to update, delete, and add a new employee) on the server side.

Right-click on the Employee entity in the Design view of the Modeler. Note the section Data Types above the function names (see Figure 12-5). Because the Employee entity has the data from only one table, you'll see Employee as the only data type there. In a more generic case, you might have several data types there.

Right-click on the Employee data type and select the menu Generate Form. The resulting pop-up window asks you to select either Flex Form or Model Driven Form. If you select Flex Form, the generated code will contain only basic Flex form attributes; this form can be used in non-LCDS 3 applications.

You can also select the Model Driven Form option so that the code generator can use the extended attributes of the model (such as validations and associations). In either case, you'll see newly generated form next to the `DataGrid`. The form has the same fields as the `Employee` entity. Switch to the source code perspective and bind it to the `DataGrid` by adding to the `<forms>` tag the following property:

```
valueObject="dataGrid.selectedItems as Employee"
```

where `dataGrid` is an `id` of the `DataGrid` with employees.

Run the application and you'll see that selecting a row in the `DataGrid` shows all the data about this employee, as seen in the form in Figure 12-6.

If the entity Employee had an association with the entity Department, the generated form would contain a drop-down populated with departments. As you may remember, in order to achieve the same functionality with BlazeDS, we had to come up with the idea of resources (see Example 3-10), but in LCDS 3 using associations is even simpler.

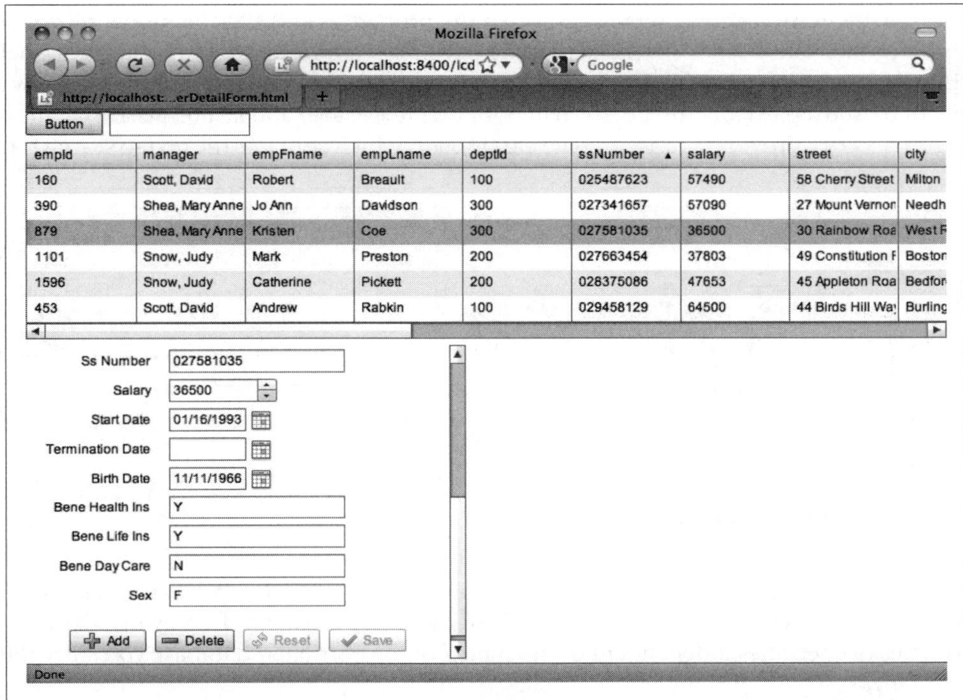

Figure 12-6. Master/detail view

The generated form displays all required form items in one column. The good news is that you can customize the template used for the form generation to make it as fancy as needed. Fiber uses templates generated by a template engine called FreeMarker (*http://freemarker.org*), and you can tweak the form's template as you wish.

Try to add a new employee using the form shown earlier. Clicking the Add button makes a server call to save a new row in the underlying database table.

Queries in this Modeler are called *filters*. Defining a filter on the entity serves the same purpose as, say, writing a `Select` statement against an RDBMS. One entity can have multiple filters, which makes sense, because you need to be able to retrieve more than one data set (for example, show all employees or show only employees from New York) on the same data entity.

Of course, you don't always want to display all the data. What if you'd like to filter the data based on some criterion? For example, you may want to find all employees who have specific letters in their names. In the SQL world, you'd use the `like` keyword for this.

The generated function `getByEmpLName()` shown previously in Figure 12-5 can help only if you know the exact last name you want, but not when you want to search just by a couple of letters.

To specify more complex filters, just open the properties sheet of the model by going back to the Data Model view, clicking the Employee model and referring to the panel in the bottom left, and creating a new filter as shown in Figure 12-7. In this case, we want to find a particular text pattern in both first (`empFname`) and last (`empLname`) names. The Flex code provides the argument `searchModel`, which contains the text to search for.

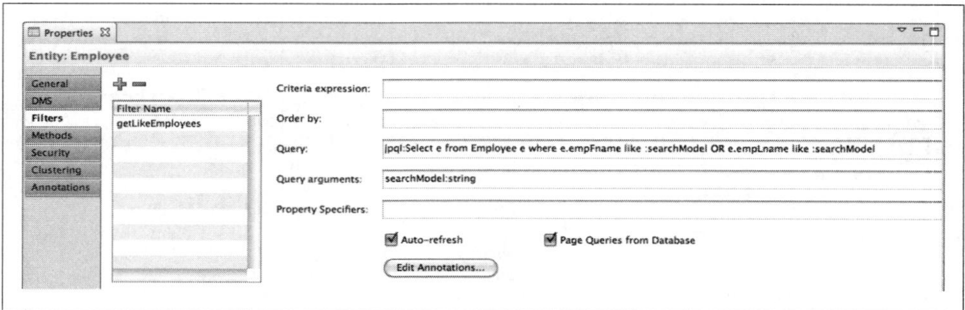

Figure 12-7. Adding a filter query

Java EE developers may recognize the `jpql` prefix in the Query expression. Yes, this is the Java Persistence Query Language used in the Java persistence framework to define queries over entities independent of the syntax of the particular database you store the data in.

You could've specified the search criteria in the Criteria Expression field shown in Figure 12-7, but JPQL allows you to create a lot more complex queries, which are also called *pass-through filters*. To get familiar with the expression syntax for filters, refer to the online manual "Application Modeling Technology Reference" (*http://help.adobe.com/en_US/livecycle/9.0/lc_ds_list.html*).

The DMS tab from Figure 12-7 enables you to configure pagination, which is a useful feature for large result sets. The LCDS server will feed you the data in chunks based on the configured number of records in the page and the size of the visible portion of the UI control, that is, `DataGrid`.

The Modeler generates an appropriate function with a call responder for the filter defined earlier. The rest is simple. Add a button and a text field (say, `MySearchText`) on the top of the view as shown in Figure 12-8.

On the click event of the button, make the call to the newly generated filter function passing `"%" + MySearchText.text + "%"` as an argument to the filter expression defined in Figure 12-7.

Don't forget to modify the `dataProvider` of the `DataGrid` to use the `lastResult` not from the `getAll()` method as it was done originally, but from the method generated for the

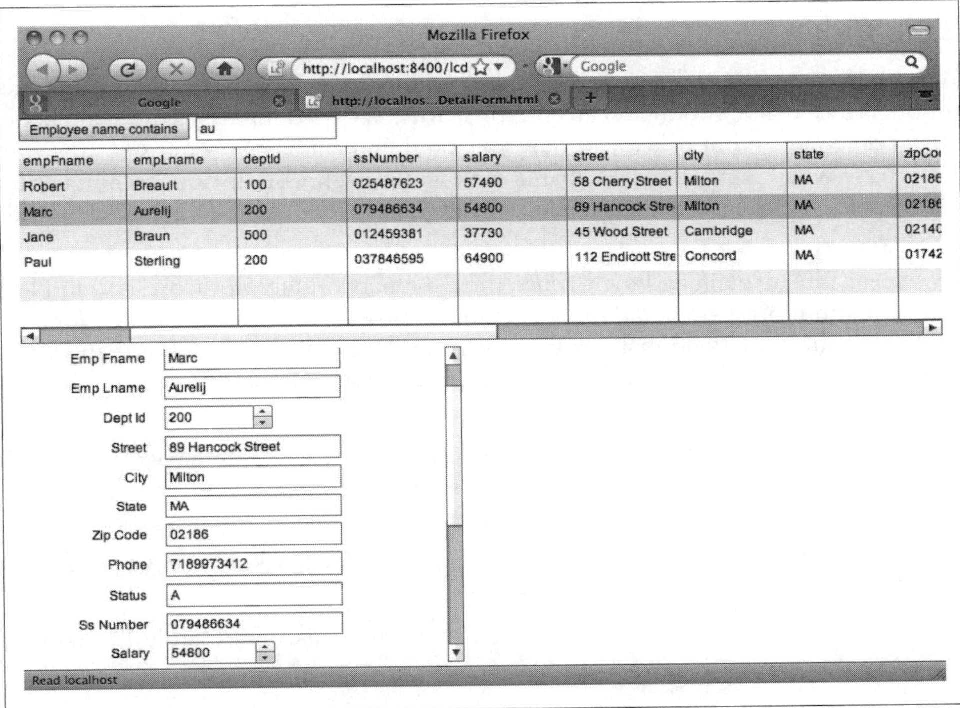

Figure 12-8. Adding a search with filter criteria

filter expression. With Fiber, the result returned by the service call is placed into the property `lastResult` of the corresponding class `CallResponder`. The `dataProvider` of your `DataGrid` should get the data there.

Summary

Overall, the model-driven development workflow with LCDS 3 is a great move toward automation of creating data-driven enterprise RIA, but it is a work in progress.

After reading the first chapter of this book, you most likely got the feeling that we don't see too much value in introducing MVC frameworks in a Flex RIA. By creating the Fiber architecture and this new model-driven design workflow, Adobe may be sending a similar message. Of course, you can use the generated view with Flex/LCDS/DBMS in conjunction with the MVC framework of your choice, but does it make much sense?

In this chapter, we've reviewed just one aspect of LCDS 3—model-driven development—but LCDS 3 has a number of other great improvements that will definitely make it a valuable addition to any enterprise application built with Flex and Java EE. As a matter of fact, now you don't even have to know Java to create LCDS-based applications.

Epilogue

The book is over. We tried to discuss the most important subjects that Flex/AIR practitioners face while working on an enterprise RIA. We tried not to just give you better Flex components, but to explain how *you* can build similar or better ones for your enterprise-wide framework. We shared with you some not-so-obvious techniques for establishing communication between a Flex or an AIR client and the server-side systems.

We spent time explaining how to customize the networking protocols used in Flex/Java communications. We did this even though most of you can happily develop Flex RIAs without bothering much about what's traveling over the wire. But if and when you are facing a challenge that requires changing the way Flex and Java communicate, this book will help make your project a success.

Adobe software engineers did a great job designing the Flex framework, but what's more important is that they left all the doors open. Step in and enhance, extend, improve, and add more stuff to this great product as you see fit. Don't be afraid!

The authors of this book would really appreciate your feedback. Please send your constructive critique and praises of this book our way.

—Yakov Fain, Victor Rasputnis, and Anatole Tartakovsky

Index

Symbols

A

We'd like to hear your suggestions for improving our indexes. Send email to *index@oreilly.com*.

B

C

D

E

G

H

L

M

N

O

P

Q

R

S

T

U

V

W

X

Y

About the Authors

Yakov Fain is a managing director at Farata Systems, a company that provides consulting services in the field of development of enterprise rich Internet applications. A certified Adobe Flex instructor and developer as well as the leader of the Princeton Java Users Group, he has authored several technical books and dozens of articles on software development. Sun Microsystems awarded Yakov the title of Java Champion, which is presented to only 100 people worldwide. Yakov also holds a BS and an MS in applied math. You can reach him at *yfain@faratasystems.com* and follow him on Twitter at *@yfain*.

Dr. Victor Rasputnis is a managing director at Farata Systems. He spends most of his time providing architectural design, implementation management, and mentoring to companies migrating to Flex and J2EE technologies. Victor has authored several books and dozens of technical articles. A certified Adobe Flex instructor and developer, Victor holds a PhD in computer science. Reach him at *vrasputnis@faratasystems.com*.

Anatole Tartakovsky is a managing director at Farata Systems. He has spent more than 20 years developing complex distributed systems. In the last 10 years, his focus has been on creating frameworks and business applications for dozens of enterprises ranging from Wal-Mart to Wall Street firms. Anatole has authored a number of books and articles on AJAX, Flex, XML, the Internet, and client-server technologies. He holds an MS in mathematics. You can reach him at *atartakovsky@faratasystems.com*.

Colophon

The animals on the cover of *Enterprise Development with Flex* are red-crested wood-quails (*Rollulus roulroul*), more commonly known today as crested wood partridges or Roul-roul partridges. The birds live in small flocks in the lowland rainforests of Myanmar, Thailand, Malaysia, Sumatra, and Borneo. They forage on the ground for fruit, seeds, and insects, and often follow wild pigs through the forest to feed on any leftovers. If disturbed, these plump birds can fly for short distances, but, as is common in many quail species, they tend to run instead.

Male and female red-crested wood-quails have vastly different appearances. Males sport a white spot at the base of the bristling red-crested head for which the bird is named, as well as iridescent blue-green plumage and a dark blue underbelly. In contrast, the female is pea green, with brown wings and a gray head. Both have red feet, red skin around the eyes, and black bills.

The red-crested wood-quail nests on the forest floor in a dome-like construction of leaves and twigs that completely conceals its eggs and the nesting female. Unusually for a galliform (fowl-like) species, the chicks are fed bill-to-bill by their parents rather than pecking their food from the ground. This bird's call is a plaintive, whistled *si-ul*, most often heard at dawn. In 2004, the red-crested wood-quail was listed as a near threatened species due to heavy logging activity in Southeast Asia.

The cover image is from *The Riverside Natural History*. The cover font is Adobe ITC Garamond. The text font is Linotype Birka; the heading font is Adobe Myriad Condensed; and the code font is LucasFont's TheSansMonoCondensed.

Related Titles from O'Reilly

Web Programming

ActionScript 3.0 Cookbook
ActionScript 3.0 Design Patterns
ActionScript for Flash MX: The Definitive Guide, *2nd Edition*
Adobe AIR 1.5 Cookbook
Adobe AIR for JavaScript Developer's Pocket Guide
Advanced Rails
Ajax Design Patterns
Ajax Hacks
Ajax on Rails
Ajax: The Definitive Guide
Apache 2 Pocket Reference
Apache Cookbook, *2nd Edition*
Building Scalable Web Sites
Designing Web Navigation
Dojo: The Definitive Guide
Dynamic HTML: The Definitive Reference, *3rd Edition*
Essential ActionScript 3.0
Essential PHP Security
Ferret
Flash CS4: The Missing Manual
Flash Hacks
Head First HTML with CSS & XHTML
Head First JavaScript
Head First PHP & MySQL
High Performance Web Sites
HTTP: The Definitive Guide
JavaScript & DHTML Cookbook, *2nd Edition*
JavaScript Pocket Reference, *2nd Edition*
JavaScript: The Definitive Guide, *5th Edition*
JavaScript: The Good Parts
JavaScript: The Missing Manual
Learning ActionScript 3.0
Learning PHP and MySQL, *2nd Edition*
PHP Cookbook, *2nd Edition*
PHP Hacks
PHP in a Nutshell
PHP Pocket Reference, *2nd Edition*
Programming ColdFusion MX, *2nd Edition*
Programming Flex 2
Programming PHP, *2nd Edition*
Programming Amazon Web Services
Rails Cookbook
The ActionScript 3.0 Quick Reference Guide
Twitter API: Up and Running
Universal Design for Web Applications
Upgrading to PHP 5
Web Database Applications with PHP and MySQL, *2nd Edition*
Website Optimization
Web Site Cookbook
Webmaster in a Nutshell, *3rd Edition*

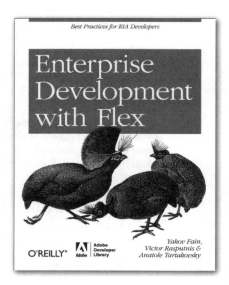